English Society in the Seventeenth-Century Chesapeake

JAMES HORN

Adapting to a New World

Adapting to a New World

Published for the

Omohundro Institute

of Early American

History and Culture,

Williamsburg, Virginia,

by the University of

North Carolina Press

Chapel Hill & London

Adapting to

James Horn

English
Society
in the
Seventeenth-
Century
Chesapeake

a New World

The Omohundro Institute of

Early American History and

Culture is sponsored jointly by

the College of William and Mary

and the Colonial Williamsburg

Foundation.

Library of Congress
Cataloging-in-Publication Data
Horn, James P. P.
   Adapting to a new world : English
society in the seventeenth-century
Chesapeake / by James Horn.
      p.   cm.
   Includes bibliographical references
and index.
   ISBN 0-8078-2137-3 (cloth :
alk. paper)
   ISBN 0-8078-4614-7 (pbk.: alk. paper)
   1. Chesapeake Bay Region (Md.
and Va.)—Emigration and
immigration—History—17th century.
2. British—Chesapeake Bay Region
(Md. and Va.)—History—17th
century. 3. Kent (England)—
Emigration and immigration—History
—17th century. 4. Gloucestershire
(England)—Emigration and
immigration—History—17th century.
I. Omohundro Institute of Early
American History and Culture
(Williamsburg, Va.) II. Title.
F187.C5H66   1994
975.5'18—dc20   93-38421
                                    CIP

The paper in this book meets the
guidelines for permanence and
durability of the Committee on
Production Guidelines for Book
Longevity of the Council on Library
Resources.

*This volume received indirect support from
an unrestricted book publication grant
awarded to the Institute by the L. J. Skaggs
and Mary C. Skaggs Foundation of Oakland,
California.*

FOR SALLY

Preface

This is not a conventional history of the early Chesapeake. It is not intended to be a description of the peculiar characteristics of plantation society, although description is involved. Its aim is not to chart the growth of the tobacco industry or unravel the origins of chattel slavery, although both are considered. It embraces both Virginia and Maryland, but no attempt is made to be comprehensive. It adopts a local and regional approach, but the choice of areas is highly selective and perhaps uneven. The interpretive focus lies not in emphasizing the distinctiveness of Chesapeake society compared to New England or other mainland English colonies. Neither is there any effort to locate social developments within a model of increasing independence from or, alternatively, dependence on the parent society. The study is as much about the evolution of *English* societies and cultures overseas as about the formation of early *American* society, although, in a sense, it may be construed as either or both.

A single object motivates the work: to explore the degree to which English attitudes, values, and traditions shaped settlers' adaptation to the New World during the seventeenth century. At its heart is an attempt to reconstruct experiences of English immigrants—how they adjusted to conditions in America—by way of a comparison of local society in England and the Chesapeake. English attitudes and behavior are examined through consideration of aspects of daily life in the two societies (sex, marriage, community, work, living standards, order and disorder, and religion), studied against the backdrop of particular locales in England, Virginia, and Maryland, representing regions from which colonists emigrated and to which they came. It is argued that the period from 1607 to the 1690s represented a peculiarly English phase of settlement. Chesapeake society was an immigrant society. The overwhelming majority of settlers were born and raised in England, and the tide of large-scale immigration remained substantially unabated until after 1670. Driven by the same imperatives that persuaded countless thousands of people to move within England, emigration was an expression of migratory flows that linked English villages and towns to cities and ports—and beyond, to Europe, Ireland, and the plantations.

Maryland and Virginia are seen, not as radically different societies owing little to English society or as incipient states of the new nation to be, but as far-flung provinces overseas, intimately linked to the parent society by strong and enduring political, cultural, social, and economic ties. The Chesapeake colonies were extensions of Old World society in the New. In creating governing institutions, temporal and spiritual, in their efforts to establish orderly society at local and provincial levels, and in their assumptions about the proper relationship between rulers and ruled, settlers looked to England for guidance and inspiration. The intensity of cultural ties varied considerably from one part of English America to another and across time, but there can be no doubt that in tone and temperament England's New World colonies were emphatically English.

The argument advanced is not an exercise in "little Englandism" or manifest destiny, a eulogy of English expansion and imperialism. Stress given to settlers' English background and worldview is not intended to obscure the crucial contribution of other peoples to the development of early American society, especially Indians and Africans. Neither is the intention to create a bland and featureless landscape of cultural uniformity reaching across English counties, kingdoms, and colonies. Throughout the study, the dynamic interplay of distinctive cultures is recognized and given close attention, both in differences between English colonists themselves and between English and non-English cultures. Out of this admixture emerged various, sometimes exotic Anglo-American hybrids, integral to the Atlantic world of the seventeenth century. The perspective, however, is that of the English immigrant, not of the Indian or black slave, and is adopted in the conviction that early American historians have seriously underestimated the significance of English settlers' attitudes and values in shaping English societies in the New World. Immigrant experience should be seen as a whole, embracing English origins and heritage as well as their responses to conditions in America. One without the other makes little sense.

During the course of my research I have incurred many academic debts on both sides of the Atlantic. I would like to thank the staff of the Gloucestershire Record Office, particularly Brian Smith (former county archivist), Linda Beard, and Margaret Richards, who generously helped me with my initial forays into sixteenth- and seventeenth-century handwriting and Latin. I am indebted also to archivists and librarians at the Gloucester City Library, Kent Archives Office, the Bristol Record Office, the Public Record Office, the Greater London Record Office, the Guildhall Library in London, the Royal Society, the British Library, and the Bodleian Library and to the Trustees of the Berkeley family muniments at Berkeley Castle, Gloucestershire, for permission to use their archives.

The staff of the Hall of Records, Annapolis, was unfailingly helpful and supportive when I began research in Maryland, and I would like to thank also the staff at the Colonial Williamsburg Foundation's superb research library in Williamsburg, Virginia. I am grateful to Cary Carson for permission to use records of the Colonial Virginia Records Project, the York County Project, and other sources. Staff at the Institute of Early American History and Culture have provided much encouragement during the course of this research, especially during my residency as an American Council of Learned Societies–Fulbright Fellow in 1985–1986. I am grateful to Institute fellows and colleagues for friendship and conversation and for making my stay in Virginia so pleasant. In particular, I owe Thad Tate an enormous debt of gratitude as a friend and mentor since my first ventures into Chesapeake history. My thanks are extended also to archivists of the Virginia State Library and Archives in Richmond.

No one working in the field of Chesapeake history over the last twenty years could have failed to benefit from the rich seam of scholarship associated with Lois Green Carr and her colleagues of the St. Mary's City Commission, notably Lorena Walsh, Russell Menard, P. M. G. Harris, Allan Kulikoff, and Jean Russo. My debt to the Commission will be evident from what follows, but I would like to record my warm thanks to Carr and Walsh for help and encouragement they have given since I first started my research. Without their generosity and support I doubt whether this book could have been written. I would also like to thank other Chesapeake practitioners, Warren Billings, Paul Clemens, Gloria Main, Philip Morgan, Kevin Kelly, the late James Perry, Barbara Carson, Henry Miller, Julie King, Anne Smart Martin, and Kathleen Brown for sharing unpublished research, insights, and ideas.

Undertaking research on both sides of the Atlantic is expensive, and I would like to thank those institutions and organizations that have generously assisted my work: The Johns Hopkins University, the American Council of Learned Societies, the Fulbright Commission, the American Philosophical Society, the American Historical Association, the Virginia Center for the Humanities, and the University of Brighton. Most of this work was written while I was a Fellow at the Charles Warren Center for Studies in American History, Harvard University, 1989–1990, and I am grateful to Bernard Bailyn and Fellows for making my residence so congenial.

Numerous friends and colleagues have helped along the way: Colin Brooks supervised my doctoral dissertation at the University of Sussex, from which this book grew, and I have profited over many years from the advice and encouragement of Richard Dunn, Jack Greene, and Tim Breen. I would also like to thank (in no particular order) Jerry Handler, Cynthia Carter Ayres, Edward Ayres, Gil Kelly, Alan Taylor, Ida Altman, Philip

Gura, David Ammerman, John McCusker, Nicholas Canny, Michael McGiffert, Hank Gemery, Walter Jackson, David Jaffee, Noel Currer-Briggs, Edward Papenfuse, Ken Morgan, David Souden, James Axtell, Peter Clark, and Karen Kupperman. Fredrika Teute has been an ideal editor, and I thank her for her hard work, perceptive comments, and, above all, humor.

The book is dedicated to my wife, Sally, who reminds me there are other worlds to be explored.

Contents

Illustrations and Tables

TABLES

Adapting
to a New
World

Introduction

In winter of 1636, the *Tristram and Jane* of London arrived at the busy little port of Kecoughtan (Elizabeth City), at the mouth of the Chesapeake Bay. She carried a varied cargo of Spanish wine, strong waters, sugar, cheese and other foodstuffs, clothing, shoes, candles, and nails as well as two paying passengers and seventy-four indentured servants. Most of the goods and the servants were sold or consigned to planters over the next few months as she traded along the Bay before returning to England in the spring with ninety-nine hogsheads of tobacco in her hold. It was a successful voyage. The seven partners who financed it grossed more than 73,000 lbs. of tobacco, worth about £1,000 at London prices in the late 1630s, which, although not all profit (the cost of the cargo, provisions, hiring the ship and men, duties, fees, and other expenses had to be deducted), undoubtedly represented a healthy return on the original investment.[1]

There was nothing exceptional about the voyage. Hundreds of other merchantmen, mainly from London, carrying a vast range of manufactured goods and provisions, made similar journeys to the tobacco coast in this period. But it serves to introduce a number of important themes relating to England's emerging transatlantic world and the development of colonial trade: the exchange of European manufactured goods and foodstuffs for New World staples and primary produce; the manner by which people were transported across the Atlantic; the establishment of English settlements in America, both providing a market for English wares and producing commodities in demand at home; and the vital role of the mercantile community in connecting the financial and human resources of England to the American hinterland. Singly, the voyage of the *Tristram and Jane* was of little account. Cumulatively, thousands upon thousands of such trading ventures brought about a profound transformation in English society and economy and laid the foundations of a Greater England that embraced the British Isles, the Caribbean, and the colonies of the eastern seaboard of North America.[2]

1. Martha W. Hiden, ed., "Accompts of the Tristam and Jane," *Virginia Magazine of History and Biography*, LXII (1954), 424–447. The price of leaf fluctuated between 3.25d. and 2.8d. per pound between 1637 and 1639: see Russell R. Menard, "The Tobacco Industry in the Chesapeake Colonies, 1617–1730: An Interpretation," *Research in Economic History*, V (1980), appendix, 157.

2. Bernard Bailyn and Philip D. Morgan, eds., *Strangers within the Realm: Cultural*

By 1650 it is possible to speak, not of English society, but of English *societies*. New societies developed rapidly in New England, the Chesapeake, Bermuda, and the English Caribbean, all closely linked to England by political, economic, social, and cultural ties. At midcentury, Virginia and Maryland had a population of about 12,000–13,000, New England 23,000, and the West Indies 59,000 (including 14,000 slaves). Within a generation after their foundation, the population of England's colonies in the New World approached 100,000; thirty years later the number had nearly doubled. By premodern standards, emigration was massive. More than 250,000 people left England in the first six decades of the century (including those drawn to Ulster and Munster), a figure all the more impressive given the relatively small size of the domestic population.[3] The great majority settled permanently in America. Whether or not they were fully aware of it at the time, most English men and women who made the Atlantic crossing in this period went, not to trade and then return home: they went for good.

The establishment of England as one of the great colonial powers by 1660 could not have been foreseen half a century earlier. Informed observers might have predicted that the Dutch, with their powerful mercantile marine, wealthy merchant elites, and growing influence in the Far East, would develop as the main challenge to Iberian monopoly of transoceanic trade routes, but not the English. England appeared to be literally on the periphery of new developments in extra-European trade. At the death of Elizabeth I,

Margins of the First British Empire (Chapel Hill, N.C., 1991), 1–11; Kenneth R. Andrews, *Trade, Plunder, and Settlement: Maritime Enterprise and the Genesis of the British Empire, 1480–1630* (Cambridge, 1984).

3. Jack P. Greene, *Pursuits of Happiness: The Social Development of Early Modern British Colonies and the Formation of American Culture* (Chapel Hill, N.C., 1988), 7–8, 178; John J. McCusker and Russell R. Menard, *The Economy of British America, 1607–1789*, rev. ed. (Chapel Hill, N.C., 1991), 103, 136, 153, 154, 172, 203 (tables 5.1, 6.4, 7.1, 7.2, 8.1, 9.4); Henry A. Gemery, "Emigration from the British Isles to the New World, 1630–1700: Inferences from Colonial Populations," *Res. Econ. Hist.*, V (1980), 179–231; R. J. Dickson, *Ulster Emigration to Colonial America, 1718–1775* (London, 1966), 3; Michael McCarthy Morrogh, "The English Presence in Early Seventeenth-Century Munster," in Ciaran Brady and Raymond Gillespie, eds., *Natives and Newcomers: Essays on the Making of Irish Colonial Society, 1534–1641* (Dublin, 1986), 171–172; E. A. Wrigley and R. S. Schofield, *The Population History of England, 1541–1871: A Reconstruction* (Cambridge, Mass., 1981), 219–224; Ida Altman and James Horn, eds., *"To Make America": European Emigration in the Early Modern Period* (Los Angeles, 1991), 3–4; Bernard Bailyn, *Voyagers to the West: A Passage in the Peopling of America on the Eve of the Revolution* (New York, 1986), 24.

there was little to show for forty years of piracy and plunder in the Caribbean or for the effort to find a northwestern passage to the Orient. Plans to establish a permanent English presence in the New World came to nothing. The first concerted effort, at Roanoke in the 1580s, ended in complete failure. Only in Ireland did colonizers meet with some success, and there at considerable cost in men and money.[4]

England's backwardness in colonial enterprises was deceptive, however. During the second half of the sixteenth century, merchants began to look beyond traditional European markets and sought new avenues of trade in Russia, the Levant, West Africa, and the Far East. The Venice and Turkey companies, chartered in the 1580s, facilitated direct trading with the great Turkish cities that served as entrepôts for a vast range of goods from the Levant and Asia, and, in the opening years of the new century, traders began making voyages around the Cape of Good Hope to the Indian Ocean and the Malay Archipelago to compete with the Portuguese and Dutch for the spice trade. Westward, an opportunity to reap the wealth of the New World by preying on Spanish shipping and the annual treasure fleets arose with the deterioration in Anglo-Spanish relations after 1580. In the last twenty years of the century, English seamen and merchants, with the government's blessing, systematically plundered Spanish possessions in the Caribbean and along the Spanish Main. The privateering war marked an important stage in the nation's maritime history. Upward of a hundred, and sometimes nearer two hundred, ships set out every year to pillage Spanish galleons on the high seas. With the possible exception of West Country fleets to the Newfoundland fisheries, never before had English ships been so prevalent

---

4. J. Holland Rose *et al.*, eds., *The Old Empire: From the Beginnings to 1783* (Cambridge, 1929), vol. I of *The Cambridge History of the British Empire*, chaps. 2–4; James A. Williamson, *A Short History of British Expansion: The Old Colonial Empire*, 3d ed. (London, 1961), pt. 2, chaps. 7–9; T. O. Lloyd, *The British Empire, 1558–1983* (Oxford, 1984), 1–14; Andrews, *Trade, Plunder, and Settlement*; David Beers Quinn, *England and the Discovery of America, 1481–1620* . . . (New York, 1974), chap. 11; Quinn, *Set Fair for Roanoke: Voyages and Colonies, 1584–1606* (Chapel Hill, N.C., 1985); Karen Ordahl Kupperman, *Roanoke: The Abandoned Colony* (Totowa, N.J., 1984); Nicholas P. Canny, *The Elizabethan Conquest of Ireland: A Pattern Established, 1565–76* (Hassocks, 1976); Canny, *From Reformation to Restoration: Ireland, 1534–1660* (Dublin, 1987), 108–187; T. W. Moody *et al.*, eds., *A New History of Ireland*, III, *Early Modern Ireland, 1534–1691* (Oxford, 1976), chaps. 3–7; David Beers Quinn, *The Elizabethans and the Irish*, Folger Monographs on Tudor and Stuart Civilization (Ithaca, N.Y., 1966), chap. 10; Steven G. Ellis, *Tudor Ireland: Crown, Community, and the Conflict of Cultures, 1470–1603* (London, 1985), chaps. 8–9.

in the Atlantic. By the early seventeenth century, mariners had gained considerable experience of practical problems involved in transatlantic crossings as well as a growing corpus of knowledge about the West Indian islands and the North American seaboard. This experience was to prove indispensable to the planting of colonies that followed the end of war.[5]

For all the individual successes of English privateers, the plunder of Spanish shipping did not compensate for England's lack of colonies. Privateering was viable only during a period of open hostility between the two countries, which ended with the peace of 1604. In national terms it was of limited economic significance, bringing wealth to a few investors who had the means or luck to be associated with lucrative ventures but not affecting the material lives of the great majority of the population.

An altogether broader conception of empire was put forward by a small group of men in the late sixteenth century who argued that colonization and colonial trade would benefit the entire nation and ensure lasting prosperity at home and overseas. Adopting earlier ideas that promoted projects—new industries and the cultivation of new crops—that would reduce the country's reliance on imports and encourage the development of the domestic economy, their comprehensive plan was intended to appeal not only to merchants and financiers but also to the government, whose support in the long term would be vital.[6] Writers such as Sir George Peckham, Christopher Carleill, and the two Richard Hakluyts stressed social benefits as well as the purely commercial. Overpopulation and rising poverty would be alleviated by putting the poor and unemployed to productive use in the colonies, and those who, for one reason or another, had been marginalized in England had

5. On trade to the East: C.G.A. Clay, *Economic Expansion and Social Change: England, 1500–1700*, II, *Industry, Trade, and Government* (Cambridge, 1984), 126–130; Williamson, *Short History of British Expansion*, pt. 2, chap. 7, pt. 3, chap. 6; Ralph Davis, *English Overseas Trade, 1500–1700* (London, 1973), chap. 5; K. N. Chaudhuri, *The Trading World of Asia and the English East India Company, 1660–1760* (Cambridge, 1978).

On western trade: Kenneth R. Andrews, *Elizabethan Privateering: English Privateering during the Spanish War, 1585–1603* (Cambridge, 1964); Arthur P. Newton, *The European Nations in the West Indies, 1493–1688* (London, 1933), chaps. 6–8; Quinn, *England and the Discovery of America*, chap. 10. For transatlantic routes, see Ian K. Steele, *The English Atlantic, 1675–1740: An Exploration of Communication and Community* (Oxford, 1986), 45–51.

6. A. P. Newton, "The Beginnings of English Colonization, 1569–1618," in Rose *et al.*, eds., *Cambridge History of the British Empire*, I, 67–70; E.G.R. Taylor, ed., *The Original Writings and Correspondence of the Two Richard Hakluyts*, 2 vols., Hakluyt Society, 2d Ser., LXXVI–LXXVII (London, 1935), II, 211, 327–335, 347.

an opportunity to make a new start in America. The prescience of their vision is striking. The export of manufactured goods to the colonies in return for raw materials was the basis of colonial trade down to the American Revolution and helped to reduce significantly England's dependence on traditional sources of imports. During the seventeenth century, measures were taken to get rid of unwanted elements of society (vagrants, the poor, criminals, and political prisoners) by transporting them overseas. Larger numbers, mainly the poor and unemployed, emigrated of their own volition in response to the plantation colonies' voracious demand for labor. American staples were raised, not by indigenous peoples supervised by small immigrant elites, but by English men and women together with (especially in the West Indies) African slaves. The huge flow of people who moved to America in this period can be explained only in terms of the transferal of a massive labor force. Rather than conquerors or colonial administrators, the vast majority of English immigrants who made their way to the New World became planters, farmers, and agricultural field hands.[7]

It is unlikely, notwithstanding their foresight, that advocates of colonial expansion in the 1580s could have predicted the magnitude of change that took place in English trade during the following century. In 1622, 93 percent (by value) of London's imports were from Europe and the Baltic, less than 6 percent from Asia, and less than 1 percent from America. By the end of the century, two-thirds of imports were from Europe, compared to 16 percent from Asia and 18 percent from America. Transoceanic trade now accounted for a third of all imports. Expansion was maintained by two major developments. First was a sharp rise in reexports. While the value of exports barely doubled between 1640 and 1699–1701, reexports quadrupled from an estimated £500,000 to £2,000,000. By midcentury, London shipped East Indian calicoes, pepper, and spices to Russia, Germany, the Netherlands, Italy, and the Levant and Virginia tobacco to Amsterdam and Hamburg. With the increasing volume of reexports after 1650, London emerged as one of the great

7. Newton, "Beginnings of English Colonization," in Rose *et al.*, eds., *Cambridge History of the British Empire*, I, 69; Taylor, ed., *Original Writings and Correspondence of the Two Richard Hakluyts*, II, 315, 319; Edmund S. Morgan, *American Slavery, American Freedom: The Ordeal of Colonial Virginia* (New York, 1975), 15–17, 28–31; Joan Thirsk, *Economic Policy and Projects: The Development of a Consumer Society in Early Modern England* (Oxford, 1978); McCusker and Menard, *Economy of British America*, chaps. 1–4, 6; Richard S. Dunn, "Servants and Slaves: The Recruitment and Employment of Labor," in Jack P. Greene and J. R. Pole, eds., *Colonial British America: Essays in the New History of the Early Modern Era* (Baltimore, 1984), 157–194.

entrepôts of the world. Second, there was a dramatic rise in domestic demand for consumer goods such as tobacco, sugar, calicoes, wine, and dried
fruits. Tobacco was the first of the American staples to emerge. Imports rose
from 1,250 lbs. in 1616 to more than 500,000 by 1634, 15,000,000 by 1669,
and 28,000,000 by the end of the century.[8] Much was reexported, but there
can be no doubt that, as the retail price of leaf fell, so demand in England
rapidly increased. The same principle governed the rise of the West Indian
sugar industry. Retail prices of sugar were halved between 1630 and 1680 as
a result of the massive rise in production and expansion of the market. Sugar
imports rose from about eight thousand tons in 1663 to more than twenty-
three thousand by 1700. During the century, tobacco and sugar established
themselves as the two leading colonial commodities, worth £249,000 and
£630,000 per year, respectively, by 1699–1701.[9]

Expansion of the tobacco and sugar industries was largely export-led.
Economies in production, transportation, and marketing reduced prices of
staples and thus created a steady rise in demand. Mass markets and increasing demand in England and Europe were vital both for the development of
colonial trade and to the development of plantation societies. If production
had been limited to supplying a small luxury market, neither the Chesapeake
colonies nor the West Indian islands would have required large labor forces,
and consequently very different societies would have emerged. Large-scale
production of tobacco and sugar had an enormous influence on the sorts of

8. Clay, *Economic Expansion*, II, 125, 142–145, 160, 163–182 (tables 10, 11–14, 20);
D. C. Coleman, *The Economy of England, 1450–1750* (Oxford, 1977), tables 12, 13, p. 138;
Davis, *English Overseas Trade*, chap. 5; F. J. Fisher, "London's Export Trade in the Early
Seventeenth Century," in W. E. Minchinton, ed., *The Growth of English Overseas Trade in
the Seventeenth and Eighteenth Centuries* (London, 1969), 75. Tobacco figures are derived
from Menard, "Tobacco Industry," *Res. Econ. Hist.*, V (1980), appendix, 157–161.

9. Richard S. Dunn, *Sugar and Slaves: The Rise of the Planter Class in the English
West Indies, 1624–1713* (Chapel Hill, N.C., 1973), table 21; Ralph Davis, "English Foreign Trade, 1700–1774," in Minchinton, ed., *Growth of English Overseas Trade*, 119. The
development of the tobacco trade in England is outlined in C. M. MacInnes, *The
Early English Tobacco Trade* (London, 1926). Tobacco retailing spread rapidly throughout England and Wales and was not restricted to London and major towns. In 1634
alone, licenses permitting the sale of leaf were issued to 293 individuals in 42 counties (C66/2640, Pat. Roll, 9 Chas. I, pt. 26; C66/2646, Pat. Roll, 10 Chas. I, pt. 5; C66/
2659, Pat. Roll, 10 Chas. I, pt. 18, Public Record Office, London; references are derived
from the Colonial Virginia Research Project, nos. 10911–10913, Colonial Williamsburg
Foundation Research Library, Williamsburg, Virginia).

societies that developed in the Chesapeake and Caribbean and the relationship they had with England.[10]

Rapid growth in output of colonial products and their impact on English trade and domestic consumption patterns are worth emphasizing. Not only did imports from America rise from insignificant amounts in the 1620s to nearly one-fifth of all imports by value in 1700, but exports from England to the colonies increased massively in response to growing demand from colonial populations. By the second half of the century, impressive fleets left London, Bristol, and other outports carrying a vast array of manufactured goods, foodstuffs, and settlers on a nine- or ten-week journey across the Atlantic, returning laden with rich cargoes of tobacco, sugar, dyestuffs, cotton, skins, and timber. The number of ships engaged in Atlantic commerce rose from fewer than one hundred per year in the 1660s to between two and three hundred by the 1680s.[11]

English awareness of newly established societies across the Atlantic was aroused primarily through the import and distribution of colonial products. From its inception England's empire was an "empire of goods." The most important colonies (from England's point of view) were those that produced the major staples and consumed the most goods from England. Colonial trade had a significant impact on English society, not only in stimulating domestic industry, transforming traditional patterns of imports and exports, and encouraging new consumer tastes but also in the development of a consciousness of a wider world on the other side of the ocean. In previous centuries, English ambitions had been focused on the neighboring kingdoms of Scotland and Ireland, the absorption of Wales, and above all on maintaining a territorial presence in France. During the seventeenth century, efforts to impose tighter control over Scotland and Ireland continued, but, with the end of England's attempt to retain a beachhead on the Continent, projectors, merchants, and statesmen began looking westward rather than to Europe for expansion. The foundation of colonies in America heralded the beginnings of the most important expansionist phase in English history.[12]

10. McCusker and Menard discuss the staple theory of colonial economic development in *Economy of British America*, 18–32.

11. Ralph Davis, *The Rise of the English Shipping Industry in the Seventeenth and Eighteenth Centuries* (London, 1962), 17–18; Dunn, *Sugar and Slaves*, 210–211; Steele, *English Atlantic*, 41, 45–51, 262, 291. Steele estimates that 10,000–15,000 English-speaking seamen manned transatlantic merchantmen and fishing vessels by the 1680s.

12. Hugh Kearney, *The British Isles: A History of Four Nations* (Cambridge, 1989),

Conventionally, the emergence of England's North American empire has been described from the standpoint of the mainland colonies that later made up the United States, usually treated separately from contemporaneous developments in the parent society or other parts of the English Atlantic such as the Caribbean. Scholars of Anglo-American politics and those engaged in studies of changing trends in trade have been most successful in adopting transatlantic approaches, exploring in depth and with considerable subtlety the interaction between English and colonial society.[13]

Social historians have not been so assiduous. In the main, they have been less concerned with transatlantic comparisons than with identifying and illustrating themes related to particular colonies or regions in America, which may (or may not) have contributed to the development of distinctively American forms of provincial society. For the seventeenth century, a series of counterpoints has emerged. Stable, consensual societies of New England have been contrasted to the chaotic, shallow societies of Virginia and Maryland; coherent New England communities, to dispersed settlement and lack of community in the Chesapeake; long lives and large families in the North, to short lives and broken families in the South. The profound importance of religion in the Bible Commonwealth has been compared to irreligion and secularism in the tobacco colonies; small independent farmers relying on family labor in New England, to plantation agriculture and slave labor along the Bay. Whereas the northern colonies approximated Old World society in the New, the Chesapeake was a grotesque parody. New England society has been interpreted as normative, the South as deviant.[14]

---

chaps. 6–7. The quoted phrase is taken from T. H. Breen, "An Empire of Goods: The Anglicization of Colonial America, 1690–1776," *Journal of British Studies*, XXV (1986), 467–499.

13. Bailyn and Morgan, eds., *Strangers within the Realm*, 1–3; Richard R. Johnson takes issue with the view that Andrews was of the "imperial school," in "Charles McLean Andrews and the Invention of American Colonial History," *William and Mary Quarterly*, 3d Ser., XLIII (1986), 519–541. Numerous examples of studies of Anglo-American colonial politics and commerce could be given, but see, for example, the works by Andrews, Bailyn, Barrow, Beer, Christie, Gipson, Greene, Harper, Kammen, Olson, Osgood, Pole, Sosin, Steele, Thomas, Webb, and Wood listed in David L. Ammerman and Philip D. Morgan, comps., *Books about Early America: 2001 Titles* (Williamsburg, Va., 1989), 10–11, 14–16, 28–29, 38; and in *Books about Early America: A Selected Bibliography*, 4th ed. (Williamsburg, Va., 1970), 8, 19–20, 22, 24–26. Discovery and exploration are, of course, another field where transatlantic perspectives are well established.

14. For examples of tendency to overdraw studies between North and South,

Such contrasts are frequently placed within the broader and highly influential paradigm of exceptionalism. Whether one takes reflection, simplification, or fragmentation as the model of the transmission of European cultures to early America, the essential point remains the same: colonial society diverged significantly from its parent cultures. This is not the place to describe at length the major tenets of exceptionalist theories. They have tended to revolve around the selectivity of European immigration, the mixing of European and non-European cultures in America, and the transforming impact of the novel environmental conditions encountered. Although immigrants sought to recreate their societies in the image of those they left behind, in practice, the argument goes, their experience in the New World rapidly led them away from traditional attitudes and patterns of behavior inherited from the Old World. An abundance of cheap land and the perceived opportunities for relatively poor men to make a good living accentuated the aggressively materialistic traits already discernible in the mother country. Colonial society, less attenuated by extremes of wealth and poverty and less dominated by inherited rank and status, developed an egalitarian ethos, reinforced by a homespun independence bred of widespread landownership and distrust of central government. The outcome, according to Robert Mitchell, was that early settlers were "liberalist, individualistic, and capitalist . . . to a degree rarely encountered in Europe."[15]

Evident differences between European and American societies in the seventeenth century have imbued exceptionalist arguments with a compelling logic. Immigration *was* selective (though not necessarily in the way that

see Gary B. Nash, "Social Development," in Greene and Pole, eds., *Colonial British America*, 233–238, 242–247; Greene, *Pursuits of Happiness*, 5, 8–27; T. H. Breen, *Puritans and Adventurers: Change and Persistence in Early America* (New York, 1980), chaps. 4, 6–7.

15. R. Cole Harris, "The Simplification of Europe Overseas," Association of American Geographers, *Annals*, LXVII (1977), 469–483; Michael Kammen, *People of Paradox: An Inquiry concerning the Origins of American Civilization* (New York, 1972), 6; Oscar Handlin, "The Significance of the Seventeenth Century," in James Morton Smith, ed., *Seventeenth-Century America: Essays in Colonial History* (Chapel Hill, N.C., 1959), 4. Quote in Robert D. Mitchell, "The Formation of Early American Cultural Regions: An Interpretation," in James R. Gibson, ed., *European Settlement and Development in North America: Essays on Geographical Change in Honour and Memory of Andrew Hill Clark* (Folkestone, 1978), 69. On individualism, see also James T. Lemon, "The Weakness of Place and Community in Early Pennsylvania," in *European Settlement*, 195, 203; Breen, *Puritans and Adventurers*, 106–126; and Morgan, *American Slavery, American Freedom*, 169–198.

exceptionalists have argued), and few would deny that the environment played an important part in shaping settlers' lives in America. Considering the many adaptations that colonists were forced to make in the New World, it is perhaps unsurprising that historians have been more impressed by change than continuity. The problem is one of emphasis. The stress given to discontinuity has resulted in a seriously flawed view of American society. European settlers did not suddenly become *Americans*, ineluctably brought together as a new people by shared experiences and conditions in the New World. Neither did they abruptly shed their heritage in the face of change. Attitudes, values, and norms, shaped by Old World backgrounds, were just as important in forging their adaptation to colonial society as the environment they encountered. Their intention to create a society resembling the one they left behind might not have been realized, but it cannot be doubted that settlers were highly successful in transferring significant elements of Old World culture to America. The centrality of what Jack P. Greene and J. R. Pole term "inheritance" in the formation of New World societies has lent greater sensitivity to the "traditions, cultural imperatives, and conceptions of the proper social order" that colonists brought with them from Europe.[16] Arguably, cultural continuities have been at least as important as discontinuities in the evolution of American society.

The reluctance of social historians to engage in sustained transatlantic comparisons is perplexing in view of the recognized contribution of Old World cultures to New World society. Immigrants' regional origins have not been prominent in accounts of the development of early America, and with one or two exceptions the significance of English provincial cultures has largely been ignored.[17] The reasons are both methodological and conceptual. Practical difficulties involved in undertaking research on both sides of

16. Greene and Pole, eds., *Colonial British America*, 15–16.

17. The notable exceptions are Sumner Chilton Powell, *Puritan Village: The Formation of a New England Town* (Middletown, Conn., 1963); David Grayson Allen, *In English Ways: The Movement of Societies and the Transferal of English Local Law and Custom to Massachusetts Bay in the Seventeenth Century* (Chapel Hill, N.C., 1982); and, more recently, David Hackett Fischer's massive and idiosyncratic *Albion's Seed: Four British Folkways in America* (Oxford, 1989). Other important studies include Barry Levy, *Quakers and the American Family: British Settlement in the Delaware Valley* (New York, 1988); Ned C. Landsman, *Scotland and Its First American Colony, 1683–1765* (Princeton, N.J., 1985); David Cressy, *Coming Over: Migration and Communication between England and New England in the Seventeenth Century* (Cambridge, 1987); Greene, *Pursuits of Happiness*; Stephen Foster, *The Long Argument: English Puritanism and the Shaping of New England Culture, 1570–1700* (Chapel Hill, N.C., 1991).

the Atlantic and the sheer volume of published work on colonial America and early modern England are daunting. Consequently, American historians have tended to rely on the English canon of social history and on readily available printed sources for comparative perspectives, a practice that has had the serious drawback of allowing, for the most part, only general considerations of the relationship between Old and New World societies. On their side, English social historians have shown little interest in the evolution of colonial societies, believing it to be the province of American, not English, scholars. Few, if any, conceive of colonies as overseas variants of English society. English history is delimited by the historic borders of the kingdom, based on the "premise that English history takes place only in England." Beyond lies terra incognita, different countries with their own historic contexts and agendas. In a number of areas academic isolationism has begun to break down, but Hugh Kearney's opinion expressed in the 1970s, that "nationalist assumptions in English and American historiography are still strong on both sides of the Atlantic," nevertheless remains valid today.[18] Discrete interpretations of English and American history according to the differing emphases (one might say styles) of English and American historians would have made little sense to contemporaries—and make no sense of the vital interconnections between the diverse components of the English Atlantic world.

This work aims to describe the evolution of English society in the seventeenth-century Chesapeake through a comparison of local societies in England, Virginia, and Maryland. The approach and argument depend upon a key aspect of Chesapeake society. Virginia and Maryland were *immigrant* societies: down to the final decades of the century the majority of settlers were born and raised in England, a factor that had far-reaching consequences for social development in the two colonies. The study reconstructs examples of English local society from which settlers came as well as emergent societies along the Bay to which they went, to provide a picture of both the migrants' backgrounds and their adjustment to life in America. Emphasis is given to their experiences: the sorts of backgrounds they came from and the reasons

18. J.G.A. Pocock, "The Limits and Divisions of British History: In Search of the Unknown Subject," *American Historical Review*, LXXXVII (1982), 324; Hugh Kearney, "The Problem of Perspective in the History of Colonial America," in K. R. Andrews *et al.*, eds., *The Westward Enterprise: English Activities in Ireland, the Atlantic, and America, 1480–1650* (Liverpool, 1978), 290. See also Ida Altman, *Emigrants and Society: Extremadura and America in the Sixteenth Century* (Los Angeles, 1989), 1–7.

that encouraged, or forced, them to leave England; their impressions of the Chesapeake; how they adapted to the novel conditions they faced; their experience of family life, the local community, and work; their perceptions of the social order, disorder, and religion. From a transatlantic perspective, a number of questions come to mind: What did immigrants make of their new society? How did it compare to their native communities in England? In what ways did their lives change? How did their English origins shape responses to conditions in the Chesapeake? How successful were they in recreating aspects of life they had left behind?

The method adopted should be made clear. A comparative study linking the social origins of a particular group, or groups, of emigrants from locales in England to the development of particular communities in the Chesapeake is not possible. Immigration to Virginia and Maryland took a different form from that to New England. In the latter, relatively large numbers of people who left from the same areas in England relocated themselves, at least initially, in the same region, or even town.[19] Understandably, the New England town has been an essential focus of study, and the fact that people frequently emigrated in groups from their native communities in England has greatly eased the problem of making comparisons between specific locales in the two societies. Chesapeake settlers typically did not emigrate in groups. Although it has been possible to identify cities such as London and Bristol as major contributors, the great majority of emigrants came from all over central and southern England. Ships arriving in the Chesapeake Bay, as in the case of the *Tristram and Jane*, deposited their human cargo at numerous locations along the tobacco coast; and, since many of the newcomers were poor and young, it has proved difficult to trace them. Because the likelihood of recovering the local English origins of large numbers of settlers of particular Chesapeake counties is remote, this study adopts an indirect comparison between areas in England and the Chesapeake not necessarily related by particular groups of settlers. What can be examined are the cultural terrains of emigrants, whose varied experiences were brought to bear on life in a New World setting.[20]

19. Allen, *In English Ways*, 163–204, 245–290. Richard Archer argues that the family orientation of New England emigration has been exaggerated and that 30%–33% of immigrant males were single when they arrived, in "New England Mosaic: A Demographic Analysis for the Seventeenth Century," *WMQ*, 3d Ser., XLVII (1990), table 3, 482, 487. Differences between Chesapeake and New England immigration might have been less pronounced than some historians have claimed.

20. A few settlers are known to have linked the English and Chesapeake societies selected in this study. Thomas Willoughby (ca. 1599–1657), from Rochester, and

The choice of two regions in England—the Vale of Berkeley, Gloucestershire, and central Kent—was not arbitrary. Both have adequate local and county records for detailed studies, but, more important, they both had strong links with the Chesapeake. Emigrants left from the Vale of Berkeley as early as 1619 to establish a plantation at Berkeley Hundred on the James River. The entire Severn Valley, in which the Vale is located, was a prime recruiting ground for immigrants to Ireland, the West Indies, New England, Virginia, and Maryland. Over the century, and especially during the peak period of emigration from the 1640s to 1660s, the proximity of Bristol encouraged hundreds of young men and women to take ship for America. Kent, especially the area along the Thames Valley, was also an important recruiting ground for emigrants. The county produced a number of highly influential early explorers, colonists, and governors, such as Captain Nathaniel Powell, Samuel Argall, George Sandys, Sir Francis Wyatt, Henry Fleet, and William Claiborne. Moreover, a number of prominent Kentish families, such as Eppes, Digges, Gookins, Filmer, Willoughby, and Brodnax, established important dynasties along the tobacco coast.[21]

Lower Norfolk and Lancaster counties, Virginia, were selected primarily because of the survival of records (both have good sets of court records for the seventeenth century) and also because they represent two quite different regions of the tidewater. Lower Norfolk, south of the James at the entrance of the Chesapeake Bay, was created formally in 1636, and Lancaster County in the Northern Neck, fifteen years later. Their respective locations and dates of settlement had an important bearing on their subsequent development, a point explored in detail below. In addition, material from St. Mary's County, Maryland, has been drawn upon to provide a broader context. These areas do not embrace the entire range of regional variation in the early Chesapeake—historians are aware of important local differences in economic and social structure—but there can be little doubt that together these regions suggest something of the diversity as well as the broad similarities of local society in this period.

Daniel Tanner, from Canterbury, Kent, both settled in Lower Norfolk County, as possibly did Thomas Harding of Thornbury, Gloucestershire, an indentured servant. Henry Fleet of Chartham, Kent, was a prominent gentleman-merchant of early Lancaster County and had connections with St. Mary's County, Maryland. John Catlett, from Sittingbourne, Kent, lived further up the Rappahannock River in the freshes. His half-brother, Ralph Rouzee (Rousey), who emigrated at the same time and settled nearby, was from Ashford in the same county.

21. James Horn, Biographical files for Vale of Berkeley, Gloucestershire, Lower Norfolk and Lancaster counties, Virginia, and immigrants (free and unfree).

No attempt is made to trace the transference of distinctive characteristics of southern Gloucestershire or Kent to the Chesapeake. Owing to the nature of emigration from England and the pattern of settlement along the tobacco coast, no identifiable English provincial culture established itself in, or exerted extensive influence on, Virginia and Maryland society. Certain regions supplied more emigrants than others, of course, and in the first half of the century many areas of the tidewater may have had a decidedly southern or southeastern flavor. Nevertheless, provincial cultures did not have the same impact in the Chesapeake as they apparently did in parts of New England. Neither are the Vale of Berkeley and central Kent conceived as microcosms of English society in toto. Society in both regions was influenced by the general political, economic, and cultural changes that affected other parts of the country in the seventeenth century, but southern Gloucestershire and central Kent do not, nor could, represent the totality of experience of English local communities. The Vale shared a range of characteristics with other wood-pasture areas in southern and central England, and therefore conclusions drawn from an analysis of its society and economy can be placed in the wider context of woodland parishes in other parts of Bristol's hinterland. Central Kent's mixed economy shares similarities with other parts of southern England where a variety of soils encouraged both pastoral and arable husbandry and where, as in woodland regions, manufacturing was important. These broad similarities should not disguise a central feature of early modern local society, however: the sheer diversity of local customs, traditions, and patterns of life that together made up a rich and variegated culture at local and provincial levels.

As will be argued throughout this study, understanding the English context and the cultural assumptions that guided settlers' adaptation to life in Virginia and Maryland is crucial to an analysis of the factors that shaped immigrant experience. Such a perspective provides a means to assess cultural continuity and change in early America and locates the social development of Virginia and Maryland in the broader setting of the seventeenth-century Anglophone world. What might appear to be a distinctively local development in the tidewater might prove on closer inspection to be a variant of contemporary English behavior. The ways by which particular forms of English behavior, values, and attitudes were transplanted and, possibly, transmuted in America are given sharper focus by transatlantic comparison, and the impact of changes in England upon Chesapeake society may better be understood. Although historians usually treat the social history of England and her colonies separately, that approach makes little sense for the lives of the settlers themselves. Immigrant experience was all of a piece, not divided into irreconcilable halves, one English and the other American. Continuing associations between settlers in America and family, kin, and business partners in England, frequently overlooked in national or regional narratives, testify to the enduring significance of transatlantic connections and to the underlying unity of English-American society.

The work falls into three sections. Part I considers the English origins of settlers, first by way of a general description of the different sorts of people who emigrated, where they were from, and what motivated them to leave England (Chapter 1), and second (in Chapter 2) through case studies of the Vale of Berkeley and central Kent that provide a more detailed and vivid impression of their social origins than is possible in a nationwide survey. These two chapters examine both the national and local factors that influenced emigration and portray the types of communities from which settlers came. Part II begins with an interpretive overview of the development of Chesapeake society in the seventeenth century (Chapter 3) and introduces many of the themes considered later. The intention is to explain how new arrivals might have perceived the tidewater and to describe the major social and economic influences that shaped their lives. Chapter 4 returns to the local level and takes a worm's-eye view of the formation of local society along the Bay by focusing on the settlement of Lower Norfolk and Lancaster counties. Parts I and II comprise discrete studies of English and Chesapeake society, and the focus is more descriptive and contextual than analytical. Part III adopts a different approach. Here, the chapters are explicitly comparative; that is, they all draw directly on English as well as Chesapeake material to illustrate their particular themes. Chapter 5 considers attitudes in the two societies toward sex, marriage, the family, and the wider community. Chapter 6 considers working lives and contrasts the experience of work, or what might be termed work culture. Chapter 7 explores material culture through a comparison of standards of living and the domestic environment in the two societies. Chapter 8 examines concepts of order and disorder and patterns of crime, social protest, and rebellion. Finally, Chapter 9 examines the spiritual world of settlers through an investigation of the church, established religion, radicalism, and popular belief. Throughout Part III, the argument is that, while material conditions changed dramatically, inherited attitudes and values did not.

The early history of the Chesapeake is about this disjunction. Traditional attitudes, inherited from their English backgrounds, influenced powerfully the way settlers thought about themselves, social relations, and the institutions of state and church they sought to establish. In Virginia and Maryland, however, inherited values and norms were not easily translated into accepted patterns of social and political behavior as practiced in England. There was no readily available template whereby English society could be duplicated in America. What emerged were improvisations and accommodations. Settlers adapted familiar English ways as best they could to suit themselves and the new conditions. Here is a familiar theme in colonial historiography: European cultures, transformed under the impact of New World environments, gradually gave way to the emergence of a rich diversity of Euro-American cultural hybrids. Undeniable in its central assumptions, this line of reasoning in fact explains little. To argue that moving to America brought significant changes to immigrants' lives, or that settlers were forced into unforeseen adaptations, would appear, on the face of it, obvious. Altogether more remarkable would have been no change. The key questions relate to the nature and pace of adaptation in different parts of English America. Understanding the forms that adaptation took, conditioned by novel circumstances, depends on knowledge of the cultural habits, perceptions, and institutions that English immigrants brought with them to the American shore.

English immigrants did not expect to find a mirror image of England in the Chesapeake. They went to make money, and money was made from tobacco, not from English grains or manufactures. Yet for all the changes, tidewater society was emphatically English, not just in name but in temperament. This is not to deny the importance of the presence of native peoples and Africans, but Anglo-Saxon immigrants thought of themselves as English, were governed by English laws and institutions, followed English religious practices, and shared the same general outlook of English people back home. Consequently, changes that occurred in Virginia and Maryland were molded (interpreted) by English assumptions and attitudes and channeled in peculiarly English forms. Emigration did not constitute a conscious desire to throw off old ways of thought or behavior. It was not a rejection of Old World life. Men and women who moved to the Chesapeake in the seventeenth century saw themselves, not as social outcasts exiled to a foreign land or as a chosen people on God's errand, but as participants in a vibrant and interconnected transatlantic world. This study explores that world.

One

The English Context of Emigration

1

Contrast and Diversity: The Social Origins of

Chesapeake Immigrants

Joseph Bridger immigrated to Virginia in the 1650s and settled in Isle of Wight County, south of the James River, where he quickly established himself as a leading planter-merchant. At his death in 1686 he was one of the wealthiest men in the colony, one of the lucky few who gambled on making a fortune in America and succeeded. He was, however, no threadbare adventurer seeking a new start overseas. Joseph was the third son of Samuel Bridger, a minor gentleman of Dursley, Gloucestershire, whose family had been established in the region for generations. The small market town in which he grew up lies about eighteen miles northeast of Bristol, bordering the rich dairy pastures of the Vale of Berkeley to the west and the broken sheep country of the Cotswold Hills to the east. From the steep hill overlooking the parish, Bridger would have been able to see far across the checkerboard fields, commons, and woodland of the Vale to the broad waters of the River Severn, busy with traffic, and the brooding presence of the Forest of Dean and Cambrian Mountains beyond. In fine weather, the masts and spars of oceangoing vessels awaiting entry to or leaving Bristol for European ports, Ireland, and America would have been just visible in the distance to the south. The particular circumstances that led Bridger to emigrate are unknown, but it is possible that his father's death in 1650 prompted him to cash in his legacy and set himself up in the colonies. Like many of his contemporaries—younger sons, merchants, and petty retailers—he was attracted by the opportunities that beckoned in the New World.[1]

1. John Bennett Boddie, *Seventeenth Century Isle of Wight County, Virginia* . . . (Chicago, 1938), chap. 22; John Smyth, *A Description of the Hundred of Berkeley in the County*

1. View of the Vale of Severn. *By J. Burden. Courtesy of Gloucester City Library*

Elizabeth Johnson was also attracted to the New World, but her story is very different. A spinster of twenty-one years from Sevenoaks, Kent, she sailed from London in 1684 after contracting to serve for four years in Virginia as an indentured servant. Sevenoaks lies thirty miles southeast of London on a greensand ridge known as the Chartland: a poor, hilly country of infertile soils and belts of woodland and waste. The town was an old market center and locally renowned as a rallying point in times of popular unrest. Men from the neighborhood had joined Sir Thomas Wyatt's march on London in 1554 in an abortive attempt to bring down Mary Tudor's government, and nearly a century later the area was repeatedly up in arms—in both senses— against parliamentary rule during the civil wars. Elizabeth was not even born in the 1640s, but it is possible that her parents remembered the "time of troubles." Again, the particular reasons that prompted emigration remain a mystery (nothing is known about her apart from the bare personal details recorded on her indenture), but we can surmise that she left her hometown to find work in London, just as tens of thousands of other young men and women tramped the roads on their way to the capital in this period. She

---

of Gloucester and of Its Inhabitants, vol. III of *The Berkeley Manuscripts*, ed. Sir John Maclean (Gloucester, 1883–1885), 387. The main branch of the Bridger family lived in Slimbridge, a few miles away.

may have fallen on hard times and chosen to try her luck overseas as a last resort, or she may have been persuaded to go by one of the many agents ("spirits") who scoured the taverns and poorer quarters of the city seeking recruits for the colonies. In any event, after leaving England she disappears from the records without trace.[2]

Joseph Bridger and Elizabeth Johnson came from small towns of 1,100–1,600 inhabitants, comprising little more than a few streets arranged haphazardly around a marketplace or green. From any vantage point, the surrounding countryside would have been immediately apparent, and the close interdependency between town and country would have been equally obvious in the everyday meetings between townspeople and villagers. London, by contrast, was qualitatively and quantitatively in a class of its own: a rapidly expanding metropolis of thousands of streets and 400,000 inhabitants by the second half of the century. New arrivals from the provinces gazed in wonder, or shock, at the crowded thoroughfares and markets crammed with merchandise, the seemingly endless vista of houses, shops, stately buildings, and churches, all contained in a few square miles between Westminster and Limehouse. A city of stark contrasts: great wealth and abject poverty, plenty and want, magnificence and squalor coexisted side by side and were taken for granted by contemporaries with little comment.[3]

2. C.D.P. Nicholson, "Some Early Emigrants to America," *Genealogists' Magazine*, XII, nos. 1–16 (1955–1958), XIII, nos. 1–8 (1959–1961), entry 636; Alan Everitt, *Continuity and Colonization: The Evolution of Kentish Settlement* (Leicester, 1986), 50; Everitt, *The Community of Kent and the Great Rebellion, 1640–60* (Leicester, 1966), 190–194, 196–197, 200, 216; Peter Clark, *English Provincial Society from the Reformation to the Revolution: Religion, Politics, and Society in Kent, 1500–1640* (Hassocks, 1977), 88. Indentured servants, like Johnson, usually served from four to seven years (but sometimes much longer), in payment for the cost of their passage, board, lodging, and freedom dues. "Spinster" was the legal term of the period.

For migration within England and its connection with transatlantic emigration, see David Souden, " 'Rogues, Whores, and Vagabonds'?: Indentured Servant Emigrants to North America and the Case of Mid-Seventeenth-Century Bristol," *Social History*, III (1978), 23–41; James Horn, "Servant Emigration to the Chesapeake in the Seventeenth Century," in Thad W. Tate and David L. Ammerman, eds., *The Chesapeake in the Seventeenth Century: Essays on Anglo-American Society* (Chapel Hill, N.C., 1979), 73–74; John Wareing, "Migration to London and Transatlantic Emigration of Indentured Servants, 1683–1775," *Journal of Historical Geography*, VII (1981), 356–378.

3. C. R. Elrington, "The Surveys of Church Livings in Gloucestershire, 1650," *Bristol and Gloucestershire Archaeological Society*, LXXXIII (1964), 85–98; E179/247/13, 14, 16 (Hearth Tax), Public Record Office; C. W. Chalklin, *Seventeenth-Century Kent: A Social and Economic History* (London, 1965), 36. Ralph Bigland, *Historical, Monumental, and*

2. View of the River Thames. *By Wenceslaus Hollar. Permission of the British Library*

For as many as three-quarters of immigrants to Virginia and Maryland, the bustling streets, markets, and docks of the city were their final memory of England. Their backgrounds varied enormously. Those at the very bottom of society either lived on the streets or scratched out a precarious existence in the slums before indenturing themselves. Thomas Poyner and Mary Tate were "taken up late at night," probably for vagrancy, and committed to New Prison in the summer of 1685. Since no charges were made against them and "they were not married nor apprentices," they were allowed to contract themselves for four years' labor in Maryland. William Sommersett, "lately living in Whitechappell not knowing where to find his father or how to get his living," was bound to John Seaman of Virginia in 1684, and James Rither,

Genealogical Collections Relative to the County of Gloucester, ed. Richard Bigland, 2 vols. (London, 1791–1792), I, 511; A. L. Beier and Roger Finlay, eds., *London 1500–1700: The Making of the Metropolis* (London, 1986), 2–4. See also Roger Finlay, *Population and Metropolis: The Demography of London, 1580–1650* (Cambridge, 1981), 51; Jeremy Boulton, *Neighbourhood and Society: A London Suburb in the Seventeenth Century* (Cambridge, 1987), 1–5; E. Anthony Wrigley, "Urban Growth and Agricultural Change: England and the Continent in the Early Modern Period," *Journal of Interdisciplinary History*, XV (1984–1985), 683–728; Bernard Bailyn, *Voyagers to the West: A Passage in the Peopling of America on the Eve of the Revolution* (New York, 1986), 273–274.

who emigrated at the age of thirteen, was described as "having no friends." At the other end of the social scale, provincial merchants and gentlemen such as Henry Fleet or Henry Corbin developed important connections and financial backing in the City before eventually settling in the Chesapeake.[4]

4. Michael Ghirelli, *A List of Emigrants from England to America, 1682–1692* (Baltimore, 1968), 66; Lord Mayor's Waiting Books, XIII, entry for July 14, 1684, XIV, fol. 459, Guildhall Library, London; Henry Fleet, "Henry Fleet of Fleet's Bay, Virginia, 1600–1660," *Northern Neck Historical Magazine*, XII (1962), 1068–1076; Darrett B. Rutman and Anita H. Rutman, *A Place in Time: Middlesex County, Virginia, 1650–1750* (New York, 1984), 50–51.

The proportion of immigrants to Virginia and Maryland includes migrants from other parts of the country who took ship from London. For a modern estimate of the proportion of London emigrants who went to the Chesapeake, see Russell R. Menard, "British Migration to the Chesapeake Colonies in the Seventeenth Century," in Lois Green Carr, Philip D. Morgan, and Jean B. Russo, eds., *Colonial Chesapeake Society* (Chapel Hill, N.C., 1988), 123.

Quotations from primary sources follow original spelling, punctuation, and capitalization with the following exceptions: thorns and ampersands are expanded, tildes are omitted, letters are brought down to the line, initial and terminal ellipses are omitted, and the resultant syntactic sentences are punctuated and capitalized conventionally.

Wealthy emigrants might have occasionally suffered discomfort staying in London en route to the colonies, but they inhabited a different world, compared to the hardships endured by poor migrants.

South Gloucestershire, Kent, and London hardly do justice to the diversity of local cultures from which emigrants came, but they serve as three examples of areas that produced large numbers of Chesapeake settlers in the seventeenth century and suggest something of the profound differences between colonists—their social backgrounds, regional origins, and reasons for leaving England—all of which had a vital influence on their prospects and opportunities in America and how quickly, if ever, they adapted to the New World.

A Diverse Multitude: Social Characteristics

"*English* ground in *America*" is how one contemporary described Virginia in 1649. It was an apt description. The great majority of men and women who settled in North America during the seventeenth century were of English origin, despite significant contributions from other parts of Britain as well as Europe and Africa. Of the 500,000 or so people who left England in the period, approximately 400,000 went to America, a ratio of emigrants to domestic population greater than from any other part of Europe. Most went to colonies that produced the major staples of colonial trade, tobacco and sugar: some 225,000 went to the Caribbean, 120,000 to the Chesapeake, and the remainder to New England and the Middle Colonies. In the context of the emergent transatlantic economy, New England remained a backwater, compared to the plantation colonies to the south.[5]

5. Colonel [Henry] Norwood, *A Voyage to Virginia* (1649), in Peter Force, comp., *Tracts and Other Papers, Relating Principally to the Origin, Settlement, and Progress of the Colonies in North America, from the Discovery of the Country to the Year 1776*, 4 vols. (1836–1846; Gloucester, Mass., 1963), III, no. 10, p. 47; Bailyn, *Voyagers to the West*, 24; Henry A. Gemery, "Emigration from the British Isles to the New World, 1630–1700: Inferences from Colonial Populations," *Research in Economic History*, V (1980), 179–231; John J. McCusker and Russell R. Menard, *The Economy of British America, 1607–1789*, rev. ed. (Chapel Hill, N.C., 1991), 102–103, 214–217; Gloria L. Main, *Tobacco Colony: Life in Early Maryland, 1650–1720* (Princeton, N.J., 1982), 10–16; E. A. Wrigley and R. S. Schofield, *The Population History of England, 1541–1871: A Reconstruction* (Cambridge, Mass., 1981), 469–472. On New England, see Daniel Vickers, *Farmers and Fishermen: Two Centuries of Work in Essex County, Massachusetts, 1630–1850* (Chapel Hill, N.C., 1994).

The peak period of emigration occurred within a single generation, from 1630 to 1660, but the rapid growth of the tobacco industry created a constant demand in the Chesapeake for cheap labor and capital throughout the century. Virginia and Maryland were consequently *immigrant societies*, highly sensitive to the social composition of new arrivals and closely attuned to demographic and social changes in England. Like London, the two colonies depended on large-scale immigration from English provinces to maintain their populations and allow economic growth. Without sustained immigration they would have collapsed.[6]

Emigrants generally fell into two categories: those who paid their own passage and those who could not afford the fare and went under some form of labor contract, such as indentured servants. The size of free emigration is conjectural, but between twenty thousand and thirty-five thousand is the probable range (toward the lower end is more likely, around twenty-five thousand). This figure implies that, across the century, indentured servants outnumbered free emigrants by about three or four to one.[7]

Free emigrants shared a number of similarities with servants. The majority were young, male, and single and came predominantly from the same regions: London, the Southeast, and a broad band of counties stretching from the Thames Valley to the West Country. Factors that influenced free migration also influenced unfree migration: the propensity to move while young and unmarried, contacts with mercantile communities, and proximity to major ports. These considerations suggest that free migration was not autonomous of the general forces that shaped the movement of people within England and abroad in this period.[8] There were also obvious differences,

6. Horn, "Servant Emigration," in Tate and Ammerman, eds., *Chesapeake in the Seventeenth Century*, 51; Menard, "British Migration," in Carr, Morgan, and Russo, eds., *Colonial Chesapeake Society*, 99–132; Menard, "The Tobacco Industry in the Chesapeake Colonies, 1617–1730: An Interpretation," *Res. Econ. Hist.*, V (1980), 109–177.

7. These estimates are based on the assumption that approximately 120,000 settlers immigrated to Virginia and Maryland in the 17th century, of whom 70%–85% were indentured servants. If, as is likely, the proportion of servants is nearer the upper bound, then a figure of about 25,000 free emigrants is probable. For a discussion of free emigrants, see James Horn, " 'To Parts beyond the Seas': Free Emigration to the Chesapeake in the Seventeenth Century," in Ida Altman and Horn, eds., *"To Make America": European Emigration in the Early Modern Period* (Los Angeles, 1991), 85–130.

8. E. E. Rich, "The Population of Elizabethan England," *Economic History Review*, 2d Ser., II (1949–1950), 263–264; Horn, "Servant Emigration," in Tate and Ammerman, eds., *Chesapeake in the Seventeenth Century*, 66–74; Souden, " 'Rogues, Whores, and Vagabonds'?" *Soc. Hist.*, III (1978), 23–41; Anthony Salerno, "The Social Background

notably higher social status, the possession of capital, and important business or kinship connections with planters, merchants, and officials, which
set the free settlers apart from indentured servants decisively.

Evidence from a wide range of primary and secondary sources yields more
than six hundred biographies of free emigrants whose English origins are
known.[9] What is immediately striking about the occupations and status of
male emigrants is the high proportion claiming gentry origins (see Table 1).
This is partly a reflection of the high visibility of gentry in the sources and
the tendency of scions of the middling classes to accord themselves gentry status in America. However, sons of gentlemen were prominent in the
early years of settlement. Captain John Smith, an early governor of Virginia,
wrote of the multitude of "Masters" and "Gentlemen" who "could doe nothing but complaine, curse, and despaire." "One hundred good labourers," he

---

of Seventeenth-Century Emigration to America," *Journal of British Studies*, XIX (1979),
31–52; Peter Clark and David Souden, eds., *Migration and Society in Early Modern
England* (London, 1987), chap. 1.

9. Biographical files of free emigrants were compiled from a wide range of sources.
An enormous amount of genealogical material exists, much of which can be found in
the *Virginia Magazine of History and Biography*, the *William and Mary Quarterly*, 1st and
2d series, and *Tyler's Quarterly Historical Magazine*, besides specialist family histories.
Testamentary evidence is also voluminous but less readily accessible; the same can
be said of court records both in England and in the Chesapeake. Literary sources—
letters, journals, diaries—are much less common, but see the *WMQ* for some examples of 17th-century correspondence. Especially valuable for tracing free emigrants
(besides the above) are W. G. Stanard, comp., *Some Emigrants to Virginia* . . . , 2d
ed. (Richmond, Va., 1915); William Hand Browne et al., eds., *Archives of Maryland*,
72 vols. to date (Baltimore, 1883–) (hereafter *Md. Arch.*); Susan Myra Kingsbury, ed.,
The Records of the Virginia Company of London . . . , 4 vols. (Washington D. C., 1906–
1935); Alexander Brown, *The Genesis of the United States*, 2 vols. (Boston, 1890); H. R.
McIlwaine, ed., *Minutes of the Council and General Court of Colonial Virginia* . . . (Richmond, Va., 1924); [Annie Lash Jester and Martha Woodroof Hiden, eds.], *Adventurers
of Purse and Person, Virginia, 1607–1624/5*, 3d ed., rev., ed. Virginia M. Meyer and John
Frederick Dorman (Richmond, Va., 1987); and Nell Marion Nugent, comp., *Cavaliers
and Pioneers: Abstracts of Virginia Land Patents and Grants*, 2 vols. (Richmond, Va., 1934,
1977). More evidence would be unlikely to alter the fact that the backgrounds of the
vast majority are forever lost. The key question, then, is, To what extent is this sample
representative of free emigration as a whole? There is an obvious bias toward wealthy
and high-status immigrants; middling groups and poorer elements are less visible,
as are women, who make only fleeting appearances in the records. Nonetheless, sufficient material exists to construct an outline of free settlers' origins and the main
impulses that governed emigration in this period.

TABLE 1

Occupational Status of Free Male Emigrants from England to the Chesapeake,
1607–1699

Status or Occupational Group	All Emigrants		London Emigrants		As % of All Emigrants
	No.	%	No.	%	
Gentry	132	30.6	21	11.5	15.9
Professions	34	7.9	7	3.8	20.5
Merchants	119	27.6	52	28.6	43.7
Mariners	19	4.4	5	2.7	26.3
Food, drink, and supply trades	38	8.8	34	18.7	89.5
Clothing and allied trades	41	9.5	32	17.6	78.0
Leather trade	7	1.6	4	2.2	57.1
Building trades and woodworking	15	3.5	14	7.7	93.3
Metalworking trades	9	2.1	7	3.8	77.7
Agriculture	14	3.2	6	3.3	42.9
Semiskilled and unskilled labor	3	.7	0		
Overall	431	99.9	182	99.9	42.2

Note: Deviations from 100.0% in tables are due to rounding.

Sources: W. G. Stanard, comp., *Some Emigrants to Virginia . . .* , 2d ed. (Richmond, Va., 1915); William Hand Browne *et al.*, eds. *Archives of Maryland*, 72 vols. to date (Baltimore, 1883–); Susan Myra Kingsbury, ed., *The Records of the Virginia Company of London . . .* , 4 vols. (Washington, D.C., 1906–1935); Alexander Brown, *The Genesis of the United States*, 2 vols. (Boston, 1890); H. R. McIlwaine, ed., *Minutes of the Council and General Court of Colonial Virginia . . .* (Richmond, Va., 1924); [Annie Lash Jester and Martha Woodroof Hiden, eds.], *Adventurers of Purse and Person, Virginia, 1607–1624/5*, 3d ed., rev., ed. Virginia M. Meyer and John Frederick Dorman (Richmond, Va., 1987); Nell Marion Nugent, comp., *Cavaliers and Pioneers: Abstracts of Virginia Land Patents and Grants*, 2 vols. (Richmond, Va., 1934, 1977).

remarked, would have been "better than a thousand such Gallants as were sent me." More than half of the 105 men and boys who founded Jamestown in 1607 were described as gentlemen, and 33 men who arrived in the following year were from gentry stock. Some came from aristocratic families. George Percy, who sailed with the first expedition, was the eighth son of the earl of Northumberland. He was about twenty-six when he arrived in Virginia and had previously served as a soldier in the Netherlands. George Sandys, treasurer of Virginia in the 1620s, was the son of the archbishop of Canterbury and brother of Edwin, an influential member of the Virginia Company and important London merchant.[10]

The founders of Maryland in 1634 included a number of wealthy Catholic gentry, such as the Calverts, Thomas Cornwallis, and Jerome Hawley, all of whom invested heavily in the new colony. Lord Baltimore's vision was to erect a New World aristocracy that would control land, labor, and political office. To ensure the development of a well-ordered society, it was considered vital to attract men of substance and status to oversee the transfer of English institutions to America, enforce the law, and provide governance. The Calverts sought to attract gentry immigrants by granting manorial privileges with large tracts of land and thereby to create a hierarchical society based on land and rents familiar to them in England and Ireland. The attempt failed. Baltimore's plans foundered during the 1640s owing to internal dissension and the phenomenal growth of the tobacco industry, which led to a rapid rise in the fortunes of small and middling planters. Efforts to promote a rigidly stratified society collapsed as new wealth brought about the emergence of a homegrown elite that challenged the political power of Baltimore's aristocracy.[11] Similarly, in Virginia, important gentry who arrived in the first couple of decades rarely stayed more than a few years before returning home. Throughout the rest of the century there was a steady if small flow of gentlemen to the Chesapeake, mainly younger sons, but no direct transfer of England's ruling classes.

In the absence of a *nobilitas major*, an elite emerged out of the fusion of minor or middling gentry and men from mercantile backgrounds. There was frequently no clear distinction between them. The younger son of a provincial squire commonly took up trading and became, in Moll Flanders's words, a "Gentleman-Tradesman." Maurice Thompson, one of the greatest colonial merchants of his day, was born in 1604 to a Hertfordshire gentry family. His brother-in-law, William Tucker, was also a leading London merchant but

10. William A. Reavis, "The Maryland Gentry and Social Mobility, 1637–1676," *WMQ*, 3d Ser., XIV (1957), 418–428. Philip L. Barbour, ed., *The Complete Works of Captain John Smith (1580–1631)* (Chapel Hill, N.C., 1986), II, 140–142, 160–162, III, 272; Bernard Bailyn, "Politics and Social Structure in Virginia," in James Morton Smith, ed., *Seventeenth-Century America: Essays in Colonial History* (Chapel Hill, N.C., 1959), 92.

11. Russell Robert Menard, "Economy and Society in Early Colonial Maryland" (Ph.D. diss., University of Iowa, 1975), 32–35, 38, 70–71, 111–141; Garry Wheeler Stone, "Manorial Maryland," *Maryland Historical Magazine*, LXXXII (1987), 5–6; Russell R. Menard et al., "Opportunity and Inequality: The Distribution of Wealth on the Lower Western Shore of Maryland, 1638–1705," *Md. Hist. Mag.*, LXIX (1974), 181.

styled himself "Esquire" in his will.[12] By virtue of immigrating to the tobacco coast, most gentry became merchants and active managers of plantations, and some large merchants dignified themselves with the title of gentleman.

A large group of merchants from the lower and middling echelons of England's trading community, however, had no pretensions toward gentility. America opened up bright new horizons for small traders because, unlike the Levant and Far Eastern trades dominated by powerful mercantile monopolies, transatlantic commerce was free to all comers. By 1640, from London alone 330 merchants were involved in the tobacco trade, compared to only 57 active Levant merchants. A great expansion of commerce took place at midcentury owing to the rapid growth of the tobacco industry and the increasing involvement of merchants from English outports, notably Bristol. Most new merchants of mid-seventeenth-century London came from the middle tiers of society and frequently spent the early part of their careers in a variety of City occupations—as shopkeepers, domestic tradesmen, mariners, or smaller merchants in noncolonial trades.

Since the tobacco trade involved the production of leaf as well as its marketing, many colonial merchants found themselves settling temporarily or permanently in the Chesapeake. Thomas Burbage and George Menefie, two important planter-merchants, led quasiamphibious lives crossing and recrossing the Atlantic on numerous occasions. They were as at home in the busy streets of the metropolis as in the land-water expanse of the tidewater. Another merchant, George Faulkner, deposed in the late 1650s that he had traded to Virginia for sixteen years and after the first voyage had lived in the colony for twelve months. He returned to London and then moved to nearby Deptford, where he had only a small estate, "having suffered great losses at sea." There was often a close connection between merchants and men involved in the victualing trades: cheesemongers, grocers, brewers, fishmongers, and salters. William Harris and Thomas Deacon, London cheesemongers, formed partnerships with both Maurice Thompson and William Tucker in the late 1630s and settled briefly in Virginia about the same time.[13] As noted above, many merchants had themselves been involved in provisioning or shopkeeping before moving into colonial trade.

12. Daniel Defoe, *Moll Flanders*, ed. Edward Kelly (New York, 1975), 48; Robert Paul Brenner, "Commercial Change and Political Conflict: The Merchant Community in Civil War London" (Ph.D. diss., Princeton University, 1970), 113–115, 126–127, 132; Stanard, comp., *Some Emigrants*, 83–84.

13. Brenner, "Commercial Change," 76–77, 83–84, 115, and chap. 3 generally; Jacob M. Price and Paul G. E. Clemens, "A Revolution of Scale in Overseas Trade: British Firms in the Chesapeake Trade, 1675–1775," *Journal of Economic History*, XLVII

TABLE 2

Age of Free Male Emigrants from England to the Chesapeake, 1607–1699

Age Group	No.	%	Cumulative %
0–15	3	3.1	3.1
15–19	10	10.2	13.3
20–24	26	26.5	39.8
25–29	17	17.3	57.1
30–34	18	18.4	75.5
35–39	11	11.2	86.7
40–44	7	7.1	93.8
45+	6	6.1	99.9
Total	98	99.9	

Sources: See Table 1.

Other occupations (Table 1) are largely unremarkable. Forty-one settlers had been engaged in clothing or textile trades before emigrating, including five haberdashers, three tailors, two pointmakers, two sergemakers, a silkweaver, clothworkers, and a linen draper. It is doubtful that they hoped to practice their crafts in Virginia or Maryland. Tailors could expect to find employment part-time, but there was little domestic cloth production until the end of the century. More probably, they had fallen on hard times and converted their remaining funds into capital to finance setting up a modest tobacco plantation. A small proportion of emigrants (5.6 percent) came from artisanal backgrounds, such as carpenter, joiner, mason, and blacksmith. Plantation economy did not require numerous specialist crafts, and conditions in the colonies were not attractive enough to encourage skilled workers to emigrate in large numbers while there was plenty of work in England. Neither did the tobacco coast hold much appeal for men from farming backgrounds. Yeomen and husbandmen were reluctant to exchange their holdings in England for Chesapeake plantations. Those who chose or were forced to give up their land may have been too poor to afford the cost of setting up a plantation of their own and joined the ranks of indentured servants, laboring for a living.

One analysis of free men suggests that about two-fifths were under twenty-five and three-fifths were under thirty (Table 2). Free emigrants were

(1987), 2–4, 9–27, 37; Peter Wilson Coldham, ed., *English Adventurers and Emigrants, 1609–1660* (Baltimore, 1984), 23, 76, 78, 158.

typically older than indentured servants, many of whom left England while still in their teens. Older age is a reflection of the higher status of free emigrants and the fact that they had usually established themselves in a trade before moving to the colonies. What little evidence exists suggests most were single. Of 169 settlers, male and female, free and unfree, who left London for Virginia in 1635, only 7 (4.1 percent) were members of family groups, compared to more than half the New England emigrants who sailed for Massachusetts in the same year. Single men formed the largest proportion of free immigrants into Maryland from 1634 to 1681: of 122 men studied, 71 were single, 49 were married, and 2 were widowers. Bachelors who settled in the Chesapeake commonly married women servants or, in some cases, returned to England for a bride. The sex ratio among free emigrants (239.2 men per 100 women) did not compensate for the imbalance between male and female indentured servants, which for most of the century was about 3 men for every woman.[14]

The social character of indentured servants was much commented upon during the seventeenth century. "Virginia and Barbadoes," according to Sir Josiah Child, "were first peopled by a sort of loose vagrant People, vicious and destitute of means to live at home, (being either unfit for labour, or such as could find none to employ themselves about, or had so mis-behaved themselves by Whoreing, Thieving, or other Debauchery, that none would set them to work)." William Bullock agreed. Servants, he wrote in 1649, were "idle, lazie, simple people . . . such as have professed idlenesse, and will rather beg then work." "Among those who repair to Bristol from all parts to be transported for servants to his Majesty's plantations beyond seas," the mayor of Bristol complained in 1662, "some are husbands that have forsaken their wives, others wives who have abandoned their husbands; some are children and apprentices run away from their parents and masters; oftentimes unwary and credulous persons [that] have been tempted on board by men-stealers, and many that have been pursued by hue-and-cry for robberies, burglaries, or breaking prison, do thereby escape the prosecution of law and justice."[15] Political writers in favor of emigration, as well as those opposed, concurred that servants were low, base people.

14. Horn, "Servant Emigration," in Tate and Ammerman, eds., *Chesapeake in the Seventeenth Century*, 57–59, 63; Menard, "British Emigration," in Carr, Morgan, and Russo, eds., *Colonial Chesapeake Society*, 117–121.

15. Sir Josiah Child, *A New Discourse of Trade* . . . (London, 1693), 170; William Bullock, *Virginia Impartially Examined* . . . (London, 1649), 14; W. Noel Sainsbury *et*

Servants came from a broad spectrum of working people, ranging from the destitute and desperate to the lower-middle classes.[16] From the occu-

---

al., eds., *Calendar of State Papers*, Colonial Series, *America and West Indies* (London, 1860–), V, no. 331, cited by Abbot Emerson Smith, *Colonists in Bondage: White Servitude and Convict Labor in America, 1607–1776* (Chapel Hill, N.C., 1947), 82–83.

16. Lists of men and women who sailed for America from Bristol, London, Liverpool, and minor outports provide the most important source for reconstructing the social origins of indentured servants. Since much research has been done on this subject, there is no need to go into detail. What is presented here is a summary of the main findings.

The Bristol lists are contained in four manuscript volumes: "Servants to forraign plantations, 1654–1663," 04220 (1), "Servants to forraign plantacons, 1663–1679," 04220 (2), "Actions and Apprentices," 04355 (6), and "Actions and Apprentices," 04356 (1), Bristol Record Office. These lists have been partially transcribed by N. Dermott Harding and R. Hargreaves-Mawdsley, eds., *Bristol and America: A Record of the First Settlers in the Colonies of North America, 1654–1685* (London, 1929). A more recent and accurate transcript has been made by Noel Currer-Briggs, ed., "Indentured Servants from Bristol to America, 1654–1686" (MS). I am grateful to Mr. Currer-Briggs for allowing me to use his transcript. The London list of servants of 1682–1692 may be found in the Lord Mayor's Waiting Books, XIII–XV, in the Guildhall Library, London. They have been transcribed by Ghirelli, *List of Emigrants*. The original indentures of the servants who left London between 1683 and 1684 are in the Greater London Record Office, but see the transcripts by Nicholson, "Some Early Emigrants," and by John Wareing, "Some Early Emigrants to America, 1683–84; A Supplementary List," *Genealogists' Magazine*, XVIII (1975–1976), 239–246. The Liverpool list has been transcribed by Elizabeth French, in "List of Emigrants to America from Liverpool, 1697–1707," *New England Historical and Genealogical Register*, LXIV (1910), LXV (1911). Finally, a list of more than 2,000 emigrants who went to Virginia in 1635 can be found in John Camden Hotten, ed., *The Original Lists of Persons of Quality . . . and Others Who Went from Great Britain to the American Plantations, 1600–1700* (London, 1874), 35–138. Seminal studies are A. E. Smith, *Colonists in Bondage*; and Mildred Campbell, "Social Origins of Some Early Americans," in J. M. Smith, ed., *Seventeenth-Century America*, 63–89. See also David W. Galenson, " 'Middling People' or 'Common Sort'?: The Social Origins of Some Early Americans Reexamined," *WMQ*, 3d Ser., XXXV (1978), 499–524; Galenson, *White Servitude in Colonial America: An Economic Analysis* (Cambridge, 1981); Souden, " 'Rogues, Whores, and Vagabonds'?" *Soc. Hist.*, III (1978), 23–41; Horn, "Servant Emigration," in Tate and Ammerman, eds., *Chesapeake in the Seventeenth Century*, 51–95; Salerno, "Social Background of Seventeenth-Century Emigration," *Jour. Brit. Stud.*, XIX (1979), 31–52; Wareing, "Migration to London," *Jour. Hist. Geog.*, VII (1981), 356–378; Menard, "British Emigration," in Carr, Morgan, and Russo, eds., *Colonial Chesapeake Society*, 99–132; Henry A. Gemery, "Markets for Migrants: English Indentured Servitude and Emigration in the Seventeenth and Eighteenth Centuries," in P. C. Emmer, ed., *Colonialism and Migration: Indentured Labour before and after Slavery* (Dordrecht, 1986), 33–54.

pational background of servants who emigrated from Bristol and London between 1654 and 1686 (summarized in Table 3), four main groups stand out: farmers, laborers, men from skilled trades and services, and youths apparently without trades. Approaching half the servants who emigrated from Bristol, 1654–1686, described themselves as coming from agricultural backgrounds. The next-largest group came from the semiskilled and unskilled category, of which laborers formed the majority. This distribution was not constant over time. In the 1650s and 1660s, the largest group of male servants with registered occupations was from farming backgrounds, followed by men from the textile industry and clothing trades. By the 1680s, the numbers of Bristol servants from farming occupations had dropped significantly while men from textile and clothing trades, together with laborers, increased.[17]

The London servants of 1683–1684 portray a different occupational structure. Semiskilled and unskilled workers formed the largest category, with 28 percent of the total, followed by men from farming backgrounds with 24 percent. Like the Bristol servants, clothing and textile workers composed 15 percent of the men listed, but, unlike Bristol, a much larger proportion came from low-grade professional work such as accounting and clerical work. To an extent, differences in occupational structure between Bristol and London servants reflect the much higher proportion of men from urban backgrounds in the London sample, but they may also suggest that servants who emigrated during the last twenty years of the century were of lower status, compared to the earlier period. The short-term decrease of England's population after 1650, generally favorable harvests, and rising wage rates compelled fewer poor to look abroad for work, and the pace of emigration declined. Consequently, by the 1680s and 1690s, colonial merchants may have had to look lower down the social scale to the unskilled and youths for indentured servants.[18]

From the earliest years of colonization, destitute men, women, and children had been rounded up from London's streets and shipped to the colonies. Between 1640 and 1660, when large numbers of laborers were recruited for the West Indies, merchants shipping servants to Virginia and Maryland

17. Horn, "Servant Emigration," in Tate and Ammerman, eds., *Chesapeake in the Seventeenth Century*, 57–59; Galenson, *White Servitude*, 34–50. Of the occupations of the fathers of 129 servants who emigrated from London between 1682 and 1686, 11.6% were from agricultural origins, 17.8% from food, drink, and distributive trades, 18.6% from the clothing and textile industries. Nearly a quarter came from unskilled jobs (Ghirelli, *List of Emigrants*).

18. Galenson, *White Servitude*, 48–50; Gemery, "Markets for Migrants," in Emmer, ed., *Colonialism and Migration*, 40–45.

TABLE 3

Occupational Status of Male Indentured Servant Emigrants from Bristol and London to the Chesapeake, 1654–1686

| | Emigrants | | | |
| | To Chesapeake | | To All Colonies | |
Status or Occupational Group	No.	%	No.	%
Bristol Servants, 1654–1686				
Gentry and professions	9	1.7	44	2.3
Food, drink, and supply trades	15	2.8	55	2.9
Clothing and allied trades	78	14.5	282	14.9
Leather trade	26	4.8	101	5.3
Building trades and woodworking	29	5.4	125	6.6
Metalworking trades	14	2.6	62	3.3
Agriculture	252	46.9	910	48.0
Semiskilled and unskilled labor	112	20.9	310	16.4
Miscellaneous	2	.4	6	.3
Total	537	100.0	1,895	100.0
London Servants, 1683–1684				
Gentry and professions	16	12.2	28	11.0
Food, drink, and supply trades	3	2.3	10	3.9
Clothing and allied trades	19	14.5	36	14.2
Leather trade	10	7.6	14	5.5
Building trades and woodworking	10	7.6	22	8.7
Metalworking trades	2	1.5	17	6.7
Agriculture	31	23.7	59	23.2
Semiskilled and unskilled labor	37	28.2	59	23.2
Miscellaneous	3	2.3	9	3.5
Total	131	99.9	254	99.9

Sources: Bristol servants, 1654–1686: "Servants to forraign plantations, 1654–1663," Bristol Record Office 04220 (1); "Servants to forraign plantacons, 1663–1679," BRO 04220 (2); "Actions and Apprentices," BRO 04355 (6); "Actions and Apprentices," BRO 04356 (1); Noel Currer-Briggs, ed., "Indentured Servants from Bristol to America, 1654–1686" (MS). London servants, 1683–1684: C.D.P. Nicholson, "Some Early Emigrants to America," *Genealogists' Magazine,* XII, nos. 1–16 (1955–1958), XIII, nos. 1–8 (1959–1961), and John Wareing, "Some Early Emigrants to America, 1683–84; A Supplementary List," XVIII, no. 5 (1975–1976), 239–246.

probably had to take whomsoever they could get, even the poor and un-skilled. The social character of Chesapeake servants was therefore influenced not simply by supply factors but also by the competition for laborers from other colonies. While the volume of servant recruitment was higher in the first half of the century than the second, so was demand. Across the entire period, merchants routinely recruited from the lowest echelons of the working classes as well as from the middling and upper tiers of working people. Accurate estimates of changes in the social origins of servants during the century will remain elusive, given the paucity of reliable evidence for London (the major port of embarkation) and changes in the registration of servants in both Bristol and London.[19]

Age at emigration confirms the generally humble social standing of indentured servants.[20] The most likely age was 15–24, with 20–21 predominating (Table 4), but servants who were not registered at their port of departure and who consequently served according to the "Custome of the Country" were even younger. Only 32 of 296 servants without indentures who arrived in Lancaster County, Virginia, between 1662 and 1680 were 19 or over. The median age was 16, although 133 (45 percent) were younger. Eight "Irish boyes" transported to Maryland in 1654 were "not above tenn yeares of age and many of them not neere soe much." Four were "soe little" that the wife of one of the purchasers was surprised they did not have "Cradles to have Rocked

19. The issue is further complicated by changes in the registration of servant occupations. Available figures (Table 3) are based on registered occupations only and do not take into account the large proportion of men (between 30% and 60%) whose occupations were not recorded. In the Bristol list, for example, laborers were recorded much less frequently than other occupations after 1655. Reasons for changes in registration are obscure. Possibly as the volume of work increased, clerks began abbreviating entries by omitting the occupations of unskilled men or those who had no obvious trade. If so, the figures greatly underestimate the number of unskilled laborers and youths. As many as half the servants who emigrated from Bristol may have fallen into this category, and a similar, if not larger, proportion of London servants. Thus, only 36% of men from London, 1683–1684, had their former occupations recorded. Bristol registration was higher (64.5% between 1654 and 1660), but within these years fluctuations are severe; see Galenson, " 'Middling People' or 'Common Sort'?" *WMQ*, 3d Ser., XXXV (1978), 499–524.

20. The length of a servant's period of servitude gives a rough idea of age at emigration. Adults usually served four or five years, and children served until they reached majority. On this basis, 84% of servants leaving Bristol from 1654 to 1660 were over age 21; see David Souden, " 'To Forraign Plantacons': Indentured Servant Emigration, c. 1650–1660" (B.A. diss., Cambridge University, 1976), table 3:2, p. 24.

TABLE 4

Age of Indentured Servant Emigrants from London and Liverpool to the Chesapeake,
1635–1707

Age	% of London Servants, 1635 (N)		% of London Servants, 1682–1686 and 1683–1684 (N)		% of Liverpool Servants, 1697–1707 (N)	
	Males (1,740)	Females (271)	Males (414)	Females (159)	Males (518)	Females (284)
0–15	3.8	3.0	6.5	1.9	23.0	4.2
15–19	27.4	30.0	21.0	25.8	32.0	30.6
20–24	39.9	48.1	51.0	57.2	26.8	46.5
25–29	14.2	11.1	12.6	11.9	9.5	13.6
30–34	8.5	4.1	8.0	2.5	5.4	3.5
35–39	3.2	1.5	.2	.6	1.9	1.4
40–44	1.6	.7	.2	0	1.0	.4
45+	1.4	1.5	.5	0	.4	0
Total	100.0	100.0	100.0	99.9	100.0	100.0

Sources: London servants, 1635: John Camden Hotten, ed., *The Original Lists of Persons of Quality . . . and Others Who Went from Great Britain to the American Plantations, 1600–1700* (London, 1874), 35–138. London servants, 1682–1686, 1683–1684: Michael Ghirelli, *A List of Emigrants from England to America, 1682–1692* (Baltimore, 1968); C.D.P. Nicholson, "Some Early Emigrants to America," *Genealogists' Magazine*, XII, nos. 1–16 (1955–1958), XIII, nos. 1–8 (1959–1961), and John Wareing, "Some Early Emigrants to America, 1683–84; A Supplementary List," XVIII, no. 5 (1975–1976), 239–246. Liverpool servants, 1697–1707: Elizabeth French, "List of Emigrants to America from Liverpool, 1697–1707," *New England Historical and Genealogical Register*, LXIV (1910), LXV (1911).

them in."[21] Generally, the young age of servants suggests that they had little stake in society, little substance of their own. About half, by virtue of their parents' occupations or acquired skills, came from the lower-middle ranks of English society, and the rest were children, adolescents, the poor, and the unemployed, who had nothing to lose—or were powerless to choose—by emigrating.

Far fewer female servants emigrated than male (Table 5). For every woman who left London for Virginia in 1635, there were 6 men, and although the

21. Edmund S. Morgan, *American Slavery, American Freedom: The Ordeal of Colonial Virginia* (New York, 1975), 216; *Md. Arch.*, XLI, 477–478.

TABLE 5

Sex Ratios of Groups of Servant Emigrants from England to the Chesapeake, 1635–1707

Emigrant Group	Males per 100 Females
London servants, 1635	642.1
Maryland headright sample, 1646–1657	312.5
Virginia headright sample, 1648–1666	341.8
Bristol servants, 1654–1686	308.1
Servants in Maryland inventories, 1658–1679	320.1
Maryland headright sample, 1658–1681	257.1
Servants in Maryland inventories, 1680–1705	295.1
London servants, 1682–1686	245.7
Virginia headright sample, 1695–1699	296.4
Liverpool servants, 1697–1707	236.0

Note: This table is adapted from Russell Robert Menard, "Economy and Society in Early Colonial Maryland" (Ph.D. diss., University of Iowa, 1975), 194.

Sources: London, 1635: John Camden Hotten, ed., *The Original Lists of Persons of Quality . . . and Others Who Went from Great Britain to the American Plantations, 1600–1700* (London, 1874), 35–138.   Maryland, 1646–1647: Russell R. Menard, "Economy and Society in Early Colonial Maryland" (Ph.D. diss., University of Iowa, 1975), 156, 217–221. Virginia, 1648–1666: Wesley Frank Craven, *White, Red, and Black: The Seventeenth-Century Virginian* (Charlottesville, Va., 1971), 27.   Bristol, 1654–1686: Herbert Moller, "Sex Composition and Correlated Culture Patterns of Colonial America," *William and Mary Quarterly*, 3d Ser., II (1945), 117–118.   Maryland, 1658–1679: St. Mary's City Commission, "Social Stratification in Maryland, 1658–1705" (National Science Foundation Grant, GS-32272).   Maryland, 1658–1681: see Maryland, 1646–1647.   Maryland, 1680–1705: see Maryland, 1658–1659.   London, 1682–1686: Michael Ghirelli, *A List of Emigrants from England to America, 1682–1692* (Baltimore, 1968); C.D.P. Nicholson, "Some Early Emigrants to America," *Genealogists' Magazine*, XII, nos. 1–16 (1955–1958), XIII, nos. 1–8 (1959–1961), and John Wareing, "Some Early Emigrants to America, 1683–84; A Supplementary List," XVIII, no. 5 (1975–1976), 239–246.   Virginia, 1695–1699: Edmund S. Morgan, "Slavery and Freedom: The American Paradox," *Journal of American History*, LIX (1972–1973), 27.   Liverpool, 1697–1707: Elizabeth French, "List of Emigrants to America from Liverpool, 1697–1707," *New England Historical and Genealogical Register*, LXIV (1910), LXV (1911).

number of women servants increased sharply during the middle decades of the century, even by the 1680s and 1690s the sex ratio was still heavily skewed at 2 or 3 men per woman. Men and boy servants were more attractive to merchants and planters, because their labor potential was considered greater. Although women were sometimes put to work in the fields alongside the men, it is improbable that they were as consistently applied to the production of tobacco as were male hands. As in England, their duties may have revolved around "Howseholdworke" and tending the garden plot. Little is known about their backgrounds. Of the 226 women who left Bristol between 1654 and 1686 whose occupation or status was recorded, 214 were described simply as "spinsters," 10 were widows, and 2 were wives of male servants. The London lists occasionally reveal a glimpse of their lives before leaving England. Mary Read, formerly a servant of Jane Corfield, had been committed to Bridewell for "pilfering" two chickens from the shop of her master, John Corfield, a deed that presumably accounts for her mistress's decision "to part with her." Elizabeth Day bound herself for four years in Virginia with the "consent of her husband," Stephen Day, sawyer. Was this a means of arranging an informal separation, a recognition of the breakdown of their marriage, or did her husband intend to follow her at some later date? Hester Speed, reduced to destitution and desperation after the death of her husband, "slaine in the rebellion in the West" (a reference to Monmouth's uprising), opted to start a new life in the colonies.[22]

Like most male servants, the majority of emigrating women were of ages 15–24. However, relatively more women came from this category and fewer from the older age range (Table 4). Throughout the seventeenth century approximately 30 percent of women left England when under 20 and a further 50 percent under 25 years. Given that the average age of first marriage was commonly around 24, it appears that most female servants were not older women who went to the colonies in search of husbands. Most emigrated at or below marrying age.[23]

22. On men: Horn, "Servant Emigration," in Tate and Ammerman, eds., *Chesapeake in the Seventeenth Century*, 62; Menard, "Economy and Society," 193–194. See also Bullock, *Virginia Impartially Examined*, 52, 60–62; *A Relation of Maryland; Together, with a Map of the Countrey, the Conditions of Plantation, His Majesties Charter to the Lord Baltemore, Translated into English* (London, 1635), 52.

On women: Lois Green Carr and Lorena S. Walsh, "The Planter's Wife: The Experience of White Women in Seventeenth-Century Maryland," *WMQ*, 3d Ser., XXXIV (1977), 542–577. Some women had clauses written into their indentures that they would not work in the fields. Margaret Prou was bound to Richard Bray to serve for four years in Virginia, "Working in the Ground excepted." Mary Goldsmith, from Southwark, who sailed for Maryland in 1684, bound herself to "serve on Howsholdworke." See Nicholson, "Some Early Emigrants," *Gen. Mag.*, XIII, nos. 1–8 (1959–1961), 49, 177.

Only 32 women of the 120 who left London, 1683–1684, had their occupation or status recorded: 28 were described as single women, 2 were dairymaids, 1 a widow, and the other a wife; see Ghirelli, *List of Emigrants*, 23, 69, 76.

23. For the average age of women at first marriage, see Peter Laslett, *The World We*

Town and Country: Geographical Origins and Migration

Apart from London and Bristol, no community regularly contributed large numbers of settlers throughout the century, but two regions stand out as especially important: the counties surrounding London and Bristol—areas in proximity to the two major colonial ports where business and social connections between country and city were closest. Of those who paid their own passage, nearly a third came from London and just under half from the metropolis and southeastern counties combined; another fifth came from a broad sweep of counties stretching from the Thames Valley to the Bristol Channel (Figure 1). That many (almost 60 percent) were from urban backgrounds strongly suggests that aspiring colonial merchants and planters first moved from their own county town or parish to one of the two major colonial ports before eventually taking ship to America.[24]

Indentured servants exhibit a similar geographical pattern. Again, London and the Southeast provided the bulk of emigrants. During the first four decades of colonization, 80–90 percent of servants sailed from London. In the second half of the century London's share of the servant trade dropped to about 60 percent, owing to the rise of importance of other tobacco ports, such as Bristol and Liverpool. Until the 1680s, Bristol, together with surrounding counties and parts of southern Wales, was the second most important source of servants, but in the last two decades of the century Liverpool's growing

---

Have Lost (London, 1965), 85–86; J. A. Sharpe, *Early Modern England: A Social History, 1550–1760* (London, 1987), 39–41. The idea that women over the usual age at first marriage could find husbands in the colonies was popular even in the 17th century. George Alsop described women's opportunities in Maryland as follows: "The Women that go over into this Province as Servants, have the best luck here as in any place of the world besides; for they are no sooner on shoar, but they are courted into a Copulative Matrimony, which some of them (for aught I know) had they not come to such a Market with their Virginity, might have kept it by them untill it had been mouldy." *A Character of the Province of Maryland* (1666), in Clayton Colman Hall, ed., *Narratives of Early Maryland, 1633–1684*, Original Narratives of Early American History (New York, 1910), 358.

24. Horn, "Servant Emigration," in Tate and Ammerman, eds., *Chesapeake in the Seventeenth Century*, 66–74; Horn, " 'To Parts beyond the Seas,' " in Altman and Horn, eds., *"To Make America,"* 97–101. Of the emigrants, 197 were from London and 94 from the surrounding counties of Kent, Surrey, Sussex, Essex, Middlesex, and Hertfordshire. Counties from the Thames Valley to Bristol are as follows: Bedfordshire, Berkshire, Buckinghamshire, Oxfordshire, Gloucestershire, Wiltshire, Hampshire, Dorset, and Somerset. See Horn, "To Parts beyond the Seas," 96–98 (and table 4.2); Brenner, "Commercial Change," 76–77, 83–84.

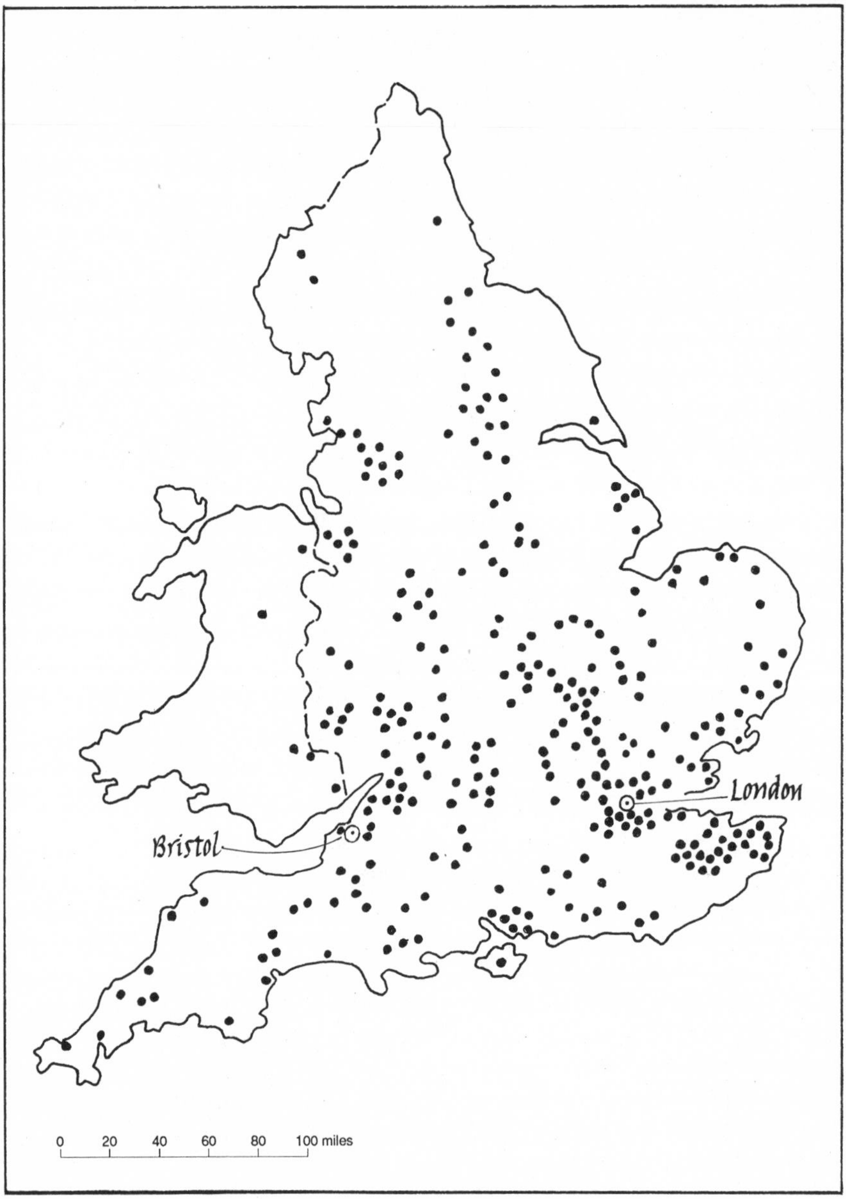

Figure 1. Origins of Free Immigrants to the Chesapeake
in the Seventeenth Century

share of the tobacco market made the Northwest of England and northern Wales important regions for the recruitment of bound laborers.[25]

The Bristol list provides the best evidence for locating the geographical origins of servants, the majority of whom were from near the city (see Figure 2). More than 60 percent were from communities within a forty-mile radius (Table 6), and Bristol itself provided ninety-four servants (13 percent of all those whose origins can be traced), although some of these might have first come from elsewhere. Together, the West Country, southern Wales, and the Severn Valley contributed 87 percent of the total. Proximity was a major factor in determining the prospective servant's port of departure.[26]

Bristol servants came from a wide variety of urban and rural backgrounds. Slightly fewer than half were from villages, about a quarter had lived in market towns, and the rest were from county towns or provincial capitals. There was no clustering of emigrants from particular communities as in the case of immigration to New England. Aside from the cities and larger towns, servants traveled to Bristol in ones and twos from hundreds of parishes scattered throughout the West. Other than Bristol itself, no single community produced more than twenty emigrants. The same can be said of servants who emigrated from Liverpool at the end of the century. Approximately 45 percent were from villages, 38 percent from market towns, and 17 percent from county towns or cities. Although large numbers came from areas surrounding the rapidly expanding industrial town of Manchester, the overwhelming impression one gets is of the scattered nature of their places of origin.[27]

25. Menard, "British Emigration," in Carr, Morgan, and Russo, eds., *Colonial Chesapeake Society*, 123; Wareing, "Migration to London," *Jour. Hist. Geog.*, VII (1981), 356–387; Horn, "Servant Emigration," in Tate and Ammerman, eds., *Chesapeake in the Seventeenth Century*, 66; W. E. Minchinton, "Bristol—Metropolis of the West in the Eighteenth Century," Royal Historical Society, *Transactions*, 5th Ser., IV (1954), 69–85; Minchinton, ed., *The Growth of English Overseas Trade in the Seventeenth and Eighteenth Centuries* (London, 1969), 33–34; Paul G. E. Clemens, "The Rise of Liverpool, 1665–1750," *Econ. Hist. Rev.*, 2d Ser., XXIX (1976), 211–225; Price and Clemens, "A Revolution of Scale," *Jour. Econ. Hist.*, XLVII (1987), 1–38.

26. Villages and market towns were defined and located on the basis of descriptions contained in John Adams, *Index Villaris; or, An Exact Register, Alphabetically Digested, of All the Cities, Market Towns, Parishes* . . . (London, 1690). Of the servants, 237 were from the West Country, 317 from the Severn Valley, and 167 from South Wales; see Horn, "Servant Emigration," in Tate and Ammerman, eds., *Chesapeake in the Seventeenth Century*, 66–74.

27. The exact percentages for Bristol servants are as follows: from villages, 44.4; from market towns, 26.0; from county towns and provincial capitals, 29.6 (on the

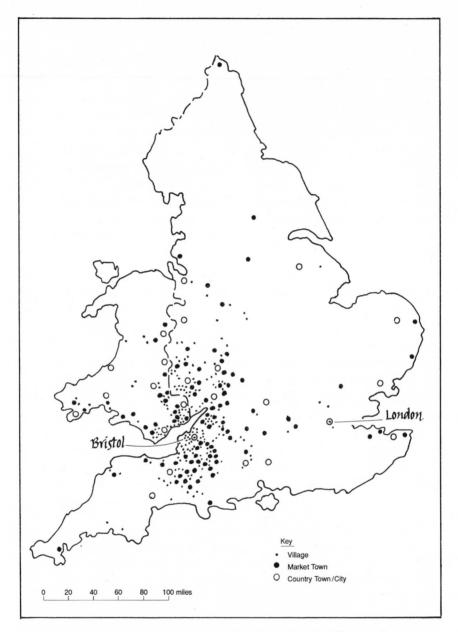

Figure 2. Origins of Servants Emigrating from Bristol to the Chesapeake, 1654–1686

TABLE 6

Distances Traveled to Bristol, Liverpool, and London by Servant Emigrants to the Chesapeake, 1654–1707

Distance Traveled (Miles)	To Bristol, 1654–1686		To Liverpool, 1697–1707		To London, 1682–1686	
	No.	%	No.	%	No.	%
0–9	140	20.0	51	6.5	185	52.3
10–19	105	15.0	122	15.6	9	2.5
20–39	188	26.8	375	47.8	14	4.0
40–59	138	19.7	80	10.2	31	8.8
60–79	39	5.6	39	5.0	10	2.8
80–99	21	3.0	14	1.8	19	5.4
100–149	45	6.4	38	4.9	40	11.3
150–199	13	1.9	52	6.6	26	7.3
200–249	11	1.5	7	.9	9	2.5
250+	1	.1	6	.8	11	3.1
Total	701	100.0	784	100.0	354	99.9

Sources: Bristol, 1654–1686: "Servants to forraign plantations, 1654–1663," Bristol Record Office 04220 (1); "Servants to forraign plantacons, 1663–1679," BRO 04220 (2); "Actions and Apprentices," BRO 04355 (6); "Actions and Apprentices," BRO 04356 (1). Liverpool, 1697–1707: Elizabeth French, "List of Emigrants to America from Liverpool, 1697–1707," *New England Historical and Genealogical Register,* LXIV (1910), LXV (1911). London, 1682–1686: Michael Ghirelli, *A List of Emigrants from England to America, 1682–1692* (Baltimore, 1968); C.D.P. Nicholson, "Some Early Emigrants to America," *Genealogists' Magazine,* XII, nos. 1–16 (1955–1958), XIII, nos. 1–8 (1959–1961), and John Wareing, "Some Early Emigrants to America, 1683–84; A Supplementary List," XVIII, no. 5 (1975–1976), 239–246.

Urban backgrounds figure prominently in the social origins of the servants who emigrated from the outports. At a time when about four-fifths

---

problems of categorizing urban communities, see Peter Clark and Paul Slack, eds., *Crisis and Order in English Towns, 1500–1700; Essays in Urban History* [London, 1972], 1–55). Of those places that could be identified, 231 servants were from 31 county towns and provincial capitals, an average of 7.5 per town/capital (excluding Bristol the figure is 4.7); 207 were from 97 market towns, an average of 2.1; and 258 were from 207 villages, an average of 1.3. Of Liverpool servants whose place of origin could be traced, 161 came from 31 county towns and cities, an average of 5.2 per city/town; 334 came from 87 market towns, an average of 3.8; and 289 were from 170 villages, an average of 1.7.

of England's population lived in the countryside, only half that proportion of emigrants came from rural communities. If one must be careful not to make too much of a contrast between rural and urban life in the seventeenth century, neither should the differences be ignored. In the larger towns there was a greater variety of occupations that had their own system of manu-facture and distribution, markedly different from those of rural trades. The higher density of population brought with it more heterogeneity, since town people were more likely to have come from diverse social backgrounds.[28] Market days brought an influx of people from neighboring parishes to sell their produce and buy essential goods that only the town provided. These occasions gave an opportunity not only to exchange goods but also to trade local news and gossip. Markets and fairs were essential in the dissemination of information from one locality to another, a factor of some importance with regard to the spread of news about the colonies.

The geographical origins of servants who emigrated from London were different from the origins of either the Bristol or the Liverpool group. More than half of them came from the metropolis, but the rest came from widely dispersed communities throughout England (see Figure 3). The majority were from urban backgrounds, including London; only 29 percent came from villages. Almost all the servants from London itself had lived on the periphery of the city or in the suburbs. Districts surrounding the inner city together with outlying suburbs to the south and east contained the great-est concentrations of poor people and were the fastest growing areas of the metropolis. By 1700 their population exceeded 200,000, composing about 40 percent of London's entire population. "In passing through the City's gates," A. L. Beier remarks, "one entered another world. The sights and smells of the busy, rambling extra-mural parts must have presented a sharp contrast to the well-ordered world of merchants and professional men within." Extra-mural parishes were the "workshops of the capital." Shipbuilders, leather-workers, smiths, cutlers, tailors, and weavers were located in St. Botolph Aldgate. St. Giles Cripplegate was known for its clothing and leather trades (weavers, cobblers, and glovers), as was St. Olave Southwark. Whereas the East End in 1550 was a rural area with little urban development, a century

28. Clark and Slack, eds., *Crisis and Order*, 6; John Patten, "Village and Town: An Occupational Study," *Agricultural History Review*, XX (1972), 8–9. For general devel-opments in the period, see Peter Clark and Paul Slack, *English Towns in Transition, 1500–1700* (Oxford, 1976); and Jonathan Barry, ed., *The Tudor and Stuart Town: A Reader in English Urban History, 1530–1688* (London, 1990).

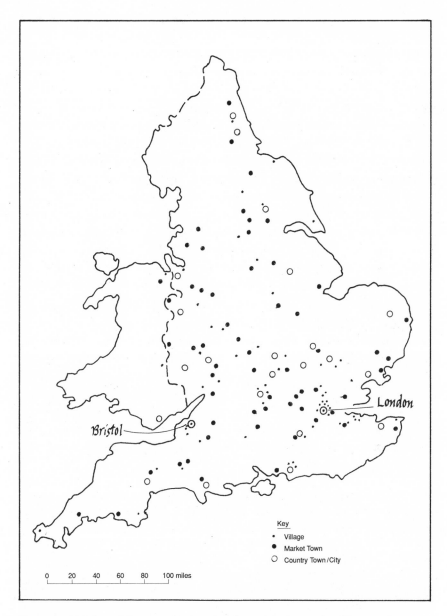

Figure 3. Origins of Servants Emigrating from London to the Chesapeake, 1682–1686

later it was characterized by important shipbuilding, textile, and distributive industries.[29]

The "Queene of Cities" was, in fact, less one city than several cities close together. Within the walls was the ancient City of London, the heart of the capital, where the wealthiest districts were situated. To the west, the city of Westminster was becoming an increasingly fashionable suburb for the rich, a spacious open area providing relief from the hurly-burly of urban life in central London. East and south lay less salubrious neighborhoods. The East End, one of the fastest-growing suburbs, developed as a patchwork of rough open ground, crowded streets, filthy courts, and squalid alleys, "no small blemish," according to the antiquary John Stow, "to so famous a city." South-wark, across the Thames, had a population of about nineteen thousand in 1603 and approaching thirty-two thousand by 1678. It too contained some of the poorest quarters in London, especially along the riverside, which were generally the least healthy. The growth of the capital, "one of the most strik-ing and important of the changes which occurred within English society" between 1500 and 1700, exhibited a dark side reflected in terrible poverty and abject living conditions found in many parts of the city.[30]

Population rose from about 200,000 at the beginning of the century to 490,000 by 1700, at which time it was the largest city in western Europe. Given the excess of deaths over births, the whole of this increase may be attributed to immigration. To sustain its rate of growth, London must have absorbed at least 8,000 persons per year from 1650 to 1700. A similar figure, 7,000–10,000, has been suggested for the first half of the seventeenth cen-tury. Put another way, about half the natural increase of provincial England fueled the rapidly expanding metropolis.[31]

29. Thus, of London servants, 185, or 52.3%, were from London, although, as will be argued below, many were born elsewhere. Only 2.0% were from county towns or provincial capitals, 16.6% came from market towns, and 29.1% were from villages.

On London: M. J. Power, "East London Housing in the Seventeenth Century," in Clark and Slack, eds., *Crisis and Order*, 237–262; A. L. Beier, "Engine of Manufacture: The Trades of London," in Beier and Finlay, eds., *London, 1500–1700*, 153–154; Peter Earle, *The Making of the English Middle Class: Business, Society, and Family Life in London, 1660–1730* (London, 1989), chap. 3; M. J. Power, "The East and West in Early Modern London," in E. W. Ives *et al.*, eds., *Wealth and Power in Tudor England: Essays Presented to S. T. Bindoff* (London, 1987), 167–185.

30. John Stow, *A Survay of London* . . . (London, 1598); Beier and Finlay, eds., *London, 1500–1700*, 199, 202–206; Boulton, *Neighbourhood and Society*, chap. 2; C.G.A. Clay, *Economic Expansion and Social Change: England, 1500–1700*, 2 vols. (Cambridge, 1984), I, 212–213.

31. E. A. Wrigley, "A Simple Model of London's Importance in Changing English

Long-distance migrants accounted for much of this movement. Of deponents from Stepney in the East End who came before the archidiaconal courts of the diocese of London between 1580 and 1640, 74 percent were born outside London and the Home Counties. Only 13 percent were born within the city itself. One study of London apprentices who took up service in the 1630s finds that only one-third to one-half came from the metropolis and neighboring counties. There was considerable variation from company to company, but in no case was the proportion of apprentices from London higher than 25 percent. In Stuart England, London's migration field was nationwide.[32]

It would appear, therefore, that the number of servants who emigrated from London and gave their place of origin as the city itself exaggerates the number of them born there. At least half of them had probably been born elsewhere and lived in the capital a few months or years before moving to the colonies. Charles Parker from Staffordshire, for example, resided "half a yeare" in Aldgate before taking ship in 1685. Henry Gray, who lived "a considerable time" in London before emigrating, was from Durham. Outside London, the pattern of migration displayed by servants is similar to that of other lower-class migrant groups who moved to the city. Beyond the concentration of emigrants from the metropolis and the Home Counties, they came from communities all over England in roughly equal numbers. The high proportion from urban backgrounds suggests that individuals had first moved from their native parishes to the local town. Finding little or no work there, or simply following the lure of the capital, they moved to London.[33]

Society and Economy, 1650–1750," *Past and Present*, no. 37 (July 1967), 44–49; John Patten, "Rural-Urban Migration in Pre-Industrial England," School of Geography, University of Oxford, *Research Paper*, no. 6 (1973), 27.

32. David Cressy, "Occupations, Migration, and Literacy in East London, 1580–1640," *Local Population Studies*, no. 5 (1970), table 2, p. 58. S. R. Smith, "The Social and Geographic Origins of London Apprentices, 1630–1640," *Guildhall Miscellany*, IV, pt. 3 (1973), 204. See also A. L. Beier, *Masterless Men: The Vagrancy Problem in Britain, 1560–1640* (London, 1985), chap. 3, appendix, tables 1, 2; John Wareing, "Changes in the Geographical Distribution of Apprentices to the London Companies, 1486–1750," *Jour. Hist. Geog.*, VI (1980), 241–249.

33. Wareing, "Migration to London," *Jour. Hist. Geog.*, VII (1981), 360. For the attraction of the city, or "great centres of commerce," see E. G. Ravenstein's classic study, "The Laws of Migration," Royal Statistical Society, *Transactions*, XLVIII (1885), 167–235, esp. 198–199. See also Paul A. Slack, "Vagrants and Vagrancy in England, 1598–1664," *Econ. Hist. Rev.*, 2d Ser., XXVII (1974–1975), 360–379; Beier, *Masterless Men*, chap. 3; and Clark and Souden, eds., *Migration and Society*, 22–26.

Immigration to America was merely one aspect of much broader migratory patterns within early modern England. Men and women who eventually ended up in Virginia and Maryland migrated to London with tens of thousands of their contemporaries who, for one reason or another, had chosen to live and work in the nation's capital. For those who found conditions in the crowded suburbs harsh, the prospect of work, food, and shelter, albeit overseas, was no doubt tempting. Thus, the decision to emigrate may frequently have been taken, not when persons left their home community, but after they had arrived in one of the country's principal towns or ports. Indentured servants who immigrated to the Chesapeake should be viewed as a subset of a much larger group of young and single people who moved from town to town in search of greater opportunities than were to be had at home. Arriving in cities and ports such as London, Bristol, and Liverpool, they found plenty of people like themselves looking for work and precious little available. Some eked out a living as best they could; others moved elsewhere or returned home; still others decided to try their luck in a new setting and embarked for the colonies.[34]

Poverty and Profit: Motives for Emigration

Settlers' backgrounds and the general reasons that prompted migration have attracted much research and debate.[35] If some early adventurers dreamed of finding fortunes in gold, or perhaps discovering the fabulously wealthy cities foretold in legends and myth, others had more modest ambitions of finding work, earning a living, and perhaps eventually securing a smallholding. Still others looked to combine profit with faith and sought to create a religious sanctuary for those whose convictions, whether Puritan, Quaker, or Catholic, encouraged them to leave England. Some settlers intended to stay for good; others remained only a year or two. Emigration was not a single, concentrated outpouring of people united by a common vision of a new start in America, but, rather, a multilayered, multitextured phenomenon comprising wave upon wave of colonists who found their way

34. Needless to say, this explanation does not assume that all servants left England in this way. Doubtless there were many who had particular reasons for leaving the country. But for the vast majority of emigrants the decision to take ship for America came after a period (possibly prolonged) of movement within England.

35. Altman and Horn, eds., *"To Make America,"* 1–29; Menard, "British Emigration," in Carr, Morgan, and Russo, eds., *Colonial Chesapeake Society,* 99–132; Gemery, "Markets for Migrants," in Emmer, ed., *Colonialism and Migration,* 33–54.

to the Chesapeake from very different backgrounds and for very different reasons.

There is no need to detail the changes that transformed English society in the sixteenth and seventeenth centuries, but it is worth highlighting those aspects that had a significant bearing on migration and helped shape the colonial societies that emerged along the eastern seaboard of North America. First and foremost, since so much stemmed from it, was demographic growth. England's population rose by about a third, from three to four million, between 1550 and 1600 and to just more than five million by 1650. Contemporaries were perplexed and alarmed. There is "nothing more dangerous for the estate of commonwealths," Robert Gray observed in 1609, "than when the people do increase to a greater multitude and number than may justly parallel with the largeness of the place and country." Authorities condemned the burgeoning armies of "masterless men"—vagrants, the idle and dissolute—that (in their view) infested the highways and swarmed into towns and villages bringing disease and disorder in their wake. Spiraling food prices and a concomitant decline in real wages led to a disastrous drop in the living standards of the poorer sections of society, and recurrent harvest failure and dearth brought widespread misery as well as sporadic food and enclosure riots throughout southern and central England. By the mid-seventeenth century, the *third world* of the poor had risen in some regions, particularly protoindustrial areas, to between one-third and one-half of the population. The rough-and-ready homogeneity of village life in the late medieval period, insofar as it had ever existed, broke down irrevocably as society became increasingly polarized.[36]

36. Wrigley and Schofield, *Population History of England*, table A3.1, p. 528; Keith Wrightson, *English Society, 1580–1680* (London, 1982), 122–123; Robert Gray, *A Good Speed to Virginia* (London, 1609), quoted in Joan Thirsk and J. P. Cooper, eds., *Seventeenth-Century Economic Documents* (Oxford, 1972), 757; Beier, *Masterless Men*, chaps. 1–2; Christopher Hill, *The World Turned Upside Down: Radical Ideas during the English Revolution* (London, 1972), chap. 3. Good general accounts of the changes are Joyce Youings, *Sixteenth-Century England* (London, 1984); Wrightson, *English Society*; Clay, *Economic Expansion*; and Sharpe, *Early Modern England*.

On decline of living standards and rural life: R. B. Outhwaite, *Inflation in Tudor and Early Stuart England*, 2d ed. (London, 1982), 11–17; Buchanan Sharp, *In Contempt of All Authority: Rural Artisans and Riot in the West of England, 1586–1660* (Berkeley, Calif., 1980); Andrew Charlesworth, ed., *An Atlas of Rural Protest in Britain, 1548–1900* (London, 1983), 8–82; Anthony Fletcher and John Stevenson, eds., *Order and Disorder in Early Modern England* (Cambridge, 1985), 1–15; Roger B. Manning, *Village Revolts: Social Protest and Popular Disturbances in England, 1509–1640* (Oxford, 1988), pt. 1.

Far-reaching social changes were accompanied by equally important economic changes. One of the most notable developments was the emergence of a national market for foodstuffs and manufactured goods centered in London. Local markets retained their vitality, but producers also looked to more distant horizons and became more closely involved, via provincial capitals, major ports, and London, in national and international trade. The steady advance of commercial agriculture in pastoral and arable areas was encouraged by the growing population and production for expanding metropolitan and overseas markets. Innovations in land use and husbandry by large capitalist farmers were motivated more by a desire to raise output and profit than by an intention to benefit the commonweal. Enclosure, the improvement of wastes and commons, deforestation, and the drainage of marshland and fens frequently met with fierce local protest from commoners who had nothing to gain and possibly everything to lose. Nevertheless, the trend toward an increasingly market-oriented society was irresistible.[37]

Much interest, too, was shown in initiatives to develop industries in the countryside, particularly in marginal areas. The growth of domestic manufactures such as iron production, coal mining, glassmaking, linen weaving, and stocking knitting, among others, eroded England's traditional reliance on foreign imports, provided new avenues of investment for entrepreneurs, and put the poor to work. Similar principles governed experiments with a range of industrial crops—rape, flax, hemp, woad, and tobacco—promoted enthusiastically by agricultural improvers of the age. Many experiments were subsequently transferred to the colonies, where efforts were made to establish industries and crops that had already met with some success in England, an extension of attempts by projectors to maximize the profitability of marginal land and utilize a vast pool of cheap, underemployed labor.[38]

An opportunistic spirit and a willingness to experiment in new economic ventures are striking characteristics of the period. Nowhere was this more apparent than among the mercantile community. As England emerged from the periphery of a predominantly intra-European trading system, so London developed as one of the great centers of transatlantic and long-distance

37. Joan Thirsk, *Economic Policy and Projects: The Development of a Consumer Society in Early Modern England* (Oxford, 1978); H.P.R. Finberg and Joan Thirsk, eds., *The Agrarian History of England and Wales* (Cambridge, 1967–), V, pt. 2, chaps. 16, 19; Keith Lindley, *Fenland Riots and the English Revolution* (London, 1982); Brian Manning, *The English People and the English Revolution, 1640–1649* (London, 1976), chap. 6.

38. Thirsk, *Economic Policy and Projects*, 101–105. This point is developed further in Chapter 3, below.

oceanic commerce. In response, merchants and gentry flocked to join the new joint-stock companies that mushroomed in the City. Whether in London or in the provinces, men with capital eagerly sought to invest their money in trading schemes that offered potentially rich rewards, if at high risk. Consequently, important elements of England's ruling classes, together with merchants and retailers large and small, became closely involved in overseas ventures and colonizing projects. The steady expansion of England's empire was not orchestrated by a small clique of wealthy merchants insulated from the general community, but was supported by broad sections of the middle and upper classes.[39] This breadth of support imparted overseas enterprises with a vigor and energy they would have otherwise lacked and brought colonial developments into the mainstream of English social and economic life.

The impact of these general changes was, of course, mediated and very much determined by local experience. Change was conditioned by the manner in which it was interpreted by different social groups in thousands of small-scale communities across the country. At the national level, however, the cumulative effect is reasonably clear. English society in the early seventeenth century was characterized by growing social differentiation, increased mobility, and an emphasis on market forces, competition, materialism, acquisitiveness, and individualism. Social contrasts were brought into sharp focus in the teeming cities and ports, where vagrancy, destitution, and the basest poverty existed side by side with riches and opulence enjoyed by the gentry and mercantile elite. Throughout England, in the smaller towns and villages, the same motif of plenty and want was endlessly repeated. While the middle and upper classes became increasingly wealthy from the opportunities provided by the quickening pace of commercial and agrarian capitalism, the ranks of the poor steadily swelled.[40]

The rapid changes that gave English society its "unique dynamism" in this period exerted an enormous influence on the development of colonial

39. Jack P. Greene, *Pursuits of Happiness: The Social Development of Early Modern British Colonies and the Formation of American Culture* (Chapel Hill, N.C., 1988), 34–35; Brian Dietz, "Overseas Trade and Metropolitan Growth," in Beier and Finlay, eds., *London, 1500–1700,* 115–140; F. J. Fisher, "London's Export Trade in the Early Seventeenth Century," in Minchinton, ed., *Growth of English Overseas Trade,* 64–77; Brenner, "Commercial Change," chap. 3; Theodore K. Rabb, *Enterprise and Empire: Merchant and Gentry Investment in the Expansion of England, 1575–1630* (Cambridge, Mass., 1967).

40. Wrightson, *English Society,* 125–148, 222; Greene, *Pursuits of Happiness,* 30–36; Beier, *Masterless Men,* chaps. 1–2; Paul Slack, *Poverty and Policy in Tudor and Stuart England* (London, 1988), chap. 3.

society. They shaped the character and timing of emigration and largely determined the types of societies that evolved. Most important, their influence was *continuous*. Social and economic forces that worked upon English society throughout the century also worked upon American society. From this point of view, colonies are better conceived as far-flung English provinces, closely linked to metropolitan society by ties of politics, commerce, kinship, and a common culture rather than as incipient independencies. Understanding the close and continuing interrelationship of English and American social developments is vital to unraveling the full complexity of Anglo-American society in this formative period and assessing the relative degrees of continuity and change.[41]

Motives that prompted free settlers to emigrate were diverse. In the early years of colonization many gentry were attracted by the prospect of easy wealth and military adventure; exploration and conquest of foreign lands were deemed worthy and honorable pursuits for gentlemen, especially when allied with the propagation of the Protestant faith. Hopes that North America would furnish the English with fabulous riches, however, faded in the face of hardships during the first years of settlement. Virginia was no Mexico or Peru. "It was the spaniards good hap," lamented William Simmonds in 1612, "to happen in those parts where were infinite numbers of people, whoe had manured the ground with that providence that it afforded victuall at all times; and time had brought them to that perfection [that] they had the use of gold and silver. . . . But we chanced in a lande, even as God made it. Where we found only an idle, improvident, scattered people, ignorant of the knowledge of gold, or silver, or any commodities; and carelesse of anything but from hand to mouth . . . nothing to encourage us but what accidently wee found nature afforded."[42] Tobacco, not gold and silver, saved Virginia

41. Jack P. Greene and J. R. Pole, eds., *Colonial British America: Essays in the New History of the Early Modern Era* (Baltimore, 1984), 13–16; J.G.A. Pocock, "The Limits and Divisions of British History: In Search of the Unknown Subject," *American Historical Review*, LXXXVII (1982), 318. The phrase "unique dynamism" is taken from Charles Wilson and Bruce Lenman, "The British Isles," in Charles Wilson and Geoffrey Parker, eds., *An Introduction to the Sources of European Economic History, 1500–1800* (Ithaca, N.Y., 1977), 153.

42. Wesley Frank Craven, *The Southern Colonies in the Seventeenth Century, 1607–1689* (1949; Baton Rouge, La., 1970), chap. 3; Morgan, *American Slavery, American Freedom*, chap. 4; Simmonds in Warren M. Billings, ed., *The Old Dominion in the Seventeenth Century: A Documentary History of Virginia, 1606–1689* (Chapel Hill, N.C., 1975), 27.

from collapse. Gentlemen of fortune had to hang up their swords and take up the hoe if they wished to strike it rich. As it became evident that the high risks involved in moving to the Chesapeake were not matched by quick wealth, the aristocracy lost interest in the New World.

If the tobacco coast failed to meet expectations of an El Dorado, and the English *conquista* proved very different from the Spanish, nevertheless possibilities of making a modest profit remained. A number of early arrivals may best be described as *hobereaux*, impoverished gentry who gambled on Virginia to recoup dwindling fortunes at home. Sir John Berkeley of Beverston, Gloucestershire, who immigrated to Virginia in 1620 to erect an ironworks, was described as "estranged from his friends and reduced to poverty." He died in the Indian uprising two years later. A near neighbor, George Thorpe, esquire, of Wanswell Court, Berkeley, "did seccretlie flie out of England to Virginia" in 1620 to avoid creditors, as did his associate Arnold Oldisworth, esquire, who reputedly owed the crown six thousand pounds in 1631. Another Gloucestershire gentleman, William Tracy of Hailes, was jailed for debt on the eve of his departure for Berkeley plantation on the James River and had to be bailed out by friends. Financial problems were not confined to the upper classes. The case of George Grace, a merchant of London, provides a good example. During the late 1620s or early 1630s he shipped to Delft "a great quantity" of cloths, but, owing to plague in the city, his servants were not able to sell his merchandise and exchanged cloth for Bibles, "being the best bargain they could make." The Bibles, worth three hundred pounds, were exported to London, where they were seized, and Grace was unable to pay his debts. He fled to Virginia, where, according to his wife, "he now lives in a poor condition."[43] Throughout the century Virginia and Maryland provided a distant refuge for immigrants fleeing from creditors.

The Chesapeake also provided a sanctuary for religious refugees. Perry Miller exaggerated in proposing that religion "was the really energizing propulsion" in the founding of Virginia, but he was surely correct to suggest that

43. "Berkeley Manuscripts," *WMQ*, 1st Ser., VI (1897–1898), 135; William Clayton Torrence, "Henrico County, Virginia: Beginnings of Its Families," pt. 2, *WMQ*, 1st Ser., XXIV (1915–1916), 205; Henry J. Berkeley, "The Berkeley-Berkley Family and Their Kindred in the Colonization of Virginia and Maryland," *WMQ*, 2d Ser., III (1923), 186; C24/525 part 2/17 [1626]; C24/572 part 1; C2 Chas. I, W99/38, Public Record Office; Eric Gethyn-Jones, *George Thorpe and the Berkeley Company: A Gloucestershire Enterprise in Virginia* (Gloucester, 1982), 147; State Papers, Domestic, Chas. I, 16/475, no. 60, Public Record Office (CW VCRP, 3244); Nugent, comp., *Cavaliers and Pioneers*, I, 104, 109, 123–124.

it was an important instrumental stimulus. Despite the pious exhortations of the Virginia Company, there was little sustained effort to bring the Protestant faith to indigenous peoples of the Chesapeake. Unlike Spanish and French colonies, settlement in English America was not followed by a vigorous attempt to convert Indians, and thus there was no large-scale movement of Anglican missionaries to the tobacco coast. In fact, until the early eighteenth century, there were insufficient ministers to serve the needs of English colonists, let alone convert Indian peoples.[44] Rather than becoming a New World forum for a Protestant (Anglican) crusade, Virginia and Maryland attracted men and women whose religious beliefs were becoming marginalized in England—Puritans and Catholics—or proponents of new radical sects such as Quakers.

From its inception Maryland was intended as a haven for Catholics. By the early seventeenth century, despite modest growth, the Catholic community in England existed as "a tiny and embattled minority," and, although there was no organized campaign against Catholics, they were generally excluded from the highest offices in local and central government and lived under increasing surveillance by the church courts and quarter sessions. Maryland provided a refuge from religious and civil disabilities suffered in England and gave Catholics an opportunity to practice their religion openly as well as enjoy the benefits of important political office. During the first fifteen years of the colony's existence, Baltimore's highest-ranking supporters came from Catholic backgrounds. Five of the six major initial investors were Catholics. Thomas Cornwallis contributed the largest share. His motives for immigrating were varied, a combination of ambition, enterprise, and faith, but "Securety of Contiens," he confided to Lord Baltimore, "was the first Condition that I expected from this Government." He threatened to leave the colony rather than "Consent to anything that may not stand with the Good Contiens of A Real Catholick." There was no possibility, however, that Maryland would become an exclusively Catholic province; not enough Catholics emigrated from England, and, even if they had, an entirely Catholic colony was politically unacceptable to the English government. Nevertheless, down to the Glorious Revolution, Catholics dominated the political life of Maryland in a way that would have been impossible in the parent country. Baltimore may have been disappointed that more of his coreligionists chose not to settle

44. Perry Miller, *Errand into the Wilderness* (Cambridge, Mass., 1956), 101; William H. Seiler, "The Anglican Parish in Virginia," in J. M. Smith, ed., *Seventeenth-Century Virginia*, chap. 6; Morgan, *American Slavery, American Freedom*, chap. 3; Craven, *Southern Colonies*, 142–145, 177–182.

in the Chesapeake, but sufficient numbers emigrated or were converted to maintain an important presence in the colony.[45]

Puritans also found their way to the early Chesapeake. On August 28, 1618, Thomas Locke of London wrote to William Trumbull in Brussels, "The last weeke there were some 100 or verie neere of Brownists shipped to Virginia, and shortlie there wilbe twice as many puritans, god speede them well." The scale of Puritan immigration was far smaller than to New England but was nonetheless significant and deserves consideration. Separatist settlements in Virginia were guided by the same impulses that led the Pilgrims to Plymouth. Like the Pilgrims, early leaders of Virginia's Puritan movement—Edward Bennett, Christopher Lawne, and Francis Blackwell—were associated with the separatist church in the Netherlands before immigrating to America. Bennett probably moved to Holland in the first years of the seventeenth century, residing initially at Delft and then at Amsterdam, where he became one of the elders of the Ancient Church. He may have begun shipping colonists to Virginia about the same time that Blackwell emigrated in 1618. By 1620 he was a wealthy merchant in London and one of the principal pillars of Puritan emigration to America. In 1622 he financed the establishment of a plantation at Warraskoyack (later Isle of Wight County) and moved there himself four years later. When he returned to England in 1629, his nephew, Richard Bennett, assumed the leadership of the Puritans in the colony.[46]

Christopher Lawne, from Blandford, Dorset, was born about 1580. As a young man he moved to Norwich and followed the trade of a buttonmaker, and he possibly came into contact with Dutch separatists fleeing from per-

45. Martin Ingram, *Church Courts, Sex, and Marriage in England, 1570–1640* (Cambridge, 1987), 85, 86; Christopher Haigh, "From Monopoly to Minority: Catholicism in Early Modern England," Royal Hist. Soc., *Trans.*, 5th Ser., XXXI (1981), 129–147; John Bossy, *The English Catholic Community, 1570–1850* (London, 1975), 182–194, 278–282; Bossy, "Reluctant Colonists: The English Catholics Confront the Atlantic," in David B. Quinn, ed., *Early Maryland in a Wider World* (Detroit, Mich., 1982), chap. 6; Menard, "Economy and Society," 36 (Cornwallis quote, 33–34); David W. Jordan, "Political Stability and the Emergence of a Native Elite in Maryland," in Tate and Ammerman, eds., *Chesapeake in the Seventeenth Century*, 249–250; Lois Green Carr and Jordan, *Maryland's Revolution of Government, 1689–1692* (Ithaca, N.Y., 1974), 37; Jordan, *Foundations of Representative Government in Maryland, 1632–1715* (Cambridge, 1987); Michael Graham, "Meetinghouse and Chapel: Religion and Community in Seventeenth-Century Maryland," in Carr, Morgan, and Russo, eds., *Colonial Chesapeake Society*, 242–274.

46. Trumbell MSS, no. 101, Berkshire Record Office (VCRP R10); Boddie, *Isle of Wight County*, chap. 2.

secution in their own country. In 1610, or before, he immigrated to Amsterdam and became a prominent critic of the internal feuds between different branches of the separatist church. Eight or nine years later he transported himself to Virginia and settled at Lawne's Creek on the south side of the James River a few miles downstream from Jamestown. Francis Blackwell, another elder of the Ancient Church, was responsible for organizing the expedition of 1618, when approximately 180 Brownists took ship in the *William and Thomas*. He and 130 others died en route in one of the most terrible crossings of the century.[47]

The impact of Puritan immigration upon Chesapeake society was considerable. By midcentury there were large numbers of Nonconformists in Isle of Wight, Nansemond, and Lower Norfolk counties. Mr. Thomas Harrison, a Puritan minister of Lower Norfolk County, was said to have 118 members in his church in 1648, which represented about a quarter of the adult population: a formidable "schismaticall party, of whose intentions," the colony's assembly declared, "our native country of England hath had and yet hath too sad experience." Several hundred Puritans migrated northward to Providence on the Severn River, Maryland, in the following year. At the same time, Nonconformists from the Eastern Shore of Virginia began moving to Maryland. The Eastern Shore, like the area south of the James, was a stronghold of Puritanism. Notable among the early settlers of Northampton County were William Stone, nephew of a wealthy London merchant, who became governor of Maryland in 1648 and who promoted the exodus of the Puritans from Virginia, and Obedience Robins, born in Brackley, Northamptonshire, one of the colony's leading Nonconformists.[48]

Quakerism arrived in America in the mid-1650s. George Fox wrote in his diary in 1655, "About this time several Friends went beyond the seas to declare the everlasting Truth of God." Fifty-nine, nearly half of whom were women, migrated between 1656 and 1663 alone. Most Quakers went to New

---

47. Boddie, *Isle of Wight County*, 15–26.

48. Lower Norfolk County, Virginia, Wills and Deeds B, 1646–1651, 92–93. There were 334 tithables in 1648 (tithables were taxable members of the community, that is, slaves and males over sixteen: see Morgan, *American Slavery, American Freedom*, 400–401); Craven, *Southern Colonies*, 229.

On Maryland and the Eastern Shore: Stanard, comp., *Some Emigrants*, 71, 78; Jennings Cropper Wise, *Ye Kingdome of Accawmacke; or, The Eastern Shore of Virginia in the Seventeenth Century* (1911; Baltimore, 1967), 105–109; Clayton Torrence, *Old Somerset on the Eastern Shore of Maryland: A Study in Foundations and Founders* (Richmond, Va., 1935); Babette M. Levy, "Early Puritanism in the Southern and Island Colonies," American Antiquarian Society, *Proceedings*, LXX (1960), 122–123, 130–133, 140.

England, but some missionaries, like Thomas Thurston, ended up in the Chesapeake after first proselytizing in Massachusetts. Owing to a greater freedom of conscience in religion than elsewhere in the colonies, Maryland "was the scene of the first substantial convincements in Quakerism on the mainland of the New World."[49] In the absence of a strong Anglican presence, Quakerism, like other Nonconformist sects, flourished.

Quaker links with Bristol may have been especially close. The West Country was an important center of Quakerism, and the Society of Friends in Bristol was in regular contact with friends in Virginia from at least 1667. Edward Beare of Bristol, "a maker of apparell," emigrated in 1673, and Jonathan Packer sought a "speedy effecting" of his request to marry in 1678, "being sudenly bound away to Virginia." The movement was not all one-way. William Bressie, a Quaker from Isle of Wight County, was described in 1672 as "now resident in Bristoll." Quakerism evidently appealed to men and women of middling status, especially those involved in mercantile activities, skilled work of various kinds, and the clothing trade. Some 29 percent of Bristol Friends were involved in commerce or food and drink processing, and clothing trades accounted for another 40 percent. Relative to their numbers, Quakers were well represented in occupations associated with transatlantic commerce.[50]

Nonconformists of another kind, political rather than religious, settled in the Chesapeake in the 1640s and 1650s, as echoes of the civil wars and overthrow of the monarchy reached the colonies. Susana Chidley wrote to her uncle, John Ferrar, in October 1649 and reported that four ships were about to sail to Virginia, "and abundance of quality go in them." She met with few people who did not know of some who were going, or resolved to go, to America. According to the earl of Clarendon, Sir William Berkeley "invited many gentlemen and others thither, as to a place of security

49. J. Reaney Kelly, *Quakers in the Founding of Anne Arundel County, Maryland* (Baltimore, 1963), 1, 2, 29; B. Reay, "Quakerism and Society," in J. F. McGregor and B. Reay, eds., *Radical Religion in the English Revolution* (Oxford, 1984), 141, 145; Kenneth L. Carroll, "Thomas Thurston, Renegade Maryland Quaker," *Md. Hist. Mag.*, LXII (1967), 170–192; Aubrey C. Land, *Colonial Maryland: A History* (New York, 1981), 65; Graham, "Meetinghouse and Chapel," in Carr, Morgan, and Russo, eds., *Colonial Chesapeake Society*, 242–272.

50. Russell Mortimer, ed., *Minute Book of the Men's Meeting of the Society of Friends in Bristol, 1667–1686* (Bristol Record Society, XXXVI [1971]), xii, xxvi, xxvii, 11, 21, 26, 49, 70, 92, 127–128, 194, 206; "Isle of Wight County Records," *WMQ*, 1st Ser., VII (1898–1899), 228; Reay, "Quakerism and Society," in McGregor and Reay, eds., *Radical Religion in the English Revolution*, 143–144.

which he could defend against any attempt, and where they might live plentifully, [and] many persons of condition, and good officers in the war, had transported themselves, with all the estate they had been able to preserve." Among prominent royalist settlers were Sir Henry Chicheley, Sir Thomas Lunsford, Sir Grey Skipwith, Sir Dudley Wyatt, Sir Philip Honeywood, John and Lawrence Washington (whose father had been turned out of his benefice in 1643 for being a "malignant loyalist"), Henry Randolph, John Brodnax of Godmersham, Kent, colonels Guy Molesworth, George Mason, and Henry Norwood, General Mainwaring Hammond, John Carter, and Richard Lee.[51]

Cavalier immigration to Virginia during the 1640s and 1650s was not large; no more than a couple of hundred arrived in this period. The great majority remained in England either in retirement or fomenting plots against Parliament and the Republic. Others fled to the Continent. But although Virginia did not become a royalist bastion as Berkeley hoped, a number of Cavaliers in the colony established prominent families that dominated the political and economic life of their respective localities for the rest of the century. Numerically, royalists were insignificant, but in local as well as provincial politics they exercised an influence disproportionate to their numbers.[52]

Whatever settlers' religious or political persuasion, a striking feature of free immigration is the importance of kinship connections. Emigration tended to be organized privately rather than through official recruitment or

51. Ferrar Papers, box II, no. 102, Magdalen College, Cambridge, (VCRP, C22); Edward Hyde, earl of Clarendon, *The History of the Rebellion and Civil Wars in England Begun in the Year 1641*, ed. W. Dunn Macray, 8 vols. (Oxford, 1888), V, 263; Richard L. Morton, *Colonial Virginia*, 2 vols. (Chapel Hill, N.C., 1960), I, 167–168; "Virginia in 1641–49," *Virginia Magazine of History and Biography*, XVII (1909), 26–33; Norwood, *Voyage to Virginia*, in Force, comp., *Tracts and Other Papers*, III, no. 10, p. 49; Philip Alexander Bruce, *Social Life of Virginia in the Seventeenth Century* (1907; New York, 1964), 61.

52. See, for example, Everitt, *Community of Kent and the Great Rebellion*, chaps. 6–8; David Underdown, *Royalist Conspiracy in England, 1649–1660* (New Haven, Conn., 1960); Craven, *Southern Colonies*, 247; Morton, *Colonial Virginia*, I, 166–168; Bruce, *Social Life*, 76, 79. John Carter established a powerful dynasty in Lancaster County in the 1650s; Richard Lee and Henry Chicheley settled across the Rappahannock about the same time. Edward Digges patented land in York County, George Mason in Northumberland, Joseph Bridger in Isle of Wight County. David Hackett Fischer lists many more "cavalier" immigrants in *Albion's Seed: Four British Folkways in America* (Oxford, 1989), 207–418, but I do not believe they influenced the social and cultural development of the colony to the extent that he claims (see my critique in "Cavalier Culture? The Social Development of Colonial Virginia," *WMQ*, 3d Ser., XLVIII [1991], 240–245).

state sponsorship, and "it was the family that in many senses provided structure and coherence to the entire process." The decision to move to America was often related to a range of familial considerations: position within the family (younger sons, for example), contacts with relatives in London or other major ports, and kinship connections in the Chesapeake.[53] Although relatively few settlers emigrated in family groups, family and kinship were significant in influencing the decision to emigrate, facilitating the move, and sometimes determining where individuals finally settled.

The importance of family ties can be illustrated by a few examples. Henry Fleet was born in the small Kentish village of Chartham in the Stour Valley, a few miles southeast of Canterbury in 1600. At the age of twenty-one he took ship for Virginia, where he was captured by Anacostan Indians and held prisoner for five years. After his release he returned to England but was soon back in America trading along the Chesapeake Bay as well as further afield to New England. In the same year that he first set sail, his kinsman, Sir Francis Wyatt, from Boxley, Kent, took up residence in Jamestown as the new governor of Virginia. Fleet was also related through marriage to the Kentish families of Argall and Filmer and more distantly to the Horsmandens, Codds, and Culpepers, all of whom were represented in the Chesapeake during the early and middle decades of the century. From another part of the county, Thomas Warren of Ripple, in East Kent, settled at Smith's Fort in Surry County in 1642. He was related to the Gookin family of the same parish. Daniel Gookin, a Puritan, had arrived in Virginia in 1621 and lived first at Newport News before moving to Nansemond and, later, to Maryland and Massachusetts. Warren might have heard about opportunities in the Chesapeake through his kinsman. Two other kinsmen of Warren's also moved to Virginia: Nicholas Merriwether settled in Surry, and David Crafford at James City. Linked by marriage in England, these families continued to intermarry in the Chesapeake.[54]

53. Ida Altman, "Emigrants and Society: An Approach to the Background of Colonial Spanish America," *Comparative Studies in Society and History*, XXX (1988), 182. Martin H. Quitt emphasizes the lack of support given by kin and family to gentry emigrants, in "Immigrant Origins of the Virginia Gentry: A Study of Cultural Transmission and Innovation," *WMQ*, 3d Ser., XLV (1988), 639–642.

54. Henry Fleet, "Henry Fleet of Fleet's Bay, Virginia, 1600–1660," *Northern Neck Historical Magazine*, XII (1962), 1068–1076; [Jester and Hiden], eds., *Adventurers of Purse and Person*, 248–286, 718–723; Peter Laslett, "The Gentry of Kent in 1640," in T. H. Breen, ed., *Shaping Southern Society: The Colonial Experience* (New York, 1976), 32–47; James D. Alsop, "Sir Samuel Argall's Family, 1560–1620," *VMHB*, XC (1982), 478–484; Stanard, comp., *Some Emigrants*, 24; Will of Samuel Filmer, 1670 (VCRP,

A number of kin (usually brothers) emigrated together. William and George Fitzgeffrey, born in Bedfordshire, sailed for Virginia in 1623; Hugh and Justinian Yeo of Harton, Devon, settled on Virginia's Eastern Shore in the 1650s; and John and Lawrence Washington moved to the Northern Neck in the mid-1660s. Thomas Lygon arrived in Virginia with Sir William Berkeley in 1642 and settled in Henrico County. A branch of the family had experimented with tobacco production in England during the 1620s, and it is possible that Lygon's interest in the Chesapeake sprang from this ultimately unsuccessful venture. More likely, however, he was taking advantage of his kinship with Governor Berkeley to secure an advantageous position in the colony. Perhaps similar reasons induced George Sandys to emigrate with his kinsman Sir Francis Wyatt in 1621.[55]

Some free settlers emigrated because they already had kin living in America. John Beheathland left for Virginia in 1636 to join his mother. He was probably related to Robert Behethland, gentleman, a member of the first expedition of 1607. Henry Fleet's three brothers settled in Maryland during the 1630s and 1640s, and his nephews in Virginia around the same time. Colonel Henry Norwood could have followed fellow Cavaliers into exile in Europe or the West Indies in 1649 but instead chose Virginia. "The honour," he wrote, "I had of being nearly related to Sir *William Barkeley* the governor, was no small incitation to encourage me with a little stock to this adventure." Gentlemen went to the colonies with capital and connections. In Virginia and Maryland, relatives, friends, or former neighbors in England provided introductions to prominent planters and local grandees. One of the most striking characteristics of the gentry in this period was the resilience of family ties—a bond sufficiently strong and flexible to survive the Atlantic crossing.[56]

3730); John B. Boddie, *Colonial Surry* (Richmond, Va., 1948), 67–72; William Berry, *County Genealogies: Pedigrees of the Families of the County of Kent* (London, 1830).

55. Stanard, comp., *Some Emigrants*, 34, 86, 93–94; John Bennett Boddie, "Lygon of Madresfield, Worcester, England, and Henrico, Virginia," *WMQ*, 2d Ser., XVI (1936), 302–303, 307–308, 310–311; Joan Thirsk, "Projects for Gentlemen, Jobs for the Poor: Mutual Aid in the Vale of Tewkesbury, 1600–1630," in Patrick McGrath and John Cannon, eds., *Essays in Bristol and Gloucestershire History: The Centenary Volume of the Bristol and Gloucestershire Archaeological Society* ([Bristol], 1976), 153; Stanard, comp., *Some Emigrants*, 73; Boddie, *Colonial Surry*, 36–40.

56. Will of John Beheathland, Prerogative Court of Canterbury (PCC) PROB 22, October 22, 1639 (VCRP, 3985); [Jester and Hiden], eds., *Adventurers of Purse and Person*, 105–106; Billings, ed., *The Old Dominion*, 18; Lois Green Carr, Russell R. Menard, and Lorena S. Walsh, *Robert Cole's World: Agriculture and Society in Early Maryland* (Chapel Hill, N.C., 1991), chap. 1; Fleet, "Fleet of Fleet's Bay," *Northern Neck Hist.*

Kinship was significant also in forging links between English provinces and major mercantile centers, particularly London. William Ferrar, born at Croxton, Lincolnshire, in 1583, left London with Lord De La Warr's expedition of 1618. He was related to Nicholas Ferrar, Sr., "a merchant of great eminence" in the city and a leading member of the Virginia Company. Henry Corbin was the third son of Thomas Corbin, esquire, of Hall End, Warwickshire. He moved to London in his early twenties, where he joined his brothers, Gawain and Thomas, who may have been already involved in the tobacco trade. Shortly after receiving a four-hundred-pound legacy from his father, he sailed for Maryland in 1654 "to serve as the American arm of a transatlantic merchant partnership." As we have seen, George Sandys of Norbonne, Kent, had City connections through his elder brother, Sir Edwin, leader of the liberal faction of the Virginia Company. George Fitzgeffrey's brother, William, was of Staple Inn, London, at the time of their departure for America, and William Stone from Northamptonshire, who emigrated in 1663, was a nephew of Thomas Stone, haberdasher and merchant of the City.[57]

Although it is difficult to gauge the influence of London connections upon an individual's decision to emigrate, it is evident that many future settlers first arrived in the capital to take up apprenticeships or work before moving on to the colonies. Younger sons of gentry, yeomen, and provincial tradesmen flocked to London and, to a lesser extent, other colonial ports, seeking opportunities in the burgeoning transatlantic trade. It made good sense for one member of the family to supervise business in America while other members remained in England. Many partnerships operated on this basis during the century. As representatives of provincial families established themselves in London and Bristol, they facilitated the movement of brothers, nephews, and cousins from the shires. London and the outports served as staging posts en route to the New World and constituted a vital link in the chain that took people from their native parishes across the Atlantic to the shores of the Chesapeake Bay.

Mag., XII (1962), 1068–1076; Stanard, comp., *Some Emigrants*, 34; VCRP, 3730; Norwood, *Voyage to Virginia*, in Force, comp., *Tracts and Other Papers*, III, no. 10, p. 4; Laslett, "Gentry of Kent," in Breen, ed., *Shaping Southern Society*, 45–46.

57. [Jester and Hiden], eds., *Adventurers of Purse and Person*, 273–274; Darrett B. Rutman and Anita H. Rutman, *A Place in Time: Middlesex County, Virginia, 1650–1750* (New York, 1984), 50–51; Stanard, comp., *Some Emigrants*, 34, 73, 78; Boddie, *Colonial Surry*, 36–40.

Poverty was the principal influence on servant emigration in the seventeenth century. Possibly because it was one of the most obvious features of servants—few who were able to pay the cost of their own passage would have willingly emigrated under indentures—or because it was at the center of much government legislation, poverty appears again and again as a key determinant in the experiences of individuals. Robert Redman, for example, was sent to London to be put on board the *Hopewell* in 1684. "If 9 years or tenn yeares service be required," his uncle wrote, "I am contented provided he have his bellefull of food, with cloathes to keep him warm and warm lodgin at night." "I could keep him no longer," he added. Jonathan Cole, "a poor boy," had been left in the parish of Coleshurst, London, before indenturing himself to Thomas Gadsen, mariner, of Limehouse, in 1685, and George Fawne's parents of the "Isle of Garnsey" consented to his emigrating at the age of ten because, "being very poore," they were "not able to maintaine him." [58]

Loss of one or both parents was common among poor emigrants. Nearly two-thirds of servants under twenty-one who left London between 1682 and 1686 were orphans. Thomas Martin, born in Morpeth, Northumberland, was only eight when his father died. He moved to Newcastle upon Tyne with his mother and, when she died two years later, was placed in the care of the parish. At the age of sixteen he journeyed to London, where he took ship to Maryland. John Fitch of Cambridgeshire, aged about twenty, testified on oath before magistrates that his parents were dead before he signed up for four years in Virginia in the summer of 1684. Parishes routinely rid themselves of the expense and trouble of caring for unwanted children by indenturing them for service in the colonies. John Browne, an orphan from Essex, was "desired by the parish to be sent to sea," and the overseers of the poor of Thornbury, Gloucestershire, paid £1 11s. "for Linen and woolen and other necessarys for Thomas Harding when he was going to Virginia," in 1672.[59]

58. Campbell, "Social Origins," in J. M. Smith, ed., *Seventeenth-Century America*, 77; Ghirelli, *List of Emigrants*, 18, 30. There is little direct evidence why the vast majority of immigrants to Virginia and Maryland, indentured servants, chose to leave England. Most servants did not (or could not) record their thoughts in letters, diaries, and memoirs that might have provided glimpses of the immediate factors that led to their decision to take ship for America. Consequently, much of the evidence is circumstantial.

59. Nicholson, "Early Emigrants," *Gen. Mag.*, XIII, nos. 1–8 (1959–1961), 12–13. Horn, "Servant Emigration," in Tate and Ammerman, eds., *Chesapeake in the Seventeenth Century*, 83; Ghirelli, *List of Emigrants*, 18–19; Lord Mayor's Waiting Books, XIV,

Loss of parental support, for one reason or another, encouraged many poor young people to leave home and seek opportunities elsewhere. Emigrants were merely a small part of an enormous volume of movement from one part of the country to another, and especially to London. A continual flow of unskilled workers, domestics, and casual laborers from the provinces expanded the vast pool of underemployed cheap labor that already existed in the capital, concentrated in the poorer quarters and slums. Large numbers were arrested for vagrancy and sent to London's Bridewell Hospital. During the 1620s, an average of about fifteen hundred vagrants per year were admitted, most of whom, according to A. L. Beier, were migrants. London was said to have been the best recruiting ground in the country for the military and American colonies. A report of the mid-eighteenth century commented that, if newcomers "cannot get such employment as they expected or chuse to follow, many of them will not go home again to be laughed at . . . but enlist for soldiers, go to the plantations etc. if they are well enclined; otherwise they probably commence thieves or pickpockets." Sir Josiah Child believed, if the urban poor had not been employed overseas, they "could probably never have lived at home to do Service for their Country, but must have come to be hanged or starved, or dyed untimely of some of those miserable Diseases, that proceed from want and Vice, or else have sold themselves for Soldiers."[60]

Out of work and on the streets, it is hardly surprising that some young people found themselves the unwanted attention of legal and illegal recruitment for the colonies. In 1618 John Chamberlain reported that the City was about to ship to Virginia "an hundred younge boyes and girles that [had] bin starving in the streetes which is one of the best deeds that could be don with so little charge not rising to above £500." Several hundred more were sent out in succeeding years. Sir Edwin Sandys commented in 1620 that some of the children, "who under severe masters in Virginia may be brought to goodness, and whom the City is especially desirous to be disburdened, declare their unwillingness to go." He urged the government to grant the Virginia Company the authority to transport them against their will if necessary.[61]

---

fol. 459. For Harding, see P330, OV2/7, GRO; Currer-Briggs, ed., "Indentured Servants," entry for Thomas Harding, Nov. 2, 1672; and Nugent, comp., *Cavaliers and Pioneers*, II, 168, 185.

60. Bailyn, *Voyagers to the West*, 274; Beier, *Masterless Men*, 42; Child, *A New Discourse of Trade*, 170–171; Joseph Massie quoted in M. Dorothy George, *London Life in the Seventeenth Century* (London, 1925), 355, n. 2.

61. SP14/103, no. 33, Public Record Office (CW, microfilm, reel 404); A. E. Smith, *Colonists in Bondage*, 148–149; *Cal. State Papers*, Col. Ser., I, 19.

Generally, governments of the day were quite content to support measures that rid the country of its poor. Vagrants and the destitute were regularly sent to the colonies from the Bridewell Hospital throughout the century even though few had been formally sentenced to transportation. In 1656, the Council of State ordered that "lewd and dangerous persons, rogues, vagrants, and other idle persons, who have no way of livelihood, and refuse to work" should be shipped to "the English plantations in America." This order was followed a few years later by comprehensive proposals "for the better accomodating the Forreigne Plantations with servants." The newly created Council of Foreign Plantations recommended that "all Sturdy Beggars as Gypsyes and other incorrigible Rogues and wanderers may be taken upp by Constables and imprison'd untill at the next Assizes or Sessions they shall either bee acquitted and assigned to some settled aboade and course of life here or bee appointed to bee sent to the plantacons for five years under the Condition of Servants." It was suggested: "Whereas there are divers Towns Villages and Parishes in this Nacon where the numbers of poore and idle debauched Persons are exceeding great and where there is either noe meanes for the setting them on worke or by their parents or themselves they are applyed to Stealing and other idle or evill Courses to the great Scandall and inconvenience of the Nacon. It may be advisable that a provision bee made for the inviteing and recruiting or compelling (if it shall bee Judged fitt by the Law . . .) some few out of such Towns Villages or p[ar]ishes yearly" to be consigned to labor in the colonies.[62]

In fact, these proposals were only voicing official support for measures that had been practiced for years. A Somerset justice of the peace, Sir Edward Hext, complained to the Privy Council in 1618 of one Owen Edwards, who had commanded the constable of Whitleigh among others to press "maidens" to be sent out to Bermuda and Virginia. He had given money to several people to bring him girls despite having no commission or power to do so. Owen was imprisoned, but the rumors had so alarmed the neighborhood that forty poor girls had fled from one village alone. Nine years later, a contemporary noted, "There are many ships now going to Virginia, and with them, some 1400 or 1500 children, which they have gathered up in diverse places." In the 1630s, numbers of poor were summarily despatched from

---

62. *Cal. State Papers*, Col. Ser., I, 410–411, 447; George Chandler, *Liverpool under Charles I* (Liverpool, 1965), 411–412; Egerton MSS, 2395, 277–278, British Library, London.

Kent and Essex, and in 1656 several hundred prostitutes were sent to the West Indies from London, apparently to boost the birthrate.[63]

How much did the poor know about opportunities in the colonies? Should we interpret indentured servitude as mass emigration of the poor and ignorant, or did servants have sufficient knowledge of conditions in America to make informed choices about where they wished to settle and for how long? Did they seek a chance to better their condition and start a new life, attracted by the abundant cheap land of the tidewater, or did they have little choice about leaving and little idea of what the future held? Were servants merely another species of commodity in the international trade in laborers, or were they able to negotiate individual conditions of service with merchants and recruiting agents on the basis of the value of their skills and potential return of their labor?

Emphasizing the role of the market in influencing labor contracts, one argument stresses that "servants were not simply passive victims of a process beyond their control." In a competitive market, they retained a significant degree of leverage in determining their terms of service. Thus older, literate, and skilled servants received shorter terms than the young and unemployed, as did men and women going to the West Indies, where mortality rates were high and opportunities for the poor comparatively limited. Length of service was directly related to the expected return on the planter's investment. Skilled men repaid their master's initial outlay more quickly than unskilled and hence did not serve as long. Servants, it is argued, were broadly aware of conditions in America, since rumors and stories about the colonies were widespread in England. Potential emigrants could judge for themselves what their prospects were in different parts of America and bargain accordingly.[64]

The argument is suggestive but not convincing. Skilled men with trades in high demand in the colonies sometimes served shorter terms than usual, and servants going to the West Indies were on average more likely to serve slightly shorter terms than their counterparts going to the mainland, but the

63. SP14/103, no. 42, Public Record Office (CW, microfilm, reel 404); Beier, *Masterless Men*, 163; D/P 50/12/1, Writtle, Overseers of the Poor Accounts, 1631, Essex Record Office, (VCRP, no. Es. 3).

64. Menard, "British Migration," in Carr, Morgan, and Russo, eds., *Colonial Chesapeake Society*, 107–108 (quote), 131–132; Galenson, *White Servitude*, 102–113; Galenson, "Labor Market Behavior in Colonial America: Servitude, Slavery, and Free Labor," in David W. Galenson, ed., *Markets in History: Economic Studies of the Past* (Cambridge, 1989), 58–61.

leeway for individual bargaining was severely circumscribed and should be considered within the general context of servant recruitment. Most servants (73–95 percent), whether bound for the Chesapeake or the Caribbean, signed up for four or five years (Table 7) in conformity with colonial legislation and English custom. Adult servants usually served four years, and minors contracted until age twenty-four. Generally speaking, the younger one was, the longer one served; but this practice was not just a reflection of market value, or "age-earnings profile": it was wholly in accordance with English expectations of service. Young men and women from lower social classes commonly served as domestics or servants in husbandry until they reached majority or married. The long terms given to teenage boys and girls in Virginia and Maryland should be interpreted in this light. Having entered their master's family, they were expected to work for their keep until they were old enough to form their own household. The initial payment by planters for the cost of transportation made some form of legal contract necessary to ensure that the servant repaid the debt with labor over a specified period, hence the evolution of the indenture system.[65]

Most men and women servants, whether laboring in tobacco fields or on sugar plantations, had to work four or five years before being granted freedom. Aggregate differences in length of service from one colony to another do not imply that servants commonly negotiated contracts individually, but suggest that a general going rate existed at various times for various colonies; thus by the 1680s it was rare to serve more than five years in the West Indies. The large numbers of emigrants that made consideration of individual cases impossible, the widespread acceptance of four to five years as the standard term, the passage of colonial legislation that codified the usual length of service in the "custom of the country," and the role of the mercantile community in directing the flow of servant traffic significantly reduced flexibility in the negotiation of contracts.

The view that servants played a minor role in deciding where they eventually ended up is further supported by the abrupt change of destinations of Bristol servants between 1654 and 1662. From the beginning of registration until 1659, the great majority went to the West Indies, notably Barbados, but thereafter immigration to the islands fell dramatically. As demand in the West Indies declined, so the number of servants transported to Virginia and Maryland steadily increased. The twin peaks of 1659 and 1662

65. Galenson, "Labor Market Behavior in Colonial America," in Galenson, ed., *Markets in History*, 59; A. E. Smith, *Colonists in Bondage*, 17, 229–231; Morgan, *American Slavery, American Freedom*, 216.

TABLE 7

Length of Contract of Indentured Servant Emigrants from Bristol and London to America, 1654–1686

Destination (N)	Length of Contract in Years				Total
	0–3	4–5	6–9	10+	
	Percent				
From Bristol, 1654–1680					
West Indies					
Males (3,346)	12.0	73.9	13.9	.2	100.0
Females (914)	6.1	84.8	8.6	.4	99.9
Chesapeake					
Males (3,839)	4.2	81.4	13.5	.8	99.9
Females (1,242)	2.6	89.8	7.3	.3	100.0
From London, 1682–1686					
West Indies					
Males (553)	2.7	89.3	7.4	.5	99.9
Females (150)	1.3	95.3	3.3	0	99.9
Chesapeake					
Males (596)	0	72.7	24.3	3.0	100.0
Females (242)	0	91.7	7.9	.4	100.0

Source: Figures compiled from data presented in Farley Grubb, "The Long-Run Trend in the Value of Indentured Servants: 1654–1831," Working Paper, no. 90-25, Department of Economics, University of Delaware (June 1990), appendix, 44–61.

stand out clearly (Figure 4), representing the changing direction of English immigration from the West Indies to the Chesapeake. It is hard to reconcile this turnabout with the emphasis on servant choice.

An alternative argument stressing labor demands and different types of labor employed is more convincing: the increasing reliance of sugar planters on slave labor led to a severe fall in demand for indentured servants, whereas in the Chesapeake tobacco planters continued to depend on white laborers until the end of the century. Several historians have suggested a correlation between the pace of immigration to the Chesapeake and the price of tobacco: "When the price of tobacco was high," Russell Menard comments, "merchants actively recruited servants and produced a boom in investment; when tobacco was low, they were reluctant to invest in labor and the rate of immi-

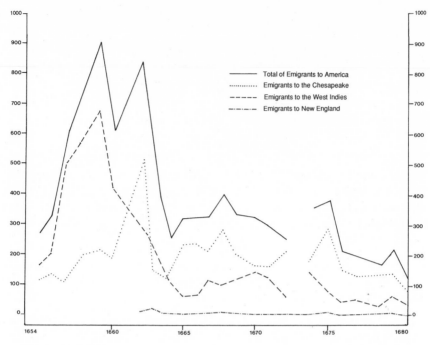

Figure 4. Destinations and Annual Totals of Servants Emigrating from Bristol to America, 1654–1680

gration declined." The rapid growth of the tobacco industry between 1620 and 1680 created and maintained the need for a continuing supply of cheap labor, most of which was met by a massive influx of poor English workers. Thus choice of destination was largely dictated by the labor demands of the colonies; indentured servants went where planters needed workers and merchants could get the best price.[66]

The bulk of the servant trade was based on the principle of supplying servants to the colonies in much the same way as any other marketable commodity. Merchants, mariners, and small traders typically paid about £6 each for servants' transportation and shipped them to the tobacco coast in the expectation of a handsome profit. John Pope and Henry Gough, merchants of Bristol, informed their factor in 1661 that they had placed £249 worth of goods on the *Providence* for sale in Virginia. After receiving detailed instructions, he was told: "You are Alsoe to take note of one Servant that is aboard and to dispose [of him] there to our best Advantage for which we

66. Menard, "Economy and Society," 164; Horn, "Servant Emigration," in Tate and Ammerman, eds., *Chesapeake in the Seventeenth Century*, 91–92.

have paid his passage." [67] For many merchants who had an interest in transatlantic trade, the transportation of servants was simply one aspect of the main business of importing tobacco and exporting their own merchandise.

Not all servants were the victims of demographic pressures, economic recessions, and the demand for contract labor in the plantations. Doubtless there were those, like Stephen Barrow and "a fellow servant" from Clapton, Somerset, who sought a new life and opportunities "beyond the sea." Little is known about them. Some men from rural backgrounds may have decided to swap casual laboring on English farms for working in the tidewater, where at least there was a possibility of one day setting up their own smallholding. Others, impressed by stories of the profits to be made from tobacco, may have been attracted by the prospect of becoming landowners after what they construed as an apprenticeship in tobacco husbandry. Landownership was extremely attractive to men inculcated with the symbolic as well as the economic value of land in the Old World. But to argue that generally servants considered emigration in terms of perceived "life expectancies, wage rates, job opportunities, access to land and credit, the costs of starting a farm or entering a trade, and the like" is misleading.[68] Most poor did not have the luxury of considering their future in such a detached manner, and it is highly unlikely that they had sufficient information to weigh their options in such a calculated way. If they had, it is improbable that so many would have left England: the risk of early death was too great.

On the Margins: Forests, Heath, and Woodland

Further clues about the social and economic factors that influenced servant emigration can be found from a more detailed examination of the sorts of backgrounds from which they came. Thus, the significant social and cultural differences between wood-pasture and downland areas in early modern England have been emphasized. Such an approach greatly oversimplifies the diversity of provincial society but nevertheless remains a valuable means of exploring regional differences.[69]

67. Westmoreland County, Virginia, Deeds, Wills Etc. (1661–1662), 34, Virginia State Library, Richmond; Lancaster County, Virginia, Orders Etc. (1655–1666), 93 (CW, microfilm, reel M 117-1).

68. E. H. Bates, ed., "Quarter Sessions Records for the County of Somerset, III, Commonwealth, 1646–1660," *Somerset Record Society*, XXVIII (1912), 358–359; Menard, "British Migration," in Carr, Morgan, and Russo, eds., *Colonial Chesapeake Society*, 106.

69. Alan Everitt, "Farm Labourers," in Finberg and Thirsk, eds., *Agrarian History of England and Wales*, IV, 409–412, 462–464; Christopher Hill, *Religion and Politics in*

Downland society tended to be organized around the parish church, manor, and ancient customs governing land use and husbandry. Open-field agriculture, which held sway across large areas of central, southern, and eastern England, encouraged a cooperative village community. By contrast, communal activities were much less in evidence in pastoral and woodland regions. Compared to downland society, wood-pasture parishes were less cohesive and more divided: "divided physically (because they were so often larger in area), divided socially (because of the influx of poor), and divided in religion (because of the frequent presence of knots of Puritan reformers)." Family farming and domestic industry were not regulated by village tradition to anywhere near the extent they were in downland communities. By 1600, David Underdown argues, two very different Englands coexisted uneasily side by side. "In one, roughly coterminous with the surviving areas of open-field arable husbandry, the old conception of the stable, harmonious village community based on deference and good neighbourhood retained some vitality. In the other, comprising many of the towns . . . the industrializing regions devoted to cloth-making, mining, and metal-working, the ideal was increasingly threatened."[70]

An examination of the places of origin of Bristol servants (for whom the best evidence survives) reveals that their distribution was not random. Many came from communities clustered in a linear pattern along roads or rivers or concentrated near the coast. At the hub of a broad communications network, Bristol was linked northward via the Severn Valley to the Midlands and Border Counties, west across the Bristol Channel to the Vale of Glamorgan and the south Wales coastal plain, southwest along the coast to Somerset, Devon, and Cornwall, and east to London. All these regions had strong trading connections with Bristol in the seventeenth century.[71]

Most servants were from lowland areas surrounding Bristol, which may be divided into three regions: the Severn Valley, the south Wales coastal plain, and the low-lying districts of Somerset (Figure 5). These regions were mainly woodland and pastoral areas devoted to dairy farming, stock rearing and the cultivation of a variety of crops. Dairying was especially common in the

---

Seventeenth-Century England (Brighton, 1986), vol. II of *The Collected Essays of Christopher Hill*, 91–98; Sharp, *In Contempt of All Authority*, chap. 6; David Underdown, *Revel, Riot, and Rebellion: Popular Politics and Culture in England, 1603–1660* (Oxford, 1985), chap. 4.

70. Underdown, *Revel, Riot, and Rebellion*, 4–8, 18, 82, 88–89, 103–105.

71. Horn, "Servant Emigration," in Tate and Ammerman, eds., *Chesapeake in the Seventeenth Century*, 76–77; Souden, " 'To Forraign Plantacons,' " 34.

Severn Valley, the Vale of Glamorgan, and eastern Somerset. The heavy clay soils of the vales of Berkeley and Gloucester were unsuitable for extensive tillage, and most farmers grew only limited amounts of cereals and fodder. Like the dairying districts of eastern Somerset, settlement was dispersed, and small to middling farms were the basic unit of production. Along the coast of Somerset and in the Vale of Taunton Deane (Norden's "Paradise of England") agriculture was more mixed. Farmers reared cattle and sheep for market, engaged in dairying, and produced a number of crops, of which wheat was the most important. There was also limited pig rearing and horse breeding, and in the fen country of the Somerset Levels fowling and fishing supplemented stock rearing. Lowland regions around Bristol were characterized too by a good deal of rural industry. Weaving and spinning were widespread, and heavier industries, such as iron ore extraction and coal mining (in the forests of Dean and Kingswood, respectively) made significant contributions to the prosperity of the area.[72]

In comparison with upland regions, woodlands and vales tended to be very populous. East Somerset, the vales of Gloucester and Taunton Deane, and pastoral parishes of West Wiltshire experienced dramatic population growth in the latter half of the sixteenth century and the early seventeenth century as a consequence both of natural increase and immigration. Partly owing to the growing number of people and partly because of changes in the structure of the local economy, it appears that lowland areas were finding it progressively difficult to support their populations. One reason for this was the slow conversion of arable to pasture farming. In the century after 1640, a gradual expansion of meadow and pasture in the Southwest reflected the increasing importance of dairying and stock rearing in the region and a trend toward specialized production tailored to a national food market centered in London. Change was by no means universal, and certain areas were affected more than others. In some areas population pressure led to further and further subdivision of landholdings. Whereas about one-half of farmers in the cheese country of Wiltshire owned less than twenty acres in the period 1540–1590, by the eve of the Civil War the proportion had risen to 70 percent. Of tenants on the Berkeley manors in south Gloucestershire, 30 percent rented

72. Finberg and Thirsk, eds., *Agrarian History of England and Wales*, V, pt. 1, chaps. 6, 11; Joan Thirsk, "Industries in the Countryside," in F. J. Fisher, ed., *Essays in the Economic and Social History of Tudor and Stuart England in Honour of R. H. Tawney* (Cambridge, 1961), 70–88; Thirsk, "Seventeenth-Century Agriculture and Social Change," in Thirsk, ed., *Land, Church, and People: Essays Presented to Professor H. P. R. Finberg*, suppl. to *Agricultural History Review*, XVIII (Reading, 1970), 148–175.

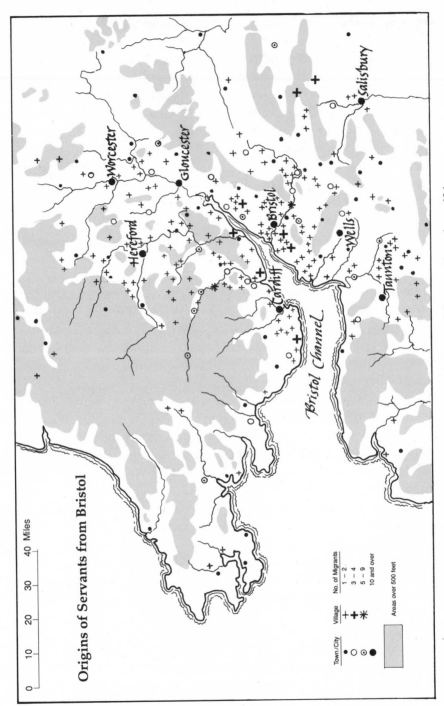

Origins of Servants from Bristol

| 0 | 10 | 20 | 30 | 40 Miles |

Worcester
Gloucester
Hereford
Bristol
Cardiff
Wells
Taunton
Salisbury
Bristol Channel

	No. of Migrants
Town/City	Village	1 – 2
• ○ ⊙ ●	+ ✚ ✳	3 – 4
		5 – 9
		10 and over

Areas over 500 feet

Figure 5. Origins of Bristol Servants to the Chesapeake, by Number and Community, 1654–1686

less than four acres in 1667, and nearly 60 percent had less than twenty. In the densely populated northeastern part of Somerset the introduction of artificial grasses began to take over from arable farming after 1640, and in other areas the cultivation of orchards gradually replaced the production of more traditional crops. The effect of these changes is clear. In the context of a period of rapid population increase, the contraction of the relatively labor-intensive arable sector led to a steady rise in rural unemployment.[73]

An integral part of the local economies of Gloucestershire, Wiltshire, and Somerset in the seventeenth century was cloth production. The industry was dispersed in a wide arc stretching from Ilminster in southern Somerset, through Yeovil, Shepton Mallet, Frome, and Mere to Wotton under Edge and Stroud in Gloucestershire. Along with parts of Lancashire, Yorkshire, East Anglia, and Devon, it was one of the main centers of manufacture in the country. All these regions encountered difficulties in the first half of the century owing to a series of setbacks: the failure of an attempt to export finished cloth to Europe in place of undressed broadcloth, the rise in demand for new, lighter fabrics produced in the Low Countries, and the disruption of trade and loss of markets caused by the Thirty Years' War and the English upheavals of the 1640s.[74]

The depression was particularly severe in the West. In rural areas such as southern Gloucestershire, northwestern Wiltshire, and northern Somerset, many smallholders depended on weaving and spinning to supplement their income from farming and sustain members of the family who would not otherwise have been employed. Some areas attracted numerous poor because of the hope of work in the industry. The Somerset-Wiltshire border, from which many emigrants came, was described in 1623 as being "forest and woodlands, and the rest very barren for corn . . . the people of the country (for the most part) being occupied about the trade of cloth-making,

---

73. Horn, "Servant Emigration," in Tate and Ammerman, eds., *Chesapeake in the Seventeenth Century*, 79; Finberg and Thirsk, eds., *Agrarian History of England and Wales*, IV, 72, 144–145, V, pt. 1, 358–366; Salerno, "Social Background of Seventeenth-Century Migration," *Jour. Brit. Stud.*, XIX (1979), 47–49; J.P.P. Horn, "The Distribution of Wealth in the Vale of Berkeley, Gloucestershire, 1660–1700," *Southern History*, III (1981), 81–109.

74. B. E. Supple, *Commercial Crisis and Change in England, 1600–1642: A Study of a Mercantile Economy* (Cambridge, 1959); J. de L. Mann, *The Cloth Industry in the West of England from 1640 to 1880* (Oxford, 1971), xiii–xviii; G. D. Ramsay, *The Wiltshire Woollen Industry in the Sixteenth and Seventeenth Centuries* (London, 1943), 71–84, 111–114, 124–125; David Rollison, *The Local Origins of Modern Society: Gloucestershire, 1500–1800* (New York, 1992), chap. 1.

spinning, weaving, and tucking. Also we find that by reason of the trade of cloth-making, and the increase of people working about that trade, there have been very many cottages erected . . . for them to work in, which have no means of living but about that trade." The depression was equally severe in the towns, which may account for the large number of indentured servants from cloth centers such as Wells, Frome, Bradford upon Avon, Bath, and Malmesbury.[75]

Certain lowland regions were notorious for the numbers of poor they supported. The large numbers of virtually propertyless wage earners and pieceworkers who inhabited forest and wood-pasture areas depended on wastes and commons for subsistence. Poverty in the eastern part of the Vale of Tewkesbury, for example, was particularly deep-rooted. According to Thomas Dekker, at a beggar's fair held annually near Tewkesbury "you shall see more rogues than ever were whipped at a cart's arse through London, and more beggars than ever came dropping out of Ireland." Poor laborers had flocked to Winchcombe following the introduction of tobacco cultivation in 1621. The parish's overseers of the poor claimed that there were twenty families begging for alms for every householder able to bestow them. Further south, the expansive commons of Slimbridge encouraged an influx of poor, who squatted on land outside the jurisdiction of neighboring landowners. Commenting on the parish in 1639, John Smyth complained, "The more large the wast grounds of a manor are, the poorer are the inhabitants; such comon grounds, comons, or wast grounds, used as comonly as they are . . . drawe many poor people from other places, burden the township with beggerly Cotages, Inmates, and Alehouses, and idle people; where the greater part spend most of their daies in a lazy idlenes and petite theeveries, and fewe or none in profitable labour."[76]

Forests and woodlands were traditional havens for the poor and indigent. The forests of Dean and Kingswood in Gloucestershire and Frome-Selwood in Somerset all produced large numbers of emigrants. Frome and its environs were especially susceptible to harvest failures and were well known for poverty. In 1631, a year of severe dearth, the county's justices reported an

75. Finberg and Thirsk, eds., *Agrarian History of England and Wales*, IV, 80; Sharp, *In Contempt of All Authority*, 161–164; Campbell, "Social Origins," in J. M. Smith, ed., *Seventeenth-Century America*, 84–85; Salerno, "Social Background of Seventeenth-Century Migration," *Jour. Brit. Stud.*, XIX (1979), 31–52, disagrees.

76. Thirsk, "Projects for Gentlemen, Jobs for the Poor," in McGrath and Cannon, eds., *Essays in Bristol and Gloucestershire History*, 148; and "Seventeenth-Century Agriculture," *Agr. Hist. Rev.*, XVIII (1970), 165–166; Smyth, *Hundred of Berkeley*, 51, 328.

invasion of poor cottagers who had congregated in Frome and the nearby forest. Forest dwellers in general seemed to have been held in contempt by contemporaries, who viewed them as addicted to crime and violence. The "mean people," John Aubrey observed, "lived lawless, nobody to govern them." Inhabitants of the Forest of Dean were described by other contemporaries as "people of very lewd lives and conversations, leaving their own and other countries, and taking this place for a shelter and a cloak to their villanies." Their numbers had so increased by 1640 that it was feared that "the poor people there would impoverish the richer sort." Aubrey commented that "the Indigenae" of Wiltshire's wood-pasture regions were "melancholy, contemplative, and malicious," prone to Puritanism, superstition, and litigiousness.[77]

Heath and woodland parishes were attractive to the poor because of the relative ease with which they could establish temporary—or permanent— dwellings while avoiding paying rent to the local landlord and because of opportunities for casual work on nearby farms or in local industries. If no work was available, they could abandon their temporary refuge and move elsewhere. In contrast to the more stationary population of the surrounding champion country (or downlands), where stronger manorial control and a less diverse economy prevailed, there was continual movement in and out of marginal lowland areas. Many poor moved from these regions to Bristol at one time or another. Significantly, woodland areas were under pressure in the mid-seventeenth century as an increasing emphasis by the crown and landlords on profit encouraged the improvement of commons, wastes, and royal forests. The deforestation of Frome-Selwood and Neroche in Somerset, for example, undermined an important shelter for the poor and led to serious rioting in the 1640s. Similarly, the Forest of Dean suffered considerable spoliation during the Civil War.[78]

The Bristol evidence suggests that the great majority of indentured servants came from the second of Underdown's Englands: wood-pasture, forest, and marginal areas together with market and clothing towns. What characterized them all in the mid-seventeenth century were declining opportunities for the poor owing to the relative contraction of the labor market. Three especially important factors may be singled out: first, substantial

77. Finberg and Thirsk, eds., *Agrarian History of England and Wales*, IV, 80; Sharp, *In Contempt of All Authority*, 161–162; John Aubrey cited by Underdown, *Revel, Riot, and Rebellion*, 7, 73; William Bradford Willcox, *Gloucestershire: A Study in Local Government, 1590–1640* (New Haven, Conn., 1940), 157n.

78. Finberg and Thirsk, eds., *Agrarian History of England and Wales*, V, pt. 1, 191.

demographic growth, which placed increasing pressure on natural resources and provoked a marked increase in urban populations; second, the gradual conversion of arable to pasture farming in those parts of the South, West Country, and the Midlands that had formerly supported mixed agriculture; and, third, the recession in the cloth industry, on which many people, particularly in the towns, depended for their support.

Diversity, a distinguishing feature of emigrants' social backgrounds, characterizes their motives for leaving England. From the urban poor and destitute who had little choice in moving to America to the commercial classes and wealthy who looked for handsome profits from tobacco and merchandising, the colonies offered quite different expectations and experiences. Men with capital and connections were enmeshed in a transatlantic world of commerce, an expansive world that was bound together by continual correspondence—social, economic, and political. Planters and merchants were able to keep in touch with family, friends, and business partners by letter or word of mouth, carried with the ebb and flow of shipping. Thousands of miles away in Virginia, they may have sometimes felt on the sidelines of events taking place in England, but they were not completely cut off from metropolitan society, and many planters visited England periodically or returned for good, to continue merchandising or perhaps retire. For wealthier settlers, moving to America did not invariably mean a one-way ticket.

By contrast, the social world of the poor was far more circumscribed. Population increase and the growing magnitude of poverty forced tens of thousands of young men and women to leave their homes and go on the tramp in search of subsistence and shelter. Poverty and the search for work were the compelling and confining determinants of everyday life. After a period of traveling the roads and byways or living on the streets in the slums of London and Bristol, some of the poor and out-of-work chose to labor in the colonies for the same reason they might have signed up in the army or navy: the future was mortgaged in return for the immediate benefit of food, lodgings, and regular work. Not every servant left England with the preconceived idea of becoming a tobacco planter or staying in the Chesapeake for good. The poorest emigrants indentured themselves to escape from their *immediate* situation—destitution, homelessness, unemployment—rather than because they had a clear concept of what life would be like in America. For many servants, short-term, not long-term, imperatives were the driving force behind immigration to the New World.

Underlying differences between free and unfree emigrants had a profound impact on the development of colonial society. Even small amounts of capital allowed individuals to pay their own transportation costs and escape the rigors of four to seven years hard labor in the tobacco fields serving someone else. Capital and, possibly, the help of kin, friends, or business connections enabled the free immigrant to establish himself immediately as a small planter or merchant, patent a few hundred acres, set up a plantation, and perhaps buy a few laborers. Money gave the free settler an enormous advantage over the mass of poor who arrived as bound laborers and created the most fundamental divisions in white society: between freedom and bondage, master and servant, independence and dependence.

2

English Landscapes

English settlers came, not simply from "England," but from London and the Home Counties, the Southeast, the Midlands, the West Country, and the North. They came from wood-pasture regions, clay vales, forests, small towns, large ports, and, in lesser numbers, the wolds and downs. The impact of migration, both on the societies that received settlers and the societies from which they came, can be understood only in the context of the rich variety of colonists' own local cultures and backgrounds. Such specificity provides the starting point for a discussion of the contribution of English local and provincial cultures to the social development of the early Chesapeake and the settlers' adaptation to their new society. Two regions are here considered in detail: the Vale of Berkeley, in Gloucestershire, and central Kent.

Gloucestershire and Emigration

John Smyth spent most of his life managing the financial affairs and estates of the lords Berkeley of Berkeley, Gloucestershire. In the course of more than fifty years' service, spanning the final years of Elizabeth's reign to the eve of the Civil War, he acquired an intimate knowledge of the lower half of the Vale of Severn, where the bulk of their property lay and where he lived in his new-built mansion at Smalcombe Court. With the loving care of a true enthusiast he sketched the peculiarities of each parish and manor, variations in local customs, notable historical events, current proverbs, genealogies, and holdings of the major landowners, all of which he gathered together toward the end of his life in his three-volume history of the Berkeley family. By temperament he was a traditionalist. His view of society was governed by a strong sense of hierarchy, honor, and place—a world where the lowly owed deference to their superiors, where a family's worth was judged by its pedigree and how long it had owned land in the area, and where lordship and governance were interchangeable. He paid scant attention to the changes that were going on around him, except to grumble about the laziness and insolence of servants, the cupidity of townspeople, the fanaticism of Puritans, and a general decline in the morals and standards in which he believed.[1]

At first sight, Smyth's conservatism and attachment to localism make him an unlikely candidate for extensive involvement in entrepreneurial activities. But, in fact, he was far from being the insular, rustic squire that he initially appears. In the mold of a gentleman-capitalist, he was at one and the same time a sharp lawyer frequently involved in litigation in the London courts, a shrewd businessman and "assiduous accumulator of property" who, backward-looking in his social values, was very much in touch with contemporary economic realities and opportunities. While lauding the virtues of old fashioned country life—thrift, self-sufficiency, honesty, and neighborliness—he had his fingers in numerous financial pies, one of which linked him closely to the expanding world of colonial commerce and colonization. Through his business interests, the several worlds of John Smyth came together: the Vale of Berkeley, London, and the James River, Virginia.[2]

Smyth was one of four principal sponsors, all from the region, behind an effort to establish a plantation on the James River in 1619. A number of prominent Gloucestershire gentry were involved, mostly providing financial backing, but some, like George Thorpe of Wanswell, Berkeley, Arnold Oldisworth of Wotton under Edge, and William Tracy of Hailes, in the Vale of Tewkesbury, set sail to make a new start in the fledgling colony. Smyth used his extensive contacts and knowledge of the local population to recruit colonists from the villages and hamlets around him: a husbandman, a gardener, and a glover from Wotton, a shoemaker and a smith from North Nibley, a joiner from Wanswell. Additionally, twenty men and women were rounded up "from the parts of Hailes." In all, about one hundred settlers from the region were transported to the banks of the James in 1619 and 1620. The project was a disaster. Most of the new arrivals, including Thorpe and

1. Irvine Gray, *Antiquaries of Glouchestershire and Bristol* (Gloucester, 1981), 36–40; James Herbert Cooke, "The Berkeley Manuscripts and Their Author—John Smith," *Bristol and Gloucestershire Archaeological Society*, V (1880–1881), 212–217; John Smyth, *A Description of the Hundred of Berkeley in the County of Gloucester and of Its Inhabitants*, vol. III of *The Berkeley Manuscripts*, ed. Sir John Maclean (Gloucester, 1883–1885), 4–33, 43, 349.

2. David Rollison, "The Bourgeois Soul of John Smyth of Nibley," *Social History*, XII (1987), 309–330.

Tracy, died of disease or were killed in Indian attacks; by the summer of 1622 only nineteen were alive. After periodic efforts to resurrect the plantation proved unsuccessful, Smyth and his partners eventually sold out to a group of London merchants in 1637, leaving only the name, "Burckley hundred," as a reminder of the men and women from Gloucestershire who lived and died there.[3]

Smyth's interest in Virginia faded with the collapse of the venture—too much time, energy, and money had been wasted—but the failure did not discourage others from emigrating. How many left the region during the 1630s and 1640s is unknown. Approximately 75 settlers from the county went to New England between 1620 and 1650, of whom the majority came from the Severn Valley and Bristol, and there was also a considerable movement of people to Ireland. Bristol merchants were already significantly involved in transatlantic trade, though not to the same extent as later in the century, and it is likely that there was a steady, if modest, flow of settlers to the Caribbean and Chesapeake from the West Country during these years. After midcentury the evidence is more certain. Of 113 indentured servants from Gloucestershire who immigrated to Virginia and Maryland in 1654–1661 and 1684–1686, 62 were from parishes and towns bordering the Severn River below Gloucester, 25 of whom were from the Vale of Berkeley. In the same periods, an additional 48 servants from the Vale immigrated to the West Indies. Since the places of origin of servants were not recorded in the Bristol registers for most of the peak period of emigration (1660s and 1670s), we may surmise that several hundred more left the region during this time, the great majority ending up in the Chesapeake.[4] For at least thirty or forty years,

3. Wesley Frank Craven, *The Southern Colonies in the Seventeenth Century, 1607–1689* (1949; Baton Rouge, La., 1970), 161–162; Joan Thirsk, "Projects for Gentlemen, Jobs for the Poor: Mutual Aid in the Vale of Tewkesbury, 1600–1630," in Patrick McGrath and John Cannon, eds., *Essays in Bristol and Gloucestershire History: The Centenary Volume of the Bristol and Gloucestershire Archaeological Society* ([Bristol], 1976), 147–169; Eric Gethyn-Jones, *George Thorpe and the Berkeley Company: A Gloucestershire Enterprise in Virginia* (Gloucester, 1982), 272–273; Smyth of Nibley Papers, V, fol. 65, Gloucester City and County Library; Nell Marion Nugent, comp., *Cavaliers and Pioneers: Abstracts of Virginia Land Patents and Grants*, 2 vols. (Richmond, Va., 1934, 1977), I, 53.

4. On 1630s and 1640s: Charles Edward Banks, *Topographical Dictionary of 2885 English Emigrants to New England, 1620–1650*, ed. Elijah Edward Brownell (Philadelphia, 1937), 55–59; Carl Bridenbaugh, *Vexed and Troubled Englishmen, 1590–1642* (New York, 1968), 465; Nicholas Canny, "Migration and Opportunity: Britain, Ireland, and the New World," *Irish Economic and Social History*, XII (1985), 7–32.

After 1650: "Servants to forraign plantations, 1654–1663," 04220 (1), "Servants to

parishes along the Severn Valley were regular contributors to the servant trade centered on Bristol.

Evidence of free settlers from the region is more scarce. Joseph Bridger came from the hamlet of Woodmancote in the parish of Dursley, and Richard Nelme, a planter of Northumberland County, Virginia, in the 1650s, probably came from the neighboring parish of North Nibley (where John Smyth lived). Thornbury, an early center of Quakerism, was the birthplace of Thomas Thurston, the "renegade Maryland Quaker," who immigrated to New England in 1656 and to Maryland two years later. He may have been related to the Daniel Thurston, also from Thornbury, who settled in Newbury, Massachusetts, before 1650. In his will of 1664, Throgmorton Trotman left fifty pounds to his "Cozen" Edward Trotman's daughter "in Vergena." The Trotmans were an important family in the Vale, and Throgmorton, though a wealthy merchant in London, appears to have maintained close ties with relatives and friends there. John Trotman, who owned land in Accomack County in the 1660s, may have been related to another branch of the family.[5]

As with servants, a key factor encouraging free migration was the proximity of Bristol. Just as the poor and unemployed were drawn to the city, so were young men seeking openings in trade and commerce; and since Bristol had long been the departure point for western voyages, it is understandable that they extended their search for work across the Atlantic.[6] Twelve weeks away by sea to the west, the Chesapeake offered an alternative range of opportunities to men and women who preferred not, for one reason or another, to remain at home or settle in neighboring towns, Bristol, or London.

As contemporaries were well aware, Gloucestershire consists of three distinctive regions. "The east part," wrote Sir Robert Atkyns in 1712, "is hilly, and not so very fertile . . . it is called Cotswold, and generally fed by sheep which yield an excellent sort of wool; it is parted from the Vale by a long ridge of hills, reaching from Campden near Worcestershire to Lansdown near Somersetshire. . . . The middle part is a rich vale, lying on each side

---

forraign plantacons, 1663–1679," 04220 (2), "Actions and Apprentices," 04355 (6), and "Actions and Apprentices," 04356 (1), Bristol Record Office; Noel Currer-Briggs, ed., "Indentured Servants from Bristol to America, 1654–1686" (MS).

5. John Bennett Boddie, *Seventeenth Century Isle of Wight County, Virginia* . . . (Chicago, 1938), chap. 22; Banks, *Topographical Dictionary*, ed. Brownell, 58; Nugent, comp., *Cavaliers and Pioneers*, I, 434.

6. Bernard Bailyn, *The Peopling of British North America: An Introduction* (New York, 1986), 26.

the great navigable river of Severn. . . . The west part, or forest division, is sufficiently fruitful, in good enclosed grounds, and well furnished with woods and iron."[7] These different landscapes, as Atkyns recognized, produced quite different local economies and social organization.

The broken hills of the Forest of Dean, "the famousest and best wooded forest in all England," were notable for blast furnaces, timber, poverty, and insularity. A rapidly growing population, supported by the iron industry, mining, and woodcrafts, guarded its local privileges and independence with a determination unusual even by the standards of the day. Throughout much of the period between 1600 and 1660, the forest was the scene of bitter and violent clashes between inhabitants and enclosers, which gave the area a reputation for unruliness and disorder. An "isolated outpost of the Welsh mountains," the region had more in common with the uplands to the west than with the rest of the county, but, in a sense, it belonged to neither: it was quite literally a law unto itself.[8]

Contrasts with the Cotswold Hills could not have been more stark. A broad plateau of gently rolling countryside, for the most part between 250 and 500 feet, the Cotswolds run diagonally across the county from the outskirts of Bristol in the south to the border with Warwickshire in the north and cover the whole eastern part of the county. In the sixteenth and seventeenth centuries it was famous for extensive pastures and "innumerable numbers of sheepe," which, John Smyth remarked with evident satisfaction, excused "the barrennes of the soile with a large profit drawne from them." By the Restoration, the more substantial yeomen possessed flocks of four to five hundred head and produced, according to Defoe, the finest wool in England. It was an open region with few woods and generally compact settlement: "stone villages nestled in small valleys" interspersed with small decayed clothing towns such as Stow on the Wold, Northleach, and Cirencester.[9]

Intersecting these two very different landscapes is the Vale of Severn, extending roughly from Evesham in the north to Bristol in the south, which in

7. Sir Robert Atkyns, *The Ancient and Present State of Glocestershire* (London, 1712), 17.

8. William Bradford Willcox, *Gloucestershire: A Study in Local Government, 1590–1642* (New Haven, Conn., 1940), 6; Buchanan Sharp, *In Contempt of All Authority: Rural Artisans and Riot in the West of England, 1586–1660* (Berkeley, Calif., 1980), 175–219, 252–255.

9. Smyth, *Hundred of Berkeley* 4; H.P.R. Finberg and Joan Thirsk, eds., *The Agrarian History of England and Wales* (Cambridge, 1967–), V, pt. 1, 179; Daniel Defoe, *A Tour through the Whole Island of Great Britain*, ed. Pat Rogers (Harmondsworth, England, 1971), 260–264.

the seventeenth century was given over, for the most part, to dairying, fruit production, and various manufactures. A wide, undulating country in the north, it narrows rapidly below Gloucester so that the "feet of the hills, in many places, stretch a considerable way towards the river; raising the surface into inequalities." At Berkeley, the hills of Dean and the Cotswolds Edge are no more than seven miles apart. Rather than uniformly flat, the Vale on the eastern side of the river can be envisaged as rising gently in a series of tiers from the Severn to the Cotswolds, a feature which encouraged considerable diversity among parishes only a few miles apart. Most observers were impressed by the fertility of the region. Writing of Berkeley Hundred, John Smyth commented: "The Soile is for the most part bountefull; ritch in pasture and meadow, fruitfull in procreation of divers and different kindes of trees. . . . The lowe and fat grounds doe yield such abundance of pasture for kyne and oxen, as sufficeth the greedines of those beasts, and covetousnes of their owners." Nearly a century later, following "the course of the famous River Severn," Defoe described the area as "the richest, most fertile, and most agreeable part of England; the bank of the Thames only excepted."[10]

Despite the emphasis on the richness of soils, there remained significant pockets of marginal land throughout the Vale. East of Tewkesbury and around Winchcombe, for example, where soils were poor, the local population turned to the production of tobacco, mustard, hemp, and flax and made a living from intensively cultivated small plots of land. Tobacco cultivation, in particular, attracted large numbers of casual laborers to the area. Similar principles governed the employment of the poor in manufactures. The lower half of the Vale was a rapidly developing industrial region notable for broadcloth production along the Cotswolds escarpment and coal mining in Kingswood Chase, just north of Bristol. Employment in manufacturing was not merely supplemental to farming. In many parishes a large proportion of inhabitants were wholly dependent on wages from industry, a fact that contributed heavily to poverty and unrest in these areas.[11] The dynamic aspects

10. Finberg and Thirsk, eds., *Agrarian History of England and Wales*, V, pt. 1, 187–191; William Marshall, *The Rural Economy of Gloucestershire . . .* , 2 vols. (Gloucester, 1789), II, 86; Smyth, *Hundred of Berkeley*, 4, 10; Defoe, *Tour through Great Britain*, ed. Rogers, 364.

11. Finberg and Thirsk, eds., *Agrarian History of England and Wales*, V, pt. 1, 170–172; Rollison, "Bourgeois Soul," *Soc. Hist.*, XII (1987), 316–317; Sharp, *In Contempt of All Authority*, chap. 6; Robert W. Malcolmson, " 'A Set of Ungovernable People': The Kingswood Colliers in the Eighteenth Century," in John Brewer and John Styles, eds., *An Ungovernable People: The English and Their Law in the Seventeenth and Eighteenth*

of social and economic change in the region were tied closely to the fortunes of its manufactures and trade. Much of the area's history in the seventeenth century can be explained through the interplay of agrarian and industrial sectors.

Plenty and Want: The Vale of Berkeley

No obvious topographical or social boundaries define the Vale of Berkeley. The area discussed here comprises fifteen contiguous parishes on the eastern bank of the Severn midway between Gloucester and Bristol (see Figure 6). Like the rest of the Severn Valley, it was very populous: the "houses in it are almost innumerable, the churches passing fair, and the towns standing very thick." Population growth had been rapid in the fifty years following the accession of Elizabeth I, rising from seven or eight thousand to about twelve thousand, but growth was not sustained in the seventeenth century, and by the 1670s the region's population had increased little, if at all.[12]

This pattern is not unique to the Vale—it has much in common with the general course of population change in England from 1550 to 1700—but regional as well as national factors played an important role in influencing changes. Atkyns believed that the lack of increase in the county during the seventeenth century could be "attributed to the many persons which go

---

Centuries (London, 1980), 85–127; John S. Moore, ed., *The Goods and Chattels of Our Forefathers: Frampton Cotterell and District Probate Inventories, 1539–1804* (Chichester, 1976), 13, 16.

12. Willcox, *Gloucestershire*, 3. Occupying 7.4% of the total area of Gloucestershire, the Vale supported between 12% and 13% of the county's population in the 17th century. The land areas of the Vale and entire county were derived from the national census of 1801 (William Page, ed., *The Victoria History of the County of Gloucester*, II [London, 1907], 175–176, 180–181, 183, 185–186).

For population estimates, 1548: see John Maclean, "Chantry Certificates, Gloucestershire (Roll 22)," *BGAS*, VIII (1884), 229–308 (communicants multiplied by 1.67). 1551: James Gairdner, "Bishop Hooper's Visitation of Gloucester," *English Historical Review*, XIX (1904), 98–121 (communicants multiplied by 1.67). 1563: Bodleian MSS, Rawlinson C. 790, Bodleian Library, Oxford (families multiplied by 4.5). 1603: Harleian MSS 594, British Library (communicants multiplied by 1.67). 1650: C. R. Elrington, "The Survey of Church Livings in Gloucestershire, 1650," *BGAS*, LXXXIII (1964), 85–98 (households multiplied by 4.5). 1664 and 1672: E179/247/16, E179/247/13, E179/247/14, Hearth Tax returns (households multiplied by 4.5), Public Record Office. 1676: Compton Census, photocopy, 37/7, Gloucestershire Record Office (communicants multiplied by 1.67). 1712: Atkyns, *Ancient and Present State* (households and total populations).

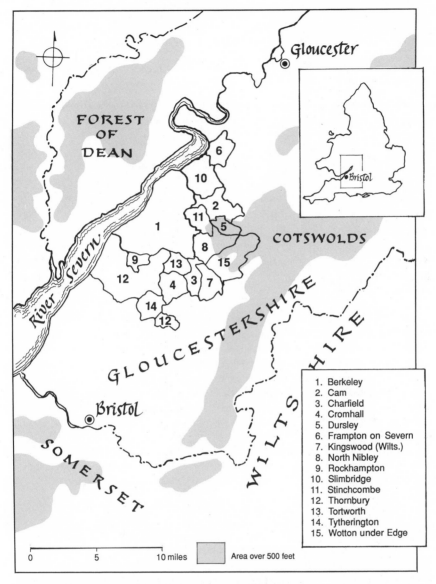

Figure 6. The Vale of Berkeley. *Drawn by Richard Stinely*

away yearly to the cities of London and Bristol, and from Bristol to Ireland, and into the foreign plantations."[13] The region surrounding Bristol was a major recruiting ground for emigrants, but it is unlikely that out-migration

13. E. A. Wrigley and R. S. Schofield, *The Population History of England, 1541–1871: A Reconstruction* (Cambridge, Mass., 1981), 531–534; Atkyns, *Ancient and Present State*, 22.

TABLE 8

Population in the Vale of Berkeley, 1563–1712

Parish	1563	1603	1650	1676	1712
Berkeley	1,825	2,890	2,034	2,210	2,900
Cam	325	670	900[a]	735[b]	800
Charfield	125	180	150	140	145
Cromhall	200	405	360	130	360
Dursley	865	875	1,100	1,340	2,500
Kingswood	—	235	—	850	1,200
North Nibley	405	690	810	975	1,000
Slimbridge	455	500	405	—	560
Stinchcombe	195	370	ca. 400	418[c]	500
Thornbury	1,215	1,910[d]	1,665	1,390	1,450
Tortworth	190	310	305	285	240
Wotton under Edge	620	2,030[e]	1,500[f]	2,885	3,500

Notes: [a]The return gives a figure of 1,300 but probably includes the 400 inhabitants of Stinchcombe; if removed, a more plausible total of 900 results.   [b]The return of 1,135 included Stinchcombe; again, 400 inhabitants were deducted.   [c]Return for 1695: P 312, MI/3, Gloucestershire Record Office.   [d]The returns for Thornbury and the tithings of Falfield, Morton, Oldbury on Severn, Kington, and Rangeworthy give a combined total of 3,580 inhabitants, which is clearly a mistake. Since the figure for Thornbury is probably 705, not 1,705 as given in the returns, the overall population of the parish would be reduced to 1,910.   [e]This figure is suspiciously high.   [f]The "5000 souls" given in the return is an error.

Sources: 1563: Bodleian MSS, Rawlinson C. 790, Bodleian Library, Oxford (families multiplied by 4.5). 1603: Harleian MSS 594, British Library (communicants multiplied by 1.67). 1650: C. R. Elrington, "The Survey of Church Livings in Gloucestershire, 1650," *Bristol and Gloucestershire Archaeological Society*, LXXXIII (1964), 85–98. 1676: Compton Census, photocopy, 37/7, Gloucestershire Record Office (communicants multiplied by 1.67). 1712: Sir Robert Atkyns, *The Ancient and Present State of Glocestershire* (London, 1712).

alone accounts for the lack of growth. Although there was a significant and fairly constant flow of people out of the Vale during most of the century, as a wood-pasture region with a number of important manufactures it was also a major receptor of migrants. Explanations of population change must therefore be sought in a closer analysis of the relationship between demography and economic developments.

The general trend of population change in eleven parishes across 150 years (from 1563 to 1712) is clear, although there are some difficulties in interpreting individual figures (see Table 8). Dursley, described by John Leland in the late 1530s as "a praty clothinge towne," hardly grew at all down to 1600, but thereafter the increase was dramatic: from fewer than 900 in the early seventeenth century to about 2,500 at the beginning of the eighteenth. Wotton under Edge, the chief clothing town in the Vale, grew even more rapidly, from fewer than 1,000 in the 1550s to more than 3,000 by 1712 and 4,000 twenty years later. Other clothing centers, such as North Nibley, Cam, Stinchcombe, and Kingswood, also show impressive growth over the period, their populations either doubling or tripling.[14]

Different factors contributed to growth (see Figure 7). North Nibley, "pleasantly seated on a comely hill," experienced continuous natural increase throughout the period despite severe visitations of the plague in the 1560s and late 1630s and heavy mortality in the 1590s. Baptisms consistently outnumbered burials by a wide margin (Table 9), perhaps giving credence to John Smyth's conviction that no village "in the county or scarce in the kingdome standeth in a sweeter aire." Cam exhibits a similar pattern, except that the surplus of baptisms over burials is more impressive in the late sixteenth than in the seventeenth century. Wotton under Edge, by contrast, has a different pattern. There is respectable, if not spectacular, natural increase down to the 1660s, but thereafter the gap between baptisms and burials narrows significantly. Unlike Cam and North Nibley, immigration rather than natural increase was the major factor that contributed to Wotton's large population rise during the period.[15]

Parishes that were mainly devoted to farming experienced little, if any, increase during the seventeenth and eighteenth centuries. Berkeley and Thornbury, the largest towns and important markets in the 1550s, gradually lost their dominance in the following hundred years. The signs of decline had been obvious for some time. Both had once been active in cloth production, but even when Leland passed through the county the trade was in decay. "There hathe bene good clothing in Thornebyry," he remarked, "but now idlenes muche reynithe there," while the "towne of Berkeley is no great thynge." According to John Smyth, Berkeley had never recovered from the plundering of the Wars of the Roses during the fifteenth century. Although

14. Lucy Toulmin Smith, ed., *The Itinerary of John Leland in or about the Years 1535–1543 . . .* , 6 vols. (London, 1910), V, 96. See note 12, above, for sources relating to population growth in Dursley, Wotton under Edge, North Nibley, Cam, Stinchcombe, and Kingswood.

15. Demographic data for Cam, North Nibley, and Wotton under Edge supplied by the Cambridge Group for the Study of Population and Social Structure, to whom I am most grateful. Smyth, *Hundred of Berkeley*, 260–261.

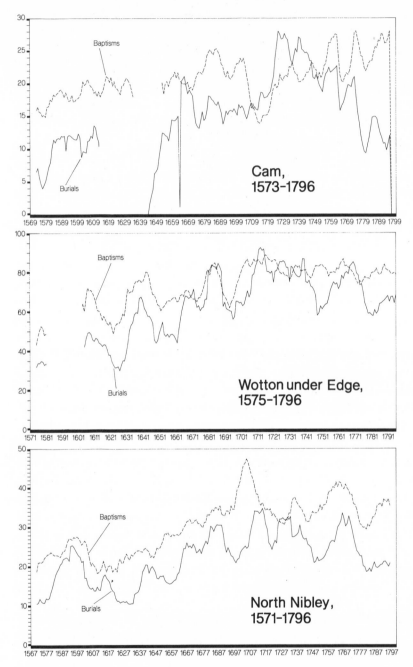

Figure 7. Baptisms and Burials in Gloucestershire, 1571–1796

TABLE 9

Baptisms and Burials, Vale of Berkeley, 1581–1640

Time Span	Cam		North Nibley		Wotton under Edge	
	Baptisms	Burials	Baptisms	Burials	Baptisms	Burials
1581–1600	361	228	498	434	—	—
1601–1620	387	—	409[a]	320[a]	1,174	836
1621–1640	378	—	461[a]	240[b]	1,276	887
1641–1660	270[a]	—	508	348	1,373	1,037
1661–1680	416	340[c]	610	484	1,359	1,236
1681–1700	452	328	690	535	1,493	1,398
1701–1720	365	330	811	584	1,717	1,590
1721–1740	419	500	683	580	1,605	1,627

Notes: [a]Underregistration owing to defective registers.   [b]Plague in 1638–1639.
[c]Plague in the 1660s.

Sources: Data supplied by the Cambridge Group for the Study of the History of Population and Social Structure.

its population grew rapidly in the latter half of the sixteenth century, the increase was not sustained in the seventeenth and, in fact, may have declined by 1650. After the Restoration, burials substantially outnumbered births for twenty-two of the thirty-five years between 1660 and 1695. A century later, Ralph Bigland observed that "few alterations have taken Place, either as to the Appearance or Extent of the Town," since John Smyth's day.[16]

Berkeley and Thornbury, with their small market centers and rich meadows, pasture, and arable lands, gradually moved more and more toward an emphasis on dairy farming, as did parishes such as Slimbridge, Frampton on Severn, and Tortworth and a few minor clothing villages in the Vale that could not compete with the rapidly growing towns of the Cotswolds Edge. During the seventeenth century there was an increasing division between predominantly agricultural parishes bordering the Severn, which occupied the low-lying grounds and contained the best pasture and arable land, and a

16. Smith, ed., Itinerary of John Leland, V, 100–101; Smyth, Hundred of Berkeley, 84; P42 (Berkeley parish registers), GRO. Between 1660 and 1695, an average of 60 persons were buried per year, compared to 50 baptized: see Ralph Bigland, Historical, Monumental, and Genealogical Collections Relative to the County of Gloucester, 2 vols. (London, 1791–1792), I, 151–512.

group of expanding industrial towns and villages located in the northeastern part of the Vale on, or just below, the Cotswold Hills.[17]

Similar changes were taking place elsewhere in the region. Seven parishes just north of Bristol in the early seventeenth century reveal the same emerging distinction between agricultural and industrial villages. In the former, 70–80 percent of the male population were involved in farming, compared to fewer than 10 percent in manufactures, while in the mainly industrial parishes farming accounted for only 30–40 percent of the population and textiles and coal mining for 20–30 percent. Industries stimulated demographic growth. Throughout the county the population of clothing centers increased on average by four times during the sixteenth and seventeenth centuries, and Kingswood Chase, where there was a rapid increase in the number of collieries, grew by six times between 1600 and 1800.[18]

Shifts in the local economy and population in the Vale demonstrate the difficulty of generalizing about factors that might have led individuals to migrate. Men and women who immigrated to America came from declining market towns, pastoral parishes, and proto-industrial villages, not from any single type of community. The changing balance of population within the region suggests that people who left from towns such as Berkeley and Thornbury had the option of moving to expanding cloth-producing centers nearby if they chose not to leave the area. Growing industrial communities such as Wotton under Edge offered migrants an alternative to seeking opportunities beyond the Vale and absorbed some of the surplus population that might otherwise have increased the number of immigrants who found their way to Ireland and the plantations. Especially evident is the complexity of migratory patterns within the area. Atkyns was correct in identifying a significant movement of people out of Gloucestershire, but he paid less attention to in-migration from other provinces and to the considerable volume of short-range mobility within the region. Migration from the Vale of Berkeley to America should be seen against high levels of intra- and interregional movement.

What kind of society did emigrants from the Vale of Berkeley leave? For much of the early modern period the twin pillars of the local economy were pasture farming and broadcloth production. The significance of industry in

17. F. V. Emery, "England circa 1600," in H. C. Darby, ed., *A New Historical Geography of England before 1600* (London, 1976), 277–278.

18. Moore, ed., *Goods and Chattels*, 11–18; David Rollison, "Bourgeois Soul," *Soc. Hist.*, XII (1987), 316–317; Rollison, *The Local Origins of Modern Society: Gloucestershire, 1500–1800* (New York, 1992), chap. 1.

TABLE 10

Occupational Status of Males in the Vale of Berkeley and in Gloucestershire, 1608

	Vale of Berkeley		Gloucestershire	
Status or Occupational Group	No.	%	No.	%
Gentry and professions	45	2.2	390	2.1
Merchants and dealers	0		53	.3
Official positions	0		21	.1
Food and drink trades	95	4.6	872	4.7
Textile industry	856	41.0	3,534	19.0
Leather trade	105	5.0	729	3.9
Building trades and woodworking	103	4.9	981	5.3
Metalworking trades	44	2.1	576	3.1
Agriculture	529	25.4	6,146	33.0
Mining, quarrying, and charcoal burning	0		186	1.0
Semiskilled and unskilled labor	254	12.2	3,318	17.8
Miscellaneous	10	.5	65	.3
Unidentified	0		34	.2
Occupation not stated	45	2.2	1,719	9.2
Total	2,086	100.0	18,624	100.0

Sources: John Smyth, *Men and Armour for Gloucestershire in 1608*, ed. Sir John Maclean (London, 1902); John Wyatt, unpublished research.

the region is underlined by the occupations of males in the early seventeenth century (Table 10). More than 40 percent of working men from the Vale were engaged in woolen manufacture, compared to 19 percent for the whole county. The next-largest category, agriculture, occupied about a third of the work force. Cloth production was firmly established in Gloucestershire by the early Middle Ages, and the county quickly established itself as one of the most important regions of manufacture in England. By the early seventeenth century, more than twenty thousand men, women, and children were employed in the industry throughout Gloucestershire, nearly a quarter of the entire population of the county.[19]

19. Occupational structure derived from John Smyth, *Men and Armour for Gloucestershire in 1608*, ed. John Maclean (London, 1902). Figures do not include Kingswood, which in the 17th century was located in a detached part of Wiltshire. J. de L. Mann, *The Cloth Industry in the West of England from 1640 to 1880* (Oxford, 1971), xiii–xiv; R. Perry, "The Gloucestershire Woollen Industry, 1100–1690," *BGAS*, LXVI (1945), 49–137; Jennifer Tann, *Gloucestershire Woollen Mills* (Newton Abbot, 1967), 29.

The industry was organized on a putting-out basis. According to Defoe, interspersed between the main market towns are "a very great number of villages, . . . hamlets, and scattered houses, in which, generally speaking, the spinning work of all this manufacture is performed by the poor people; the master clothiers who generally live in the greater towns, sending out the wool weekly to their houses, by their servants and horses, and, at the same time, bringing back the yarn that they have spun and finished, which then is fitted for the loom." The clothier was key to the system. It was he who purchased the raw wool, distributed it to his carders and spinners and then to the weavers. After fulling, drawing, and shearing, the cloth was either sold locally or, more commonly, taken by packhorse to Blackwell Hall, London.[20]

Production was increasingly dominated by big capitalists. Clothiers needed large amounts of money to purchase the raw materials, pay their employees' wages, and extend credit, sometimes for long periods, to prospective buyers. Although the village freeholder or copyholder who was also a small-scale clothier was still in evidence, he was generally of a dying breed. The fall in exports of unfinished cloth, the rising price of fine wool, the necessity to provide long-term credit, and the growing complexity of farming, which made it more profitable to concentrate on agriculture than to engage in two occupations at once, progressively weakened the position of the small producer. While the industry offered considerable opportunities to men who had inherited or could acquire capital, the vast majority of textile workers had no other resources than their labor.[21]

Dependent on the clothier for their work and the market for food, weavers and clothworkers were among the poorest groups of workers in preindustrial society. Hardship was caused by chronic underemployment and periodic and prolonged unemployment owing to abrupt and severe fluctuations in the trade. John Barnesdale, minister of Cam, commented in 1666 "that the generality of the poore and meane people of our Parish (wch are many) [who] had their dependence uppon the trade of cloathing . . . are now almost wholly out of imployment, whereby the number of those who are inforc't to cast themselves uppon us for relief is intollerably increased." One consequence of the serious recession of the 1660s and 1670s was a steady increase in paupers in Kingswood, to the extent that there were "near three times as many families receiving alms as there were housekeepers." Annual disbursements to the poor continued to rise in the early 1690s, from £166 in

20. Defoe, *Tour through Great Britain*, ed. Rogers, 261; Tann, *Woollen Mills*, 20–25.
21. Mann, *Cloth Industry*, 89–98.

1692 to £219 in 1695. Numerous entries in the parish's Overseers of the Poor accounts testify to the problem of unemployment, describing recipients of relief as "haveing no worke." Such was the severity of fluctuations in the industry that annual payments to those thrown on the parish could rise by nearly a third over four years. The depression was so bad that a group of justices wrote to the Privy Council drawing their attention to the plight of the starving unemployed, "as their faces (to our griefs) do manifest."[22]

In hard times textile workers had little to fall back on. As early as 1597 the majority of householders in Kingswood (100 of 170) had insufficient land to support their families and were entirely dependent on spinning and weaving for their living. The problem of unemployment was exacerbated by the increasing numbers of textile workers, especially weavers. Richard Stephens of Gloucestershire complained at the end of the century that "many years since (as I have heard) a Weaver was esteemed a good Trade, but now one of the poorest, it being now commonly practised by Parishes to bind out their poor boyes to weavers." In the same letter, he continued, "The Practice of Clothiers to turn off their workemen upon any deadness of Trade and paying them in comodities above the market price is a great mischief to the countrey."[23]

To poor clothworkers living in cramped tenements and cottages in the bustling towns along the Cotswolds Edge, the spacious pastures and meadows of the countryside nearby must have seemed like a different world. Rural parishes of the Vale of Berkeley had much in common with the dairying regions of Hampshire, Wiltshire, Dorset, and Somerset and formed part of that area of England described by contemporaries as "woodland" or wood-pasture, characterized by fertile clay soils, dairying or mixed agriculture, numerous family farms, scattered settlement, and a good deal of old enclosure. During the late sixteenth and seventeenth centuries, farmers increasingly specialized in the production of high-quality cheese for the local market, Bristol, and London, a trend that continued in the eighteenth century. "All the lower part of . . . Gloucestershire," Defoe reported, "is full of large feeding farms, which we call dairies, and the cheese thay make . . . is excellent good of its

22. "A Booke of actes, rates and monuments of the parish of Cam . . . ," Berkeley MSS, General Series, no. 95, p. 50; Historical Manuscripts Commission, *Report on Manuscripts in Various Collections*, [15th Report] (London, 1901), I, 154; P193, OV 2/1, GRO; Tann, *Woollen Mills*, 38.

23. Sharp, *In Contempt of All Authority*, chap. 6; Stephens cited in Mann, *Cloth Industry* 90, 105.

TABLE 11

Size of Dairy Herds, Vale of Berkeley, 1611–1699

	Farms					
	1611–1640		1641–1670		1671–1699	
Cattle per Farm	No.	%	No.	%	No.	%
0	10	33.3	13	28.9	58	27.5
1–4	11	36.7	7	15.6	20	9.5
5–9	7	23.3	14	31.1	34	16.1
10–19	2	6.7	8	17.8	57	27.0
20+	0		3	6.7	42	19.9
Total	30	100.0	45	100.1	211	100.0

Note: Average cattle per farm: 1611–1640: 5.1. 1641–1670: 8.9. 1671–1699: 15.8.
Source: Probate Inventories, 1611–1699, Gloucestershire Record Office.

kind. . . . A vast quantity is every week . . . carried . . . to London." William Marshall was of the same opinion. The hundred of Berkeley, he commented, "has ever been celebrated for the superior quality of its cheese."[24]

Probate inventories illustrate the growing concentration on dairying in the seventeenth century. Average numbers of milk cows owned by farmers rose steadily from 5.1 in the period 1611–1640, to 8.9 in 1641–1670, and 15.8 in 1671–1699 (see Table 11). Yeomen with herds in excess of 20 head, rare or nonexistent in the early part of the century, were numerous by the 1680s and 1690s and during the eighteenth century became more numerous still. These were the large capitalist farmers of the area, producing cheese by the hundredweight. Richard Collins of Thornbury, who died in 1682, furnishes a good example. At his death he owned eighteen cows, ten "Young Beasts," and a bull together valued at £83 (just under a third of his total estate). In his "Cockloft" were fifteen hundredweight of cheese and three "flitches" (sides) of bacon worth £13. Thomas Weare of Charfield, who died a few years later, had 272 cheeses in his loft, which, with a few other goods, came to £26. Production was not confined to big farmers. Nearly 70 percent of inventories of yeomen and husbandmen in the Vale in the second half of the century contained references to cheese or cheese-making implements

24. Finberg and Thirsk, eds., *Agrarian History of England and Wales*, IV, 1–112; William Harrison, *A Description of England*, ed. George Edelen (Ithaca, N.Y., 1968), 259; Defoe, *Tour through Great Britain*, ed. Rogers, 264; Marshall, *Rural Economy*, II, 103.

TABLE 12

Livestock, Crops, and Products in Inventories, Vale of Berkeley, 1660–1699

Item	Farmers Owning (N=254)		Nonfarmers Owning (N=188)	
	No.	%	No.	%
Fauna				
Cattle	204	80.3	55	29.3
Horses	182	71.7	81	43.1
Swine	166	65.4	63	33.5
Sheep	132	52.0	36	19.1
Poultry	18	7.1	3	1.6
Bees	13	5.1	4	2.1
Cheese-making equipment	174	68.5	32	17.0
Flora				
"Corn"	80	31.5	21	11.2
Wheat	69	27.2	19	10.1
Barley	24	9.4	13	6.9
Oats	11	4.3	5	2.7
Rye	2	.8	0	
Beans	34	13.4	11	5.9
Pease	22	8.7	6	3.2
Maslin	7	2.8	4	2.1
Pulse	4	1.6	0	
Vetches	3	1.2	0	
Turnips	1	.4	0	
Apples	14	5.5	3	1.6
Cider	32	12.6	9	4.8

Note: Farmers are here defined as yeomen and husbandmen; nonfarmers are all other male occupations.

Source: Probate inventories, 1660–1699, Gloucestershire Record Office.

(Table 12). Single or double Gloucester cheese was "an almost ubiquitous commodity on local farms."[25]

Besides their cattle, most farmers owned a few sheep, horses, and pigs.

25. Probate Inventories, 1660–1700, GRO; Prerogative Court of Canterbury (PCC) PROB 4, 5, 522, 1541, Public Record Office; Marshall, *Rural Economy*, II, 98; Moore, ed., *Goods and Chattels*, 29.

Large flocks of sheep were uncommon, pastures being generally reserved for milk cows, but in most parishes there could be found a few farmers who owned fifty to one hundred head of sheep, or even a couple of hundred. They were raised for their wool but also served as an occasional source of meat for local consumption. Horses were found on more than 70 percent of estates and were mainly kept for transportation or carting, since the heavy clays of the Vale encouraged the use of oxen for plowing. Only on the lighter soils of the Cotswolds Edge were horses routinely used as plow beasts. Swine were raised primarily for meat and were fed on the by-products of cheese production. Farmers, according to Defoe, "send a very great quantity of bacon up to London. . . . This bacon is raised in such quantities here, by reason of the great dairies . . . the hogs being fed with the vast quantity of whey, and skimmed milk, which so many farmers have to spare, and which must, otherwise, be thrown away."[26] Flitches of bacon, salted down, as well as Gloucester cheese were also sent to Bristol, where demand rose rapidly in the second half of the seventeenth century in response to the victualing trade and the requirements of transatlantic shipping.

Arable husbandry played a relatively minor role in the agriculture of the Vale. Acreages of crops sown, where given, were small (usually fewer than ten acres), and crops, either on the ground or in store, were not present in inventories with anything near the same frequency as livestock (Table 12). "Corn" was mentioned in fewer than a third of estates, wheat in just more than a quarter, and barley in fewer than a tenth. The balance between arable and pasture is indeterminable, but findings from south of the area suggest that the proportion of arable was usually less than 20 percent of the total holding and probably nearer 10 percent.[27]

Despite the drift to large-scale capitalist production, it is clear that the region was not dominated by big farms. On ten manors belonging to the lords Berkeley in 1667, half of copyholders (not counting cottagers) rented fewer than twenty acres, and a further 31 percent had fewer than fifty. Only 6 percent farmed more than one hundred acres. Other parts of the Severn Valley

26. Defoe, *Tour through Great Britain*, ed. Rogers, 264.

27. The time of year when an inventory was made must be taken into account, since crops might not be mentioned because they had just been sown or sold. Acreages were itemized in only 59 inventories (23.2% of the total sample). Of these, 27 farms had fewer than 5 acres (45.8%); 12 had 5–9 acres (20.3%); 7 had 10–20 acres (11.9%); 11 had 20–50 acres (18.6%); 1 had 50–100 acres (1.7%); and 1 had more than 100 acres (Probate Inventories, 1660–1700, GRO).

On arable versus pasture: Moore, ed., *Goods and Chattels*, 30; Bigland, *Collections*, n.p. (see Tortworth).

followed a similar pattern, with yeomen's farms averaging between 60 and 160 acres. Most were family farms owned or held on long leases. Only a few large farms employed agricultural workers.[28]

Much of the region was enclosed by the seventeenth century. In 1646, "diverse disorderly persons, taking advantage of the late warres," pulled down enclosures and burnt cottages in Slimbridge and Frampton on Severn. Four years later, a troop of horse was stationed in the area "for preventing the rude multitude who are gathered there from doing any further prejudice to the proprietors and estates of particular persons in those parts, by throwing down the fences of their grounds." The reference may be to Diggers, but there had been trouble in the area for years stemming from attempts to enclose the New Warth (three hundred acres of rich, fertile land newly gained from changes in the course of the Severn), which was hotly contested by inhabitants of the two parishes that claimed right of commons. Such violence was untypical. The lords Berkeley were not aggressive landlords and generally favored negotiation rather than confrontation with their tenants. Enclosure, whether undertaken by villagers or manorial lords, was usually preceded by agreement between the various parties involved and was seen as a means of protecting valuable lands from depredations by squatters and poor migrants.[29]

Consolidation of holdings encouraged improvements by allowing farmers greater flexibility in the use of their lands and thereby helped raise output. It would have been virtually impossible to accommodate the concentration on pasture farming within the traditional open-field system, which placed much greater emphasis on arable.[30]

---

28. "A booke of rentalls of all the Lord Berkeleys Lands [1634]," Gloucestershire Collections MSS, 16066, Gloucester City Library; "Rentals of Different Manors, 1667," Berkeley MSS, unbound books, no. 50, Berkeley Manor Court Books, 1656–71, 1676–82, 1680–88, 1688–93, 1694–1702, General Series, nos. 50, 52, 55, 57, 60, Berkeley Castle muniments room. Evidence of land owned by freeholders is not available in the 1660s, but in 1634 about a third of 227 individuals paying chief rent on nine Berkeley manors had more than 20 acres, and, of these, only 13% had more than 50. Thirsk and Moore in Finberg and Thirsk, eds., *Agrarian History of England and Wales*, V, pt. 1, 190–191; and in Moore, ed., *Goods and Chattels*, 13–15.

29. Mary Anne Everett Green, ed., *Calendar of State Papers*, Domestic Series, [Commonwealth, II], *1650* (London, 1876), 218; Smyth, *Hundred of Berkeley*, 328–330; Sharp, *In Contempt of All Authority*, 173, 243; Roger B. Manning, *Village Revolts: Social Protest and Popular Disturbances, 1509–1640* (Oxford, 1988), 127–129.

30. Joan Johnson, *Tudor Gloucestershire* (Gloucester, 1985), 69–73; Moore, ed., *Goods and Chattels*, 29; J. A. Yelling, *Common Field and Enclosure in England, 1450–1850* (Lon-

Society in the Vale was open and fluid and was characterized by large inequalities in wealth. At the very top of the social hierarchy were the lords Berkeley: peers of the realm, the greatest landowners in the region, and representatives of one of the oldest and most distinguished families in England.[31] Family prestige and wealth were symbolized by the massive presence of Berkeley Castle, dominating the landscape roundabout, where the Berkeleys had lived since the reign of Henry II and where they still held courts leet and baron in the seventeenth century, five hundred years later. If their wealth had declined substantially since medieval times, nevertheless they were still the most prominent family in the region and retained "a very great estate in the county." John Smyth recounted an old saying of the Vale: "Hee is a hughy proud man, hee thinks himselfe as great as my lord Berkeley," adding, "Our simple ancient honesties knewe not a greater to make comparison by, when this proverbe first arose." After much financial retrenchment during the seventeenth century the family's income from all sources was about five thousand to six thousand pounds in the 1680s.[32]

Whether because of their preoccupation at court or their travels abroad, the Berkeleys paid little attention to the running of local affairs, and, instead, leadership passed to a group of about forty gentry families. There was considerable variation among them. A minority, like the Thorpes, Sanigers, Freames, and Bassets, had lived in the region for centuries; and others, such as the Smyths of Nibley, the Hales, Fusts, Wises, and Hookes, were relative newcomers, arriving in the sixteenth and seventeenth centuries. Wealth, however, was far more important in determining a gentleman's status than lineage. The top rank of squires held lordships of numerous small manors scattered throughout the area or owned large amounts of freehold (and frequently both). Land, let rather than farmed, was the basis of their wealth and power, which was conspicuously displayed in the provincial magnificence of their family seats: Smyth of Smalcombe Court, Fust of Hill, Dawes of Bradley, and Ducie Morton of Tortworth. Lesser gentry possessed smaller estates, perhaps as little as a few hundred acres and some tenements. Their holdings were usually concentrated in one or two parishes, within which their influence was largely confined, such as the Bridgers and Essingtons

don, 1977), 27, 34, 175; W. E. Tate, "Gloucestershire Enclosure Acts and Awards," *BGAS*, LXIV (1943), 1–70.

31. Lawrence Stone, *Family and Fortune: Studies in Aristocratic Finance in the Sixteenth and Seventeenth Centuries* (Oxford, 1973), chap. 8.

32. Smyth, *Hundred of Berkeley*, 26; Stone, *Family and Fortune*, 267.

of Slimbridge, the Lawrences of Berkeley, the Hardings of Cam, and the Archards of North Nibley.[33]

As in other parts of the country, the gentry monopolized the most important offices at county, hundred, and parish level. But they did not form a Venetian oligarchy; their ranks were open to those who could afford to pay the entry fee. Clothiers and mercers, among the wealthiest men in Gloucestershire, were frequently accepted into the squirearchy. "It was no extraordinary thing," Defoe reported, "to have clothiers in that county worth, from ten thousand, to forty thousand pounds a man, and many of the great families, who now pass for gentry . . . have been originally raised from, and built up by this truly noble manufacture." In the Vale, the gentry families of Hicks, Purnell, Webb, and Witchel were all closely connected with the woolen industry.[34]

The richest groups in society—gentry, clothiers, and large farmers—made up 10–15 percent of the region's householders in the second half of the seventeenth century (Table 13). Below them a broad range of men and women of middling status (worth £50–£250 in personalty at death), engaged in farming, rural trades, food and drink processing, and small-scale manufacturing, constituted just less than a third of the population. The yeomanry formed the core of this group. At the top end of the wealth spectrum their way of life was virtually indistinguishable from that of the lesser gentry while at the bottom they differed little from husbandmen. Ownership of their farms, however, set them apart from most of the region's inhabitants; the large amounts of capital required to buy land and stock were beyond the means of most men.

The majority of people at the bottom end of the middling range (£50–£99)—husbandmen, innholders, victuallers, carpenters, cordwainers, and blacksmiths—earned a living by working smallholdings, providing goods and services to the local community, or both. There was sometimes no clear division between them and their poorer neighbors, but, in general, the possession of a skill, a little land, or age and experience placed them above those at "the Feet of the Body Politique" and ensured a degree of independence. John Corbet summed up the "whole middle ranke of the people" in 1647

33. James Horn, biographical files, Vale of Berkeley; Thomas May, *The Visitation of the County of Gloucester . . . 1682–83*, ed. T. Fitz-Roy Fenwick and Walter C. Metcalfe (Exeter, 1884); Atkyns, *Ancient and Present State* (see engravings of family seats); Smyth, *Hundred of Berkeley*.

34. Defoe, *Tour through Great Britain*, ed. Rogers, 262.

TABLE 13

Personal Wealth in the Vale of Berkeley, 1660–1699

| | % of Decedents (N=983) | | | | |
| | Wealth | | | | |
Time Span	0–£9	£10–£49	£50–£99	£100–£249	£250+
	Unadjusted				
1660–1669	5.0	32.5	23.8	22.5	16.3
1670–1679	9.2	34.8	24.1	20.6	11.3
1680–1689	4.8	30.3	23.6	24.7	16.6
1690–1699	9.9	32.6	18.8	24.7	14.1
1660–1699	7.0	31.8	22.2	23.9	15.1
	Adjusted: 50% of Population Too Poor to Pay Hearth Tax				
1664	55.0	14.4	11.1	12.0	7.5
	Adjusted: 33% of Population Too Poor to Pay Hearth Tax				
1672	42.2	17.0	14.8	15.9	10.0

Sources: Probate Inventories, 1660–1669, GDR Consistory Court Act Books, Gloucestershire Record Office; PCC PROB 4, 5; E179/247/13, 14, 16, Public Record Office.

as "a generation of men truely laborious, jealous of their Properties, whose principall ayme is Liberty and Plenty, . . . the Country-man had of his owne, and did not live by the breath of his great Land-lord." [35]

If these estimates of the size of the upper and middling wealth categories are correct, then at least half of the Vale's householders (worth less than £50 or judged too poor to pay the hearth tax in the 1660s and 1670s) lived on the poverty line. They included weavers and clothworkers, laborers, servants, cottagers, poor widows, the unemployed, the old, and the sick. Few owned more than a tenement and garden, and most probably rented smallholdings on short-term leases or lodged in other people's houses. By no means were

35. J.P.P. Horn, "The Distribution of Wealth in the Vale of Berkeley, Gloucestershire, 1660–1700," *Southern History*, III (1981), 81–109; John Corbet, *A True and Impartiall History of the Military Government of the Citie of Gloucester from the Beginning of the Civil War* . . . (London, 1647), 9, Thomason Tracts, microfilm, reel E402, British Library, London.

all paupers. As Charles Wilson says, "The collective title by which the least fortunate of the lower orders of society were known—'the Poor'—did not mean that they were all destitute. It meant that they had little or nothing to save them from destitution when times were bad or as they grew old: that a proportion of them was therefore always destitute, another proportion potentially destitute."[36]

The hard core of the poor were too old, young, or sick to work and consequently were completely dependent on parish relief. Sometimes the problem could become overwhelming. In 1634 the inhabitants of North Nibley complained to the justices sitting at Chipping Sodbury of the "great payments wherwith this village above others is yearly burdened." Their petition gave the names of fifty-three "poore mens children of this parish fitt to be placed apprentices" and offered to take in twenty-three of them; the remaining thirty were to be placed in other parishes. Generally, however, those receiving relief rarely formed more than a small minority of the disadvantaged. Adult poor in Slimbridge and Stinchcombe who received relief between 1635 and 1692 constituted 6–15 percent of the total adult population; in Thornbury, between 1656 and 1688, they never exceeded 10 percent, and in Frampton on Severn, in the 1680s and 1690s, only 3–6 percent. Even in Kingswood, notorious for its poverty, only 13 percent of the population received alms between 1674 and 1694.[37]

They were merely the tip of the iceberg. Men and women "on the parish" were the official poor: those deemed worthy of relief in the sense of being respectable or longtime inhabitants of the community. During periods of high unemployment, however, people "haveing no worke"—able-bodied poor, usually ineligible for the parish dole—swelled the ranks of the region's destitute enormously. In Cam, forty pounds was paid to the poor in 1669 as part of a bequest by Throgmorton Trotman. The accounts show that sixteen persons regularly received relief, but a further forty-one, variously described as "poore," "aged," and "decayed," were also given money from the bequest. Those on the fringes of destitution outnumbered the official poor by at least two or three times, and in periods of especial hardship probably by much more.[38]

36. Horn, "Distribution of Wealth," *So. Hist.*, III (1981), 87–97; Charles Wilson, *England's Apprenticeship, 1603–1763* (London, 1965), 17.

37. Smyth of Nibley Papers, IV, fols. 4, 19, Gloucester City Library; "A booke of actes," 42, Berkeley MSS, General Series, no. 173, Berkeley Castle muniment room; P193 OV2/1, P298a OV2/1, 2/2, P312 OV2/1, D688/1, P330 OV2/1, GRO.

38. *Ibid.*

TABLE 14

Hearth Tax, Vale of Berkeley, 1664, 1672

Parish	Chargeable Households		Nonchargeable Households	
	No.	%	No.	%
	1664			
Berkeley	360	58.3	257	41.7
Cam	72	44.7	89	55.3
Charfield	26	78.8	7	21.2
Cromhall	59	54.1	50	45.9
Dursley	127	41.6	178	58.4
North Nibley	105	55.6	84	44.4
Rockhampton	26	76.5	8	23.5
Slimbridge	80	50.6	78	49.4
Stinchcombe	24	25.8	69	74.2
Tortworth	27[a]	51.9	25	48.1
Wotton under Edge	147	37.7	243	62.3
Overall	1,053	49.2	1,088	50.8
	1672			
Berkeley	421	71.0	172	29.0
Cam	84	73.7	30[b]	26.3
Charfield	25	86.2	4	13.8
Cromhall	68	77.3	20	22.7
Dursley	113	44.8	139	55.2
Frampton on Severn	47	45.6	56	54.6
North Nibley	116	74.8	39	25.2
Rockhampton	27		—	
Slimbridge	70		—	
Stinchcombe	32	45.7	38	54.3
Thornbury	349	92.8	27[c]	7.2
Tortworth	40	69.0	18	31.0
Tytherington	36	63.2	21	36.8
Wotton under Edge	214	58.5	152[b]	41.5
Overall[d]	1,196	63.4	689	36.6

Notes: There are no returns for Thornbury, Tytherington, Frampton on Severn, and Kingswood in 1664 and for Kingswood in 1672.   [a]Chargeable returns incomplete by approximately 8 households.   [b]Not clear whether nonchargeable total is complete. [c]Nonchargeable total incomplete.   [d]Excludes Thornbury.

Sources: E179/247/13, 14, 16, Public Record Office.

Widespread poverty is confirmed by taxation records. In hearth tax returns for 1664 (literally a tax on fire hearths), half of all householders were exempted because they were considered too poor to pay (Table 14). The proportion of nonchargeables was especially high in parishes heavily dependent on the cloth industry—Stinchcombe, 74 percent; Wotton under Edge, 62 percent; Dursley, 58 percent; and Cam, 55 percent.[39]

These proportions may seem implausibly high. No one likes paying taxes, and the hearth tax, owing to its broad brief (theoretically all householders, unless too poor, were to pay), was particularly unpopular; consequently, evasion was rife. But other evidence suggests that local conditions were very bad in the mid-1660s. John Smyth, a justice of the peace and son of John who was steward to the Berkeleys, justified his defense of poor householders who could not afford to pay the tax in 1666 by a thinly veiled suggestion that any attempt to collect outstanding money could lead to serious unrest. He and other justices had been deluged with "numberlesse" complaints about the collection of the tax, "the complaynants beinge generally of the poorer sort dependinge upon the trade of clothinge of which number I am well informed there are more than 10000 liveinge within 10 miles of my house that want worke by reason of the stoppe of trade." Smyth claimed he averted a riot the previous year only by giving in to the demands of a crowd "of nigh one hundred people" to return the money or property of those who believed they had been unfairly assessed.[40]

Even assuming that there was wholesale evasion in the 1660s and that the 1672 returns are more reliable, the proportion of nonchargeables throughout the Vale was still well more than a third, and in some parishes (Dursley and Stinchcombe, for example) more than a half (Table 14). There is little reason to doubt that during the 1660s and 1670s at least a third, and in many parishes nearer a half, of all householders lived near or below subsistence level; and while the contours of poverty may have softened during the final years of the century, continuing fluctuations in the textile industry ensured that there would be no dramatic improvement.[41]

39. Rollison, "Bourgeois Soul," *Soc. Hist.*, XII (1987), 324; E179/247/16, Public Record Office.

40. See the complaints of Samuel Yeeds and Richard Morse, both of Thornbury, collectors of the Hearth Tax in 1665, to the Lord Treasurer, Southampton, Add. MSS 33589, fol. 33, British Library, and statement of Smyth, fol. 49.

41. E179/247/13, E179/247/14, E179/116/544, Public Record Office. Poverty was less widespread in the Cotswolds. Of a sample of 51 rural parishes and tithings, 28.2% of all householders were exempted in 1672. By contrast, of a sample of 9 parishes

A "Much Diversified Country": Kent

Kent, no less than Gloucestershire, is a county of rich contrasts. A traveler following one of the old droveways from north to south would cross half a dozen distinct countrysides in the space of thirty or forty miles, from the marshes and fertile soils of the Thames Valley, over the Downs capped with woods and heath, through the fertile Vale of Holmesdale and barren hills of the Chartland, to the broad expanse of the Weald dotted with shaws, copses, and small, enclosed fields stretching as far as the eye can see into Sussex (Figure 8). This variety of landscapes and soils in turn encouraged a rich diversity of settlement patterns, types of husbandry, and manufactures, always seen as a principal characteristic of the county.[42]

Following national trends, the population of the county rose rapidly in the sixteenth century, from about 85,000 in 1500 to 130,000 one hundred years later; but growth slowed considerably after 1600, and by the 1670s there were probably about 150,000 inhabitants. The most densely settled areas were in northwestern Kent, along the coastal plain (apart from the marshes), the Isle of Thanet, and parts of the Weald, where either natural fertility, industry, or trade attracted and supported large numbers of people.[43]

The Weald, divided into the heavy clays of the Low Weald and the lighter sands of the High Weald, forms the core of the region, stretching more than seventy miles from the Sussex-Hampshire border to Romney Marsh, and thirty miles at its widest extent north to south. Anciently, the Weald of Andred formed a huge tract of dense, unbroken forest separating London and North Kent from the Saxon kingdoms to the south. Despite extensive colonization and clearance during pre-Conquest and medieval times, large

---

in the Forest of Dean, 41.9% were exempted (D383, GRO). For a comparison with other parts of the country, see Keith Wrightson, *English Society, 1580–1680* (London, 1982), 148. See also Tom Arkell, "The Incidence of Poverty in England in the Later Seventeenth Century," *Soc. Hist.*, XII (1987), 23–47.

42. A. M. Everitt, "The Making of the Agrarian Landscape of Kent," *Archaeologia Cantiana*, XCII (1976), 6; *Continuity and Colonization: The Evolution of Kentish Settlement* (Leicester, 1986), 43.

43. Peter Clark, *English Provincial Society from the Reformation to the Revolution: Religion, Politics, and Society in Kent, 1500–1640* (Hassocks, 1977), 6; C. W. Chalklin, *Seventeenth-Century Kent: A Social and Economic History* (London, 1965), 27–29; Harleian MSS, 280, fol. 165, British Library; Phyllis Deane and W. A. Cole, *British Economic Growth, 1688–1959* (Cambridge, 1967), 103.

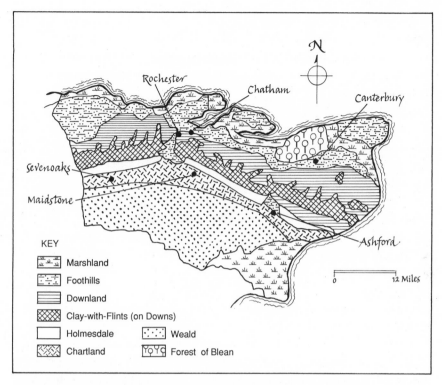

Figure 8. Natural Regions of Kent. *After Alan Everitt,* Continuity and Colonization: The Evolution of Kentish Settlement *(Leicester, 1986). Drawn by Richard Stinely*

tracts of woodland remained in the early modern period, especially in the High Weald.[44]

During the sixteenth and seventeenth centuries the area was a major industrial region, noted for iron production, gun founding, and broadcloth manufacture besides a variety of lesser industries. The Kentish broadcloth industry was located around Cranbrook and Tenterden, but by the outbreak of the Civil War only the latter could be classed as a major center, and the industry as a whole was in a steady decline throughout the century, bringing considerable poverty to the locality. Workers in iron manufacture fared little better: they too experienced difficult times with the contraction of the industry after 1640. Both industries relied upon vast amounts of timber

44. The Weald covers 260,000 acres and makes up about one-quarter of the total land surface of the county; see Everitt, *Continuity and Colonization,* 45.

and competed with the equally large quantities transported via the Medway River to the naval dockyards at Chatham, Woolwich, and Deptford.[45]

Husbandry revolved around stock rearing and fattening, much Wealden beef finding its way to markets in Southwark and London. Small farmers usually possessed herds of ten to twelve head, mainly local breeds, while wealthier men fattened stock from both the locality and from further afield— the North of England, Wales, or "scotch" cattle purchased in London—and commonly owned herds of up to fifty head. Arable farming was of less importance. The main crops grown were wheat and oats, mostly for local consumption, together with a variety of fodder crops.[46]

Across the "stony and infertile" Chartland, which marks the northern boundary of the Weald, and the narrow band of more fertile soils of Holmesdale lies the second major region of Kent, the North Downs. Running the entire length of the county from the Surrey border to Dover, the chalk hills rise in places to more than eight hundred feet and rarely fall below six hundred and cover nearly 30 percent of the total area of the county. Extensive deposits of clay-with-flints account for the thick woods and heath that cover much of the region (in contrast to the broad sheep pastures of the South Downs in East Sussex), and thin chalk soils account for the general infertility of large areas, especially on the upper slopes. Further down on the lower slopes (or dipslope), where the clays mix with chalk or where river valleys have cut through the hills, soils tended to be more fertile and provided good "corn land." Merging into the rich loams of the Thames Valley and coastal plain, the lower reaches of the Downs were given over mainly to wheat and barley.[47]

Perhaps accounting for the legendary wealth of Kent, the Thames Valley and north coastal plain, the third major natural region, were unquestionably the richest part of the county in this period. A combination of fertile

45. Peter Brandon and Brian Short, *The South East from AD 1000* (London, 1990), 185–190; Short, "The De-industrialisation Process: A Case Study of the Weald, 1600– 1850," in Pat Hudson, ed., *Regions and Industries: A Perspective on the Industral Revolution in Britain* (Cambridge, 1989), 156–174.

46. Chalklin, *Seventeenth-Century Kent*, 96–99; Finberg and Thirsk, eds., *Agrarian History of England and Wales*, V, pt. 1, 270–273, 308–309; Michael Zell, "A Wood-Pasture Agrarian Regime: The Kentish Weald in the Sixteenth Century," *So. Hist.*, VII (1985), 73, 80, 90–91; Brandon and Short, *The South East from AD 1000*, 170–173, 203–206.

47. Everitt, *Continuity and Colonization*, 47; Edward Hasted, *The History and Topographical Survey of the County of Kent . . .* , 3d ed., 12 vols. (Yorkshire, 1972; rpt. of 2d ed., Canterbury, 1797–1801), IX, 224; Chalklin, *Seventeenth-Century Kent*, 78–81; Finberg and Thirsk, eds., *Agrarian History of England and Wales*, V, pt. 1, 277–278, 292.

and easily worked soils, proximity to London, good lines of communication along the coast by road and river, and numerous ports and boroughs gave the region unrivaled advantages over other parts of the county. William Camden had North Kent in mind when he described the county as abounding "with meadows, pastures, and corn fields, . . . wonderfully fruitful in apples as also cherries." As on the Downs, wheat and barley were the chief crops. Huge amounts were sent by hoy, or barge, each year from Sandwich, Faversham, Milton, Rochester, and Dover to feed London's enormous population. Before the Civil War, wheat and malt from Kent frequently constituted more than half of the capital's imports. Other produce sent up to London included cattle and sheep pastured on the rich marshlands bordering the Thames, fruit from the orchards of northwestern Kent and around Canterbury, hops from the vicinity of Sittingbourne, and vegetables from market gardens located within easy reach of the capital such as at Greenwich and Gravesend.[48]

Prosperity was closely tied to demand from London, and, as demand rose throughout the sixteenth and seventeenth centuries, the region expanded and diversified its output. Besides agricultural produce there were a number of important manufactures and industries—shipbuilding, paper, lime, glass, brewing, copperas, wrought iron, gunpowder, cloths, and silks— many, along the Thames, only a few miles from the city. Large quantities of fish and oysters were sent up to the London markets and constituted a leading industry among riverine parishes and along the coast. Camden was impressed by the industriousness of farmer-fishermen on the coast who lived "like amphibious animals both by sea and land, making the most of both elements, being both fishermen and ploughmen, farmers and sailors . . . [and] expert in both professions."[49]

Prosperity was represented, too, by the number of important towns and ports in the region. Apart from Maidstone in the Medway Valley and Dover, every sizable town (more than twenty-five hundred people) was located in North Kent, including the county capital, Canterbury, which had about seven thousand inhabitants by the 1670s, and the naval dockyard towns, whose populations mushroomed during the century with the massive expan-

48. William Camden, *Kent*, ed. Gordon J. Copley (London, 1977), 3; Chalklin, *Seventeenth-Century Kent*, 81–82, 88–95, 173–177; Finberg and Thirsk, eds., *Agrarian History of England and Wales*, V, pt. 1, 275, 280–283, 291.

49. Chalklin, *Seventeenth-Century Kent*, 113–116, 140–146, 150–156; Finberg and Thirsk, eds., *Agrarian History of England and Wales*, V, pt. 1, 307; Camden, *Kent*, ed. Copley, 55.

sion of shipbuilding and provisioning. The ports along the Thames estuary and coast provided vital channels of trade for the export of foodstuffs and manufactures produced throughout the county to the capital, other parts of the country, and abroad as well as the import of all sorts of goods from Europe. "Kent," remarked Leland, "is the key [quay] of al Englande."[50]

Contemporary enthusiasm about the wealth of the county, however, overlooked a bedrock of poverty that became an increasingly serious problem in the late sixteenth and seventeenth centuries. In the 1590s, it was claimed that the county was "overspread not only with unpunished swarms of idle rogues and of counterfeit soldiers but also with numbers of poor and weak but unpitied servitors." Kentish towns, as Peter Clark has shown, experienced the worst problems during the period as they came under virtual siege by poor and desperate migrants who tramped the highways in search of work, but the problem was almost as bad in the countryside. Although conditions improved slightly in the early decades of the new century, the decay of the cloth industry and intermittent harvest failures brought renewed hardship for the poor after 1620.[51]

Patchy evidence suggests that the majority of emigrants from Kent came from parishes along the coast and Thames Valley, the two major urban centers of Canterbury and Maidstone, and a cluster of parishes below the scarp face of the Downs between Maidstone and Ashford.[52] This account focuses

50. Chalklin, *Seventeenth-Century Kent*, 30–33, 161–188; A.J.F. Dulley, "People and Homes in the Medway Towns," in Margaret Roake and John Whyman, eds., *Essays in Kentish History* (London, 1973), 101–117; Smith, ed., *Itinerary of John Leland*, IV, 57.

51. D. C. Coleman, "The Economy of Kent under the Later Stuarts" (Ph.D. diss., University of London, 1951), 300, 317; Peter Clark, "The Migrant in Kentish Towns, 1580–1640," in Clark and Paul Slack, eds., *Crisis and Order in English Towns, 1500–1700: Essays in Urban History* (London, 1972), 117; Finberg and Thirsk, eds., *Agrarian History of England and Wales*, V, pt. 1, 308. See also A. E. Newman, "The Old Poor Law in East Kent, 1606–1834: A Social and Demographic Analysis" (Ph.D. diss., University of Kent, 1979), 65–66, 81, 219–221, 233–265.

52. Currer-Briggs, "Indentured Servants"; Michael Ghirelli, *A List of Emigrants from England to America, 1682–1692* (Baltimore, 1968); C.D.P. Nicholson, "Some Early Emigrants to America," *Genealogists' Magazine*, XII, nos. 1–16 (1955–1958), XIII, nos. 1–8 (1959–1961), no. 284; Lord Mayor's Waiting Books, XIII, XIV, entries for July 4, 1684, Oct. 10, 1685, City of London Record Office, Guildhall. For sources regarding the geographical origins of free emigrants, see above, Chapter 1, n. 9.

Unlike for the Bristol region, no comprehensive source details the origins of Kentish servants during the main period of emigration from the 1630s to the 1670s. Nor can it be assumed that the pattern of migration from the county in the 1680s is represen-

on eleven parishes located in central Kent, along the river valleys of the Medway, Len, and Stour. Soils and landscape are extremely varied, ranging from the poor clay-with-flints soils of the Downs escarpment to the fertile and well-watered countryside of the Vale of Holmesdale and the thin soils, scrub, and woods of the Chartland a few miles to the south.[53] Most identifiable emigrants from this area were from well-connected and wealthy families and played a prominent part in the early history of the Chesapeake.

At the base of the Downs, near Maidstone, is Boxley, formerly the home of Sir Francis Wyatt, who served twice as the governor of Virginia, 1621–1625 and 1638–1642 (Figure 9). His brother, Haute, also emigrated and was an Anglican minister in Jamestown during the 1620s before returning to Boxley in 1632. A few miles away, on the high road from Maidstone to Ashford, lies Leeds Castle, "a magnificent pile of building . . . pleasantly situated in the midst of a beautiful park," which was the home of Thomas, Lord Culpeper, governor of Virginia from 1677 to 1683, and a proprietor of the Northern Neck (a huge tract of more than two million acres in the northernmost part of the colony). The Culpepers, a royalist family, were related to a number of important Kentish families in the neighborhood and, through the marriages of Lord Thomas to Katherine St. Leger and of their daughter Frances to Sir William Berkeley, were also connected to numerous influential Virginian families, such as the Byrds, Carters, Beverleys, and Ludwells.[54]

Just to the south of Leeds is East Sutton, in the Stone Hills, the birthplace of Henry and Samuel Filmer (sons of Sir Edward), who emigrated to James City, Virginia, in the early 1640s. Their uncle, Samuel Argall, from the same parish, had emigrated thirty years earlier and had served as deputy governor

---

tative of an earlier period. While it is probable that there was considerable migration from the area bordering London, riverside parishes, and important towns, there is little indication of the scale of the movement or whether certain communities were more prominent in despatching emigrants than others were. Large areas of the county do not figure at all in the evidence from the 1680s. This gap might be understandable in the case of the relatively sparsely populated Downs, but the complete absence of emigration from the Weald is curious, especially considering the economic difficulties the region experienced throughout the 17th century and the substantial contribution it made to New England settlement before 1650. (Nearly a third of the 197 Kentish emigrants who sailed for New England before 1650 were from Wealden parishes. Other main centers were Canterbury [22], Sandwich [17], and Ashford [17]. See Banks, *Topographical Dictionary*, ed. Brownell, 74–86.)

53. Everitt, *Continuity and Colonization*, 50.

54. Descriptions of parishes are from Hasted, *History and Topographical Survey*, IV, 335–365, 490.

Figure 9. Central Kent. *Detail. By John Speed*

of the colony before the arrival of his "countryman" Sir Francis Wyatt. Adjoining East Sutton, Ulcombe was the home of Warham Horsmanden, who moved to Virginia in the 1650s and who was related to St. Leger Codd of Lenham. Sir Philip Honeywood, who emigrated in 1649, came from Charing, a parish lying "partly below and partly above the upper range of chalk hills"; Major John Brodnax was from Godmersham, Edward Digges from Chilham, and Henry Fleet from Chartham (situated in the fertile Stour Valley).[55]

Most parishes were small, from two to six hundred inhabitants, and of dispersed settlement (Table 15). This pattern was typical of the county as a whole, whether in the Weald, in Holmesdale, or on the Downs. A village, consisting of the parish church surrounded by a few houses and possibly

55. *Ibid.*, V, 375, VII, 429.

TABLE 15
Population in Central Kent, 1563–1676

Parish	Number of Inhabitants		
	1563	1640	1676
Boxley	270	—	300
Langley	68	92	133
Leeds	315	—	383
East Sutton	135	216[a]	192
Ulcombe	270	375	312
Lenham	540	667	500[b]
Charing	270	617	507
Ashford	—	1,050	1,667[c]
Godmersham	248	405	567
Chilham	338	628	580
Chartham	270	500	333

Notes: [a]1648.   [b]Clearly an underestimate: the Hearth Tax returns of 1664 indicate a population of about 850.   [c]In 1664 the population was about 1,150.

Sources: 1563: Harleian MS 594, fols. 63–84, British Library. 1640: Edward Hasted, *The History and Topographical Survey of the County of Kent . . .* , 3d ed., 12 vols. (Yorkshire, 1972; rpt. of 2d ed., Canterbury, 1797–1801). 1676: C. W. Chalklin, "The Compton Census of 1676: The Dioceses of Canterbury and Rochester," in *A Seventeenth-Century Miscellany*, Kent Records, XVII, 153–174.

a tavern, provided the nucleus of the community and was surrounded by numerous outlying farms and homesteads. In very few rural parishes in Kent was settlement concentrated in a single center, and there is little evidence that villages served as centers for communally organized farming as in the Midlands. Husbandry, like crafts and small-scale manufacturing, tended to be organized around individual holdings.[56]

Even within short distances there were considerable differences between villages. Some parishes, either because they were off the main roads or because there was little to attract visitors, existed in a quiet, somnambulant isolation. East Sutton commanded "a most beautiful and extensive view southward" across the Weald but would have been "little known or frequented was it not for the residence of the Filmer family in it." The small market town of Lenham, situated in "a poor unfertile country," was described as "a dull and unfrequented place, and of but little traffic," and similarly Ulcombe lay

56. Everitt, *Continuity and Colonization*, 40–41.

in "rather an obscure and unfrequented district, having but little thorough-fare." Boxley and Charing, on the edge of the Downs, had thin chalky soils and extensive woodlands, composing a "barren dreary country." By contrast, from the parishes of Godmersham, Chilham, and Chartham, lying in the Downs above the Ashford-to-Canterbury road, there was "a beautiful view over the spacious vale of Ashford, through which the Stour directs its course; the valley comprehending a most enchanting prospect, diversified by seats, parks, towns and churches." Here, on the sides of the hills along the river valley, fertile meadows provided pastures for large flocks of sheep, which fertilized the rich loams of this prime corn-producing country.[57]

As befitted a region of mixed soils and varying topography, agriculture depended on a range of activities, with a bias toward the production of cereals. Most farmers raised cattle (for fattening as well as dairying), sheep, and swine and also produced significant quantities of wheat, barley, and oats (Table 16). Income was supplemented by the cultivation of fruit, hops, and hemp and the sale of timber.[58] Richard Heneker of Charing, for example, owned a cow, 4 milk cows, 28 ewes, and 20 lambs besides having 24 acres of wheat on the ground and 76 quarters of wheat, barley, and oats in his barn. He also had 3 gallons of butter, 20 small cheeses, and 10 quarters of wool ready for sale at the time of his death in 1639. John Young of Godmersham, who died in the same year, possessed 6 cows and 45 ewes, lambs, rams, and young sheep and had 28 acres of wheat and barley on the ground as well as 12 quarters of wheat, barley, oats, and hemp, 10 loads of wood, and 3 "tonne of sawen lumber." Few men were large-scale farmers. The majority (more than three-quarters) owned herds of fewer than 10 head and flocks of fewer than 50 sheep and generally had about 15–40 acres under the plow.[59]

Farming was the major economic activity in the area (just more than half the men in a small sample of inventories were yeomen or husbandmen),

57. Hasted, *History and Topographical Survey*, V, 375–376, 415–416; W. H. Ireland, *England's Topographer; or, A New and Complete History of the County of Kent*, 4 vols. (London, 1828–1830), II, 521, 535, 543.

58. Probate Inventories, PRC 27/5/54–27/26/176, Kent Archives Office, Maidstone, Kent.

59. PRC 27/6/127, 27/7/95, KAO; Chalklin, *Seventeenth-Century Kent*, chap. 5. (A quarter is one-fourth of a hundredweight, about 28 pounds.) Of a sample of 46 farmers from central Kent, 1633–1676, 76.1% owned fewer than 10 head of cattle, and 80.4% had fewer than 50 sheep. Only 3 men owned more than 300 sheep. Of 25 farms, the mean average arable was 26 acres and the median 16.5. The range was from 3 to 102 acres (PRC 27/5/54–27/26/176, KAO).

TABLE 16

Livestock, Crops, and Products in Inventories, Central Kent, 1633–1676

Item	Farmers Owning (N=46)		Nonfarmers Owning (N=54)	
	No.	%	No.	%
Fauna				
Cattle	46	100.0	26	46.4
Oxen	10	21.7	3	5.4
Horses	35	76.1	20	35.7
Swine	38	82.6	25	44.6
Sheep	35	76.1	13	23.2
Poultry	12	26.1	5	8.9
Cheese	17	37.0	8	14.3
Cheese-making equipment	19	41.3	7	12.5
Milk	8	17.4	4	7.1
Butter	16	13.4	5	8.9
Flora				
"Corn"	6	13.0	5	8.9
Wheat	41	89.1	18	32.1
Barley	28	60.9	9	16.1
Oats	27	58.7	9	16.1
Beans	2	4.3	5	8.9
Pease	20	43.5	7	12.5
Podware (beans and peas)	3	6.5	2	3.6
Tares	16	34.8	2	3.6
Hops	1	2.2	2	3.6
Hemp	15	32.6	11	19.6
Apples	10	21.7	2	3.6

Source: Probate Inventories, PRC 27/5/54–27/26/176, Kent Archives Office.

but there was a locally important branch of the cloth industry in the vicinity of Boxley and along the River Len, which was a principal source of fuller's earth used for cleansing wool. Chalk from the Downs provided the raw material for another small industry, lime burning, and the clays and brick earths at the foot of the Downs and ragstone of the Chart were the basis of tile making and quarrying. Many of these products were marketed at Maidstone, described by Defoe as "a considerable town, very populous, and the inhabitants generally wealthy."[60] The town served as an entrepôt for much of central Kent, channeling goods from the Weald and adjoining region down the Medway to the Thames estuary and thence to London. Alternatively, in the eastern part of the Len Valley and upper reaches of the Stour, farmers and manufacturers could send their produce to markets in Ashford, Canterbury, or Faversham.

Town life provided many contrasts to rural society. Rochester and Maidstone both had populations of about three thousand in the mid-seventeenth century but were quite different in character. The development of the naval dockyards was largely responsible for the populousness and prosperity of Rochester and Chatham in the period and accounts for the relatively low proportion of poor in the two towns, since the docks and service trades provided a good deal of casual work throughout the year. Along the busy high street, seamen, naval personnel, and dockyard workers jostled with servants and maids who worked in the numerous taverns and inns and with victuallers, retailers, and travelers passing through on their way to London or the coast.

Contemporary observers were unimpressed by either town. "There's little remarkable in Rochester," Defoe commented, "except the ruins of a very old castle, and an antient but not extraordinary cathedral." Later in the century, Edward Hasted found Chatham "like most sea ports, a long, narrow, disagreeable, ill-built town, the houses in general occupied by those trades adapted to the commerce of the shipping and seafaring persons." Very much working towns, there was little in the way of fashionable or genteel company. Despite being a cathedral city, the clergy played a minor role in the affairs of Rochester, and, like the bishop, many ministers were nonresident. Neither was there a large gentry community. Too far from London to be a part of the fashionable fringe that included Greenwich and Eltham, Rochester offered little in the way of natural advantages (a healthy aspect or pleasant countryside) and was much too devoted to the navy and commerce to develop assembly rooms and other entertainments that would have attracted large numbers of gentry. Instead, Kentish gentlemen visited Canterbury, the new spa at Tunbridge Wells, or went up to London.[61]

---

60. Defoe, *Tour through Great Britain*, ed. Rogers, 130. Just over 14% of a sample of 78 men from central Kent who died between 1633 and 1676 earned a living primarily from the cloth industry (clothiers, weavers, clothworkers, and fullers), but many farmers and tradesmen also possessed woollen or linen wheels for spinning (PRC 27/5/54–27/26/176, KAO).

61. Hasted, *History and Topographical Survey*, IV, 192; Defoe, *Tour through Great Brit-*

Maidstone, straddling the Medway, had more of the atmosphere of an important market town. Sucking in migrants from the surrounding area, it grew rapidly in the second half of the sixteenth and in the early seventeenth century with mixed results. A diversified economy embracing cloth manufacture, distributive trades, service industries, retailing, and jobs associated with the port attracted large numbers of poor from a rural hinterland about fifteen miles in radius, but, unlike Rochester and Chatham, there was never enough work to go around. In 1596, Maidstone's magistrates protested that "the number of poor people inhabiting within this town . . . (by means of the long time of scarcity and dearth . . .) is now grown and come to be very great . . . [so] that the lamentable cries and miserable estate and condition of the said poor people do require rapid and speedy relief." Sixty years later, fully one-half of all householders were deemed too poor to pay the hearth tax.[62]

In addition to being a port and market town, Maidstone was an administrative center. Both quarter sessions and assizes were held there, and it served as a general forum for county business. It rapidly developed its educational and legal services and became locally fashionable as a meeting place for the gentry. Defoe thought it "a very agreeable place to live in, and where a man of letters, and of manners, will always find suitable society, both to divert and improve himself; so that here is, what is not often found, namely, a town of very great business and trade, and yet full of gentry, of mirth, and of good company." This variety of functions assured it a prominent place in Kent's urban hierarchy, and by the outbreak of the Civil War the town had assumed the role of a second county capital serving central and western lathes (administrative divisions) while Canterbury served the east.[63]

Comparisons: Provincial and Local Cultures

Comparing Kent and Gloucestershire, one is first struck by similarities. Both counties exhibited sharply contrasting landscapes—forest, wood-pasture, downlands, and river valleys—which had an enormous influence on the development of local society and economy. Short-range differences are

ain, ed. Rogers, 123; Dulley, "People and Homes in the Medway Towns," in Roake and Whyman, eds., *Essays in Kentish History*, 109–110.

62. Chalklin, *Seventeenth-Century Kent*, 31; Clark, "Migrant in Kentish Towns," in Clark and Slack, eds., *Crisis and Order*, 125; Clark, *English Provincial Society*, 233, 236, 243; Coleman, "Economy of Kent," 403–410.

63. Defoe, *Tour through Great Britain*, ed. Rogers, 132. See also Clark, *English Provincial Society*, 311, 400.

significant because they underline the fact that, even when narrowed down to a particular county, the backgrounds of emigrants might be quite varied. Both counties experienced impressive demographic growth and, largely as a result, underwent considerable social and economic readjustment involving periodic, and sometimes severe, social stress.

Two trends are worth highlighting: the increasing divergence between rural and industrial regions and the growth of poverty. One must be careful not to exaggerate, but it is clear that certain areas, such as the Forest of Dean, Kingswood Chase, and the Cotswolds escarpment in Gloucestershire and the Weald and Thames estuary in Kent, were far more industrialized by the early seventeenth century than they had been one hundred years earlier. Manufacturing was no longer the monopoly of towns. But, like towns, industrial areas in the countryside attracted large numbers of people, migrants from predominantly agricultural parishes usually within the county but sometimes from further afield, who sought work and a place to live, if only temporarily before moving on. Unsurprisingly, these areas suffered some of the highest levels of poverty, especially where the cloth industry was in decline or subject to severe slumps. In the 1660s about half of their adult populations lived on the breadline, compared to nearer a third for other areas. If industrial areas avoided the terrible subsistence crises that affected France and parts of northern England in this period, nonetheless it requires little effort to imagine the hardships that the poor endured during bad years.[64]

Above the ranks of the poor, the middle classes and gentry in both counties prospered. Capitalist farmers, merchants, and manufacturers for the most part benefited from the expansion of commerce and rising profitability of agriculture and industry. London and Bristol were not only the foremost ports in England, vital channels to other parts of the country and abroad, but were also virtually insatiable in their demand for local goods. Producers were therefore closely integrated into provincial, national, and ultimately international markets. Gloucestershire cheeses and Kentish hops found their way to America and Europe as well as to the tables and brewing vats of more immediate surroundings, and in both counties there were men who were equally content to sell their produce locally or send it to more distant destinations.

64. Andrew B. Appleby, *Famine in Tudor and Stuart England* (Liverpool, 1978); John Walter and Keith Wrightson, "Dearth and the Social Order in Early Modern England," *Past and Present*, no. 71 (May 1976), 22–42; Paul Slack, *Poverty and Policy in Tudor and Stuart England* (London, 1988), chap. 3.

An emerging "ethos of agrarian and commercial capitalism" accounts in large measure for the growing self-confidence and independence of middling groups in the two societies. John Corbet and William Lambarde stressed both the wealth of the middle classes and their freedom from seigneurial obligations; neither in Kent nor in Gloucestershire were they tied to the purse strings of their social superiors. While the notion of a finely graded hierarchy of status remained a powerful icon in seventeenth-century society, it did not, as contemporaries realized, conform to social reality, and still less to structured relations between the classes in any other way than a very broad sense.[65] Although manorialism may have been more important in rural society in Gloucestershire than in Kent, this fact does not imply that society was more hierarchical, deferential, or archaic in the former. Both counties were governed ("managed" might be a better word) by groups of gentry rather than aristocratic grandees and relied largely on the consent of the ruled rather than force. The gentry were well aware of how much they depended on the support of the respectable middle classes for the maintenance of the king's peace and the orderly administration of local affairs.

A comparison also reveals important differences between the two societies. Most significant was the influence of London on the economic development of Kent. Sustained population increase and the growth of London's overseas trade acted as a massive stimulus to the county's economy, far beyond Bristol's impact on Gloucestershire. Throughout most of the seventeenth century, Kent regularly ranked fourth or fifth in national tax assessments, compared to Gloucestershire's fourteenth to twenty-second.[66] In commercial terms, just as Bristol was a pale reflection of London, so the Severn was a pale reflection of the Thames: similar influences were at work, but the scale was wholly different. The Severn was an increasingly busy waterway in this period, but it came nowhere near rivaling the volume of traffic entering the Thames. Kent's long coastline and proximity to London and the Continent gave it obvious natural advantages in coastal and overseas trade, which, in turn, were an important factor in giving the Southeast the lead

65. Keith Wrightson, "The Social Order of Early Modern England: Three Approaches," in Lloyd Bonfield *et al.*, eds., *The World We Have Gained: Histories of Population and Social Structure* (Oxford, 1986), 177–202; Wrightson, "Estates, Degrees, and Sorts: Changing Perceptions of Society in Tudor and Stuart England," in Penelope J. Corfield, ed., *Language, History, and Class* (Oxford, 1991), 30–52.

66. James E. Thorold Rogers, *A History of Agriculture and Prices in England . . .* , 7 vols. (Oxford, 1866–1902), V, 118–119; for the assessments of 1341, 1453, and 1503, see IV, 89.

in adopting new ideas, crops, and manufacturing techniques from Europe. Such innovations often took decades to reach other parts of the country.

But most important, from the viewpoint of this study, were cultural differences. Culture is here understood as a set of shared values, attitudes, and norms, inherited and experienced, which shaped daily behavior and social interaction and conditioned individuals' conception of themselves, their place in society, and their outlook on life and the afterlife.[67] Using these criteria, it is hard to pin down a distinctively Kentish or Gloucestershire culture in this period. County loyalties manifested themselves from time to time, in the reluctance of militias to serve outside their own boundaries and more obviously in the emergence of self-conscious county elites with their elaborate genealogies and histories, but it is doubtful whether the majority of ordinary people had any well-formulated sense of their county heritage. The county, after all, was an administrative, not a social, unit. As far as daily routine is concerned, a laborer in the Kentish Weald would have had much more in common with his neighbor across the Sussex border than with his fellow countryman from the Downs or near London. This is not to imply that provincial cultures did not exist, but, rather, that the county was neither the principal locus of cultural expression below the national level nor its principal determinant.

A more revealing way of conceiving cultural influences and identities is through a number of overlapping cultural horizons, radiating outward from the local to the national. Local cultures, or subcultures, might embrace a couple of dozen or more parishes united by a common pattern of agriculture,

---

67. This is a very complex problem. My thinking has been influenced by a number of historical, geographical, and anthropological studies, notably, Louis Hartz, *The Founding of New Societies: Studies in the History of the United States, Latin America, South Africa, Canada, and Australia* (New York, 1964); James R. Gibson, ed., *European Settlement and Development in North America: Essays on Geographical Change in Honour and Memory of Andrew Hill Clark* (Folkestone, Kent, 1978); T. H. Breen, "Creative Adaptations: Peoples and Cultures," in Jack P. Greene and J. R. Pole, eds., *Colonial British America: Essays in the New History of the Early Modern Era* (Baltimore, 1984), 195–232; D. W. Meinig, *The Shaping of America: A Geographical Perspective on Five Hundred Years of History*, I, *Atlantic America, 1492–1800* (New Haven, Conn., 1986), pts., 1 and 2; Alan R. Beals, *Culture in Process* (New York, 1967), ix, 5, 33; David L. Sills, ed., *International Encyclopedia of the Social Sciences* (New York, 1968), III, 529, 555, 560–561; Yehudi A. Cohen, ed., *Man in Adaptation: The Cultural Present*, 2d ed. (Chicago, 1974), 3–4, 45–68; F. R. Vivelo, *Cultural Anthropology Handbook: A Basic Introduction* (New York, 1978), 5, 16–19; Robert A. LeVine, *Culture, Behavior, and Personality* (London, 1973), 3–4; David Kaplan and Robert A. Manners, *Culture Theory* (Englewood Cliffs, N.J., 1972), 75–87.

industry, trade, local history, folklore, and customs. John Smyth's description of the hundred of Berkeley provides one example, the distinctiveness of society in the Forest of Dean another. In Kent, pronounced physical differences created a variety of local cultures in the Weald, Downs, coastal region, and marshes, and there was also a significant difference in tone between the western part of the county, heavily influenced by London, and the east, centered on Canterbury. An understanding of these highly localized cultures avoids overlooking the rich diversity of local life in England and emphasizes the importance of humdrum everyday occurrences that played such a large part in shaping community and individual experience.

While local traditions and customs exerted a powerful influence on daily life, it would be myopic to assume that people did not at the same time share in a broader culture. Beyond immediate horizons (the group of parishes that a person's "country" comprised) was an awareness of a wider regional identity—the West Country, Midlands, Southeast, East Anglia, Northwest, and so on: vague groupings of counties that corresponded either to large-scale geographical features, patterns of trade and social activities focused on particular cities, traditions and customs peculiar to an area, or speech patterns and dialect, some or all of which located an individual within a much wider cultural context. Thus indentured servants originally from the Southeast who sailed from Bristol in the 1650s must have been well aware of a different regional identity when they moved to the West Country before emigrating, just as John Smyth would have missed the gentle cadences of his native dialect when he visited London.

Markets at Bristol, Norwich, York, and Exeter provided outlets for all sorts of farm produce and manufactured goods from their respective regions and served as forums for buyers and sellers to discuss prices and trade as well as to pass on the latest news and gossip from the vicinity. In the inns and taverns one could eat local delicacies and drink the local ales. Crowded streets gave an opportunity to those who could afford it to display new fashions that were popular locally. Artisans produced clothing, furniture, household goods, and other commodities, often from local materials to vernacular designs. Provincial capitals gave coherence to English regions, linking the parishes and market towns of their hinterlands to the nation at large and providing a focus for social and economic exchange and cultural expression. Between the sixteenth and eighteenth centuries, provincial capitals played a crucial role in the development of regional identity.[68]

68. Alan Everitt, "Country, County, and Town: Patterns of Regional Evolution in England," Royal Historical Society, *Transactions*, 5th Ser., XXIX (1979), 90.

Emigrants from Gloucestershire, Kent, and other parts of England carried both their local cultures and broader regional identities to America. They came from a multitude of "countries" in the Southeast, West Country, and Midlands or, put differently, from the regions around London, Bristol, Exeter, and Liverpool. Memories of the Severn and Thames valleys, central Kent and Gloucestershire, and other local countrysides must have remained long in the minds of settlers as they adjusted to the novel conditions encountered in America. An understanding of colonists' regional origins is therefore crucial to an assessment of the problems and challenges they confronted in the process of adaptation and to an awareness of the differences among English people who found themselves living together in new societies along the Chesapeake Bay.

Two

The Formation of Chesapeake Society

3

The Great Bay of Chesupioc

What would have passed through the minds of immigrants as their ship rounded Cape Henry and entered the great expanse of the Chesapeake Bay? Relief that the long Atlantic crossing was over? Curiosity and wonder at their first sight of the great rivers busy with traffic, exotic flora and fauna, and plantations and tobacco wharves bustling with people dotted along the shoreline? How quickly settlers adjusted to their new surroundings depended to a large extent on the circumstances in which they arrived and their immediate prospects.[1] Luck, good or bad, dictated whether indentured servants would find themselves working for a hard taskmaster or a reasonable man; the majority had little say about where or whom they would serve and under what conditions. Free settlers, on the other hand, had the cushion of money and perhaps connections—relatives, friends, or other contacts—to help them adjust. Timing was also important. Chesapeake society of the 1670s and 1680s had changed beyond recognition compared to the tenuous settlement of half a century earlier. But no matter whether rich or poor, free or bound, all immigrants shared one thing: all would be profoundly influenced by the environment encountered in the tidewater.

1. Stephen Greenblatt argues that "wonder" was a dominant response of Europeans to encounters with the New World in *Marvelous Possessions: The Wonder of the New World* (Oxford, 1991). For a discussion of the ecology of the southern colonies in the early modern period, see Timothy H. Silver, *A New Face on the Countryside: Indians, Colonists, and Slaves in South Atlantic Forests, 1500–1800* (Cambridge, 1990); for New England, see William Cronon, *Changes in the Land: Indians, Colonists, and the Ecology of New England* (New York, 1983).

3. Map of Virginia and Maryland. *By John Speed. Permission of the British Library*

"A Lande, Even as God Made It"

By English standards, the tidewater of Virginia and Maryland covers a huge area. Superimposed on a map of England, it stretches from the south coast north to the Humber and east-west from the Wash (the Lincolnshire coast) to the Midland Plain. The central feature of the region, dividing the Western and Eastern shores, is the Chesapeake Bay, a massive drowned river valley, ten to twenty miles across and two hundred miles long (see Figure 10), which provided a superb harbor for oceangoing vessels and was navigable nearly its entire length. Four major rivers—the James, York, Rappahannock, and Potomac—have carved the Western Shore into a series of peninsulas stretching out into the Bay while myriad small tributaries, creeks, and islands give the shoreline a highly irregular appearance. Numerous secondary rivers, such as the Elizabeth, Chickahominy, and Patuxent on the Western Shore and the Choptank on the Eastern, provided further access for shipping and coastal vessels into the interior.

Colonists were impressed by the scale and extensiveness of waterways. The James was described as "one of the famousest Rivers that ever was

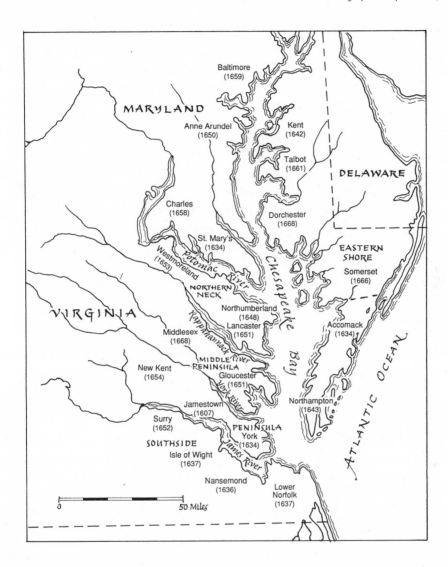

Figure 10. The Seventeenth-Century Chesapeake. *Drawn by Richard Stinely*

found by any Christian, it ebbes and flowes a hundred and threescore miles where ships of great burthen may harbour in saftie." Father Andrew White considered the Potomac "the sweetest and greatest river I have seene, so that the Thames is but a little finger to it." Rivers and the long coastline of the Bay opened up the region for settlement and allowed relatively quick, easy, and cheap transportation throughout the tidewater, the potential benefits of which were not lost on settlers and merchants familiar with the advantages of river and coastal traffic in England.[2] "The number of Navigable Rivers, Creeks, Inlets," wrote a visitor at the end of the century, "render it so Convenient for Exporting and Importing goods into any part . . . by Water Carriage, that no Country can Compare with it." In fact, it may not be too fanciful to conceive of two interconnected riverine worlds: the ports and rural hinterlands of the Thames and Severn valleys on the one hand, linked by transatlantic trade and shipping to the thousands of square miles of the tidewater on the other.[3]

Aside from rivers and the Bay itself, the other natural feature of Virginia and Maryland frequently commented upon by new arrivals was the richness and diversity of woodlands. From a distance, one traveler thought that the Virginia shore looked "like a forest standing in water," and the Reverend Hugh Jones found Maryland "Very Woody like one continued forest, no part Cleared but what is Cleared by the English." Some areas were so densely wooded, he reported, that although "we are pretty Closely seated together, yet wee cannot see our Neighbours House for Trees." In other areas, according to another account, trees were "commonly so farre distant from each other as a coach and fower horses may travale without molestation." An abundance of different kinds of trees—pines, hickories, white oaks, cedars, cypresses, poplars, black walnuts, and maples, "the Trunks of which are often Thirty, Forty, Fifty, some Sixty or Seventy Foot high, without a Branch or Limb"—spread over the land in wild profusion down to

2. Warren M. Billings, ed., *The Old Dominion in the Seventeenth Century: A Documentary History of Virginia, 1606–1689* (Chapel Hill, N.C., 1975), 22, 24; Father Andrew White, *A Briefe Relation of the Voyage unto Maryland* (1634), in Clayton Colman Hall, ed., *Narratives of Early Maryland, 1633–1684*, Original Narratives of Early American History (New York, 1910), 40; T. S. Willan, *The English Coasting Trade, 1600–1750* (Manchester, 1938); Willan, *The Inland Trade* . . . (Manchester, 1976); J. A. Chartres, *Internal Trade in England, 1500–1700* (London, 1977); Willan, "Food Consumption and Internal Trade," in A. L. Beier and Roger Finlay, eds., *London, 1500–1700: The Making of the Metropolis* (London, 1986), 168–196.

3. Arthur P. Middleton, *Tobacco Coast: A Maritime History of the Chesapeake Bay in the Colonial Era* (Newport News, Va., 1953), 33; "Part of a Letter from the Rev. Mr Hugh Jones to the Rev. Dr. Benjamin Woodruff, F.R.S., concerning Several Observables in Maryland," Jan. 23, 1698 [1699], LBC II (2), 247, 248, Royal Society Archives, London. Jones, with a touch of exaggeration, expressed the view that gentlemen of Virginia received goods from "London, Bristol, etc. with less trouble and cost, than to one living five miles in the country in England," in Jones, *The Present State of Virginia . . .* , ed. Richard L. Morton (Chapel Hill, N.C., 1956), 73. According to Lyon G. Tyler, the "plantations were mere suburbs of London and Bristol," in "Washington and His Neighbors," *William and Mary Quarterly*, 1st Ser., IV (1895–1896), 28.

the water's edge. Even in "the Swamps and sunken Grounds" were trees, opined Robert Beverley, "as vastly big, as I believe the World affords."[4]

This seemingly endless sweep of forest covered a landscape of generally low relief rarely above a few hundred feet, except in the interior where the coastal plain gradually rises to the higher elevation of the piedmont and, beyond, to the yet higher Blue Ridge Mountains. On the Western Shore, the ridges, or "necks," that form the spines of peninsulas give the landscape a gently rolling quality of "pleasant plaine hils and fertle valleyes," in contrast to the Eastern Shore, which is mostly flat and prone to flooding along the low-lying waterfront.[5]

First impressions guided a variety of responses to the land—awe, wonder, fear—but more important in the long run were the cultural assumptions that influenced settlers' interpretations of the natural setting, assumptions very different from those of Indian inhabitants. Viewed through English eyes, the landscape was bestowed with qualities and potentialities that reflected the expectations and aspirations of colonists. "To perceive a landscape," J. H. Elliott points out, "was to endow it in the mind's eye with a distinctive shape and purpose, suggesting what it might become if put to 'proper' use."[6] As far as the vast majority of immigrants, sponsors, and merchants were concerned, "proper use" meant, and in the context of European colonial expansion could mean only, sustained exploitation of the region's natural resources for profit. The land was seen in terms of the commodities it would in time yield.

Two contradictory images were initially influential. One depicted America as a wilderness, the other as a newfound Eden.[7] Captain John Smith,

4. "Report of the Journey of Francis Louis Michel from Berne, Switzerland, to Virginia, October 2, 1701–December 1, 1702," *Virginia Magazine of History and Biography*, XXIV (1916), 16; Jones, "Part of a Letter," 247; White, "A Briefe Relation," in Hall, ed., *Narratives of Early Maryland*, 40; Robert Beverley, *The History and Present State of Virginia*, ed. Louis B. Wright (Chapel Hill, N.C., 1947), 124; Silver, *A New Face on the Countryside*, 14–23, 25.

5. Capt. John Smith, *A Map of Virginia, with a Description of the Countrey . . .* (1612), in Philip L. Barbour, ed., *The Complete Works of Captain John Smith (1580–1631)*, 3 vols. (Chapel Hill, N.C., 1986), I, 145.

6. Keith Thomas, *Man and the Natural World: Changing Attitudes in England, 1500–1800* (London, 1983); Cronon, *Changes in the Land*, 19–22; John H. Elliott, "Introduction: Colonial Indentity in the Atlantic World," in Nicholas Canny and Anthony Pagden, eds., *Colonial Identity in the Atlantic World, 1500–1800* (Princeton, N.J., 1987), 10.

7. Michael Kammen, *People of Paradox: An Inquiry concerning the Origins of American Civilization* (New York, 1972), 151; Howard Mumford Jones, *O Strange New World: American Culture, the Formative Years,* (New York, 1964), chaps. 1–2.

although describing Virginia in favorable terms, viewed the country as "over-growne with trees and weedes being a plaine wildernes as God first made it." William Simmonds was more critical and characterized the colony as "Salvage" and "barbarous" but, like Smith, stressed its primordial nature: "a lande, even as God made it." Fifty years later, colonists were still described as living in a "Wildernesse" surrounded by "Heathen." The counterimage was equally important in early propaganda tracts. George Percy described his impressions of Virginia in the spring of 1607 in rapturous prose. Here were "faire meddowes and goodly tall Trees, with such Fresh-waters running through the woods, as I was almost ravished at the first sight thereof. . . . Going a little further we came into a little plat of ground full of fine and beautifull Strawberries, foure times bigger and better then ours in England." The James River contained "great plentie of fish of all kindes; as for Sturgeon, all the World cannot be compared to it. In this Countrey I have seene many great and large Medowes having excellent good pasture for any Cattle. There is also great store of Deere both Red and Fallow." Rivers teemed with fish, forests abounded with game, and skies were darkened with innumerable birds: abundance and plenty, Virginia offered a cornucopia of earthly delights, "as in the first creation, without toil or labor."[8]

Wilderness or Eden, images common in European literature of the sixteenth century and adopted by English propagandists for and against new colonies in the early years of settlement, dovetailed neatly with the notion of "improvement," a trend in English political economy that developed in the second half of Elizabeth's reign but that was considerably more influential by the 1640s and 1650s. A basic tenet was set out by Walter Blith in *The English Improover*: "All sorts of Lands, of what nature or quality soever they be, under what Climate soever, of what constitution or condition soever, of what face or character soever they be . . . will admit of a very large Improve-

---

8. Smith, *Map of Virginia*, in Barbour, ed., *Works of Smith*, I, 145; Simmonds in Billings, ed., *The Old Dominion*, 27; R. G., *Virginia's Cure; or, An Advisive Narrative concerning Virginia* (1662), in Peter Force, comp., *Tracts and Other Papers, Relating Principally to the Origin, Settlement, and Progress of the Colonies in North America*, 4 vols. (1836–1846; Gloucester, Mass., 1963), III, no. 15, 3–4; George Percy, "Observations" (1607), in Lyon Gardiner Tyler, ed., *Narratives of Early Virginia, 1606–1625*, Original Narratives of Early American History (New York, 1907), 9–10, 11, 15, 18; Michael Zuckerman, "Identity in British America: Unease in Eden," in Canny and Pagden, eds., *Colonial Identity*, 123. See also an "Extract from a Letter of Captain Thomas Yong to Sir Toby Matthew" (1634), in Hall, ed., *Narratives of Early Maryland*, 60. For a similar emphasis on abundance in New England, see Cronon, *Changes in the Land*, 22–31.

ment."[9] Careful husbandry and management could lead to higher yields and hence bigger profits. Improvement took a number of forms: more intensive farming of prime cornlands, introducing new crops in mixed farming or pastoral areas, and bringing under cultivation hitherto marginal areas such as forests and fens.

The last were given special prominence. " 'Improvement of the wastes and forests,' " Joan Thirsk says, "became the slogan of the age." Important social issues were involved. Not only did schemes such as the drainage of fenlands and improvement of forests and waste promise great profits to the investors; they also held out the possibility of employing substantial numbers of poor. John Stratford argued in 1619 that cash crops provided an opportunity to put to better use "mean land such as the uplands of remote forests, chases and other commons which doth now increase and nourish idle people." Whereas at present the poor "are an intolerable burden to the abler sort by begging and stealing, they would contrariwise become profitable to the commonwealth." Silvanus Taylor believed that one-fifth more people might be fed if wastes were enclosed, an opinion supported by Blith. "As for your Heathes, Moores, and Forrest Lands," he wrote enthusiastically, "I shall onely speak thus much, That vast and Incredulous are their Capacities of Improvement in generall." Not only would the cultivation of forests and fens "produce a great encrease of all things that the Land brings forth," according to Henry Robinson, but there were opportunities too for the exploitation of natural resources: woodcrafts, mining, and a variety of manufactures in woodland regions; fishing, fowling, reeds for thatching, and turf cutting in the fens.[10] Marginal lands could be improved, and they could also be more fully exploited, and in both cases it was expected that the poor would play a central role to the benefit of themselves and the common good. At least, that was the ideal.

Improvement, in this sense, was the guiding principle behind English settlement in the Chesapeake. Clearance of woodlands, planting cash crops, employment of the poor, and plans for towns, villages, markets, and manu-

---

9. *The English Improover; or, A New Survey of Husbandry* . . . (London, 1649), 11.

10. Joan Thirsk, "Seventeenth-Century Agriculture and Social Change," in Joan Thirsk, ed., *Land, Church, and People: Essays Presented to Professor H. P. R. Finberg*, suppl. to *Agricultural History Review*, XVIII (Reading, 1970), 167, 169, 171; Thirsk, *Economic Policy and Projects: The Development of a Consumer Society in Early Modern England* (Oxford, 1978), 102–104; Blith, *English Improover*, 49; Henry Robinson, *Certain Proposalls in Order to the Peoples Freedome and Accommodation* . . . (London, 1652), 19.

factures drew upon ideas, experiments, and precedents initiated in England. Efforts to create a diversified economy in Virginia, based on the cultivation of a variety of new crops and the development of industries, were a direct consequence of similar economic experiments at home. Hemp and flax, dye crops, tobacco, vines, and mulberry trees for silk production, enthusiastically promoted by English projectors, had an equally enthusiastic reception among investors in colonial ventures and settlers. American colonies were the testing grounds for all sorts of new projects being tried simultaneously in the parent country.[11]

In addition, products imported into England from Europe and Asia could instead be procured at much lower cost from the colonies. Richard Hakluyt the younger considered that America "will yelde unto us all the commodities of Europe, Affrica, and Asia, as far as wee were wonte to travell, and supply the wantes of all our decayed trades." The northern parts would supply timber, masts, clapboard, pitch, tar, cordage, and naval supplies, and the southern parts wine, silk, fruits, oil, sugar and salt.[12] While supporters of colonization expected that trade with indigenous populations would reap rewards, all were convinced that, to produce the goods that England required, large numbers of men and women would have to be transported to the plantations. This scheme was doubly advantageous. Supplying colonists overseas with English goods would greatly stimulate manufactures in the parent country while, for their part, colonists would produce commodities that England needed. An expansive new market for English manufactured goods in the colonies would be created, thereby encouraging production and providing relief for the poor who depended on those trades, and the country would also benefit from the import of a growing volume of colonial products that could be sold at home and in Europe.

Promoters of colonies were quick to emphasize the tangible financial rewards that colonial trade would bring to the home country and the much-needed boost it would give to ailing domestic manufactures. They also stressed social benefits. America offered a golden opportunity to put the country's surplus population to work. The able-bodied poor, unemployed,

11. Thirsk, *Economic Policy*; Wesley Frank Craven, *The Southern Colonies in the Seventeenth Century, 1607–1689* (1949; Baton Rouge, La., 1970), chaps. 3–5; Edmund S. Morgan, *American Slavery, American Freedom: The Ordeal of Colonial Virginia* (New York, 1975), chaps. 3–6.

12. E.G.R. Taylor, ed., *The Original Writings and Correspondence of the Two Richard Hakluyts*, 2 vols., Hakluyt Society, 2d Ser., LXXVI–LXXVII (London, 1935), II, 211, 327–335, 347.

and idle, an "altogether unprofitable" drain on the country's resources, could be found work in the colonies to their own and the nation's advantage. If England, as Hakluyt believed, was "swarminge at this day w[i]th valiant youthes rustinge and hurtfull by lacke of employement," the solution was to transport them overseas, where plenty of jobs were to be had. Petty thieves, vagabonds, and criminals who "for trifles may otherwise be devoured by the gallowes" could redeem themselves by laboring in America. Overpopulation would be avoided and England's mounting social problems associated with poverty, vagrancy, and underemployment alleviated.[13]

A couple of points are worth underlining. The adoption of industrial crops in America, notably tobacco, was not an entirely new departure reserved for colonial expansion. Tobacco had been grown in small quantities in England since the 1570s. What was different was the scale of production and the practice of extensive, rather than intensive, farming in the land-rich tidewater. New crops introduced into England in the second half of the sixteenth and the early seventeenth centuries were usually cultivated in small plots on marginal lands, often as a supplement to arable or pasture farming, whereas in the Chesapeake tobacco dominated the region's economy and land use throughout the century. Yet despite significant differences in methods of cultivation and husbandry, the economic and social principles that guided improvement of marginal lands in England were similar to those adopted in Virginia and Maryland. In fact, from an English perspective, the entire eastern seaboard was seen as a vast marginal expanse of forest and fen ripe for exploitation.

In one important respect, however, the idea of improvement was broadened in America to embrace the concept of civility. Whether subscribing to a view of America as primordial garden or savage wilderness, settlers had no desire to divorce economic improvement from social and political development. In practice, this entailed civilizing the New World, whereby society would be transformed from a state of nature to "one that was not wild, barbaric, irregular, rustic, or crude, but, like England itself, . . . settled, cultivated, civilized, orderly, developed and polite."[14] The absence of what the English conceived of as civilized indigenous peoples and the lack of cities, towns, European types of agriculture, manufactures, and trade confirmed the view that the Chesapeake was a tabula rasa on which a new English society could be inscribed. The land would be cleared and cultivated for

13. *Ibid.*, 315, 319.

14. Jack P. Greene, "Changing Indentity in the British Caribbean: Barbados as a Case Study," in Canny and Pagden, eds., *Colonial Identity*, 228–229.

profit, towns and roads built to encourage trade, manufactures established, English laws and institutions adopted to promote order and social harmony. Over time, society in Virginia and Maryland, it was believed, would come to resemble metropolitan society. In the event, the degree to which Chesapeake society fell short of these expectations was to be a continuous source of frustration and disappointment to settlers, colonial officials, and improvers alike.

While colonists might have preferred settling virgin territories ready for the taking, they in fact entered a land that had been occupied and cultivated for centuries by native peoples. Recent estimates suggest that from twenty-six thousand to thirty-four thousand Algonquian Indians lived in the Chesapeake tidewater at the time the English arrived, scattered throughout the region in about two hundred villages. In addition, the powerful Susquehannocks occupied tribal lands along the river that bears their name in northern Maryland, and other Iroquoian tribes, Nottaways and Meherrins, inhabited large areas of the Southside below the Appomattox River down to the Virginia–North Carolina border.[15]

What did settlers make of their new neighbors? From the beginning there was little effort to create a biracial society where the English and Indian could live together on equal and mutually beneficial terms. Such a vision was beyond the grasp of a nation intent on colonial expansion and assured of its own cultural superiority. Justifications legitimizing (in English eyes) the conquest and dispossession of Catholic Irish and the enslavement of Africans for use in the colonies were tailored to justify English responses to indigenous peoples in America. From the mid-sixteenth century, vital elements of English racism were hammered out in the context of territorial expansionism and contact with alien peoples. In Ireland and along the coast of West Africa native peoples were described in strikingly similar terms as uncivilized, pagan, savage, barbarous, lascivious, treacherous, inconstant, bestial, and

15. Estimates are derived from Christian F. Feest, in Bruce G. Trigger, ed., *Northeast* (Washington, D.C., 1978), 241, 242, 255, 256, vol. XV of William C. Sturtevant, ed., *Handbook of North American Indians*; E. Randolph Turner, "Socio-Political Organization within the Powhatan Chiefdom and the Effects of European Contact, A.D. 1607–1646," in William W. Fitzhugh, ed., *Cultures in Contact: The Impact of European Contacts on Native American Institutions, A.D. 1000–1800* (Washington, D.C., 1985), 193; Helen C. Rountree, *The Powhatan Indians of Virginia: Their Traditional Culture* (Norman, Okla., 1989), 15. This compares to an English population in the Chesapeake of about 1,300 in 1625 (see Morgan, *American Slavery, American Freedom*, 404).

On Susquehannocks and Iroquoian tribes: Trigger, ed., *Northeast*, 282–289, 362–367.

belonging "to a lower order of humanity." Negative stereotypes of American Indians drew upon a common reservoir of racial and cultural prejudice that developed as a functional and increasingly consistent set of ideas to explain obvious differences between races and affirm the unquestionable superiority of the English. The perception of Gaelic Irish, Africans, and Indians as subhuman liberated the English from adhering to European conventions governing warfare and legitimized any actions undertaken by settlers and soldiers against savages, from stealing corn to genocide.[16]

English reactions to peoples inhabiting the Chesapeake were not simply determined by existing stereotypes, however; they were shaped too by the exigencies of colonial life and the attitudes of Indians they encountered. Colonists who arrived in Virginia at the beginning of the century found themselves in the midst of about thirty tribes united under the "small-scale monarchy" of Wahunsenacawh (Powhatan), a powerful chief (*mamana-towick*) who had been steadily consolidating his influence in the region over the previous twenty years. Initially content to allow a small English contingent to establish itself at Jamestown, Wahunsenacawh and his successor, Opechancanough, soon found that settlers' increasingly insistent and bellicose demands for corn and land caused more trouble than they were worth. Convinced that the colonists' "comming hither is not for trade, but to invade my people, and possesse my Country," Wahunsenacawh launched the first Anglo-Powhatan war of 1609–1614.[17]

16. My thinking, expressed briefly here, has been influenced by the following: Nicholas P. Canny, "The Ideology of English Colonization: From Ireland to America," *WMQ*, 3d Ser., XXX (1973), 575–598; Winthrop D. Jordan, *White over Black: American Attitudes toward the Negro, 1550–1812* (Chapel Hill, N.C., 1968), pt. 1; Alden T. Vaughan, "The Origins Debate: Slavery and Racism in Seventeenth-Century Virginia," *VMHB*, XCVII (1989), 311–354, esp. 344–354; Peter Fryer, *Staying Power: The History of Black People in Britain* (London, 1984), 4–12, 14–32; Roy Harvey Pearce, *The Savages of America: A Study of the Indian and the Idea of Civilization*, rev. ed. (Baltimore, 1965), chap. 1; Gary B. Nash, "The Image of the Indian in the Southern Colonial Mind," *WMQ*, 3d Ser., XXIX (1972), 197–230; Bernard W. Sheehan, *Savagism and Civility: Indians and Englishmen in Colonial Virginia* (Cambridge, 1980). For two important interpretive reviews of English-Indian relations, see J. Frederick Fausz, "The Invasion of Virginia: Indians, Colonialism, and the Conquest of Cant: A Review Essay on Anglo-Indian Relations in the Chesapeake," *VMHB*, XCV (1987), 133–156; and James H. Merrell, " 'The Customes of Our Countrey': Indians and Colonists in Early America," in Bernard Bailyn and Philip D. Morgan, eds., *Strangers within the Realm: Cultural Margins of the First British Empire* (Chapel Hill, N.C., 1991), 117–156.

17. J. Frederick Fausz, "Patterns of Anglo-Indian Aggression and Accommodation

Land, as he astutely observed, was the key issue. Once it became clear that the English were not so much interested in establishing a trading outpost as in a permanent colony, the contest between two very different conceptions of using the land began in earnest. "Our first worke," declared Sir Francis Wyatt shortly after the great Indian uprising of 1622 nearly wiped out the colony, "is expulsion of the Salvages to gaine the free range of the countrey for encrease of Cattle, swine etc which will more then restore us, for it is infinitely better to have no heathen among us, who at best were but thornes in our sides, then to be at peace and league with them." His plan for Virginia's development over the following seven years entailed "extirpating of the Salvages, winning of the Forrest, encrease of cattle, swine etc building houses convenient for both seasons, planting gardens and orchards for delight and health setting vines and Mulberry trees for raising those two excellent comodities of wine and Silke." What colonists wanted from their Indian neighbors, Francis Jennings comments, "was *cleared* land. It was the Indian farmer, not the Indian hunter, who stood in the way." [18]

In reality, English policy was somewhat more flexible, involving reducing friendly Indians to tributary status, dependent on the English rather than the Powhatans, developing links with tribes, like the Susquehannocks, that had access to the profitable beaver trade, and supporting frontier tribes as buffers between English settlements and potentially hostile Indians from outside the region. Nevertheless, the rapid expansion of English population after 1630 and the spread of settlement from the James-York peninsula up the Bay was a source of continual friction between settlers and local tribes and posed an insoluble problem to colonial governors seeking to minimize frontier violence. Efforts to contain hostilities by segregating English and Indian communities, protecting Indians in the courts, and making formal peace treaties eventually broke down in the Anglo-Indian conflagration of the mid-1670s during Bacon's Rebellion and brought about the virtual destruction of tidewater Indians. [19] Seventy years of conflict with the English,

---

along the Mid-Atlantic Coast, 1584–1634," in Fitzhugh, ed., *Cultures in Contact*, 235–254; Fausz, "An 'Abundance of Blood Shed on Both Sides': England's First Indian War, 1609–1614," *VMHB*, XCVIII (1990), 3–56.

18. "Letter of Sir Francis Wyatt, Governor of Virginia, 1621–1626," *WMQ*, 2d Ser., VI (1926), 118–119; Francis Jennings, "Virgin Land and Savage People," *American Quarterly*, XXIII (1971), 520–521.

19. On accommodation with Indians: J. Frederick Fausz, "Merging and Emerging Worlds: Anglo-Indian Interest Groups and the Development of the Seventeenth-Century Chesapeake," in Lois Green Carr, Philip D. Morgan, and Jean B. Russo, eds., *Colonial Chesapeake Society* (Chapel Hill, N.C., 1988), 47–98; Trigger, ed., *North-*

European diseases, wars with other tribes, and migration reduced the Indian population to a fraction of its original size by the last quarter of the century. "Att the first coming of the English," wrote Thomas Glover in 1675, "divers [Indian] Towns had two or three thousand Bow-men in them, but since they [the English] seated themselves there, they have destroyed many of them, partly by their own army, and partly by setting them together by the ears amongst themselves . . . now, in the Southern parts of Virginia . . . they are so universally thinned . . . I verily believe there are not above three thousand left." Although more numerous in Maryland, they "are like shortly to be reduced to as small numbers as the former." By 1705, according to Robert Beverley, the Indians were "almost wasted."[20]

Indian culture influenced the adaptation of English settlers to their new environment in several crucial respects. The Chesapeake economy depended on an Indian plant, tobacco, and the English adopted a variety of Indian foods such as maize, squash, and various types of beans, as well as herbs for medicinal purposes. Indian words for fauna and flora entered the English vocabulary, and Indian placenames for rivers and other natural features described the landscape. A small number of colonists and traders joined Indian tribes or learned Indian ways while held captive and frequently acted as go-betweens ("cultural brokers") during treaty or trade negotiations. Less concrete but much more important was the impact of Indian culture on the minds of settlers. If the general framework of Anglo-Indian relations was structured by English ethnocentrism and aggression and by the wary and

---

east, 364; Wesley Frank Craven, *White, Red, and Black: The Seventeenth-Century Virginian* (Charlottesville, Va., 1971), 39–72; Craven, "Indian Policy in Early Virginia," *WMQ*, 3d Ser., I (1944), 65–82; W. Stitt Robinson, "Tributary Indians in Colonial Virginia," *VMHB*, LXVII (1959), 49–64.

On English expansion: Craven, *Southern Colonies*, 231–232, 365–393; Morgan, *American Slavery, American Freedom*, 230–233, 250–270; Stephen Saunders Webb, *1676: The End of American Independence* (New York, 1984), 14–16, 20, 21–24, 29–30, 127, 131, 132, 143–144, 160; Wilcomb E. Washburn, *The Governor and the Rebel: A History of Bacon's Rebellion in Virginia* (Chapel Hill, N.C., 1957), 19–30, 32–48, 162–165; Billings, ed., *The Old Dominion*, 205–213.

20. Thomas Glover, "An Account of Virginia . . . ," Cl.P., vii (i), 18, Royal Society Archives, London (an edited version, which omits the passages describing the English destruction of Indian tribes, appears in *Philosophical Transactions*, XI [1676], 623–636; subsequent references are taken from this version); Beverley, *History and Present State of Virginia*, 232. See also Turner, "Socio-Political Organization within the Powhatan Chiefdom," in Fitzhugh, ed., *Cultures in Contact*, 193–217; and Helen C. Rountree, *Pocahontas's People: The Powhatan Indians of Virginia through Four Centuries* (Norman, Okla., 1990), chaps. 4–6.

sometimes hostile attitude of Indians toward settlers, this mutual antipathy did not preclude contact between the peoples in thousands of everyday routine meetings. Informal encounters—at court days, during hunting trips, when men from nearby tribes visited plantations with trade goods, or when whites sought the help of Indians to locate prime tobacco lands or for other reasons—had an important influence on settlers' lives.[21]

The cumulative effect of these ordinary contacts on Anglo-Indian relations at the local level is uncertain. How did living with the Indians, if only experienced through fear of attack, military expeditions, or taxes to pay for forts, shape English identity, the settlers' perceptions of themselves and their environment? Did notions of Indian savagery and heathenism reinforce the sense of a collective identity among the English, thereby helping to erode regional differences between settlers? Did the behavior and proximity of Indians provide a tangible warning of what might happen to them if they slipped from civilized European standards? During the course of the seventeenth century, English settlers, whether they liked it or not, shared their environment with a large and culturally diverse native American population; their reaction was considerably more complex than the rhetoric of colonial leaders or propagandists might suggest, and the impact of Indian culture on English life considerably greater than they might have cared to admit.[22]

White Immigration, Population, and Settlement

As the numbers of Indians inhabiting the Chesapeake rapidly declined, the white population grew by leaps and bounds, from 105 men and boys who settled at Jamestown in 1607 to about 900 in 1620, 8,000 in 1640, 25,000 in 1660, 60,000 in 1680, and 85,000 by 1700. Virginia was the most populous

21. James Axtell, "The White Indians of Colonial America," *WMQ*, 3d Ser., XXXII (1975), 55–88; Axtell, *The European and the Indian: Essays in the Ethnohistory of Colonial North America* (Oxford, 1981), 275–297; J. Frederick Fausz, "Middlemen in Peace and War: Virginia's Earliest Indian Interpreters, 1608–1632," *VMHB*, XCV (1987), 41–64; Karen Ordahl Kupperman, *Settling with the Indians: The Meeting of English and Indian Cultures in America, 1580–1640* (London, 1980), pt. 2.

On encounters, see James H. Merrell, "Cultural Continuity among the Piscataway Indians of Colonial Maryland," *WMQ*, 3d Ser., XXXVI (1979), 558–559.

22. Kupperman, *Settling with the Indians*, pt. 2; Zuckerman, "Identity in British America," in Canny and Pagden, eds., *Colonial Identity*, 144–149; T. H. Breen, "Creative Adaptations: Peoples and Cultures," in Jack P. Greene and J. R. Pole, eds., *Colonial British America: Essays in the New History of the Early Modern Era* (Baltimore, 1984), 195–232.

of the mainland colonies throughout the century, although dwarfed by the scale of demographic growth in the Caribbean. In both Virginia and Maryland the flow of immigrants surged after 1650. During the 1630s and 1640s immigration averaged about 8,000–9,000 per decade, but from 1650 to 1680, 16,000–20,000 people entered the Chesapeake each decade—the equivalent of the population of England's second city, Bristol. Half the total number of immigrants who settled along the tobacco coast in the seventeenth century arrived in these three decades.[23]

Despite this impressive growth, immigrants did not enter a healthy environment. Whereas about 120,000 settlers immigrated to the Chesapeake over the whole century, the white population in 1700 was not even 90,000. Unlike the northern colonies, growth in the South was sustained only by continuous immigration to compensate for the massive wastage of life and, increasingly after 1675, a significant movement of people out of the region. Contemporaries were well aware of the deleterious effect of the Chesapeake environment on English settlers. Colonists, wrote George Gardyner in 1650, were subject to "much sickness or death. For the air is exceeding unwholesome, insomuch as one of three scarcely liveth the first year at this time." He attributed the high mortality to "the changeableness of the weather, which is mighty extream in heat and cold," to "the Swamps, standing-waters and Marshes, and mighty store of Rivers, and the low lying of the land," to a disease called "Country Duties" (probably syphilis) caught from the Indians, and, finally, to rattlesnakes. Anthony Langston believed that salt-water was chiefly responsible for "those ill Sents, and Foggs, and vapors"

23. On population: Russell R. Menard, "Immigrants and Their Increase: The Process of Population Growth in Early Colonial Maryland," in Aubrey C. Land *et al.*, eds., *Law, Society, and Politics in Early Maryland* (Baltimore, 1977), 88; John J. McCusker and Russell R. Menard, *The Economy of British America, 1607–1789*, rev. ed. (Chapel Hill, N.C., 1991), 136, 154; Menard, "The Tobacco Industry in the Chesapeake Colonies, 1617–1730: An Interpretation," *Research in Economic History*, V (1980), appendix, 157–160; Jack P. Greene, *Pursuits of Happiness: The Social Development of Early Modern British Colonies and the Formation of American Culture* (Chapel Hill, N.C., 1988), table 8.1, 178–179. The population of the British Caribbean Islands in 1660 was approximately 81,000, of whom 40% were black slaves.

On immigration: Gloria L. Main, *Tobacco Colony: Life in Early Maryland, 1650–1720* (Princeton, N.J., 1982), 10; Henry A. Gemery, "Emigration from the British Isles to the New World, 1630–1700: Inferences from Colonial Populations," *Res. Econ. Hist.*, V (1980), 179–231, esp. 215; Russell R. Menard, "British Migration to the Chesapeake Colonies in the Seventeenth Century," in Carr, Morgan, and Russo, eds., *Colonial Chesapeake Society*, 103–105.

which "breeds those Agues, Feavers, Dropsies, and Lethargies, which in the Country they call the Seasonings."[24]

The association of sickness with tidal and low-lying regions was not accidental. English marshes and fenlands were also characterized by high rates of mortality and morbidity. In northern Kent, for example, the area along the Thames between Erith and the Isle of Sheppey was described as very "unwholesome" owing to "large tracts of low swampy marsh ground" and "stagnating waters." Mortality rates in the tidewater, however, were even greater. Up to 40 percent of new arrivals may have died in their first couple of years, commonly of a variety of ailments associated with malaria and intestinal disorders. Malaria occasionally reached pandemic proportions among settlers and frequently left survivors in poor health, easy prey to a variety of other diseases.[25] Even if the outcome was not fatal, most immigrants experienced a period of sickness (seasoning) in their first year. Moving to Virginia

24. George Gardyner, *A Description of the New World* . . . (London, 1650), 99–100; "Anthony Langston on Towns and Corporations; and on the Manufacture of Iron," *WMQ*, 2d Ser., I (1921), 102; Menard, "Immigrants and Their Increase," in Land *et al.*, eds., *Law, Society, and Politics*, 93; J. P. Horn, "Moving On in the New World: Migration and Out-Migration in the Seventeenth-Century Chesapeake," in Peter Clark and David Souden, eds., *Migration and Society in Early Modern England* (London, 1987), 197–200; Lorena S. Walsh and Russell R. Menard, "Death in the Chesapeake: Two Life Tables for Men in Early Colonial Maryland," *Maryland Historical Magazine*, LXIX (1974), 211–227; Daniel Blake Smith, "Mortality and Family in the Colonial Chesapeake," *Journal of Interdisciplinary History*, VIII (1977–1978), 403–427; Darrett B. Rutman and Anita H. Rutman, " 'Now-Wives and Sons-in-Law': Parental Death in a Seventeenth-Century Virginia County," in Thad W. Tate and David L. Ammerman, eds., *The Chesapeake in the Seventeenth Century: Essays on Anglo-American Society* (Chapel Hill, N.C., 1979), 153–182; Rutman and Rutman, *A Place in Time: Middlesex County, Virginia, 1650–1750* (New York, 1984), 113–120; Lois Green Carr, "Emigration and the Standard of Living: The Seventeenth Century Chesapeake," *Journal of Economic History*, LII (1992), 272–275.

25. Mary Dobson, " 'Marsh Fever'—The Geography of Malaria in England," *Journal of Historical Geography*, VI (1980), 357–389; Philip MacDougall, "Malaria: Its Influence on a North Kent Community," *Archaeologia Cantiana*, XCV (1979), 256; John Duffy, *Epidemics in Colonial America* (Baton Rouge, La., 1953), 214, 215, 237–247; Lorena Seebach Walsh, "Charles County, Maryland, 1658–1705: A Study of Chesapeake Social and Political Structure" (Ph.D. diss., Michigan State University, 1977), 46; Darrett B. Rutman and Anita H. Rutman, " 'Of Agues and Fevers': Malaria in the Early Chesapeake," *WMQ*, 3d Ser., XXXIII (1976), 31–60; Carville V. Earle, "Environment, Disease, and Mortality in Early Virginia," in Tate and Ammerman, eds., *Chesapeake in the Seventeenth Century*, 96–125; Karen Ordahl Kupperman, "Apathy and Death in Early Jamestown," *Journal of American History*, LXVI (1979–1980), 24–40.

and Maryland, like moving from the provinces to London, was risky and amounted to a calculated gamble on survival. For those who survived and lived long enough, the rewards could be considerable, but that very success was predicated in part on a rapid turnover of population caused by the high death rate.

Natural population growth was retarded also by the considerable sexual imbalance that existed throughout the century. Chesapeake society was dominated by males not only in the conventional sense but simply in sheer numbers. At no time in the century did the sex ratio improve upon two to three men for every woman. Such an imbalance had far-reaching practical effects (quite apart from the psychological stress it must have caused). A shortage of women restricted family formation and forced many males to remain single. More than a quarter of men from the lower Western Shore of Maryland who died leaving estates between 1658 and 1705 were unmarried. The problem was exacerbated by the relatively late age at which women married. Since the vast majority of women arrived in the Chesapeake as servants and were usually obliged to finish their term of service before marrying, they were unable to take a husband until their mid-twenties: about the same age they would have married in England. A shortage of women did not, therefore, lead to a lower age of marriage, which would have increased their reproductive lives and the birthrate. Any one of these factors (high rates of mortality and morbidity, sexual imbalance, and a late age at first marriage), Russell Menard points out, could have severely restricted natural increase, but, with all acting together, "demographic failure along the tobacco coast was inevitable."[26] Not until the final years of the seventeenth century did the white population of Virginia and Maryland become self-sustaining.

One of the most obvious differences between English and New World society immediately apparent to early settlers and, indeed, its main attraction was an "abundance of land and absence of people." Covering about half the land area of England, the Chesapeake had a population at midcentury that could have quite easily been accommodated in a small English county or London suburb. The lower Western Shore of Maryland, for example, occupies about sixteen hundred square miles, and yet its population at the end of the seventeenth century of about thirteen thousand was the same as that of the Vale of

26. Lois Green Carr and Russell R. Menard, "Immigration and Opportunity: The Freedman in Early Colonial Maryland," in Tate and Ammerman, eds., *Chesapeake in the Seventeenth Century*, 211; Menard, "Immigrants and Their Increase," in Land *et al.*, eds., *Law, Society, and Politics*, 97.

Berkeley, which covers less than one hundred square miles.[27] Low population density was a function of both the small size of local populations and a scattered pattern of settlement. Given the cheapness of land and the nature of the economy, it made sense for planters to take up large tracts of land (by European standards) and seat themselves on or near convenient shipping routes. Water carriage not only provided the best means of transporting bulky tobacco leaf packed in hogsheads, but it was also favored by English merchants, who preferred to trade directly with individual producers: manufactured goods, liquor, and servants brought from London, Bristol, or other outports could be exchanged on the spot for tobacco. The system bypassed the need for market towns in the tidewater, because trade was as dispersed as settlement.[28]

An unfortunate consequence, as commentators never tired of repeating, was that Chesapeake society failed to develop urban communities. "Townes and Corporations have likewise been much hindred," Anthony Langston wrote of Virginia in the 1650s,

> by our manner of seating the Country; every man having Liberty . . . to take up Land (untaken before) and there seat, build, clear, and plant without any manner of restraint from the Government in relation to their Religion, and gods Service, or security of their persons, or the peace of the Country, so that every man builds in the midst of his own Land, and therefore provides beforehand to take up so much at the first Patent, that his great Grandchild may be sure not to want Land to go forward with any great design they covet, likewise the conveniency of the River from Transportation of their Commodities, by which meanes they have been led up and down by these famous Rivers . . . to seate in a stragling distracted Condition leaving the inside of the Land from the Rivers as wast for after Comers.[29]

27. Morgan, *American Slavery, American Freedom*, 158; Russell R. Menard, P.M.G. Harris, and Lois Green Carr, "Opportunity and Inequality: The Distribution of Wealth on the Lower Western Shore of Maryland, 1638–1705," *Md. Hist. Mag.*, LXIX (1974), 170; James Horn, "Adapting to a New World: A Comparative Study of Local Society in England and Maryland, 1650–1700," in Carr, Morgan, and Russo, eds., *Colonial Chesapeake Society*, 165. For the population of the Vale of Berkeley, see Chapter 2, above. The land surface of the Vale is based on acreages given in William Page, ed., *The Victoria History of the County of Gloucester*, II (London, 1907), 175–186.

28. Durand of Dauphine, *A Frenchman in Virginia: Being the Memoirs of a Huguenot Refugee in 1686*, trans. Fairfax Harrison ([Richmond, Va.], 1923), 22–23; Walsh, "Charles County," 34–35.

29. "Anthony Langston on Towns," *WMQ*, 2d Ser., I (1921), 101.

Thirty years later, the French Huguenot Durand of Dauphine commented, there was "neither town nor village in the whole country, save one named Gemston [Jamestown], where the Council assembles. All the rest is made up of single houses, each on its own plantation." In 1678, Charles, Lord Baltimore, described St. Mary's City, the capital of Maryland, as consisting of "not above thirty houses, and these at considerable distances from each other." No other place in the province was even worthy of being called a town.[30]

In terms of first impressions, it is worth stressing that to English eyes what was missing in Virginia's and Maryland's landscape was as significant as what was present. Immigrants, whether from urban or rural backgrounds, were used to living in a society where there was a hierarchy of interdependent and interrelated communities: village, market town, provincial capital, and city. Few people in England lived more than a few miles from a local town—an hour, if that, by road or across country. Along the tobacco coast, only the cluster of dwellings and other buildings located in the colonies' capitals resembled small towns, and for most of the century even they were nearer in size, if not character, to English villages. The absence of towns inclined English commentators to view the Chesapeake as undeveloped and uncivilized. Missing, too, was the bustle of fairs and market days, crowded taverns and inns, and busy roads bringing people and goods to trade. Approximations existed, but nothing that could compare to the crowd of people and places familiar to English men and women in their native communities.[31] Getting used to the *absence* of significant aspects of everyday life that were taken for granted in England was probably the most difficult part of adapting to conditions in the Chesapeake.

Tobacco and the Chesapeake Economy

Little can be understood of the development of Virginia and Maryland society without reference to tobacco. Considered a luxury in the early seventeenth century, it could be produced cheaply in the tidewater and sold initially for a handsome profit in European markets. From the early 1620s, when

30. Durand of Dauphine, *A Frenchman in Virginia*, trans. Harrison, 90; W. Noel Sainsbury *et al.*, eds., *Calendar of State Papers*, Colonial Series, *America and West Indies* (London, 1860–), X, *1677–1680*, no. 633, p. 226. Settlement patterns will be discussed in more detail in the next chapter.

31. Darrett B. Rutman, "Assessing the Little Communities of Early America," *WMQ*, 3d Ser., XLIII (1986), 168–169.

extensive production began, tobacco governed the character and pace of immigration, population growth, settlement patterns, husbandry and land use, transatlantic trade, the development of the home market, manufactures, opportunity, standards of living, and government policy. Settlers used leaf as local money, paid their taxes, extended credit, settled debts, and valued their goods in it. "We have [no] trade at home and abroad," a contemporary stated at the end of the century, "but that of Tobacco . . . [it] is our meat, drink, clothes, and monies." [32] Without tobacco, a very different kind of society would have evolved.

The advantages of tobacco production were many: its yield per acre was high, and its keeping qualities were good; it fetched a better price per pound than English grains, and the soils and climate of the Chesapeake were, for the most part, suitable for its cultivation. A plantation required relatively little capital to set up, and a man's labor, or that of his family and a couple of servants, was sufficient to run it. Last, there was a potentially expansive market for tobacco in England, which the monopoly granted to the Virginia Company in 1619 recognized and protected. [33] The very success of the "Weede," in fact, would later cause problems in both colonies owing to overproduction.

There is general agreement about the broad pattern of economic growth and its link with immigration and settlement, which will be briefly summarized here. An extraordinary expansion of the tobacco industry took place in the middle decades of the century, when output rose from about 400,000 pounds (weight) in 1630 to 15,000,000 pounds by the late 1660s. The growth rate slowed in the 1670s and was followed by stagnation for thirty years after 1680, during which output fluctuated around 20,000,000–30,000,000 pounds. In good times, such as the 1620s, mid-1630s, 1645 to 1654, and mid-1670s, planters sought to increase production by acquiring more land and

32. McCusker and Menard, *Economy of British America*, 118–127; Main, *Tobacco Colony*, 16–27; Morgan, *American Slavery, American Freedom*, chap. 6; Thomas J. Wertenbaker, *The Planters of Colonial Virginia* (1922; New York, 1958), 23–24; Jones, "Part of a Letter," 250–253.

33. Philip Alexander Bruce, *Economic History of Virginia in the Seventeenth Century: An Inquiry into the Material Conditions of the People . . .* , 2 vols. (New York, 1896), I, 211–255; Wertenbaker, *Planters of Colonial Virginia*, 64–71; Avery Odelle Craven, *Soil Exhaustion as a Factor in the Agricultural History of Virginia and Maryland, 1606–1860* (1926; Gloucester, Mass., 1965), 30–39; Morgan, *American Slavery, American Freedom*, chap. 6. The most thorough treatment of 17th-century Chesapeake agriculture can be found in Lois Green Carr, Russell R. Menard, and Lorena S. Walsh, *Robert Cole's World: Agriculture and Society in Early Maryland* (Chapel Hill, N.C., 1991), chaps. 2–3.

labor. When the price of leaf was high, the number of ships trading to the tobacco coast rose, and greater numbers of servants were imported. Settlement expanded into new areas where land was inexpensive and plentiful, and free immigrants and ex-servants alike took advantage of the availability of cheap credit to set up their own plantations; thus output increased not only because the same planters were producing more but also because the number of units of production rose.[34]

The long-term decline in the price of leaf, from 1 or 2s. per pound in the boom times of the 1620s to 5d. in the mid-1630s, to 2 or 3d. in the early 1650s, to 1 or 2d. in the 1660s, and to less than 1d. after 1680, was not simply the result of overproduction. As the cost of producing and marketing tobacco fell during the century, merchants and planters were able to lower the price of tobacco and reach a larger market. The creation of a mass market was crucial, because without it Chesapeake tobacco would have remained a high-priced luxury item in limited demand. Consequently, there would have been no expansion of output and, therefore, no need for significant population growth. Stagnation set in after 1680 because planters were unable to lower the costs of production any further: freight charges ceased to fall as quickly after 1660, the amount of tobacco being produced by each worker reached a maximum such that increased productivity required more labor (more capital investment), and the price of both land and servants rose steadily in the 1670s and 1680s. Any economies in the costs of transportation and marketing of leaf could no longer be passed on to the consumer; instead, they helped planters absorb rising production costs. The result was thirty years

34. Russell Robert Menard, "Economy and Society in Early Colonial Maryland" (Ph.D. diss., University of Iowa, 1975), 285; McCusker and Menard, *Economy of British America*, 119–123; Menard, "Tobacco Industry," *Res. Econ. Hist.*, V (1980), 109–177; Paul G. E. Clemens, *The Atlantic Economy and Colonial Maryland's Eastern Shore: From Tobacco to Grain* (Ithaca, N.Y., 1980), 29–40; Lois Green Carr, "Diversification in the Colonial Chesapeake: Somerset County, Maryland, in Comparative Perspective," in Carr, Morgan, and Russo, eds., *Colonial Chesapeake Society*, 342–388. For recent critiques of the "boom and bust" model, see Charles Wetherell, " 'Boom and Bust' in the Colonial Chesapeake Economy," *Jour. Interdisc. Hist.*, XV (1984–1985), 207–208; and Anita H. Rutman, "Still Planting the Seeds of Hope: The Recent Literature of the Early Chesapeake Region," *VMHB*, XCV (1987), 5–7. The timing of economic cycles was different in the case of areas producing sweet-scented tobacco. During the 1680s, for example, the price of sweet-scented leaf may have remained steady or have risen in contrast to the low price fetched by oronoco. However, the same general pattern of expansion and contraction is believed to have prevailed. I am grateful to Lorena S. Walsh for this information.

of depression until the end of the War of Spanish Succession and renewed demand after 1715.[35]

Despite the dominance of tobacco, planters did develop other commodities. Toward the end of the century, the cultivation of wheat, barley, oats, and rye became more common, albeit in relatively small quantities, and reflected an effort to seek alternative sources of income in a period of low and declining tobacco prices. As returns from tobacco slumped, many planters, already self-sufficient in foodstuffs, sought to maximize income from the sale of surplus meat, corn, fruit, and cider locally and, if possible, initiate activities such as raising cereals, manufacturing homespun cloth, and producing naval stores. The significance of this development is twofold. First, the trend toward diversification underlined the obvious fact that soils and land varied enormously in quality and in access to the main shipping routes. Planters were acutely aware of these factors, but, while the price of leaf was high, the economic impact of such variation was less apparent. During depressions, differences between regions came into sharper relief. Slumps affected everyone, but they hit men on marginal soils, in the interior, or on the frontier much harder than planters possessing the best land by the major rivers. Thus while the ebb and flow of tobacco prices exerted a powerful influence on the Chesapeake economy as a whole, important differences in soil, location, timing of settlement, and links with English merchants distinguished regions and communities from one another and in large part determined how they would respond to the long depression after 1680. In Virginia, the best soils were to be found between the James and Rappahannock rivers, for example, in York and Middlesex counties, where the highly valued sweet-scented tobacco was grown mainly for the London market. In Maryland, the lower Western Shore, particularly Anne Arundel County, was the prime tobacco area and produced the lower-priced oronoco. Mediocre or poor soils were found on the Eastern Shore and on the southern bank of the James in counties such as Surry and Lower Norfolk (Figure 10). Unsurprisingly, these were the first areas to move away from tobacco cultivation.[36]

35. Menard, "Economy and Society," 285; Clemens, *The Atlantic Economy,* 34–35; McCusker and Menard, *Economy of British America,* 123–124; Lois Green Carr and Russell R. Menard, "Land, Labor, and Economies of Scale in Early Maryland: Some Limits to Growth in the Chesapeake System of Husbandry," *Jour. Econ. Hist.,* XLIX (1989), 407–418.

36. Gloria L. Main, "Maryland and the Chesapeake Economy, 1670–1720," in *Land et al.,* eds., *Law, Society, and Politics,* 141–143; P.M.G. Harris, "Integrating Interpretations of Local and Regionwide Change in the Study of Economic Development and Demographic Growth in the Colonial Chesapeake, 1630–1775," *Regional Economic*

Second, the impetus for change was nothing new. From the beginning of settlement, investors, projectors, and officials had tried to encourage the production of a range of commodities that would lay the foundation for healthy economic growth. Sir William Berkeley was convinced that such staples could "be easily raised in *Virginia*" and would make the colony wealthier in the long run than even Barbados. In 1649, the writer of *A Perfect Description of Virginia* mentioned that indigo "thrives wonderfully well" and that every planter "begins to get some of the seeds, and know it will be of ten-times the gaine to them as Tobacco." They grew "much Hempe and Flax" and "make Pitch and Tarre," and "Iron Ore and rich Mine" were "in abundance in the Land." Edward Williams was equally enthusiastic: potash had risen in price from "ten to fifty pound the Tunne," pipe staves and clapboard sold for twenty pounds per thousand in the Canaries, iron mills would "raise to the Adventurer foure thousand pound yearely," and Virginia, when well peopled, would match Spain in the output of wine. But his most optimistic predictions were reserved for silk production. The colony was naturally endowed with "infinities of Mulberry-trees . . . why may not Virginia in her future felicity of Silke be a new China and Persia to Europe?" Arguments in favor of silk seemed overwhelming. It brought a vastly higher return than tobacco, was not labor-intensive, required little capital, and could be transported easily. Edward Digges was confident when he wrote to his friend John Ferrar in 1654 that he had "conquered all the great feared difficulty of this rich commodity, and made its sweet easy and speedy Profitt so evident to all the Virginians . . . that now I doubt not (nor they) but that in a short time here will be great quantities made of Silke."[37]

History Research Center, *Working Papers*, I, no. 3 (1978), 35–71; Main, *Tobacco Colony*, 69–91; Lois Green Carr and Lorena S. Walsh, "Economic Diversification and Labor Organization in the Chesapeake, 1650–1820," in Stephen Innes, ed., *Work and Labor in Early America* (Chapel Hill, N.C., 1988), 144–188; Carr, "Diversification in the Colonial Chesapeake," in Carr, Morgan, and Russo, eds., *Colonial Chesapeake Society*, 342–382; Lorena S. Walsh, "Plantation Management in the Chesapeake, 1620–1820," *Jour. Econ. Hist.*, XLIX (1989), 393–400; Russell R. Menard, Lois Green Carr, and Lorena S. Walsh, "A Small Planter's Profits: The Cole Estate and the Growth of the Early Chesapeake Economy," *WMQ*, 3d Ser., XL (1983), 171–196; Carr, Menard, and Walsh, *Robert Cole's World*, chaps. 2–4; Carr and Menard, "Land, Labor, and Economies of Scale," *Jour. Econ. Hist.*, XLIX (1989), 407–418.

37. William Berkeley, *A Discourse and View of Virginia* (London, 1663), 2, 12; in Force, comp., *Tracts and Other Papers: A Perfect Description of Virginia* . . . (1649), II, no. 8, pp. 4–6; E. W., *Virginia: More Especially the South Part Thereof* . . . (1650), III, no. 11, pp. 12–16, 19–45; *The Reformed Virginian Silk-Worm* . . . (1655), III, no. 13, pp. 5–27, 33, 36, 37.

The great majority of tobacco planters did not share this enthusiasm. Despite the tumbling price of leaf, an established market for tobacco remained, and most men could not afford the capital outlay and risk involved in raising new crops or producing the kinds of goods espoused in promotional literature. While leaf remained above a penny a pound, a bare living could be made, which when supplemented by the local sale of surplus food or undertaking casual work was sufficient to ensure subsistence. The movement away from tobacco, when it did come, was the result of economic imperatives, not political planning, and it took a different form from that envisaged by earlier writers. On Maryland's Eastern Shore, planters gradually turned to the cultivation of English grains, notably wheat, for export and the manufacture of cheap coarse woolen cloth for domestic consumption. In Lower Norfolk County, tobacco cultivation largely came to a halt in the 1680s and was replaced by the production of tar and the sale of livestock and foodstuffs to the West Indies. There was no rapid or wholesale switch to the sorts of commodities that Governor Berkeley had in mind, and large-scale manufacturing remained conspicuous by its absence. Yet, to critics of the Chesapeake's overdependence on tobacco, the gradual move away from tobacco cultivation was a step in the right direction. Regional differentiation mitigated the worst effects of the tobacco depression of the late seventeenth century and produced an economic diversity along the tobacco coast not present two generations earlier. If economic salvation did not take the form of the silkworm, viticulture, or bar-iron, nevertheless important new sectors had been established that would play a leading part in the transformation of the economy during the eighteenth and early nineteenth centuries.[38]

See also Hammond, *Leah and Rachel; or, The Two Fruitfull Sisters Virginia and Mary-Land* (1656), in Hall, ed., *Narratives of Early Maryland*, 296.

38. On continuing with tobacco: Joan de Lourdes Leonard, "Operation Checkmate: The Birth and Death of a Virginia Blueprint for Progress, 1660–1676," *WMQ*, 3d Ser., XXIV (1967), 44–74; Menard, Carr, and Walsh, "A Small Planter's Profits," *WMQ*, 3d Ser., XL (1983), 171–196.

On movement away from tobacco: Carr, "Diversification in the Colonial Chesapeake," in Carr, Morgan, and Russo, eds., *Colonial Chesapeake Society*, 342–388; Clemens, *The Atlantic Economy*, chap. 6; Main, *Tobacco Colony*, chap. 2; Morgan, *American Slavery, American Freedom*, 139–140. Trade from Lower Norfolk County to the West Indies started at least as early as the 1650s. Tar production probably began in earnest in the 1660s.

On the transformation: Allan Kulikoff, *Tobacco and Slaves: The Development of Southern Cultures in the Chesapeake, 1680–1800* (Chapel Hill, N.C., 1986), chaps. 3–4; Richard L. Morton, *Colonial Virginia*, 2 vols. (Chapel Hill, N.C., 1960), II, 444–453,

Inequality and Opportunity

Chesapeake society differed from that of England in many important respects. Entire sections of English society were missing. There was little in the Chesapeake to attract men of established fortune from the parent country, despite the efforts of promotional writers to convince them otherwise. In the absence of towns and industry and with a relatively small, dispersed population, Virginia and Maryland did not require (and could not support) the range of specialist trades and crafts to be found at home. Consequently, social status associated with most Old World occupations was not transferred to the New. Colonial society lacked the complexity and subtlety of European social hierarchies.[39]

Yet this is not to imply that the Chesapeake developed as a rough-hewn, undifferentiated society. As in England, those with the greatest estates were judged the fittest to govern, and the precept that political power followed economic power was generally accepted, if not always practiced. The absence of a traditional ruling class undoubtedly weakened social cohesion and was exacerbated by the high turnover of officeholders owing to heavy mortality, the difficulty of establishing ruling dynasties, and the return of gentry to England. In these uncertain conditions, it is hardly surprising that colonial rulers appealed time and time again to English precedents to justify and legitimize their actions. Assemblies were loosely modeled on Parliament, county courts on quarter sessions, and the church (in Virginia, not Maryland) on parochial organization in England. Virginia governors were enjoined in their oath of office to adhere as closely as possible "to the common law of England, and equity thereof." Justices were commanded to "do justice as near as may be" to English precedent and were granted extensive powers similar to those of their counterparts in English shires.[40] Injunctions and

---

536–598; Greene, *Pursuits of Happiness*, chap. 4; Clemens, *The Atlantic Economy*, pt. 2; Walsh, "Plantation Management in the Chesapeake," *Jour. Econ. Hist.*, XLIX (1989), 393–406.

39. Walsh, "Charles County," 365–378.

40. Warren M. Billings, "The Growth of Political Institutions in Virginia, 1634 to 1676," *WMQ*, 3d Ser., XXXI (1974), 225–235; Billings, "The Transfer of English Law to Virginia, 1606–1650," in K. R. Andrews *et al.*, eds., *The Westward Enterprise: English Activities in Ireland, the Atlantic, and America, 1480–1650* (Liverpool, 1978), 215–244. For a different emphasis, see David Thomas Konig, " 'Dale's Laws' and the Non-Common Law Origins of Criminal Justice in Virginia," *American Journal of Legal History*, XXVI (1982), 354–375.

appeals to the past, to tradition, were intoned endlessly throughout the century.

Problems arose, of course, and it is in this respect that important differences between colonial and metropolitan society quickly emerged. Considering the heterogeneous origins of settlers, who was to say what was traditional? To people from towns or areas populated mainly by freeholders, the attempt by Lord Baltimore to create a society of manorial lords and tenants must have seemed archaic, a throwback to medieval times. To men and women brought up in the Church of England, used to attending divine service on Sundays whether they wanted to or not and celebrating the vital religious rituals associated with birth, marriage, and death, the absence of the Anglican church and parochial organization in Maryland must have seemed equally strange. Inevitably, colonial officials encountered serious difficulties in trying to recreate, overnight, governing institutions that had evolved over centuries in England. Neither Virginia nor Maryland developed viable manorial structures, and in both colonies the county court absorbed the functions of English borough, manor, and church courts, becoming the key governing institution at the local level. The rich particularity of the past could not be replicated in America; what emerged were compromises and approximations.[41]

Chesapeake society, therefore, developed as a simplified version of English society, but also a highly aberrant one. One of the most obvious social dif-

41. Essays in Bruce C. Daniels, ed., *Town and County: Essays on the Structure of Local Government in the American Colonies* (Middletown, Conn., 1978): Lois Green Carr, "The Foundations of Social Order: Local Government in Colonial Maryland," 72–110, Robert Wheeler, "The County Court in Colonial Virginia," 111–133, William H. Seiler, "The Anglican Church: A Basic Institution of Local Government in Colonial Virginia," 134–159; Craven, *Southern Colonies*, 169, 172, 179; Walsh, "Charles County," 310–311, 315, 344, 351, 355, 365–371; Lois Green Carr and David William Jordan, *Maryland's Revolution of Government, 1689–1692* (Ithaca, N.Y., 1974), chap. 1; Lois Green Carr, "County Government in Maryland, 1689–1709" (Ph.D. diss., Harvard University, 1968), 10–11, 13–15, and chaps. 5, 7; Virginia Bernhard, "Poverty and the Social Order in Seventeenth-Century Virginia," *VMHB*, LXXXV (1977), 147; Russell R. Menard, "Maryland's 'Time of Troubles': Sources of Political Disorder in Early St. Mary's," *Md. Hist. Mag.*, LXXVI (1981), 125; Jon Kukla, "Order and Chaos in Early America: Political and Social Stability in Pre-Restoration Virginia," *American Historical Review*, XC (1985), 275–298; Lois Green Carr, "Sources of Political Stability and Upheaval in Seventeenth-Century Maryland," *Md. Hist. Mag.*, LXXIX (1984), 44–70; David W. Jordan, *Foundations of Representative Government in Maryland, 1632–1715* (New York, 1987). Billings discusses modifications to English law in Virginia in "The Transfer of English Law," in Andrews *et al.*, eds., *The Westward Enterprise*, 215–244.

ferences was the presence of slaves. Numerically insignificant throughout most of the century, the black population increased enormously in the final two decades. From a couple of thousand in 1670 (6 percent of the total population), numbers shot up to about thirteen thousand (13 percent of the population) by 1700. Half the bound labor force was enslaved by the beginning of the eighteenth century.[42]

As suggested earlier, English attitudes toward blacks were molded by a similar ragbag of racial and cultural prejudice adopted against Indians and other alien peoples. They were savage, heathen, lascivious, shifty, lazy, and apelike, in every way inferior to whites. Apart from emigrants from London or Bristol, most settlers probably encountered blacks for the first time in the Chesapeake and in this context made the indelible connection between slavery and race. Yet, like English reactions to Indians, the everyday response to blacks was more complex than the general framework of prejudice and institution of slavery might lead one to expect. Especially in the early years of settlement, down to 1660, when numbers were small and blacks worked alongside servants and masters to bring in the tobacco crop, relations between the two races may have been relatively relaxed. Occasionally slaves were freed or purchased their liberty. Some acquired property and were able to live peaceably side by side with their white neighbors.[43]

But one should not exaggerate even the limited opportunities for blacks, slave or free, to improve their condition in this period. From the 1660s, Virginia began legislating "stringent racial laws" designed to regulate white-black relations and provide planters with greater powers to discipline their slaves. Possibly this development represented an effort by the recently restored royal government to tighten up generally on bound laborers in the

42. Greene, *Pursuits of Happiness*, table 8.1, 178–179; Kulikoff, *Tobacco and Slaves*, 319–320; Morgan, *American Slavery, American Freedom*, 305–308, 422–423; Russell R. Menard, "The Maryland Slave Population, 1658 to 1730: A Demographic Profile of Blacks in Four Counties," *WMQ*, 3d Ser., XXXII (1975), 29–54. Figures are drawn from McCusker and Menard, *Economy of British America*, table 6.4, 136.

43. Fryer, *Staying Power*, chaps. 1–7; Jordan, *White over Black*, particularly pt. 1; Philip D. Morgan, "British Encounters with Africans and African-Americans, circa 1600–1780," in Bailyn and Morgan, eds., *Strangers within the Realm*, 157–219. For the changing fortunes of free blacks, see T. H. Breen and Stephen Innes, *"Myne Owne Ground": Race and Freedom on Virginia's Eastern Shore, 1640–1676* (New York, 1980); Ross M. Kimmel, "Free Blacks in Seventeenth-Century Maryland," *Md. Hist. Mag.*, LXXI (1976), 19–25; Douglas Deal, "A Constricted World: Free Blacks on Virginia's Eastern Shore, 1680–1750," in Carr, Morgan, and Russo, eds., *Colonial Chesapeake Society*, 275–305.

colony: to highlight the distinctions between free and unfree and clarify their respective rights and privileges. In this fashion, social position was defined and the preeminence of the elite confirmed. But measures enacted against slaves had no parallel among the white population, and it is certain that conditions for blacks began to deteriorate sharply as a consequence. Mass importation after 1680 and the changing origin of slaves (brought directly from Africa rather than the Caribbean) served only to intensify discriminatory legislation. Chesapeake society took on a new character as planters became irrevocably wedded to slavery and shifted from incoherent racial prejudice to full-blown racism.[44]

In his description of Virginia published in 1705, Robert Beverley thought it necessary to clarify the distinction between slavery and servitude: "Slaves are the Negroes, and their Posterity, following the condition of the Mother. . . . They are call'd Slaves, in respect of the time of their Servitude, because it is for Life. Servants, are those which serve only for a few years, according to the time of their Indenture, or the Custom of the Country." Male servants and slaves toiled together in the fields, "but the Work of both," Beverley assured his readers, "is no other than what the Overseers, the Freemen, and the Planters themselves do." In fact, neither servant nor slave was "worked near so hard, nor so many Hours in a Day, as the Husbandmen, and Day-Labourers in *England*." The rapid expansion of tobacco production after 1620 created an insatiable demand for cheap labor, which was met almost wholly, until the conversion to slavery, by indentured servants. White servants, recruited in England, constituted the Chesapeake's main source of labor during the seventeenth century, in contrast to the West Indies, where by 1660 approaching half the total population was black. Servants' work and conditions will be dealt with later, although we might note that some servants, such as Richard Frethorne (who would have gladly sacrificed a limb to get back to England) or Thomas Best (who considered that he was treated like "a damned slave"), would have found Beverley's distinction meaningless.[45] In terms of social development, however, the crucial issue was whether the huge numbers of young men and women who ended up laboring in Virginia

44. On the origins of racism in early America, see Vaughan, "The Origins Debate," *VMHB*, XCVII (1989), 311–354; Warren M. Billings, "The Law of Servants and Slaves in Seventeenth-Century Virginia," *VMHB*, XCIX (1991), 45–62.

45. Beverley, *History and Present State of Virginia*, ed. Wright, 271–272; Morgan, *American Slavery, American Freedom*, 130. Lois Green Carr suggests that field laborers probably worked on average a longer day in the Chesapeake (8–10 hours) than in England (6 hours): "Emigration and the Standard of Living," *Jour. Econ. Hist.*, LII (1992), 281–282.

and Maryland could be absorbed into society once they had completed their period of service.

Throughout the Chesapeake, servants formed a large proportion of local populations—as much as half in some counties in the 1650s and 1660s—but as Beverley and others emphasized, service was temporary, not permanent, and was closely linked to life cycle. As in England, servants were the youngest section of the working population and had usually finished their period of service by their early twenties. Women were then free to marry, and men could take up work for wages until they had sufficient capital to establish their own plantations. Of course, the reality was somewhat different. High mortality rates dictated that large numbers of servants never lived to achieve freedom. Others, possibly after a few years of laboring, may have returned to England or moved on to neighboring colonies. Nevertheless, there existed numerous men who, having survived servitude, joined the ranks of free society. Initially they occupied an intermediate stage between servitude and independent planters and played an important role in the local economy as tenants, agricultural workers, craftsmen, or overseers for wealthier planters. Lois Green Carr and Russell R. Menard have estimated that about 18 percent of male decedents from southern Maryland who were inventoried between 1658 and 1705 were inmates of established planters, but the proportion of recently freed inmates in the living population was probably greater. It was estimated in 1676 that a quarter of Virginia's population consisted of "merchants and single freemen and such others as have noe land." Tenancy provided an alternative to living in. Ex-servants frequently rented tracts on short-term leases (six or seven years) as a step toward establishing themselves on their own land. By the final decades of the century about a third of householders in southern Maryland were tenants, a proportion similar to other parts of the Chesapeake.[46]

What did the future hold for recently freed men and women? What were their chances of establishing themselves as freeholders? How much opportunity was there for people with little or no capital to earn a living as independent planters? Two different interpretations dominate the literature.

46. Beverley, *History and Present State of Virginia*, ed. Wright, 271–272 (see also George Alsop's and John Hammond's descriptions, respectively, of servitude, in Hall, ed., *Narratives of Early Maryland: A Character of the Province of Maryland* [1666], 358, *Leah and Rachel*, 289–291, 295); Lois Green Carr and Russell R. Menard, "Immigration and Opportunity: The Freedman in Early Colonial Maryland," in Tate and Ammerman, eds., *Chesapeake in the Seventeenth Century*, 210–212. For the growth of tenancy, see Menard, "Economy and Society," 244–246, 425–428; Morgan, *American Slavery, American Freedom*, 220–223.

Maryland historians, such as Carr, Menard, and Lorena Walsh stress the abundant opportunities for ex-servants, at least down to the end of the 1670s, in access to land, wealth, and public office. Historians of Virginia, particularly Edmund S. Morgan and T. H. Breen, on the other hand, are more pessimistic and emphasize instead the enormous difficulties freedmen faced in establishing themselves. To some extent, differences of interpretation may reflect genuine differences between the experiences of ex-servants in the two colonies; for a variety of reasons, conditions may have been harsher in Virginia than Maryland.[47] But that is not the whole answer. A review of the evidence suggests that the Maryland interpretation may be overly optimistic.

If much of what immigrants encountered in the Chesapeake was new, there were yet familiar aspects of society. In the second half of the seventeenth century the tidewater was characterized by levels of poverty that would not have been out of place in England. Along the lower Western Shore of Maryland, during Menard's "age of the small planter" in the late 1650s and 1660s, nearly 10 percent of decedents whose estates were inventoried had less than £10 in personal goods, and nearly 60 percent had less than £50 (Table 17). Even allowing that £50 is too much to describe someone as poor, between 36 and 39 percent of inventoried planters had less than £30. In a study of six Maryland counties embracing both sides of the Bay, Gloria Main found that 40 percent of decedents who died between 1656 and 1696 were worth less than £35 and more than half had less than £50. These figures represent a generalized slice through society and do not measure social mobility or individual opportunities. Neither do they include land. But, even so, it is indisputable that by the second half of the century a significant proportion of the ex-servant and planter population lived in hardship.[48]

Estimating wealth distribution from Virginia's probate inventories is prob-

47. Menard, Harris, and Carr, "Opportunity and Inequality," *Md. Hist. Mag.*, LXIX (1974), 169–184; Russell R. Menard, "From Servant to Freeholder: Status Mobility and Property Accumulation in Seventeenth-Century Maryland," *WMQ*, 3d Ser., XXX (1973), 37–64; Carr and Menard, "Immigration and Opportunity," in Tate and Ammerman, eds., *Chesapeake in the Seventeenth Century*, 206–242; Carr, "Emigration and the Standard of Living," *Jour. Econ. Hist.*, LII (1992), 271–291; Morgan, *American Slavery, American Freedom*, bk. 3; and T. H. Breen, "A Changing Labor Force and Race Relations in Virginia, 1660–1710," *Journal of Social History*, VII (1973–1974), 3–25; Joseph Douglas Deal III, "Race and Class in Colonial Virginia: Indians, Englishmen, and Africans on the Eastern Shore during the Seventeenth Century" (Ph.D. diss., University of Rochester, 1981), 105–117.

48. Menard, Harris, and Carr, "Opportunity and Inequality," *Md. Hist. Mag.*, LXIX (1974), 171–178; Main, *Tobacco Colony*, table 2.5, 60.

TABLE 17

Personal Wealth on the Lower Western Shore of Maryland, 1638–1705

Total Estate Value in £	% of Decedents			
	1638–1642 (N=25)	1658–1665 (N=92)	1683–1687 (N=245)	1658–1705 (N=1738)
0–9	12.0	9.8	9.4	9.5
10–49	56.0	48.9	42.9	41.7
50–99	12.0	17.4	21.6	20.0
100–249	12.0	16.3	14.3	17.1
250+	8.0	7.6	11.8	11.7
Total	100.0	100.0	100.0	100.0

Sources: William Hand Browne *et al.*, eds., *Archives of Maryland*, 72 vols. to date (Baltimore, 1883–), IV, 30–33, 43–49, 73–113. Figures for 1658–1705 were compiled from data supplied by St. Mary's City Commission.

lematic, because they are nowhere near as representative of the total decedent population as Maryland's. However, Lancaster and Lower Norfolk counties suggest that poverty was similarly entrenched. A contemporary observed in the early 1660s that three-quarters of Virginia planters were so poor they would have to become servants to others: an exaggeration, but indicative of an awareness of the high incidence of poverty, and its attendant problems, along the tobacco coast.[49]

49. For the representativeness of Maryland and Virginia inventories, see Carr, "Diversification in the Colonial Chesapeake," in Carr, Morgan, and Russo, eds., *Colonial Chesapeake Society*, appendix 1, 383–386. I am grateful to Lois Carr and Lorena Walsh (and the St. Mary's City Commission) for help in compiling estimates for Lancaster and Lower Norfolk counties. Darrett and Anita Rutman found that nearly a third of inventoried decedents were worth less than £20 in personalty in Middlesex County, 1650–1699: *A Place in Time: Explicatus* (New York, 1984), table 2.8, 129. Landownership is dealt with in James P. P. Horn, "Social and Economic Aspects of Local Society in England and the Chesapeake: A Comparative Study of the Vale of Berkeley, Gloucestershire, and the Lower Western Shore of Maryland, c. 1660–1700" (D.Phil. diss., University of Sussex, 1982), 136–143; Menard, "Economy and Society," 81–83, 241–246, 422–426; and Walsh, "Charles County," 388–396, 399–420; Kevin Peter Kelly, "Economic and Social Development of Seventeenth-Century Surry County, Virginia" (Ph.D. diss., University of Washington, 1972), 124–139; Robert Anthony Wheeler, "Lancaster County, Virginia, 1650–1750: The Evolution of a Southern Tidewater Community" (Ph.D. diss., Brown University, 1972), 36–43, 62–63, 67, 87–98.

The causes are not hard to find. The massive scale of immigration after 1640 meant that every year hundreds of ex-servants sought to set themselves up as smallholders. When the price of leaf was high, they could borrow money to get a start, and good returns on their crop might allow them to buy or hire extra hands to increase output. After a few years, hard work and luck enabled some to establish themselves as prosperous and, possibly, locally influential householders. Undoubtedly, opportunities for poor men to make their mark existed in this period. Of 158 ex-servants who had entered Maryland before 1642, at least 90–92 (57 percent) eventually acquired land in the Chesapeake, 75–76 (48 percent) served in local office, and 22 (14 percent) became major officeholders, as justices, sheriffs, militia officers, and even councillors. It is extremely unlikely they would have done so well had they remained in England. But there is another side to the story. In all, 275 male servants were brought into Maryland before 1642, of whom 117 (43 percent) disappeared without trace. Most of those who disappeared fell victim to the disease environment before their terms were completed. Others may have moved out as soon as they could. Either way, including those who died or did not stay produces rather different results: fewer than a third became landowners or held local office during one of the most prosperous periods of the region's history. Those who, for the most part, did succeed acquired only small tracts, from fifty to four hundred acres, and served in minor offices (jurymen, constables or sergeants in the militia). Even these achievements were much harder to come by for servants who entered the province after 1670.[50]

In Virginia, opportunities for servants after 1660 were considerably less bright. Settled a generation earlier than Maryland, Virginia's boom years had passed by midcentury; consequently, conditions for the poor were tougher. Fewer than 10 percent of servants freed between 1662 and 1678 in Lancaster appear as householders in the county in 1679. On the Eastern Shore only 17 and 9 percent, respectively, who arrived in Accomack and Northampton counties between 1663 and 1697 eventually became landowners. Some may have moved to neighboring counties or other parts of the Bay, but, nevertheless, few were able to achieve the status of independent planters in the

50. Menard, "From Servant to Freeholder," *WMQ*, 3d Ser., XXX (1973), 37–64; Menard, "Population, Economy, and Society in Seventeenth-Century Maryland," *Md. Hist. Mag.*, LXXIX (1984), 82–83; Carr and Menard, "Immigration and Opportunity," in Tate and Ammerman, eds., *Chesapeake in the Seventeenth Century*, 206–242; Lorena S. Walsh, "Servitude and Opportunity in Charles County, Maryland, 1658–1705," in Land *et al.*, eds., *Law, Society, and Politics*, 111–133.

locality where they had lived and worked as bound laborers. Assuming that migration by the poor is frequently subsistence-driven, it appears that a majority of ex-servants, like casual laborers in England, were commonly forced to go on the tramp in search of opportunities. During the last quarter of the century many moved out of the region altogether. Like the lotteries that initially helped finance the settlement of Virginia, poor men and women who immigrated under indentures entered a gigantic human lottery themselves. Losers met an early death or lived in poverty for the rest of their lives. Winners secured a comfortable income and independence and in a few cases attained a level of wealth and social standing unthinkable for men and women of humble origins at home. The logic of the lottery, however, dictated that, for every ex-servant who made it into the ranks of the middling or upper classes, tens of others, who left barely a trace in the records, died in poverty and obscurity.[51]

Opportunity for all planters was closely attuned to the ebb and flow of the tobacco economy. During the early 1660s the price of leaf dipped below two pennies per pound and then hovered just above one penny for the rest of the decade. There was no improvement in the years that followed; if anything, conditions worsened. English officials were bombarded by a chorus of complaints. Sir William Berkeley wrote in 1662 that prices had fallen so low that tobacco would not "bear the charge of freight and customs, answer the adventure, give encouragement to the traders and subsistence to the inhabitants." A few years later, Thomas Ludwell told Lord Arlington that tobacco was "worth nothing." He elaborated to one of Sir William's kinsmen, Lord John Berkeley, in 1667. "Twelve hundred pounds of tobacco is the medium of men's crops," he wrote, "and half a penny per pound is certainly the full medium of the price given for it, which is fifty shillings out of which when the taxes . . . shall be deducted, is very little to a poor man who hath perhaps a wife and children to cloath and other necessities to buy. Truly so much too little that I can attribute it to nothing but the great mercy of God . . . that keeps them from mutiny and confusion." Governor Berkeley made the con-

---

51. Morgan, *American Slavery, American Freedom*, 226; Deal, "Race and Class in Colonial Virginia," 114; Horn, "Moving On in the New World," in Clark and Souden, eds., *Migration and Society*, 185–186, 197–200; Lorena S. Walsh, "Staying Put or Getting Out: Findings for Charles County, Maryland, 1650–1720," *WMQ*, 3d Ser., XLIV (1987), 89–103. Whether or not "losers" would have done better in England is an open question. The lottery analogy emphasizes the degree of chance involved in emigrating: the chances of survival and whether servants were lucky or unlucky in their conditions of service. Handicaps could be introduced to allow for timing and place of arrival.

nection between poverty and rebellion more explicit in 1673. "A large part of the people are so desperately poor," he said, "that they may reasonably be expected upon any small advantage of the enemy [the Dutch] to revolt to them in hopes of bettering their condition by sharing the plunder of the colony with them."[52]

Exaggeration is to be expected in petitions of this sort, but planters had cause for complaint. The massive expansion in production, while impoverishing planters, brought a handsome return in duties to the English government (about £100,000 by 1675), but little was plowed back into the two colonies, and Whitehall showed little interest in economic projects in the Chesapeake. Planters also resented the exclusion of the Dutch from the tobacco trade, which gave English merchants a monopoly and kept prices artificially low. Berkeley spoke for many when he asked why "forty thousand people should be impoverish'd to enrich little more than forty Merchants, who being the only buyers of our *Tobacco*, give us what they please for it."[53]

Poverty wore a different face in the Chesapeake. Unlike Europe, where poverty manifested itself in malnutrition, chronic underemployment, vagrancy, and slums in major cities, along the tobacco coast unemployment was not a serious blight upon the economy, and relatively high wages enabled most able-bodied workers to feed and clothe themselves adequately. Few Virginia or Maryland counties supported anywhere near the number of paupers typical of English rural parishes. Poverty in the Chesapeake had its own distinctive character, expressed by severe material deprivation (poor housing and low standards of living), the inability of many small planters in Virginia after 1660 and Maryland after 1680 to escape from a living of bare subsistence, and the movement out of the region after 1675 of thousands of ex-servants for whom the Chesapeake held no future. As the price of tobacco spiraled downward, the transition from servant to smallholder

52. Prices are based on Menard's figures, in "Tobacco Industry," *Res. Econ. Hist.*, V (1980), appendix, 157–159. It should be kept in mind, however, that falling costs of production helped mitigate the impact of the decline in prices. Menard's figures provide a general picture of fluctuations in tobacco prices and do not reflect local variations. Sweet-scented tobacco may not have been so susceptible to the overall downturn in prices in this period. Berkeleys and Ludwell are cited by Wertenbaker, *Planters of Virginia*, 89–91. See also the petition of Henry Chichley, John Jeffreys, Edward Digges, and Francis Moryson to the Privy Council in 1664: CO 1/18, fol. 313, Public Record Office.

53. Morgan, *American Slavery, American Freedom*, 197; Leonard, "Operation Checkmate," *WMQ*, 3d Ser., XXIV (1967), 64–74; Berkeley, *Discourse and View of Virginia*, 6–7.

brought neither the well-being nor economic independence anticipated. At the level of the individual holding, landowners, big and small, had complete freedom to manage their affairs as they felt fit, perhaps limiting the amount of tobacco grown and turning to other products. But economic opportunities for smallholders were considerably limited by the grip of tobacco on the economy and low returns from leaf. The stint placed on Virginia tobacco production in 1668, for example, meant that planters "not able to remove from their ould and over worne grounds, are Kepte by the Limitacon of a certen number of plants per poll in Perpetuall poverty." Hedged in by meager profits and dependence on merchants and wealthy planters for credit to buy essentials, the world of the small planter became increasingly constricted as the going got tougher in the last third of the century.[54]

A sure sign of worsening economic conditions is the growing evidence of serious social tensions and a hardening of class lines in Maryland and Virginia after 1660. Isaac Friend, servant of John Parkes of York County, described as possessing "a turbulent and unquiett spiritt," was alleged to have said in 1661 that he could get "fforty of them [servants] together, and get Armes and he would be the first and have them cry as they went along, 'who would be for Liberty, and free from bondage,' and that there would enough come to them and they would goe through the Countrey and kill those that made any opposition, and that they would either be free or dye for it." Two years later another servant uprising was narrowly avoided in Gloucester County.[55] Such examples might be dismissed as unimportant. Most servants, despite Governor William Berkeley's fears, were not rebellious troublemakers. And even if servants were occasionally ill disciplined and fractious, what did it matter so long as the majority of planters were relatively contented?

Bacon's Rebellion and echoes of unrest in Maryland in 1676 prove beyond doubt the existence of widespread discontent, at all levels of society, with

54. This assessment of opportunity for ex-servants and small planters is based upon evidence from petitions and contemporary observations together with my reading of evidence from Maryland probate records and aggregate career studies (elucidated in the text). For a recapitulation of what I consider the optimistic view of immigrant opportunity, see Carr, "Emigration and the Standard of Living," *Jour. Econ. Hist.*, LII (1992), 282–287. For examples of petitions, see H. R. McIlwaine, ed., *Journals of the House of Burgesses of Virginia, 1659/60–1693* (Richmond, Va., 1914), 55, 101, 105, 109, 112, 158–159, 228–229 (quote from 53).

55. York County, Virginia, Deeds, Orders, and Wills, no. 3 (CW, York County Project); "Proceedings in York County Court," *WMQ*, 1st Ser., XI (1902–1903), 34–36; Morgan, *American Slavery, American Freedom*, 246.

the privileged elites clustered around Berkeley and Baltimore. "Wee confess a great many of us came in servants to others," the petitioners of the "Complaint from Heaven with a Huy and crye and a petition out of Virginia and Maryland" wrote, "but wee adventured owr lives for it, and got owr poore living with hard labour out of the ground in a terrible Willdernis." References to the poor being "robbed" and "cheated" by their "supperiors" and to the gentry as "Grandees," "the great ones," and "great men" in petitions and lists of grievances in the wake of Bacon's Rebellion suggest that ordinary planters saw themselves (or, at least, attempted to present themselves) as virtuous, hardworking, and loyal subjects, unjustly oppressed by rapacious, self-interested colonial aristocrats. Whereas Bacon characterized his followers as patriotic volunteers, prepared at their own "hazard and charge" to rid the country of barbarous savages and concerned only for the common good, Virginia's Council denounced them as a "Rabble Crue," "only the Rascallity and meanest of the people . . . there being hardly two amongst them that we have heard of who have Estates or are persons of Reputation and indeed very few who can either write or read." Thomas Notley, deputy governor of Maryland, had a similar opinion of the protesters in his colony: never was a "Body . . . more repleat with Malignancy and knavery then our people were in August last," he wrote to Baltimore in January 1677.[56]

As economic conditions worsened throughout the Chesapeake in the 1670s and opportunities for the poor and middling planters declined, so social divisions and attitudes hardened. It is difficult to avoid the conclusion that many of those at the pinnacle of colonial society viewed the majority of planters as merely a source of revenue to mulct dry. Unable to command the labor of the poor indefinitely, elites devised numerous strategies for siphoning off the small profits of planters into their own coffers. Bacon's Rebellion gave a clear warning that the people could not be pushed any further but did not bring about any improvement in their lot. Lord Culpeper, the new governor, wrote from Virginia in 1680 that the "low price of tobacco staggers . . . the continuance of it will be the fatal and speedy ruin of this noble Colony with-

---

56. William Hand Browne *et al.*, eds., *Archives of Maryland*, 72 vols. to date (Baltimore, 1883–), V, 140; "Proclamations of Nathaniel Bacon," "Bacon's Rebellion," *VMHB*, I (1893–1894), 59–60, 169, 179; "Causes of Discontent in Virginia, 1676," *VMHB*, II (1894–1895), 167, 170; "Charles City County Grievances, 1676," *VMHB*, III (1895–1896), 135–147; McIlwaine, ed., *Journals of the House of Burgesses of Virginia, 1659/60–1693*, 101–103, 109, 112–114. Morgan, *American Slavery, American Freedom*, 258–259; Webb, *1676*, 71; Warren M. Billings, "The Causes of Bacon's Rebellion: Some Suggestions," *VMHB*, LXXVIII (1970), 409–435, esp. 435. A fuller discussion of Bacon's Rebellion will be found in Chapter 8.

out the application of a remedy." "Our most formidable enemy, poverty," Colonel Nicholas Spencer observed, "is falling violently on us through the low value, or rather no value, of tobacco." A few years later, the colony was described as "a Barbarous and Malancholy part of the world."[57] If rebellion had tempered the worst excesses of government corruption, it did nothing to alleviate the poor planter's problem of making a living. The last two decades of the century were locust years.

Chesapeake society underwent profound changes during the course of the seventeenth century. Evolving from fragile frontier outposts in the early years, the adoption of plantation agriculture and subsequent massive immigration ensured the survival of the Chesapeake Bay colonies and led to the spread of English settlement across thousands of square miles of the tidewater. Gradually the landscape was transformed. The first colonists had envisioned a land of limitless promise where towns and cities would push back the forest, manufactures would thrive, and well-cultivated farms would tap the natural abundance of the earth. The outcome, however, was very different. Plentiful cheap land and plantation agriculture led to the evolution of a form of husbandry excoriated as slovenly and wasteful by English commentators who misunderstood its advantages, the tobacco trade retarded the development of urban centers because marketing and distribution took place in Europe, and no important manufactures took root. These shortcomings were a constant source of frustration and disappointment to colonial officials, who blamed planters' slavish dependence on tobacco for Virginia's and Maryland's failings.

If the Chesapeake did not live up to the expectations of early settlers or projectors, nevertheless during the middle decades of the century the region provided opportunities for poor immigrants who survived the disease environment and the rigors of servitude to earn a modest livelihood and perhaps move a few rungs up the social ladder. With hard work, or perhaps a good marriage, male and female servants might themselves eventually become smallholders and employ their own servants. Potentially, even greater rewards were to be had: a fortunate few enjoyed spectacular success and moved from servitude into the ranks of the local gentry within a few years, a degree of social mobility unthinkable in England. But opportunities for the poor should not be exaggerated. During the 1660s and 1670s,

57. W. Noel Sainsbury *et al.*, eds., *Cal. State Papers*, Col. Ser., *America and West Indies*, X, *1677–1680*, 568–569, XI, *1680–1685*, 47; McIlwaine, ed., *Journals of the House of Burgesses of Virginia, 1659/60–1693*, 228.

first in Virginia and then in Maryland, opportunities for the poor declined. Ex-servants experienced increasing difficulty in establishing themselves as independent planters, and many smallholders were relentlessly pushed to the brink of poverty by the steady decline in income as the price of tobacco fell. The distinctive features of the Chesapeake's social structure slowly took shape. About half the population was made up of servants, slaves, and recently freed men and women (dependents of established planters): the equivalent of servants in husbandry, day laborers, and domestics in England, although, of course, there was no equivalent of the slave field hand. Small and middling planters, including tenant farmers, who used their own family labor to work their holding or who possessed a few servants, made up about 40 percent of the population, while the rest were wealthy planters, merchants, gentry, and a small group of artisans.[58]

From the 1660s, especially in older-settled regions, the social order became increasingly articulated and social distinctions increasingly visible. Social rank became more predictable and rigid, more like that in England. At the same time, and probably related, settlers' tolerance of nonwhite elements of the population declined. Indian peoples were marginalized, and conditions for blacks rapidly deteriorated. By the turn of the century, the political and economic consolidation of colonial elites in both Maryland and Virginia and the switch from white to slave labor heralded the emergence of the "slave-based, gentry-dominated society" characteristic of the Chesapeake's golden age.[59]

---

58. David Hackett Fischer, *Albion's Seed: Four British Folkways in America* (Oxford, 1989), 374–382. For economic activities of large planters, see Main, *Tobacco Colony*, 79–81. There were, of course, important regional variations in social structure; see Harris, "Integrating Interpretations," Regional Econ. Hist. Research Center, *Working Papers*, I, no. 3 (1978), 43–50.

59. Menard, "Economy and Society," 449; Carr, Menard, and Walsh, *Robert Cole's World*, chap. 6.

4

Settling the Land

Before the Indian uprising of 1622, English settlements in the tidewater were established along the James River from Point Comfort at the mouth of the Bay to the falls in the west (the site of present-day Richmond), a distance of more than seventy miles (see Figure 11). Both sides of the river experienced growth, but upriver from Jamestown tended to be favored as healthier and safer from Spanish attack than farther down toward the Bay, and the majority of "particular plantations" founded between 1617 and 1622, including Berkeley Hundred, were located there. The only plantations of note below Jamestown were Martin's Hundred, devasted in the Indian attack of 1622, and Kecoughtan, founded in 1610 on the Hampton River near the entrance to the James. During the 1620s and 1630s, as the pace of immigration increased, settlement along the James thickened, and the Peninsula (between the James and York rivers) filled in. Further north, Kent Island was settled in the early 1630s as a trading post, and Maryland was founded in 1634. Land was also gradually taken up across the Bay on the Eastern Shore, to form Accomack County, one of the eight original shires in 1634.[1]

1. Charles E. Hatch, Jr., *The First Seventeen Years: Virginia, 1607–1624*, Jamestown 350th Anniversary Booklet (Williamsburg, Va., 1957), 32–33, 38–110; Wesley Frank Craven, *The Southern Colonies in the Seventeenth Century, 1607–1689* (1949; Baton Rouge, La., 1970), 169 n. 72. The other counties were Henrico, Charles City, James City, Warwick River, Charles River, Warraskoyack, and Elizabeth City.

The expansion of English settlement throughout the tidewater in the seventeenth century is reasonably well documented: Edward B. Mathews, ed., *The Counties of Maryland: Their Origin, Boundaries, and Election Districts* (Baltimore, 1907); Morgan P. Robinson, "Virginia Counties: Those Resulting from Virginia Legislation," Virginia State Library, *Bulletin*, IX (1916), 1–283; Richard L. Morton, *Colonial Virginia*, 2 vols. (Chapel Hill, N.C., 1960), I, 52, 58, 62–65, 122–130, 155–158, 163, 242; Robert D.

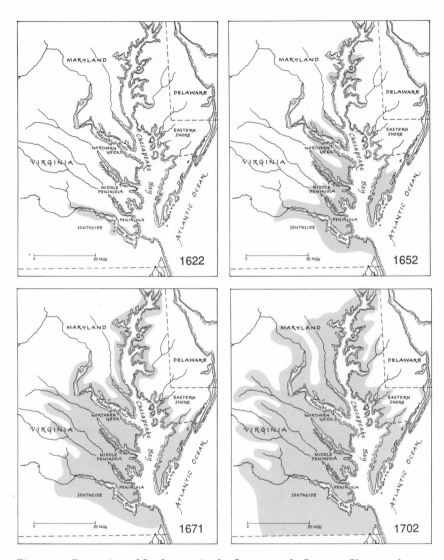

Figure 11. Expansion of Settlement in the Seventeenth-Century Chesapeake.
Drawn by Richard Stinely

By the mid-seventeenth century a substantial movement of settlers had taken place northward beyond the York River on the Middle Peninsula (Gloucester and Middlesex counties) and the Northern Neck (embracing

Mitchell, "American Origins and Regional Institutions: The Seventeenth-Century Chesapeake," Association of American Geographers, *Annals*, LXXIII (1983), 404–420.

Lancaster, Rappahannock, Northumberland, and Westmoreland counties). Large numbers of Virginia planters crossed the Potomac into Maryland, the Chesapeake frontier of the 1650s and 1660s, moving up the Western Shore to Anne Arundel while others pushed up the Eastern Shore into Somerset County. In the middle years of the century, the most expansive in the region's history, eight new counties were formed in Maryland and Virginia between 1648 and 1654 and another seven during the next decade, in response to the floodtide of immigration. Whereas almost all the growth in Maryland before the 1650s occurred along the lower Western Shore, after 1660 there was a major movement of settlers into the Eastern Shore and frontier counties such as Baltimore. In the half-century after 1630, therefore, the axis of population shifted decisively from the older-settled region of the James River basin to the more northerly rivers of the York, Rappahannock, and Potomac as well as across the Bay.[2]

The spread of settlement throughout the region, so much a feature of early Chesapeake history, came to a halt about the same time that the flow of immigrants from England dried up. By the beginning of the long tobacco depression (around 1680), settlement had virtually reached its seventeenth-century limits. In the rest of the century less desirable land was taken up in the interior of established counties, and there was a drift of population westward across the fall line, foreshadowing the major impulse of the following century. There was relatively little movement into new areas of the tidewater, because the best tobacco lands had already been patented and the depression, which would last about thirty years, did not encourage further expansion. Instead of seeking new land on the frontier of Maryland and Virginia, thousands of settlers began moving to other colonies, such as Pennsylvania, the Carolinas, Delaware, and the Jerseys.[3] In the best tradition of migration within England, when opportunities declined, the poor moved on.

2. Russell Robert Menard, "Economy and Society in Early Colonial Maryland" (Ph.D. diss., University of Iowa, 1975), 216, 223; Clayton Torrence, *Old Somerset on the Eastern Shore of Maryland: A Study in Foundations and Founders* (Richmond, Va., 1935), 257–281, 297–334, 435–460; Gloria L. Main, *Tobacco Colony: Life in Early Maryland, 1650–1720* (Princeton, N.J., 1982), 10; Russell R. Menard, "The Tobacco Industry in the Chesapeake Colonies, 1617–1730: An Interpretation," *Research in Economic History*, V (1980), 133, 134; Edmund S. Morgan, *American Slavery, American Freedom: The Ordeal of Colonial Virginia* (New York, 1975), table 4, 414.

3. Morgan, *American Slavery, American Freedom*, chaps. 11–14; Menard, "Tobacco Industry," *Res. Econ. Hist.*, V (1980), 137–142, 153–156; Thomas J. Wertenbaker, *The Planters of Colonial Virginia* (1922; New York, 1958), 139–147.

General discussions of the spread of settlement, however, tell us little about how the Chesapeake was first peopled by English immigrants. Lower Norfolk and Lancaster counties, in Virginia, furnish two examples of contrasting social and economic developments. Lower Norfolk was settled a generation earlier than Lancaster and, owing to its generally poor soils, was never an important tobacco-producing area, despite its situation at the mouth of the Chesapeake Bay and excellent natural harbors. Like other parts of the southern James basin (Surry, for example), it lost out to regions elsewhere that produced better-quality leaf. Lancaster was formed in the early 1650s, following the great northward expansion of settlement (described above), which opened up the whole of the Northern Neck to English settlers in this period. A region of mixed soils, it quickly established itself in the mainstream of tobacco production and supplied both sweet-scented and oronoco to English markets. The different timing of settlement was a critical influence on the subsequent development of local society and economy in these two areas.[4]

Lower Norfolk

English settlement of the region that later became Lower Norfolk lagged about a decade behind the movement of people to other parts of the James's southern bank. Several plantations were founded across the river from Jamestown in the early 1620s (Edward Bennett, for example, established his Puritan colony at Warrascoyack in the winter of 1621), but apart from a short-lived expedition to the Nansemond River in the summer of 1609 there was little effort to colonize the region between the Nansemond and the Atlantic coast before the late 1620s.[5]

4. For Lancaster County, see Robert Anthony Wheeler, "Lancaster County, Virginia, 1650–1750: The Evolution of a Southern Tidewater Community" (Ph.D. diss., Brown University, 1972); and Darrett B. Rutman and Anita H. Rutman, *A Place in Time: Middlesex County, Virginia, 1650–1750* (New York, 1984), which deals with the county until the late 1660s. For Lower Norfolk, see Florence Kimberly Turner, *Gateway to the New World: A History of Princess Anne County, Virginia, 1607–1824* (Easley, S.C., 1984), chaps. 1–2.

5. Hatch, *The First Seventeen Years*, 32–33, 77–90; John Bennett Boddie, *Seventeenth Century Isle of Wight County, Virginia* . . . (Chicago, 1938), 34–35. More than 1,600 acres, on the "Southside of the maine River against Elizabeth Cittie," were patented in the early 1620s, but little actual settlement took place (CO 1/4, fol. 27, Public Record Office, London). Of the seven original patentees, five resided in Elizabeth City in 1624, one died at Warraskoyack in the 1622 uprising, and one could not be traced (*Colonial*

The reasons for this are not altogether clear. Throughout the 1620s the English conducted numerous raids on local Indians south of the James, in particular the Nansemonds and Warrasquoakes, but little mention is made of the "Chesapeacks," who, according to Captain John Smith's account of 1612, were able to muster a hundred fighting men. It is unlikely, therefore, that colonists were deterred by the presence of hostile Indians.[6] There may have been fears that the region was dangerously exposed to attack from the sea, but the threat of Spanish incursions had not prevented settlement along the Eastern Shore, equally exposed, some years before. A more plausible explanation lies in the rapid growth of Kecoughtan (Elizabeth City) and adjacent communities. By 1625, the town, together with neighboring plantations, numbered 359 persons and was by far the most populous area in Virginia. Although the Corporation of Elizabeth City included the south side of the James, it appears that immigrants were sucked into the Hampton River area, where a number of large planter-merchants, such as William Tucker and Daniel Gookin, had established themselves.[7] Any new settlements across the James would have to compete with powerful interests in Elizabeth City and Newport News.

Two principal factors account for the movement of people into Lower

---

Records of Virginia [1874; Baltimore, 1964], 51–53, 66). Settlers may have begun moving into the region in larger numbers after 1625.

6. Boddie, *Isle of Wight County*, 84–87; Capt. John Smith, *A Map of Virginia, with a Description of the Countrey* . . . (1612), in Philip L. Barbour, ed., *The Complete Works of Captain John Smith (1580–1631)*, 3 vols. (Chapel Hill, N.C., 1986), I, 145–146; Lower Norfolk County, Virginia, Minute Book, transcript of Wills and Deeds A, 2 vols. (1637–1646), I, fol. 35, II, fols. 33, 59 (Colonial Williamsburg, microfilm, reel M 1365-2; references to CW microfilm will be given only with the first citation); H. R. McIlwaine, ed., *Minutes of the Council and General Court of Virginia* . . . (Richmond, Va., 1924), 151, 193. For the general background to hostilities, see J. Frederick Fausz, "Patterns of Anglo-Indian Aggression and Accommodation along the Mid-Atlantic Coast, 1584–1634," in William W. Fitzhugh, ed., *Cultures in Contact: The Impact of European Contacts on Native American Institutions, A.D. 1000–1800* (Washington, D.C., 1985), 227–231, 241–250; Fausz, "An 'Abundance of Blood Shed on Both Sides': England's First Indian War, 1609–1614," *VHMB*, XCVIII (1990), 3–56. The Chesapeakes appear to have been virtually wiped out by Powhatan's warriors about the time of the arrival of the English at Jamestown; see Helen C. Rountree, *The Powhatan Indians of Virginia: Their Traditional Culture* (Norman, Okla., 1989), 120–121.

7. Hatch, *The First Seventeen Years*, 93–101; [Annie Lash Jester and Martha Woodroof Hiden, eds.], *Adventurers of Purse and Person, Virginia, 1607–1624/5*, 3d ed., rev., ed. Virginia M. Meyer and John Frederick Dorman (Richmond, Va., 1987), 50–68; Morgan, *American Slavery, American Freedom*, 119–121.

Norfolk in the 1630s: continuing population increase and the English government's clarification of its land policy. The growing population of the lower James-York peninsula encouraged planters and new arrivals in search of abundant cheap land to look further afield, either northward to the York or south across the James. No longer tied to the restrictive policies of the Virginia Company, dissolved in 1624, planters had more freedom in deciding where they wished to settle. Uncertainty about the government's recognition of individual property rights in Virginia, however, discouraged the expansion of settlement until the issue was cleared up in 1634, after which a return to the system of granting patents initiated by the Virginia Company sparked a flood of applications for new land.[8]

One such applicant was Captain Adam Thorowgood, a wealthy and well-connected gentleman from East Anglia, who arrived in Virginia in 1621 and lived at Elizabeth City. Probably through his brother's connections at the Caroline court, he managed to solicit from the Privy Council an "espetiall recommendation" for a grant on "the Chesapeakean River to the southward of the Bay, where it may be most convenient for him." Accordingly, he patented 5,350 acres in 1635, in return for the transportation of himself, his wife, and 105 persons, who became the nucleus of Lynnhaven Parish and opened up the whole region to settlement. Thorowgood's initiative appears to have been decisive. Previously a commissioner and burgess for Elizabeth City, his decision to move, probably taken in conjunction with a number of other prominent planters and gentlemen from his neighborhood, ensured the orderly settlement of the region and was doubtless instrumental in the creation of the new county: a group of experienced planters and commissioners conducted the affairs of the county from its inception.[9]

Just fewer than a hundred individuals were granted patents or certifi-

---

8. Craven, *Southern Colonies*, 174–175; James R. Perry, *The Formation of a Society on Virginia's Eastern Shore, 1615–1655* (Chapel Hill, N.C., 1990), 38–39.

9. "Abstracts of Virginia Land Patents," *Virginia Magazine of History and Biography*, II (1894), 415–416; [Jester and Hiden, eds.], *Adventurers of Purse and Person*, xxi, 607–608; Nell Marion Nugent, comp., *Cavaliers and Pioneers: Abstracts of Virginia Land Patents and Grants*, 2 vols. (Richmond, Va., 1934, 1977), I, 22, 23. Lower Norfolk was created from the division of New Norfolk (formed 1636) into Upper and Lower County of New Norfolk in 1637. Upper County of New Norfolk was renamed Nansemond by 1642. The first court of Lower Norfolk County was held on May 15, 1637, probably at Thorowgood's house. Of the commissioners who sat with Thorowgood that day, Francis Mason, Capt. John Sibsey, and William Julian were from Elizabeth City and had been in the colony at least a decade before settling in Lower Norfolk. The origins of the two other commissioners, Edward Windham and Robert Camm, are uncertain.

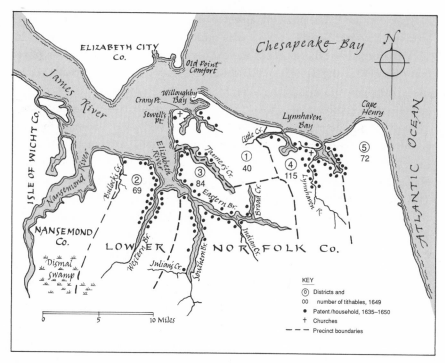

Figure 12. Lower Norfolk County in the Mid-Seventeenth Century.
Drawn by Richard Stinely

cates in Lower Norfolk between 1620 and 1650, the great majority of whom
settled in the county. One can approximate the location of plantations (see
Figure 12). Lynnhaven was the most populous area; half the county's 380
tithables lived between Little Creek and the eastern side of Lynnhaven River
in 1649. In central and western parts of the county, land along the three
main branches of the Elizabeth River was also quickly taken up.[10] Unsurprisingly, there was little effort to settle on the coast or in the interior. The dunes
and pine barrens of the littoral, together with the absence of safe anchorage,
did not encourage the settlement of the coastal region, and inland planters
would have been too far from convenient access to the major rivers and lines
of communication. Virtually all the land patented in this period was located
on creeks and rivers within a few miles of the Bay or the James.

10. Lower Norfolk County, Wills and Deeds B (1646–1651), fols. 128–129. Of 94
individual landowners of Lower Norfolk, only 6 have been identified as nonresi-
dents. Abstracted from Nugent, comp., *Cavaliers and Pioneers,* I, 21–222; and Lower
Norfolk County, Minute Book (1637–1646), 2 vols.; Wills and Deeds B (1646–1651), C
(1651–1656) (CW, microfilm, reels M 1365-2, 1365-17).

An exception is the puzzling absence of settlement in the vicinity of Willoughby Bay and Sewell's Point, which had significantly fewer tithables in 1649 compared to other parts of the county (Figure 12). There may be obvious reasons for this (poor soils and the tendency of shipping to anchor in the Lynnhaven and Elizabeth rivers, for example), but there could have been social factors involved too. Of the four prominent planters who settled in the area—Captain Thomas Willoughby, Captain John Sibsey, Lieutenant Francis Mason, and Mr. Henry Sewell, all formerly of Elizabeth City and all on the bench by 1638—three, Willoughby, Sibsey, and Mason, built up considerable estates and transported at least 130 persons over the next two decades. The area appears to have been dominated by large planters, and many of the forty tithables listed in 1649 were probably servants working on large plantations.[11]

Social differences between four areas of the county—Willoughby Bay and Tanner's Creek, the Western Branch of the Elizabeth River, the Eastern and Southern branches, and Lynnhaven (Western and Eastern branches here combined) are highlighted by the size of landholdings held by individuals (Figure 12). Nearly half the planters residing along the Elizabeth River (areas 2 and 3) had fewer than 300 acres (Table 18), and another quarter had fewer than 500. This was evidently a region that attracted smallholders; only 4 of 51 men patented more than 1,000 acres. The pattern is slightly different in the Lynnhaven area (4 and 5), where just more than a third of landowners fell into the small planter category and a half owned 300–750 acres. Of 34 men, 4 had 750–1,500 acres, and 1 man, Adam Thorowgood, had more than 6,500. Men of middling rank (500–1,000 acres) were more numerous in the Lynnhaven region than on the Elizabeth River. Across the entire county, however, the proportion of small planters among landowners is striking. Only 9 men (10 percent) had patented more than 1,000 acres before 1650. This feature of early Lower Norfolk society is confirmed by the number of headrights (50 acres for every person transported to the colony) granted to

11. Thomas Willoughby patented 3,000–4,000 acres between 1620 and 1654 and transported at least 58 people from 1635 to the mid-1650s. Francis Mason owned about 1,500 acres by his death in 1648 and brought 26 people into the colony. Capt. John Sibsey patented 3,000 acres near Crany Point on the Western Branch of the Elizabeth River but appears to have lived in the Willoughby Bay area, where he owned another 370 acres. He transported at least 66 persons between 1635 and 1649 (James Horn, biographical files, Lower Norfolk County, 1635–1680; Lower Norfolk County, Wills and Deeds B [1646–1651], fols. 128–129). Conversely, Adam Thorowgood's huge grant of 1635 did not form the nucleus of a large planter enclave on the Lynnhaven River.

TABLE 18

Landholdings in Lower Norfolk County, 1635–1651

| | % of Estates | | | | |
| | Area of County | | | | |
No. of Acres	1	2	3	4 and 5	Overall
0–299	40.0	44.0	46.2	35.3	41.1
300–499	20.0	28.0	23.1	20.6	23.3
500–749	0	16.0	19.2	29.4	21.1
750–999	0	0	7.7	5.9	4.4
1,000–1,499	20.0	4.0	0	5.9	4.4
1,500–1,999	0	0	3.8	0	1.1
2,000–2,999	0	4.0	0	0	1.1
3,000–4,999	20.0	4.0	0	0	2.2
5,000+	0	0	0	2.9	1.1
Total	100.0	100.0	100.0	100.0	99.8

Note: The areas of the county are (1) Willoughby Bay and Tanner's Creek; (2) Western Branch of Elizabeth River; (3) Eastern and Southern branches of Elizabeth River; (4 and 5) Lynnhaven (Western and Eastern branches combined). The acreages include an individual's holdings in each area only, and figures include nonresident county landholders.

Sources: Nell Marion Nugent, comp., *Cavaliers and Pioneers: Abstracts of Virginia Land Patents and Grants*, 2 vols. (Richmond, Va., 1934, 1977), I, 21–222; Lower Norfolk County, Virginia, Minute Book, transcript, 2 vols. (1637–1646), Wills and Deeds B (1646–1651), C (1651–1656) (Colonial Williamsburg, microfilm, reels M 1365-2, 1365-17); James Horn, biographical files, Lower Norfolk County, Virginia.

individuals. Between 1635 and 1651, 891 headrights were issued to 85 men, half of whom transported only 1–5 persons.[12]

Given the small number of settlers living between Tanner's and Little Creek (area 1), the main centers of population developed around the two major rivers and their tributaries, a pattern recognized by the creation of Elizabeth River and Lynnhaven parishes, serving the two halves of the

12. Acreages and headrights computed from Nugent, comp., *Cavaliers and Pioneers*, I, 21–222. For a discussion of headrights, see Edmund S. Morgan, "Headrights and Head Counts: A Review Article," *VMHB*, LXXX (1972), 361–371; Russell R. Menard, "Immigration to the Chesapeake Colonies in the Seventeenth Century: A Review Essay," *Maryland Historical Magazine*, LXVIII (1973), 323–329.

county.[13] By 1650, settlement stretched thirty miles from Bullock's Creek in the west to Lynnhaven in the east, and about twelve miles from Willoughby Bay at the mouth of the James to Julian's Creek on the Southern Branch of the Elizabeth River. Individual plantations were not widely dispersed; rather, settlement tended to cluster around certain creeks, rivers, and already-occupied areas. Even within a few years of the original settlement of the county it would have been possible for planters on Lynnhaven to visit at least a dozen neighbors living a few miles away. In other parts of the county, settlement was not so tightly grouped, but neighborhoods were gradually taking shape along the Elizabeth River, at Clark's Creek and Crany Point on the Western Branch, for example. Few planters, unless by choice, lived in isolation.

Where did early settlers come from? Of 56 men who patented land in the county by 1650, at least 23 (41.1 percent) formerly resided in Elizabeth City County (most at Kecoughtan), about the same proportion probably came directly from England, and the rest were from other parts of Virginia. The last included planters from the counties of Warrascoyack, Nansemond, James City, Charles City, Henrico, and possibly Accomack.[14]

Elizabeth City County played a key role, supplying a large contingent of settlers and a number of influential men who brought capital and experience of local government to the new county. Lower Norfolk, in its early days, was virtually a colony of Elizabeth City, but what should be emphasized too is the mix of different people who came to live in the county. Settlers who had already spent many years in Virginia were joined by growing numbers of men and women who paid their own passage, or were transported, directly from England. The exact proportions are difficult to determine, but among free settlers of the 1640s it is likely that between one-third and one-half were newcomers to the colony. Among servants the proportion would

---

13. Mr. John Wilson was appointed minister of Elizabeth River in 1637, and the construction of a church at Sewell's Point was begun almost immediately. Adam Thorowgood's house served as a place for divine worship until a church was built at Church Point, on Lynnhaven River, about the same time. A third parish, Southern Shore, existed briefly in the early 1640s, but little is known about it. Lower Norfolk County, Minute Book (1637–1646), I, fols. 3, 18, 59, 104; Charles B. Cross, Jr., *The County Court, 1637–1904, Norfolk County, Virginia* (Portsmouth, Va., 1964), 49; George Carrington Mason, "The Colonial Churches of Norfolk County, Virginia," *William and Mary Quarterly*, 2d Ser., XXI (1941), 139–148.

14. The missing 70 men appear neither in the musters of the 1620s nor as landowners elsewhere or as headrights.

have been much higher.[15] County populations were therefore amalgams of Virginia settlers and newly arrived English immigrants, the proportion varying according to time and place. Initially, the former were most prominent but rapidly gave way to incoming migrants and servants from England as the county began to fill up.

Where many of the people came from in England will remain a mystery, but the origins of those traced suggest a rich mix of backgrounds. Adam Thorowgood, born in 1603, was the son of a vicar from Grimston, Norfolk. His wife, Sarah, was from London, the daughter of an important merchant and leading member of the Virginia Company. They were married in Blackfriars in 1627 while Thorowgood was visiting London and returned to Virginia shortly after. Thomas Willoughby, from Rochester, Kent, was born about 1601 and emigrated as a young boy in 1610, settling at Kecoughtan. He patented one hundred acres in the vicinity of Willoughby Bay in the early 1620s but probably did not move there until a decade later. In the meantime, he served as a militia captain, commissioner, and burgess for Elizabeth City. Both he and Thorowgood established ruling dynasties in Lower Norfolk, their sons and grandsons serving as sheriffs, militia officers, and commissioners throughout the second half of the century. Another immigrant from Kent, Daniel Tanner of Canterbury, also lived in Elizabeth City County during the 1620s before moving to Tanner's Creek, not far from Willoughby's plantation, sometime before November 1637. Mr. John Hill, who immigrated to Virginia in the early 1620s, formerly lived "in the University of Oxford of the trade of a Bookebinder . . . the sonne of Stephen Hill of Oxford aforesaid Fletcher." Cornelius Lloyd and Thomas Burbage were merchants from London; Thomas Reynolds, mariner, came from East Smithfield; and Stephen Hicks was born in Southampton.[16]

Colonists had a variety of connections with other parts of England. William Jermy, clerk of the court, moved to "Kettlebaston," Suffolk, in 1658 but returned to Virginia a few years later; John Turner of Little Creek assigned to John Shute of Bristol "a house and shop in Ham, Essex in the occupation of

15. Lower Norfolk County, Wills and Deeds B (1646–1651), fols. 128–129; Horn, biographical files, Lower Norfolk County.

16. [Jester and Hiden, eds.], *Adventurers of Purse and Person*, 458–460, 607–619, 688–692; Lower Norfolk County, Wills and Deeds B (1646–1651), fols. 61, 202–203, C (1651–1656), fol. 158, D (1656–1666), fols. 145–146 (CW, microfilm, reel M 1365–18); W. G. Stanard, comp., *Some Emigrants to Virginia . . .*, 2d ed. (Richmond, Va., 1915), 53; Peter Wilson Coldham, ed., *English Adventurers and Emigrants, 1609–1660* (Baltimore, 1984), 23.

Goodman Cooke and all other lands etc in England" in 1663; Thomas Reynolds had a sister in Bristol; Robert Hodge, a brother in Dartmouth, Devon.[17] These references suggest that, although most settlers came from the southern counties of England and major ports, their particular backgrounds were considerably diverse. Settling down in Virginia entailed getting used to near neighbors from many different parts of the country.

To the mix of settlers from England and Virginia were added other peoples: Indians, blacks, and, to a limited extent, other Europeans. For reasons already explained, Chesapeake Indians did not play a large role in the early development of Lower Norfolk County. No mention is made of settlers' taking up Indian land or bargaining with local tribes for desirable tracts. Of the few references to Anglo-Indian contacts, most relate to war. During the 1630s and 1640s, men from the county took part in expeditions against the Nanticoke, Pamunkey, Chickahominy, and tribes to the south located in "Yawopyn" and "Rowanoake." Increased tithes and the expense and inconvenience of periodic marches against "the savages" were how the majority of settlers experienced contacts with the Indians. Only a couple of brief glimpses—the friendship between Christopher Burroughs of Lynnhaven and an Indian who "usually did abide" with him and the fining of Richard Owens for "unlawful entertaining of Indians" (probably trading)— suggest that occasionally there may have been more relaxed relationships between the two peoples.[18]

English attitudes and everyday contacts with blacks are equally difficult to recover. The first blacks recorded in Lower Norfolk were three "Negroes" registered by Adam Thorowgood in February 1638. These were followed by at least another thirty, transported by five other planters, down to 1650. Captain Richard Parson claimed three hundred acres in 1643 for "John, the negro, his wife and child" and "Basteano, a negro." A few years later, Captain Francis Yeardley transported "Simon a Turke and John a Negro" and in 1649 bought another eleven blacks, five from Daniell Pierce of Barbados to serve "for ever."[19] Owing to their expense, most were owned by large planters and worked in the tobacco fields alongside white servants, but

17. Lower Norfolk County, Wills and Deeds D (1656–1666), fols. 145–146, 208, 320, 369, E (1666–1675), fols. 146, 177 (CW, microfilm, reel M 1365–18).

18. Lower Norfolk County, Minute Book (1637–1646), I, fols. 9, 10, 35, II (1637–1646), fols. 2, 33, 59–60, 83, 87–88, Wills and Deeds C (1651–1656), fol. 12 (see also fols. 180, 224, Wills and Deeds D [1656–1666], fol. 293); Boddie, *Isle of Wight County*, 98.

19. Hatch, *The First Seventeen Years*, 93; Nugent, comp., *Cavaliers and Pioneers*, I, 79, 129, 182; Lower Norfolk County, Minute Book (1637–1646), I, fol. 219, Wills and Deeds B (1646–1651), fols. 50, 115–116.

sometimes they were given particular tasks. Mingo, described in 1645 as "a negro cowkeeper," had charge of cattle belonging to the orphans of Adam Thorowgood.

How much opportunity for contact and how frequently whites and blacks came into contact are unknown. Will Watts and Mary, "Mr Cornelius Lloyds negar woman," were ordered in April 1649 to do penance in the chapel of Elizabeth River Parish by standing in white sheets with a "white Rodd in their hands in the face of the congregation" on the next Sabbath day, the usual method of punishing fornication. Although relatively few, blacks constituted an important element of the local population, emphasizing differences between English and colonial society and between large and small planters. As slaves became more numerous in the second half of the century, such differences were accentuated.[20]

Just before Christmas 1647, a decade after the founding of the county, an exceptionally detailed tithe account was drawn up by the court: 360 tithables (suggesting a total population of about 750–900) lived in the region, clustered in distinct neighborhoods. Householders owned 546 head of cattle, 121 goats, and 5 horses and had seated 36,560 acres of the county's best land. It was a young society in every sense. Of 84 adults who deposed before the county court between 1637 and 1647, 43 (51.2 percent) were under thirty, and 55 (65.5 percent) were under thirty-five years old. Another 18 (21.2 percent) were of ages thirty-five to forty.[21] Most servants would have been in their

20. Capt. Francis Yeardley paid 2,000 lbs. of tobacco each for six slaves in 1649, which at 3d. per lb. would have amounted to £25 per slave (Lower Norfolk County, Wills and Deeds B [1646–1651], fol. 116). For Mingo and the Will Watts case, see Minute Book (1637–1646), II, fol. 53, Wills and Deeds B (1646–1651), fol. 106. Fornication in Lower Norfolk is discussed in Chapter 7.

Lower Norfolk was never a major tobacco-producing region, and hence slaves were not imported in large numbers. The largest single recorded consignment was 22 by Major Adam Thorowgood (son of Adam) in May 1670 (Wills and Deeds E [1666–1675], fol. 49).

21. Lower Norfolk County, Wills and Deeds B (1646–1651), fols. 55–57. Estimating total populations from numbers of tithables is difficult, because the proportions of different elements—free householders, servants (male and female), wives and children—are unknown. The ratio of total population to tithables in 1699 was 3.3 in Norfolk County and 3.2 in Princess Anne (created out of the eastern half of Lower Norfolk in 1691) (Morgan, *American Slavery, American Freedom*, 412–413). Numbers of wives and children were probably larger at the end of the century than in the early years of the county's history, however, and it is likely that the ratio for midcentury was nearer 2.0–2.5. All estimates should be treated with caution.

On ages: Charles F. McIntosh, "Ages of Lower Norfolk County People," *WMQ*,

teens and early twenties. The great majority of the population, therefore, was either young or very young. Immigration, servitude, and the disease environment dictated that there were few greybeards in the new societies taking shape along the Bay. English settlers, mainly from southern and eastern parts of the country, many of whom had lived in Virginia for years before moving to Lower Norfolk, were joined by a few Dutch merchants, Indians, and blacks to create a mix of peoples that had no parallel in the Old World.[22]

Lancaster County

Interest in the Northern Neck dates from the early 1640s. In 1642 the Assembly at Jamestown restricted movement into the "Rapohanok River" region for fear of igniting an Indian war with northern tribes, but by the summer the Assembly had relented, probably under pressure from self-interested burgesses, and allowed individuals the right to patent land, if not to seat it. Under these terms, the first grants along the Rappahannock were made to John Carter and the Puritans Richard Bennett, William Durand, and Daniel Gookin, all from Nansemond County. Tracts taken up for speculation were frequently extensive. Captain Samuel Matthews, for example, patented four thousand acres on the north side of the Rappahannock in 1643, one of the largest grants of the period, and eight of the thirteen patents issued for the Piankatank-Rappahannock area in 1642 and 1643 were for more than one thousand acres. Wealthy and well-connected planters took up land in the expectation of handsome returns when the region came to be settled. The colony's rulers—governors, burgesses, and members of the Council— were in an especially advantageous position to assess the possibilities of new lands for settlement and by making full use of the headright system could patent large areas at relatively small initial expense.[23]

1st Ser., XXV (1916–1917), 36–38. For age structures in England, see E. A. Wrigley and R. S. Schofield, *The Population History of England, 1541–1871: A Reconstruction* (Cambridge, Mass., 1981), 215–219, 528–529.

22. T. H. Breen, "Creative Adaptations: Peoples and Cultures," in Jack P. Greene and J. R. Pole, eds., *Colonial British America: Essays in the New History of the Early Modern Era* (Baltimore, 1984), 198, 216–217.

23. Thomas Hoskins Warner, *History of Old Rappahannock County, Virginia, 1656–1692* (Tappahannock, Va., 1965), 13–14; "The Virginia Assembly of 1641: A List of the Members and Some of the Acts," *VMHB*, IX (1901–1902), 53; Nugent, comp., *Cavaliers and Pioneers*, I, 132–148. The lands of Bennett, Durand, and Gookin were contiguous, about 35 miles up the Rappahannock River on the south bank, probably on the sites of Indian villages and clearings. It is possible that a Puritan settlement was planned in northern Virginia. In the event, most Puritans who left the south side of the James

Large-scale movement into the region would probably have taken place shortly after, had it not been for the Anglo-Indian war of 1644–1646 and continuing tension between the two peoples. The peace treaty of October 1646 prohibited the English from settling land north of the York River, in return for the Indians' removal from the James River basin. A confident Assembly claimed in the same year that Opechancanough's forces were "so routed and dispersed that they are no longer a nation, and we now suffer only from robbery by a few starved outlaws." This was an exaggeration. The Powhatan Chiefdom, embracing much of Virginia's tidewater, had collapsed, but a number of powerful tribes, whose allegiance to the Powhatans had never been unqualified, were still in existence. During the third quarter of the century the cockpit of Anglo-Indian tension shifted northward with migrating English settlers to the frontier region of the upper Rappahannock.[24]

Efforts to keep the English and Indians physically apart in different areas of the tidewater were bound to fail, in view of the increasing tide of immigration and the land hunger of colonists. The great attraction of the Chesapeake, after all, was plentiful land. By 1648 any pretense to following the letter of the peace treaty had disappeared with the formation of Northumberland County, which secured the settlements on the southern bank of the Potomac for Virginia. Movement into this area had begun about 1640, when John Mottrom of York County, who traded up the Bay to Maryland, settled at Chicacone. The south side of the Potomac became a refuge for people fleeing the political and social turmoil of Maryland during Richard Ingle's Rebellion, and John Mottrom's house developed as a refuge for Protestants hostile to Baltimore's government. Men like Richard Thompson, who formerly worked for William Claiborne on Kent Island, also established themselves there.[25]

---

moved further north into Maryland, many settling at Providence on the Severn River (the future Anne Arundel County); see Boddie, *Isle of Wight County*, chap. 4. John Mottram, gent., formerly of York County, patented 1,900 acres on the Piankatank River in 1642. See Rutman and Rutman, *A Place in Time: Middlesex County*, 74, for land speculation.

24. Morton, *Colonial Virginia*, I, 153–156; Ben C. McCary, *Indians in Seventeenth-Century Virginia*, Jamestown 350th Anniversary Booklet (Williamsburg, Va., 1957), 80–81; W. Stitt Robinson, "Tributary Indians in Colonial Virginia," *VMHB*, LXVII (1959), 49–64; E. Randolph Turner, "Socio-Political Organization within the Powhatan Chiefdom and the Effects of European Contact, A.D. 1607–1646," in Fitzhugh, ed., *Cultures in Contact*, 215–216; Warner, *History of Old Rappahannock*, chaps. 3–4.

25. "Mottrom—Wright—Spencer—Ariss—Buckner," *WMQ*, 1st Ser., XVII (1908–1909), 53, 58; Walter Briscoe Norris, ed., *Westmoreland County, Virginia, 1653–1983* (Montross, Va., 1983), 40–42.

Further south, settlers poured into the region. By the end of 1650, sixty patents had been granted along the Rappahannock totaling more than 53,000 acres. During the next two years a further 123,000 acres were patented along the north bank of the Piankatank, both sides of the Rappahannock, and inland along the major tributaries and creeks. Well more than half the total area of Lancaster County, as created in 1651, had been patented by the time of the first division of the county in 1656, and, as the land boom continued, virtually all the rest was taken up by the late 1660s.[26]

Settlers found a countryside of gently rolling hills, heavily wooded apart from Indian clearings and dissected by numerous streams and creeks. Fertile soils and excellent lines of communication ensured that the county quickly emerged as a prime tobacco-growing area. Population increase was rapid: from 380 tithables in 1653, to 663 in 1656, and 945 by 1663. In just a couple of years, Lancaster had the same population that Lower Norfolk had taken more than a decade to achieve. Settlement tended to cluster along both shores of the Rappahannock, frequently on the former sites of Indian villages. Ralph Wormeley, for example, patented 3,200 acres in June 1649 along the southern bank of the river, which included the "Indian Townes of old and new Nimcock." Thomas Brice took up 1,650 acres on the north bank three years later, "being part of an Indian Habitation called Old Moraticond," and another group of settlers patented land forty miles upriver on an old Indian village near present-day Tappahannock.[27]

Some idea of how land was seated can be gained from this description by Rowland Haddaway of an expedition in 1651:

> Going in company with Thomas Gaskins Richard Budd Abraham Moone and John Dennys our desire was to take up land in Fleets bay and we went into Corotomen Creek where we looked upon land and took up some, afterwards going into a Creek where Hugh Brent now liveth we gave it the name of Haddaways Creek and I this depont. did take up the land that Hugh Brent now lives upon there being three Indian Cabbins upon

26. Nugent, comp., *Cavaliers and Pioneers*, I, 177–209; Wheeler, "Lancaster County," 16–17, 27, 36–42, 62, 87.

27. Lancaster County, Virginia, Deeds Etc., no. 1 (1652–1657), 90–94, 302–307, Orders Etc. (1655–1666), 236–238 (CW, microfilm, reels M 1363-1, M 117-7; Lancaster County records are paginated, not foliate); Wheeler, "Lancaster County," 17; Nugent, comp., *Cavaliers and Pioneers*, I, 181–182, 272; Rutman and Rutman, *A Place in Time: Middlesex County*, 46. During the period 1653–1663 the total number of tithables in Virginia increased from just more than 7,000 to 12,500 (Menard, "Tobacco Industry," *Res. Econ. Hist.*, V [1980], appendix, 158–159).

the sd. Land. Going over a run above the sd. Hugh Brents house and we coming upon the land upon the sd. run Abraham Moone asked Thomas Gaskins whether he liked the sd. land or would have any of the same. The sd. Gaskins answered no for he thought it would drown, the sd. Moone answered if you wil not, I wil have it myselfe, the sd. Moone likewise took a book out of his pocket and did set down the bounds of the sd. land.[28]

The apparently casual attitude toward claiming land and lack of concern about Indian settlements is revealing. In some cases an accommodation was reached with local tribes, and land was purchased. Colonel Moore Fauntleroy and Francis Brown came to such agreements with the Rappahannocks and Mattaponis, respectively, in the late 1650s, although subsequently there was considerable doubt whether the Indians would recognize their claims. A few years earlier, following an order by the Assembly, the court defined the boundaries of Indian lands and affirmed that "Indians inhabitinge within this Countie" would be protected by (as well as be subject to) English laws. Even so, English settlers appear to have taken the view that, once they moved into an area, resident Indians would soon move out. As the south bank of the Rappahannock filled up, the Mattaponis moved in the 1660s from the Southern Branch of Piscataway Creek to near the head of the Western Branch, before moving again to the Mattaponi River. Similarly, under pressure from advancing English settlements, the Moraticoes moved out of the area around the Corotoman River sometime before 1652 and established a new town on Moratico Creek (see Figure 13). They resettled again later in the decade on the eastern side of Totuskey Creek and finally moved out of the region altogether in 1672. Despite declining Indian populations and the movement of some tribes beyond the limits of English settlement, competition for land and the proximity of whites and Indians were a constant source of friction down to Bacon's Rebellion.[29]

In 1653, ninety-one households stretched across forty-five miles from the freshes upriver to Stingray Point at the mouth of the Bay (Figure 13). Approximately twenty households, accounting for eighty-three tithables, were seated around the Corotoman River, the most populous part of the northern bank of the Rappahannock, where a number of important planters and mer-

28. Lancaster County, Deeds Etc., no. 2 (1654–1666), 363: deposition of Rowland Haddaway, Jan. 25, 1659/60 (CW, microfilm, reel M 1363-1). In the quotation, periods have been added at end of sentences and initial letters capped.

29. Warner, *History of Old Rappahannock*, 27–49, 55–60, 63–65, 71; Norris, ed., *Westmoreland County*, 18–33, 48–50; Rutman and Rutman, *A Place in Time: Middlesex County*, 45; Lancaster County, Orders Etc. (1655–1666), 125–126.

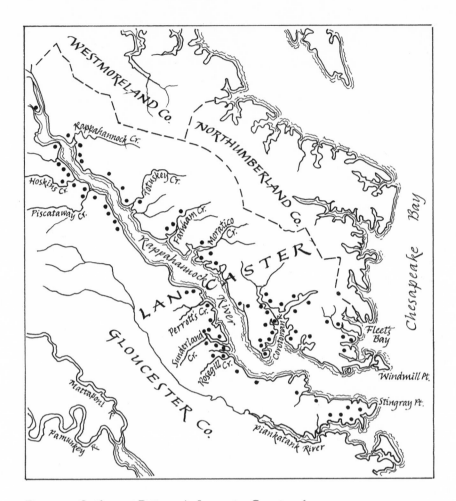

Figure 13. Settlement Patterns in Lancaster County, 1653.
Drawn by Richard Stinely

chants such as Major John Carter, Mr. Thomas Brice, and Dominic Therriott
were located; fourteen households (eighty-two tithables), including several
of the largest plantations in the county, were situated between Rosegill and
Perrott's creeks on the southern bank. The rest of the population was distributed in small clusters around major creeks (such as Moratico, Farnham,
and Piscataway), on Fleet's Bay (where Captain Henry Fleet from Chartham,
Kent, lived), and near the mouth of the Piankatank River.[30]

30. Lancaster County, Deeds Etc., no. 1 (1652–1657), 65–66, 91–94; James Horn,
biographical files, Lancaster County, Virginia, 1652–1700.

TABLE 19
Tithables per Household in Lancaster County, 1653

| Neighborhood (N) | % of Households | | | | |
| | Tithables per Household | | | | |
	1–4	5–6	7–9	10+	Total
Fleet's Bay (5)	80.0	0	0	20.0	100.0
Corotoman (20)	55.0	40.0	0	5.0	100.0
Moratico to Totuskey (18)	66.7	16.7	11.1	5.6	100.1
Upper south side of Rappahannock (20)	80.0	15.0	5.0	0	100.0
Rosegill (8)	25.0	25.0	0	50.0	100.0

Source: Lancaster County, Virginia, Deeds Etc., no. 1 (1652–1657), 90–94, Colonial Williamsburg, microfilm, reel M 1363-1.

The number of tithables owned by each family in 1653 suggests that, with one exception, there were no major differences in the social composition of these various neighborhoods (Table 19). Commonly, each area had one or two large planters and a majority of smaller households. In the Corotoman area, for example, John Carter was assessed on 12 tithables, 8 families had 5–6, and the rest had 1–4. Along the northern side of the Rappahannock between Moratico and Totuskey creeks, Mr. David Fox had 10 tithables, 2 families were assessed on 8, 3 households had 5, and 12 had fewer than 5. The upper reaches of the southern side of the Rappahannock had the fewest large households: 16 of 20 families had 4 or fewer tithables. Only one planter, Ralph Rouzee, had as many as 8.

By contrast, one area that stands out clearly from all the others was dominated by big plantations and was located in the vicinity of Rosegill and Sunderland creeks. Four men, Mr. Edmond Kemp, Colonel Richard Lee, Sir Henry Chicheley, and Captain William Brocas, together owned 57 tithables. The largest plantation was Rosegill, patented by Captain Ralph Wormeley on Nimcock Creek (renamed Rosegill) in return for transporting 69 persons, including 17 "Negroes." Shortly after his death in 1651, his widow married Sir Henry Chicheley, who had recently arrived from England. Another recent arrival was Sir Thomas Lunsford, who took up 3,423 acres in 1649 near Rosegill and served as a member of the Council and lieutenant general of Virginia before his death in 1653 (his widow was assessed on 12 tithables in 1654). Edmond Kemp, a merchant, was the nephew of Richard Kemp, secretary of the colony from 1637 to 1640. The latter's death in 1649 probably prompted

Edmond's move to the colony in the following year. Brocas and Lee, formerly of York County, were influential planter-merchants who served in a number of high-ranking offices as commissioners, burgesses, and members of the Council during the 1640s and 1650s. Both speculated extensively in land in Lancaster and other parts of Virginia. The area around Rosegill developed as an aristocratic enclave, where the chief gentry were closely associated with the upper echelons of the colonial elite surrounding Governor Berkeley and usually kept themselves aloof from ordinary planters around them.[31]

Early settlers came from a variety of backgrounds. At least 50, and probably nearer 80, of the 141 householders who appear on the 1655 tithing list entered the county directly from England, a ratio suggesting a higher proportion of new arrivals than that estimated for Lower Norfolk. They included a number of politically influential men of high status. Chicheley, Lunsford, and Sir Grey Skipwith were royalist officers who had left England after the execution of Charles I. Lunsford had a tempestuous history. From Wilegh, Sussex, he shocked county society in 1632 by attempting to murder his respected and influential neighbor Sir Thomas Pelham and spent a year in Newgate before fleeing to France. His appointment to the lieutenantship of the Tower of London in 1641 was met with horror and disbelief by the House of Commons, who voted for his immediate removal. A group of City petitioners described him as "a man of decayed and desperate fortune, most notorious for outrages," an opinion reflected by the earl of Dorset's view that he feared "neither God nor man." He fought for the king in both civil wars and may have met Sir Henry Chicheley, a fellow officer, while imprisoned in the Tower following the collapse of the antiparliamentarian uprising of 1648. Another Cavalier émigré, Colonel Henry Norwood, described meeting both Lunsford and Chicheley at Ralph Wormeley's plantation on the York River in early 1650, where they passed an evening "feasting and carousing" with other ex-royalist officers "lately come from England."[32]

31. Lancaster County, Deeds Etc., no. 1 (1652–1657), 91–94; "Tithables of Lancaster County, Virginia, 1654, with Notes," *VMHB*, V (1897–1898), 159; Nugent, comp., *Cavaliers and Pioneers*, I; Rutman and Rutman, *A Place in Time: Middlesex County*, 46, 48, 49, 53–55.

32. Lancaster County, Deeds Etc., no. 1 (1652–1657), 234–239; Morton, *Colonial Virginia*, I, 167; Steven D. Crow, " 'Your Majesty's Good Subjects': A Reconsideration of Royalism in Virginia, 1642–1652," *VMHB*, LXXXVII (1979), 158–173; Anthony Fletcher, *A County Community in Peace and War: Sussex, 1600–1660* (London, 1975), 54–55; Brian Manning, *The English People and the English Revolution, 1640–1649* (London, 1976), 74–76; C. V. Wedgwood, *The King's War, 1641–1647* (New York, 1959), 49–53, 59; "Note—Sir Thomas Lunsford," *VMHB*, XVII (1909), 26–33; Colonel [Henry] Norwood, *A Voy-*

Other immigrants, like John Cox, William Ball, David Fox, and Thomas Powell, were merchants from London and the outports. Ball first appeared in the county in the 1650s and quickly developed an extensive trade provisioning deepwater shipping in the Corotoman River. Despite his evident success, it does not appear that he was initially committed to staying in the Chesapeake, since his wife and children remained in London until the mid-1660s. During part of this period his eldest son, William, was responsible for running the English end of the family business. Similarly, Henry Corbin, a wealthy planter seated on the south side of the Rappahannock, had emigrated in the mid-1650s while his two brothers, merchants in London, remained in England. Further up the river, in the freshes, lived John Catlett from Sittingbourne, Kent, who arrived in 1650 with his son and two half-brothers, Ralph and Edward Rouzee, from Ashford in the same county. Catlett became a leading figure in Rappahannock County (formed in 1656) and held the offices of justice, burgess, sheriff, and colonel. Much involved in Indian affairs, he was killed defending the fort at Port Royal in 1670. Not all immigrants were from the southern counties of England. Ralph Wormeley, the Lawsons, and Cuthbert Potter were from Yorkshire; Chicheley, from Wimpole, Cambridgeshire; and Edmond Kemp, from Gissing, Norfolk.[33]

About a third of the householders who had arrived in Lancaster by 1655 were from other parts of Virginia. Two regions contributed the majority of Virginian settlers. Of 36 families for whom reliable evidence exists, half came from the counties immediately to the south (11 from York and 6 from Gloucester), and 13 were from the three easternmost counties south of the James (8 from Isle of Wight, 4 from Nansemond, and 1 from Lower Norfolk). Of the remaining 6 families, 2 were from Charles City County, 1 was from Elizabeth City, and 3 were from the Eastern Shore. The proximity of York and Gloucester counties and the general south-to-north direction of migra-

---

age to Virginia (1649), in Peter Force, comp., *Tracts and Other Papers, Relating Principally to the Origin, Settlement, and Progress of the Colonies in North America from the Discovery of the Country to the Year 1776*, 4 vols. (1836–1846; Gloucester, Mass., 1963), III, no. 10, p. 49.

33. N. T. Mann, "William Ball, Merchant," *Northern Neck Historical Magazine*, XXIII (1973), 2523–2529; Rutman and Rutman, *A Place in Time: Middlesex County*, 50; J. M. Sosin, *English America and the Restoration Monarchy of Charles II: Transatlantic Politics, Commerce, and Kinship* (Lincoln, Nebr., 1980), chap. 1; William Carter Stubbs, *A History of Two Virginia Families Transplanted from County Kent, England* (New Orleans, La., n.d.), 1, 5–6; Horn, biographical files, Lancaster County (I am grateful to Warren M. Billings for allowing me to use his unpublished research on prominent Virginia planters).

tion in the 1640s and early 1650s explain the prominence of families from this area. Settlements along the York River and Mobjack Bay, which had spread rapidly in the previous decades, provided an excellent springboard for the exploration of lands on the Piankatank and Rappahannock rivers. Rowland Haddaway and his four companions, for example, set out from York in 1651 to explore Fleet's Bay. The opening up of new regions was generated in part by the movement of established planters and their families from contiguous counties that themselves had been frontier settlements a few years earlier.[34]

Migration from the counties south of the James is less easily explained. Considerable distances were involved. A family migrating from Isle of Wight County faced a journey of about twenty miles downriver to Old Point Comfort, forty miles up the Bay to the mouth of the Rappahannock, and possibly another twenty to thirty miles upriver before reaching its final destination. The lower James basin was a low-grade tobacco area. John White, a London merchant, explained to Robert Shepard of Surry in 1646 that, although his crop was "sound good Leafe," it was "of the common sort" and would not fetch as high a price as the more favored "Sweetsentes" variety. Planters in the know may well have feared, justifiably as it turned out, that with the expansion of settlement north of the York, where there was an abundance of prime soils, the Southside would become more and more marginal.[35] They would have also been aware that the Rappahannock basin was the last extensive region of unclaimed land in the tidewater (short of moving further up the Bay into Maryland, which many did) and that migrating to the Northern Neck was probably their last chance to obtain the pick of the best land in a new region that clearly had enormous potential. The expansion of opportunities on the Virginia frontier explains why men with connections and resources moved so quickly.

These suppositions are supported by a range of clues about the influences that lay behind the decisions of individuals and families to migrate. First, political connections were important in alerting planters to opportunities elsewhere in the Chesapeake. Toby Smith, Captain Moore Fauntleroy, and

34. Rutman and Rutman, *A Place in Time: Middlesex County*, 44–49, provides an excellent account of the settlement of the south side of the Rappahannock (the future Middlesex County). Approximately a third of all patents issued in 1642 were for lands north of the York River. Twenty individuals took up patents in the Mobjack Bay region of the future Gloucester County (Nugent, comp., *Cavaliers and Pioneers*, I, 130–142).

35. Eliza Timberlake Davis, comp., *Surry County Records, Surry County, Virginia, 1652–1684* ([Baltimore, 1980]), 11; Kevin Peter Kelly, "Economic and Social Development of Seventeenth-Century Surry County, Virginia" (Ph.D. diss., University of Washington, 1972), 139.

John Carter arrived in Virginia about the same time, in the early 1640s, and settled in Nansemond. All three served regularly in the Assembly. Carter may have discussed with Smith and Fauntleroy his speculative venture of 1642 (he had patented thirteen hundred acres on the north side of the Rappahannock) and the possibility of moving north. Smith and Fauntleroy probably knew Rowland Burnham and Richard Lee, of York County, who also sat in the assemblies of the 1640s. At meetings of the colonial legislature and Council in Jamestown and on court days in the counties at large, there would have been plenty of occasions to gather information and discuss the potential of the lands beyond the York.[36]

Second, kinship and neighborliness appear to have played an important role in encouraging migration, or at least in influencing the choice of destination. Smith was married to Fauntleroy's sister, and when Smith and Fauntleroy migrated to Lancaster in 1650, they chose to settle near one another on Farnham Creek, about thirty miles upriver. Epaphroditus Lawson, who settled in Nansemond before 1635, was the brother of Rowland and Richard Lawson, who also moved to Lancaster in the early 1650s. One of the wealthiest men in the county and a member of the bench, Epaphroditus Lawson was well known to other prominent planters in Nansemond. Moore Fauntleroy was a close neighbor, and John Carter had assigned him land in the early 1640s. In Lancaster, Carter and the Lawsons became neighbors again on the Corotoman River. Ralph Wormeley, William Brocas, and Rowland Burnham were brothers-in-law and settled close to one another between Rosegill and Sunderland creeks. In fact, of twenty-four families who settled on the south side of the Rappahannock by 1653, more than half had lived in a cluster of households along the York River, and just fewer than half had known each other previously as relatives or acquaintances.[37] The south side of the county may have been more closed to new arrivals without existing kinship or business ties than the northern bank of the river, settled mainly by planters from the James River region and new immigrants from England.

Again and again, one is struck by the small world inhabited by Chesapeake planters of this rank. Linked by a "tangled web of cousinry," friendship, political and business connections, planters were brought into frequent face-

---

36. H. R. McIlwaine, ed., *Journals of the House of Burgesses of Virginia, 1619–1658/59* (Richmond, Va., 1915), xvi–xx; Nugent, comp., *Cavaliers and Pioneers*, I, 132.

37. Beverley Fleet, abs., *Virginia Colonial Abstracts*, XXII, *Lancaster County, 1652–1655* (Baltimore, 1961), 36–38; Horn, biographical files, Lancaster County, Virginia; Nugent, comp., *Cavaliers and Pioneers*, I, 135, 151; Rutman and Rutman, *A Place in Time: Middlesex County*, 48–49.

to-face contact with one another. Such links helped to shape the pattern of migration and would profoundly influence the development of society in new areas. Settlers chose to move to Lancaster not only because of the plentiful fertile land but also because they had kin and friends there. As experienced tobacco planters, merchants, and county rulers, they persuaded English merchants to reroute their shipping, export English goods, and extend credit and marketing outlets for their crops, thereby ensuring the economic growth of the region; and they helped to establish orderly rule on the frontier through their monopoly of local offices and links with provincial government. Kinship and friendship minimized the potential for conflict and encouraged cooperation in meeting the myriad problems and challenges during the initially uncertain early years of the new society's formation. In the process, not only did they consolidate their own position in the new county hierarchy, but they also played a crucial role in helping newcomers from England (of their own rank) acclimatize to conditions in the Chesapeake.

The majority of new arrivals in Lancaster, as elsewhere along the tobacco coast in the second half of the seventeenth century, were indentured servants. Between 1653 and 1656 the number of laborers rose from approximately 350 to 550, or about half the total population of the county. Planters "lived in a sea of servants." At the time of the formation of Middlesex County in 1668, on the south side of the Rappahannock, 45 percent of the population were servants and slaves. Little is known about the origins of servants. The majority were probably recruited in London, since most merchants trading to the Rappahannock were from the capital, but, in view of English migratory patterns, this does not imply that servants invariably came from the city itself. A large proportion were in their midteens or younger and served at least seven years. Some became householders in the county: Clement Herbert, transported in the 1650s, patented several hundred acres of land on the south side of the Rappahannock, and Charles King, who took up forty acres at the mouth of the Corotoman in 1657, had been brought into the colony by Mordecai Cooke of Mobjack Bay, Gloucester County, seven years earlier. John Bell, formerly a servant of Rice Jones, sued in court for his freedom dues in January 1652/3 and was awarded "3 barrels of Corn and Cloaths according to custom together with an Ax and hoe." He patented 350 acres on the south side of the Rappahannock before his death in 1657.[38]

38. Wheeler, "Lancaster County," 22; Rutman and Rutman, *A Place in Time: Middlesex County*, 71–72 (quote); Morgan, *American Slavery, American Freedom*, 216, 226–227; Nugent, comp., *Cavaliers and Pioneers*, I, 200, 254, 308, 346, 348, 350, 354; Lancaster County, Deeds Etc., no. 1 (1652–1657), 24, Orders Etc. (1655–1666), 26, 42.

Owing to the later date of settlement and immigration of several wealthy planters with substantial capital, slaves were imported in much greater numbers than in Lower Norfolk. At least 69 entered the county between 1649 and 1654, and another 141 in the rest of the decade. Most were transported singly or in small groups, but Colonel John Carter claimed headrights for 21 slaves in 1665, and Thomas Chetwood for 23 in the same year. At his death in 1655, Captain William Brocas owned 14 slaves (most of whom were old or diseased) worth about ninety pounds, and Mr. David Fox bequeathed 14 slaves and their children in his will ten years later. Although it is not certain how many planters owned slaves, 23 of 429 householders in 1657 (5.4 percent) claimed that they had been overcharged "for many yeres past" by "retourneing their Negroe weomen" in the annual levies. In all likelihood, more slaves would have been purchased by Lancaster planters if they had been available. Francis Cole made a provision in his will in 1658 for 2 slaves to be bought out of his present crop if "negroes do come in this year." Limited supplies and the ready availability of white servants retarded the growth of slavery in the region until the final decades of the century.[39] Even so, on large plantations bordering the Corotoman River and Rosegill and Moratico creeks, slaves toiling in the fields or laboring around the plantation would have been a familiar sight to neighboring planters from the very beginning of the county's settlement.

Finally, Lancaster's population included a number of non-English immigrants. A few Scottish, Welsh, and Irish servants were transported in the 1650s and early 1660s, often identified, like slaves, by their forenames only: David a "Scott," "Morose a Scott," Patrick a "Highlander," and "Daniell an Irishman." Dominic Therriott, a merchant, was from France. Eppy, or Abia, Bonnison, who arrived sometime before December 1653, was Dutch, as was Doodes Minor, who settled in Nansemond before moving north.[40]

Evidence from other parts of the Chesapeake suggests that the manner in which Lower Norfolk and Lancaster were settled was not exceptional. James Perry's study of the Eastern Shore in the first half of the century reveals the rapid but orderly taking up of land after 1635, as planters spread out from

39. Nugent, comp., *Cavaliers and Pioneers*, I; Lancaster County, Deeds Etc., no. 1 (1652–1657), 10–11, 191–192, 202–204, no. 2 (1654–1666), 56, 68–71, 72–73, 121–122, 283–285, Orders Etc. (1655–1666), 36, 38.

40. Nugent, comp., *Cavaliers and Pioneers*, I, 200, 242, 253, 256, 437, 440, 536; Lancaster County, Deeds Etc., no. 1 (1652–1657), 10–11; Horn, biographical files, Lancaster County, Virginia.

the earliest settlements near the southern tip of the peninsula and moved northward, establishing plantations on rivers, creeks, and inlets along the bayside. Colonists preferred to patent land that adjoined or was close to other planters, a pattern that "maximized the possibility for contact," and they frequently opted to settle near relatives if they had any. The tendency of newcomers to take up land in areas of older settlement meant that, despite the high population turnover, new landowners never represented more than half the total number of landowners in any particular locale after the initial phase of colonization had passed.[41]

Farther north and across the Bay in Maryland, planters began moving out along the rivers and creeks from the original site of settlement at St. Mary's City in the 1630s and 1640s, although the political problems and catastrophic decline in population during Ingle's Rebellion restricted the spread of settlement until the early 1650s. Lord Baltimore's attempt to encourage the growth of a manorial society, which might have resulted in a very different pattern of landholding, was largely a failure. Settlers took up land in much the same way as in Virginia, considering first the quality of the soils, convenience of access for shipping, and proximity of other households.[42]

All along the tobacco coast, the formation of local societies was conditioned by the mixture of settlers from different parts of England who came into contact, variously, with Indians, blacks, other Europeans—and one another. Early settlers of York County came from London, Kent, Surrey, Essex, Middlesex, Bedfordshire, East Anglia, Wiltshire, Gloucestershire, Devon, Somerset, and Yorkshire. A group of colonists who settled in Westmoreland County in the middle years of the century came from Bristol, Plymouth, Somerset, Shropshire, Bedfordshire, Middlesex, and London. Counties south of the James River, such as Surry, Isle of Wight, and Lower

41. Perry, *Formation of a Society*, 37–42, 68–70, 89–97. For Surry County, see Kevin P. Kelly, "'In Dispers'd Country Plantations': Settlement Patterns in Seventeenth-Century Surry County, Virginia," in Thad W. Tate and David L. Ammerman, eds., *The Chesapeake in the Seventeenth Century: Essays in Anglo-American Society* (Chapel Hill, N.C., 1979), 183–205.

42. Lorena S. Walsh, "Community Networks in the Early Chesapeake," in Lois Green Carr, Philip D. Morgan, and Jean B. Russo, eds., *Colonial Chesapeake Society* (Chapel Hill, N.C., 1988), 200–241; Lois Green Carr, Russell R. Menard, and Lorena S. Walsh, *Robert Cole's World: Agriculture and Society in Early Maryland* (Chapel Hill, N.C., 1991), chap. 5; Garry Wheeler Stone, "Manorial Maryland," *Md. Hist. Mag.*, LXXXII (1987), 3–27; Russell R. Menard, P.M.G. Harris, and Lois Green Carr, "Opportunity and Inequality: The Distribution of Wealth on the Lower Western Shore of Maryland, 1638–1705," *Md. Hist. Mag.*, LXIX (1974), 169–184.

Norfolk, had closer links with Bristol than with London and therefore received more settlers from the West Country than usual elsewhere; but, even so, colonists who settled on the south bank of the James came from a broad spread of counties in central and southern England.[43]

In a period when local customs and traditions were a vibrant force in shaping daily life and experience in England, the formation of communities in Virginia and Maryland, which suddenly brought together men and women from a multitude of different English backgrounds, constituted an abrupt break with the past. Far removed from the familiar surroundings of their native societies, settlers began to reconstruct a Chesapeake version of English local society that accommodated the diversity of their provincial origins and recognized the presence of a number of non-English cultures. If the impact of non-English cultures should not be exaggerated—there was no melding of the races in Virginia or Maryland during the seventeenth century—neither should those cultures be ignored. From this mixing of diverse English people and their contact with profoundly different Indian and African cultures, an English culture peculiar to the Chesapeake eventually emerged, analogous to regional cultures elsewhere in the Anglo-American world of the seventeenth century yet still within the dominant national culture that encompassed England and all its colonial dependencies. Much of the peculiar richness of immigrants' own provincial backgrounds was lost, but contact with other English peoples and other races provided an equally rich source for the forging of new cultural hybrids.

County and Parish

Vitally important to the development of society in the early Chesapeake were the adoption and evolution of English institutions of local government. Following the establishment of the eight original counties in Virginia in 1634, the founding of county courts recognized and gave official sanc-

43. *WMQ*, 1st Ser.: "Pedigree of a Representative Virginia Planter," I (1892–1893), 80–88, 140–154; "Temple Farm," "The Calthorpes," "Libraries in Colonial Virginia," II (1893–1894), 3, 106–111, 169, 171; "Washington and His Neighbors," IV (1895–1896), 31; "Isle of Wight County Records," VII (1898–1899), 212, 215, 221–228, 259; "Westmoreland County Records," XV (1906–1907), [176]. Boddie, *Colonial Surry*, 38–40, 67–72, 75, 80, 91; Boddie, *Isle of Wight County*, chaps. 2–7. For the origins of English immigrants who settled in Henrico County, see William Clayton Torrence, "Henrico County, Virginia: Beginnings of Its Families," pt. 2, *WMQ*, 1st Ser., XXIV (1915–1916), 205–210; John Bennett Boddie, "Lygon of Madresfield, Worcester, England, and Henrico, Virginia," *WMQ*, 2d Ser., XVI (1936), 302–303.

tion to the creation of new communities as settlement spread throughout the tidewater. In both Virginia and Maryland the county court and justice of the peace became the keystone of local government: the great majority of colonists acknowledged the efficacy of local rule and shared assumptions about their own role within it. Critical to the "conservation of the peace and quiet government" was the recognition that "everyone had a basic duty to maintain order." [44]

In addition, colonists were familiar with the principle that the area of government that affected them most directly—the everyday conduct of their affairs—should be conducted by men who, although bearing the king's commission and usually of higher status, by and large shared their interests and were neighbors of the people they judged. In a society deeply imbued with patriarchal values, county justices assumed the role of fathers of their communities, dispensing justice, regulating local business, and ensuring the continuance of "the Amity, Confidence and Quiet that is between men." [45]

The powers and jurisdiction of Virginia's county courts developed over several decades. Initially, they had authority to judge civil causes involving less than ten pounds, decide petty offenses and disputes, and administer local affairs as occasion arose; but they soon took on wider responsibilities, partly owing to the decentralization of powers from Jamestown and partly in response to the exigencies of the times. During the 1640s and 1650s, courts were empowered to decide criminal cases not involving loss of life and limb, to consider capital offenses before referral to the General Court in Jamestown, and to adjudicate all causes at common law and equity involving local parties. They also took on the functions of English church, manor, and admiralty courts in considering moral offenses, testamentary business, ophans' estates, parochial affairs, poor relief, land grants, deeds, shipping, and salvage. Administrative duties included setting and collecting the annual tithe, laying out parish and county boundaries, registering cattle marks, ordering the construction of bridges, maintaining highways and ferries, licensing taverns, inspecting weights and measures, holding elections for burgesses,

44. Warren M. Billings, "The Growth of Political Institutions in Virginia, 1634 to 1676," *WMQ*, 3d Ser., XXXI (1974), 225–235; Lois Green Carr, "The Foundations of Social Order: Local Government in Colonial Maryland," in Bruce C. Daniels, ed., *Town and County: Essays on the Structure of Local Government in the American Colonies* (Middletown, Conn., 1978), 72–110, esp. 99; Robert Wheeler, "The County Court in Colonial Virginia," in Daniels, ed., *Town and County*, 111–133; Craven, *Southern Colonies*, 169–179; Walsh, "Charles County," 312.

45. Craven, *Southern Colonies*, 72; Billings, "Growth of Political Institutions," *WMQ*, 3d Ser., XXXI (1974), 227.

supervising the militia, regulating Anglo-Indian relations, and enforcing acts passed by the Assembly.[46]

The evolution of local government in Virginia and Maryland was, of course, significantly influenced by local conditions. English courts did not have to address the kinds of issues that routinely arose in new communities on the Chesapeake frontier. But the development of Chesapeake institutions was not entirely autonomous of developments in England. During the sixteenth and seventeenth centuries, as a consequence of complex and interrelated political and social developments, central government began strengthening the authority of local rulers appointed by the state. The crown's courts (assizes and quarter and petty sessions) and officers (lord lieutenant, sheriff, and justice of the peace) emerged as the primary means of maintaining law and order and enforcing government policies. At the same time, the parish became the most important agency of social discipline and regulation below the county, assuming a wide range of powers for the supervision and maintenance of the poor, punishment of the idle, and care for the very young, elderly, and sick. The influence of manor courts and, to a lesser extent, church courts gradually waned.[47]

46. Billings, "Growth of Political Institutions," *WMQ*, 3d Ser., XXXI (1974), 227–235; Lois Green Carr and David William Jordan, *Maryland's Revolution of Government, 1689–1692* (Ithaca, N.Y., 1974), 8–12; Philip Alexander Bruce, *Institutional History of Virginia in the Seventeenth Century: An Inquiry into the Religious, Moral, Educational, Legal, Military, and Political Condition of the People . . .* , 2 vols. (New York, 1910), I, 478–549; William Waller Hening, ed., *The Statutes at Large: Being a Collection of All the Laws of Virginia . . .* , 13 vols. (1809–1823; Charlottesville, Va., 1969), I, 125, 127, 132, 168–169, 224, 273.

47. This account, of course, simplifies complex events. Both manor and church courts remained important with respect to certain offenses throughout the 17th and early 18th centuries. However, there can be little doubt that, with the strengthening of the state in the Tudor period, spiritual and private (manorial) courts gradually lost ground to the crown's courts, central and provincial. See, for example, Penry Williams, *The Tudor Regime* (Oxford, 1979); D. M. Palliser, *The Age of Elizabeth: England under the Later Tudors, 1547–1603* (London, 1985); Alan G. R. Smith, *The Government of Elizabethan England* (London, 1967); Anthony Fletcher, *Reform in the Provinces: The Government of Stuart England* (New Haven, Conn., 1986). J. H. Shennan, *The Origins of the Modern European State, 1450–1725* (London, 1974); and Norbert Elias, *State Formation and Civilization*, trans. Edmund Jephcott (Oxford, 1982), provide broader perspectives, as do works examining problems confronted by centralizing states, such as Trevor Aston, ed., *Crisis in Europe, 1560–1660* (London, 1965); Geoffrey Parker and Lesley M. Smith, eds., *The General Crisis of the Seventeenth Century* (London, 1978); and Yves-Marie Bercé, *Revolt and Revolution in Early Modern Europe: An Essay on the History of Political Violence*, trans. Joseph Bergin (Manchester, 1987), 163–183.

Only those institutions that in England were reinforced by central government became functional in the Chesapeake. The development of the English magistracy after 1500 was echoed by the growth of magistracy in Maryland and Virginia during the seventeenth century. While the small populations of Chesapeake counties did not require the complex array of courts available in England, it was hardly a coincidence that the linchpin of local government was modeled on English county government rather than on manor, borough, or sheriffs' courts or that a powerful colonial gentry mirrored the emergence of powerful gentry communities in English shires.[48] The timing of colonization, during a period when the gentry was consolidating its political power at local and national levels in England, partly accounts for the rapid extension of gentry control in the tobacco colonies.

Comparisons with English institutions and precedents should not lead us to an overly grandiose view of Chesapeake courts, however. There was little of the ritual, ceremony, and provincial splendor that commonly accompanied meetings of the assizes or quarter sessions in English county towns. In the early years of county formation the bench, usually consisting of eight to twelve justices appointed by the governor and Council, convened every few months as the volume of business, weather, and convenience dictated.[49] Before the construction of courthouses they tended to meet at a variety of locations: in their own houses, local taverns, or the dwellings of prominent planters. Lower Norfolk's first court, in May 1637, was held at Adam Thorowgood's house and, subsequently, at the houses of other magistrates, such as Thomas Willoughby, John Sibsey, Henry Sewell, Francis Mason, and William Julian. We can imagine half a dozen justices seated around a table in

48. The "rise of the gentry" theory and subsequent controversy is reviewed in J. H. Hexter, "Storm over the Gentry," in his *Reappraisals in History* (London, 1961), 117–162. See also J. T. Cliffe, *The Yorkshire Gentry: From the Reformation to the Civil War* (London, 1969); Alan Everitt, *The Community of Kent and the Great Rebellion, 1640–60* (Leicester, 1966); Fletcher, *A County Community at Peace and War*; G. E. Mingay, *The Gentry: The Rise and Fall of a Ruling Class* (London, 1976); Ann Hughes, *Politics, Society, and Civil War in Warwickshire, 1620–1660* (Cambridge, 1987). The resurgence of the aristocracy after the Restoration is considered in J. V. Beckett, *The Aristocracy in England, 1660–1914* (Oxford, 1986); and John Cannon, *Aristocratic Century: The Peerage of Eighteenth-Century England* (Cambridge, 1984).

49. The act of March 5, 1623/4, that established local courts stipulated that they were to meet once a month. In 1642, the Assembly provided that courts meet at least six times a year (Cross, *The County Court, Norfolk County*, 1–2; Craven, *Southern Colonies*, 168–170). In early Lower Norfolk and Lancaster counties, courts met at irregular intervals throughout the year but usually sat from five to nine times.

the main room of the house discussing the cases brought before them while plaintiffs and defendants sat or stood outside waiting to be called. Use of a justice's house or Will Shipp's tavern for the monthly court was merely an extension of the practice of a single justice's dealing with minor complaints in his own parlor, a practice followed in England that helped clear up a great deal of petty business before it came to court. Courts tended to be held alternately near Elizabeth River and near Lynnhaven, recognizing the most populous areas of the county. Evidently this arrangement suited residents, since plans to build a courthouse were not initiated until 1660, more than twenty years after the formation of the county. Similarly in Lancaster, early courts were usually held in the houses of justices, but steps were quickly taken to erect two courthouses, one at Corotoman and another upriver at Mr. William Underwood's plantation, the latter becoming the venue for Rappahannock's court at the formation of the county in 1656.[50]

Aside from settling local disputes and maintaining the peace, the most important function of courts was to provide an official record of county and residents' affairs. Particularly significant, for obvious reasons, was a record of land transactions. With the rapid growth of population after 1630, the county courts provided a convenient means of handling the voluminous business of recording patents, headrights, sales, and leases. To avoid a chaotic land rush, it was imperative for settlers to have recognized and acceptable procedures for seating land and registering their titles. A few examples illustrate the routine business that came before the courts. In autumn 1641, the Lower Norfolk court recorded the sale of 100 acres on the Elizabeth River by Captain John Sibsey to Robert Taylor and Henry Hawkins. Two years later Sibsey sold another 100 acres to Henry Catlin. Sibsey was land-rich, having patented 3,000 acres near Crany Point in 1635, and was evidently selling off part of his initial investment. The subdivision of large tracts was common. John Lankfield's original patent of 500 acres on Bennett's Creek, taken up in 1638, was divided between five men, owning 28–182 acres by 1673. Leasing land was also common, even from the early days of settlement. Henry Hill, a blacksmith of Lynnhaven, leased a tract (which he had rented from Mrs. Sarah Gookin) to Andrew Warner in 1644, agreeing, as part

50. Wheeler, "County Court in Colonial Virginia," in Daniels, ed., *Town and County*, 114; Cross, *The County Court, Norfolk County*, 49–53; Lower Norfolk County, Wills and Deeds A (1637–1646), B (1646–1651), C (1651–1656), D (1656–1666); Lancaster County, Deeds Etc., no. 1 (1652–1657); for the construction of courthouses, see 172, 201, 212, 233, 239–240; for the division of the county and the formation of Rappahannock County, see 310, 315–316, 317.

of the contract, to repair the house by making "a partition, two chimneys" and laying "the loft." [51]

On a more mundane level, reflecting the bulk of the court's business, Richard Owens was granted a certificate for 300 acres for transporting himself, his wife, and four servants in August 1650, and Richard Foster, who later moved to St. Mary's County, Maryland, received a certificate for 250 acres in November for himself, his wife and daughter, and two other persons. Having acquired the rights to land, planters then chose where they wished to settle, had the tract surveyed, and formally registered their claim or patent.[52] The turnover of land might have caused untold confusion without the court's involvement. Eppy Bonnison first appeared in Lancaster County in October 1652, when he was assigned 350 acres at "Muskeeto poynt" by Edward Patterson, who had acquired it from Rice Jones. In the following January he was granted a certificate for transporting six persons, including himself. There was then a lull for a few years before he bought 550 acres from Henry Rye on the south side of Haddaway's Creek near Fleet's Bay in late 1658, which he promptly assigned to Ever Peterson a few months later. In February 1659 he sold his tract at Muskeeto Point to Peterson but acquired the rights to 350 acres in the summer and bought 200 acres from William Thatcher in November. He last appears in a sale of 200 acres to Hugh Brent and Tobias Horton, both neighbors, in 1662.[53]

Captain Henry Fleet's history is equally complex. Like Bonnison, he arrived in the county about 1652 and during the next five years received certificates for fifty-one headrights. Between 1655 and 1657 he bought 2,700 acres, leased an unspecified amount from a neighbor, and sold 347 acres upriver in the freshes. Such transactions were typical, especially in the early years of settlement. As planters moved into new counties, land was sold to pay debts or realize profits or was transferred to consolidate holdings. The large volume of sales kept the land market fluid after the best tracts had been taken, gave smallholders a chance to get started, and encouraged the development of local social and economic exchanges.[54]

51. W. Stitt Robinson, Jr., *Mother Earth—Land Grants in Virginia, 1607–1699*, Jamestown 350th Anniversary Booklet (Williamsburg, Va., 1957); Nugent, comp., *Cavaliers and Pioneers*, I, 22; Lower Norfolk County, Minute Book (1637–1646), I, fols. 127–128, II, 37, Wills and Deeds E (1666–1675), fols. 142, 147; Rutman and Rutman, *A Place in Time: Middlesex County*, 73–76.

52. Lower Norfolk County, Wills and Deeds B (1646–1651), fols. 153, 155.

53. Lancaster County, Deeds Etc., no. 1 (1652–1657), 26, 39, no. 2 (1654–1666), 174–176, 188, 245–246, 363–364, Orders Etc. (1655–1666), 86.

54. Lancaster County, Deeds Etc., no. 1 (1652–1657), 89, 132, 186, 198, 229, no. 2

Orderly settlement of the land was a key responsibility of courts; another was the collection of annual levies. First introduced in 1619, tithes were rated on all males over the age of sixteen (and later on female slaves) and became a regular assessment in the 1620s. They met the cost of the administration at Jamestown and also local charges.[55] During the 1630s sheriffs were given the task of enforcing payment, but the courts appear to have played a prominent role in the supervision of the levy, drawing up lists of tithables and appointing collectors. Courts found it convenient to divide counties into a number of limits or precincts ("hundreds" in Maryland) comparable to English tithings, for which individual or sometimes a couple of collectors were responsible.

The earliest example in Lower Norfolk dates from 1646, but there is little reason to doubt that the system had been in operation for some time. Six precincts were originally created: Lynnhaven, Little Creek, the Eastern Branch of the Elizabeth River, the Western Branch, from Tanner's Creek to Broad Creek, and from Daniel Tanner's to Thomas Willoughby's. Two years later the boundaries were redrawn, splitting the growing population of Lynnhaven and combining the Eastern and Southern branches (Figure 12). Lancaster County was divided into fourteen precincts for the collection of the 1654/5 levy, representing small groups of five to thirteen households, indicating a more dispersed pattern of settlement than in Norfolk.[56] In both cases, the designation of precincts suggests the courts' early recognition of neighborhoods as well as a need for administrative units below the level of the county.

Precincts were not the only subdivisions within counties. Constables, who took on the broad policing powers of their English counterparts, aiding justices and sheriffs in their official duties, were also designated certain "lymitts." Initially, two or three men were appointed for entire counties. In

---

(1654–1666), 119, 144, Orders Etc. (1655–1666), 21, 34. Sixty thousand acres changed hands between 1653 and 1656, compared to 90,000 from 1657 to 1669 (Wheeler, "Lancaster County," 39). Inevitably, given rudimentary surveying techniques and the rapidity with which the land was taken up, numerous disputes arose about boundaries and size of tracts. See, for example, Lancaster County, Orders Etc. (1655–1666), 58, 164, 203, 208, Deeds Etc., no. 1 (1652–1657), 171, no. 2 (1654–1666), 370–371.

55. Bruce, *Institutional History*, II, 534–539, 556–569; Craven, *Southern Colonies*, 165–166; Hening, *Statutes*, I, 142, 143, 160, 171–172, 176–177, 196, 201, 220, 265–267, 342–343, 354, 356, 521, 551. For Maryland, see Lois Green Carr, "County Government in Maryland, 1689–1709" (Ph.D. diss., Harvard University, 1968), 410–432.

56. Lower Norfolk County, Wills and Deeds B (1646–1651), fols. 14, 92 (see also Minute Book [1637–1646], I, fol. 140); Lancaster County, Deeds Etc., no. 1 (1652–1657), 174–178.

1652, for example, William Clapham, Sr., and Mr. Anthony Jackson were responsible for the north and south side of the Rappahannock, respectively. Within a few years, however, men were appointed annually to serve specific areas that included but were not necessarily identical with precincts. Similarly, groups of households placed under the authority of particular militia officers in Lower Norfolk County might be located in several neighborhoods. Lieutenant Colonel Cornelius Lloyd commanded families inhabiting the area between Willoughby's plantation and the mouth of the Eastern Branch of the Elizabeth River together with householders of the Western Branch, comprising two distinct settlements.[57] Different subdivisions were therefore created for different purposes and generally took the form of one or more neighborhoods identified in the lists of tithables.

The most important subdivision below the county in Virginia was the parish. When the first court met in Lower Norfolk, two congregations had already been organized, one at Lynnhaven where services were held at Adam Thorowgood's house and the other at John Sibsey's, both served by the Reverend Mr. John Wilson. Inhabitants were not content to use private houses for divine services for long and quickly organized the construction of churches. By 1640 the two congregations were formally organized into separate parishes and officers appointed. Mr. Thomas Harrison, a young Puritan minister who replaced Wilson, was described as "well liked of" by "the pishoners of the Parrishe Church at mr Sewell's Pointe who to testifie their zeale and willingness to promote gods service" promised to pay him one hundred pounds a year. Besides preaching at the church on Sewell's Point, he agreed to "teach evie other Sunday amongst the Inhabitants of Ellizabeth River at the house of Robert Glascocke untill a convenyent Church be built and Erected there for gods Service." This arrangement was confirmed the following year by the governor and Council. Sewell's Point was the parish church, but a "Chappell of Ease" was ordered to be built on the Elizabeth River "at the Charges of paticular famalies Situated in the Aforesaid River by Reason of the Remote Plantations from the aforesaid pish Church." To distinguish between the two it was expressly stipulated that the vestry "shall ever heereafter be chossen and held" at the church. Two churchwardens, Lieutenant Francis Mason and Mr. Thomas Meares, one a justice and the other appointed to the bench a few years later, served Elizabeth River Parish in July

57. Joan R. Kent, *The English Village Constable, 1580–1642: A Social and Administrative Study* (Oxford, 1986); Lancaster County, Deeds Etc., no. 1 (1652–1657), 2, 44, 62, 141, 146, 269, 284, 285; Lower Norfolk County, Minute Book (1637–1646), I, fol. 130, II, fol. 49, Wills and Deeds C (1651–1656), fol. 21.

1640. In the eastern part of the county, Lynnhaven Parish church was built on Church Point near Thorowgood's plantation. Mr. Robert Powis officiated as minister, assisted by ten members of the vestry and two churchwardens.[58]

In Lancaster County the development of parishes was more complex. Alexander Cooke, clerk, was engaged to serve from March 1653, but little evidence survives from this early period. In August 1654 "the inhabitants being summoned therto" voted to divide the county into two parishes, an upper and a lower half, along the Moratico River, which was later the boundary between Lancaster and Rappahannock counties. About the same time, householders on the south side of the Rappahannock were beginning to group themselves into parishes. In November 1657, an "agreement made and concluded at the house of Mr. Henry Corbyn . . . between Samuel Cole Clark and the major part of the Inhabitants of the parish of Lancaster" provided for Cole to serve the new parishes of Lancaster and Piankatank, preaching on alternate Sundays and performing "all Christenings, burials, marriages, Churchings, and what else is proper to his office." A church was to be built on Boswell's Point, just to the south of Corbin's house, "with all convenient speed." Cole had earlier agreed to be the minister of the whole county, but the shortage of ministers in Virginia in the seventeenth century often led to one minister's serving several parishes. During the next ten years, further developments saw Lancaster and Piankatank united to form Christ Church Parish, and on the north bank "Christchurch" and St. Mary's "White Chappell" were created by 1669.[59]

The vestry, modeled on English precedent, was the governing body of

58. Mason, "Colonial Churches of Norfolk County," *WMQ*, 2d Ser., XXI (1941), 140–148; Lower Norfolk County, Minute Book (1637–1646), I, fols. 1–3, 18, 27, 50, 55, 59, 92, 104; Hening, *Statutes*, I, 154–161, 240–242. The chapel was about eight miles from the church.

59. Lancaster County, Deeds Etc., no. 1 (1652–1657), 41–42, 99, 152; Orders Etc. (1655–1666), 1, 6, 53, 56, 158; Deeds Etc., no. 2 (1654–1666), 141; C. G. Chamberlayne, ed., *The Vestry Book of Christ Church Parish, Middlesex County, Virginia, 1663–1767* (Richmond, Va., 1927), 1–8; Lancaster County, Orders Etc., no. 1 (1666–1680), 81, 140, 143, 156, 218, 252–253 (CW, microfilm, reel M 117-8).

Piankatank Parish was formed shortly before Lancaster Parish; see Rutman and Rutman, *A Place in Time: Middlesex County*, 52–53, 55–57. For the development of the Anglican church in Virginia generally, see George Maclaren Brydon, *Virginia's Mother Church and the Political Conditions under Which It Grew*, 2 vols. (Richmond, Va., 1947–1952); and William H. Seiler, "The Anglican Parish in Virginia," in James Morton Smith, ed., *Seventeenth-Century America: Essays in Colonial History* (Chapel Hill, N.C., 1959), 119–142.

the parish and had five principal duties: to secure ministers, organize the construction and maintenance of churches and chapels, oversee the moral welfare of the congregation, provide care for the elderly, sick, and poor, and set the parish levy. Some idea of the range of responsibilities can be gained from the vestry minutes of Christ Church Parish (formed in 1666 on the south side of the Rappahannock). At a meeting early in the new year, the fourteen vestrymen present ordered that John Blaike, "a poore Decriped Man of This prish," be granted one thousand pounds of tobacco "Towards The Maintenance of his Wife and Family." Mr. Richard Morris was "Dismist from being our Minister any longer," and Mr. Gabriell Comberland was appointed as "Reader" for the year: to "read Divine Service Each Sabboth Day in the fore-Noon" in the parish church " 'till we can be provided of a Minister." In 1672, the parish accounts reveal sixteen thousand pounds of tobacco paid to Mr. John Shepherd, the minister, ten thousand pounds to Mr. William Dudley "for Compleating the Chappell," two hundred pounds for the nursing of "a Bastard Childe," five hundred pounds to Robert Thompson "a poore Man," and four hundred pounds to David Barrick for two "prish Children." Payments were made also for communion wine, "Cleaning the Church Yard," and "work done to the Gleabe house."[60] Major expenses were the salaries of ministers and parish clerks (readers) and the building or repair of the church and chapels. Amounts paid for the upkeep of the poor and children on parish relief were never large, rarely more than a few thousand pounds of tobacco per year, generally less than 20 percent of the total charge.[61]

The relationship between the vestry and court was close. It was common for vestrymen to serve as justices, sheriffs, and burgesses, and the court's authority was vital for the creation and recognition of the vestry. There was frequently a good deal of overlap in their respective duties. Whereas, in England, churchwardens' presentments were made to a church court (archdeaconry or consistory), in Virginia they were forwarded to the county court via the grand jury. Both detected and punished a variety of moral lapses,

60. Bruce, *Institutional History*, I, 62–144; Virginia Bernhard, "Poverty and the Social Order in Seventeenth-Century Virginia," *VMHB*, LXXXV (1977), 148–149, 151; Chamberlayne, ed., *Vestry Book of Christ Church Parish*, 8–9, 20. The total charge for 1672 was 46,536 lbs. tobacco, or 81.5 lbs. per poll.

61. Chamberlayne, ed., *Vestry Book of Christ Church Parish*, 18–21, 23–24, 26, 29–36, 39–41, 44–48, 51, 56–60, 63–68, 71–76, 78–91. For other 17th-century vestry books, see Chamberlayne, ed., *The Vestry Book of Petsworth Parish, Gloucester County, Virginia, 1677–1793* (Richmond, Va., 1933); and Chamberlayne, ed., *The Vestry Book and Register of St. Peter's Parish, New Kent and James City Counties, Virginia, 1684–1786* (Richmond, Va., 1937).

notably the "heinous and odious sinne of fornicacon," bastardy, and defamation. Dual jurisdiction was reflected in punishments meted out to culprits.
Offenders were often required to ask the forgiveness of the court and do
penance in their parish church, but sometimes the punishment was more
severe. Agnes Holmes, for example, was convicted of speaking "certaine
slanderous words tending to the great disparragement of Captain Thomas
Willoughby Esq." by Lower Norfolk's court shortly before Christmas 1646.
She was ordered to receive fifteen lashes and "allsoe to weare a paper upon
her head with these words written in Capitall letters (vizt) for slander-
ing Capt. Willoughby Esq" for one hour at Lynnhaven and Elizabeth River
churches.[62]

Parish and county were also responsible for the upkeep of roads, bridges,
and ferries, an important concern in the early years of settlement. One of
the first measures passed by the Lower Norfolk court was the provision of
ferries, at public charge, across Tanner's Creek, "the two creeks at Lieutenant Mason's and the little creek at Linhaven." They were justified on the
grounds that "all or the most part of the inhabitants resident within this
County do sustain many inconveniences for want of free passage over these
creeks." In Lancaster County ferries were quickly established on Sunderland
Creek, and across the Rappahannock from Captain Brocas's plantation to
Major John Carter's on the Corotoman River.[63]

Planters used Indian paths and bridges to travel around their neighborhoods on foot, but early in the 1660s there appears to have been an effort
to improve overland communications. Justices were required to supervise
"the layeing out of highwayes . . . for the more convenient travelling of
strangers as alsoe the inhabitants" and, accordingly, appointed surveyors
of the highways to clear the roads. They probably followed old routes as
much as possible, but occasionally new roads were created. In response to
the petition of Nicholas Hale, Dominic Therriott, William Ball, Jr., "and the
rest of the neighbourhood," for example, the Lancaster court ordered that a
roadway for horse and foot be laid out from the "new church" to Mr. Fox's
mill dam. Lower Norfolk planters were less enthusiastic. In August 1669
the court commented on the "Extraordinary badnesse of the Severall high

62. Bruce, *Institutional History*, I, 73–93, 478–534; William H. Seiler, "The Anglican
Church: A Basic Institution of Local Government in Colonial Virginia," in Daniels,
ed., *Town and County*, 134–159; Hening, *Statutes*, II, 48, 51–53, 240; Lower Norfolk
County, Minute Book (1637–1646), I, fols. 5, 13, 37, 54, 69–70, 99–100, 101, 137, 187,
Wills and Deeds B (1646–1651), fol. 15.

63. Lower Norfolk County, Minute Book (1637–1646), I, fols. 18, 31, 192, 196, 209;
Lancaster County, Deeds Etc., no. 1 (1652–1657), 101, Orders Etc. (1655–1666), 3, 36.

ways of this County in some of wch noe man Eyther on foot or horseback Cann have Safe passage," the chief cause being the "greate neglect of the Survayers formerly Chosen by the Court." Population growth and an increasing volume of traffic made the improvement of roads a necessity, but, as in England, many householders were reluctant to give up their time for such laborious work.[64]

County and parish were the backbone of local society in Virginia. They provided political and religious organization, official sanction, and links with the wider society as well as the setting for vital events in the everyday lives of colonists. Despite adaptations, the duties of courts and vestries (and the principles that underpinned them) would have been broadly familiar to English immigrants and reminiscent of a variety of jurisdictions in England. Most important, local institutions instilled a sense of order and stability in societies where population turnover and mortality rates were high. Individuals might come and go, but institutions remained, and, consequently, methods of governance and patterns of response and obligation gradually emerged.[65]

Lower Norfolk and Lancaster counties suggest the factors that shaped local societies throughout the early Chesapeake: the mix of colonists from different parts of England and their contact with Indians, blacks, and other Europeans; the quality of soils and the lines of communication that dictated the growth of the local economy; and the development of neighborhoods and the establishment of formal political and religious institutions that administered local affairs. Differences in timing of settlement were reflected in the varying composition of immigrants. Counties founded in the 1630s had a higher proportion of settlers from other parts of Virginia (as opposed to directly from England) than counties created in the 1650s. Indian relations

64. For Indian paths, see Lower Norfolk County, Wills and Deeds C (1651–1656), fol. 15; Lancaster County, Deeds Etc. (1652–1657), no. 1, 226, (1654–1666), no. 2, 287. For the laying out of roads and appointment of surveyors, see Lancaster County, Orders Etc. (1655–1666), 224, 226, no. 1 (1666–1680), 88, 120, 202, 209, 242, 298; Lower Norfolk County, Wills and Deeds D (1656–1666), fols. 363, 410. For complaints, see Lower Norfolk County, Wills and Deeds E (Orders) (1666–1675), fols. 29, 38, 103, 112.

65. Lower Norfolk County, Minute Book (1637–1646), I, fols. 159–160; Lois Green Carr, "Sources of Political Stability and Upheaval in Seventeenth-Century Maryland," *Md. Hist. Mag.*, LXXIX (1984), 44–70; J. P. Horn, "Moving On in the New World: Migration and Out-Migration in the Seventeenth-Century Chesapeake," in Peter Clark and David Souden, eds., *Migration and Society in Early Modern England* (London, 1987), 183–185, 195–196.

and the numbers of black slaves imported had a crucial influence on how societies evolved. During the second half of the century, settlers' fears of Indian attacks were much more immediate in the frontier settlements of the Northern Neck than in the lower James basin, for example. Large planters located in prime tobacco-growing regions along the Rappahannock turned to slave labor much more quickly than planters in marginal areas of the Southside.[66]

The initial years of settlement had an enduring impact on county development. Early neighborhoods became foci for subsequent settlement as new arrivals sought land in proximity to established plantations. Population increase led small groups of households to evolve into parishes and, in some cases, separate counties. Among early immigrants, wealthy planters laid claim to the best lands and consolidated their political power. Without exaggerating the longevity or political influence of locally prominent families, it is striking that Thorowgoods, Willoughbys, and Masons continued to serve on the Lower Norfolk bench throughout the rest of the century, just as Carters, Balls, and Foxes regularly served Lancaster as burgesses and justices in the second half of the seventeenth and in the early eighteenth centuries. Opportunity for newcomers with capital and connections remained, but early arrival in a new county undoubtedly gave rich planter-merchants an advantage. The number of wealthy immigrants who moved into a region had an important bearing on local society. From the beginning, the Rappahannock attracted more wealthy men than the lower James; hence, social divisions were more prominent.[67]

If the early years stamped a certain character on future developments, far-reaching social and economic changes that occurred after 1660 irrevocably altered the fabric of pioneer settlements. The continuing influx of settlers and expansion of settlement in the tidewater, the vicissitudes of the tobacco economy, the widening gulf between rich and poor, the increasing volume of African slave importations, war, and social unrest were to change society profoundly at local and provincial levels by the final decades of the century.

66. Carr, "County Government in Maryland," 313, 528–538, and chap. 7. Anglican parishes were not established until 1692.

67. Horn, biographical files, Lower Norfolk County and Lancaster County; Darrett B. Rutman and Anita H. Rutman, *A Place in Time: Explicatus* (New York, 1984), table 28, 129, 130; Morgan, *American Slavery, American Freedom*, 227–230; Wheeler, "Lancaster County," 101–104.

Three

Comparative Themes

5

The Social Web: Family, Kinship,

and Community

"The naturalest and first conjunction of two towards the making of a further societie of continuance," wrote Sir Thomas Smith in 1565, "is of the husband and of the wife. . . . And without this societie of man, and woman, the kinde of man would not long endure." The formation of new societies in Virginia and Maryland depended above all on the family. In the Chesapeake, as in England, the family was the means by which society reproduced itself, the primary unit of production and consumption, and the major agency for the upbringing and education of children. It provided individuals with identity, support, and protection as well as the legitimate fulfillment of emotional and physical needs. In less happy cases, it was an arena for frustration, bitterness, and violence. Everywhere throughout the Anglo-American world of the seventeenth century the family was fundamental.[1]

That colonial society, once past the stage of trading outposts or military garrisons, was based on the family unit is not surprising. Civil society was unthinkable without it. The problem was how best to achieve settled family life in the uncertain conditions encountered. In New England a large proportion of immigrants arrived in families; and, in the absence of serious

1. Ralph A. Houlbrooke, *The English Family, 1450–1700* (London, 1984), 19; Keith Wrightson, *English Society, 1580–1680* (London, 1982), 66; Lawrence Stone, *Road to Divorce; England, 1530–1987* (Oxford, 1990); Darrett B. Rutman, "The Social Web: A Prospectus for the Study of Early American Community," in William L. O'Neill, ed., *Insights and Parallels: Problems and Issues of American Social History* (Minneapolis, Minn., 1973), 71.

demographic disruption and wholesale servitude, new households prolif-
erated, and population grew rapidly. Society in the plantation colonies to
the south and in the islands was very different. Immigration was dominated
by young, single males. High mortality rates, the unbalanced sex ratio, and
relatively late age at marriage dictated by servitude acted in concert to restrict family formation and limit the number of children per household. Early
death of parents meant that many children were brought up in the homes
of stepparents or friends; few adults saw all their children reach majority.[2]
In the face of such formidable obstacles it might be wondered whether any
meaningful family life was possible in early Virginia and Maryland. But the
degree of disruption should not be exaggerated, nor the differences between
Old and New World experience overdrawn. Settlers adapted to the environment as best they could by modifying the attitudes and practice of England.
Patterns of behavior associated with sex, betrothal, and marriage were not
developed anew in the Chesapeake; they were variants of English behavior, although not always what the authorities, church and state, deemed
acceptable.

Sex and Marriage

In an ideal world, at least according to moralists and the church, young
men and women would be virtuous and chaste before marriage. After an
extended period of courtship properly supervised by elders and peers, and
when the male was able to support a wife, the couple might decide to marry.
Betrothal was followed by publication of banns, a formal ceremony in the

2. On New England: Jack P. Greene, *Pursuits of Happiness: The Social Development
of Early Modern British Colonies and the Formation of American Culture* (Chapel Hill,
N.C., 1988), 19–20; Terry L. Anderson and Robert Paul Thomas, "White Population,
Labor Force, and Extensive Growth of the New England Economy in the Seventeenth
Century," *Journal of Economic History*, XXXIII (1973), 639–642.

On the South: Russell R. Menard, "Immigrants and Their Increase: The Process
of Population Growth in Early Colonial Maryland," in Aubrey C. Land *et al.*, eds.,
Law, Society, and Politics in Early Maryland (Baltimore, 1977), 88–110; Lorena S. Walsh,
" 'Till Death Us Do Part': Marriage and Family in Seventeenth-Century Maryland,"
in Thad W. Tate and David L. Ammerman, eds., *The Chesapeake in the Seventeenth Century: Essays on Anglo-American Society* (Chapel Hill, N.C., 1979), 126–152; Darrett B.
Rutman and Anita H. Rutman, " 'Now-Wives and Sons-in-Law': Parental Death in
a Seventeenth-Century Virginia County," in Tate and Ammerman, eds., *Chesapeake
in the Seventeenth Century*, 153–182; Rutman and Rutman, *A Place in Time: Middlesex
County, Virginia, 1650–1750* (New York, 1984), 113–120.

parish church, celebration, and consummation. The holy state of wedlock, a union made before God, was for life and to be undertaken only after careful thought and guidance from parents, kin, and friends, giving due weight to considerations of property and family status as well as love and affection. Marriage and the creation of a household represented a vital transition for newlyweds from dependence to independence and conferred a higher social position in the community and new responsibilities. Husbands took their place in a hierarchy of heads of households and were responsible for the maintenance of their families, their moral and religious supervision, discipline, payment of tithes and taxes, and various services to the local community. Wives were primarily responsible for the care and upbringing of children, running the household, supplementing the family income, and providing comfort and support for their spouse.

Marriage was viewed as a partnership, but an unequal one. Scripture and conventional values reinforced the dominant role of the male. Wives were supposed to be obedient, submissive, and wholly dependent on their husbands, "both in judgement and will." The authority of the husband over his family was the same in principle as that of a monarch over his people. William Gouge asserted in the 1620s that the husband was "as a Priest unto his wife. . . . He is the highest in the family, and hath both authority over all and the charge of all is committed to his charge; he is as a king in his owne house." English society in the seventeenth century was traditionally conceived in terms of a hierarchy of families, from rich to poor, governed according to similar precepts.[3]

In reality, as contemporaries realized and to a certain extent accepted, sexual behavior, marriage, and family relations were far from uniform and only approximated the ideal. Attitudes toward sex and family life in the Chesapeake and England were influenced by tensions between conventional wisdom and state mores on the one hand, and social position and local experience on the other. The extent to which social reality deviated from the ideal can be assessed from a number of perspectives. In neither society

3. Houlbrooke, *English Family*, chaps. 4–7; Peter Laslett, *The World We Have Lost* (London, 1965), chap. 1; Christopher Hill, "Sex, Marriage, and the Family in England," *Economic History Review*, LXXX (1978), 450–463; John R. Gillis, *For Better, for Worse: British Marriages, 1600 to the Present* (Oxford, 1985), chaps. 1–2; Lawrence Stone, *The Family, Sex, and Marriage in England, 1500–1800* (London, 1977), 158; Susan Dwyer Amussen, *An Ordered Society: Gender and Class in Early Modern England* (Oxford, 1988), chap. 2; Wrightson, *English Society*, 90, and chaps. 3–4; Martin Ingram, *Church Courts, Sex, and Marriage in England, 1570–1640* (Cambridge, 1987), chap. 4; Alan Macfarlane, *Marriage and Love in England, 1300–1840* (Oxford, 1986), chap. 13.

was marriage universal. About 10 percent of women remained unmarried throughout their lives in England, and a much greater proportion, perhaps a third at any one time, were either widows or spinsters. In Virginia and Maryland, owing to the shortage of women, the roles were reversed: 20–30 percent of male testators in various parts of the tidewater died bachelors, and 12–14 percent went to the grave as widowers. Eligible spinsters and widows were virtually unknown.[4] Emotions usually reserved for wives and children were either suppressed or invested in close friendships and relations with quasi kin.[5]

In England most people followed a number of stages to matrimony. First, the decision to initiate courtship was usually taken by the couple themselves, not by parents or family, and was strongly influenced by personal attraction, affection, or love as well as by considerations of property. The freedom of individuals to choose their own prospective spouses had a long history and can be traced back at least until the end of the twelfth century. Marriage was conceived as essentially involving only the couple concerned; "no rights of either lordship or family" were acknowledged as binding. In contrast to other parts of Europe, where Roman law endowed parents with considerable formal power over their offspring, in England parents could neither prevent their children from marrying nor force them to marry against their will. As long as the couple were old enough (fourteen years for men and twelve for women), no one could legally prevent them from marrying.

4. Wrightson, *English Society*, 67; Stone, *Road to Divorce*, chaps. 2–3; Gillis, *For Better, for Worse*, 11; E. A. Wrigley and R. S. Schofield, *The Population History of England, 1541–1871: A Reconstruction* (Cambridge, Mass., 1981), 257–265; Walsh, " 'Till Death Us Do Part,' " in Tate and Ammerman, eds., *Chesapeake in the Seventeenth Century*, 127. In Lower Norfolk County, Virginia, bachelors constituted 20.6% of male testators and widowers 13.6%, and in Lancaster 29.4% and 12.5%, respectively. In southern Maryland, about a quarter of testators died unmarried. These figures suggest considerable regional variation.

5. Russell R. Menard and Lorena S. Walsh, "The Demography of Somerset County, Maryland: A Progress Report," *Newberry Papers in Family and Community History*, 81-2 (1981); Lancaster County, Virginia, Deeds Etc., no. 2 (1654–1666), 42; Lower Norfolk County, Virginia, Wills and Deeds C (1651–1656), fol. 18, E (1666–1675), fols. 78–79 (Colonial Williamsburg, microfilm, reels M 1363-1, 1365-17, 18; references to CW microfilm will be given only with the first citation). In Lower Norfolk County, of 252 wills probated between 1639 and 1689, 21 (8.3%) were widows, 2 (.8%) were wives, and 1 (.4%) was a single woman. In Lancaster, 4.2% of 143 estates probated between 1652 and 1699 belonged to widows. There were no wives or single women. On the importance of emotional bonds between friends and peers, see Gillis, *For Better, for Worse*, 34–35.

In most cases, however, the choice of a partner and courtship tended to be guided by the advice of parents and friends. Courtship fulfilled the important purpose of allowing a man and woman to get to know one another before the irrevocable step of marriage. Time spent together "eating, and walking, working, and playing, talking, and laughing, and chiding too," John Dod and Robert Clever wrote in 1612, enabled a man to "know all his wives qualities" and her to "perceive her husband's dispositions, and inclination." During this period it became clear whether the couple were committed to one another and whether they were compatible. Courtship followed a common pattern, starting with "talking," then "walking," and, only much later, evolving to the most intimate stage of "keeping company." Small gifts, or love tokens, were often exchanged as testimony of their earnestness and to bind themselves one to the other. These took a variety of forms: pieces of silver, rings, whistles, coins, gloves, handkerchiefs, "carved knitting sticks, spindles, and bobbins," and, of course, love letters. The exchange of gifts was important and was construed as a formal declaration of intent to marry, that is, as a form of engagement.[6]

Steps toward marriage, like the marriage itself, were therefore largely conducted by people themselves. It was not necessary to be married in church or to be married by a clergyman; all that was required was the mutual consent of both partners freely given. In fact, technically the church ceremony was merely a public expression of the private betrothal that constituted the marriage proper. Across the medieval and early modern periods the church made strenuous efforts to bring the whole ritual of marriage under its control. But it was only partially successful. If the majority of people by Elizabeth's reign accepted the desirability of a church wedding to confirm publicly the solemn union of a couple, a large minority eschewed the standard marriage in their parish church. Others combined private betrothal and public ceremony.

William Whiteway, for example, "concluded the marriage" with Eleanor Parkins, his "best beloved," in early April 1620. This, however, was only the beginning. A month later, he noted in his diary that they were "bewrothed in my father Parkins his hall about 9 of the clock at night, [by] Mr. John White in the presence of our parents." And, finally, on June 14 they were married by Mr. John White "in the Church of the Holy Trinity in Dorchester, in the presence of the greatest part of the town." English canon law recognized that vows made in the presence of witnesses without solemnization in church

6. Macfarlane, *Marriage and Love*, 124–131, 293–304; Gillis, *For Better, for Worse*, 31, 33.

were a binding, if irregular, form of union. Anxiety about the expense of a wedding or about the attitude of parents, masters, and parish worthies may have induced couples to enact their own marriages ("spousals") and avoid the church altogether. Such couples were "married but not churched." How many people chose not to marry in church is impossible to determine, but in some areas, especially regions where manufactures were located, the practice was common. In Tetbury, Gloucestershire, between 1696 and 1699, "almost half of the marriages entered in the register were in an irregular form." According to one authority, by the early eighteenth century irregular unions and marriages by license ("little weddings") were "almost as numerous as big weddings." Throughout England it was possible for couples to bypass the local church and be married outside of their neighborhood by clergymen who did not scruple to perform clandestine marriages or, if they could afford it, by opting for a license.[7]

Whatever form of marriage was adopted, betrothal was often seen as legitimizing sexual intercourse. During the sixteenth and seventeenth centuries between 10 and 30 percent of brides in English rural parishes were pregnant at marriage. While neither the church nor state tolerated sexual intercourse before marriage, popular attitudes were evidently more flexible.[8]

7. This paragraph relies heavily on John R. Gillis, *For Better, for Worse*, 16–17, 38, 50, 84–98; Gillis, "Married but Not Churched: Plebeian Sexual Relations and Marital Nonconformity in Eighteenth-Century Britain," in Robert P. Maccubbin, ed., *Unauthorized Sexual Behavior during the Enlightenment (Eighteenth-Century Life*, IX [1985]), 31–41; Lawrence Stone, *Uncertain Unions: Marriage in England, 1660–1753* (Oxford, 1992); Stone, *Road to Divorce*, chap. 4; and Macfarlane, *Marriage and Love*, 309–317. Martin Ingram argues that spousals were not commonly accepted by any social group as properly constituted marriage and that they declined across the 16th and 17th centuries even as a preliminary to church weddings. The increasing incidence of clandestine marriages, he suggests, "reflected the enhanced social and legal importance of solemnisation, which made eloping couples eager to secure at least the semblance of a church wedding." See *Church Courts*, 131–134. For Tetbury, see E. A. Wrigley, "Clandestine Marriage in Tetbury in the Late Seventeenth Century," *Local Population Studies*, no. 10 (Spring 1973), 16.

8. P.E.H. Hair, "Bridal Pregnancy in Rural England in Earlier Centuries," *Population Studies*, XX (1966–1967), 233–243; Hair, "Bridal Pregnancy in Earlier Rural England Further Examined," *Population Studies*, XXIV (1970), 59–70; R. M. Smith, "Marriage Processes in the English Past: Some Continuities," in Lloyd Bonfield *et al.*, eds., *The World We Have Gained: Histories of Population and Social Structure* (Oxford, 1986), 90, 99; Macfarlane, *Marriage and Love*, 304–307. For a contrary view, see Martin Ingram, *Church Courts*, chaps. 4, 6–8; and Ingram, "The Reform of Popular Culture? Sex and

Plenty of examples of informal unions and premarital sex survive, mainly from records of unfortunates who found themselves before the church courts. John Morris of Frampton on Severn was presented in 1625 "for begetting his wife w[i]th childe *ante nuptias.*" A few years later Richard and Ann Kite of East Sutton, Kent, were charged with "incontinency before their marriage," but claimed that they were "contracted together long before their offence comitted." Similarly, Thomas Barker and Elizabeth Dove of Bersted, Kent, presented for the same offense in 1621, objected that they were "lawfully contracted together in matrimonye and were man and wyffe." Edward Webb's case was somewhat different. Accused in 1632 of living "incontinently" with Mary Cossham of Marden in the Weald and getting her with child, he claimed that "before carnall knowledge of her body he had an intencon to marry w[i]th her and for that purpose p'cured a licence out of the Com[missary]'s Court at Cant[erbury] to have beene before her deliverie married to her in Malden Church." He later found out, however, that Cossham "had had a childe formerly unlawfully begotten on her body in Sussex w[hi]ch much altered his purpose."[9]

In seventeenth-century England, not one, but several types of "marriage" existed: spousals, clandestine marriages, and church weddings; the conventional "big marriage" did not have a monopoly. Among all classes the church wedding was probably the preferred mode, and the importance of a public celebration should not be underestimated, both in official legitimization and community recognition. But the survival throughout the period and into the eighteenth and nineteenth centuries of "little weddings" suggests that alternative views of marriage and sexual union persisted, particularly among the lower classes, who may have had a more relaxed attitude than the church or respectable propertied classes.

To what extent did conditions in the Chesapeake—the pressures of the sex ratio, rapid population turnover, large numbers of servants, and lack of family ties—alter attitudes and behavior toward courtship and marriage? Most modern historians have stressed the "profound disruption in the pat-

---

Marriage in Early Modern England," in Barry Reay, ed., *Popular Culture in Seventeenth-Century England* (London, 1985), 129–165.

9. Gloucester Diocesan Registers, Dursley Deanery, 1619–1641, June 27, 1625 (vol. CXXXVII), Gloucestershire Record Office; Consistory Court, Ex Officio, Coperta and Detecta, Deanery of Sutton, 1620–1635, 5, 213, 216, Canterbury Cathedral Library (CCL), Canterbury, Kent.

terns of family life" and the development of a "milieu of relative sexual freedom," reflected in high rates of bridal pregnancy and bastardy, short marriages, and pervasive orphanhood. In Somerset County, Maryland, in the second half of the century, more than a third (36.8 percent) of immigrant women were pregnant at marriage, and illegitimate births were at least two or three times the figure common in England. Servants were particularly vulnerable. A fifth of all female servants in Charles County, Maryland, were presented to the court between 1658 and 1705 for bearing bastards. In numerous cases throughout the tidewater the father of the child was the servant's master. Simon Cornix, of Lower Norfolk, was fined five hundred pounds of tobacco in 1653 for getting his "woeman servant" with child. Clement Theobald of Lynnhaven was presented by the churchwardens of his parish "for living and continuing in apparent fornication" with Elizabeth Hall, his servant, "so as a bastard son was lately born of her." She received twenty lashes for "divers misdemeanours and apparent whoredom." The problem was sufficiently common to force the Virginia Assembly to address the issue in 1662. Women bearing bastards usually served an extra two years, which penalty inclined "some dissolute masters" to get "their maides with child, and yet claime the benefitt of their service." Concerned that freeing women in such cases would encourage "loose persons to lay all their bastards to their masters," the Assembly required that offending servants be placed in the custody of the churchwardens and sold for two years, the money going to the parish.[10]

10. Walsh, " 'Till Death Us Do Part,' " in Tate and Ammerman, eds., *Chesapeake in the Seventeenth Century*, 126–127, 128; Lois Green Carr and Lorena S. Walsh, "The Planter's Wife: The Experience of White Women in Seventeenth-Century Maryland," *William and Mary Quarterly*, 3d Ser., XXXIV (1977), 542–543, 547–549, 553–554; Rutman and Rutman, "Now-Wives and Sons-in-Law,' " in Tate and Ammerman, eds., *Chesapeake in the Seventeenth Century*, 158–167; Menard and Walsh, "Demography of Somerset County," *Newberry Papers in Family and Community History*, 81-2 (1981). Daniel Blake Smith considers similarities between Old World and New World experience in "Mortality and Family in the Colonial Chespeake," *Journal of Interdisciplinary History*, VIII (1977–1978), 425–427.

On Somerset County: Menard and Walsh, "Demography of Somerset County," *Newberry Papers in Family and Community History*, 81-2 (1981); Peter Laslett and Karla Oosterveen, "Long Term Trends in Bastardy in England . . . ," *Population Studies*, XXVII (1973), 267, 274, 276–280; Keith Wrightson, "The Nadir of English Illegitimacy in the Seventeenth Century," in Peter Laslett *et al.*, eds., *Bastardy and Its Comparative History* (London, 1980), 177–179. Bastardy in four parishes in southern Gloucestershire ranged between zero and 7.2% of all births, 1601–1700. The mean ratio was 1.8% (I am indebted to John S. Moore for this information).

If sexual relations outside marriage were more widespread in Virginia and Maryland than England, attitudes toward sex and marriage did not necessarily differ radically. Such behavior can be largely attributed to the peculiar demographic pressures of the early Chesapeake, the huge numbers of servants, and the lack of ministers and churches. In these conditions settlers adopted popular forms of courtship and marriage prevalent in the parent society, which frequently brought them into conflict with colonial authorities attempting to enforce the letter of English law.

The fact that servants were not allowed to marry without the consent of their masters or mistresses posed an especially thorny problem in view of the relative shortage of women and the length of service involved. "Secret marriages" between servants (probably in the form of an exchange of vows in front of witnesses without reference to masters, the church, or local magistrates) were outlawed by the Virginia Assembly in 1643. Elopement was another option for lovesick swains not prepared to wait until the end of their own or their partner's period of service. Michael Lawrence was charged by the Lower Norfolk court in 1650 with "conveying Rose, Mrs Phillipps maid sarvant, to Lynhaven with an intent to have Married her." To prevent clandestine or irregular unions, ministers were instructed to conduct all marriages "according to the laws of England" and "booke of common prayer": banns were to be published in the parish (or parishes), of the couple's usual abode on three successive Sundays, and the ceremony was to be conducted "only betweene the howers of eight and twelve in the forenoone." An act of 1662 spelled out the consequences for disobedience. Any "pretended marriage hereafter made by any other than a minister be reputed null, and the children borne out of such marriage of the parents, be esteemed illegitmate and the parents suffer such punishment as by the laws prohibiting fornication ought to be inflicted." Nevertheless, the problem of clandestine marriages persisted.[11]

Undoubtedly, women servants in the Chesapeake were more vulnerable

---

On servants: Lower Norfolk County, Wills and Deeds C (1651–1656), fol. 46; Minute Book, transcript of Wills and Deeds A, 2 vols. (1637–1646), II, fols. 110, 113 (CW, microfilm, reel M 1365-2); William Waller Hening, ed., *The Statutes at Large: Being a Collection of All the Laws of Virginia . . .* , 13 vols. (1809–1823; Charlottesville, Va., 1969), II, 114–115, 167.

11. Hening, *Statutes*, I, 156–157, 252–253, II, 28, 49–51; Lower Norfolk, Wills and Deeds B (1646–1651), 147 (CW, microfilm, reel M 1365-17); H. R. McIlwaine, ed., *Journals of the House of Burgesses of Virginia, 1659/60–1693* (Richmond, Va., 1914), 60; Kathleen Mary Brown, "Gender and the Genesis of a Race and Class System in Virginia, 1630–1750" (Ph.D. diss., University of Wisconsin–Madison, 1990), 132–137.

to sexual exploitation than their English counterparts (although studies of Somerset and Essex, England, reveal that female servants were also often the victims of the unwanted sexual attention of their masters). Not uncommonly, masters married their servants—an arrangement that may have suited both parties—and sometimes a planter might buy a woman's remaining time, again, with her consent. In these cases, as in England, the crucial point was that consent was freely given. No one could be forced into marriage. Since many women servants doubtless arrived with an intention to marry sooner or later, if a suitable match could be made with a free man who was willing to buy her freedom, she may have considered the opportunity too good to miss. The high incidence of premarital sex reflects not only illicit relations between servants but also betrothals between servant women and free men.[12]

Courtship followed a pattern similar to that in England. Thomas White of Maryland told John Piper that he "Came to Gather Some Hasell nuts for Margaret William Marshalls maid" and that they "had past their faith and troth together." He told another neighbor that he had "been in Leage" with her for "two yeares or thereabouts," and, when he asked "her good will," she said "She Loved him." White intended to "buy her off" with three hogsheads of tobacco he had saved, but "if it pleased God" that he "Should dye, before he married . . . he would give her all he had." Somewhat more dramatically, Grace Molden, "the now Wife of Henry Mitchel," "confidently declared" before the provincial court that Mitchel "did not Steale her away (as the Court is informed) But rather more willingly shee went away w[i]th him; then hee did w[i]th her: for that shee was before th[a]t time resolved to marry him, bearing love and affection to him." Love and mutual attraction were key criteria for marriage to the extent that both couples were prepared to challenge the authority of the bride's master.[13] In view of contemporary practice in England, lack of parental guidance for most young couples in Virginia and Maryland was less important than might at first appear. Friends and fellow servants played the same role in giving advice and support that their counterparts did in English society. What mattered most was the couple's determination to marry.

Chesapeake legislators had no more success than English authorities in eradicating irregular marriages. Bridgett Nelson deposed before the Provin-

12. J. A. Sharpe, *Early Modern England: A Social History, 1500–1760* (London, 1987), 44; Carr and Walsh, "Planter's Wife," *WMQ*, 3d Ser., XXXIV (1977), 549–550.

13. William Hand Browne *et al.*, eds., *Archives of Maryland*, 72 vols. to date (Baltimore, 1883–), XLI, 26–27, 336–338 (hereafter cited as *Md. Archives*).

cial Court of Maryland in 1661 that she had exchanged a "peice of Silver" with Quintin Counyer, who had promised to marry her. Before the marriage could be officially sanctioned, however, Counyer fell sick and "did upon his death Bedd relate that he . . . was marryed before God" to Nelson "by breakeing of the aforesd Silver Betweene them." Four years later, Gils Tomkinson of Charles County, accused of fathering an illegitimate child, claimed that the woman he lived with "is and was befor the Getting of her with Child his lawfull wiffe and . . . that his marriage was as good as possibly it Coold bee maed by the Protestants hee beeing one becaus that befor that time and ever since thear hath not bin a protestant Minister in the Province and that to Matrimony is only necessary the parties Consent and Publication thearof befor a Lawfull Churchman and for their Consents it is Apparent and for the worlds Satisfaction thay hear publish them selves Man and wife till death them doe part."[14] Mutual consent, the publication of their vows before a respectable "churchman," social recognition, and commitment for life were the key requirements for marriage in Tomkinson's eyes.

Virginia's rulers found themselves in the same dilemma. They insisted that marriages, other than by license, should be conducted by the Anglican church but recognized that "the scarsity of ministers" made such unions "(att present) impossible." Whether or not a minister was available, many couples did not care to go to the trouble or expense of a formal wedding. Lower Norfolk's grand jury regularly presented men and women for "liveing together unmarried." James Steward was charged on "suspicion of Incontynencie w[i]th Alice Young they liveing together" in December 1654. Richard Barrett and Ellenor "his p'tended wife" were presented "for livinge in adultery under p'tence of marriage" a few years later, as were Will Cooke and Eliza Copeland. Unlawful marriages were sometimes the result of a casual attitude toward illegal separations from former unions. Francis Plomer was accused in 1678 of unlawfully marrying a woman whose husband was still alive, and Robert Woody lived with Daniel Lenier's spouse "as Comon man and wife." Lawrence Arnold was presented the following year "for having of two wifes and his wife for haveing another husband."[15]

14. Walsh, " 'Till Death Us Do Part,' " in Tate and Ammerman, eds., *Chesapeake in the Seventeenth Century*, 129–130; *Md. Archives*, XLI, 456–457, LIII, 599.

15. Hening, ed., *Statutes*, II, 28, 54–55; Lower Norfolk County, Minute Book (1637–1646), II, fol. 141, Wills and Deeds C (1651–1656), fols. 113–114, D (1656–1666), fols. 392, 435 (CW, microfilm, reel M 1365-18), Deed Book, no. 4 (1675–1686), fols. 40, 48, 119 (CW, microfilm, reel M 1365-1). After 1661, couples could obtain a license from their local court if sufficient security was given that there was no lawful impediment

Far more common were charges of "Incontynencie" before marriage. Of twenty-six separate presentments made to the Lower Norfolk court in 1654, more than a third were for prenuptial sex. From the court's point of view, it had been a long-standing problem. One of the earliest cases to come before the bench concerned Sarah Parfitt, a widow, who "being big with child and destitute of any place of abiding" petitioned to marry Thomas Hughes, the reputed father, "man servant" of Captain Thomas Willoughby. Accordingly, they were ordered to be married by Mr. John Wilson, minister of Elizabeth River Parish, Captain Willoughby giving Sarah a bushel of corn for her maintenance and allowing Hughes "to go to the said Sarah Parfit at convenient times, not hindering his master's business."[16]

This was an unusually lenient and humane response, but in following years the court was not so accommodating. Christopher Burroughs and Mary Soames, his wife, were presented for having their first child four months after their marriage and ordered to do penance. Similarly, Thomas and Eady Tooker were found "guilty of fornication" early in 1641 and ordered to do penance in their parish church "the next sabbath the minister preacheth . . . standing in the middle ally of the said church upon a stool in a white sheet, and a white wand in their hands, all the time of divine service and shall say after the minister such words as he shall deliver unto them before the congregation." One can sense the resentment of couples who, although married, still found themselves convicted of moral offenses because they began sexual relations after betrothal instead of after obtaining a license or church ceremony. Eady Tooker, for example, evidently did not believe she had committed "the foul crime of fornication." When admonished by the minister to be sorry for her offense, she "like a most obstinate and graceless person, did cut and mangle the sheet wherein she did penance," for which she was sentenced to twenty lashes and to repeat her penance "according to the tenor of the said spiritual laws and form of the Church of England in that case provided."[17]

Immigration, the breaking of ties with home communities, the constant coming and going of settlers, mariners, and merchants, the shortage of

---

to marriage. Before 1660, couples had to apply directly to the governor for a license (Hening, ed., *Statutes*, I, 156–157).

16. Lower Norfolk County, Wills and Deeds C (1651–1656), fols. 113–114, Minute Book (1637–1646), I, fol. 3.

17. Lower Norfolk County, Minute Book (1637–1646) I, fols. 85, 100, 101, 112–113, 122. See also Wills and Deeds D (1656–1666), fols. 392, 417, E (Orders) (1666–1675), fols. 1–2 (CW, microfilm, reel M 1365-18), Deed Book, no. 4 (1675–1686), fols. 40, 48, 119.

women, and the vulnerability of female servants—all unquestionably provided opportunities for those so inclined to indulge in a form of sexual license possible in England only in the larger ports, towns, and cities. How many women found themselves in the position of Joane Langford, who sued George Harris of Charles County in 1668 "for begetting a Bastard Child on her Body, and for Nonperformance of his promise to Marry her," or Mrs. Susan Warren, widow, who, believing Captain William Mitchell was sincere in his promises to marry her, later found he was already married, is impossible to determine.[18] But despite the potential for a looser sexual milieu, there was no fundamental breakdown of conventional attitudes toward marriage, if by conventional we embrace popular as well as official mores.

Official responses were governed by the imperative of maintaining social order and the desire to conform, as closely as possible, to spiritual and temporal laws in England. Colonial legislators found themselves struggling with the same problem that had bedeviled English courts since medieval times: while canon law recognized irregular marriages, common law did not. The ambiguity that surrounded informal unions could be a fertile source of litigation and ultimately oblige the parish to support abandoned wives and children. A church wedding, solemnized by a minister, became the critical test of a legal marriage, enforceable at law. From this perspective, colonial rulers' insistence on marriage according to English laws can be viewed as an effort to reduce the number and cost of unmarried women and bastards, precisely the same concern of parish officials burdened with increasing numbers of poor in England. It can also be seen as an effort to control the servant population and guarantee that a servant remained a subordinate member of the master's household, a dependent member of the planter's family. That elites were intent upon a "reformation of manners" comparable to the efforts of godly rulers in English parishes such as Terling, Essex, and Cranbrook in the Weald seems, on the face of it, unlikely.[19]

There is little evidence in the Chesapeake of a sustained campaign against

18. *Md. Archives*, X, 173–185, LIII, 141. Mitchell was charged with atheism, blasphemy, and inducing an abortion as well as bigamy.

19. David Levine and Keith Wrightson, *Poverty and Piety in an English Village: Terling, 1525–1700* (New York, 1979), 127–133; Wrightson and Levine, "The Social Context of Illegitimacy in Early Modern England," in Laslett *et al.*, eds., *Bastardy and Its Comparative History*, 158–175; Martin Ingram, "Reform of Popular Culture?" in Reay, ed., *Popular Culture*, 140–146; Ingram, "Religion, Communities, and Moral Discipline in Late Sixteenth- and Early Seventeenth-Century England: Case Studies," in Kaspar von Greyerz, ed., *Religion and Society in Early Modern Europe, 1500–1800* (London, 1985), 177–193.

moral abuses by Puritan magistrates and local officials, who, given the drive against Nonconformity by Sir William Berkeley in Virginia and the Catholic tenor of Maryland, were in any case relatively rare. More likely is that Virginia governors saw the Anglican church, backed by the county courts, as the principal vehicle for the enforcement of moral discipline. The touchstone of acceptable behavior as far as they were concerned was, not some idealized godly society, but conformity to the English church and common law.

Family and Inheritance

A distinctive feature of marriage along the tobacco coast was its short duration. Owing to high mortality rates, half the marriages in one Maryland county lasted no longer than seven years before one of the partners died. Of 239 children born in Middlesex County during the second half of the seventeenth century, a quarter had lost one or both parents by their fifth birthday, more than a half by their thirteenth birthday, and approaching three-quarters by the time they were twenty-one or at marriageable age. Children were usually left in the care of affines, steprelatives, friends, or neighbors, and in extreme cases the courts were forced to appoint guardians and supervise their estates. "From the standpoint of children," Darrett and Anita Rutman conclude, "parents were ephemeral. A father might give way to a stepfather, an uncle, a brother, or simply a friend of the deceased father; a mother might well be replaced by an aunt, an elder sister, or a father's 'now-wife.'" That rapid population turnover did not destroy the family as a social unit owed, in large part, to the compensatory role played by "a larger collectivity of kin and friends—the collective family of the neighborhood." Ultimately, "stability for children as well as for adults lay not so much in the transitory family of the household but in the permanent network of friends and relations within which the family was embedded."[20]

To modern sensibilities, the continual disruption of family life by death or remarriage is difficult to comprehend. How did people cope with the emo-

20. Houlbrooke, *English Family*, 20; Peter Laslett, ed., *Household and Family in Past Time . . .* (Cambridge, 1972), 138. Mean household size in the Vale of Berkeley in 1712 was 4.44 (Robert Atkyns, *The Ancient and Present State of Glostershire* [London, 1712]), compared to 4.70 for 45 parishes throughout England, 1650–1749, and 4.43 for 34 Kentish parishes in 1705. For the Chesapeake, see Walsh, "'Till Death Us Do Part,'" in Tate and Ammerman, eds., *Chesapeake in the Seventeenth Century*, 128, and Rutman and Rutman, "'Now-Wives and Sons-in-Law,'" 153–175; Rutman and Rutman, *A Place in Time: Middlesex County*, 118–120; Smith, "Mortality and Family," *Jour. Interdisc. Hist.*, VIII (1977–1978), 403–427.

tional trauma of frequent bereavement? Did familial turnover induce less affectionate or loving relationships between husbands and wives, parents and children? One answer is provided by the Rutmans. Seventeenth-century Chesapeake society exhibited less of a separation between family and local community—"the larger collectivity of kin and friends"—than today. Families survived even though their composition might often change. The very frequency of remarriages served to strengthen ties with the locality and create ever-widening circles of relations in the neighborhood.

"Living with death" was a fact of life in the early Chesapeake and England. The premodern family, Lawrence Stone observes, "was, statistically speaking, a transient and temporary association, both of husband and wife and of parents and children." In England the median length of marriage was from seventeen to twenty years, compared to a mean duration of thirteen years in Somerset County, Maryland, in the case of immigrants, and nearly twenty years where one partner was an immigrant and the other native-born. A man living in England in the seventeenth century who married at the age of thirty could expect to live another twenty-five years, "not long enough to ensure he would see his own son married." Peter Laslett estimates that between two-fifths and two-thirds of women had lost their fathers by the time they married in their mid-twenties. Nearly two-thirds of indentured servants aged under twenty-one who emigrated from London to the Chesapeake in the 1680s had lost one or both parents. Low life expectancy, especially for child-bearing women, meant that at least half the population would spend part of their lives with a stepparent. Many immigrants to Maryland and Virginia who died leaving minor children themselves experienced orphanhood as young children in England.[21]

Immigrants who lived in London would have found little difference in the extent of family disruption along the tobacco coast. A sample of 104 London marriages between 1580 and 1640 reveals that more than a third (36 percent) lasted fewer than eight years and more than a half (55 percent) fewer than ten. Only 16 percent of marriages lasted longer than twenty years. As in the Chesapeake, loss of a spouse or children was frequent. By 1610, at

21. Stone, *Family, Sex, and Marriage*, 55; Menard and Walsh, "Demography of Somerset County," *Newberry Papers in Family and Community History*, 81-2 (1981); Peter Laslett, *World We Have Lost*, 98, 100, 103–104; Laslett, *Family Life and Illicit Love in Earlier Generations* (Cambridge, 1977), 162–163; James Horn, "Servant Emigration to the Chesapeake in the Seventeenth Century," in Tate and Ammerman, eds., *Chesapeake in the Seventeenth Century*, 83 n. 96; Alan Macfarlane, *The Family Life of Ralph Josselin: A Seventeenth-Century Clergyman* (Cambridge, 1970), 126.

the age of thirty-eight, Thomas Ivie, a blacksmith of St. Olave's Hart parish, had buried three daughters and two sons from his first marriage, his first wife, two daughters from his second marriage, and his second wife. Remarriage was frequent. Frances Medewell married in 1605 when she was twenty-nine. A month later she was a widow but married again at the age of thirty-one to Thomas Chambers, a widower aged forty-six. Widowed two years later with an infant son, her third marriage in 1611 ended sometime before 1620, when she married a fourth time, after which she disappears from the records. No wonder that family size was small and that "the permanent residents of London had little likelihood of replacing themselves."[22]

Expectations of the respective duties of husbands and wives in England appear similar to expectations in Virginia and Maryland. The "reinforcement of patriarchy" was just as much a feature of Chesapeake society as it was of England's. Families were conceived of as units of residence embracing a married couple, their children, and servants, ruled by the husband as the head of the household. An act passed by the Virginia Assembly in 1644 stated that masters of families "shall be responsible for all the publique duties, tithes and charges, due from all persons in their familys." They were also held responsible for the conduct of the members of their household regarding religious observance, moral education of the young, and proper behavior. And, like their counterparts in England, they were expected to fulfill a variety of obligations: militia service, local office, and essential tasks undertaken by the community. The family was a political as well as a social and economic unit, and orderly family life, it was believed, ensured an orderly society.[23]

Order and discipline were the twin watchwords. Husbands provided security for the good behavior of their wives and servants and were legally entitled to apply moderate correction to enforce compliance to their will. Male authority was backed by the courts through a series of measures that defined the master's rights to punish his servants and slaves and through measures stipulating compensation where he had been seriously inconvenienced. Punishments usually took the form of beatings or, in the case of theft or running away, an extra period of service. As in England, special punishments, intended as shaming rituals, were reserved for women who consistently spoke out of turn to their husbands, masters, neighbors, or

---

22. Examples and findings are taken from Vivien Brodsky, "Widows in Late Elizabethan London: Remarriage, Economic Opportunity, and Family Orientations," in Bonfield *et al.*, eds., *World We Have Gained*, 136–139.

23. Hening, *Statutes*, I, 286, 311–312, 433, 525, 542, II, 103; Rutman and Rutman, *A Place in Time: Middlesex County*, 51–52.

social superiors and who transgressed acceptable behavior as judged by the local community. Ducking (immersing in water) women convicted of being "scolds" was practiced in Virginia from at least the 1620s. In 1654, Lower Norfolk's court ordered "one duckeing or Cookeing stoole" to be built "in some convenient place in the Little Creeke in the p'rish of Lynhaven." Six years later the Assembly ordered that every county should have a ducking stool for the punishment of women with "slanderous and brawling tongues."[24]

The establishment of patriarchy was not simply related to mortality rates, the sex ratio, and similar male-female work routines, all of which, it has been argued, restricted patriarchalism in the seventeenth-century Chesapeake. Whether or not women had more familial power than women in England is still an open question, but it cannot be assumed that the low life expectancy of men or the fact that women had plenty of prospective partners to choose from necessarily weakened patriarchal values. Patriarchy was above all a political system and as such was incorporated into the familial politics of Maryland and Virginia society as surely as it was in England. Conditions along the Bay undoubtedly mediated its impact, but there can be no question of the importance of its influence on relationships between men and women.[25]

Colonists, Lorena Walsh suggests, "considered normal and exclusive

24. The "limits" of order are discussed more fully in Chapter 8. Hening, *Statutes*, I, 358, II, 26, 116–118, 254, 266, 270, 273–274, III, 451, 460–461; Philip Alexander Bruce, *Institutional History of Virginia in the Seventeenth Century: An Inquiry into the Religious, Moral, Educational, Legal, Military, and Political Condition of the People . . .* , 2 vols. (New York, 1910), I, 620–621; Lower Norfolk County, Wills and Deeds C (1651–1656), fol. 82, E (Orders) (1666–1675), fols. 16–17, Order Book (1675–1686), fol. 6 (CW, microfilm, reel M 1365-25). For comparisons with England, see D. E. Underdown, "The Taming of the Scold: The Enforcement of Patriarchal Authority in Early Modern England," in Anthony Fletcher and John Stevenson, eds., *Order and Disorder in Early Modern England* (Cambridge, 1985), 123–125.

25. On patriarchy, see Gordon J. Schochet, *Patriarchalism in Political Thought: The Authoritarian Family and Political Speculation and Attitudes, Especially in Seventeenth-Century England* (New York, 1975); Allan Kulikoff, *Tobacco and Slaves: The Development of Southern Cultures in the Chesapeake, 1680–1800* (Chapel Hill, N.C., 1986), chap. 5; Mary Beth Norton, "The Evolution of White Women's Experience in Early America," *American Historical Review*, LXXXIX (1984), 597–598. A distinction should be made between patriarchal thought in its most general political forms, and domestic patriarchy, which relates to power relations between man and wife within and beyond the family. Kulikoff, for example, is concerned with the latter. But one should not overdraw differences between attitudes and values of the public world and the private world of domestic polity. To a large extent they reflected and influenced one another.

sexual union, peaceful cohabitation, and economic support of the wife by the husband the minimal duties that spouses must perform." Kenelm Cheseldyne and Mary Phippard did not marry in church or by license, but he considered her "his Lawfull wife," and so did his neighbors. Sarah Turner, a midwife who delivered their three children, related that he was present "at the birth of the second and seemed very fond of the child." He called Mary "his wife and took care of her as such and Owned the Children." Benjamin Reeder, a neighbor, recalled that Cheseldyne "came with her publickly to Church and helped her off and on her Horse and shewed her the respect due to a wife." Another neighbor, Thomas Bolt, described him "walking in his Hall" with one of his children "in his Armes and in discours about a certaine Mr. Donaldson who had been [at the house] but a small time before and was angry about [Mary's] . . . giving the said Donaldson's Child Indian Bread in boiled Milk . . . Cheseldyne sayd that he thought his wife knew what was best for children for says he our own Children Eat the same." Cheseldyne's marriage was acceptable to the community because he behaved in ways conceived as appropriate for a husband. He acknowledged her in public as his wife, supported her and their children according to his means, treated her with respect, and showed affection and love for his family. Their union also conformed to the expectations of the church and Scriptures in the "procreation of children, the regulation of sexual activity, and mutual comfort and support."[26]

An idea of what was usually expected of wives can be gained negatively from the following examples. Eady Hawkins (later Tooker), of Lower Norfolk, ridiculed Matthew Hayward's wife by saying that she "did live as brave a life as any woman in Virginia for she could lie abed every morning 'til her husband went a milking and came back again and washed the dishes and skimmed the milk, and then Mr. Edward Floide would come in and say 'Come neighbour, will you walk?' and so they walk abroad and left the children crying that her husband was fain to come home and leave his work to quiet the children." Similarly, there was widespread disapproval of Mrs. Mary Woodhouse's behavior toward her husband. In 1655, Lower Norfolk's court, "haveing heard many Compl[ain]ts concerning the unkinde usuage of Mrs Woodhowse towards her husband Mr. Woodhowse in his present sickness," suggested that "some adjacent Neighbor . . . shall have full lib[er]tie to resorte to the howse of Mr Woodhowse to see that he have what shalbe both sufficient and necessarie for him dureing his sicknes, and

---

26. Walsh, " 'Till Death Us Do Part,' " in Tate and Ammerman, eds., *Chesapeake in the Seventeenth Century*, 139–140; Houlbrooke, *English Family*, 96.

according to his quallitye." Woodhouse died six months later, and his widow quickly remarried. Generally speaking, wives were expected to rear children, run the household, tend the garden plot, and supplement the family income by occasionally helping their husbands in the fields or with preparing tobacco for shipment.[27]

The church warned that few marriages were "without chidings, brawlings, tauntings, repentings, bitter cursings, and fightings." Couples, however, were expected to work out their differences and enjoined to exercise the Christian virtues of patience and forgiveness. Those pushed beyond the limits of patience and forgiveness, however, frequently could not contain their frustrations and stepped outside the bounds of marriage into illicit relationships. John Norton, a married man of Maryland, fell in love with Jane Palldin, a neighbor's servant and got her with child in 1657. When his wife found out, he attacked her with a knife, crying: "Damned whore . . . I thought you were my Bosom friend, and have you betrayed me? Gods wounds I will run my knife through you." George Edgerton was ordered to "forbeare to frequent the house and company of Anne Bennett or any wayes to allowe her maintenance she absentinge herselfe from her husband." Frances, wife of John Dyer of the same county, was found guilty of committing adultery with Hugh Wood "at several times as appears by divers testimonies" and was ordered to "ask Almighty God forgiveness" upon her "bare knees in the presence of this court for their said heinous offence against His Divine Majesty." Both she and Wood received fifteen lashes.[28]

Annulment of marriages was uncommon, but adultery could be the basis for legal separation. Robert Robins of Charles County accused his wife of adultery in 1658, but the court did not support his charge and ordered that he "take the sayd Elisa: his wife againe, and provid for her and her children." The court added, however, that should it subsequently appear "that the child now in her Armes was not begotten by her sayd housband but by some other that then hee shal not bee charged either to mayntaine her or her Sayd Child." In a rare example of divorce, a couple from Lower Norfolk, "lawfully married in Virginia," for "se[ver]all occasions, p[ar]ticulerly for Adultery manifestly committed on the womans p[ar]te . . . findinge there is noe possible way or meanes of reconciliacon to be made betweene us whereby wee may be agayne agreed and enioy either the other as man and

27. Lower Norfolk County, Minute Book (1637–1646), I, fols. 54, 57–58, Wills and Deeds C (1651–1656), fols. 157–158, 171, 181, 221.

28. *Md. Archives*, XLI, 15–16; Lower Norfolk County, Wills and Deeds D (1656–1666), fol. 370, Minute Book (1637–1646), I, fol. 180.

wife ought to doe havinge used all possible meanes to accomplish the same for the space of neere seaven yeres, w[hi]ch tyme we have spent w[i]thout Cohabitacon or access either to other, We have now both of us consented and agreed to peticon to Whosoever it may be done by, that we may obtayne a divorse."[29] Sexual exclusivity and cohabitation were considered the sine qua non of marriage. In the face of abandonment or adultery, there was little that the courts could do apart from punish the offenders, promote reconciliation, and in the last resort recognize the separation.

How many marriages broke down as a result of irreconcilable conflict, violence, adultery, or one partner's running away, and whether breakdown was more common in the Chesapeake than England, is unknowable. We can suggest, however, that community mores appear broadly the same in both societies. Certain types of behavior (private marriages and prenuptial sex, for example) frowned upon by the state were often tolerated by local communities where couples were known and whose families had lived in the parish for some time. Similar behavior by strangers would not be condoned. The community and the courts came together as one to outlaw blatant promiscuity, sexual infidelity, excessive brutality, and bastardy. Warnings of the consequences of "scandalous" behavior were voiced initially by friends or neighbors before being reported to churchwardens or local justices. In England various forms of popular theater (notably "ridings" and "rough music") were sometimes used to express the community's disapproval of wifely insubordination or gross immorality, but more usually public scorn and, ultimately, presentment to the courts were adopted. In these cases, popular morality and official attitudes were, not at odds, but complementary and mutually reinforcing.[30]

Because the family was a primary economic unit, the devolution of property by householders represented a number of critical decisions. A major responsibility of parents was providing for their children, but at what point and in what proportions were land and movable estate to be distributed? Behind

29. *Md. Archives*, LIII, 4; Lower Norfolk County, Wills and Deeds D (1656–1666), fol. 35.

30. E. P. Thompson, *Customs in Common* (London, 1991), chap. 8; Martin Ingram, "Ridings, Rough Music, and the 'Reform of Popular Culture' in Early Modern England," *Past and Present*, no. 105 (November 1984), 79–113; Ingram, "Ridings, Rough Music, and Mocking Rhymes in Early Modern England," in Reay, ed., *Popular Culture*, 166–197; Ingram, *Church Courts*, chaps. 7–8; G. R. Quaife, *Wanton Wenches and Wayward Wives: Peasants and Illicit Sex in Early Seventeenth Century England* (London, 1979), chaps. 5–9.

such decisions lay a complex substratum of assumptions about the relationship of parents to children (or the older generation to the younger), the
role of wives within family polity and economy, distinctions between sons
and daughters and between elder and younger children, the preservation
of the family holding within the bloodline, and a host of mundane practical
considerations governed by the particular circumstances in which property
was passed on. Lands and chattels, in the form of deeds of gift or dowries,
were commonly given to children when they were about to marry and set
up their own households. Property "could be broken up and distributed to
children over very long periods of time," as offspring successively left the
family home or gifts were made to minor children in trust.[31] In other cases,
the distribution of the family's estate occurred at a single moment after the
death of the head of the household. Who got what depended, among other
things, on whether a will had been made, whether property was subject to
intestacy laws or manorial custom, the types of property involved, the number, age, and sex of children, the relationship between husband and wife,
and the judgment of parents of what was best for their children.

English intestacy laws, codified under the Statute of Distributions in 1671,
dictated that real estate should descend to the eldest son or, in the absence of
sons, to daughters equally. If there were no children, then land went to next
of kin in the following order: (1) parents, (2) brothers and sisters, (3) grand-
parents, (4) nephews, nieces, uncles, and aunts, and (5) cousins. According
to the custom of "thirds," a widow was entitled to a third of the annual revenue from her husband's lands for life as well as any land she might have in
her own name. Movable property was distributed more equitably, a third to
the widow and the rest in equal proportions to children. Thus intestacy laws,
with the exception of particular local customs such as Kentish gavelkind (see
below), emphasized primogeniture. "The Eldest Son," Edward Chamberlayne commented in the mid-seventeenth century, "inherits all Lands, and
to the Younger Children are disposed Goods and Chattels." These principles
were adopted with minor changes in both Virginia and Maryland.[32]

31. Jack Goody *et al.*, eds., *Family and Inheritance: Rural Society in Western Europe,
1200–1800* (Cambridge 1976), introduction, chaps. 1, 5–7; Wrightson and Levine,
Poverty and Piety, 96.

32. 22 and 23 Car. II, c. 10; Sir William Blackstone, *Commentaries on the Laws of
England . . .* , 11th ed., 4 vols. (London, 1791), II, 208, 212, 214, 216–217, 218,
220, III, 496–515; Danby Pickering, ed., *The Statutes at Large . . .* , 24 vols. (Cambridge,
1762–1763), VIII, 347–350; Edward Chamberlayne, *Angliae Notitia; or, The Present State
of England . . .* , 2d ed. (London, 1669), 460–461; Lois Green Carr, "Inheritance in the
Colonial Chesapeake," in Ronald Hoffman and Peter J. Albert, eds., *Women in the Age*

Intestacy laws governed the majority of householders (between one-half and four-fifths) in both societies who, for one reason or another, did not make a will. Some may have considered their estates too inconsiderable to merit the effort, since relatively few poor are represented among testates, or simply did not wish the bother and expense. But many men and women nearing the end of their days chose not to make a will because provisions under the law for intestates satisfied their own family requirements. In theory, therefore, primogeniture was the norm in England and the Chesapeake, although there is no way of knowing whether in practice estates were distributed strictly according to the letter of the law.[33]

In England manorial customs provided another method of providing for widows and children. The majority of tenants on the Berkeley estates in Gloucestershire, for example, like other parts of the West Country and central England, held land by copyhold for ninety-nine years determinable on three lives. Tenants could add or substitute lives when they pleased by surrendering the lease into the hands of the lord and paying a fine for a new copy, thereby ensuring that the succession of holdings suited changing family circumstances such as the birth or death of children. Wives could be counted as one of the "lives" but usually inherited the holding by custom of freebench, which allowed widows of copyholders to retain the holding until death or remarriage. John Smyth, steward of the Berkeley manors in the first half of the seventeenth century, noted "that the wife of every such copihold tenant dyinge seized and in possession, shall, after the decease of her husband hold the same so longe as she shall live chast and unmarried." The custom of freebench probably accounts for the relatively low number of reversions to wives. Between 1656 and 1688, 219 estates on the Berkeley manors reverted to the next in line, of which 26.9 percent went to wives,

---

of the American Revolution (Charlottesville, Va., 1989); Marylynn Salmon, *Women and the Law of Property in Early America* (Chapel Hill, N.C., 1986), 9–11, 149–156; and, generally, Carole Shammas, "English Inheritance Law and Its Transfer to the Colonies," *American Journal of Legal History*, XXXI (1987), 145–163; Carole Shammas, Marylynn Salmon, and Michel Dahlin, *Inheritance in America: From Colonial Times to the Present* (New Brunswick, N.J., 1987), chaps. 1–2.

33. In the Vale of Berkeley at least 70% of householders died intestate, compared to 53%–76% in various parts of the Chesapeake. James P. P. Horn, "Social and Economic Aspects of Local Society in England and the Chesapeake: A Comparative Study of the Vale of Berkeley, Gloucestershire, and the Lower Western Shore of Maryland, c. 1660–1700" (D. Phil. diss., University of Sussex, 1982), 230–234; Carr, "Inheritance in the Colonial Chesapeake," in Hoffman and Albert, eds. *Women in the Age of the American Revolution*, appendix 1.

40.2 percent to sons, 7.8 percent to daughters, 4.1 percent to siblings, and 2.8 percent to grandchildren and other kin.[34]

Local custom makes generalizations about the transfer of land hazardous. In Kent, gavelkind governed the division of lands to sons equally; in Sussex the custom of borough English dictated that land went to the youngest son. A single manor might include a variety of quite different tenures: chief tenants, whose title was virtually the same as that of freeholders; copyholders, whose tenure might be subject to variable terms or "lives"; and tenants who held indenture leases and were not protected by the customs of the manor. Conditions surrounding freebench also varied.[35] Individuals might possess combinations of freehold, copyhold, and leasehold property, acquiring and discarding tracts as need dictated. There was often no simple division in English landed society between freeholders on the one hand and manorial tenants on the other. Yet certain basic similarities in English local customs stand out: the assumption that a wife's interest was restricted to a form of guardianship during her life or widowhood, after which the land would devolve to the next in line; and, second, that holdings were retained, where possible, in the bloodline by favoring sons over daughters.

A third means of devising property was by last will and testament. Interpreting patterns of bequests in wills is complicated not only because practices varied according to the wealth, social status, occupation, and age of the testator or testatrix but also because of differences conditioned by family life cycle and composition. A poor man with a wife and several young sons and daughters might divide the family estate very differently than a wealthy widower with married daughters only. Wills do not necessarily include all family

34. Eric Kerridge, *Agrarian Problems in the Sixteenth Century and After* (London, 1969), 17–64; Horn, "Social and Economic Aspects," 262–265; John Smyth, *A Description of the Hundred of Berkeley in the County of Gloucester and of Its Inhabitants*, vol. III of *The Berkeley Manuscripts*, ed. Sir John Maclean (Gloucester, 1883–1885), 17; Berkeley Manor Court Books, 1656–1688, General Series, 50, 52, 55–56, Berkeley Castle muniments. Eleven percent of reversions went to people with no obvious kinship with the former tenant. Fines could run into hundreds of pounds and represented a considerable financial outlay, tantamount to a bequest in a will or some other form of settlement.

35. Kerridge, *Agrarian Problems*, 17–64; C. W. Chalklin, *Seventeenth-Century Kent: A Social and Economic History* (London, 1965), 55–57; C. Thomas Stanford, ed., *An Abstract of the Court Rolls of the Manor of Preston*, Sussex Records Society (Sussex, 1921), xxvi–xxvii. See also Cicely Howell, "Peasant Inheritance Customs in the Midlands, 1200–1700," and Margaret Spufford, "Peasant Inheritance Customs and Land Distribution in Cambridgeshire from the Sixteenth to the Eighteenth Centuries," in Goody et al., eds., *Family and Inheritance*, 112–155, 157–176.

property, since manorial land was commonly omitted and previous inter vivos settlements, such as marriage portions or deeds of gift, do not usually appear. In some cases, wills represent merely the final stage in the transmission of property to the next generation. Married children were frequently given only a token bequest or were left out altogether. Occasionally the testator was explicit. John Barber of North Nibley, Gloucestershire, left his married daughter, Elizabeth, two shillings and explained, "I having already given unto her fforty pounds and more at her marriage," and Thomas Bushell of St. Mary's County, Maryland, when asked whether he would remember his brother, replied, "No, I shall not give him anything, for I have given enough allready by setting of him free."[36]

Finally, owing to the practice of leaving unspecified property ("residue") to the executor or other heirs, it is not always clear precisely how the estate was divided between legatees. George Ashall of Little Creek, Lower Norfolk County, bequeathed land, household goods, livestock, and a slave to his two sons; household goods and livestock to two daughters; and the dwelling plantation to his wife for her life together with the residue of the estate. Without a detailed reconstruction of landholdings and personal wealth at the time of his death early in 1673, it is impossible to say who received the bulk of the estate.[37] Testators were not required by law, and did not feel it necessary in practice, to itemize every single piece of property bequeathed.

With these limitations in mind, the following section compares patterns of testation as revealed by wills in the Vale of Berkeley, Lower Norfolk and Lancaster counties in Virginia, and St. Mary's County, Maryland. It explores attitudes of male householders toward their wives and children in relation to family property and, in a broader context, "the sexual division of labour, the importance of land and the conception of social hierarchy" in these different societies.[38]

One indication of the trust that husbands had in the capacity of their wives to manage family affairs after their death lies in the decision of whom to appoint as executor. The position carried considerable responsibilities. Executors were accountable for ensuring that the intent of the testator was carried

---

36. Horn, "Social and Economic Aspects," 228–240; Amussen, *An Ordered Society*, 76–81; Lloyd Bonfield, "Normative Rules and Property Transmission: Reflections on the Link between Marriage and Inheritance in Early Modern England," in Bonfield *et al.*, eds., *World We Have Gained*, 155–176; Wills and Deeds, 1682/3, Gloucestershire Record Office; St. Mary's County, Wills and Deeds, transcript courtesy of SMCC.

37. Lower Norfolk County, Wills and Deeds E (1666–1675), fol. 134.

38. Amussen, *An Ordered Society*, 81.

TABLE 20

Wives Appointed Executrix of Husband's Estate in England and the Chesapeake, 1640–1750

Area, Period (No. of Widows)	Sole Executrix	Joint Executrix
Vale of Berkeley, 1660–1700 (276)[a]	73.2%	5.8%
Norfolk (England),		
selected parishes, 1590–1750 (325)[b]	61.5	15.0
St. Mary's and Charles		
counties, 1640–1710 (404)[b]	80.5	8.2
Lancaster County, 1652–1699 (80)[a]	60.0	11.3
Lower Norfolk County		
1639–1675 (40)[a]	72.5	10.0

Notes: [a]Samples include only testators with children. [b]Samples include all testators, whether or not they had children.

Sources: Vale of Berkeley: Wills, 1660–1699, Gloucestershire Record Office; PCC PROB 11, Public Record Office. Norfolk, England: Susan Dwyer Amussen, *An Ordered Society: Gender and Class in Early Modern England* (Oxford, 1988), table 3, 82–83. St. Mary's and Charles counties: courtesy of Lois Green Carr and Lorena S. Walsh. Lancaster: transcripts of wills, SMCC. Lower Norfolk: Minute Book, transcript, 2 vols. (1637–1646), Wills and Deeds B (1646–1651), C (1651–1656), D (1656–1666), E (1666–1675), Colonial Williamsburg, microfilm, reels M 1365-2, M 1365-17, M 1365-18.

out as fully as possible, with respect to the payment of legacies (if any), maintenance of children, and management of the estate. Wives, no longer junior partners in the family economy, took over as heads of household in charge of all aspects of family affairs. That testators sometimes appointed two or more executors, including the wife, might reflect the claims of an elder son or daughter or, perhaps, recognize that the widow was incapable of managing the estate by herself. In more extreme cases, wives were excluded from executorship completely. The great majority of men in both societies (ranging from 60 to 80 percent), presumably, trusted their wives' ability to supervise the family's estate (see Table 20). If wives who were designated joint executors are added, the proportion of estates wholly or partially supervised by women is even more impressive, ranging from 71 percent to 88 percent. The only significant difference between English and Chesapeake practice relates to families with adult children. In the Vale of Berkeley, testators whose children had reached majority made their wives sole executors in fewer than half of all cases. Husbands in Virginia and Maryland were not usually in a position to choose between adult children and their wives, because the great majority of men died while their children were below age.[39]

Not only were a large majority of wives given the responsibility of overseeing their late husband's estate, but they were frequently granted a substantial interest in family property, real and movable. In St. Mary's County and the Vale of Berkeley approximately three-quarters of wives with children received land, usually the dwelling plantation or house for life and possibly some other tracts. A life interest in land was the most common form of bequest in both societies, but a variety of other strategies were also employed. Arthur Bridger of Slimbridge, gentleman, who died in 1662, bequeathed all his lands to his eldest son but allowed his wife the profits of the land for ten years in order to raise their four youngest children. William Curnocke of Berkeley, yeoman, stipulated that the profits of all lands were to go to his wife, Hester, "for better bringing up, placing out, and providing for my children." Testators sometimes left their wives chattel leases or the right to share part of the dwelling house and adjoining lots with sons and daughters.[40] Overall, about one-half of widows received land for life, compared to one-quarter for lesser terms and one-fifth forever (see Table 21). Additionally, wives of copyholders could claim freebench or were granted title in their own right.

Planters in Virginia and Maryland adopted similar practices. Rowland Burnham of Lancaster County wrote his will in early 1656, shortly before making "a voyage for England." He appears to have been traditionally minded. Although all his children were minors, he left his wife Alice only a third part of his house and clear ground during her widowhood, after which she was to depart without injuring the property. The bulk of his land went to his three sons, the eldest, Thomas, being granted first choice "in regard of his birth right." His daughter and wife were compensated with bequests of livestock, servants, slaves, household goods, and money. A neighbor and "loveing friend" of Burnham's, Francis Cole, made his will a few years later and granted his wife the dwelling plantation for life if she remained a widow.

39. Vale of Berkeley: Wills and Deeds, 1660–1699, GRO; PCC PROB 11, Public Record Office, London; Norfolk, England: Amussen, *An Ordered Society*, table 3, 82–83; St. Mary's and Charles counties, Maryland, courtesy of Lois Green Carr, Lorena S. Walsh, and the St. Mary's City Commission; Lancaster County, Virginia, transcripts of Wills and Deeds, SMCC; Lower Norfolk County, Minute Book, 2 vols., (1637–1646), Wills and Deeds B, C, D, and E. See also Shammas, Salmon, and Dahlin, *Inheritance in America*, chap. 2, esp. table 2.12, 59–60.

40. Wills and Deeds, 1662/14, 1671/140, 1679/110, 1680/157, 1681/20, 1686/299, 389, 1690/238, 1692/101, 1693/258, 1697/20, 1698/111, 196, GRO.

TABLE 21

Bequests of Land to Wives with Children, Vale of Berkeley, 1660–1699

	% of Bequests				
Duration	£10–£49 (N=31)	£50–£99 (N=28)	£100–£249 (N=34)	£250+ (N=34)	Overall (N=127)
Forever	6.5	28.6	20.6	23.5	19.7
For life	58.1	53.6	47.1	50.0	52.0
During widowhood	19.4	7.1	14.7	14.7	14.2
During minority	3.2	0	5.9	11.8	5.5
For fixed term	6.4	3.6	11.8	0	5.5
Other	6.4	7.1	0	0	3.1
Total	100.0	100.0	100.1	100.0	100.0

Sources: Wills, 1660–1669, Gloucestershire Record Office; PCC PROB 11; Public Record Office.

More typical, however, is the example of Abraham Bush, also of Lancaster, who bequeathed his wife, Ann, his plantation for life, to descend to his youngest son after her death. Of thirty Lancaster widows with children who were explicitly left land, just fewer than half received a life interest, compared to a third who had possession for their widowhood or minority of the children, and a fifth who were bequeathed land forever. Men elsewhere in the Chesapeake may have been slightly more generous. In Lower Norfolk County half the widows were given land for life, but only a fifth held land for their widowhood or minority of children, and more than a quarter received land outright.[41]

Whatever the exact proportions or method by which land was passed on to wives and children, there can be no doubt that in both societies widows were the crucial link in the transmission of property from one generation to another and played a vital role in safeguarding the children's estate after the husband's death. Henry Hyde of St. Mary's County instructed his wife, Frances, to possess and manage the estate during her lifetime for the

41. Lancaster County, Deeds Etc., no. 2 (1654–1666), 46–49, 54–56, Wills and Deeds Etc., no. 5 (1674–1689), 114–115 (SMCC transcript). See Carr on regional differences of testation patterns in "Inheritance in the Colonial Chesapeake," in Hoffman and Albert, eds., *Women in the Age of the American Revolution.* A life interest was common also in St. Mary's and Charles counties.

children's use "with as much Freedom as it were myself in my lifetime." John Atwell of Cromhall, Gloucestershire, desired his wife "to be careful in the paying of all my debts and funeral expenses; And to take upon her the management of my whole estate for the good of my Children during their minority." Wives, whether married to English yeomen or Chesapeake tobacco planters, were enjoined to "sufficiently breed up" minor children, keep family property in "good repaire," and make "no waste."[42]

In Virginia and Maryland, as in England, the overwhelming concern of husbands was to provide a means of support for their immediate family. Unsurprisingly, therefore, the bulk of the estate, real and personal, almost always went to wives and children, in varying proportions. In both societies daughters commonly received land as well as movables but rarely received more land than sons; testators attempted whenever possible to keep the main holding in the male line. Thus in the Vale of Berkeley nearly three-quarters of husbands with sons and daughters bequeathed the majority of land to their sons, and even in the land-rich tidewater it was very rare for daughters to receive the bulk of the holdings. More often, daughters were compensated with personal goods, usually in the form, in the Vale, of cash legacies or household goods and, in the Chesapeake, of livestock and laborers.[43]

Women in the Chesapeake may have enjoyed a more favorable position in family life, resulting from the shortage of women, late marriages, lack of close kin, and high mortality rates, which led to greater dependency of husbands on their wives than in England.[44] Evidence from the Vale of Berkeley and elsewhere suggests there was nothing exceptional about bequest pat-

42. St. Mary's County Wills and Deeds, transcript (SMCC); Wills and Deeds 1690/ 160, 1693/137, GRO.

43. James W. Deen, "Patterns of Testation: Four Tidewater Counties in Colonial Virginia," *Am. Jour. Leg. Hist.*, XVI (1972), 154–176; Jean Butenhoff Lee, "Land and Labor: Parental Bequest Practices in Charles County, Maryland, 1732–1783," in Lois Green Carr, Philip D. Morgan, and Jean B. Russo, eds., *Colonial Chesapeake Society* (Chapel Hill, N.C., 1988), 306–341; Carr, "Inheritance in the Colonial Chesapeake," in Hoffman and Albert, eds., *Women in the Age of the American Revolution*, table 1A; Linda E. Speth, "More than Her 'Thirds': Wives and Widows in Colonial Virginia," in Speth and Alison D. Hirsch, *Women, Family, and Community in Colonial America: Two Perspectives* (New York, 1983), 5–41; Horn, "Social and Economic Aspects," 254–276; Kulikoff, *Tobacco and Slaves*, chap. 5; Howell, "Peasant Inheritance," in Goody *et al.*, eds., *Family and Inheritance*, 151–155; Wrightson and Levine, *Poverty and Piety*, 98–99.

44. Carr and Walsh, "Planter's Wife," *WMQ*, 3d Ser., XXXIV (1977), 542–571; Carr, "Inheritance in the Colonial Chesapeake," in Hoffman and Albert, eds., *Women in the Age of the American Revolution*, 155–208.

terns of male householders in Virginia and Maryland or the attitudes that underpinned them. Variations occurred because of different forms of property involved and the practice of transferring land through manorial courts in England, but the concerns of testators in both societies were the same. Wives had to be provided for during their widowhood, sons needed land or cash to establish themselves on their own holdings or in various occupations, and daughters needed legacies for dowries. The underlying assumptions were patriarchal and patrilineal. Widows supervised the family estate and were primarily responsible for passing on the main holding to sons, if any, thereby ensuring the preservation of the family name in the community. Whereas wives and daughters might join other families, only sons maintained the testators' bloodline. Yet testators did not treat daughters harshly. "If there was a single concern running through the varieties of behavior observed," Keith Wrightson and David Levine point out for testators in the Essex village of Terling, "then it was that of maximizing the opportunities of as many children as possible to set up their own family units in due course."[45] Such wishes were manifest both in England and along the tobacco coast.

Emphasis on the welfare of wives and children is all the more striking when bequests to kin outside the immediate family are taken into account (Table 22). Men in both societies were much more likely to remember friends and neighbors than siblings, nephews, nieces, cousins, or affines. In early Virginia and Maryland, dominated by immigrants and high population turnover, extensive kin networks took several generations to develop; hence bequests to friends were an expression of their importance in the lives of settlers largely cut off from a wider kin group in England. Less expected is the finding that secondary kin and affines were not frequently mentioned in the wills of English testators.[46] The reasons will be explored in the next section, but it is probable that the tendency to ignore kin beyond the immediate family in Chesapeake wills was as much a carryover of English practice as a result of the peculiar demographic environment encountered in the tidewater.

In the absence of diaries and letters, it is difficult to recapture a sense of the emotional content of relationships between husbands and wives and parents and children. Comments in wills are of value in providing a glimpse of such feelings, even though wills were first and foremost legal documents often

45. Wrightson and Levine, *Poverty and Piety*, 99.

46. See David Cressy, "Kinship and Kin Interaction in Early Modern England," *Past and Present*, no. 113 (November 1986), 38–69.

TABLE 22

Minor Bequests by Married Men with Children, Vale of Berkeley and the Chesapeake, 1640–1705

Recipient	% of Wills Making Bequest			
	Vale of Berkeley (N=276)	Lower Norfolk (N=58)	Lancaster (N=80)	St. Mary's (N=120)
Parents	1.4	0	1.3	.8
Grandchildren	18.8	5.2	5.0	5.0
Brothers	13.8	5.2	5.0	1.7
Sisters	9.7	0	6.3	0
Nephews	4.7	0	2.5	.8
Nieces	4.7	0	2.5	2.5
Uncles	1.8	0	1.3	0
Aunts	.7	0	1.3	0
Undefined kin	6.5	0	1.3	0
In-laws	22.5	8.6	4.5	7.5
Friends and neighbors	27.2	29.3	31.3	30.0
The poor	7.2	1.7	3.8	1.7

Sources: Wills, 1660–1699, Gloucestershire Record Office: PCC PROB 11, Public Record Office; Lower Norfolk County, Virginia Minute Book, transcript, 2 vols. (1637–1646), Wills and Deeds B (1646–1651), C (1651–1656), D (1656–1666), E (1666–1675), Colonial Williamsburg, microfilm, reels M 1365-2, 17, 18; transcripts of St. Mary's and Lancaster County wills courtesy of SMCC.

written in formulaic language. Edward Grimes, of Lancaster County, left his "well beloved wife" the bulk of his estate in 1653. "Beloved" and "well beloved" were common terms, but not every testator chose to use them. Nor was it common for men to be as expressive as Henry Powell, a glover from Wotton under Edge, who described his wife, Bridgett, as "truely loving and truely loved," or Thomas Warner, of Cam, who would have given his "deare and loveing wife" more "if I had it as a demonstration of my entire love to her." On his deathbed, Richard Bray of Lancaster County, told his wife, "I shall leave thee enough for I shall leave thee all, and thou mayst go to England and live like a Gentlewoman."[47]

Similar expressions of love and concern were reserved for children.

47. Lancaster County, Deeds no. 1 (1652–1657), 124–125, Wills and Deeds no. 8 (1690–1709), 1 (SMCC transcript); Wills and Deeds 1684/319, 1686/349, GRO.

William Lane of Thornbury, gentleman, left each of his three sons one pound "as a token of fatherly Love to them beseeching Almighty [God] to give Every of them his Blessing and Grace to guide them all their dayes." Mrs. Hannah Ball, widow of Colonel William Ball of Lancaster County, left the bulk of her estate to her "Loveing Son" and "Loveing Daughter" and their children, and Margaret Hattersley of Lower Norfolk, "for the naturall Love and affection I have and beare unto my Children," gave them all she had. Many parents were eager to settle their estates to avoid family feuds arising from disputes over property. Richard Woodward of Cam, yeoman, drew up his will in 1675 in the hope that "there may be noe strife amongst my wife and children after such tyme god shall have taken me." Walter Danford, a carpenter of Dursley, appointed William Nelme and John Watkins, "Loveing freinds and Masters," as overseers of his will "to see things goe freindly amongst my family."[48]

In view of the likelihood that wives would quickly remarry, male testators in Virginia and Maryland were understandably concerned about the welfare of their children. Property was bequeathed to wives to help bring up young children, not to fill the coffers of future husbands. Joseph Baley of Lancaster left all his land and goods to his wife while a widow ("and after, if her husband imbezell not the estate away") while his two sons were under age. Edward Clark, of St. Mary's, stipulated that, if his wife remarried and mistreated his son, then his overseers were to assume guardianship and supervise the estate. David Miles, gentleman, wished his daughter to remain with her mother until of age or married. "But in case my wife should marry then my will is that upon just cause of my Daughters Discontent she may have the priviledge to choose her a Guardian." Andrew Robinson, who died in 1671 worth only about twenty-six pounds, left elaborate instructions. His wife was to have the use of his plantation and goods for life, but if with child "the sd. child [was] to enjoy the estate when of age." If she remarried, her husband "may not sell anything belonging to the estate without the consent of my wife Jane: furthermore, he may not clear any ground except for the purpose of firing and fencing and security must be given so that when the child comes of age he will receive a plantation as well fenced, cleared, etc., as the other plantation."[49]

Despite these precautions, and the protection offered by local courts, ulti-

---

48. Wills and Deeds 1675/125, 1683/161, 1687/283, GRO; Lancaster County, Wills and Deeds no. 8 (1690–1709), 52–53; Lower Norfolk, Wills and Deeds E (1666–1675), fol. 181.

49. Lancaster County, Wills and Deeds Etc., no. 5 (1674–1689), 5, 6–7; St. Mary's County, Wills and Deeds, transcripts.

mately most men had to entrust their children to the goodwill and love of their wives. No one could foresee the future, and even the most detailed safeguards might be utterly irrelevant within a few years. The fact that so many testators in both societies put their wives in charge of the family's estate suggests that few doubted their capacity or willingness to do the best for their children they possibly could and provides further evidence of the durability of family ties even in the adverse conditions experienced by settlers along the Bay.

Friends and Neighbors: The Local Community

While family and household were the most intimate and important social contexts bounding the lives of individuals, in early modern England and America the local community was also crucial. Within the locality, and more particularly within the smaller clusters of households that constituted neighborhoods, friends and neighbors provided company and recreation, helped in periods of crisis, witnessed vital events in individual lives, kept watch and ward, mediated in local disputes, defined acceptable standards of behavior, lent money and tools, exchanged produce, participated in various communal activities, and carried out official duties. Individuals and families, enmeshed, to one extent or another, in a complex web of interrelationships, acted first and foremost within the local community, which also linked them to the larger world beyond.[50]

Contemporary English observers were not impressed by the development of local communities in the Chesapeake. Lacking the traditional hierarchy of village, town, and city, settlement in the tidewater appeared scattered, "solitary and unsociable." Settlers were described in 1662 as living in a wilderness, "dispersedly and scatteringly seated upon the sides of Rivers," in "great want of Christian Neighbourhood." Even in 1688, eighty years after the founding of Jamestown, Virginia was described as "thinly inhabited."[51]

50. For an introduction to the meaning and nature of community, see Rutman, "Social Web," in O'Neill, ed., *Insights and Parallels*, 57–89; and Richard R. Beeman, "The New Social History and the Search for 'Community' in Colonial America," *American Quarterly*, XXIX (1977), 422–443.

On friends and neighbors and the community: Lorena S. Walsh, "Community Networks in the Early Chesapeake," in Carr, Morgan, and Russo, eds., *Colonial Chesapeake Society*, 200–241, esp. 241, and Horn, "Adapting to a New World," 164–174; Rutman and Rutman, *A Place in Time: Middlesex County*, chap. 4; James R. Perry, *The Formation of a Society on Virginia's Eastern Shore, 1615–1655* (Chapel Hill, N.C., 1990), chap. 3; Kulikoff, *Tobacco and Slaves*, chap. 6.

51. Peter Force, comp., *Tracts and Other Papers, Relating Principally to the Origin,*

Implicit were not only a comparison with the more complex community life of English counties but also a belief that a society lacking community would necessarily lack order, social discipline, and good government.

To English eyes, as discussed earlier, there was much missing in the Chesapeake landscape. At least half, and perhaps more, of seventeenth-century immigrants had lived in market towns, cities, and ports before taking ship, but there was nothing in Virginia or Maryland that replicated English urban experience. Jamestown and St. Mary's City more closely resembled villages than towns, let alone cities. The density of interaction familiar to English people on market days, at fairs, or when the court was sitting could not be duplicated in the land-water expanse of the tidewater, where entire county populations were no larger than in a modest English market town. To suggest, however, that, because Chesapeake settlers did not group themselves into townships, they perforce led "hard, lonely lives" on isolated plantations largely cut off from kin and friends not only ignores a massive amount of evidence to the contrary but is also a misreading of the nature of local community in England.[52]

Modern discussion has emphasized the richness and importance of local society in Virginia and Maryland. As argued in the previous chapter, local communities began taking shape in the earliest years of county formation. With continuing immigration, older-settled areas became more densely populated, and new neighborhoods were created. In Lancaster County the number of households nearly doubled during the decade after 1653 and, following the breaking away of Middlesex, rose from 131 in 1673 to 250 by 1693. The best lands along the Rappahannock and major tributaries had been taken up during the 1650s and early 1660s; thereafter, waterfront locations steadily filled in, and people moved upriver into the freshes.[53]

Settlement, and Progress of the Colonies in North America . . . , 4 vols. (1836–1846; Gloucester, Mass., 1963), III, no. 12, p. 21, no. 15, pp. 3–5.

52. John C. Rainbolt, "The Absence of Towns in Seventeenth-Century Virginia," *Journal of Southern History,* XXXV (1969), 343–360; "Part of a Letter from the Rev. Mr Hugh Jones to the Rev. Dr. Benjamin Woodruff, F.R.S., concerning Several Observables in Maryland," Jan. 23, 1698 [1699], LBC II (2), 253, Royal Society Archives, London; Durand of Dauphine, *A Frenchman in Virginia: Being the Memoirs of a Huguenot Refugee in 1686,* trans. Fairfax Harrison ([Richmond, Va.] 1923), 90; Rutman, "Social Web," in O'Neill, ed., *Insights and Parallels,* 58–59; Alan Macfarlane, *Reconstructing Historical Communities* (Cambridge, 1977), chap. 1.

53. Lancaster County, Deeds Etc., no. 1 (1652–1657), 91–94, Orders Etc. (1655–1666), 236–238, Orders Etc., no. 1 (1666–1680), 275–276, no. 3 (1686–1696), 28–29, 139–140 (CW, microfilm, reel M 117-8).

TABLE 23
Tithables in Lower Norfolk County, 1653–1662

Area	1653		1657		1662	
	No.	%	No.	%	No.	%
Elizabeth River						
Western Branch	101	21.4	94	20.2	94	19.3
Eastern/Southern branches	122	25.9	60/54	24.5	56/75	26.8
Lynnhaven						
Western Shore	78	16.6	65	14.0	63	12.9
Eastern Shore	59	12.5	70	15.1	85	17.4
Little Creek	71	15.1	60	12.9	55	11.3
Tanner's Creek to Willoughby Bay	40	8.5	62	13.3	60	12.3
Total	471	100.0	465	100.0	488	100.0

Sources: Lower Norfolk County, Virginia, Wills and Deeds C (1651–1656), fols. 62–64, D (1656–1666), fols. 106–107, 355–356, Colonial Williamsburg, microfilm, reels M 1365-17, 18.

In Lower Norfolk the population fluctuated between 334 and 490 tithables during the late 1640s and 1650s but grew rapidly over the next twenty years to reach more than 800 by 1677 (Table 23). Whereas the proportion of tithables remained static or declined along the Western Branch of the Elizabeth River, tithables increased steadily on the eastern shore of Lynnhaven and Tanner's Creek areas and marginally along the Southern Branch of the Elizabeth River, which was a less densely peopled area in the early years of settlement. In regions of the tidewater where local population growth was sustained, the number of households in a given community might rise dramatically. On St. Clement's Manor, St. Mary's County, for example, a typical household in the early 1660s was within 2.5 miles of 15 other households and within 5–6 miles of about 25. Ten years later these numbers had increased to 25 and 60, respectively. Individuals now had a good deal more choice in selecting whom they wished to befriend.[54]

54. Lower Norfolk County, Minute Book (1637–1646), II, fol. 89, Wills and Deeds B (1646–1651), fols. 92–93, 158, C (1651–1656), fols. 62–64, 183–184, D (1656–1666), fols. 106–107, 355–356, 379, 412–413, E (Orders) (1666–1675), fols. 42–43, 56, 119, Order Book, no. 1 (1666–1680), fols. 47–48; Lois Green Carr, "Sources of Political Stability and Upheaval in Seventeenth-Century Maryland," *Maryland Historical Magazine*,

Five to six miles was the usual extent of local communities in Virginia and Maryland, since daily interaction was difficult beyond this limit, but the most frequent contacts occurred within a shorter range, usually two to three miles, corresponding to the neighborhood. Communities were typically bounded by physical features—rivers, bays, creeks, and infertile interior areas—or grew up around earlier settlements, near the plantations of large planter-merchants, and on old Indian town lands. In Lower Norfolk, neighborhoods developed around the three major tributaries of the Elizabeth River and on Lynnhaven Bay. In Lancaster County, settlement was more dispersed. Neighborhoods formed around Fleet's Bay, the Corotoman and Moratico rivers, and a series of large creeks on both sides of the Rappahannock. Although their form varied considerably from one part of the Cheapeake to another, according to particular conditions, local communities nevertheless shared a number of important similarities. Four examples of the pattern of local interaction from St. Clement's Manor, representing poor, middling, and wealthy planters, will serve to illustrate the scope and nature of one local community.[55]

Vincent Mansfield died in 1687 worth about eighteen pounds. He was a longtime resident of St. Clement's and possibly the younger son of John Mansfield, who died in 1660. Twenty-four "points of interaction" have been traced for the period 1672–1687 (which is obviously an absolute minimum in view of the impossibility of recovering the myriad everyday associations that went unrecorded), but the more important events in his life stood a good chance of being registered, and the range of contacts gives at least a rough impression of the social world of a small planter. Most notable is the restricted geographical extent of his world (see Figure 14). Of his contacts, 83 percent were within five miles of his plantation on Foster's Neck, and all of these were fellow residents of the manor. Nearly half were in easy walking distance, less than two miles away. He was related by marriage to two nearby families, served on a number of manor court juries, appraised the

---

LXXIX (1984), 45; Walsh, "Community Networks," in Carr, Morgan, and Russo, eds., *Colonial Chesapeake Society*, 222.

55. Walsh, "Community Networks," in Carr, Morgan, and Russo, eds., *Colonial Chesapeake Society*, 203–222; Rutman and Rutman, *A Place in Time: Middlesex County*, chap. 4; Perry, *Formation of a Society*, chap. 3; Lois Green Carr, Russell R. Menard, and Lorena S. Walsh, *Robert Cole's World: Agriculture and Society in Early Maryland* (Chapel Hill, N.C., 1991), chap. 5. I am indebted to the St. Mary's City Commission, and particularly Lorena S. Walsh and Russell R. Menard, for permission to use their unpublished research on St. Clement's Manor, St. Mary's County, Maryland.

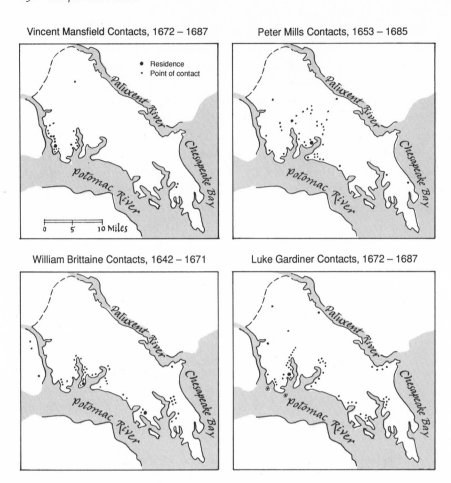

Figure 14. Contacts of Residents of St. Clement's Manor, St. Mary's County. *Drawn by Richard Stinely*

estates of a couple of neighbors, worked for a local large planter, Gerrard Slye, and was in debt to a local merchant. His few excursions beyond the manor involved him in serving at Susquehanna Fort in 1676 and acting as an Indian interpreter at a Council meeting in St. Mary's City.

Peter Mills, a middling planter-cum-carpenter, lived on the manor between 1653 and 1667 before moving to Newtown Hundred, where he eventually died in 1685. Like Mansfield, the range of his social world was very limited: 89 percent of his contacts were within five miles of his residence (Figure 14). Again, these took the form of routine tasks such as serving as a juror on the manor court, witnessing wills, appraising estates, and lending money. Interestingly, although he spent most of his life in Newtown Hundred, he appears to have maintained close ties with neighbors of his former residence at Mills Birch, where he possibly kept a plantation.

Large planters, such as William Brittaine and Luke Gardiner, present a somewhat different pattern of interaction (Figure 14). Ties beyond the locality were more numerous and significant than in the case of lesser planters. Only about half the contacts of either man fell within a five-mile radius of his home, and both were often called away from the local community to serve in public office. Brittaine served as clerk of the provincial Assembly, burgess, justice of the peace, clerk of the Council, and county coroner. Gardiner also served as a burgess and justice besides being an officer in the militia and sheriff of the county. Both men had many personal contacts beyond the locality. Brittaine had friends and kin in Poplar Hill, Harvey's, St. Mary's, and St. Michael's hundreds, and he probably had family connections in Virginia, since his second wife came from there. Even so, it would be erroneous to assume that they were divorced from the affairs of their respective neighborhoods. Brittaine's residence at "Little Brettons" developed as a focal point of the area, especially after a Roman Catholic church was built there in the early 1660s; and Luke Gardiner, too, was intimately involved in the life of St. Clement's Manor, witnessing wills, appraising inventories, acquiring land, attending manor courts, and getting into disputes with neighbors.

St. Clement's was not a typical community in Maryland. Nowhere else was the manor as prominent in local affairs. Without manors, parish, or established church, most of the colony's householders lived in communities that owed little to formal institutions. In the absence of parish administration, the county court absorbed the duties usually attached to the vestry; hence few decisions concerning the locality were made by men resident in the community itself. Although local justices played an important role in the day-to-day governance of local communities, the poor relief, care of orphans, maintenance of the highways, taxation, and various other aspects of local administration were matters formally decided at county level. Apart from the minority of Catholics and Quakers, who established their own chapels, meetinghouses, and community organization during the middle decades of the century, *informal* rather than formal ties gave the local community coherence and linked it to the wider world.[56]

56. Lois Green Carr, "County Government in Maryland, 1689–1709" (Ph.D. diss., Harvard University, 1968); Carr, "The Foundations of Social Order: Local Government in Colonial Maryland," in Bruce C. Daniels, ed., *Town and County: Essays on the Structure of Local Government in the American Colonies* (Middletown, Conn., 1978), 72–110, and Robert Wheeler, "The County Court in Colonial Virginia," 111–133, and

The importance of informal associations with friends and neighbors is amply illustrated in wills and court records throughout the Chesapeake. In St. Mary's, Lancaster, and Lower Norfolk counties, friends were most frequently mentioned in wills of married men after the immediate family and were much more likely to be left a minor bequest than either secondary kin (siblings, parents, uncles, aunts, nephews, nieces, or cousins) or in-laws (Table 22). Among single males this trend was even more striking. Between 74 and 81 percent of bachelors left the bulk of their estates to friends, neighbors, and landlords. John Gooch of Lower Norfolk gave all he had to his "loving and trusty friends," Thomas Bullock and Thomas Francis. Robert Chambers of Lancaster gave Anthony Fullgam a hogshead of tobacco "in full [of] all accounts and in remembrance of Interchangeable Love and kindness past betwixt us." Collin Mackenzie of St. Mary's, who lay sick at the house of Richard Gardiner in the winter of 1682/3, said on his death bed that "if he had lived a year or two longer his friends might have done better for [by] him but as it was he could noe otherwise" but leave his estate to Gardiner.[57]

Friends were often called upon to look after a testator's family and estate. Richard Starnell, who settled on the Western Branch of the Elizabeth River, asked his friend Edmund Bowman to take care of his three children after his death, and William Jermy of Lynnhaven appointed his "much esteemed freind," Colonel Lemuel Mason, one of his overseers. John Phillips of Lancaster County trusted his "loveing friend," Moore Fauntleroy, "to administer in behalfe of my wife and stand her friend." Oliver Seager, across the river, required his "beloved friend" Mr. Richard Loes to see to "the well ordering of the estate and to dispose of it to the best advantage of the children." Occasionally neighbors were called upon collectively, as when Arthur Thompson stipulated that his children should "chuse Six honnest Men of the Neighbourhood to Divide and Allott every one" their share of his estate.[58]

William H. Seiler, "The Anglican Church: A Basic Institution of Local Government in Colonial Virginia," 134–159; Lorena Seebach Walsh, "Charles County, Maryland, 1658–1705: A Study of Chesapeake Social and Political Structure" (Ph.D. diss., Michigan State University, 1977), chap. 4; Perry, *Formation of a Society*, chaps. 3–6; Michael Graham, "Meetinghouse and Chapel: Religion and Community in Seventeenth-Century Maryland," in Carr, Morgan, and Russo, eds., *Colonial Chesapeake Society*, 242–274. Rutman and Rutman, *A Place in Time: Middlesex County*, chap. 4.

In fact, the lord of the St. Clement's Manor, Thomas Gerrard, exercised effective control only briefly in the 1650s and early 1660s.

57. Lower Norfolk County, Minute Book (1637–1646), II, fols. 144–145; Lancaster County, Deeds Etc., no. 2 (1654–1666), 8–9; SMCC, Wills and Deeds, transcripts.

58. Lower Norfolk County, Wills and Deeds C (1651–1656), fol. 179, E (1666–1675),

Neighbors witnessed wills, listened to deathbed confessions, appraised estates, and mourned the passing of old friends. In St. Mary's County, between 1658 and 1675, at least two-thirds, and probably nearer three-quarters, of appraisers were from the same manor or hundred as the decedent, and more than 85 percent of witnesses of wills whose residence could be traced were from the same locality as the testator. Far from being solemn affairs, funerals gave local inhabitants an excuse to get together for a protracted period of drinking and feasting. At the funeral of a modest planter in Charles County in 1662 were to be found "all the neighbour[s] living about" who "had intertainment part of too days," drinking several barrels of beer and two bottles of drams and firing numerous parting volleys. When George Bateman of Lower Norfolk died in 1661, the bill for the ensuing festivities came to more than 2,000 lbs. of tobacco (worth £13 at 1.5d. per lb.): 900 lbs. for cider, 500 for beef, 300 for a barrow, 100 for a calf, and 180 for "dressing" the funeral dinner. Similarly, friends and neighbors at William Wilson's funeral the following year consumed a quarter of a cask of sack, a barrel of beer, and six gallons of rum. Little wonder that Edward Dale stated in his will that he should be buried without "any vaine drinking." [59]

Relations between householders were not, of course, always so convivial. Neighborhoods could be arenas for bitter personal rivalries and disputes. The Lower Norfolk court was informed in 1658 that Katherine, wife of John Reine, "hath abused" the wife of James Mullekens, and to prevent the abuse of "any other of her neighbors" her husband was to pay the court one thousand pounds of tobacco for good behavior. Two years later, Thomas Davis complained that the wife of a neighbor, Roger Heyward, "doth disturb him and will not suffer him to live and enjoy quietly his owne plantacon." Heyward subsequently complained of the "great abuses that people are ready to give my wife by reason of an Order of Court granted against her, upon the Complaint of Rose Lee and Elizabeth Moore, which hath Encouraged many to forment occasions of debate and Controversie to the great disturbance of this Worships Commissioners and my owne disquiett." A series of slanders and arguments between women neighbors in part explains the

---

fols. 3–4; Lancaster County, Deeds Etc., no. 2 (1654–1666), 18, 60; SMCC, Wills and Deeds, transcripts.

59. James Horn, "Adapting to a New World: A Comparative Study of Local Society in England and Maryland, 1650–1700," in Carr, Morgan, and Russo, eds., *Colonial Chesapeake Society*, 170, and Walsh, "Community Networks," 234; Lower Norfolk County, Wills and Deeds D (1656–1666), fols. 321, 345; Lancaster County, Wills and Deeds Etc., no. 8 (1690–1709), 55–56.

background to a number of witchcraft allegations in the county. Owing to "scandalous speeches [which] have been raised by some p'sons concerneing sev'all women in this Countie, termeing them to be Witches, whereby theire reputations have beene much impaired, and theire lives brought into question," the court imposed a fine of one thousand pounds of tobacco on anyone making false accusations.[60] Local disputes over land boundaries, payment of debts, damage done to crops by wandering livestock, cattle marks, and scandalmongering kept the courts busy throughout the period.

Less dramatic but more important in the daily lives of planters and their wives were visits, chance meetings, and occasional gatherings. Durand of Dauphine commented in 1686, "The land is so rich and so fertile that when a man has fifty acres of ground, two men-servants, a maid and some cattle, neither he nor his wife do anything but visit among their neighbors." Women, he noted, "spend most of their time visiting one another." Most married women, tied to the house by the demands of housework, caring for children, and tending the garden plot, probably did not venture far beyond the immediate vicinity, the ten to twenty plantations within a few miles. The social world of women was generally more confined than that of men, but much depended on particular circumstances: length of time in the neighborhood, social standing, intermarriage, and the presence of in-laws and kin. When Elizabeth Blaze, a longtime resident of Middlesex County, died in 1708, she was related, through her own marriages and those of her children, to about three-quarters of the householders in her locality. By contrast, Sarah Williamson and her husband of the same county appear to have led a solitary existence. They had few friends or relatives nearby and devoted themselves to raising a large family. When her husband died, Sarah remained on the plantation with three of her sons (a fourth married and moved away), but she does not appear to have been any more involved in the neighborhood than when she and her husband first moved to the county nearly twenty years before.[61]

Whatever their status, when an opportunity arose to escape from the drudgery of routine work, men and women were usually ready to have a drink, light a pipe, and perhaps join in a dance. They could meet at a local ordinary, such as Will Shipp's on the eastern side of the mouth of the Eliza-

60. Lower Norfolk County, Wills and Deeds C (1651–1656), fol. 157, D (1656–1666), fols. 137, 237, 267, 280, 284.

61. Walsh, "Community Networks," in Carr, Morgan, and Russo, eds., *Colonial Chesapeake Society*, 225, 233; Durand of Dauphine, *A Frenchman in Virginia*, trans. Harrison, 96–97; Rutman and Rutman, *A Place in Time: Middlesex County*, 95–113.

beth River or Dominic Therriott's at the courthouse on the Corotoman River, or they could simply gather at a neighbor's house. When William Memox, John Queen, and their wives arrived at Captain William Carver's house, together with Captain Robert Jordan, Carver asked Richard Harris, who had been there "all the forenoon," "to take a bottle and make them drinck a dram for hee was glad of their Comp[an]y." In Henrico County on a hot August afternoon, a group of freemen, servants, and "Negroes" at work on the plantation of a local gentleman stopped to drink cider and were joined by Katherine, the wife of a neighbor, who drank so much that it "turned her braines."[62]

Other visits were occasioned by the exchange of food, bartering local produce, or caring for sick neighbors. Oliver Hancock, who lived on the eastern side of Lynnhaven, "did borrow of Thomas Cheely half a barrel of corn, in his great necessity." William Johnson and Thomas Hayes bought a barrel of "Indian Peas" from Henry Catlin, and William Lucas hired a cow from Thomas Davys. On the frontier, settlers depended on each other for help in times of sickness or when supplies ran low and for company and the witnessing of important events. Cooperation was vital for survival.[63]

Besides casual face-to-face meetings and visits, neighbors frequently acted together collectively. In Virginia, they were expected to attend church or their local chapel on Sundays, which besides spiritual and moral edification provided opportunities for engaging in gossip, picking up news, and socializing after the service. Local communities, organized into parishes, employed their own ministers, built churches, and supported the poor, sick, and elderly. Throughout the tidewater, men were occasionally called together for militia musters, to march against Indians, to repair the "Roades and wayes," or for jury service. When Toby Horton and Thomas Humphreys of Fleet's Bay became involved in a dispute over land boundaries, the court summoned "foure of the ablest and neerest inhabitants" to arbitrate. Similarly, juries of

62. Lower Norfolk County, Minute Book (1637–1646), I, fols. 180–181, Wills and Deeds E (1666–1675), fol. 127; Lancaster County, Orders Etc. (1655–1666), 2; Colonel [Henry] Norwood, *A Voyage to Virginia* (1649)," in Force, comp., *Tracts and Other Papers*, III, no. 10, p. 49; Warren M. Billings, ed., *The Old Dominion in the Seventeenth Century: A Documentary History of Virginia, 1606–1689* (Chapel Hill, N.C., 1975), 163; Durand of Dauphine commented that "women show the way in drinking and smoking" (*A Frenchman in Virginia*, trans. Harrison, 96–97).

63. Lower Norfolk County, Minute Book (1637–1646), I, fols. 5, 182, Wills and Deeds B (1646–1651), fol. 10; Lancaster County, Orders Etc. (1655–1666), 136; Walsh, "Community Networks," in Carr, Morgan, and Russo, eds., *Colonial Chesapeake Society*, 206.

the neighborhood were empaneled to assess damages done to crops by cattle or to view the body of anyone who died in mysterious circumstances.[64]

Far from living on isolated plantations, the great majority of planters were embedded in an intricate network of friends and neighbors. In some cases, marriage and remarriage created complex circles of in-laws. Kin, like friends, "out of Christian piety and charity," were called upon to see the wishes of a testator performed and were sometimes appointed as attorneys to collect debts or carry out other duties. Small gifts were given to neighboring relatives. Colonel John Carter, "for the Love that I bear towards my neice Eltonheade the Daughter of Edwyn Connaway," gave her a heifer and its increase in the spring of 1656, and Henry Nicholas, also of Lancaster, gave his "kinsman" David George a cow and a bull calf. Most planters were not in touch with relatives regularly and may not have been close to in-laws they hardly knew, particularly those living outside the community. Friends and neighbors, not kin, gave structure to everyday life at the local level.[65]

Although settlement was more dense than in the tidewater, many parts of rural England, especially wood-pasture, forested, and upland regions, exhibited a scattered settlement pattern. In the Vale of Berkeley, parish populations were frequently composed of numerous hamlets and tithings. North Nibley, for example, had eleven hamlets or neighborhoods with between five and thirty families each, and Berkeley was a conglomeration of at least twenty different subunits in the form of chapelries, tithings, and farmsteads. Isaac Taylor's map of 1777 on the eve of the Industrial Revolution gives an impression of the region's dispersed settlement, which had changed little since the previous century.[66] Face-to-face contact in these areas did not take

64. Hening, ed., *Statutes*, I, 123, 144, 155, 180; Rutman and Rutman, *A Place in Time: Middlesex County*, 122–125; Virginia Bernhard, "Poverty and the Social Order in Seventeenth-Century Virginia," *Virginia Magazine of History and Biography*, LXXXV (1977), 147–151; C. G. Chamberlayne, ed., *The Vestry Book of Christ Church Parish, Middlesex County, Virginia, 1663–1767* (Richmond, Va., 1927), 52; Lancaster County, Orders Etc. (1655–1666), 8; Lower Norfolk County, Wills and Deeds B (1646–1651), fol. 156, E (1666–1675), fol. 127, E (Orders) (1666–1675), fols. 104, 129.

65. Lower Norfolk County, Wills and Deeds C (1651–1656), fol. 203; Lancaster County, Deeds Etc., no. 2 (1654–1666), 151, 169, 267–268, Orders, no. 1 (1666–1680), 191; Rutman and Rutman, *A Place in Time: Middlesex County*, 100; Walsh, "Charles County," 303.

66. Horn, "Adapting to New World: A Comparative Study of Local Society in England and Maryland, 1650–1700," in Carr, Morgan, and Russo, eds., *Colonial Chesapeake Society*, 164–175; Atkyns, *Ancient and Present State*, 139–141, 251–252, 304, 363–364; *A Gloucestershire and Bristol Atlas* (London, 1961), 10–11.

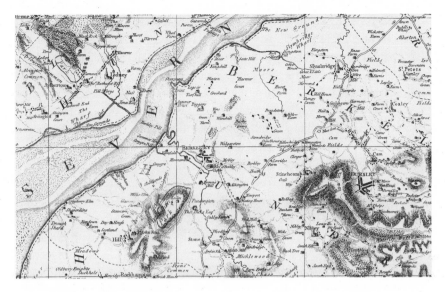

4. The Parish of Berkeley and Environs. *By Isaac Taylor.*
Permission of the British Library

place in the busy streets, lanes, or surrounding fields of compact villages, but
in the yards of small clusters of houses and in scattered closes and pastures
of each neighborhood and tithing.

As in the Chesapeake, kin in England played a less important role in the
lives of most people than friends and neighbors. Although relatives outside
the immediate family were recognized more often by married male testators
than was typical in Virginia and Maryland, in-laws and grandchildren were
mentioned in only one-fifth of wills, siblings in fewer than 14 percent, and
other relatives in fewer than 7 percent (Table 22). Of course, bequests might
represent very small amounts of money, or other "tokens," and need not
reflect the importance of a tie, but this begs the question why kin were not
frequently bequeathed minor gifts. A person's trust in friends was often expressed by appointing them overseers or executors. William Potter of Wood-
ford, Berkeley, made his "loveing neybours," Robert Davis and John Nelme,
overseers of his will, as did Roger Wilson of Lower Stone in the same parish.
George Martin left ten pounds to his overseer and "dearly Beloved and faith-
ful friend," Edward Smyth, esquire, and Sarah Clutterbuck, widow, gave
one pound each to Edward Saniger, his son, and John Pincott, her executors
in trust, to buy rings "in memory of me their derest freind."[67]

67. Wills and Deeds 1663/145, 1678/172, 1684/90, 1688/143, GRO.

The argument that kinship played an insignificant role in the daily affairs of local communities is supported by the case of Terling, Essex. Of 122 householders in 1678, about half had no kin resident in the village apart from immediate family, and the majority of inhabitants who did have kin nearby had only one such link. "Households were either isolated or relatively isolated in the village in kin terms," according to Wrightson and Levine. Beyond the nuclear family, "there is little evidence that kinship was an important independent element in the structuring of social relations." Similarly, Alan Macfarlane suggests, there "was no effective kin 'group' " in the social world of Essex clergyman Ralph Josselin. "Although there were frequent visits and occasional small loans between kin, economic and ritual activities were not carried out by them. When help was needed either in sickness, in economic undertakings, or in the celebration of birth, marriage and death, relatives were only infrequently called upon. We may therefore wonder where such help was found. The answer seems to be, amongst groups of friends and neighbours."[68]

A number of reasons account for the relative unimportance of kin ties in English communities. One was geographical mobility. Even during the second half of the seventeenth century, when the incidence of migration was declining, 60–75 percent of people moved at least once in their lives. Migration, Peter Clark comments, "was not the exception but the social and demographic norm, indeed the usual way of life, in early modern England." Most of this movement was local, possibly less than ten miles, but sufficient to take individuals out of the immediate orbit of their families of birth. Earlier in the century, poor migrants who eventually ended up as indentured servants and who typically traveled much longer distances might well have been cut off from kin for some time before taking ship to the colonies. They would have been used to relying on themselves or friends in the absence of nearby relatives. Another factor inhibiting the development of dense kinship links was the high age of marriage and low life expectancy. The tiny proportion of bequests made to parents, uncles, and aunts was not just a consequence of mobility; it was also a reflection of the high mortality rates that prevailed in early modern England. Thus most contact with adult kin was necessarily with members of the individual's own generation: siblings and cousins.[69]

68. Wrightson and Levine, *Poverty and Piety*, 102; Macfarlane, *Family Life of Ralph Josselin*, 148–149. For a critique of this view, see Cressy, "Kinship and Kin Interaction," *Past and Present*, no. 116 (November 1986), 38–69.

69. Peter Clark, "Migration in England during the Late Seventeenth and Early Eigh-

Friends and neighbors appear to have fulfilled largely the same roles in English communities as they did in the tidewater. Thomas Vidler of Cromhall witnessed the nuncupative will of his "neere neighbour," Edward Goodman, in 1671; Thomas Payne of North Nibley visited his neighbor, Thomas Croome, "when he was sick"; and Agnes Hill, a "neighbour" of Anne Turner of Dursley, spoke up on her behalf when she was called "a whore and a common whore" by Eliza Curtis. When Peter Hicks declared before his neighbors at a court leet of the manor of Tytherington that he would give all he had to his son-in-law, Edward Horrod, in consideration of all the "kindnesses" he had received from him, he knew that he could rely on his neighbors to remember his words and testify to that effect in court if necessary. In fact, one neighbor recalled that he not only "took notice of these words" but wrote them down when he got home.[70]

Informal associations between friends and neighbors were a vital aspect of daily life in the local community, and in this respect there is an important continuity between Old World and New World experience. Yet formal institutions generally had more of an impact on the lives of English villagers than on their Chesapeake counterparts. Without exaggerating the importance of the Anglican church, especially in view of the growth of dissent in the sixteenth and seventeenth centuries, it had vastly more influence at the local level in England than in Virginia or Maryland. The parish emerged as the principal unit of local government below the county in England during this period. Through its various officers it was in many respects self-governing, and if only a small proportion of people actually took part in the running of local affairs (about one in five male householders), nevertheless, decisions taken by the vestry, churchwardens, and overseers of the poor affected everybody. In some areas, such as the Vale of Berkeley, manorial courts retained vigor well into the eighteenth century, providing another tier of structured relations between neighbors. To various degrees, then, parish and manor were important influences shaping the lives of men and women and underpinning informal interaction. Hence in English rural society the parish and local community were usually coterminous.[71]

teenth Centuries," *Past and Present*, no. 83 (May 1979), 57–90; Laslett, *Family Life and Illicit Love*, chap. 5.

70. GDR 221, May 26, 1671, 232, Nov. 18, 1679, Oct. 4, 1681, Jan. 10, 1681/2, GRO. See also Horn, "Adapting to a New World," in Carr, Morgan, and Russo, eds., *Colonial Chesapeake Society*, 165–169.

71. Horn, "Adapting to a New World," in Carr, Morgan, and Russo, eds., *Colonial Chesapeake Society*, 168–189; David Underdown, *Revel, Riot, and Rebellion: Popular*

Change was a fundamental and continuous aspect of immigrant experience in the Chesapeake. It was apparent in the constant influx of new arrivals, the death of established householders, and the movement of people out of the community. Of 44 adult males who lived on St. Clement's Manor in 1659–1661, only 8 (18 percent) resided there ten years later, and only 10 of 84 males living there in 1672 were sons or sons-in-law of residents of a decade earlier. In Lancaster County, approaching a third of householders who lived between Fleet's Bay and the Moratico River on the northern side of the Rappahannock in 1655 had either died or left the county five years later, and nearly a half were no longer resident in the area by 1664. Every year a small but steady stream of planters returned to England or left for regions where opportunities seemed brighter. In 1687, Colonel St. Leger Codd in "a Privately Clandestine manner Conveyed himselfe and his wife and family out of . . . [Lancaster] County with what of his estate he could," allegedly to escape creditors. Edward Lloyd, along with other Puritans, left Lower Norfolk seeking religious refuge and settled on the "Seavern in An arrandell County in the pr'vince of Marreland." Francis Anketill, Clement Theobald, Richard Foster, and Job Chandler, of the same county, sought better prospects "up the baye" and took up land in "Patuxon," "Portobac," and on St. Clement's Manor. Beginning in the late 1660s Lower Norfolk settlers also began moving south to the "County of Carolina."[72]

Change was reflected too in local social structure. Single tithable households in Lancaster County rose from 10 percent of all householders in 1653 to more than 40 percent by 1687. In other Virginia counties, such as Accomack, Northampton, and Surry, there was a similar increase in poor households; by the eve of Bacon's Rebellion half the landowning population in these areas was taxed on a single laborer. Poverty was evident in the growing numbers in receipt of parish relief. No more than a few poor were given aid in Christ Church Parish, Middlesex County, in the late 1660s and 1670s, but during

---

Politics and Culture in England, 1603–1660 (Oxford, 1985), chaps. 2–4; Walsh, "Charles County," chap. 6.

72. Walsh, "Community Networks," in Carr, Morgan, and Russo, eds., *Colonial Chesapeake Society*, 215, 220; James Horn, biographical files, Lancaster County; Horn, "Moving On in the New World: Migration and Out-Migration in the Seventeenth-Century Chesapeake," in Peter Clark and David Souden, eds., *Migration and Society in Early Modern England* (London, 1987), 184–185, 196, Lancaster County, Orders Etc. (1655–1666), 52, 86, no. 4 (1696–1702), 18 (CW, microfilm, reel M 117-8); Lower Norfolk County, Wills and Deeds C (1651–1656), fols. 72, 111, 210, D (1656–1666), fol. 116, E (1666–1675), fols. 27, 77, 78, 98, 152.

the next two decades there was a dramatic increase. The accounts tell their own story: 500 lbs. of tobacco to "a poore old Decriped Man," 1,000 lbs. to Richard Watts, "a poore Aged and Impotent man," 1,500 lbs. to Mary Thompson, "a poore Woman (a very object of Charity)," 400 lbs. to Henry Baskett, described variously as "a Cripple" and "a poore Lame Ladd." In 1689, 8,500 lbs. spent on poor relief represented by far the largest outlay of parish funds after the payment of the minister's salary. Expenditure was not always this high, but there can be no doubt that by the 1680s provision for the poor was a major responsibility of Virginia vestries. The development of a permanent substratum of poverty was one expression of the growing social distance between rich and poor in the colony after the Restoration.[73]

The composition of the labor force changed, more so in some regions than others; but, nevertheless, its impact was felt in all areas of the Bay. During the 1680s, the Royal African Company began transporting slaves to Virginia in "cargoes" of several hundred at a time. Two hundred Gambian "negroes" were sent to the Potomac, 190 to the James River, and "about" 200 to the York in 1686 alone. In the belief that "Blacks can make [tobacco] cheaper than Whites," the planter elite bought as many slaves as they could afford and get hold of. In counties such as Middlesex, committed to tobacco husbandry and producing high-quality leaf, blacks overtook white servants as the main source of labor by the end of the century, by which time they composed a fifth of the county's population. Even in poorer regions, such as Surry, where tobacco cultivation was less profitable, slaves represented about a third of the bound labor force in 1684 and nearly half by 1699. Slaveownership was not confined to the elite; plenty of middling planters also purchased slaves. But the sight of dozens of blacks toiling on the plantations of big planters was not only a very obvious indication of wealth; it also confirmed that the elite had no need of casual labor supplied by surrounding whites. If they chose, they could be fully independent of poorer neighbors. Rising numbers

73. Lancaster County, Deeds Etc., no. 1 (1652–1657), 91–94, Orders Etc., no. 3 (1686–1696), 28–29; Edmund S. Morgan, *American Slavery, American Freedom: The Ordeal of Colonial Virginia* (New York, 1975), 226–229; Russell R. Menard, P.M.G. Harris, and Lois Green Carr, "Opportunity and Inequality: The Distribution of Wealth on the Lower Western Shore of Maryland, 1638–1705," *Md. Hist. Mag.*, LXIX (1974), 182–184; Chamberlayne, ed., *Vestry Book of Christ Church Parish*, 9–28, 39–114; Darrett B. Rutman and Anita H. Rutman, *A Place in Time: Middlesex County*, chap. 6, 115–200; Rutman and Rutman, *A Place in Time: Explicatus* (New York, 1984), 129–130; Walsh, "Charles County," 420. Social hierarchy in relation to order and challenges to constituted authority will be considered in Chapter 8.

of slaves and their concentration in the hands of the elite were another factor that contributed to the growing social distinctions that fissured local society in the last quarter of the century.[74]

Rapid change was a determining characteristic of life in the seventeenth-century tidewater. But change did not undermine the central role played by family, neighborhood, and local community in the lives of settlers; rather, it did the opposite. In the face of uncertainties about the future, and for the most part cut off from kin and friends in England, men and women looked for support and stability by creating their own households and establishing themselves in a web of relationships within the surrounding community. Despite the turnover of population, the flexibility of informal associations and demands of frontier life encouraged friendships to develop quickly and play a vital part in all aspects of daily life. For those who did not fall victim to the disease environment, marriage and the companionship of neighbors offered some recompense for the hardships endured in moving to the Chesapeake.

74. CW, VCRP 5754 (PRO T 70/61); Rutman and Rutman, *A Place in Time: Middlesex County*, 165–167; Morgan, *American Slavery, American Freedom*, 295–307; Gloria L. Main, "Maryland and the Chesapeake Economy, 1670–1720," in Land *et al.*, eds., *Law, Society, and Politics*, 134–142; Kulikoff, *Tobacco and Slaves*, 6, 33–38, 319–321, 330–332.

6

Adam's Curse: Working Lives

In *The Man in the Moone*, published in 1638, Francis Godwin described an imaginary society where there "is no want of any thing necessary for the use of man. Food groweth every where without labour, and that of all sorts to be desired. For rayment, howsing, or any thing else that you may imagine possible for a man to want, or desire, it is provided. . . . There is never any raine, wind, or change of the Ayre, never either Summer, or Winter, but as it were a perpetuall Spring, yeelding all pleasure, all content." The theme was common in utopian accounts of a previous Golden Age, Arcadia, or kingdoms yet to come. In Sir Thomas More's *Utopia* no one worked more than six hours each day. During the English Revolution some radical millenarians anticipated that the return of King Jesus would herald an earthly paradise where there would be "no painfull labour" and where, in the words of older prophesies, "honey in abundance shall drip from the rocks, [and] fountains of milk and wine shall burst forth."[1]

Similar myths were applied to America. The New World was described as a land where people were immortal, where it was always summer, where food was abundant, and where nobody had to work. In England projectors such as Richard Hakluyt and Samuel Purchas and poets such as Edmund Spenser and Michael Drayton eulogized the land of plenty, earth's "onely paradise," across the Atlantic. More's *Utopia* and Francis Bacon's *New Atlantis* were located in terra incognita in the West, and Godwin's wise and just inhabitants of the moon, the "Lunars," traded with North America, "whose people," he wrote, "I can easily beleeve to be wholly descended of them."[2]

1. [Francis Godwin], *The Man in the Moone* (London, 1638), 102, 105, 109; Keith Thomas, "Work and Leisure in Pre-Industrial Society," *Past and Present*, no. 29 (December 1964), 57; Norman Cohn, *The Pursuit of the Millennium* (Fairlawn, N.J., 1957), 11–12.

2. Howard Mumford Jones, *O Strange New World: American Culture, the Formative*

That Old World myths of abundance and ease should be transposed to the New World is not surprising, considering the political and cultural context in which Europeans discovered and learned about America. Instead of Cathay, early explorers found new lands inhabited only by (to their eyes) simple agrarian peoples, untainted by the corruption and vices of Old World society, who appeared to live in happiness and sufficiency in a kind of primordial Eden. Here, then, was proof that heaven did exist on earth, or so it seemed. It was a vision, however, that proved short-lived. Far from being an earthly paradise, America quickly became a testing ground for some of the most brutal, oppressive, and exploitative labor systems ever devised, entailing the wholesale enslavement of indigenous populations and the transportation of millions of African slaves and hundreds of thousands of poor whites to labor in the mines and on the plantations of New World colonies. Slaves, servants, and poor free immigrants found, not abundance and ease, but backbreaking work, disease, and early death. In one of history's most tragic turn of events, the American paradise rapidly turned into a living hell. The New World, it was soon realized, no more than the expected millennium, offered escape from the harsh realities of life.[3]

This chapter considers one aspect of these realities, the experience of work and its impact on the lives of early Cheasapeake settlers. Few colonists by the 1630s, apart from the gullible and credulous, believed that America offered them a life of opulence and idleness, but most must have seen some advantages in emigrating, whether in terms of regular work, board and lodging, or perhaps the chance eventually to possess land of their own. For others (as discussed earlier), Maryland and Virginia held out favorable prospects of handsome profits from tobacco and merchandising in return for the modest investment needed to set up a plantation. The Chesapeake might not be a paradise, but the twin themes of abundance and opportunity persisted in promotional literature of the period, as did the hope of finding a subsistence by those who had found one elusive in England.[4]

Years (New York, 1964), chap. 1; Christopher Hill, *Puritanism and Revolution: Studies in Interpretation of the English Revolution of the Seventeenth Century* (London, 1958), 54–55; Jeffrey Knapp, *An Empire Nowhere: England, America, and Literature from "Utopia" to "The Tempest"* (Los Angeles, 1992); [Godwin], *Man in the Moone*, 109.

3. For an interesting example of how quickly the American paradise turned sour, see George Percy, "Observations" (1607), in Lyon Gardiner Tyler, ed., *Narratives of Early Virginia, 1606–1625*, Original Narratives of Early American History (New York, 1907), 9–22.

4. See Chapter 1, above.

The Necessity of Work

Official attitudes toward work, expressed through sermons, the courts, and parliamentary statute during the sixteenth and seventeenth centuries, exhibited a number of common themes.[5] Foremost was an emphasis on order and discipline. The Statute of Artificers of 1563 (5 Eliz. I, c. 4) set the tone for the next century and a half. Under its provisions, justices and magistrates were empowered to regulate wages, hours, and conditions and put the able-bodied unemployed to work. Masters were not allowed to dismiss their servants unless for good reason, but neither could the poor refuse work or leave employment before their term was completed. If they did, they risked prosecution under the vagrancy acts passed during the period. The governing class viewed the growing numbers of vagrants and poor primarily as a problem of order rather than a serious social and economic problem generated by population increase and economic dislocation. Unemployment was an offense not just because the unemployed were a drain on society's resources but because they lived beyond the control of a master and were therefore viewed as a threat to the hierarchy of householders that bound society together. Out of work and on the tramp, the poor migrant was perceived as masterless, willfully idle, rootless, lawless, and corrupt. Hence the government supported schemes that put the poor to work at home or, better still, shipped them to the colonies. This was the background of measures to transport vagrants and other felons to America that began in the early seventeenth century.[6]

Tudor and Stuart legislation made a distinction, however, between the able-bodied poor and those who could not, for one reason or another, support themselves and deserved aid. The parish was given the major responsibility of providing for its aged, sick, and orphaned young. An evident concern of parochial authorities was to ensure that orphans were placed in

5. For example of official attitudes, see R. H. Tawney and Eileen Power, eds., *Tudor Economic Documents* . . . (1924; London, 1965), III, 62–63, 405–458; G. R. Elton, ed., *The Tudor Constitution: Documents and Commentary*, 2d ed. (Cambridge, 1982), 478–482; Dorothy Marshall, *The English Poor in the Eighteenth Century: A Study in Social and Administrative History* (London, 1926), 15–44; Hill, *Puritanism and Revolution*, 215–238.

6. Elton, ed., *Tudor Constitution*, 478–482; A. L. Beier, *Masterless Men: The Vagrancy Problem in Britain, 1560–1640* (London, 1985), 3–28, 162–164; Hilary McD. Beckles, *White Servitude and Black Slavery in Barbados, 1627–1715* (Knoxville, Tenn., 1989), 46–52; Abbot Emerson Smith, *Colonists in Bondage: White Servitude and Convict Labor in America, 1607–1776* (Chapel Hill, N.C., 1947), chap. 6; Paul Slack, *Poverty and Policy in Tudor and Stuart England* (London, 1988), chap. 7.

households and brought up to work. Typically, overseers of the poor either paid an annual wage to families who had taken in young children or laid out a certain sum for them to be apprenticed. Pauper apprenticeship was the immediate predecessor of the system of indentured servitude adopted in the colonies and very likely served as a blueprint. Churchwardens and overseers, "or the greater Part of them," with the permission of two justices, were allowed to "bind any such children . . . to be Apprentices, where they shall see convenient, till such Man-child shall come to the Age of four and twenty Years, and such Woman-child to the Age of one and twenty Years, or the time of her Marriage; the same to be as effectual to all Purposes, as if such Child were of full Age, and by Indenture of Covenant bound himself or herself." [7]

Service and apprenticeship were integral aspects of working life in early modern England. A majority of adolescents and young adults spent much of their youth in service as domestics, servants in husbandry, and apprentices. A stage in growing up, it marked the vital transition from childhood and living with parents to adulthood, marriage, and living with spouse and children. But pauper apprenticeship was different in several fundamental respects. First, unlike service in husbandry, where a contract was voluntarily entered into by the servant to serve usually for a year in return for board, lodging, and a small wage, the pauper in most cases did not have any choice about whom he or she would serve. Conventionally, paupers served until adulthood or marriage without being paid. (Keep and training were considered sufficient recompense.) Orphans apprenticed in early childhood were theoretically eligible to serve for ten to fifteen years or more, depending on their age. Second, in the absence of family or kin to look after them, poor children were vulnerable to all sorts of abuses from their masters: insufficient food and clothing, ill-treatment, inadequate training, excessive work, and abandonment. Parish overseers and the courts provided little protection, and in many cases the servant's only recourse was to run away, thereby adding to the increasing numbers of poor and homeless on the streets. [8] Hardships suffered by pauper apprentices in England and servants in the colonies stemmed from common causes: poverty, the determination of parish, county, and government to put the idle to work with small regard

7. 43 Eliz. I, c. 2 (1601); John Pound, *Poverty and Vagrancy in Tudor England* (London, 1971), chap. 4; Slack, *Poverty and Policy*, 118–119, 126–131; Marshall, *English Poor*, 182; Richard B. Morris, *Government and Labor in Early America* (New York, 1946), 384–385.

8. Ann Kussmaul, *Servants in Husbandry in Early Modern England* (Cambridge, 1981), 3, 11, 31; Marshall, *English Poor*, 194–205.

for the poor themselves, and the vulnerability of those with no resources, family, or friends to help them.

Aside from pragmatic considerations of how to employ the poor—in workhouses, through apprenticeships, various projects in England, or transportation to the colonies—a number of writers emphasized the moral and spiritually regenerative effect of work. Peter Chamberlen argued in 1649, "It is certain that employment and competencies do civilize all men, and makes them tractable and obedient to Superiors commands." Another reformer, Adam Moore, thought that the poor could be "reclaimed and refined to loyall and laudable courses" if they were given a stake in society, such as a four-acre plot taken from wastes and commons. William Perkins, a Calvinist minister, believed that "every person of every degree, state, sexe, or condition without exception, must have some personall and particular calling to walke in." His ideal was industrious small producers, who "rise early to their businesse, lest night overtake them." Those who deliberately avoided work put themselves outside "civill societie" as well as outside the church and were a "cursed generation."[9]

The necessity of work, then, was based on a number of assumptions besides the obvious need to earn a living. Whereas "Idleness in Youth" was conceived as "the Weed plot of the Hangmans Harvest," work engendered responsibility, sobriety, and conformity, a sure route to "Gods kingdome." Work conferred a place within the status-conscious social hierarchy of the late sixteenth and the seventeenth centuries and was the basis of one of the most fundamental social divisions in early modern society: between the gentry who did not involve themselves in manual labor, and the "inferior sort of people" who did. Contemporary commentators acknowledged the value of labor and emphasized the importance of a populous and industrious society. John Bellars, writing in the early eighteenth century, stated that "regularly labouring People are the Kingdom's greatest Treasure and Strength, for without Labourers there can be no Lords; and if the poor Labourers did not raise much more Food and Manufacture than what did subsist themselves, every Gentleman must be a Labourer, and every idle Man must starve." But they did not concede that, as a consequence, working people should be accorded more than a basic subsistence. To men of property, the working classes had a God-given duty to perform their allotted labor, "for it was God, not man, that had created social inequality and assigned individuals to their various social positions" and roles. Laboring people were expected to accept their

9. Joyce Oldham Appleby, *Economic Thought and Ideology in Seventeenth-Century England* (Princeton, N.J., 1978), 142–144; Hill, *Puritanism and Revolution*, 226, 227, 231.

position and not to question their social superiors why they were destined to a life of hard work.[10]

Earning a Living

In the early modern period the great majority of men and women experienced work as unremitting physical labor, in the form of long hours of tedious routine or sporadic bouts of tough, backbreaking tasks.[11] The working lives of people who left England for America were no exception. Immigrants to the Chesapeake came from a multiplicity of backgrounds and included representatives of virtually every major occupation and status in English society.

A large proportion of indentured servants who took ship for Maryland and Virginia from Bristol in the 1650s and 1660s came from agricultural backgrounds (Table 3 above). Given that the majority would have been in their late teens or early twenties at their departure, it is highly unlikely that they were independent farmers fallen on hard times. Most had probably worked as hired hands or servants in husbandry, shifting from farm to farm before making the move to Bristol. Their experiences would have varied considerably, depending on the type of farming region they were from and the sort of work they engaged in. Men and women from the Severn Valley and northwestern Somerset would have worked mainly with cattle, tending milk cows, rearing livestock, and dairying. In addition, many farms kept a few swine and sheep. The great majority of farmhands from lowland areas of the Bristol region, like the Vale of Berkeley, came, not from arable zones, but predominantly from pastoral districts. By contrast, agricultural laborers from the South and Southeast would have been familiar with a range of cereals produced for the London market, notably wheat, barley, oats, and rye, as well as a variety of cash crops such as hops, flax, hemp, and tobacco. Market gardening was important in the vicinity of London, as was dairying. Moving from region to region, some laborers may have encountered a number of different kinds of farm work while others may have stayed mostly in one type. In looking at servant emigration from rural areas throughout the country, then, no one type dominated. What should be stressed is the sheer diversity

10. Appleby, *Economic Thought*, 142; Robert W. Malcolmson, *Life and Labour in England, 1700–1780* (London, 1981), 12–17.

11. J. A. Sharpe, *Early Modern England: A Social History, 1500–1760* (London, 1987), 206.

of farming backgrounds of emigrants, which makes descriptions of particular work experiences of servants before they migrated virtually impossible.[12]

Service in husbandry is of particular interest because of its parallels with indentured servitude. Three characteristics distinguished service throughout the period, all of which largely apply to indentured servants: (1) it "was not an adult occupation, but a status and occupation of youths"; (2) it was a contractual institution; and (3) servants in husbandry were maintained by the farmer's family. Farm servants in southern and eastern England were usually hired around Michaelmas (late September), following the harvest, and were generally taken on for a year or two. Under the terms of the contract, servants obliged themselves to serve and obey their master in return for board and lodging and an agreed wage. Although technically enforceable at law, in reality contracts were often no more than oral agreements that could be terminated at any time by the mutual consent of both parties.[13]

Although particular work routines varied according to the different types of husbandry, certain generalizations can be made. Work tended to be task-centered, servants labored for the most part singly or in small groups, and the range of daily tasks was highly influenced by the seasonal rhythms of the year. During the winter months, men worked at hedging, ditching, setting trees, felling timber, plowing, and harrowing in preparation for spring sowing and looked after draft animals, cattle, and sheep. Women servants were primarily responsible for the dairy, milking cows, and tending the farmyard poultry and garden plot as well as various chores associated with running the household: cooking, brewing beer or cider, washing, and cleaning. During busy periods they also commonly worked in the fields alongside the men. In the spring, oats, barley, and vetches were sown, and sheep farmers began the lambing season. June and July brought another round of tasks—manuring the fields, summer plowing, haymaking, washing and shearing sheep—before the onset of the busiest time of the year in August and early September, when the harvest had to be gathered in, threshing done, and

12. H.P.R. Finberg and Joan Thirsk, eds., *The Agrarian History of England and Wales* (Cambridge, 1967–), IV, chaps. 1, 5, 7, 9, V, pt. 1, introduction, chaps. 6–9. See also C.G.A. Clay, *Economic Expansion and Social Change: England, 1500–1700*, 2 vols. (Cambridge, 1984), I, chap. 3; Malcolmson, *Life and Labour*, chap. 2; Kussmaul, *Servants in Husbandry*, chap. 3; K.D.M. Snell, *Annals of the Labouring Poor: Social Change and Agrarian England, 1660–1900* (Cambridge, 1985), chap. 4. No attempt is made here to consider work patterns in detail. See Chapter 1, above, for a description of servants' occupations before they left England.

13. Kussmaul, *Servants in Husbandry*, 31–34, 50.

livestock bought and sold at the local fair. In October and November, as winter approached once more, rye and wheat were planted and preparations made for housing livestock during the worst of the weather. Meanwhile, the farmer's wife salted down meat and stored away grains, cheese, and fruit for household consumption over the winter months. Christmas festivities provided a welcome break before the whole cycle began again.[14]

Work could be hard and long, especially during busy summer months. According to Gervase Markham, farm workers were to rise no later than four in the morning, feed and water the cattle, tend to the horses and tackle, and clean the stable before breakfast at six. Plowing started at seven and continued until midafternoon, at which point workers were given half an hour for dinner. After dinner, they returned to the stables and attended to the animals until about half past six, when supper was ready. Evenings were spent repairing tackle and farm tools, threshing corn, beating hemp, preparing fruit for cider and perry, and working at a variety of other tasks. After a final visit to the stables to clean the stalls, replace fodder, and bed down the livestock, the servant was permitted to retire.[15]

In practice, it is doubtful that such an arduous regimen could be sustained for long. Servants had to be continually supervised if they were to be kept hard at work all day. As one contemporary put it, "Men can worke yf they list and soe they can loyter." Masters were always complaining about the laziness of their servants. John Smyth of North Nibley, recounting the proverb, "The mice will play when the catt is away," added, "Servants will loyter when the master is absent: This my experience in my longe abodes abroad, all my life longe, hath prooved too true for my profitt." Robert Loder was convinced, "All workemen . . . will play legerdemaine with theyr masters and favour themselves." Servants slept in the corn fields, absconded to the local alehouse, and sang and played games in the stable after supper. Work, as Keith Thomas points out, was "discontinuous," punctuated by bad weather, the seasonality of tasks, visits to markets, and the feasts of the church. Hence the work pattern of many servants alternated between "bouts of intense labour and of idleness." [16]

14. Mildred Campbell, *The English Yeoman under Elizabeth and the Early Stuarts* (New Haven, Conn., 1942), 209–210; Kussmaul, *Servants in Husbandry*, 34–35; Finberg and Thirsk, eds., *Agrarian History of England and Wales*, IV, 431, 533; Alice Clark, *Working Life of Women in the Seventeenth Century* (1919; New York, 1968), 60–64.

15. E. P. Thompson, "Time, Work-Discipline, and Industrial Capitalism," *Past and Present*, no. 38 (December 1967), 77.

16. *Ibid.*, 73, 78; John Smyth, *A Description of the Hundred of Berkeley in the County of Gloucester and of Its Inhabitants*, vol. III of *The Berkeley Manuscripts*, ed. Sir John Maclean

Food and lodging was a form of payment in kind and supplemented wages. Again, conditions must have varied considerably from farm to farm, but generally servants shared the meals of and often sat at the same table as the farmer and his family. Robert Loder, who owned a large farm near the Berkshire Downs, estimated that he spent £9 16s. 6d. on meat and drink for each of his three men and two maids in 1614, and £11 18s. 6d. the following year, the same as he spent on himself and his wife and daughter. Their diet consisted primarily of wheaten bread, cheese, bacon and other "meate or flesh," "beanes and pese," fruit, and occasionally fish, washed down with beer or milk. On the Toke estates of East Kent, a sheep-looker, or shepherd, in Romney Marsh was paid £5 in wages and £10 for his keep, and £36 was laid out in one year for the food of two men and two boys. During the harvest, workers were usually given an additional payment for beer or cider and, when the harvest was completed, were invited to a feast of "beef and bacon, puddings and apple-pies, and hot cakes and ale" at the farmer's expense. William Marshall might believe that bread and cheese were good enough fare for laborers, but it appears that servants were generally well fed and enjoyed a varied diet including regular meat dishes.[17]

There is little direct evidence of the lodging arrangements of servants. On larger farms men and women servants had their own rooms. In the "Mens Chamber" of Thomas Brodnax of Godmersham, Kent, were two beds, two cupboards, and a trunk; the "Maids Chamber," next to the nursery, contained a feather bed, four chairs, a clothespress, a table, a warming pan, and a "Screene." Furnishings were usually more spartan, however. The "servants Chamber" of Gabriel Piers of Charing, gentleman, in the same county, had two old bedsteads, two flockbeds, bedding, one "little table," and "one old Chaire." Similarly, in the house of Stephen Court, a wealthy farmer of Reculver, the servants' chamber contained only four beds and an old chest.[18] It appears common for servants (of the same sex) to have been housed together, sleeping two, three, or four to a room. Among smaller farmers, servants probably slept in lofts and garrets. Conditions would have been cramped but were preferable to lodging in the outhouses or stable.

Given the expense of board and lodging, monetary wages were low. In

---

(Gloucester, 1883–1885), 33; G. E. Fussell, ed., *Robert Loder's Farm Accounts, 1610–1620*, Camden Society, 3d Ser., LIII (London, 1936), 25; Thomas, "Work and Leisure," *Past and Present*, no. 29 (December 1964), 52; Kussmaul, *Servants in Husbandry*, 43.

17. Finberg and Thirsk, eds., *Agrarian History of England and Wales*, IV, 437–438; Fussell, ed., *Robert Loder's Farm Accounts*, xxix, 86–87, 107, 122; Eleanor C. Lodge, ed., *The Account Book of a Kentish Estate, 1616–1704* (London, 1927), xxxvii.

18. PRC 27/13/1, 27/21/78, 27/25/36, Kent Archives Office, Maidstone, Kent.

Gloucestershire a common "servant of husbandry" received £3 per year in 1655 and a woman servant £1 15s. Toke's servants received £1–£1 10s. for a boy, £2 10s. or £3 for women, and £3–£7 10s. for men, but he may have been unusually generous. Women, apart from cooks and favored personal maids, were always paid less than men, even when they did the same tasks. Wages varied also according to the particular work involved. Sir Roger Twysden of Kent paid his plowman £6, threshers £3–£4 each, and a boy and a gardener £2 10s. in the 1650s. Sir John Knatchbull paid his general maids £2 10s., his cook £6 10s., and his daughter's maid £4. While his lowest-paid male servants received £4–£5, his experienced groom received £6, and his butler and keeper £6 10s. each.[19]

Overall, the conditions that servants in husbandry experienced were relatively good. They had reasonable food and shelter and were not usually expected to work longer than customary hours. Wages were low, but so were expenses, and the thrifty could probably save most of their yearly earnings if they chose. If they fell ill, their master was obliged to look after them and not turn them out. This is not to paint too rosy a picture, for abuses did occur. Servants were beaten, wages were not paid, and women were subjected to unwanted attention by their masters. But servants could appeal to a local justice, find alternative employment, or return home, and it was unlikely that they would be forced to continue working under such conditions.[20] Service did not imply social stigma. Especially where young workers were drawn from the local community, a period of employment on neighboring farms was seen as preparation for the time to come when the servant would form his or her own family.

The life of common day laborers, on the other hand, was more precarious. Wages averaged about 10d.–1s. 4d. per day in the mid-seventeenth century, "without meat and drink," depending on the work, season, and region. Laborers were also paid at varying rates for piecework: 1s.–1s. 4d. the score for shearing sheep, 2d.–3d. per score for washing them, 1s.–5s. per acre for plowing, 2d.–9d. per rod for hedging and ditching, 4s.–5s. for reaping fodder crops, 3s. 4d.–5s. 6d. for wheat, and 1s. 8d. for haymaking. From the farmer's point of view, the great advantage of day labor was its flexibility.

---

19. James E. Thorold Rogers, *A History of Agriculture and Prices in England* . . . , 7 vols. (Oxford, 1886–1902), VI, 694; Finberg and Thirsk, eds., *Agrarian History of England and Wales*, IV, 436; C. W. Chalklin, *Seventeenth-Century Kent: A Social and Economic History* (London, 1965), 248. Thomas Baskerville remarked that Kentish laborers received "the best wages . . . of any in England" (Finberg and Thirsk, eds., 436).

20. For examples from Kent, see "Calendar of Quarter Sessions Records, Sessions Papers, 1639–1677" (KAO Q/SB 1–12), 5, 6, 16, 25, 39, 78.

Men could be hired for a few days for a particular job and then released. The master had no other obligations than paying the agreed wage. Sir John Knatchbull, for example, employed about forty workers during 1693–1694 by the day or by piece, most of whom worked for a few days here and there during the summer months. Only seven men worked more than half the year. Nicholas Toke regularly employed pieceworkers to help with harvesting, haymaking, felling timber, ditching, and dressing hops, even though he had a permanent work force of between eight and twelve laborers.[21]

When plenty of work was available and bread was cheap, day laborers could live moderately well off their wages, especially if supplemented by income from a smallholding. Growing numbers of laboring men and women, without land or access to commons, however, found their wages insufficient for subsistence. Although wages in some parts of the country doubled over the span 1550–1650, they had not kept pace with a sixfold increase in the price of food or rising rents. At 1s. per day, 200–300 days work represented only £10–£15 annually, barely more than the average allowance for the keep of a servant in husbandry. In fact, wages were not much higher than weekly poor relief payments paid by the parish to the destitute.[22]

Contemporary opinion adopted the fiction that wages were merely supplemental to a worker's income from his own holding, a little extra revenue on the side. Others, like Francis Gardiner, believed that wages had to be kept low in order to force the poor to work: "The Poor, if Two Dayes work will maintain them, will not work Three." High wages, it was argued, would lead to idleness, vice, and too much time spent drinking in the local tippling house. As a result of the sustained downward spiral in real wages, by the early seventeenth century full-time wage labor in many rural communities was synonymous with pauperism. The casualization of farm labor, low wages, and irregular work encouraged a steady drift of young people out of arable and mixed farming regions to wood-pasture districts and towns. Many poor emigrants probably experienced several years of shifting from one job to another before leaving for the colonies.[23]

21. Finberg and Thirsk, eds., *Agrarian History of England and Wales*, IV, 436; Chalklin, *Seventeenth-Century Kent*, 248; Lodge, ed., *Account Book*, xxxvi–xxxix.

22. Chalklin, *Seventeenth-Century Kent*, 251–254; Finberg and Thirsk, eds., *Agrarian History of England and Wales*, IV, 857, 862, 865 (tables 8, 13, 16); R. B. Outhwaite, *Inflation in Tudor and Stuart England*, 2d ed. (London, 1982), 11–17; Clark, *Working Life*, 69–73. See, for example of such wages, P193 OV2/1, D688/1, P330 OV2/7, P149 OV 2/1, P298 OV2/1, 2/2, P312 OV2/1, Gloucestershire Record Office.

23. Christopher Hill, *Change and Continuity in Seventeenth-Century England* (London, 1974), 220; Appleby, *Economic Thought*, 145–146; James Horn, "Servant Emigration to

In the towns and cities, men and women on the tramp sought work as building workers, porters, carriers, grooms, and domestics or as servants to a host of urban traders and artisans. In the port towns were to be found all sorts of opportunities for casual labor in the docks, shipyards, or victualing trades. Urban centers were attractive because of the range of potential jobs they offered, but in reality lower-class workers faced problems similar to those encountered in the countryside: wages were low, and much of the work was short-term. Unless they were fortunate enough to secure an apprenticeship (which usually involved an initial capital outlay) or some other form of contract, there could be no guarantee of regular paid employment. Menial labor in towns was just as hard, the conditions just as uncertain, and the returns just as meager as in the countryside.[24]

Free emigrants came from an equally broad range of occupations as indentured servants, and consequently their working lives are equally difficult to summarize. The majority were from mercantile backgrounds or were younger sons of gentry who had forged links with merchants in the major English ports (see Chapter 1). Large numbers were also drawn from London's victualing and clothing trades (Table 1). Relatively few men from agricultural origins appear to have been attracted to the tobacco coast, hence most free colonists had little firsthand experience of working in husbandry before their arrival in Maryland and Virginia. Immigrant gentry from farming communities would have been familiar with the annual cycle of agricultural work, but this fact did not incline them to take up manual labor themselves. Rather, they took on a variety of roles: managing their plantations or engaging in trade, moneylending, land speculation, or any other kind of entrepreneurial activity that would bring in extra income. Instead of entering a profession in England, like many of their contemporaries, younger sons who chose to emigrate became planter-merchants in the Chesapeake while retaining their claim to gentry status.[25]

The perspective of wealthy English merchants was rather different. Their

the Chesapeake in the Seventeenth Century," in Thad W. Tate and David L. Ammerman, eds., *The Chesapeake in the Seventeenth Century: Essays on Anglo-American Society* (Chapel Hill, N.C., 1979), 69–74, 84–87.

24. Thorold Rogers, *Agriculture and Prices*, VI, 695; Sharpe, *Early Modern England*, 206–212; Horn, "Servant Emigration," in Tate and Ammerman, eds., *Chesapeake in the Seventeenth Century*, 57–61.

25. James Horn, " 'To Parts beyond the Seas': Free Emigration to the Chesapeake in the Seventeenth Century," in Ida Altman and Horn, eds., *"To Make America": European Emigration in the Early Modern Period* (Los Angeles, 1991), 85–130; Gloria L. Main, *Tobacco Colony: Life in Early Maryland, 1650–1720* (Princeton, N.J., 1982), 79–91.

working lives would have been dominated by the mercantile companies, financial houses, and internal politics of England's two largest colonial ports, London and Bristol. Settling in the tidewater, as the examples of Maurice Thompson, William Tucker, and Edward Bennett illustrate, was usually a temporary measure set against the broader background of their commercial activities in America and Europe. John Bland, who visited Virginia about 1635 and sent two of his brothers to manage his plantations there, resided variously in London, Seville, and Tangier. He was continually involved in litigation to recover money lost as a consequence of the political turmoil of the 1640s and 1650s and his bitter disputes with Virginia's ruling clique during the early 1670s. The commercial interests of Samuel Vassall were equally far-flung. He was among the incorporators of the first Massachusetts Company in 1628 and developed trading links with Virginia, the West Indies, and Venice as well as New England. During the early 1630s he became interested in the possibility of settling Carolina and financed a voyage of exploration to Florida. At the age of eighty he set sail for Virginia with his son and daughter but did not survive the voyage.[26]

Few large merchants settled permanently in the Chesapeake; it made more sense to send agents to look after their affairs while they concentrated on expanding trade and shaping government policy in London. Far more numerous were smaller merchants, tradesmen, and artisans, who composed the middle and lower tiers of free immigrants. The occupations of 32 male passengers who arrived in Virginia on the *Ann* and the *Bonny Bess* in the first two weeks of September 1623 indicate the variety of backgrounds from which they came: 10 gentry, 5 carpenters, 2 joiners, a cooper, a bricklayer, 3 haberdashers, a tailor, a leather seller, 3 chandlers, a merchant, a grocer, a vintner, a goldsmith, and a student from Christ Church, Oxford.[27]

These occupations reflect the expectations of immigrants in the early years of settlement: gentlemen saw themselves as soldiers or administrators; haberdashers, tailors, and wigmakers served the gentry; carpenters, joiners, and bricklayers were needed to build dwellings for settlers in Jamestown; and the presence of a goldsmith represents the Virginia Company's lingering

26. Neville Williams, "The Tribulations of John Bland, Merchant: London, Seville, Jamestown, Tangier, 1643–1680," *Virginia Magazine of History and Biography*, LXXII (1964), 20–29; [Annie Lash Jester and Martha Woodroof Hiden, eds.], *Adventures of Purse and Person, Virginia, 1607–1624/5*, 3d ed., rev., ed. Virginia M. Meyer and John Frederick Dorman (Richmond, Va., 1987), 644–645; CW VCRP, no. 10409 (C7 494/43, Public Record Office).

27. H. R. McIlwaine, ed., *Minutes of the Council and General Court of Colonial Virginia*, 2d ed. (Richmond, Va., 1979), 6.

hope of finding precious metals. The involvement of a substantial element of England's trading classes in colonization throughout the century is, however, indisputable. Roger North's well-known observation that in Bristol "all men that are dealers, even in shop trades, launch into adventures by sea" is confirmed by the occupations of 344 masters who transported servants to Virginia and Maryland between 1654 and 1660. While two-thirds were mariners and merchants, the rest represented at least forty trades, from hosiers to barber-surgeons.[28]

The connection between mariners, merchants, and planters was frequently very close. Captain Thomas Cornwallis, an important Catholic planter of St. Mary's County, traded extensively along the Bay throughout the 1630s and 1640s, as did his fellow settler in early Maryland, Captain Henry Fleet. Mariners and merchants, like Samuel Pensax, William Ball, and Humphrey Booth, all of whom traded to Lancaster County, Virginia, took up land in the Chesapeake for either settlement or speculative purposes. Thomas Reynolds, who settled on Tanner's Creek, Lower Norfolk County, in the early 1650s, was a mariner from East Smithfield, London, and William Daynes of the same county described himself as a merchant of Bristol in 1678. These examples serve to remind us of the importance of seafaring in the backgrounds of many free settlers and of the intimate association of sea and land.[29]

From this overview of the working lives of men and women before they immigrated to America a number of points are worth emphasizing. First, to the heterogeneity of settler society that resulted from the different provincial origins of immigrants should be added differences that resulted from their occupational backgrounds. If one can generalize in saying that the majority of settlers were poor, young, male, and single, there is no easy way of summarizing their working lives. Even those from the same trades might have had very different experiences, depending on where they were from, whom they worked for, the customs and traditions associated with their trade, and when they were employed. Laboring on farms in wood-pasture districts of southern and central England, for example, involved different seasonal work

---

28. Horn, "Servant Emigration," in Tate and Ammerman, eds., *Chesapeake in the Seventeenth Century*, 87–89.

29. Raphael Semmes, *Captains and Mariners of Early Maryland* (Baltimore, 1937), 101–105, 178–180; Horn, biographical files, Lancaster County; Lower Norfolk County, Virginia, Wills and Deeds D (1656–1666), fols. 145–146, Deed Book no. 4 (1675–1686), fol. 17 (Colonial Williamsburg, microfilm, reels M 1365-18, 1365-1).

patterns compared to farms in champion country. Work in the larger towns and cities was, of course, considerably more varied and offered greater opportunities for casual employment, acquiring a skill, or setting up shop than in the countryside. Among urban workers there was often "an intense consciousness of differences in status: a closely observed gradation of privilege, authority and material benefits." One worker was not just like another, no more than all trades carried equal weight.[30]

Second, while the sorts of work undertaken by men and women were governed by conventional attitudes toward a sexual division of labor, it is worth stressing that among the lower classes there was sometimes little distinction in practice. When necessary, women farm servants were employed in the fields alongside male hands and helped with plowing, tending crops, harvesting, and haymaking. In fact, as Alice Clark suggests, "there was hardly any kind of agricultural work from which women were excluded." Women were usually barred from skilled work (or, more specifically, what men deemed skilled work) and tended to be employed in service jobs such as child care, cooking, washing, and cleaning, but among the unskilled and laboring classes there were comparatively few tasks that were considered unsuitable for women. Poor women, like poor children, commonly experienced hard physical labor, both in agriculture and manufacturing.[31]

Finally, an aspect of work that embraced virtually everyone, from day laborers to wealthy merchants, was the unpredictability of their lives. For the poor, moving from job to job, the problem of earning a living was ever present, a compelling and inescapable fact of life. Hard work, from sunup to sundown, was to be expected, but intermittent bouts of hard work rarely compensated laborers, in monetary terms, for the low wages they received, the seasonality of demand, and long periods of underemployment. Casual work brought only temporary respite from the struggle for subsistence. Even among the middling and wealthy, violent fluctuations in trade, unforeseeable disasters like fire or theft, unwise investments, political reversals, or just plain bad luck could wipe out profits at a stroke. John Bland recovered no more than a fraction of the losses he sustained during the Civil War; George

30. Malcolmson, *Life and Labour*, 54.
31. Clark, *Working Life*, 62; Kathleen Mary Brown, "Gender and the Genesis of a Race and Class System in Virginia, 1630–1750" (Ph.D. diss., University of Wisconsin–Madison, 1990), 20–26; Sharpe, *Early Modern England*, 208–209. More generally, see Lindsey Charles and Lorna Duffin, eds., *Women and Work in Pre-Industrial England* (London, 1985).

Grace fled to Virginia when he could not repay debts because his goods had been impounded by the government.[32] The working lives of English people would be different along the tobacco coast, but one aspect of life they would be familiar with was the uncertainty of getting a living.

Servants, Planters, and Merchants

"In this immigrant society," Lois Carr and Lorena Walsh write of the Chesapeake, "customs of the mother country might be modified in the light of New World conditions, usually to the detriment of the laborer, but they could not be entirely eradicated and had the concurrence of most of the local community."[33] What were the most important changes in the lives of colonists as they adjusted to the demands of tobacco husbandry and the rhythms of transatlantic commerce? To what extent did English experiences and customs influence working conditions and attitudes toward work in seventeenth-century Virginia and Maryland?

Writers of promotional tracts, as might be expected, painted a favorable picture of working conditions in the Chesapeake. John Hammond affirmed the "Country to be wholesome, healthy and fruitfull; and a modell on which industry may as much improve itself in, as in any habitable part of the World," but, he cautioned, "not such a Lubberland as the Fiction of the land of Ease is reported to be, nor such a Utopian as Sr. Thomas Moore hath related to be found out." Nevertheless, in his opinion conditions were better than in the mother country: "The labour servants are put to, is not so hard nor of such continuance as Husbandmen, nor Handecraftmen are kept at in England, as I said little or nothing is done in winter time, none ever work before sun rising nor after sun set, in the summer they rest, sleep or exercise themselves five houres in the heat of the day, Saturdayes afternoon is always their own, the old Holidayes are observed and the Sabboath spent in good exercises." As for women, they were not "(as is reported) put into the ground to worke, but occupie such domestique imployments and houswifery as in England, that is dressing victuals, righting up the house, milking, imployed about dayries, washing, sowing, etc. and both men and

---

32. Williams, "Tribulations of John Bland," *VMHB*, LXXII (1964), 20–29; CW VCRP, no. 3244.

33. Lois Green Carr and Lorena S. Walsh, "Economic Diversification and Labor Organization in the Chesapeake, 1650–1820," in Stephen Innes, ed., *Work and Labor in Early America* (Chapel Hill, N.C., 1988), 155.

women have times of recreation, as much or more than in any part of the world besides." [34]

Hammond's description is revealing in what it does not say about servitude. He advised servants to be careful in their choice of a master, but added that they should not be deterred from emigrating by the practice of selling servants, "for if a time must be served, it is all one with whom it be served, provided they be people of honest repute." Yet not only was the "buying and selling [of] men and bois" as John Rolfe observed as early as 1619, "held in *England* a thing most intolerable," but it also underlined a crucial difference between the organization and utilization of labor in the two societies. [35] In England, formal apprenticeships aside, employers relied upon a pool of casual workers for their labor needs or entered into short-term contracts that could be terminated by mutual consent. As long as plenty of laborers were available, there was no need to attempt to restrict the free operation of the market, except in setting maximum wages and minimum working hours. Given the gathering pace of commercialization in agriculture and manufacturing during the early modern period and the disappearance of most forms of feudal tied labor in the fourteenth and fifteenth centuries, a system of indentured servitude, such as developed in the Chesapeake, would have been unacceptable in England.

Indentured servitude, as has been suggested already, was more closely related to provisions for pauper children set out in the poor law of 1601 than to either service in husbandry or craft apprenticeships. The key feature of colonial servitude was the "master's quasi-proprietary interest" in his servant. It is customary to distinguish between the ownership of slaves, which was absolute, and the ownership of servants, which was not, insofar as it was the servant's labor that was purchased, not his or her person and offspring in perpetuity. The distinction is valid in the sense that there was no systematic attempt by colonial planters to enslave their white servants, but

34. John Hammond, *Leah and Rachel; or, The Two Fruitfull Sisters Virginia and Maryland* (1656), in Clayton Colman Hall, ed., *Narratives of Early Maryland, 1633–1684,* Original Narratives of Early American History (New York, 1910), 287, 290. Lois Green Carr suggests that working conditions for most servants and planters were worse than in England ("Emigration and the Standard of Living: The Seventeenth-Century Chesapeake," *Journal of Economic History,* LII [1992], 281–282).

35. Hammond, *Leah and Rachel,* in Hall, ed., *Narratives of Early Maryland,* 288–289; Edmund S. Morgan, *American Slavery, American Freedom: The Ordeal of Colonial Virginia* (New York, 1975), 128.

what might be termed the commoditization of white labor went far beyond the accepted practice in England.[36]

An indenture drawn up between George Hancocke, a Bristol servant, and Thomas Gayner, recorded in Lancaster County in 1662, illustrates a common form of contract between a servant and master. Hancocke agreed to serve for four years after his arrival in Virginia "in such service and imployment as the sd. Thomas or his assigns shall there employ him according to the Custome of the Country." For his part, Gayner consented to "pay for his passing [passage] and to find and allow him meat drink apparell Lodging with other necessarys during the sd terme and at the end of the sd terme to pay unto him one ax one hoe one years provisions double apparell [and] fifty acres of Land."[37]

At first sight the terms appear quite favorable. Four years was not an unreasonably long time to work in return for fifty acres, food, clothing, and tools. Few young laborers in England could have hoped for as much. From this perspective, servitude could be construed as a form of apprenticeship during which the servant learned the "art and mystery" of tobacco husbandry before setting up his own plantation. But the reality proved somewhat different. Hancocke had very little control over his fate. He could be sold from one planter to another and, if unfortunate enough to be assigned to a hard master, could be forced to work until he dropped, be ill fed, and be physically abused. If he tried to run away or fought back, he could be liable to corporal punishment and an extra period of service, as the county court deemed fit. Neither was there any certainty that he would receive fifty acres at the completion of his term. This stipulation was usually interpreted as a *right* to fifty acres. The cost of having a tract surveyed and patented was borne by the ex-servant, and he needed capital to clear the land, build a house, and plant a crop. Since this was beyond the means of most ex-

---

36. The quoted phrase is taken from Morris, *Government and Labor*, 399. On distinction between slaves and servants, see, for example, David W. Galenson, *White Servitude in Colonial America: An Economic Analysis* (Cambridge, 1981), 3. Warren M. Billings adopts a similar argument to the one advanced here and stresses the harshness of servitude in "The Law of Servants and Slaves in Seventeenth-Century Virginia," *VMHB*, XCIX (1991), 45–53. Christine Marie Daniels discusses the evolution of orphan apprenticeships in relation to indentured servitude in 17th-century Maryland in "Alternative Workers in a Slave Economy: Kent County, Maryland, 1675–1810" (Ph.D. diss., The Johns Hopkins University, 1990).

37. Lancaster County, Virginia, Deeds Etc., no. 2 (1654–1666), 235–236 (CW, microfilm, reel M 1363-1).

servants immediately after completing their term, they tended either to lease land or to take up laboring until they had sufficient money to buy a small holding.[38]

Besides the practice of buying and selling servants, the other aspect of servitude that gave planters license to treat their servants more or less as they wished was the adoption of "the Custome of the Country": a vague catch-all term that governed conditions of work, discipline, board and lodging, and freedom dues. Significantly, the interpretation and implementation of "Custome" and colonial law was largely left to local courts in the Chesapeake. Throughout the seventeenth century, legislation passed by provincial assemblies in both Maryland and Virginia regulated the length of service for many thousands of servants who arrived without indentures, laid down the punishment of servants for all sorts of offenses from fornication to running away, and stipulated the obligations of masters. Yet while legislation concerning discipline and punishment was extensive, relatively little consideration was given to servants' welfare. In 1705, for example, planters were enjoined to "find and provide for their servants, wholesome and competent diet, clothing, and lodging, *by the discretion of the county court*." An earlier act of 1643 gave servants the right to complain to their local justice of "harsh or unchristianlike usage or otherways for want of diet, or convenient necessaryes," but once again determination of the precise meaning of "harsh," "unchristianlike," and "want" was left to the discretion of the county bench.[39] At no point was there an attempt by provincial assemblies to define acceptable requirements for board and lodging.

An ominous sign that servants were treated badly is revealed in the tenor of colonial legislation itself. In 1662 the Virginia Assembly outlawed the private burial of servants because "of much scandall against diverse persons and sometimes not undeservedly of being guilty of their deaths." The same year, the Assembly noted that "the barbarous usage of some servants by cruell masters bring soe much scandall and infamy to the country in generall, that people who would willingly adventure themselves hither, are through feare thereof diverted, and by that meanes the supplies of particu-

---

38. Smith, *Colonists in Bondage*, chaps. 11–12; Morris, *Government and Labor*, chap. 9; Russell R. Menard, "From Servant to Freeholder: Status Mobility and Property Accumulation in Seventeenth-Century Maryland," *William and Mary Quarterly*, 3d Ser., XXX (1973), 52–53.

39. Smith, *Colonists in Bondage*, chap. 11; William Waller Hening, ed., *The Statutes at Large: Being a Collection of All the Laws of Virginia . . .* , 13 vols. (1809–1823; Charlottesville, Va., 1969), I–III, esp. I, 255, II, 117–118, III, 448 (my italics).

ler men and the well seating his majesties country very much obstructed."
Legislation was passed seeking to protect women servants from "dissolute
masters" who having "gotten their maides with child . . . yet claime the benefitt of their service," that is, the extra two years that a woman was obliged
to serve as punishment for bearing a bastard. In 1705, masters were cautioned against "immoderate correction" and forbidden from whipping their
"christian white servants naked, without an order from a justice."[40]

Cases that came before the county courts in Lancaster and Lower Norfolk
suggest that gross ill-treatment of servants, like physical abuse or inadequate diet and accommodation, was confined to a small minority of planters.
Between 1640 and 1680 only a handful of servants in both counties came
before the bench to complain of "hard and Bad usuage." Yet not only do
extreme examples present a horrifying spectacle of violence; they frequently
reveal a disturbingly casual attitude on the part of local courts to the plight
of servants. Endymion Inleherne, for example, who belonged to Richard
Price of Lancaster County "(being a comon runnaway and one that did use
to feign himselfe sicke) haveing beene switched [beaten] by his master did
very shortly after dye." A jury impaneled to view the corpse subsequently
acquitted Price, probably on the grounds that Inleherne had deserved correction for running away and that there had been no intention to murder.
Margaret Hattersley deposed before the bench of Lower Norfolk in 1661 that
John Mansfield, a servant to John Minnikin, "a little Before his death came
to her and . . . said his dame had beate him, and further saith th[a]t his
dame said that now she hoped she would be rid of him." The court concluded that "through hard usage this Child Runn away and his Runninge
away was the cause of his death." But, again, no action was taken. In the
following year, Captain William Odeon was found guilty of "hard and cruell
usage . . . towards his servants" and was required to "give security for the
well and gentle usage of his sd. servants and that he allowe them meate,
drinke and apparrell meete and sufficient." What he thought of the verdict
can be judged by the clerk's following entry that Odeon "hath in the face of
the Co[u]rt strooke and abused his servant." Only in cases where planters
repeatedly mistreated their servants in contempt of previous court orders
did justices threaten or actually remove victims from their custody.[41]

40. Hening, ed., *Statutes at Large*, II, 53, 115, 117–118, 167, III, 448.
41. Lancaster County, Orders Etc., no. 1 (1666–1680), 10 (CW, microfilm, reel M
117-8); Lower Norfolk, Wills and Deeds D (1656–1666), fols. 334–335, 343. See, as examples of extreme brutality, the cases of Charity Dallen of Lower Norfolk and William
Drake of Kent County, Maryland, in Warren M. Billings, ed., *The Old Dominion in the*

More common than physical mistreatment was the practice of extending the period of service as punishment for various offenses, based on the principle that the servant had no money to pay a fine and that masters should be compensated for any inconvenience suffered. There might seem little to object to in this, since the only alternative would have been severer forms of corporal punishment. But in reality the practice gave unscrupulous planters an opportunity to retain their servants for long periods of extra time. In 1665, Elizabeth Poore, servant of Tobias Horton, was sentenced to two years for having a bastard (probably sired by Horton) and "to bee whipped" for the "sinne of fornicacon." Three years later she was sentenced to another two years' extra service for having a second bastard child. Richard Higby, servant to Lieutenant Colonel John Carter, was convicted in the spring of 1670 of killing three marked hogs and ordered to serve an extra six years. According to law, servants were required to serve double time for running away, but planters frequently added extra service for damage done to the crop and for the expense of recovering them. Thus James Gray, another of Carter's servants, ran away for twenty-two days "in the height of the Crop," and Carter spent more than 1,200 lbs. of tobacco in finding him. The court sentenced Gray to an extra fifteen months. William Gittery, Sarah his wife, and another servant ran away from Captain William Carver's plantation in Lower Norfolk County for thirteen days and were ordered to serve an extra two years each in order to repay the 5,361 lbs. of tobacco Carver had allegedly lost "in the pursuite after them, and what they Caryed with them." [42]

Servants were sometimes forced to serve longer than they originally contracted because their indentures had been altered or destroyed, because they were sold to another master on different terms, or because they had been duped. Thomas Damer of Charles County, Maryland, agreed to serve Thomas Tolson, a merchant of London, for four years, but on his arrival in the province was sold according to the custom of the country for seven. Two brothers, Francis and Thomas Brooke, bound themselves four years each to Henry Corbin, who subsequently sold them to Colonel Nathaniel Utie. Having served him a year, they were sold to Mr. Joseph Wicks for four years,

Seventeenth Century: A Documentary History of Virginia, 1606–1689 (Chapel Hill, N.C., 1975), 136–137; and in Eugene Irving McCormac, *White Servitude in Maryland, 1634–1820*, Johns Hopkins University Studies in Historical and Political Science, 22d Ser., nos. 3–4 (Baltimore, 1904), 64. Numerous other examples could be given.

42. Lancaster County, Orders Etc. (1655–1666), 355, Orders Etc., no. 1 (1666–1680), 82, 163, 277; Lower Norfolk County, Order Book, 1675–1686, 10 (CW, microfilm, reels M 117-7, 1365-25).

a year longer than they had agreed to serve according to their indentures. Appealing to the court for their freedom, they were ordered "to returne againe" to their master and "serve him Two yeares longer, then . . . [they] first covenanted for." The Lower Norfolk court found Richard Chapman's indenture "nott to bee authentick, but only a Certificatt from some office in England nott signed by any p'son." Nine servants belonging to Colonel John Carter and Edward Carter who presented their indentures to the Lancaster Court in 1686 were informed that "not being made before the Lord Mayor or a Justice of the Peace" they were "Null and Void."[43]

It is hard to avoid the conclusion that servants were commonly regarded as a species of property. One of the most striking aspects of this attitude was their routine valuation alongside livestock, crops, and household goods in probate inventories. Robert Glascock of Lower Norfolk County, who died in 1646, valued two male servants with two years to serve at 2,000 lbs. of tobacco, two "mayd servants" with three years to serve at 2,000 lbs., a boy with six years to serve at 1,250 lbs., and a "small boy" with eleven years to serve at 800 lbs. The appraisers of the estate of David Myles (a merchant of Lancaster County who died in 1676), itemized his servants by name: John Crailes, Thomas Gibbs, and Nathaniell Bridgement were worth £13 each, Jonathan Spencer was valued at £15, and Elizabeth Boulton at £6.[44]

Servants were shipped out to the colonies as commodities to be sold like any other merchandise for the best possible price. Colonel Thomas Spekes of Westmoreland County, Virginia, bargained with Peter Ashton for "2 able men servants in the best health between 20 and 30 having full time to serve as they came in for 4 years at the least." Owing to the constant demand for labor, the servant trade remained lucrative throughout the century. Colonial merchants from English ports plied the Chesapeake's major rivers selling their servant cargoes as they went. Servants, like land, cattle, and tobacco, were alienable assets that could be freely sold or exchanged by planters to pay debts, purchase goods, or provide security for loans. John Johnson, servant to Henry Coleman of Lower Norfolk, was sold to Lancaster Lovett in 1639 for eight hundred pounds of tobacco and twenty barrels of

43. William Hand Browne *et al.*, eds., *Archives of Maryland*, 72 vols. to date (Baltimore, 1883–), XLI, 350, LX, 492–493 (hereafter cited as *Md. Archives*); Lower Norfolk County, Wills and Deeds E (Orders) (1666–1675), 21 (CW, microfilm, reel M 1365-18), Order Book (1675–1686), 15; Lancaster County, Orders Etc., no. 2 (1680–1686), 243 (CW, microfilm, reel M 117-7).

44. Lower Norfolk, Wills and Deeds B (1646–1651), fols. 45–46 (CW, microfilm, reel M 1365-17); Lancaster County, Wills Etc., no. 5 (1674–1689), 7–8 (SMCC transcripts).

corn. Saville Gaskins and Richard Kennar swapped two male servants a few years later.[45]

Servants were priced according not only to their sex, age, and length of service but also to their physical condition. In a case reminiscent of John Barth's traveling whore of Dorset, Richard Abrell deposed before the Lower Norfolk County court in January 1648 that he had purchased a man and a woman servant from John Murrey for four thousand pounds of tobacco on behalf of Mrs. Sarah Gookin. The woman, however, "did Complaine that shee was diseased," whereupon Abrell charged Murrey of selling him "an unsound wenche." Eventually, Murrey agreed to "pay for her Cure" and lowered her price to six hundred pounds, perhaps stung by the servant's accusation that he "had undone her, for by him shee had gott that disease . . . which is the poxe." Conditions of sale often stipulated that servants should be "in perfect health" or "able," and the lame and chronically sick were sometimes dubbed "refuse."[46]

Rights taken for granted in England were curtailed in the Chesapeake. In Virginia, owing to "much detriment . . . to the service of manye masters," servants were forbidden to marry without the consent of their owner, and measures were taken to prevent clandestine marriages. In most cases, servants were obliged to finish their terms before they could contemplate setting up their own households. Following the Gloucester conspiracy of 1663, an act "for better suppressing the unlawful meetings of servants" required that "all masters of ffamilies be enjoyned and take especiall care that their servants doe not depart from their houses on Sundayes or any other dayes without perticuler lycence from them." Servants found abroad without a pass were liable to be prosecuted as runaways. The effort to suppress running away had led to the introduction twenty years earlier of an act requiring recently freed servants to obtain a "certificate" from their local court proving that they had completed their service.[47]

45. Horn, "Servant Emigration," in Tate and Ammerman, eds., *Chesapeake in the Seventeenth Century*, 94; Westmoreland County, Virginia, Wills Etc. (1653–1659), 94 (I am indebted to Lorena S. Walsh for this reference); Lower Norfolk County, Minute Book, 2 vols. (1637–1646), I, fol. 38, II, fol. 10 (CW, microfilm, reel M 1365-2).

46. Lower Norfolk County, Wills and Deeds B (1646–1651), 63, Minute Book (1637–1646), II, fol. 10; Beckles, *White Servitude and Black Slavery*, 64, 70; *Md. Archives*, XLI, 270–271.

47. Hening, ed., *Statutes at Large*, I, 252–254, II, 114, 116, 195, 266, 278, 279; J. C. Ballagh, *White Servitude in the Colony of Virginia*, Johns Hopkins University Studies in Historical and Political Science, 13th Ser., nos. 5–6 (Baltimore, 1895), 50–65; McCormac, *White Servitude*, 50–67.

Many instances of casual beatings and poor diet probably never came to court. On the other hand, we cannot assume that all planters, even those determined to extract the last ounce of work from their servants, regularly beat or starved them. Thousands upon thousands of young men and women passed their years of servitude uneventfully and entered the ranks of small-holders when their time was completed. As Richard Ligon commented of conditions in Barbados: "As for the usage of the Servants, it is much as the Master is, merciful or cruel; Those that are merciful, treat their Servants well, both in their meat, drink, and lodging, and give them such work, as is not unfit for Christians to do. But if the Masters be cruel, the Servants have very wearisome and miserable lives." There is no need to interpret servitude in the Chesapeake as a form of "proto-slavery" or servants as a "Rabble Crue" constantly on the brink of armed insurrection.[48]

But allowing that many masters treated their servants humanely, conditions of service for indentured servants were undoubtedly worse than those for laborers in England. This is illustrated, not by counting numbers of runaways, beatings, or other forms of ill-treatment, but by reference to the enormous increase in the powers of masters (sanctioned by successive legislation), with respect not only to the labor of servants but also to their persons. While ill-treatment of servants, especially paupers, was common in England, the possibility of escape was much greater, either by returning home or by running away to anonymity in another town. Casual workers were not tied to a single master for such long periods of service, nor were they indebted to their master for the cost of a transatlantic passage. The fluidity of the labor market enabled them to pick up work where they could, as long as they could avoid arrest under the vagrancy laws. Young men and women in service as domestics and farm laborers could escape from work from time to time during holidays or when work was slack. They might meet in the alehouse, on market days, or at other social gatherings. Apart from when they were supposed to be at work or church, they were not denied freedom of movement in the local community.

These possibilities were increasingly restricted for indentured servants. They could legitimately leave their master's service only if they could buy their freedom, which was beyond the means of the vast majority. Some tried running away, but the penalties if caught were severe, and the chances of escape were slim. Most therefore probably accepted their fate and counted

---

48. Richard Ligon, *A True and Exact History of the Island of Barbados . . .* , 2d ed. (London, 1673; rpt., 1970), 44; Morgan, *American Slavery, American Freedom*, chaps. 12–13. The term "proto-slavery" is taken from Beckles, *White Servitude and Black Slavery*, 78.

the days until they were free again, perhaps hoping for remission of time if they behaved themselves. As with the chances of surviving the disease environment, whether a servant was indentured to a kind or to a hard master was part of the lottery involved in moving to the Chesapeake. John Hammond presented one side of the picture in the mid-1650s:

> Those Servants that will be industrious may in their time of service gain a competent estate before their Freedomes, which is usually done by many. . . . There is no Master almost but will allow his Servant a parcell of clear ground to plant some Tobacco in for himself, which he may husband at those many idle times he hath allowed him and not prejudice, but rejoyce his Master to see it. . . . And whereas it is rumoured that Servants have no lodging other than on boards, or by the Fire side, it is contrary to reason to believe it: First, as we are Christians; next as people living under a law, which compels as well the Master as the Servant to perform his duty; nor can true labour be either expected or exacted without sufficient cloathing, diet, and lodging; all which both their Indentures (which must inviolably be observed) and the Justice of the Country requires.[49]

Later writers, however, gave an entirely different view. Two travelers who journeyed through Maryland in 1679 were scathing about the conditions endured by servants. Their usual food was

> maize bread to eat, and water to drink, which sometimes is not very good and scarcely enough for life, yet they are compelled to work hard. . . . And thus they are by hundreds of thousands compelled to spend their lives here and in Virginia, and elsewhere in planting that vile tobacco, which all vanishes into smoke, and is for the most part miserably abused. . . . The servants and negroes after they have worn themselves down the whole day, and gone home to rest, have yet to grind and pound the grain, which is generally maize, for their masters and all their families as well as themselves.

As the century progressed, servants were increasingly seen as ne'er-do-wells and criminals. Sir William Berkeley described Virginia in 1670 as "an exelent schoole to make contumacious and disorderly wild youths hastily to repent of those wild and extravagant coarses that brought them hither." Durand thought the colony constituted "the galleys of England, for those who have committed any crime short of hanging may be banished and condemned to service in America. . . . As to women likewise, it is the refuge of those who

49. Hammond, *Leah and Rachel*, in Hall, ed., *Narratives of Early Maryland*, 292–293.

have been convicted of picking and stealing or have lost their reputations for chastity." [50]

All settlers, free and unfree, had to adjust to the different demands of tobacco husbandry and the ebb and flow of transatlantic trade. Very few immigrants would have had any direct contact with cultivating tobacco, although it was grown widely (and illegally) throughout England in the seventeenth century. Tobacco cultivation involved a form of husbandry and land use altogether different from that generally practiced in England. Plentiful cheap land allowed planters to take up tracts of several hundred acres at a time, a small proportion of which would be cleared immediately for tobacco and other crops and the rest held in reserve for future use and pasturing live-stock. There was no necessity for the kind of intensive cultivation common in Europe, nor was arable acreage limited by the number of livestock kept for fertilizing the fields. Rather than expending time and money improving the same piece of land, most men cleared a fresh tract every few years and shifted their tobacco fields when the old land was exhausted. Old land could be used to raise maize, English cereals, and other crops or left fallow. "Thus their Plantations," John Clayton wrote, with a degree of exaggeration, "run over vast Tracts of ground, each [planter] ambitioning to engrosse as mch as they can, that they may be sure [to] have enough to plant, and for their Stocks and herds of Cattle to range and feed in, that Plantations of 1000, 2000, or 3000 Acres are Common." This form of husbandry may have elicited the contempt of commentators "who delighted in the sprightly countrysides of England and the colonies northward," but with so much land available planters could afford to exploit its fertility to the utmost and then allow it to recuperate naturally. [51]

New arrivals had to learn how to prepare seedbeds in January and Febru-

50. Jaspar Dankers and Peter Sluyter, *Journal of a Voyage to New York and a Tour in Several of the American Colonies in 1679–80,* ed. Henry C. Murphy (*Memoirs of the Long Island Historical Society,* I [Brooklyn, N.Y., 1867]), 191–192, 217; McCormac, *White Servitude,* 72–75; Sir William Berkeley to Sir Richard Browne, Apr. 2, 1670, Add. MSS 15857, 40, British Library; Durand of Dauphine, *A Frenchman in Virginia,* ed. Harrison, 94–95. See also Carr and Walsh, "Economic Diversification," in Innes, ed., *Work and Labor,* 155–157.

51. Edmund Berkeley and Dorothy Smith Berkeley, eds., *The Reverend John Clayton: A Parson with a Scientific Mind* (Charlottesville, Va., 1965), 79–80; Carville V. Earle, *The Evolution of a Tidewater Settlement System: All Hallow's Parish, Maryland, 1650–1783,* University of Chicago, Department of Geography, Research Paper no. 170 (Chicago, 1975), 141.

ary, make "little hillocks" for planting in May, top and sucker in the summer months, judge the best time to cut the plants in September or October, dry the leaf, and strike and pack in late autumn and early winter. Mistakes could be costly and ruin all or part of the crop. If seedlings were transplanted too soon, they might be destroyed by a late frost, but if sown too late the crop might not be ready for shipment in the winter. During the growing season plants required careful attention to keep the soil clear of weeds and plants free from flies, tobacco worms, and other vermin. If plants were not topped, the plant flowered and the quality of leaf was impaired. If they were cut down too early, they would not cure properly; and if leaves were struck at the wrong time, they would either crumble during packing if too dry or rot in the casks if too damp. The price tobacco fetched therefore depended not only on fluctuating demand and how much English and European markets could absorb but also individually on the skill of the planter in producing merchantable leaf.[52]

In most counties for most of the century, tobacco, as the dominant cash crop, engaged the attention of planters, who depended on it for the bulk of their income. But there were other concerns. Planters, Gloria Main points out, were "primarily farmers—they kept cattle, cleared land, dressed timber, built fences, and pursued the myriad activities that constituted the farm tasks of the day." As in English pasture-farming districts, cattle and swine were the most common animals found on Chesapeake plantations and constituted an extremely important element of the local economy. In the second half of the seventeenth century the ownership of livestock was universal among all classes. Sheep were less common, probably because they required more care and did not flourish in open range. Thomas Glover commented in 1676 that planters "keep but few, being discouraged by the Wolves, which are all over the Countrey, and do much mischief amongst their Flocks." Cattle and swine, on the other hand, multiplied rapidly. Extensive tracts of woodland and unimproved ground provided almost limitless pasturage for animals at little cost. "They do not know what it is to save hay," observed Durand of the planters he met, "for all their animals pasture in the woods or else in that part of the plantation which has been turned out to rest." Even in winter cattle and hogs were left to fend for themselves, and livestock were often lost, owing to disease, starvation, or miring in swamps and marshes. Nevertheless, there was an impressive increase in the numbers of

---

52. Lois Green Carr, Russell R. Menard, and Lorena S. Walsh, *Robert Cole's World: Agriculture and Society in Early Maryland* (Chapel Hill, N.C., 1991), 55–70; Thomas Glover, "An Account of Virginia . . . ," *Philosophical Transactions*, XI (1676), 634–635.

animals throughout the century, and, with some attention, planters could expect their growing herds to bring them or their children at least modest wealth even if tobacco did not.[53]

Maize replaced English cereals as the "chiefest Diett." According to Hugh Jones, "This grain is of great increase and most general use; for with this is made good bread, cakes, mush, and hommony for the Negroes." In addition, it "is the best food for cattle, hoggs, sheep, and horses," which were fed on the "blades and tops." Corn was preferred to English cereals because its yield was much higher and it was easier to grow. One laborer could produce about seventeen to twenty-five bushels of shelled corn annually, compared to fewer than five of wheat. Field crops were therefore dominated by the two Indian plants, tobacco and corn, but gardens had a decidedly English flavor. Glover found that planters cultivated "all sorts of *English* Pot-herbs, and sallets; they have *Cabbages, Colworts, Colly flowers, Parsnips, Turnips,* [and] *Carrets.*" Most men also grew English fruits such as apples, quinces, pears, and cherries. The "meanest Planter," he wrote, "hath store of *Cherries,* and they are all over *Virginia* as plentiful as they are in Kent." Cultivating orchards, like clearing land, fencing tobacco and corn fields, and building up livestock, represented a principal means of improving estates in the period.[54]

Major differences in Chesapeake work patterns compared to England were evident in the dominance of tobacco husbandry, the absence of finely graded occupational hierarchies, and the importance of such institutionalized labor systems as indentured servitude and, later in the century, slavery. But settlers, especially those from rural backgrounds, would have been aware too of some broad similarities. The main unit of production and consumption, in the Chesapeake as in England, was the household. Planters, together with their wives and children (and servants and slaves, if any),

53. Main, *Tobacco Colony,* 62; Glover, "An Account of Virginia," *Philosophical Transactions,* XI (1676), 630; Durand of Dauphine, *A Frenchman in Virginia,* ed. Harrison, 115–116; Berkeley and Berkeley, eds., *The Reverend John Clayton,* 87–88; *A Perfect Description of Virginia . . .* (1649), in Peter Force, comp., *Tracts and Other Papers, Relating Principally to the Origin, Settlement, and Progress of the Colonies in North America, from the Discovery of the Country to the Year 1776,* 4 vols. (1836–1846; Gloucester, Mass., 1963), II, no. 8, pp. 3–5; Morgan, *American Slavery, American Freedom,* 136–142.

54. Hugh Jones, *The Present State of Virginia . . . ,* ed. Richard L. Morton (Chapel Hill, N.C., 1956), 40; "Narrative of a Voyage to Maryland, 1705–1706," *American Historical Review,* XII (1906–1907), 335–336; Lorena Seebach Walsh, "Charles County, Maryland, 1658–1705: A Study of Chesapeake Social and Political Structure" (Ph.D. diss., Michigan State University, 1977), 281–283; Glover, "An Account of Virginia," *Philosophical Transactions,* XI (1676), 628, 629.

worked the family holding. Just as the family was the fundamental social unit in both societies, so it was the prime economic unit. Production was primarily for the market. In adopting commercial agriculture, as Paul Clemens remarks, settlers "did nothing that had not already occurred in many of the English communities they had left."[55] Tobacco cultivation for the metropolitan market represented a form of specialization in a particular commodity that was mirrored by similar developments in the production of cereals, livestock, dairy produce, fruit, and other goods in English provinces. The Chesapeake should be viewed as a specialized agrarian region, in the same way as particular areas of England were given over to cereal production, dairying, or stock rearing.

Although tobacco cultivation and the extensive nature of agriculture created a very different kind of husbandry compared to that practiced by most English farmers, there were parallels in the seasonality of work. Land was prepared in the winter and early spring, the summer was devoted to tending crops, and harvesting took place in the autumn. Slack periods in the winter months would have been used in Virginia and Maryland to fence and clear land and carry out odd jobs around the plantation, just as in England farmers would have been occupied by hedging and ditching, plowing and harrowing, felling timber, and seeing to various repairs.

Annual work rhythms were not punctuated with the same richness of religious and customary observances as in England, but planters retained certain important English rituals that symbolized the passing of the year. The Swiss traveler, Francis Louis Michel, reported that the period following the harvest was "one of the principal festivals or times of rejoicing" in Virginia. Christmas and Easter were celebrated with feasting and time off from work. Governor Francis Nicholson noted in 1688 that among slaves it was "common practice" to visit one another "on 2 or 3 days in Christmas, Easter and Whitsuntide." For planters, Christmas represented the end of one year and the beginning of the new. By late December most would have packed their tobacco for shipment and harvested the corn. Christmas celebrations therefore provided a welcome respite before the whole process began again

55. Carr, Menard, and Walsh, *Robert Cole's World*, 75; Paul G. E. Clemens, *The Atlantic Economy and Colonial Maryland's Eastern Shore: From Tobacco to Grain* (Ithaca, N.Y., 1980), 81. An excellent discussion of the nature and limitations of Chesapeake husbandry during the colonial period is provided by Lois Green Carr and Russell R. Menard, "Land, Labor, and Economies of Scale in Early Maryland: Some Limits to Growth in the Chesapeake System of Husbandry," *Jour. Econ. Hist.*, XLIX (1989), 407–418.

with the planting of seedbeds after Twelfth Night. In Virginia a number of anniversaries and holy days were adopted commemorating deliverance from the Indian uprisings of March 22, 1619, and April 18, 1644, and the servant rebellion of September 13, 1663. Following the restoration of the Stuarts in 1660, January 30 and May 29 (Oak Apple Day) were also set aside for fasting and thanksgiving.[56] A Chesapeake calendar that amalgamated Old World rituals with New World experiences symbolized the passage of the seasons and the agricultural cycle.

In both societies, farmers and planters were helpless in the face of the weather and natural disasters. Late frosts, droughts, untimely storms, diseases, and vermin destroyed wheat and livestock in England and tobacco crops along the Bay. John Catlett wrote from the upper reaches of the Rappahannock in 1664 that it had been "a very Unseasonable yeare so th[a]t I can say nothing did prosper of the fruits of the earth." Three years later, Thomas Ludwell informed Lord Berkeley of Stretton of a series of disasters that had reached biblical proportions.

> We had a most p[ro]digeous Storme of haile many of them as bigg as Turkey Eggs wch destroyed most of our younge Mast and fruite, and forward English Graine brake all the glasse windowes and beat holes through the tyles of our houses kild many young hoggs and Cattell. . . . [On June 5th] came the Dutch upon us . . . they were not gonn before it fell to raineing and continued for 40 dayes together wch Spoiled much of what the haile had left of our English Graine, But on the 27th of August followed the most Dreadfull Hurry Cane that ever this Collony groaned under, it lasted 24 hours . . . accompanied with a most violent raine . . . the nearest computation is at least 10000 houses blowne downe all the Indian Graine laid flatt upon the grownd, all the Tobo in the fields torne to pieces and most of that wch was in the houses perished with them, the fences about the Corne fields either blown downe or beaten to the grownd by trees wch fell upon them. . . . Soe that we are at once threatened wth the Sword of the enemyes retouneing upon us, wth Exreame wante of p[ro]vision by the Storme and of cloathes, ammunition and other necessaryes by the absence of the Shipps.[57]

---

56. "Report of the Journey of Francis Louis Michel from Berne, Switzerland, to Virginia, October 2, 1701–December 1, 1702," *VMHB*, XXIV (1916), 32; Mechal Sobel, *The World They Made Together: Black and White Values in Eighteenth-Century Virginia* (Princeton, N.J., 1987), 33, 67; Hening, *Statutes at Large*, I, 123, 290, II, 24–25, 294 (I am grateful to David Cressy for bringing these latter references to my attention).

57. John Catlett of Sittingborne, Rappahannock, to Thomas Catlett of Hollingborne,

On the eve of Bacon's Rebellion in 1675, provisions were reported to be "very scarce" in Virginia after "a bad crop there this yeare" and "a very bad winter which hath destroyed most of their cattell."[58] All agricultural societies are vulnerable to natural disasters. The point emphasized here is that uncertainty and unpredictability characterized the world of tobacco planters as much as, or more than, it did the lives of their counterparts in England. Planters' dependence on European markets meant that not only did they have to contend with plagues of vermin and the vicissitudes of the weather; they also had to trust their crop to the perils of an Atlantic crossing.

If Maryland and Virginia lacked the occupational diversity of English provincial society, nevertheless individual experience of work varied enormously. For servants, much depended on the size and location of the plantation on which they worked. Small estates of 1 or 2 laborers made up a majority of plantations in most parts of the Chesapeake in the second half of the seventeenth century, but the greater proportion of servants and slaves served on plantations with 4 or more laborers. In Anne Arundel County, Maryland, 1658–1699, two-thirds of working quarters had 3 or fewer laborers, but they represented only 31–43 percent of the total work force. The trend toward larger work forces is striking. Whereas only 7 percent of laborers worked in units of 10 or more in 1658–1677, the figure rose to 24–28 percent in the last two decades of the century (Table 24). In Lancaster County, the concentration of laborers in large units is even more impressive. More than 25 percent of servants and slaves worked on plantations with 10 or more laborers as early as 1653. A decade later, 6 planters with 20 or more laborers owned 222 servants and slaves, or 28 percent of the total work force of the county. Nearly 40 percent of laborers worked on plantations with 10 or more servants and slaves.[59]

On small and middling plantations, with no more than three or four laborers, servants would have undertaken the same tasks as their master and probably worked together much of the time. John Taylor, who settled in

---

Kent, Apr. 1, 1664, Colonial Williamsburg, Original Letters; CO 1/21, 282, Public Record Office.

58. CW VCRP, nos. 6255, 6259, 6263.

59. Various definitions of small estates are possible, based on, for example, numbers of tithables, personal wealth, and landownership. Here, small estates are deemed as planters worth less than £50 in personalty at death, owning 100–300 acres, and possibly a servant or two. On Anne Arundel and Lancaster counties, see Carr and Walsh, "Economic Diversification," in Innes, ed., *Work and Labor*, table 1, 164; Lancaster County, Deeds Etc., no. 1 (1652–1657), 91–94.

TABLE 24
Work Units in Anne Arundel County, Maryland, 1658–1699

Size of Work Unit in Laborers	No. of Units	Proportion of All Units	No. of Laborers	Proportion of All Laborers
		1658–1677		
1–3	41	67%	80	43%
4–6	13	21	57	31
7–9	6	10	36	19
10+	1	2	13	7
Total	61	100	186	100
		1678–1687		
1–3	32	65%	59	31%
4–6	8	16	39	21
7–9	5	10	39	21
10+	4	8	52	28
Total	49	99	189	101
		1688–1699		
1–3	50	67%	77	31%
4–6	15	20	74	30
7–9	5	7	38	15
10+	5	7	59	24
Total	75	101	248	100

Source: Lois Green Carr and Lorena Walsh, "Economic Diversification and Labor Organization in the Chesapeake, 1650–1820," in Stephen Innes, ed., *Work and Labor in Early America* (Chapel Hill, N.C., 1988), table 1, 164. Column 5, 1658–1677, has been amended.

the Fleet's Bay area of Lancaster County in 1652, worked his four-hundred-acre plantation with the help of a servant boy and his wife, Elizabeth. In this frontier region, Taylor and his boy doubtless devoted most of their energies to clearing land for tobacco and corn while Elizabeth tended the livestock. At his death early in 1653, Taylor owned six milk cows, a bull, three "young beasts," a calf, and about two dozen hogs. Elias Edmonds of the Corotoman River patented nearly fifteen hundred acres in the early 1650s and died in 1654 worth about £150–£200. His labor force consisted of a female servant, a boy, and Mary Marshall, a widow. The women would have helped Edmonds's wife with the children and chores around the house, but in busy times during planting and harvesting they were probably expected to help in the fields. Hammond's opinion that only "wenches that are nasty" were employed in field work was unlikely to have been the case on smaller plantations, where an extra hand could make all the difference between a poor crop and a good one. As we have seen, women were not excluded from field work in England; thus "workeing in the ground" in Maryland and Virginia was not a break with tradition, although it may have been considered unusual to attempt to work women servants as hard as men. Luke Gardiner, guardian of Robert Cole's estate on St. Clement's Manor, St. Mary's County, Maryland, between 1662 and 1673, opted as soon as possible to employ only male hands. He hired a housekeeper and bought a woman servant to look after Cole's young orphans; but once the children were old enough to look after themselves, he turned to male servants to maximize tobacco output. In this case, it appears there was a clear expectation that the women would take care of young children and manage the household, thereby freeing the men for field work.[60]

A variety of *tasks* characterized the working lives of servants and inmates on small and middling plantations: clearing land for cultivation; working in the fields at the hoe; tending to crops and livestock; carrying logs and rails for fuel, fencing, and building; beating "at the mortar"; and all sorts of "domestique imployments." On larger plantations, where typically ten or more laborers worked, planters had more options in using their work force. They could assign particular jobs to individuals or could group laborers into gangs, as the nature of the work demanded. The advantages of gang work lay in optimizing the labor potential of servants and slaves by organizing work into a series of simple and discrete stages that could be carried out by teams of workers under the direct supervision of the owner or an overseer. Larger acreages of crops could be produced and a closer eye kept on workers

60. Nell Marion Nugent, comp., *Cavaliers and Pioneers: Abstracts of Virginia Land Patents and Grants*, 2 vols. (Richmond, Va., 1934, 1977), I, 192, 259; Lancaster County, Deeds, no. 2 (1654–1666), 2–4, 96–97, 107; Hammond, *Leah and Rachel*, in Hall, ed., *Narratives of Early Maryland*, 290–291; Carr and Walsh, "Economic Diversification," in Innes, ed., *Work and Labor*, 150–152; Brown, "Gender and the Genesis of a Race and Class System," 118–123. I do not intend to examine in detail the work routine of small to middling planters. The fullest account of a middling plantation can be found in Carr, Menard, and Walsh, *Robert Cole's World*, chaps. 2–4. See also Carr and Menard, "Land, Labor, and Economies of Scale," *Jour. Econ. Hist.*, XLIX (1989), 407–418.

throughout the day than was possible under a task system. Division of labor encouraged a more efficient use of workers.[61]

The distinction between task and gang labor was not as clear-cut as the above description suggests. Both systems were used interchangeably according to the work being undertaken. Servants and slaves did not spend all or even most of their time working in gangs. Many jobs, such as fencing, routine repairs to housing, portering, and looking after livestock were best done individually. Nor were large gangs of laborers common. "One of the more remarkable facts to come to light about the workaday world of Maryland slaves and servants," Gloria Main notes, "is their dispersal into small groups" generally consisting "of a core of four or five field hands supplemented by one or two women who cooked, washed, and supervised the children." Colonel Benjamin Rozer of Charles County owned 69 laborers dispersed on seven different sites in 1681; nowhere were there more than 14 men and women on the same site. Colonel John Carter, one of the wealthiest men in Virginia when he died in 1691, possessed 107 slaves and 5 servants, who worked on six different quarters spread around the home plantation at "Curritoman." In these dispersed quarters they looked after cattle and hogs as well as planting corn and tobacco and may have enjoyed a fair degree of freedom during slack periods. There was little in the seventeenth-century Chesapeake comparable to the extreme regimentation of laborers witnessed by Richard Ligon in Barbados in the 1640s.[62]

One difference that would have been immediately obvious to English servants on larger plantations, and therefore integral to their experience of work, was the presence of black slaves. Along the lower Western Shore of Maryland, 1658–1705, about 10 percent of probated estates mention both slaves and servants. Very few planters in the lower wealth brackets owned slaves; only among the rich were they common (see Table 25). In Lancaster County, 1675–1699, whereas 80 percent of planters worth more than £250 in personalty owned both slaves and servants, only 30 percent among the

61. Main, *Tobacco Colony*, 109; Philip Morgan, "Task and Gang Systems: The Organization of Labor on New World Plantations," in Innes, ed., *Work and Labor*, 189–220, and Carr and Walsh, "Economic Diversification," 161–163. Much of the evidence about gang labor pertains to the 18th and early 19th centuries, but, given the rapid development of large work units in parts of the tidewater after 1650, gang labor was probably adopted earlier on plantations using 10 or more laborers.

62. Morgan, "Task and Gang Systems," in Innes, ed., *Work and Labor*, 199–202; Main, *Tobacco Colony*, 128–133; Lancaster County, Wills Etc., no. 8 (1690–1709), 22–29, 32–34; Ligon, *A True and Exact History*, 44.

TABLE 25

Households with Servants and Slaves, by Wealth, Western Shore of Maryland,
1658–1705

Wealth Group	% of Households Owning	
	Servants	Slaves
0–£9	1.5	0
£10–£49	17.4	1.5
£50–£99	47.4	6.8
£100–£259	78.9	35.1
£260+	87.6	73.5

Source: Adapted from Russell R. Menard, "Household and Labor, Lower Western Shore of Maryland, 1658–1705" (MS, SMCC). Note the slightly different cutoff points for the two top wealth groups.

£100–£249 group and just 12 percent of the £50–£99 category did so. By the last fifteen years of the century, white servants were increasingly likely to find themselves outnumbered by slaves on big plantations (Table 26).[63]

These figures tell us little about everyday conditions for blacks and whites. Did they usually work side by side in the fields? Were white laborers favored over blacks in the tasks they were assigned? How did black and white laborers get along together? On large estates, Gloria Main argues, workers frequently lived in groups "that tended to be all white or all colored." Three of Benjamin Rozer's quarters in Charles County were run by slaves, and two other sites were operated mainly by whites. Captain John Bayne, another wealthy Maryland planter, owned twenty-four slaves and fifteen white servants when he died in 1703. Of these, eleven slaves supervised by two servants worked on his home plantation, nine servants worked at Pascataway Quarter, and four slaves ran Aberdeen Quarter. Only on one of his sites did blacks and whites work together. On plantations with fewer laborers, servants and slaves probably worked together more often. When Lieutenant Colonel Thomas Willoughby of Lower Norfolk died in 1672, he owned "two negro men and a woman and Child," one female servant, and two male servants. Assuming that the female servant's primary duties were around the house, four male hands and the female slave would have been left for field

63. Lancaster County, Deeds Etc., no. 2 (1654– 702), no. 4 (1666–1682), Wills Etc., no. 5 (1674–1689), no. 8 (1690–1709).

TABLE 26

Number of Servants and Slaves per Household, Lower Western Shore of Maryland,
1658–1700

No. of Servants and Slaves per Household	No. of Households Owning	Proportion of All Households Owning	Proportion of All Households in Class Owning Mostly Slaves
1658–1674			
1–3	2	10.5%	0%
4–6	8	42.1	37.5
7–9	5	26.3	20.0
10+	4	21.1	25.0
Overall	19	100.0	26.3
1675–1684			
1–3	8	17.8%	12.5%
4–6	18	40.0	5.6
7–9	8	17.8	25.0
10+	11	24.4	36.4
Overall	45	100.0	17.8
1685–1700			
1–3	24	28.2%	33.3%
4–6	25	29.4	48.0
7–9	12	14.1	58.3
10+	24	28.2	66.7
Overall	85	99.9	50.6

Source: Data supplied by SMCC.

work. Even if the servants adopted a supervisory role, they would have still been required to labor in the fields at busy times of the year alongside the slaves.[64]

That occasionally whites and blacks relaxed together at work can be shown by a case that came before the Henrico County court in 1681. John Aust

64. Main, *Tobacco Colony*, 130–131; Lower Norfolk, Wills and Deeds E (1666–1675), fols. 124–125.

described how in August, visiting the plantation of Mr. Thomas Cocke, he "went into his Orchard where his servants were a cutting downe weeds, whoe asked the deponent to stay and drinke." Aust's arrival appears to have been the pretext for a general downing of tools, since "Thomas Cockes Negroes" also stopped work and spent the remainder of the afternoon "a drinking of syder" with the whites. But although servants and slaves worked together, lived together, sometimes drank together, and shared hardships, one ought not infer that white servants viewed blacks as equals or that the impact of racism on the lives of Afro-Americans was any less harsh. Servants were well aware of the unbridgeable gulf separating them from slaves. They would eventually gain their liberty and become full members of society; slaves would not. Slaves were indisputably the property of their owners to do with virtually as they wished; servants retained some rights, as subjects of the crown and Christians, and were accorded a degree of protection by the courts. Servants were sometimes employed as overseers and skilled craftsmen, whereas blacks were rarely given positions of authority or responsibility. With the intensification of racism in the late seventeenth and early eighteenth centuries, the oppressions and inequalities either side of the color bar became clearer.[65]

The vast majority of servants were brought in as field hands or domestics, but a small proportion, no more than a few percent, served as apprentices to various artisans. Thomas Wilmot claimed that he had indentured himself for seven years to "bee taught to bee a taylor," although his master disagreed. Henry Haslewood of Lancaster County came in for four years "upon the Acct. of a Cooper" but was found to be "very imperfect in the sd. trade." Early in 1664 John Helme declared before the Charles County court that he had been "bound in England to sarve Mr John Meekes in th way of Chirurgery and to find and allow your petitioner meat drinck apparrell and Lodging according to the usuall Custom in England." Unluckily for Helme, his master showed little inclination to instruct him and had told him that he "might goe whether hee woold and bee damned." As in England, orphans and children of poorer families were sometimes put out as apprentices. James, the son of Edward Lanceford, deceased, bound himself to William Clement to learn "the Arte and mistrey of a blacksmith." John Pulman was apprenticed to Richard Flint to learn tailoring but was also to be taught how to read and

65. Billings, ed., *The Old Dominion*, 162–163; Main, *Tobacco Colony*, 139. See also Chapter 3, above.

write, and William Edmonds was apprenticed to John Meredith to learn the trade of a shipwright.[66]

As one might expect, most craftsmen were engaged in trades related to the demands of tobacco husbandry, farm building, and transatlantic commerce: coopers, joiners, carpenters, shipwrights, wheelwrights, and blacksmiths. But there were exceptions. The Lower Norfolk court recorded in 1673 that John Chamberlain "hath sett up a Loome and Imployeth himselfe and family in Weaving." He was exempted from levies "for his greater Encouragem[en]t in Case any poore Children present that the Court think fitt to put out aprentices they have promises to putt one or two of them to him." George Ashall, tanner, of the same county, was paid four thousand pounds of tobacco out of the annual levy in 1663 to erect a "County Tanhouse," according to the act of the Assembly, and deliver shoes at the prescribed price. Whereas weavers and shoemakers, along with other artisans, became much more numerous in the eighteenth century, full-time free craftsmen represented no more than about 5 percent of the working population in the second half of the seventeenth century, since most planters preferred to reduce expenditures by doing their own tailoring or carpentry whenever possible or else acquired skilled servants who, as well as being employed around the plantation, could occasionally be hired out.[67]

Debts owed to Edward Floyd, a carpenter and wheelwright who lived at Mr. David Fox's plantation at Moratico, Lancaster County, provide a glimpse of the sort of work a specialist was employed to do. He built several houses, including "the great house" of Captain William Ball, ceiled over chambers, added new rooms to existing dwellings, put up chimneys, fixed the windows of Mr. Joseph Ball's "great dwelling house" with white lead, repaired George Heale's tobacco house which "the thunder broke downe," built a fifteen-foot henhouse and a fifty-foot tobacco house, and made cartwheels,

66. Lower Norfolk, Wills and Deeds D (1656–1666), fols. 173, 175, 182, 381; Lancaster County, Orders Etc. (1655–1666), 110, no. 1 (1666–1680), 114, 365, 411; *Md. Archives*, LIII, 431.

67. Lower Norfolk, Wills and Deeds D (1656–1666), fol. 373, E (Orders) (1666–1675), fol. 94; Main, *Tobacco Colony*, 77–78; Gloria Lund Main, "Personal Wealth in Colonial America: Explorations in the Use of Probate Records from Maryland and Massachusetts, 1650–1720" (Ph.D. diss., Columbia University, 1972), 126; Jean B. Russo, "Self-Sufficiency and Local Exchange: Free Craftsmen in the Rural Chesapeake Economy," in Lois Green Carr, Philip D. Morgan, and Jean B. Russo, eds., *Colonial Chesapeake Society* (Chapel Hill, N.C., 1988), 389–432; Richard Beale Davis, ed., *William Fitzhugh and His Chesapeake World, 1676–1701: The Fitzhugh Letters and Other Documents* (Chapel Hill, N.C., 1963), 92, 202.

a cart, canoe, and a "Weeding Harrow." In all, he was owed at his death in 1690 nearly twenty thousand pounds of tobacco (approximately £70) by seventeen people, most of whom were prominent planters.[68]

The problems that small-scale traders and artisans like Floyd confronted were articulated late in the century by Henry Hartwell, James Blair, and Edward Chilton. "For want of Towns, Markets, and Money," they wrote, "there is but little Encouragement for Tradesmen and Artificers, and therefore little Choice of them, and their Labour very dear in the Country." In the absence of markets, a tradesman "must either make Corn, keep Cows, and raise Stocks himself, or must ride about the Country to buy Meat and Corn where he can find it. . . . Then a great deal of the Tradesman's Time being necessarily spent in going and coming to and from his Work, in dispers'd Country Plantations, and his Pay being generally in straggling Parcels of Tobacco, the Collection whereof costs about 10 *per Cent.* and the best of this Pay coming but once a Year, so that he cannot turn his Hand frequently with a small Stock, as Tradesmen do in *England* and elsewhere, all this occasions the Dearth of all Tradesmen's Labour, and likewise the Discouragement, Scarcity, and Insufficiency of Tradesmen." The lack of towns, Francis Makemie commented a few years later, inhibited both the growth of trade and the development of a vigorous artisanal class.[69]

A final category of work that played an important role in the lives of settlers was merchandising, either because they relied on Chesapeake merchants for essential goods from England or because they made a living primarily from trading. Many planters, with money and connections in England, profited from a little trading on the side, but most regions tended to rely on direct imports from London, Bristol, and other outports or were dominated by one or two large planter-merchants. Robert Slye of St. Mary's County, who arrived in Maryland in 1654, developed an extensive trading network on Bretton's Bay, at St. Clement's and Basford manors, along both sides of the Wicomico, and across the Potomac in Virginia. At his death in 1671 he was owed approximately £1,545 by more than 200 individuals: a small fortune, compared to the income of most planters. His neighbor and competitor on St. Clement's Manor, Benjamin Salley, a merchant-cum-innkeeper, took over many of Slye's former customers and was owed more than £500 by 84 people when he died in 1674. Their trade networks were expanded in the

68. Lancaster County, Wills Etc., no. 8 (1690–1709), 19–20.

69. Henry Hartwell, James Blair, and Edward Chilton, *The Present State of Virginia, and the College,* ed. Hunter Dickinson Farish (Williamsburg, Va., 1940), 9–10; [Francis Makemie], *A Plain and Friendly Perswasive . . .* (London, 1705).

last quarter of the century by Nehemiah Blackiston and William Rosewell, who had between 400 and 550 customers on their books.[70]

Similar developments took place elsewhere in the tidewater. Captain Henry Fleet, William Ball, Dominic Therriott, Cuthbert Potter, and Raleigh Travers established themselves as important planter-merchants in early Lancaster County, although on a smaller scale than Slye or Salley. Therriott was owed £400 by just fewer than 100 people in 1676; Robert Beckingham, who married Travers's widow, was owed about £700 by 140 people at his death in the same year. From his store in York County, Jonathan Newell developed one of the most extensive commercial networks in the colony during the 1660s and 1670s, trading to New Kent, James, Warwick, and Gloucester counties as well as the "Rapahannock" River. Further south, Henry Seawell, Thomas Willoughby, John Gookin, the Dutchman Simon Overzee, and Colonel Francis Yeardley dominated the trade of Lower Norfolk County from the late 1630s to the 1650s, as Captain William Odeon, William Carver, and Robert Hodge were to do in succeeding decades.[71]

Merchants faced problems similar to those experienced by tradesmen and artisans. Although, in the opinion of Hartwell, Blair, and Chilton, they lived "the best of any in that Country," they were "subject to great Inconveniences in the way of their Trade."

> For first they are obliged to sell upon Trust all the Year long, except just a little while when Tobacco is ready. *2dly*, They likewise drive a pityful retail Trade to serve every Man's little Occasions, being all in Effect but Country Chapmen, for want of Towns to be a Center of Trade and Business. *3dly*, Besides the Charge of it, they are necessitated to trust all their Concerns to their Receivers, who go about among the Planters that owe them Tobacco, and receive and mark it for them, which Receivers, if they want either Skill or Honesty, prove very fatal to the Merchant. *4thly*, They are at the Charge of carting this Tobacco . . . to convenient Landings; or if it lyes not far from these Landings, they must trust to the Seamen for their careful rolling it on board of their Sloops and Shallops; and if the Seamen roll it in bad Weather, or dirty Ways, it is expos'd to a great deal of Damage. *5thly*, It is a great while before the Ships can be loaded, their Freight lying at such Distance, and being to be brought together in this scrambling Manner. By Reason of this it is an usual thing with Ships to lye

---

70. SMCC Debt Files.

71. Lancaster County, Wills Etc., no. 5 (1674–1689), 16–18, 32–40; Billings, ed., *The Old Dominion*, 192–204; Horn, biographical files, Lower Norfolk County.

three or four Months in the Country, which might be dispatch'd in a Fortnight's Time, if the Tobacco were ready at certain Ports; and this inhances the Freight to almost double the Price of what it needed to be, if the Ship had a quick Dispatch.[72]

Virginia's Assembly attempted to create public stores and markets in the 1630s and 1640s. Following the act of 1641, the Lower Norfolk court directed that a store, sixty by twenty feet, be built at Lynnhaven near Francis Mason's Creek, and another at Thomas Willoughby's plantation. Fourteen years later, again in response to an act of the Assembly, markets were to be established in Elizabeth River and Lynnhaven parishes. In newly formed Lancaster County, four markets were to be set up along the Rappahannock in June 1655. These proposals appear never to have progressed beyond initial planning, however. As James Perry points out, county stores were bound to fail, because planters resisted the "uncomfortably close supervision of tobacco marketing" that the system would entail and because, given "the ready access of most planters to water transport and the relative shortage of labor, it made more sense to pack and ship directly."[73]

The working lives of planter-merchants therefore focused on developing links with English merchants and captains, extending trading networks in their vicinity, keeping records of who owed them money, and perhaps running their own store, as much as on tobacco cultivation. Their contacts with settlers in their own region, with other parts of the tidewater, and with Europe were both more intensive and extensive than those of lesser planters. In taking on the role of merchants, large planters were able to diversify their financial operations and provide a means of distributing English wares throughout the Chesapeake. As agriculturalists and entrepreneurs, their working lives brought together the two major elements of the economy, tobacco and trade, and spanned the transatlantic world.[74]

The move to Maryland and Virginia led to profound changes in the working lives of immigrants. Tens of thousands of poor settlers from England's

72. Hartwell, Blair, and Chilton, *Present State of Virginia*, ed. Farish, 10–11.

73. Hening, ed., *Statutes at Large*, I, 203–207, 209–212; "The Virginia Assembly of 1641: A List of Members and Some of the Acts," *VMHB*, IX (1901–1902), 57; Lower Norfolk County, Minute Book (1637–1646), I, fols. 113, 122, 136, Wills and Deeds C (1651–1656), fol. 161, D (1656–1666), fol. 313; Lancaster County, Deeds Etc., no. 1 (1652–1657), 201, 210; Perry, *Formation of a Society*, 140–141.

74. A good example of the activities of one such entrepreneur can be found in Davis, ed., *William Fitzhugh and His Chesapeake World*.

countryside, cities, and towns found themselves laboring in an unfamiliar environment and subject to an equally unfamiliar work regimen. Even those from farming backgrounds encountered a form of husbandry quite different from English agriculture. There was little reminiscent of work practices and customs reaching back "time out of mind" in England, of the carefully ordered field systems of arable regions, or of the patchwork of enclosed fields in pastoral areas. Neither was the complexity and diversity of English occupational structure reproduced in the tidewater. Servants who arrived expecting to be treated like English apprentices or laborers found that they were commonly treated merely as a form of property, to be bought and sold like any other commodity. Legislation defining the reciprocal duties of masters and servants led to an increase in the powers of masters and gave them a degree of control over their laborers unprecedented in England. Far from being a land of milk and honey, conditions for servants along the Bay were in many respects worse than those of their counterparts who stayed behind.

A tobacco planter's life was not easy, nor were the returns great. Monotonous, hard physical labor in the fields year after year was the lot of most men and many women who settled in Maryland and Virginia during the seventeenth century. Determination and luck enabled some poor immigrants to enter the ranks of middling and wealthy planters, but for the majority, especially those who arrived after 1670, profits were meager. Many poor men and women who left England seeking opportunity in America may have encountered merely another kind of poverty in the Chesapeake. On the other hand, there was the possibility, if they lived long enough, of forming their own households on their own land, which was more than England offered them. If only a fraction of servants struck it rich, nevertheless there was the satisfaction for those who made it into the ranks of the small planter class of setting up for themselves, of being in charge (subject to the vagaries of the weather and the price of tobacco) of their own fortunes. Given the choice between tramping the highways or shifting from job to job in England and being a smallholder in the colonies, it is unlikely that many would have chosen to return home.

7

House and Home: The Domestic Environment

Widow Shuter of Leeds, Kent, died in 1670, and her goods were sold at a public outcry "for the use" of her three children. Her house had at least four rooms. In the kitchen was a variety of pots, skillets, pans, and dishes besides a couple of "rush bottome Chaires," three-legged stools, and two "small formes." They may have eaten their meals there, but no mention is made of a table or board. In the "parler," the widow's bedroom, was a four-posted bed with "curtaines and valance" (providing some privacy), together with bedding and several chests containing the family's linen and clothing. The "Garrett" above was probably the children's bedroom, since a "bed-steedle" and "flockbed" (mattress) were kept there. It was also a storeroom for small quantities of wheat, wool, and wood for domestic use. Finally, in the "Drinkehouse" were a couple of tubs and a "keiller" used for salting down meat, brewing, and the household's washing. The total value of widow Shuter's goods came to £13 6s. Aside from two linen wheels, there is no indication of how she earned a living. She apparently owned no livestock or land and apart from £4 "in money" had no other assets.[1]

Thomas Reynolds died a few years later in Lower Norfolk County, Virginia, worth approximately £45 in personalty. No details are given in his inventory about his house, but there is no reason to doubt that he lived in a small wooden structure (about twenty by sixteen feet, with a couple of rooms on the ground floor and possibly a loft above) typical of the great majority of poor-to-modest planters in this period. Reynolds evidently combined tobacco husbandry with carpentry, since besides his livestock he possessed a number of saws and axes and was owed money for "building" and "making fencing." Debts, tools, cattle, and swine amounted to nearly £24; the remainder of his estate (about £22) consisted of domestic goods. His

---

1. P222, 12/1, Widow Shute(r), April 1670, Kent Archives Office, Maidstone, Kent.

standard of living can be best described as basic. He owned a couch and a table and ate from pewter dishes as well as from wooden "trenchers." He and his wife slept on a feather bed most likely placed directly on the floor; they did not have a bedstead. A "cattalye [cattail] bed" and an "old Couch bed" may have been used by children, servants, or occasional guests. There were few luxuries. He owned a Bible, a couple of devotional works, and a "small silver Beker." A chest, an "ironbound case," and two boxes, probably brought from England when he emigrated, were used for storage purposes and make-do seats. The family's linen, a few pots, bowls, pails, and vats made up the rest of the "householdstuff."[2]

These two examples, selected from thousands of English and Chesapeake inventories, make a simple point. Widow Shuter was not utterly destitute when she died—her estate provided sufficient funds for two of her children to be apprenticed—but she occupied a position close to the bottom of village society; and, in fact, an account of her goods was filed with a bundle of pauper inventories by the parish's overseers of the poor. Thomas Reynolds was certainly not a pauper at the time of his death. A personal estate of forty to fifty pounds placed him squarely in the middle ranks of Chesapeake society. Yet his standard of living, revealed by his inventory, was not markedly better than the widow's. The house he lived in was probably no larger, and his furniture and furnishings were neither more plentiful nor of superior quality. Whatever advantages moving to the tobacco coast brought for the likes of Reynolds, it did not bring domestic comfort. During the second half

2. Lower Norfolk County, Wills and Deeds E (1666–1675), fols. 156–157 (Colonial Williamsburg, microfilm, reel M 1365-18). He may have been the same Thomas Reynolds who arrived in the county about 1649/50 and took up 100 acres on Tanner's Creek in 1653: see Nell Marion Nugent, comp., *Cavaliers and Pioneers: Abstracts of Virginia Land Patents and Grants*, 2 vols. (Richmond, Va., 1934, 1977), I, 187, 285. His estate was worth approximately 11,000 lbs. of tobacco in August 1673, which at 1d. per lb. gives £45 16s. 8d. For planters' dwellings, see Lorena Seebach Walsh, "Charles County, Maryland, 1658–1705: A Study of Chesapeake Social and Political Structure" (Ph.D. diss., Michigan State University, 1977), 250–251; Fred B. Knifflin, "Folk Housing: Key to Diffusion," in Dell Upton and John Michael Vlach, eds., *Common Places: Readings in American Vernacular Architecture* (Athens, Ga., 1986), 18–19; Cary Carson, "The 'Virginia House' in Maryland," *Maryland Historical Magazine*, LXIX (1974), 185–196; Gloria L. Main, *Tobacco Colony: Life in Early Maryland, 1650–1720* (Princeton, N.J., 1982), chap. 4; and James P. P. Horn, "'The Bare Necessities': Standards of Living in England and the Chesapeake, 1650–1700," *Historical Archaeology*, XXII, no. 2 (1988), 78–79 and fig. 3. Lorna Weatherill discusses the idea of luxury in terms of material culture in *Consumer Behaviour and Material Culture in Britain, 1660–1760* (London, 1988), 14–16.

of the seventeenth century, most settlers experienced a standard of living little different from that of the lowest stratum of householders in England.[3]

The domestic environment had a profound influence on the texture of everyday life in early modern England and America. It goes without saying that much family life—coming together for meals, sleeping, procreation, leisure, and companionship—took place within the home. The home provided shelter and comfort, a refuge from inclement weather, a place where children were born and raised, the sick were cared for, friends and neighbors were entertained, and members of the family died. It was also a theater for the display of household furnishings and valued possessions. In a preliterate age, material goods had enormous symbolic and social significance and constituted a clear and tangible reflection of the family's economic well-being and rank in the community.[4]

A great variety of options was open to householders in furnishing their dwellings. They could choose from plates and dishes made of pewter or wood or from earthenware; chairs, forms, settles, and stools made in all shapes and sizes; feather, flock, or chaff beds for their chambers. They could invest in a few modest comforts: a chamberpot to avoid nightly visits to the privy or chilly trips out the backdoor; a warming pan to heat damp and cold sheets before getting into bed; and for those who could read, a Bible or other books to pass away evenings or quiet periods during the day. Choice was not unlimited. It was conditioned in large part by the availability of goods, constraints of domestic space, and competing demands on the family's income. But, nevertheless, the size and design of housing, the use or uses to which rooms were put, and the multifarious combinations of hundreds of humdrum household items could produce considerable variation in the arrangement and furnishing of domestic interiors, even within the limits of a

3. James Horn, "Adapting to a New World: A Comparative Study of Local Society in England and Maryland, 1650–1700," in Lois Green Carr, Philip D. Morgan, and Jean B. Russo, eds., *Colonial Chesapeake Society* (Chapel Hill, N.C., 1988), 151–164; Horn, " 'The Bare Necessities,' " *Hist. Arch.*, XXII, no. 2 (1988), 74–91.

4. Weatherill, *Consumer Behaviour*, 5. General studies of the cultural significance of consumerism include Mary Douglas and Baron Isherwood, *The World of Goods: Towards an Anthropology of Consumption* (London, 1979); Arjun Appadurai, ed., *The Social Life of Things: Commodities in Cultural Perspective* (Cambridge, 1986); Grant McCracken, *Culture and Consumption: New Approaches to the Symbolic Character of Consumer Goods and Activities* (Bloomington, Ind., 1988); Ian Hodder, ed., *The Meaning of Things: Material Culture and Symbolic Expression* (London, 1989). See, also, Cary Carson's wide-ranging introduction to Carson, Ronald Hoffman, and Peter J. Albert, eds., *Of Consuming Interests: The Style of Life in the Eighteenth Century* (Charlottesville, Va., in press).

much smaller range of household goods than became available in the next century.[5]

This chapter compares standards of living as expressed by houses and their furnishings in England and the Chesapeake. Householders in the Vale of Berkeley and East Kent, together with three regions of the tidewater—Lancaster and Northumberland counties in the Northern Neck, Lower Norfolk County, and St. Mary's County—have been divided into five wealth groups (less than £10, £10–£49, £50–£99, £100–£249, £250 and over) to explore differences in living standards between the poor, middling, and rich.[6] The aim is to recapture something of the reality of home life in the two societies, assess the adjustments and adaptations made by settlers to conditions encountered along the Bay, and consider continuities and discontinuities in the organization and use of domestic space. Such a discussion is important both to an understanding of the quality of life experienced by colonists and also as a preliminary to an appraisal of general social attitudes toward hierarchy, status, gender, and consumerism.

Houses, Rooms, and Room Use

Housing in the Vale of Berkeley was characterized above all by diversity. In the upper part of the Vale, cruck and half-timbered dwellings were plentiful throughout the seventeenth and early eighteenth centuries. Further south, stone and rubble were the most common building materials, with brick generally reserved for chimneys. Roofing was usually of stone, tiles, or thatch, according to local materials and traditions. Dwellings with

---

5. Weatherill, *Consumer Behaviour*, chap. 3; Lois Green Carr and Lorena S. Walsh, "Changing Life Styles in Colonial St. Mary's County," Regional Economic History Research Center, *Working Papers*, I, no. 3 (1978), 73–118; Carr and Walsh, "The Standard of Living in the Colonial Chesapeake," *William and Mary Quarterly*, 3d Ser., XLV (1988), 135–159; Carr and Walsh, "Changing Life Styles and Consumer Behavior in the Colonial Chesapeake," in Carson, Hoffman, and Albert, eds., *Of Consuming Interests*.

6. For a discussion of the technical problems involved in using probate inventories for comparative analyses of the domestic environment in England and the Chesapeake, see Horn, "'The Bare Necessities,'" *Hist. Arch.*, XXII, no. 2 (1988), 74–77. A general discussion of consumerism in early modern England and America is provided by Carole Shammas, *The Pre-Industrial Consumer in England and America* (Oxford, 1990). Northumberland County inventories were used to boost the relatively small number in the Lancaster County sample.

a through-passage were the dominant type until midcentury, but thereafter, as rebuilding went on apace, other floor plans were adopted or adapted.[7]

Little evidence exists about the dwellings of the very poor. Rudimentary shelter erected on commons, heaths, and woodlands by itinerant laborers or vagrants represented the most humble forms of housing. Since they were usually intended for temporary refuge rather than as permanent structures, very few have survived; they were a type of English "impermanent architecture."[8] A tiny squatter's cottage dating from the late seventeenth or early eighteenth century at Lark's Farm in the parish of Iron Acton, just north of Bristol, measured ten-feet square and had two stories. At Urchfont, Wiltshire, eighteen cottages erected on the wasteland in the late sixteenth and early seventeenth centuries ranged in size from eight by ten feet or six by twelve, to twelve by sixteen. The average was ten by fourteen feet. There is no indication of materials used, but the cottages were probably built of a rough timber frame, with lathe and plaster walls and a thatched roof. They may well have been of posthole construction, since an account of the building of an illegal cottage at Downton in the same county refers to a man "who holpe digge the holes for erecting the said Cottage." In many parts of southern and central England, population increase and the rising numbers of migrants put considerable pressure on existing housing stock during the fifty years after the accession of Elizabeth I. The subdivision of dwellings and tenements and the growing number of inmates accommodated by established householders absorbed much of the increase, but particularly in marginal areas the homeless commonly erected their own houses, either

7. David G. Hey, *An English Rural Community: Myddle under the Tudors and Stuarts* (Leicester, 1974), 122; Peter Smith, "Rural Housing in Wales," in H.P.R. Finberg and Joan Thirsk, eds., *The Agrarian History of England and Wales* (Cambridge, 1967–), V, pt. 2, 689–691; Lyndon F. Cave, *The Smaller English House: Its History and Development* (London, 1985), 59–60, 169; Eric Mercer, *English Vernacular Houses: A Study of Traditional Farmhouses and Cottages* (London, 1975).

Cruck-built dwellings were characterized by pairs of large timbers (crucks) that inclined inward from the line of the outer walls, meeting at the apex to support the ridge-beam (M. W. Barley, *The English Farmhouse and Cottage* [London, 1961], 289).

Through-passage dwellings, as the name implies, had a passage running through the house from front to rear; see Linda J. Hall, *The Rural Houses of North Avon and South Gloucestershire, 1400–1720* (Bristol, 1983), 1–34.

8. The phrase is taken from Cary Carson *et al.*, "Impermanent Architecture in the Southern American Colonies," *Winterthur Portfolio*, XVI (1981), 135–196; and see Shammas, *The Pre-Industrial Consumer*, 160–161.

with the intention of becoming permanent members of the community or as a temporary measure before moving elsewhere.[9]

As population growth slackened and eventually came to a halt by the outbreak of the Civil War, so the problem of homelessness gradually receded. It is improbable that flimsy or crudely constructed cottages were numerous in southern England in the post-Restoration period, and, in fact, the period after 1660 is generally seen as one of rapid improvements in the housing of smallholders and the rural poor. M. W. Barley suggests that the two- or three-roomed cottage was the smallest form of housing common in central and southern counties in this period, and evidence from probate inventories, although slight, bears out this view. Of forty-two people who died in the Vale of Berkeley worth less than £10 in personalty between 1660 and 1700, the dwellings of ten were described room by room. Four lived in two rooms, two in three rooms, one in four rooms, and three in five rooms. Agricultural laborers from the Frampton Cotterell area, to the south of the Vale, usually lived in three-room cottages. Some poor inhabitants evidently occupied unsubstantial dwellings. Anna Bence of Slimbridge was given 2s. 10d. by the overseers of the poor in 1642 "when her house was blowne downe" in a great gale. But despite their relatively small size (twenty feet by twenty to thirty-five feet), most laborers' cottages in the region were well constructed by local craftsmen and built to last.[10]

The majority of dwellings in the Vale of Berkeley had between five and seven rooms. As with the less-than-ten-pound group, little is known about room size or specific building materials. Hearth tax returns and evidence from inventories suggest that dwellings in this range (four-fifths) had one or two hearths. Room names provide clues to the layout of houses. The large number of different names testifies both to the great variety of housing

9. Hall, *Rural Houses*, 183–184; J. H. Bettey, "Seventeenth-Century Squatters' Dwellings. Some Documentary Evidence," *Vernacular Architecture*, XIII (1982), 28–30; personal communication from J. H. Bettey. Posthole construction describes dwellings where the main vertical wall timbers were placed directly into holes in the ground.

10. In Finberg and Thirsk, eds., *Agrarian History of England and Wales*: M. W. Barley, "Rural Building in England," V, pt. 2, 653, "Rural Housing in England," IV, 762; N. W. Alcock, "The Great Rebuilding and Its Later Stages," *Vernacular Architecture*, XIV (1983), 45–48; Mercer, *English Vernacular Houses*, chap. 2; J. T. Smith, "The Evolution of the English Peasant House to the Late Seventeenth Century: The Evidence of Buildings," *Journal of the British Archaeological Association*, 3d Ser., XXXIII (1970), 122–146; Probate inventories, 1660–1700, P298c, OV2/1, Gloucestershire Record Office; John S. Moore, ed., *The Goods and Chattels of Our Forefathers: Frampton Cotterell and District Probate Inventories, 1539–1804* (Chichester, 1976), 35–36; Hall, *Rural Houses*, 22.

and the confusion of terms, but certain common features emerge. A typical five-room house had a hall, kitchen, and buttery on the ground floor and two chambers on the first floor, usually over the hall and kitchen. Larger dwellings followed a similar plan, with the addition of extra chambers and possibly one or two lofts or outhouses. Extra rooms did not necessarily imply greater domestic comfort, since larger houses inhabited by working families might contain more storage rooms, necessary for keeping foodstuffs, ale and cider, various raw materials, and working tools.[11]

There was no sharp distinction between the dwellings of the middling wealth category (£100–£249) and the rich (£250 and over). Wealthy retailers and craftsmen lived in houses of nine to ten rooms, the parish gentry and substantial yeomen in houses of eight to fifteen rooms. Many appear to have followed the layout of smaller houses, with the addition of a parlor, cellar, whitehouse (dairy), and extra lofts, the last sometimes serving as auxiliary bedrooms as well as for storage. There usually were more hearths, providing warmth and light to a larger range of chambers and ground floor rooms than in humbler structures. More specialized use of domestic space was also potentially greater, but building materials and styles do not appear to have differed markedly from other housing. Only at the very pinnacle of society were differences in style and size of dwellings striking. Smalcombe Court, owned by the Smyth family of North Nibley, had at least twenty-seven rooms. Few but the county elite and aristocracy could afford to keep up with the latest fashions in architecture, ornamental gardens, and landscaped parks. Not only were building materials different—dressed stone or brick—but designs owed as much to metropolitan taste as to vernacular tradition. An impression of new styles and the remodeling of the landscape can be gained from the series of vistas of country seats illustrated in Sir Robert Atkyns's history of Gloucestershire published in 1712.[12]

In general terms, the housing of most people in eastern Kent differed little from that of southern Gloucestershire. Timber-framed dwellings were more common, and cruck construction was rarer. Houses of stone and rubble

11. Probate inventories, 1660–1700, GRO; E179/247/16, Public Record Office, London; Horn, "'The Bare Necessities,'" *Hist. Arch.*, XXII, no. 2 (1988), 77–78; Derek Portman, "Vernacular Building in the Oxford Region in the Sixteenth and Seventeenth Centuries," in C. W. Chalklin and M. A. Havinden, eds., *Rural Change and Urban Growth, 1500–1800: Essays in English Regional History Presented in Honour of W. G. Hoskins* (London, 1974), 147–152.

12. Barley, "Rural Building," in Finberg and Thirsk, eds., *Agrarian History of England and Wales*, V, pt. 2, 600–619; Robert Atkyns, *The Ancient and Present State of Glocestershire* (London, 1712).

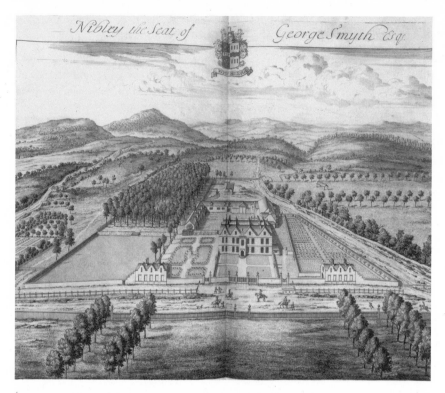

5. Smalcombe Court, Nibley. *From Sir Robert Atkyns,* The Ancient and Present State of Glocestershire *(London, 1712). Permission of the British Library*

tended to be confined to the eastern and southern parts of the county, on the borders of Sussex and Surrey. The number of rooms occupied by each wealth group was very similar to the Vale of Berkeley. The very poor inhabited dwellings of three to four rooms; poor to middling householders (£10–£99), four to seven rooms; middling to wealthy (£100–£249), six to eleven rooms; and the rich (£250 and over), seven to thirteen rooms.[13] Layout and room use were also similar: hall or kitchen, parlor, and buttery on the ground floor, with two or three chambers above and perhaps a couple of lofts or service rooms (milkhouse, drinkhouse, washhouse, or cellar) in larger dwellings.

As in Gloucestershire and many other parts of England, the hall retained

13. Cave, *Smaller English House,* fig. 10, 80, 133–134; Smith, "Rural Housing in Wales," in Finberg and Thirsk, eds., *Agrarian History of England and Wales,* V, pt. 2, 695. The mean number of rooms per house of each wealth group was as follows: less than £10: 3.3; £10–£49: 5.7; £50–£99: 6.8; £100–£249: 8.9; £250+: 11.4.

TABLE 27
Room Use in East Kent Households

Room Use	Household Wealth			
	0–£49	£50–£99	£100–£249	£250+
	Hall			
	(N=37)	(N=23)	(N=27)	(N=20)
Cooking, sitting, and eating	81.1%	69.6%	63.0%	40.0%
Cooking only	0	0	3.7	0
Sitting and eating	18.9	26.1	22.2	60.0
Storage	0	4.3	7.4	0
Sleeping	0	0	3.7	0
	Kitchen			
	(N=19)	(N=9)	(N=18)	(N=21)
Cooking only	42.1%	55.5%	38.9%	47.6%
Cooking and eating	31.6	11.1	33.3	33.3
Storage	21.1	33.3	27.8	19.0
Sitting and eating	5.3	0	0	0
	Parlor			
	(N=21)	(N=12)	(N=21)	(N=13)
Sleeping	57.1%	50.0%	38.1%	7.7%
Sitting and eating	28.6	25.0	42.9	61.5
Sleeping and sitting	14.3	16.7	9.5	30.8
Storage	0	8.3	9.5	0

Source: Consistory Court of Canterbury, Probate Inventories, 1660–1680, PRC 27/13–28, Kent Archives Office.

its importance as the principal room in the house, where a variety of activities took place: cooking, eating, relaxing, and receiving guests. Two-thirds of householders in East Kent used the hall for these purposes. Among the wealthy, however, there was a tendency to use the hall for relaxation, and possibly eating, only. Food preparation and cooking was transferred to the kitchen (Table 27). Parlors were also put to a variety of uses but were generally where people slept or sat down for meals. Whereas in poorer households parlors commonly served as a bedroom, among the rich they were usually reserved for dining and entertainment (Table 27). In larger houses rooms could be more specialized. Storage and food preparation were consigned to services areas (kitchen, buttery, cellar, loft, brewhouse, milkhouse, and so on); sleeping was confined to the upper chambers, where there was greater privacy and less likelihood of disturbance; relaxation, sitting, and eating took place in the hall and parlor, where the family's best furniture, plate, and treasured possessions would be on public display. This trend among the wealthy in the latter half of the seventeenth century foreshadowed the more general adoption of such specialized uses in the eighteenth century by an increasingly affluent middle class.[14]

A number of points from this survey are worth stressing. In Gloucestershire and Kent, like other parts of southern and central England, the medieval open-hall house had given way during the fifteenth and sixteenth centuries to the multiroomed, two-story dwelling, allowing greater specialization in the use of domestic space and greater comfort. Apart from makeshift structures on wastes and in woodlands, more common in the early decades of the seventeenth century than in later years, the smallest houses were generally three-roomed cottages, sturdily built by local craftsmen. Most people, however, lived in larger dwellings of four to seven rooms. Built of seasoned timber, stone, rubble, brick, and tile, they were sufficiently well constructed to be durable but also sufficiently flexible in plan and structure to allow the addition of new rooms, chambers, and hearths when necessary. Given reasonable maintenance, they would last for centuries.

Contrasts with Chesapeake housing could not be more dramatic. Throughout the tidewater, dwellings followed a similar formula: a wooden frame attached to heavy posts was set into holes in the ground, and riven clapboards several feet long were nailed onto the outside, providing an exterior surface and structural support. Roofs were made of wooden shingles, a convenient and cheap solution to the lack of thatch, tile, and stone. Floors sometimes had planking laid over them but more often were simply left as beaten dirt. Occasionally, clay was used to plaster inside walls and fill in gaps between clapboards to keep out drafts and rain. Partitions and ceilings provided a few rudimentary rooms in the main part of the house, and lean-tos and outhouses could be added when needed. Since bricklaying was a skill beyond

14. Weatherill, *Consumer Behaviour*, 9–13; Alan Dyer, "Urban Housing: A Documentary Study of Four Midland Towns, 1530–1700," *Post-Medieval Archaeology*, XV (1981), 207–218; Ursula Priestly and P. J. Corfield, "Rooms and Room Use in Norwich Housing, 1580–1730," *Post-Med. Arch.*, XVI (1982), 105–114.

6. A Freedman's House, St. Mary's City. *Courtesy of Historic St. Mary's City*

most planters, the majority of houses had "Welsh" chimneys, usually made of wattle and daub, attached to the gable end of the dwelling.[15]

The most obvious features of the dwellings were their small size and home-made appearance. Few were larger than about sixteen by twenty feet, and the vast majority had only a couple of rooms. They were, in fact, slightly larger and modified versions of flimsy English huts erected on commons and wastes described earlier, a comparison that has closer parallels than might first appear. Like English itinerants who built in forests and on heath-lands, most settlers along the tobacco coast were also poor migrants who had neither the skills nor money to construct larger, durable houses. It has been argued that, as a consequence of tobacco husbandry and cheapness of land, there was little reason to build permanent structures. When tobacco fields

15. Main, *Tobacco Colony*, 145–148; Carson, "The 'Virginia House,'" *Md. Hist. Mag.*, LXIX (1974), 185–196.

became exhausted, planters frequently moved to another part of their land, where a new dwelling could be quickly erected. The old house was left to decay. Given the nature of their construction, it was usually easier to erect a new dwelling or tobacco barn than to repair an old one.[16] Like the tiny squatters' huts built in marginal areas of England in the early seventeenth century, Chesapeake housing provided temporary rather than permanent shelter.

Yet similarities should not be overdrawn. Common needs—cheap, easy-to-build, and temporary accommodation—might have encouraged the adoption of structures reminiscent of the lowest types of housing in England, but this is not to suggest that vernacular building in Virginia and Maryland slavishly copied English practice. Clearly, settlers responded to the conditions they encountered and local resources. "New building materials, an unfamiliar climate, and an economy based almost exclusively on tobacco," Cary Carson points out, "began working changes in imported vernacular traditions as soon as immigrants discovered that old conventions were often poorly suited to their new way of life." Hence riven clapboards replaced wattle-and-daub infilling of walls, and wooden shingles replaced thatched roofs. Colonists borrowed from general English methods of constructing small huts, barns, and hovels for storage and farm animals, but they discarded almost entirely the infinitely varied vernacular traditions associated with their provincial backgrounds. The Chesapeake countryside exhibited no handsome timber-framed houses in the square-paneled mode of the West Midlands or jettied style of the Kentish Weald, no sturdy cottages made of rubble and stone, and only a very few brick buildings. Most planters lived in little "wooden boxes dribbled over the landscape without apparent design," which had become so universally accepted on both sides of the Potomac by the 1660s that they were commonly termed "Virginia houses." [17]

A general, and rather favorable, impression of these dwellings is provided by a traveler's description from the 1680s. Houses were usually made of wood.

16. Walsh, "Charles County," 248–250. The great number of Chesapeake inventories that do not mention rooms is not a consequence of a universal oversight on the part of appraisers to register room names; rather, it suggests small dwellings where little distinction was made between the functions to which rooms were put. See Main, *Tobacco Colony*, 152–153; and Shammas, *The Pre-Industrial Consumer*, 166–167.

17. Carson, "The 'Virginia House,' " *Md. Hist. Mag.*, LXIX (1974), 186; Main, *Tobacco Colony*, 141; Carson et al., "Impermanent Architecture," *Wint. Port.*, XVI (1981), 135–196; and, more generally, Henry Glassie, *Folk Housing in Middle Virginia: A Structural Analysis of Historic Artifacts* (Knoxville, Tenn., 1975).

They are sheathed with chestnut plank and sealed inside with the same. As they get ahead in the world they refinish the interior with plaster, for which they use oyster shell lime, making it as white as snow; so that although these houses seem poor enough on the outside because one sees only the weathered sheathing, within they are most agreeable. . . . Whatever their estates, for what reason I do not know, they build their houses consisting only of two ground floor rooms, with some closets and one or two prophet's chambers above. According to his means, each planter provides as many of such houses as he needs. They build also a separate kitchen, a house for the Christian slaves, another for negro slaves, and several tobacco barns, so that in arriving at the plantation of a person of importance you think you are entering a considerable village.

In six Maryland counties between 1660 and 1720, the bottom third of planters, worth less than £50 at death, lived in houses of one or two rooms; the middling third, worth £50–£150, usually lived in houses with three rooms; and the top third lived in houses of five or more rooms. Most small structures were probably similar to Thomas Howe's house, described in 1676 as consisting of a kitchen and hall, or Pope Alvey's, which had a new room, "Widdow alveys Room," and a kitchen. Andrew Bodman of Lower Norfolk County, who died in 1665 worth about £100, had a small lodging room, used as a bedroom and for storing linen and dishes; a "Greate Inward Roome," where members of the family slept, ate, and relaxed; and an "Outward Roome or Kitchen," used exclusively for preparing and cooking meals. Richard Russell's house had a similar plan. The lofts were used for sleeping and storage; a "little Roome" contained tools, "Old Lumber," his books, a bedstead, and various pots and kettles; and an "Outer Roome" was the main living area, where the family slept and ate.[18]

Progressing up the social scale, the middle range of housing appears little different. If we dropped in on Mr. John Martin of Lower Norfolk in the mid-1660s, we would probably have been shown into the inner room, where, besides half a dozen chairs, were a bed equipped with curtains and valances, a desk, and two chests containing his linen. The outward room was also used for sleeping, as was the "shedd." Only the closet, used for cooking, did not contain any bedding. A neighbor, Lancaster Lovett, had five rooms:

18. Durand of Dauphine, *A Frenchman in Virginia: Being the Memoirs of a Huguenot Refugee in 1686*, trans. Fairfax Harrison ([Richmond, Va.], 1923), 111–113; Main, *Tobacco Colony*, 152–153; St. Mary's County, Maryland, probate inventories, nos. 375, 557 (SMCC transcripts); Lower Norfolk County, Wills and Deeds E (1666–1675), fols. 7–8, 33.

three, including the hall, contained bedding; the kitchen was used for cooking; and a new room was used for sitting, relaxing, and storage. Similarly, in Thomas Keeling's five-room dwelling, the only room that did not contain a bed was the dairy. Even the "Dineinge Roome" had two feather beds, bedding, and a bedstead.[19] As with poorer planters, pressure on space meant that rooms served a variety of purposes. Apart from kitchens and dairies, all other rooms were employed, in various combinations, for sleeping, storage, sitting, eating, and relaxing. In dwellings as small as these, there could be little specialized use of domestic space.

Large multiroom structures were restricted to the wealthiest planter-merchants: men like William Smith, Thomas Notley, and Robert Slye of St. Mary's County, Ralph Wormeley of Rosegill, and Thomas Willoughby of Lower Norfolk. Notley's house, including garrets and cellar, had about fifteen rooms, Slye's plantation at Bushwood about twenty, and Willoughby's at least seventeen. Their design and appearance are difficult to visualize, but for the most part they were probably rambling, two-story wooden structures, possibly lofted over, with rooms added on or standing separately as outhouses. Slye had six to eight outhouses adjacent to his dwelling, used for storage, making clothes, carpentry, and dairying. Durand, the Frenchman, described Rosegill as like "a good sized town." By the end of the century the "great house" had ten rooms and was surrounded by a separate kitchen, a dairy, one or two storehouses, a smithy, a tannery yard, a barn, and a dock. As in England, the bigger the house, the more lofts and service rooms, but there was also more opportunity for specialized room use.[20]

Two points about the elite's housing should be emphasized. First, for every example of a wealthy planter's multiroom "great house," there are numerous examples of a typically small "Virginia house." And, second, there was no development in the seventeenth century of an altogether different style of housing for the colonial elite, nothing comparable to the rebuilding of country seats and the adoption of metropolitan styles by county gentry and aristocracy in England. With the exceptions of Governor Berkeley's house at Green Spring, just outside Jamestown, and Arthur Allen's brick house across

19. Lower Norfolk County, Wills and Deeds E (1666–1675), fols. 9–10, 144–145.

20. St. Mary's County, probate inventories, nos. 156, 195, 552 (SMCC transcripts); Durand of Dauphine, *A Frenchman in Virginia*, trans. Harrison, 58–59; Lower Norfolk County, Wills and Deeds E (1666–1675), fols., 124–125; Darrett B. Rutman and Anita H. Rutman, *A Place in Time: Middlesex County, Virginia, 1650–1750* (New York, 1984), 153–154.

the river in Surry County, no Chesapeake dwellings came close to matching in size, design, and quality of building materials the homes of well-to-do English squires or wealthy merchants. In Maryland and Virginia, many of the homes of leading planters, Lorena Walsh asserts, "might be mistaken for modest farm cottages in England." Not until the early eighteenth century did the Chesapeake's aristocracy, adapting English metropolitan fashions, begin building the substantial brick mansions for which the tidewater is renowned. During the first century of settlement, the overwhelming majority of dwellings, even those of the gentry, tended "to be small, inconspicuous, and inconsequential."[21]

The World of Goods: Household Possessions

In 1677 the *Humphrey and Elizabeth* cleared the port of London and set sail for Virginia. She carried a vast range of goods destined for the homes of planters, large and small. On board were all sorts of clothing and cloth: hats, hose, "bodies," suits of wearing apparel, Norwich stuffs, serges, fustians, cambrics, German linens, English bone lace, wrought silk, canvas, and lockram (a kind of linen); bed and bolster ticks, rugs, blankets, curtains, and valances; leather goods such as gloves, shoes, saddles, and horse collars; hardware such as lead shot, nails, iron, pewter, and brass; and a miscellany of other items such as gunpowder, books, cordage, and even English hops. There was nothing unusual about her cargo. Thousands of ships engaged in the transatlantic trade took similar wares to the West Indies, New England, and other colonies as well as to the Chesapeake. Among other typical imports were liquor ("strong waters" or "aquavita"), beer, cheese, raisins, spices, sugar, hard soap, furniture (chairs, tables, chests, bedsteads, and chests of drawers), pots and pans, guns, tools, and tobacco pipes. Cargoes from London, Bristol, and lesser ports remind us how dependent Virginia

21. Barley, "Rural Building," in Finberg and Thirsk, eds., *Agrarian History of England and Wales*, V, pt. 2, 600–631; Mark Girouard, *Life in the English Country House: A Social and Architectural History* (New Haven, Conn., 1978); Lorena S. Walsh, " 'A Culture of Rude Sufficiency': Life Styles on Maryland's Lower Western Shore between 1658 and 1720" (paper presented to the Society for Historical Archeologists, 1979), 7–8; Walsh, "Charles County," 258–259; Carter L. Hudgins, " 'Exactly as the Gentry Do in England': Culture, Aspirations, and Material Things in the Eighteenth-Century Chesapeake" (paper presented at conference in honor of the 350th anniversary of the founding of Maryland, 1984). See also Daniel Blake Smith, *Inside the Great House: Planter Family Life in Eighteenth-Century Chesapeake Society* (Ithaca, N.Y., 1980).

and Maryland settlers were on English manufactures throughout the colonial period and their close association with the produce and commerce of the hinterlands of English ports. Thus Hugh Jones, in the early eighteenth century, expressed the view that gentlemen of Virginia received goods from "London, Bristol, etc. with less trouble and cost, than to one living five miles in the country in England."[22]

But how many and what sort of goods did people in the various wealth categories actually own, and what were the interiors of their houses like? To what extent were their possessions purely utilitarian, having specific and often mundane practical uses, as opposed to decorative or highly valued fashionable items? The distinction between functional and fashionable, or decency and luxury, is not, of course, clear-cut. Are books, especially Bibles and devotional works, luxuries or necessities? Can we distinguish between the use of a table primarily for dining or for display or both? Even plate, ostensibly an unambiguous example of a luxury, had the important symbolic function of displaying the owner's wealth but was also a sound investment. An item regarded as a luxury by one social group might be seen as a necessity by another: furniture and furnishings, especially of rich householders, were often both functional and fashionable.[23]

Although there can be no rigorous distinction between necessities and luxuries, it is possible to suggest the sorts of goods different social groups might have expected to possess: what was basic for minimal comfort and the running of the household, and what went beyond day-to-day needs. Every household needed pots and pans for cooking but not necessarily a clock or elaborate case furniture for storage. By the mid-seventeenth century, English householders shared certain assumptions about the types of domestic goods suitable to their needs and social standing, and they were conscious of the improvement of standards of living over the previous century.[24]

22. E190/31/1, 190/59/1, 190/67/2, Public Record Office (CW VCRP, nos. 3482, 3609, 5588); Hugh Jones, *The Present State of Virginia . . .* , ed. Richard L. Morton (Chapel Hill, N.C., 1956), 73.

23. Weatherill, *Consumer Behaviour*, 14–16; Douglas and Isherwood, *World of Goods*.

24. This minimal-additional approach is adopted by Main, *Tobacco Colony*, 168–176, and chap. 7; Carr and Walsh, "Changing Life Styles and Consumer Behavior in the Colonial Chesapeake," in Carson, Hoffman, and Albert, eds., *Of Consuming Interests*. The assumptions are articulated by William Harrison, for example, in *A Description of England*, ed. Georges Edelen (Ithaca, N.Y., 1968). See also Shammas, *The Pre-Industrial Consumer*, 157–158.

THE POOR AND THE LOWER-MIDDLE CLASS

In England and the tidewater, poor and lower-middle class householders (worth less than £50 at death) formed the majority of the population.[25] There is little evidence concerning the living standards of the very poor (worth less than £10). In England that group included the aged, poor widows, paupers, and laborers, but the estates of most of these did not go through probate, and hence no inventories of their meager possessions were taken. Planters who did not live sufficiently long to get started or who simply failed to make a living from growing tobacco composed the bulk of the very poor in the Chesapeake. Based on the evidence we have, the contrast between English and Chesapeake householders in this wealth group is striking. Although at "the Feet of the Body Politique," the majority of the very poor in the Vale of Berkeley and East Kent possessed the basic necessities of domestic life. Virtually everyone had a bed, and 80–90 percent owned bedsteads (Table 28). People without bedsteads probably slept on mattresses on the floor in a fashion similar to that described by William Harrison in the sixteenth century.[26] Beds and bedding were cheap and unsophisticated. The average value of a bed, bedstead, and "appurtenances" (coverlets, rugs, blankets, and possibly sheets) was just over one pound, compared to nearly two pounds for all social groups. Four-fifths of the very poor possessed tables, and more than half had chairs, forms (benches), or stools to sit on while dining or relaxing, but other furniture was less common. About 30–50 percent had cupboards, probably either small, old, or of rough construction, since they were rarely worth more than a couple of shillings, and a few householders owned sideboards and clothespresses. Generally, there was little beyond humdrum furniture, pots, pans, and crockery: goods associated with the basic needs of sleeping, cooking, and eating. Books, pictures, chamberpots, lighting utensils, and (in the Vale of Berkeley) warming pans—items that, although not essential, made life a little more comfortable—were scarce.

If very poor householders in England owned the bare necessities, the very poor in the Chesapeake did not. The low standards of living indicated by Chesapeake housing were matched by equally low standards in domestic

25. Horn, "'The Bare Necessities,'" *Hist. Arch.*, XXII, no. 2 (1988), 79. See the discussion of social structure in Gloucestershire, Kent, and the Chesapeake in Chapters 3 and 4, above.

26. Harrison, *Description of England*, ed. Edelen, 201: "And we ourselves also, have lien full oft upon straw pallets, on rough mats covered only with a sheet, under coverlets made of dogswain or hap-harlots . . . and a good round log under their heads instead of a bolster or pillow."

TABLE 28

Standards of Living in England and the Chesapeake:
Householders Worth Less than £50

| | Percent of Households Owning, by Region and Wealth Group (N) | | | |
| | Vale of Berkeley | | St. Mary's | |
Item	0–£10 (37)	£10–£49 (155)	0–£10 (15)	£10–£49 (134)
Boiling equipment	73.0	63.9	86.7	86.6
Frying equipment	10.8	23.2	53.3	53.7
Roasting equipment	29.7	63.2	6.7	24.6
Other cooking equipment	0	3.9	6.7	.7
Brass	81.1	94.8	20.0	30.6
Pewter	83.8	96.1	53.3	70.9
Earthen or stoneware	0	9.7	13.3	35.1
Fine ceramics	0	0	0	0
Glassware	0	2.6	0	.7
Knives	0	0	0	0
Forks	0	0	0	0
Spoons	2.7	4.5	26.7	29.9
Table or tableboard	81.1	92.3	6.7	34.3
Tableframe	35.1	52.3	0	0
Chair	40.5	79.4	26.7	28.4
Bench or form	40.5	63.2	0	9.7
Stool	24.3	61.3	0	9.7
Settle	10.8	21.9	0	0
Couch	0	0	6.7	9.7
Other seating	0	0	0	0
No seats	35.1	6.5	73.3	55.2
Table linen	8.1	40.6	6.7	9.7
General linen	29.7	74.2	33.3	36.6
Beds	97.3	100.0	66.7	87.3
Bedsteads	81.1	94.2	6.7	21.6
Sheets	29.7	47.1	20.0	20.1
Curtains or valances	0	13.5	6.7	5.2
Warming pan	5.4	23.9	0	5.2

Lancaster and Northumberland		East Kent		Lower Norfolk
0–£10 (9)	£10–£49 (69)	0–£10 (22)	£10–£49 (54)	0–£50 (36)
100.0	100.0	100.0	96.3	100.0
44.4	63.8	18.2	38.9	72.2
0	34.8	36.4	38.9	25.0
0	0		14.8	5.6
33.3	47.8	54.5	75.9	13.9
66.7	79.7	59.1	88.9	66.7
33.3	36.2	18.2	22.2	36.1
0	0	0	0	0
0	1.4	0	0	0
0	0	0	0	0
0	0	0	0	0
44.4	26.1	13.6	14.8	36.1
0	37.7	77.3	92.6	47.2
0	0	0	1.9	0
0	33.3	54.5	87.0	38.9
0	23.2	45.5	68.5	36.1
0	5.8	40.9	59.3	2.8
0	0	0	7.4	0
44.4	23.2	0	0	38.9
0	0	0	0	0
55.6	49.3	4.5	0	44.4
44.4	23.2	22.7	53.7	11.1
0	46.4	22.7	63.0	11.1
66.7	92.8	100.0	100.0	100.0
0	30.4	90.9	92.6	27.8
0	30.4	72.7	74.1	13.9
0	14.5	18.2	40.7	25.0
0	7.2	45.5	57.4	2.8

TABLE 28 Continued

| | Percent of Households Owning, by Region and Wealth Group (N) | | | |
| | Vale of Berkeley | | St. Mary's | |
Item	0–£10 (37)	£10–£49 (155)	0–£10 (15)	£10–£49 (134)
Cupboard	29.7	33.5	0	9.0
Clothespress	0	20.6	0	0
Sideboard	10.8	29.0	0	0
Chest of drawers	0	1.3	0	0
Desk	5.4	5.8	0	2.2
Chest, trunk, or coffer	81.1	92.3	80.0	82.8
Lighting	2.7	29.0	20.0	26.9
Chamberpot or closestool	5.4	13.5	0	10.4
Pictures	0	0	0	.7
Books	5.4	20.6	27.7	17.2
Plate or jewels	0	9.7	0	.7
Clocks or watches	0	1.9	0	0

Note: Tables 28–30 reveal higher living standards in Kent than in Gloucestershire. This could be a function of differing compositions of the samples (the Kent sample is much smaller than that for the Vale of Berkeley), but more likely the figures represent genuine differences between the two regions. Kentish householders benefited from their proximity to London and the prosperity of the Southeast in this period (see Chapter 3). Lorna Weatherill comes to similar conclusions in her regional analysis of consumerism, 1675–1725, in *Consumer Behaviour and Material Culture in Britain, 1660–1760* (London, 1988), chap. 3.

Sources: Vale of Berkeley: Probate Inventories, 1660–1699, Gloucestershire Record Office: PCC Inventories, PROB 4, 5, Public Record Office; St. Mary's: St.

furnishings. Apart from a few chairs and couches, furniture of any kind was almost entirely missing. The great majority of householders at this level were without bedsteads, and only two-thirds owned even a proper mattress (Table 28). Rags or piles of straw served those who could not afford bedding. More than 70 percent of those in St. Mary's and 55 percent of those in Virginia were without formal seating. Presumably, they made do by squatting on the floor or sitting on upturned barrels, pails, and chests. Cooking equip-

Lancaster and Northumberland		East Kent		Lower Norfolk
0–£10	£10–£49	0–£10	£10–£49	0–£50
(9)	(69)	(22)	(54)	(36)
0	4.3	54.5	64.8	2.8
0	1.4	18.2	51.9	0
0	0	0	7.4	0
0	0	0	1.9	2.8
11.1	2.9	4.5	5.5	5.6
66.7	89.9	90.9	92.6	94.4
11.1	30.4	18.2	35.2	25.0
0	5.8	13.6	18.5	5.6
0	1.4	4.5	0	0
11.1	49.3	0	11.1	27.8
0	7.2	4.5	11.1	8.3
0	0	0	1.9	0

Mary's: St. Mary's County Inventories, 1658–1699, courtesy of SMCC. Lancaster and Northumberland: Probate Inventories, 1650–1699 (copies), Virginia State Library, Richmond. East Kent: Consistory Court of Canterbury, Probate Inventories, 1660–1680, PRC 27/13-28; Leeds Parish, Pauper Inventories, P222, 12/1, Kent Archives Office. Lower Norfolk: Minute Book, 1637–1646, II, Wills and Deeds B (1646–1651), C (1651–1656), D (1656–1666), E (1666–1675), Deed Book, no. 4, Colonial Williamsburg, microfilm, reels M 1365-2, M 1365-17, M 1365-18.

ment was limited to an iron pot or two for boiling mush and stews and, less commonly, to a frying pan. As one might expect, nonessential items, with the important exception of books, were completely absent.

Living standards of the Chesapeake poor have been described as "remarkably, almost unimaginably primitive. . . . Equipment of any kind was so scarce that we must look to aboriginal cultures to find modern analogies that even approximate these preconsumer living conditions of the seven-

7. Interior of a Freedman's House, St. Mary's City.
Courtesy of Historic St. Mary's City

teenth century." Barbara and Cary Carson provide a vivid illustration of what conditions must have been like for householders at the bottom of planter society:

> It is suppertime. A wife, husband, two children, and perhaps a servant are gathered together in the perpetual dusk of their shuttered cottage. This evening, like most evenings, their dinner is cornmeal mush boiled in an iron pot. The food is ladled into five plates or porringers, one for each person. The father sets his down on a large storage trunk which he straddles and sits on. His daughter is perched on the edge of a small chest, the only other piece of furniture in the room. The rest either stand or squat along the walls. They spoon up the food from the plates they must hold in their hands or place on the floor. They drink milk or water from a common cup, tankard or bowl passed around. No candle or lamp is lighted now or later when the room grows completely dark except for the glow of embers on

the hearth. Nightfall puts an effective end to all the day's activities. While someone rinses the bowls in a bucket of water (there being only one pot), someone else drags out a cattail mattress and arranges it in front of the fire. The husband, wife, and daughter lie down there, covering themselves with a single canvas sheet and a worn-out bed rug. The son and servant roll up in blankets on the floor. For warmth all sleep in their clothes.

As the Carsons emphasize, this is a fictional and in some respects unverifiable re-creation of the most wretched conditions in which poor planters of St. Mary's County lived, but evidence from Charles County, Maryland, and Lancaster and Northumberland counties, Virginia, only confirms their findings. Moreover, these conditions were not confined to only the very poor; they could almost equally apply to planters worth as much as fifty pounds.[27]

Although there was a slight improvement in the living standards of the lower-middle class, above ten pounds, the primitiveness of domestic conditions is nevertheless remarkable. In both Maryland and Virginia, half the householders in this group lacked any seating, and 70–80 percent were without bedsteads. Tables were found in only a third of houses. Thus few planters worth less than fifty pounds had the pleasure of sleeping on a bed and bedstead furnished with sheets and blankets, nor could they sit down to meals at a table.

Again, the contrast with English households is striking. The dwellings of weavers, clothworkers, poorer artisans, and small farmers, who made up the majority of this group in the Vale of Berkeley and East Kent, in almost every case contained beds, bedsteads, and bedding and usually had tables, chairs, forms, and stools. The possessions of Mary Martimore, a widow of Berkeley, who died in the spring of 1663 worth about sixteen pounds, furnish a good example. She owned two beds and bedsteads, with pillows and sheets; two large tableboards with frames; a side cupboard; three coffers; a chair; and another tableboard with frame. Judging by her cooking utensils, she mainly boiled her food in a "brasspot" or iron kettles and ate her meals from pewter dishes. Charles Smyth, tailor, also from Berkeley, died in the same year worth about twenty pounds. His house had at least five rooms: three on the ground floor, including his shop, and two chambers above.

27. Barbara Carson and Cary Carson, "Styles and Standards of Living in Southern Maryland, 1670–1760" (paper presented to the Southern Historical Association, 1976), 9–10, 17; Main, *Tobacco Colony*, chap. 5.

He owned three beds, bedsteads, and "appurtenances"; several tables; and various types of seating, consisting of chairs, forms, and stools. He kept his clothes in a "presse" and stored household linen in a chest in his chamber over the hall. Both chambers appear to have been used solely for sleeping and storing clothes and linen. The hall was the main living room, and the buttery served as a kitchen where meals were prepared and cooked.[28]

Cupboards, sideboards, and clothespresses, rarely found in the households of planters worth less than fifty pounds, were much more common in English houses. Such furniture provided a more convenient means of storing goods than the ubiquitous trunk or chest. There was also a greater readiness to invest in nonessential items. Nearly a quarter of the Vale of Berkeley householders and more than half of East Kent householders possessed warming pans (testifying to the superiority of beds and bedding), and approaching half of the latter adorned their best beds with curtains and valances. More householders had the means of lighting their houses in the evenings, and about 10 percent owned a small piece of silver or jewelry, perhaps a family heirloom.

MIDDLE- AND UPPER-MIDDLE CLASS HOUSEHOLDERS

The living standards of Chesapeake planters worth £50–£249 show a gradual improvement (Table 29). Planters in the £50–£99 wealth category were generally better-off leaseholders and small landowners. They generally had more furniture. Between one-half and three-quarters of decedents in the Maryland and Virginia samples owned tables, and most householders (70–90 percent) had seating of some kind. There was also a marked improvement in beds and bedding. About 60 percent in Virginia and 40 percent in Maryland owned bedsteads, and a similar proportion were able to sleep in sheets. Diet also appears to have improved. Most householders were equipped with boiling, frying, and roasting utensils. John Baley of Lancaster, who died in 1695 worth about £56, owned two brass kettles, one small spit and dripping pan, two iron kettles, a frying pan, two pots, potracks, and a pair of pothooks. John Pearse, who died in neighboring Northumberland County in 1667 worth £83, had two iron pots, a frying pan, two spits, a dripping pan, one brass pot and kettle "all very old."[29] Along with the greater variety of cooking equipment there were more implements, in contrast to the one or

28. Probate inventories, 1663/51, 1663/67, GRO.

29. Lancaster County, Wills Etc., no. 8 (1690–1709), 49; Northumberland County Records (1666–1672), 220, 228.

two pots and occasional frying pan commonly found in the inventories of planters worth less than £50.

Another notable improvement was in dining habits. One-half to two-thirds of householders were able to cover their tables with tablecloths, and almost everyone could eat from pewter plates and dishes. About half, or slightly more, owned earthen- or stoneware for keeping milk and beer cool, and a few possessed glassware, reserved perhaps for special occasions when friends came around for a drink. Nonessential items are also found in greater numbers. Lighting equipment (candles, candlesticks, lanterns, and snuffers) was much more common than in the houses of poorer planters. Being able to light the house in the evenings must have made a substantial difference to the quality of life by lengthening the day's activities, providing more time (particularly during winter evenings) for small tasks or relaxation. There may have been more time to read, since 40–60 percent of householders owned books, usually Bibles and devotional works.

If the £50–£99 group represents a transitional stage from stark poverty to modest comfort, the £100–£249 group displays the first sign of major improvements in living standards in both colonies.[30] At this level most people owned basic furniture such as tables, seats, beds, and bedsteads. The great majority owned sheets as well as table linens, and between one-half and two-thirds possessed curtains and valances. More elaborate beds, bedding, and bedsteads are reflected by their rising value. In St. Mary's County, for example, their average value across all wealth groups was about £2 10s., but planters in the £100–£249 group commonly owned beds of twice this value. Edward Fishwick owned six "feather beds and furniture" valued at £30, and John Tennison, also of St. Mary's, who died worth £209, possessed "2 old feather pillows, 1 bolster, 1 feather bed, 2 blankets, 1 Worsted Rugg, Red serge curtaines and vallens, and bedstead" appraised at £4 10s. 6d.[31] Clearly, as wealth and status increased, there was a greater readiness to invest in more expensive and comfortable bedding. Similarly, there were important improvements in other aspects of home life. Most people had the usual range of cooking equipment for boiling, frying, and roasting, but there

30. The transition, of course, was not abrupt. Many planters in the lower echelons of the £100–£249 group had living standards little different from their poorer contemporaries'. Notable too is that there is much more similarity between the £50–£99 and £100–£249 groups in Lower Norfolk County than in the other samples. This may reflect generally lower living standards in the county.

31. St. Mary's County inventories, nos. 632, 637 (SMCC transcripts).

TABLE 29

Standards of Living in England and the Chesapeake:
Householders Worth £50–£249

	Percent of Households Owning, by Region and Wealth Group (N)			
	Vale of Berkeley		St. Mary's	
Item	£50–£99 (103)	£100–£249 (111)	£50–£99 (98)	£100–£249 (67)
Boiling equipment	6.2	67.6	94.4	95.5
Frying equipment	12.6	14.4	64.0	67.2
Roasting equipment	73.8	77.5	44.9	73.1
Other cooking equipment	2.9	5.4	7.9	13.0
Brass	98.1	99.1	62.9	82.1
Pewter	98.1	96.4	89.9	95.5
Earthen or stoneware	8.7	11.7	49.4	64.2
Fine ceramics	0	0	0	0
Glassware	1.0	2.7	4.5	4.5
Knives	0	0	0	0
Forks	0	0	0	1.5
Spoons	1.9	7.2	23.6	29.9
Table or tableboard	95.1	97.3	52.8	88.1
Tableframe	48.5	61.3		
Chair	86.4	86.5	52.8	82.1
Bench or form	77.7	74.8	32.6	41.8
Stool	62.1	78.4	10.1	22.4
Settle	22.3	27.0	0	0
Couch	0	.9	30.3	38.8
Other seating	0	0	0	0
No seats	2.9	0	30.3	10.4
Table linen	49.5	60.4	46.1	74.6
General linen	75.7	84.7	64.0	83.6
Beds	100.0	100.0	97.8	98.5
Bedsteads	95.1	95.5	40.4	61.2
Sheets	45.6	40.5	43.8	67.2
Curtains or valances	23.3	27.9	28.1	49.3
Warming pan	31.1	38.7	20.2	35.8

Lancaster and Northumberland		East Kent		Lower Norfolk	
£50–£99 (41)	£100–£249 (19)	£50–£99 (36)	£100–£249 (40)	£50–£99 (25)	£100–£249 (16)
100.0	100.0	100.0	100.0	92.0	87.5
80.5	89.5	27.8	37.5	64.0	50.0
68.3	78.9	80.6	85.0	56.0	50.0
0	0	11.1	20.0	8.0	0
75.6	68.3	91.7	92.5	44.0	62.5
92.7	100.0	97.2	97.5	88.0	75.0
46.3	31.6	30.6	32.5	60.0	43.8
0	0	0	0	0	0
4.5	5.3	0	15.0	0	0
0	0	0	0	0	0
0	0	0	0	0	0
41.5	42.1	25.0	35.0	40.0	18.8
75.6	84.2	97.2	100.0	68.0	68.8
2.4		5.6	5.0	8.0	6.3
63.4	68.4	91.7	92.5	64.0	68.8
43.9	42.1	80.6	77.5	48.0	56.3
4.9	26.3	77.7	82.5	12.0	6.3
0	0	16.7	7.5	4.0	0
46.3	57.9	0	2.5	56.0	50.0
0	0	0	0	0	0
22.0	10.5	0	0	12.0	12.5
58.5	78.9	83.3	90.0	64.0	68.8
82.9	89.5	86.1	87.5	64.0	68.8
95.1	100.0	100.0	100.0	96.0	100.0
58.5	78.9	100.0	97.5	64.0	62.5
61.0	84.2	91.7	97.5	60.0	56.3
31.7	68.4	44.4	77.5	48.0	56.3
24.4	57.9	58.3	70.0	20.0	25.0

TABLE 29 Continued

| | Percent of Households Owning, by Region and Wealth Group (N) | | | |
| | Vale of Berkeley | | St. Mary's | |
Item	£50–£99 (103)	£100–£249 (111)	£50–£99 (98)	£100–£249 (67)
Cupboard	40.8	37.8	12.4	31.3
Clothespress	33.0	29.7	0	0
Sideboard	28.2	38.7	1.1	3.0
Chest of drawers	1.9	14.4	6.7	11.9
Desk	4.9	10.8	3.4	9.0
Chest, trunk, or coffer	92.2	88.3	78.7	98.5
Lighting	36.9	40.5	48.3	61.2
Chamberpot or closestool	15.5	17.1	15.7	34.3
Pictures	0	1.8	6.7	10.4
Books	22.3	26.1	39.3	52.2
Plate or jewels	21.4	27.9	12.4	22.4
Clocks or watches	6.8	13.5	0	10.4

Sources: See Table 28.

were also a few specialized implements for preparing sauces, pastries, and fish. Furnishings were more varied, with larger numbers of householders owning cupboards, chests of drawers, and writing desks. And the incidence of nonessential items also increased: warming pans, lighting equipment, chamberpots, books, plate, and clocks all become more common.

Significant as these improvements were, they nevertheless added up to a standard of domestic comfort still well below that of English counterparts. Middling and upper-middling householders in the Vale of Berkeley and East Kent generally lived in houses of five to nine rooms, compared to the three to five rooms of Chesapeake planters in these social groups. Problems of space probably account in large measure for the small incidence of domestic furniture among middle-class and relatively affluent planters. Whereas basic furniture, such as tables, chairs, and bedsteads, is to be found in virtually every household in the £50–£99 category in England, a large minority

Lancaster and Northumberland		East Kent		Lower Norfolk	
£50–£99 (41)	£100–£249 (19)	£50–£99 (36)	£100–£249 (40)	£50–£99 (25)	£100–£249 (16)
9.8	31.6	75.0	72.5	12.0	12.5
2.4	5.3	66.7	55.0	0	0
0	0	5.6	10.0	0	0
4.9	15.8	13.9	22.5	4.0	0
2.4	0	2.8	20.0	0	18.8
97.6	100.0	94.4	95.0	88.0	93.8
53.7	63.2	38.8	60.0	32.0	68.8
17.1	26.3	19.4	30.0	28.0	6.3
0	15.8	2.8	2.5	4.0	0
58.5	68.4	25.0	35.0	44.0	50.0
4.9	36.8	22.2	27.5	12.0	31.3
0	5.3	0	22.5	0	6.3

of planters in this group made do without. Among the upper-middle class (£100–£249) the gap between England and the Chesapeake closes, but case furniture is far less commonly owned in Maryland and Virginia. Little but the most ordinary furniture was found in the small and crowded rooms of most planters' houses.

RICH HOUSEHOLDERS

Among the wealthy (worth £250 and more), domestic furnishings were similar in both societies (Table 30). Ordinary furniture was present in every household and in larger numbers. Substantial wealth brought a more varied diet, greater comfort in dining and sleeping, and also a greater propensity to invest in highly valued items such as silver plate and jewelry. Nearly three-quarters of the St. Mary's elite and two-thirds of the Virginia elite owned plate, jewelry, or both. Like the rich in England, wealthy Chesapeake

8. Interior of a Middling Planter's House, St. Mary's City. *Courtesy of Historic St. Mary's City*

planters bought plate as both a sound investment and a sign of high social status. "I esteem it as well politic as reputable," William Fitzhugh of Westmoreland County opined, "to furnish my self with a handsom cupboard of plate which gives my self the present use and credit, is a sure friend at a dead lift, with out much loss, or is a certain portion for a child after my decease."[32] Few gentry in England would have disagreed.

Important differences emerge between the furnishings of the rich in the two societies, however, on closer inspection: one must not ignore the quality of goods. Hence, there might be a world of difference between an old wooden chair belonging to a Chesapeake planter and an expensive "turkey work" chair owned by one of the Vale of Berkeley's wealthiest gentlemen. In the great parlor of John Smyth's house in North Nibley, there stood "one ovill table board [with a] Turkie Karpett, a dozen and a halfe of Turkie Chairs, one

32. Quoted by Walsh, " 'A Culture of Rude Sufficiency,' " 12.

Turkie worke Couch," worth, with a few other items, more than £17. Among the wealthy in southern Gloucestershire and eastern Kent, beds, tables, and chairs might be worth two or three times more than the average valuation. Edward Warham, a yeoman from Herne in northeastern Kent, owned six feather beds, with bedsteads, curtains, valances, and coverings, appraised at more than £50. He also had forty pairs of sheets, twenty tablecloths, and ten dozen napkins, which, with other linen, were valued at £50 3s. 4d.—the equivalent of at least three or four years' wages for a common day laborer. John Tilladam of Dursley owned six joined chairs with serge coverings worth 3s. 4d. each, and Thomas Winston, a gentleman of Wotton under Edge, possessed an escritoire valued at £1.[33] The furniture of the rich was meant to be decorative as well as functional.

Expensive furniture—turkey work and leather chairs, "black walnutt" bedsteads, and more elaborate tables, chests of drawers, and cupboards—is also found in the houses of leading Virginia and Maryland planters, but so too are old, broken, or worn-out goods. Captain William Brocas of Lancaster County, a justice and former member of Virginia's Council of State, owned at his death in 1655 "a parcell of old hangings, very thin and much worn . . . a parcell of old Chairs, being 7, most of them unusefull . . . an old broken Cort Cupboard . . . 1 old rotten couch bedstead . . . 1 old broken trunk, 7 guns most unfixt," and so on. Many of the household possessions of John Godsell, a merchant who died in 1676 worth more than three hundred pounds, were described in his inventory as "old," "damnified," "motheaten," and "rotten." Virtually all the furniture owned by Thomas Wilks, whose estate was valued at about one thousand pounds, is described as "old."[34] Did the poor quality of furniture and furnishings indicate a reluctance of planters to invest their profits in household goods, or reflect problems of supply or the crudeness of material life on the Chesapeake frontier, where, perhaps, superior items lost their symbolic value?

---

33. Probate inventories, 1692/159, 1693/49, 157, GRO; PRC 27/17/1, KAO. Warham died in 1665 worth more than £1,000 in personalty alone. For the wages of laborers, see James E. Thorold Rogers, *A History of Agriculture and Prices in England* . . . , 7 vols. (Oxford, 1886–1902), VI, 694–700. I have assumed an average wage of £10–£15 a year.

34. For examples of expensive furniture, see the inventories of Col. John Carter of Lancaster, James Bowling and Capt. Joshua Doyne of St. Mary's, and Thomas Willoughby of Lower Norfolk: Lancaster County, Wills, VIII, 22–29, 32–34; St. Mary's County inventories, nos. 1067, 1315 (SMCC transcripts); Lower Norfolk County, Wills and Deeds E (1666–1675), fols. 124–125. See also Main, *Tobacco Colony*, 225–239. For worn-out furniture, see Lancaster County, Deeds Etc., no. 1 (1652–1657), 202–204, no. 2 (1654–1666), 40, Wills Etc., no. 5 (1674–1689), 19–22, 104–108.

TABLE 30

Standards of Living in England and the Chesapeake: Householders Worth £250 and More

Item	Percent of Households Owning, by Region and Wealth Group (N)				
	Vale of Berkeley (74)	East Kent (36)	St. Mary's (58)	Lancaster and Northumberland (12)	Lower Norfolk (12)
Boiling equipment	59.5	100.0	94.8	100.0	100.0
Frying equipment	13.5	52.8	72.4	83.3	58.3
Roasting equipment	81.1	91.7	77.6	91.7	83.3
Other cooking equipment	9.5	36.1	34.5	0	0
Brass	98.6	94.4	94.8	91.7	75.0
Pewter	98.6	100.0	94.8	100.0	91.7
Earthen or stoneware	14.9	38.9	75.9	50.0	66.7
Fine ceramics	0	2.8	5.2	8.3	0
Glassware	8.1	8.3	19.0	16.7	8.3
Knives	2.7	2.8	10.3	8.3	8.3
Forks	0	0	5.2	0	0
Spoons	4.1	36.1	44.8	50.0	58.3
Table or tableboard	95.9	100.0	89.7	100.0	91.7
Tableframe	62.2	2.8	0	8.3	8.3
Chair	98.6	100.0	94.8	91.7	83.3
Bench or form	71.6	66.7	34.5	50.0	58.3
Stool	85.1	91.7	31.0	25.0	50.0
Settle	43.2	19.4	1.7	0	8.3
Couch	5.4	11.1	34.5	41.7	83.3
Other seating	5.4	0	0	0	0
No seats	0	0	1.7	0	0
Table linen	73.0	94.4	94.8	100.0	75.0
General linen	95.9	97.2	96.6	100.0	75.0
Beds	100.0	100.0	98.3	100.0	100.0
Bedsteads	100.0	100.0	77.6	91.7	91.7
Sheets	54.1	94.4	93.1	83.3	75.0
Curtains or valances	40.5	69.4	72.4	66.7	66.7
Warming pan	44.6	66.7	62.1	50.0	41.7
Cupboard	39.2	86.1	37.9	50.0	66.7
Clothespress	47.3	63.9	12.1	0	0
Sideboard	51.4	19.4	5.2	0	0

TABLE 30 Continued

Item	Percent of Households Owning, by Region and Wealth Group (N)				
	Vale of Berkeley (74)	East Kent (36)	St. Mary's (58)	Lancaster and Northumberland (12)	Lower Norfolk (12)
Chest of drawers	24.3	27.8	36.2	25.0	16.7
Desk	6.2	13.9	15.5	16.7	16.7
Chest, trunk, or coffer	100.0	100.0	96.6	100.0	100.0
Lighting	47.3	44.4	75.9	83.3	58.3
Chamberpot or closestool	24.3	36.1	36.2	25.0	50.0
Pictures	4.1	11.1	17.2	8.3	25.0
Books	37.8	41.7	51.7	91.7	83.3
Plate or jewels	55.4	66.7	74.1	66.7	66.7
Clocks or watches	28.4	47.2	22.4	8.3	0

Sources: See Table 28.

Poor-quality housing and furnishings, even among the elite, have led Chesapeake historians to stress the essential similarities in living standards across all wealth groups. "All in all," the Carsons conclude, "there was a decided sameness about material life in southern Maryland throughout the seventeenth century. Partly it was a result of a limited choice of available consumer goods and partly a reflection of a community that was still more homogeneous, still less attenuated by extremes of wealth, than it became fifty years later." Being rich, they suggest, meant having more, not being different. Lorena Walsh supports this view: while "families in higher wealth levels enjoyed a greater degree of comfort than did poorer households . . . most did not use personal possessions to create a markedly different way of living from their poorer neighbors." Lois Green Carr and Walsh conclude that the Chesapeake was "a place where social elites did not develop distinct identities based on patterns of consumption very different from those of groups somewhat below them."[35]

35. Carson and Carson, "Styles and Standards of Living," 17, 21; Walsh, " 'A Culture of Rude Sufficiency,' " 7–8; Carr and Walsh, "Changing Life Styles and Consumer Behavior in the Colonial Chesapeake," in Carson, Hoffman, and Albert, eds., *Of Consuming Interests*.

This view should be qualified. Comparing the sorts of household possessions owned by different wealth groups in the Vale of Berkeley and East Kent
(Tables 28–30), one gets a similar sense of "sameness." Like most householders, the rich ate their meals from pewter plates and drank from pewter
tankards; there is little evidence that they generally owned fine ceramics or
glassware. Although the wealthy tended to have a greater range of furniture,
articles such as couches, chests of drawers, and desks were far from common, and even case furniture such as presses, sideboards, and cupboards
was not universally owned. In most cases barely half the rich had them. Differences in standards of living between the rich and middling classes were
therefore a matter of degree rather than kind. Mildred Campbell's comments
concerning the English yeomanry are just as applicable to the majority of
middle- and upper-class householders: "The inventories show . . . that the
standard of living, insofar as the quality and variety of house furnishings reveal it, was remarkably similar among the yeomen of greater and less wealth.
The difference lay in the number of rooms to be furnished rather than the
style, variety, and quality of the furnishings." [36]

Being rich meant having more, not necessarily wholly different or uniformly superior, household goods (Table 31). These considerations apply also
to the gentry. They tended to have more expensive clothing and invested
a larger proportion of their money in plate, but generally their furnishings
differed little from wealthy nongentry. An altogether different *style* of living
becomes apparent only among the top rank of gentlemen (county gentry),
who built or rebuilt large country houses and furnished them with the most
expensive and luxurious items purchased from London or the nearest city.
What is missing in the second half of the seventeenth century, outside a
tiny privileged clique, are upper-class rituals such as tea, coffee, or chocolate
drinking; eating from tables set with fine porcelain, knives, and forks (rituals
associated with studied and fashionable leisure); more varied pictures and
hangings; a range of quality ceramics; and new types of furniture made by
cabinetmakers using new woods, designs, and techniques such as veneer-
ing. These developments awaited the eighteenth century.[37] The "sameness"
of domestic possessions owned by different social groups in Maryland and
Virginia was partly a reflection of a broader homogeneity that prevailed in
seventeenth-century England.

While the limited range and poor quality of items owned by Chesapeake

36. Mildred Campbell, *The English Yeoman under Elizabeth and the Early Stuarts* (New
Haven, Conn., 1942), 238–239.

37. Weatherill, *Consumer Behaviour*, chap. 2.

TABLE 31

Furniture Items per Household, Vale of Berkeley, 1660–1699

Item	No. per Household, by Wealth (N)				
	0–£9 (19)	£10–£49 (52)	£50–£99 (35)	£100–£249 (37)	£250+ (30)
Table or board	1.3	1.9	2.7	3.8	5.1
Chair	.8	3.5	4.9	9.3	13.2
Bench or form	.9	1.2	1.6	1.7	2.1
Stool	1.0	3.0	4.8	5.3	7.6
Settle	.1	.2	.2	.3	.4
Bed	1.8	2.9	3.9	4.9	6.1
Bedstead	1.8	2.8	3.9	4.6	6.1
Cupboard	.4	.5	.6	.6	.8
Clothespress	0	.3	.5	.5	.9
Sideboard	.2	.3	.8	1.1	1.1
Chest of drawers			.1	.2	.5
Desk	.1	.1	.1	.1	.3

Sources: Probate Inventories, 1660–1699, Gloucestershire Record Office; PCC Inventories, PROB 4, 5, Public Record Office.

householders is striking, one sees significant differences in *assemblages* of household items between social groups (Tables 28–31). There would have been little doubt in the mind of Jacob Bradshaw of Lower Norfolk (who possessed no household goods apart from a few pewter dishes, "a bedd and a blankett," an iron pot, and a couple of books) that the likes of Robert Glascock (who lived in a six-room house and owned numerous feather and flock beds, bedsteads, tables, chairs, linen, and all sorts of pewter and cooking implements) were in an utterly different social class. Bradshaw slept on the floor, probably rolled up in the same blanket as his "mate" William Eady, and ate his meals (invariably mush or stew) sitting on the floor of their small hut or on a tree stump outside. Glascock could sleep comfortably in his feather bed, covered with sheets and raised off the ground on a bedstead, sit at table for his meals, and relax in the evenings in front of the fire in his "great wooden Chayre."[38]

38. Lower Norfolk County, Wills and Deeds B (1646–1651), fols. 45, 50–51 (CW, microfilm, reel M 1365-17). Glascock died in 1647 worth more than £250. Bradshaw

Wealthier planters were able to replicate at least a semblance of the domestic comfort common among English householders; the poor could not. They lived like the lowliest squatters and vagrants in England. Getting on in the Chesapeake meant being able to afford basic household furniture and utensils; poverty meant, for the most part, making do without them. Differences in the living standards of the poor, middling, and rich were so great they must have been obvious to everyone.

Elites in Maryland and Virginia were no more monolithic than in England. Even at a relatively early stage of social development there were some individuals who, by virtue of inherited status, wealth, and office, stood head and shoulders above the rest of the gentry. These men, such as the Carters, Lees, Wormeleys, Byrds, and Willoughbys, ranked alongside county magnates in English society and clearly did develop a different style as well as standard of living appropriate to their high status. As in England, a comparison of upper-middle-class and wealthy households suggests a gradual rather than dramatic improvement in living standards, with a sharp break occurring only at the very pinnacle of the social order. In both societies the distinction between top gentry and the rest of the squirearchy became clearer in the eighteenth century with the growth of magnate power.[39]

The Material World: Poverty, Class, and Gender

The most important conclusion to be drawn from a comparison of material possessions in the two societies is the great poverty experienced by the majority of Chesapeake planters. Even the very poor householders in England enjoyed living standards comparable in many respects to those of middling wealth groups along the Bay. To put it another way, only planters worth more than one hundred pounds (fewer than 30 percent of householders) had living standards that would have been accounted quite common in England. Not only were essential items of furniture often missing from planters' houses,

---

died in the same year (having been struck by lightning), worth about £26, most of which was in the form of debts owed to him.

39. Hudgins, "'Exactly as the Gentry Do in England'"; Rutman and Rutman, *A Place in Time: Middlesex County*, chap. 5; J. V. Beckett, *The Aristocracy in England, 1660–1914* (Oxford, 1986); John Cannon, *Aristocratic Century: The Peerage of Eighteenth-Century England* (Cambridge, 1984); Jack P. Greene, *Pursuits of Happiness: The Social Development of Early Modern British Colonies and the Formation of American Culture* (Chapel Hill, N.C., 1988), 92–94; Kenneth A. Lockridge, *The Diary, and Life, of William Byrd II of Virginia, 1674–1744* (Chapel Hill, N.C., 1987).

but there was often an important qualitative difference in furnishings. In general, the value of furniture (as appraised in inventories) was similar in both societies, but there was a much greater range of prices in Maryland and Virginia than in England, a consequence of the large number of very low valuations assigned to Chesapeake furnishings.[40]

Qualitative differences are also suggested by descriptions of furniture. In English inventories it is rare for items to be described as "new" or "old," whereas in the Chesapeake the term "old" is commonly applied. Old, broken, and worn goods still retained a certain value, because it might be cheaper to mend them or use them for something else (gun barrels, for example, were sometimes used as pestles) than to buy new goods. Planters had to rely on English merchants to import manufactured goods, which might be expensive. Secondhand items, however, could be acquired more cheaply at public outcries, following the death of a neighbor or when someone left the county. In this way, goods were passed on from one household to another.

Even more significant were the small size and poor quality of planters' houses. Impermanent structures—squatters' cottages or paupers' dwellings —existed in England, but they became increasingly rare in rural areas as the population stabilized during the second half of the century. Single or two-room cottages also became less common in central and southern regions as a result of the extensive rebuilding of housing that occurred in the late Tudor and Stuart periods. Thus in the Vale of Berkeley and East Kent, the poor and lower-middling classes generally lived in houses of three to five rooms, built by local craftsmen from durable materials.[41] Whereas in England the trend during the previous two centuries had been toward more specialized room use and permanent structures, in the early Chesapeake these developments were reversed: dwellings were not expected to last more than twenty to twenty-five years, and one or two rooms served a multiplicity of functions. Except perhaps in summer, when people could live partially outside, these were the physical constraints placed upon the daily routine of the great bulk of planters. The small size of Chesapeake houses dictated the adoption of furnishings that could be easily stored away if necessary. A bedstead could take up a lot of space, but a mattress could be pushed into a corner during the day and dragged out in front of the hearth at night. A large chest

40. Horn, " 'The Bare Necessities,' " *Hist. Arch.*, XXII, no. 2 (1988), 88.

41. Urban conditions for poor householders may have been worse: see M. J. Power, "East London Housing in the Seventeenth Century," in Peter Clark and Paul Slack, eds., *Crisis and Order in English Towns, 1500–1700: Essays in Urban History* (London, 1972), 237–262.

could serve as a table or seat as well as for storing goods. Neither was there much point in owning expensive furniture if there was not enough room to display it.

How is it possible to account for such a low standard of living? It has been suggested that flimsy dwellings were a response to the nature of tobacco husbandry and landownership in the tidewater. An "architecture of transience" developed because, once tobacco fields were exhausted, planters removed themselves to another part of their tract and built a new house close by.[42] This explanation is not wholly persuasive. In the case of the majority of small planters who owned two or three hundred acres, tracts were not so extensive as to necessitate building a new house in a separate location once old fields had been used up. Only a small part of a tract was devoted to tobacco, the rest being left as woodland or range for livestock, and hence planters could easily manage to cultivate new fields close to their original dwelling if they wished. Rebuilding was frequently a consequence of the poor quality of housing (wooden posts rotten with age or termites, unseasoned clapboard and shingles split and cracked after a succession of cold winters and humid summers), which often meant that it was easier to start completely over again rather than try to repair the old building.

Two obvious reasons explain the generally poor standard of housing. First, the shortage of skilled labor in the tidewater put the price of erecting substantial brick or framed houses out of reach of the vast majority of planters, even the relatively affluent. Given the lack of housewrights, bricklayers, and masons, most new arrivals desiring their own dwelling house were forced to build it themselves, possibly with the help of neighbors, or employ a local carpenter-cum-handyman. For most immigrants, constructing an elaborate multiroom house would have been well beyond their skill and pocket. People made do instead by starting off with a one- or two-room structure, adding lean-tos when required. Second, given the imperative of developing the plantation and the modest and at times uncertain returns from tobacco, most planters did not have much surplus income to invest either in the home or in household durables. Robert Cole's estate in St. Mary's County made about thirty-eight pounds a year (local currency) during the 1660s, virtually all of which was plowed back into running the plantation. Despite the family's middling status and a healthy appreciation in the value of the estate, there was little spare cash for significant home improvements or expenditure on anything other than essential consumables. In the early years of farm

42. See above, this chapter.

building, planters had to give priority to capital investment rather than to domestic comfort.[43]

Slim profit margins and lack of skilled craftsmen account in large part for the low quality of domestic furnishings. Local populations in early Virginia and Maryland counties were too small and dispersed to support specialized artisans such as joiners and carpenters, and householders could not expect to find a skilled furniture maker in the vicinity. Consequently, as the Frenchman Durand noted, planters relied on imported "wooden furniture, although they have the best and a superfluity of wood."[44] Such local woodcrafts as existed tended to be directed to coopering, fencing, and plantation work rather than to the construction of household furniture, which in any case many planters could not afford or simply did not have room for.

The social and psychological implications of this transformation in living standards have yet to be fully considered, but important changes in the style of domestic life must have resulted from the cramped conditions experienced by planters along the tobacco coast. A division of domestic space according to gender and status could not be enforced in humble Chesapeake structures where men and women, masters and servants, parents and children all lived together in physical proximity. In most English houses it was possible to escape the hubbub of a busy kitchen or living room by retiring to an upstairs bedchamber or garret. The trend toward specialized room use in wealthier households—kitchens for cooking, parlors and halls for relaxing and dining—provided further opportunities for individuals to avoid the daily activities associated with preparing food and meals and also created a growing division along status and gender lines. Domestic female servants, usually lodged upstairs out of the way in upper chambers or lofts, were increasingly confined to the working areas of the house (kitchen, hall, milkhouse, buttery, and washhouse) and, apart from cleaning duties, would have had

43. See William Fitzhugh's comment on framed houses: William Fitzhugh to Nicholas Hayward, Jan. 30, 1687, in Richard Beale Davis, ed., *William Fitzhugh and His Chesapeake World, 1676–1701: The Fitzhugh Letters and Other Documents* (Chapel Hill, N.C., 1963), 202–203. On surplus income, see Lois Green Carr, Russell R. Menard, and Lorena S. Walsh, *Robert Cole's World: Agriculture and Society in Early Maryland* (Chapel Hill, N.C., 1991), chap. 4. It should be stressed that primitive living conditions were not confined to the first years of settlement (or a frontier phase), but extended across the 17th century; see Carr and Walsh, "Changing Life Styles and Consumer Behavior in the Colonial Chesapeake," in Carson, Hoffman, and Albert, eds., *Of Consuming Interests*.

44. Durand of Dauphine, *A Frenchman in Virginia*, trans. Harrison, 100.

little reason to visit the owner's personal chambers or private rooms such as the parlor or study. Male servants were also confined to working areas but would not usually have been involved with food preparation, cleaning, and washing, which were seen as women's tasks. Depending on their master's occupation, they would have worked in the stable, barn, shop, various outhouses, or the fields. Areas of the house and around the yard devoted to cooking, dairying, brewing, storing foodstuffs for domestic consumption, washing and drying the family linen, and growing vegetables and herbs became primarily a female domain.[45]

These distinctions were difficult, if not impossible, to maintain in small Chesapeake dwellings. The planter's wife and female servants undertook the same sorts of domestic chores in Maryland and Virginia as they traditionally did in England and were more housebound than men, but there could be no clear division of social space within the home, since rooms served so many different purposes. Laborers owned by poorer and middling planters shared the same living space as their master and mistress, eating with the family and sleeping wherever they could find a convenient space. Only among the few wealthy who owned large, multiroom dwellings was it feasible to separate humdrum daily activities from more private chambers, and servants' quarters from the main part of the house.[46]

What were the social implications of small and crowded dwellings? Were family tensions exacerbated by lack of privacy? Did the proximity of servants and masters and the low standards of living among even middling and affluent planters erode traditional English social distinctions and alter perceptions of status? Did the throwaway houses that many poorer planters inhabited contribute not only to an "architecture of transience" but also to a mentalité of transience, an easy-come, easy-go attitude whereby people packed up their goods and moved on when debts became too great or the

45. Carole Shammas, "The Domestic Environment in Early Modern England and America," *Journal of Social History*, XIV (1980–1981), 5–6. More generally, see Alice Clark, *Working Life of Women in the Seventeenth Century* (1919; New York, 1968); Ivy Pinchbeck, *Women Workers and the Industrial Revolution, 1750–1850* (London, 1930), esp. chap. 1; Chris Middleton, "Women's Labour and the Transition to Pre-Industrial Capitalism," in Lindsey Charles and Lorna Duffin, eds., *Women and Work in Pre-Industrial England* (London, 1985), 181–206; Lois Green Carr and Lorena S. Walsh, "The Planter's Wife: The Experience of White Women in Seventeenth-Century Maryland," *WMQ*, 3d Ser., XXXIV (1977), 547, 561–563; Cary Carson and Lorena S. Walsh, "The Material Life of the Early American Housewife," *Wint. Port.* (forthcoming).

46. Main *Tobacco Colony*, 158, 160. See, for example, the inventories of Col. John Carter of Lancaster and Lt. Col. Thomas Willoughby of Lower Norfolk.

going too hard?[47] For the majority of English people who immigrated to the Chesapeake in the seventeenth century, one of the most important differences they would encounter in their new environment was a substantially lower standard of living. This was a consequence, not of their own humble origins and lack of aspiration to create a better way of life or of the relatively short life span that most of them experienced, but rather of the increasingly unfavorable economic climate after 1680, a simple agrarian society, and the peculiar demands of tobacco culture. During the second half of the century, most planters after years of hard work had a standard of living little different from the lowest levels of society in England. Such was the price exacted by life on the Chesapeake frontier.

47. Main *Tobacco Colony*, 153; Carson *et al.*, "Impermanent Architecture," *Wint. Port.*, XVI (1981), 135–196; J. P. Horn, "Moving On in the New World: Migration and Out-Migration in the Seventeenth-Century Chesapeake," in Peter Clark and David Souden, eds., *Migration and Society in Early Modern England* (London, 1987), 172–212.

8

Order and Disorder

A common theme in accounts of seventeenth-century Chesapeake society is the endemic disorder. Bernard Bailyn, Edmund Morgan, and T. H. Breen, among others, have stressed the chaotic individualism and chronic political instability that characterized early Virginia and Maryland. Jamestown in the 1620s is depicted as "the first American boomtown," an early Klondike in which "tobacco took the place of gold," where the elite were "tough, unsentimental, quick-tempered, crudely ambitious men" who "roared curses [and] drank exuberantly." Throughout the century, as social inequalities became entrenched, the vast majority of poor laborers who worked in the tobacco fields ("the losers") were driven further and further into poverty while the rich steadily got richer. Little wonder that Virginians were unruly. "While New Englanders lived in relative peace with one another," comments Breen, "Virginians rioted and rebelled" and "even in periods of apparent calm . . . were haunted by the specter of social unrest." Whereas society in the northern colonies "allowed the acting out of the European fantasy: order, morality, stability . . . and a long life," along the tobacco coast life was typically short, nasty, and brutish.[1]

1. Bernard Bailyn, "Politics and Social Structure in Virginia," in James Morton Smith, ed., *Seventeenth-Century America: Essays in Colonial History* (Chapel Hill, N.C., 1959), 94–98; Edmund S. Morgan, *American Slavery, American Freedom: The Ordeal of Colonial Virginia* (New York, 1975), chaps. 6, 11–13, esp. 110–111; T. H. Breen, *Puritans and Adventurers: Change and Persistence in Early America* (New York, 1980), chaps. 6–8, esp. 110–116, 128; Russell R. Menard, "Maryland's 'Time of Troubles': Sources of Political Disorder in Early St. Mary's," *Maryland Historical Magazine*, LXXVI (1981), 124–140; Nicholas Canny, "The Permissive Frontier: The Problem of Social Control in Ireland and Virginia, 1550–1650," in K. R. Andrews *et al.*, eds., *The Westward Enterprise: English Activities in Ireland, the Atlantic, and America, 1480–1650* (Liverpool, 1978), 40–42; T. H. Breen and Stephen Innes, *"Myne Owne Ground": Race and Freedom on*

This chapter examines the challenges to constituted authority in Maryland and Virginia during the seventeenth century. Earlier chapters have touched on relevant issues—social structure, laws and institutions, local communities, patriarchalism and the family, work discipline, and material expressions of status. The focus here is the establishment of order and an acceptable form of authority in the new societies along the Bay. Assessment of how volatile society was will follow from a study of social conflict at both the local and provincial levels and comparisons with English society.[2]

The Establishment of Authority

Discussions of disorder in Maryland and Virginia have usually focused on the major social upheavals that punctuated the seventeenth century, such as the collapse of Lord Baltimore's government between 1645 and 1647, the "plundering time" in Virginia during Bacon's Rebellion, and the overthrow of proprietary rule in Maryland in the Glorious Revolution of 1689. These striking demonstrations of political instability have been used to characterize Chesapeake society throughout most of the century as socially weak, cha-

---

Virginia's Eastern Shore, 1640–1676 (New York, 1980) chap. 3; Douglas Greenberg, "Crime, Law Enforcement, and Social Control in Colonial America," *American Journal of Legal History*, XXVI (1982), 302, 303; Jack P. Greene, *Pursuits of Happiness: The Social Development of Early Modern British Colonies and the Formation of American Culture* (Chapel Hill, N.C., 1988), 8–15; Kenneth A. Lockridge, *Settlement and Unsettlement in Early America: The Crisis of Political Legitimacy before the Revolution* (Cambridge, 1981), 3, 53–104; John J. Waters, "The Traditional World of the New England Peasants: A View from Seventeenth-Century Barnstable," *New England Historical and Genealogical Register*, CXXX (1976), 21.

A critique of this view can be found in Jon Kukla, "Order and Chaos in Early America: Political and Social Stability in Pre-Restoration Virginia," *American Historical Review*, XC (1985), 275–298; Lois Green Carr, "Sources of Political Stability and Upheaval in Seventeenth-Century Maryland," *Md. Hist. Mag.*, LXXIX (1984), 44–70; and James R. Perry, *The Formation of a Society on Virginia's Eastern Shore, 1615–1655* (Chapel Hill, N.C., 1990), 228–238.

2. Order and disorder are considered within a broad framework of crime, riot, tensions within communities, expressions of class conflict, and popular revolt. See, for example, essays in John Brewer and John Styles, eds., *An Ungovernable People: The English and Their Law in the Seventeenth and Eighteenth Centuries* (London, 1980); Anthony Fletcher and John Stevenson, eds., *Order and Disorder in Early Modern England* (Cambridge, 1985); and Douglas Hay et al., *Albion's Fatal Tree: Crime and Society in Eighteenth-Century England* (London, 1975); and also E. P. Thompson, *Customs in Common* (London, 1991).

otic, and conflictual. There can be little doubt that Virginia's promoters encountered enormous problems in trying to establish acceptable government in Virginia during the first two decades of the colony's existence. Factional intrigue (in the colony and in London), heavy mortality, the wars against the Powhatans and other local tribes, efforts to find profitable commodities to warrant continued investment, and the peculiar form that local government took in the early years combined and virtually overwhelmed the colony by the time the Virginia Company was disbanded in 1624.[3] But to what extent was the stamp of Chesapeake society already cast?

First, it is important to distinguish between different arenas of disorder: at the provincial level, and within certain regions or communities. Thus, Josias Fendall's "pygmie rebellion" of 1659–1660, located firmly within the tradition of "Protestant-led rebellions" in Maryland, was a coup in which one faction of the ruling elite challenged the proprietary authority of Lord Baltimore. It had little impact on daily life in the localities. Only major upheavals such as Ingle's and Bacon's rebellions had the capacity to disrupt both provincial and local society. A second and related point concerns types and social significance of disorder. Both colonies experienced protracted and at times bitter constitutional wrangling between the executive and legislative branches of government that mirrored to a certain extent developments in England. Although much of the time arguments were contained within the framework of legitimate political behavior, occasionally they took the form of violent challenges to the authority of the governor or proprietor. Provincial revolts were sparked by the breakdown of political negotiation in the assemblies and a loss of support for the governor's policies.[4]

3. Bailyn, "Politics and Social Structure," in Smith, ed., *Seventeenth-Century America*, 90–115; Breen, *Puritans and Adventurers*, chaps. 6–7; Morgan, *American Slavery, American Freedom*, chaps. 3–6, 11–13; Menard, "Maryland's 'Time of Troubles,' " *Md. Hist. Mag.*, LXXVI (1981), 124–140; Carr, "Sources of Political Stability," *Md. Hist. Mag.*, LXXIX (1984), 44–70; David Thomas Konig, " 'Dale's Laws' and the Non–Common Law Origins of Criminal Justice in Virginia," *Am. Jour. Leg. Hist.*, XXVI (1982), 354–375; Wesley Frank Craven, *The Southern Colonies in the Seventeenth Century, 1607–1689* (1949; Baton Rouge, La., 1970), chaps. 3–5; Craven, *Dissolution of the Virginia Company: The Failure of a Colonial Experiment* (New York, 1932); Charles M. Andrews, *The Colonial Period of American History*, 4 vols. (New Haven, Conn., 1934–1937), I, 180–205.

4. Lois Green Carr and David William Jordan, *Maryland's Revolution of Government, 1689–1692* (Ithaca, N.Y., 1974), chap. 1, esp. 32; Jordan, *Foundations of Representative Government in Maryland, 1632–1715* (Cambridge, 1987); J. Mills Thornton, "The Thrusting Out of Governor Harvey: A Seventeenth-Century Rebellion," *Virginia Magazine of History and Biography*, LXXVI (1968), 11–26; Richard L. Morton, *Colonial Virginia*, 2 vols. (Chapel Hill, N.C., 1960), I, 122–146; Morgan, *American Slavery, American*

At the local level, disorder took a variety of forms: challenges to the bench or minister, tax strikes, attempted insurrections by servants or freedmen, hostility between different religious groups, disputes between neighbors and within families, and criminal activity. The key consideration in these cases is whether they threatened to paralyze local government and eventually overturn the social order, or whether such conflict could be accommodated within existing structures and, in a sense, was acceptable. Finally, there is the issue of context. Disorder in Virginia and Maryland is usually compared (unfavorably) to the social harmony that is said to have prevailed in New England.[5] A more relevant comparison, however, is with old England. Levels of political violence, the incidence of rebellion, challenges to authority, and patterns of crime in the Chesapeake take on an entirely different character when compared to the parent society.

Earlier it was suggested that a vital means of establishing order in the Chesapeake was the adoption of English law. In theory, settlers retained their traditional constitutional rights and "were to be governed by laws resembling those of England as closely as circumstances would permit." Three principles were established. Colonial laws could not be "repugnant" to English law; where colonial laws were silent, the law of England applied in full force; and English laws were the colony's law except as modified by local statute. Recalling the many different branches of English law and variations in custom and practice from one region to another, the development of Virginia and Maryland laws can be interpreted as a form of "local tradition" that involved the simplification of English codes and procedures together with the addition of measures designed to meet conditions peculiar to the Chesapeake. Thus English laws governing a range of felonies from treason, murder, and rape to witchcraft, riot, and fraud were applied in Maryland and Virginia with little modification, but laws dealing with Indians and slaves were created afresh, since few English precedents existed to guide colonial legislators.[6]

Freedom, chaps. 12–13; Warren M. Billings, "The Causes of Bacon's Rebellion: Some Suggestions," *VMHB*, LXXVIII (1970), 409–435.

5. For example, Greene, *Pursuits of Happiness*, chap. 1; Timothy H. Breen and Stephen Foster, "The Puritans' Greatest Achievement: A Study of Social Cohesion in Seventeenth-Century Massachusetts," *Journal of American History*, LX (1973–1974), 5–22; Greenberg, "Crime, Law Enforcement, and Social Control," *Am. Jour. Leg. Hist.*, XXVI (1982), 293–325.

6. Arthur P. Scott, *Criminal Law in Colonial Virginia* (Chicago, 1930), 5, 22–23, 27; Warren M. Billings, "The Transfer of English Law to Virginia, 1606–1650," in Andrews *et al.*, eds., *The Westward Enterprise*, 221–234; Scott, *Criminal Law*, 27; Lois Green Carr, "County Government in Maryland, 1689–1709" (Ph.D. diss., Harvard University,

From the individual's point of view, the adherence to English laws and privileges had a number of very important implications: it guaranteed protection of person and property, freedom from arbitrary arrest or taxation, and the right to trial by jury. For their part, subjects were expected to keep the king's peace and help, if called upon, to restore order. Everyone had a duty under English law to maintain social harmony and avoid conflict. More generally, the adoption of English law linked Maryland and Virginia closely to the hierarchy of courts and governing institutions in England. Authority flowed in a theoretically unbroken chain of command from the king, Privy Council, great offices of state, committees, and Parliament, via the proprietor and governor, to the central ruling bodies at Jamestown and St. Mary's City, and thence to the county courts. Settlers (in Virginia but not Maryland) had the right of appeal to the king and Privy Council if they could not obtain justice in the provincial courts, and, of course, all subjects had the right to petition the king for redress of grievances. In moving from England to the tobacco coast, therefore, settlers were not faced with an entirely alien system of law. Local variations arose according to necessity, but the system was recognizably English in its precepts, origins, and procedures.

The establishment of order depended not simply on the transferal of English laws but on their effective implementation, and, again, colonial governors turned to English precedents, both in the universal assumption that the wealthy and well-born were the fittest to rule and in the adoption of English institutions and officers of local government. In Maryland and Virginia, as in England, the justice of the peace, usually a gentleman and always dignified by the title "Mister," was at the heart of government in the counties. "Quiet rule" in the scattered settlements of the early seventeenth-century tidewater could not be imposed by a centralized body in Jamestown or St. Mary's City. To maintain the peace it was necessary to decentralize authority and develop a simple hierarchy of courts linking the counties to provincial government. In Virginia, this development represented a decisive move away from the military style of rule that had characterized the period down to the early 1620s, in favor of a country form of government, which emphasized the role of the gentry as local rulers. Nothing testifies as clearly to the desire of provincial rulers to emulate social developments in England

---

1968), 10–15, 312–328; Carr and Jordan, *Maryland's Revolution of Government*, 5–12; Carr, "The Foundations of Social Order: Local Government in Colonial Maryland," in Bruce C. Daniels, ed., *Town and County: Essays on the Structure of Local Government in the American Colonies* (Middletown, Conn., 1978), 73, 99.

as the creation of local institutions for the maintenance of order and the enhancement of gentry power in Chesapeake counties.[7]

Lower Norfolk's first court was held just three years after the creation of the shire, or county, system of government in Virginia in 1634. Six justices— Captain Adam Thorowgood, Captain John Sibsey, Mr. Edward Windham, Mr. Francis Mason, Mr. William Julian, and Mr. Robert Came (or Camm)— gathered at Thorowgood's house in May 1637 to hear a number of complaints brought before the new court. Captain Adam Thorowgood, esquire, age thirty-four, was the largest landowner in the county, had previously served as a justice and burgess for Elizabeth City, was a vestryman of Lynnhaven Parish, and was a member of the Council. He could claim gentry status by virtue of his father's service as commissary to the bishop of Norwich and the position of his brother, Sir John Thorowgood, as secretary to the earl of Pembroke, which linked him to the court of Charles I. He was indisputably the most powerful man in the county until his death in 1640. Captain John Sibsey, also formerly from Elizabeth City, was described as a "yeoman" in 1624. Eight years later he served as burgess for the county, alongside his future fellow justices, Thorowgood, Thomas Willoughby, and Henry Sewell. He patented at least three thousand acres in Lower Norfolk by 1635 and was the second-largest landowner in the county. Less is known about Edward Windham. He arrived in Virginia in 1634 and appears as a headright in Thorowgood's huge patent of the following year. His appointment as a justice was probably a consequence of his kinship with Thorowgood (who described him in his will as his "brother-in-law"), which indicates his gentry status and possibly gave Thorowgood an ally on the bench. Francis Mason and William Julian were longtime residents of the colony who arrived in 1613 and 1608, respectively, and settled in Elizabeth County. Both were in their sixties by 1637 and, having lived in Virginia twenty to thirty years, brought a wealth of experience to the court. Mason patented approximately fifteen hundred acres by the early 1640s and lived near to Thomas Willoughby. Julian took up six hundred acres in 1635 on the Elizabeth River bordering Mason's land.[8]

7. Warren M. Billings, "Transfer of English Law," in Andrews *et al.*, eds., *The Westward Enterprise*, 223; Billings, ed., *The Old Dominion in the Seventeenth Century: A Documentary History of Virginia, 1606–1689* (Chapel Hill, N.C., 1975), 69–81; Carr, "Foundations of Social Order," in Daniels, ed., *Town and County*, 72–110, and Robert Wheeler, "The County Court in Colonial Virginia," 111–133.

8. James Horn, biographical files, Lower Norfolk County, Virginia; [Annie Lash

These men owed their positions to their wealth, inherited status, experience of governing, kin connections, and long residence in the colony. Similar factors influenced appointments to the bench throughout the century. Captain Thomas Willoughby took over as the county's leader in 1640. Like Thorowgood, he was a commissioner and burgess for Elizabeth City and served on the Council. He commanded an attack against the "Chesapiacks" in 1627 and the next year was put in charge of "Marie's Mount," near Newport News. His holdings in Lower Norfolk were initially modest, about one thousand acres by 1635, but he steadily accumulated a large estate during the next two decades and, when he died, owned more than thirty-six hundred acres. John Gookin was the son of Daniel Gookin, merchant, originally from Ripple Court, Kent, who emigrated to Newport News a few months before the Indian uprising of 1622. He moved to Nansemond County for a brief period in the mid-1630s but settled in Lower Norfolk after his marriage to Adam Thorowgood's widow in 1641. He appears to have been the senior justice in Willoughby's absence and attended courts regularly from 1642 until his death the following year. Whether by design or coincidence, Gookin, who was a Puritan, never served at the same court as the royalist Willoughby. Henry Woodhouse, who served on the bench in the 1640s and early 1650s, was the grandson of Sir Henry Woodhouse from Waxham, Norfolk, and the son of a former governor of Bermuda. He was a vestryman of Lynnhaven Parish and represented the county in the assemblies of 1647 and 1652. Francis Yeardley was the son of former governor of Virginia, Sir George Yeardley, and was the third husband of Sarah Thorowgood-Gookin, whom he married in 1647. He was also active in Maryland and was appointed to the Council there in 1652.[9]

Justices were for the most part recruited from among the gentry, prominent mercantile families, and large landowners. For 215 justices in Lower Norfolk, Lancaster, Northumberland, and York counties, together with members of the Council between 1634 and 1676, Warren Billings found the average holding to be in excess of 1,000 acres, at least double the holdings of most planters. In Middlesex County, 1650–1750, major officeholders—burgesses, justices, vestrymen, and sheriffs—typically owned about 800 acres

Jester and Martha Woodroof Hiden], eds., *Adventurers of Purse and Person, Virginia 1607–1624/5*, 3d ed., rev., ed. Virginia M. Meyer and John Frederick Dorman (Richmond, Va., 1987), 607–608; "Abstracts of Virginia Land Parents," *VMHB*, II (1894–1895), 414–424. Nothing is known of Robert Came, but he disappears from the records almost immediately.

9. Horn, biographical files, Lower Norfolk County.

and had more than six hundred pounds at the peak of their careers. Men who achieved only the most humble offices (jurors, appraisers, and processioners) had about 180 acres and eighty-five pounds. On the Eastern Shore, from 1635 to 1650, justices owned two to three times the average landholding of all planters and enjoyed economic networks "far more extensive" than most men. "Economic position, age, kin networks, and experience elevated the commissioners above their fellows on the Eastern Shore," James Perry concludes, "and allowed them to assume an elite position similar to that enjoyed by the justices of the peace in England."[10] County elites no more composed a closed oligarchy than they did in England, and men who arrived with sufficient capital, connections, or lived long enough to amass a large estate might eventually gain a place on the bench or be elected to the Assembly. The high mortality rate and return of planter-merchants to England caused a continual turnover of officeholders. But the entry qualifications for high office were established early, and relatively quickly (after 1640 in Virginia and 1660 in Maryland) the social order began to reflect both the assumptions and material reality that underpinned social hierarchy in England. Rank became more clearly articulated, social and economic differences became more pronounced, and social mobility less fluid.[11]

Perhaps the most intractable problem facing county elites in establishing their authority was the newness of society along the tobacco coast. John Smyth of North Nibley proudly related that the lords Berkeley had governed the Hundred of Berkeley since "shortly after William the Conquerors daies, (if not in his time)."[12] Chesapeake gentry could not appeal to a tradition of family rule in the community that went back "time out of mind." Nor could they depend on the ritual and theater reserved for court days at sessions

10. Warren M. Billings, "The Growth of Political Institutions in Virginia, 1634 to 1676," *William and Mary Quarterly*, 3d Ser., XXXI (1974), 236–238; Darrett B. Rutman and Anita H. Rutman, *A Place in Time: Middlesex County, Virginia, 1650–1750* (New York, 1984), 146–147; Perry, *Formation of a Society*, 196–199; Lorena Seebach Walsh, "Charles County, Maryland, 1658–1705: A Study of Chesapeake Social and Political Structure" (Ph.D. diss., Michigan State University, 1977), 383–384; Robert Anthony Wheeler, "Lancaster County, Virginia, 1650–1750: The Evolution of a Southern Tidewater Community" (Ph.D. diss., Brown University, 1972), 26–27, 50–52, 58, 101–104.

11. Russell R. Menard, "From Servant to Freeholder: Status Mobility and Property Accumulation in Seventeenth-Century Maryland," *WMQ*, 3d Ser., XXX (1973), 37–64; Morgan, *American Slavery, American Freedom*, chaps. 11–12.

12. John Smyth, *A Description of the Hundred of Berkeley in the County of Gloucester and of Its Inhabitants*, vol. III of *The Berkeley Manuscripts*, ed. Sir John Maclean (Gloucester, 1883–1885), 7.

in England. The majesty of the law was difficult to instill when played on the humble stage of one of the justice's houses, at the local ordinary, or in a recently constructed wooden courthouse. And they came face to face with men and women who did not know them and who did not always render the respect they believed was due their position. Unsurprisingly, then, there were occasional challenges to individual justices, sheriffs, burgesses, and even governors.

One of the first cases that came before the Lower Norfolk court on May 15, 1637, involved Anne, the wife of William Fowler, who, in a row over some casks found by the servants of Adam Thorowgood "by the seaside," was alleged to have said, "Let Capt. Thorougood kiss my arse." For good measure, she called Thomas Keeling, Thorowgood's agent, "Jackanapes, Newgate rogue and brigand and told him if he did not get him out of doors she would break his head." She was sentenced to twenty lashes and to ask Thorowgood's forgiveness before the court and at the next Sunday service held at Lynnhaven. Three days later, Deborah Glascock was accused of having "most falsely and after an abusive manner scandalized Capt. John Sibsey in saying his maid servant was with child by him," for which slander she was ordered to be given a hundred "stripes" and to ask forgiveness before the court and at church.[13]

As public figures, justices were vulnerable to this type of abuse, which in some cases was merely a means for servants and the poor to vent their frustrations and express their dislike of those in authority. John Jones, of Lancaster County, was fined 400 lbs. of tobacco in 1659 for "abuseing Mr. Henry Corbyn a member of this Court, by sayeing he was as good a man as the sd Corbyn with other uncivill language and taxeing the Co[u]rt in generall." James Mackmun, who ran a ferry across the Rappahannock and who appeared frequently before the Lancaster court, was found guilty of using "base scandalous and ignominious words" against Mr. Cuthbert Potter, a member of the bench, in 1660 and was fined 5,000 lbs. as well as being ordered to stand at the courthouse door for three days "with Capitall letters affixed on his brest, expresseing his sd offence w[i]th his harty sorrow for the same."[14]

13. Lower Norfolk County, Virginia, Minute Book, transcript of Wills and Deeds A, 2 vols. (1637–1646), I, fols. 1–2, 14–15, 16 (Colonial Williamsburg, microfilm, reel M 1365-2; references to CW microfilm will be given only with the first citation).

14. For more examples, see Lower Norfolk County, Minute Book (1637–1646), I, fols. 28, 37, 64, 103, 108–109, 126, 130, 134, 166, 177, 187, 210–211, 231–232, II, fol. 151, Wills and Deeds B (1646–1651), fols. 15, 52, 77, 104, 129, 152, 186, C (1651–1656),

Not all confrontations with the bench were gratuitous insults thrown at the rich by poorer planters. John Lownes, gentleman, wrote to Lieutenant Colonel Cornelius Lloyd, a justice of Lower Norfolk, in 1653 complaining, "I . . . have beene often before you . . . and instead of receaveing Justice I have had abuses by you and yo[u]r wife." Potentially more serious than personal verbal attacks on individual justices, however, were challenges to the courts' authority in general, either through a failure to comply with court orders or by defaming the bench as a whole. William Hatton slandered several justices of York County, "calling them Coopers, Hog trough makers, Pedlars, Cobblers, tailors, weavers and saying they are not fit to sit where they doe sit." Mr. Jeremiah Parkquet of Lancaster, "in a most rude and uncivill manner," exclaimed "that he never would have Justice by this Co[u]rt," and John Weblin was imprisoned during the court's pleasure for speaking "abusively of sume of the Justices" of Lower Norfolk.[15]

An unusually detailed example, taken from Lower Norfolk County, suggests why the court's authority was sometimes questioned. Early in 1641, Anne, the wife of Saville Gaskins, deposed that the wife of Richard Foster was two months pregnant before she married and that on her wedding night she had suffered a "mischance" (miscarriage) and had "privately made away" with the child. Anne had spent the night with Foster's wife on the eve of the wedding and was in the house the following night when the alleged miscarriage occurred. Her testimony was supported by her husband, who told Thomas Davis that "the wife of Richard Foster had a mischance, a child or the like" and that "he could not endure such base whores." In April, the court, finding that neither Saville nor Anne Gaskins "can bring any any testimony or proof," convicted them both of defamation and ordered them to be whipped and pay costs. Their punishment was remitted, however, by the

---

fols. 34, 38, 60, 62, 74, 84, 88, 97, 102, 126, 219, 226, 241, D (1656–1666), fols. 82, 87, 163, 193, 204, 250, 256, 263, 265, 329, 334, 335, 363, 366, 384, 385, 400, 438, E (1666–1675), fols. 41, 82, E (Orders) (1666–1675), fols. 9, 13–14, 17, 22, 34, 51, 55, 77, 81, 108, 110, 125, Order Book (1675–1686), fol. 43 (CW, microfilm, reels M 1365-1, 2, 17, 18, 25); William Hand Browne *et al.*, eds., *Archives of Maryland*, 72 vols. to date (Baltimore, 1883–), LVII, 65–67 (hereafter cited as *Md. Archives*); Perry, *Formation of a Society*, 202–206.

15. Lownes acknowledged in open court, however, that he had done Lloyd "greate wrong" and was "sorry for it." Lower Norfolk County, Wills and Deeds C (1651–1656), fol. 60, E (Orders) (1666–1675), fols. 13, 110; "Extracts from the Records of York County," *WMQ*, 1st Ser., XXVI (1917–1918), 30; Henrico County, Order Book (1678–1693), 171–173 (Virginia State Library, Richmond); Lancaster County, Order Book, no. 1 (1666–1680), 408, 419 (CW, microfilm, reel M 117-8).

entreaty of Foster and his wife, and instead they were required to ask for public forgiveness in court and the Lynnhaven church.[16]

The matter might have ended there had not Anne Gaskins refused to obey, saying that "she would never perform it." In November the court ordered her to be taken to Captain Thomas Willoughby's house and given twenty lashes; if she still refused to obey, then she would receive another thirty lashes at Mr. Henry Sewell's, then forty at Captain Sibsey's, and so on up to fifty lashes every time she refused to comply with the court's order. She remained defiant. When Philip Land came to arrest her, she said, "Let Capt. Willoughby bring me from court to court and do what he can, he shall never make me ask Anne Foster forgiveness."

The case could be interpreted as an example of the sometimes bitter rivalry that existed between neighbors, and more particularly women, but another defamation case that came before the court around the same time suggests an alternative interpretation. Christopher Burroughs petitioned the bench in July 1641 concerning a slander that he claimed had been made against him. The outcome is unclear, but evidently Burroughs was dissatisfied, since he subsequently appealed to the General Court in Jamestown charging an injustice by the Lower Norfolk bench and supporting his claim by citing "a suit then in question between Anne Foster and Anne Gaskin." Since the records for this period no longer exist, the General Court's decision is unknown; but Burroughs later apologized to the Lower Norfolk court, and the case was dropped.[17]

The protracted resistance of Anne Gaskins and the appeal of Christopher Burroughs to a higher court were unusual. By far the great majority found guilty of defamation appear to have accepted their punishment without further comment. In this case, however, there was a clear sense on the part of Gaskins, Burroughs, and perhaps others that the court had committed an injustice. Their refusal to obey the court was a consequence, not of blind obstinacy, but of a conviction that the bench was either incompetent or partial and that they had not been dealt with fairly.[18]

16. Lower Norfolk County, Minute Book (1637–1646), I, fols. 85, 87, 94, 99–101, 137.

17. *Ibid.*, fols. 117, 126, 130, 134, 166.

18. *Ibid.*, fols. 137, 159–160, 177, 181–182, 193, 209, 213, 219. A few clues suggest that the court decided to drop the matter. Gaskins had been arrested in November 1641 at "Mr Gookins his house." Gookin may have been a political rival of Willoughby's and possibly gave tacit support to Gaskins's challenge to the bench. He became chief commissioner of the court the following year in place of Willoughby. Gaskins's fate is unknown; no further references are made to her, but it is unlikely that she suffered the savage punishment ordered by the court. Burroughs's apology apparently satis-

How frequent were challenges to the authority of individual justices and the bench? Between May 1637 and December 1675, the Lower Norfolk court met on 308 occasions. During thirty-eight years there were 36 cases of contempt of court, 24 cases of abuse of individual justices, 8 cases of physical or verbal attacks on sheriffs and undersheriffs, and 1 attack on a constable. In addition, 5 people were charged for fighting in court, 11 (including several justices) for swearing, and 1 person for being drunk. Challenges to the authority of the bench composed about 12 percent of criminal causes and misdemeanors in the period (Table 32), and defamation of individual justices about 5 percent. At no time was the maintenance of law and order in the county seriously threatened.

Ten of the twenty-four slanders of justices were aimed at two men: Thorowgood and Captain William Carver.[19] Thorowgood may have been unusually energetic in prosecuting slurs on his reputation, but in the first couple of years of the court's existence there were several slanders of justices and their wives, which suggest that initially the county's leaders had to be alert in establishing their authority. Carver, however, was not a popular choice as a justice. He had been appointed to the bench in October 1663, suspended two years later, and reappointed in 1667. From then until 1670 he was slandered at least six times, culminating in "Uncivill Speaches" and "Blows" by Richard Taylor. Two years later, Carver was charged with the murder of Thomas Gilbert, who was stabbed to death at Carver's house. He did not deny that he had done it, but claimed that at the time he was in a "distracted Condition" and "Knoweth nothing of It, noe more than the Child that is now unborne, nor of any other action that day nor severall days before or after." Richard Taylor was ordered to prosecute Carver "on his Majesty's behalf," and in open court Carver called him "Cow killer," to which Taylor replied that "hee was nott a man killer neyther did hee beleive that was the first." Carver was eventually acquitted, but the suspicion that he was a violent man, capable of murder if he "might gett something by It," remained. His enemies doubtless considered that he came to a fitting end when in September 1676 he was hanged by Governor Berkeley on the Eastern Shore for his part in Bacon's Rebellion.[20]

---

fied the honor of the bench, and the remittance of his fine was perhaps a recognition that his allegations had not been entirely spurious.

19. Fifty-one justices were commissioned between 1637 and 1675.

20. Lower Norfolk County, Wills and Deeds D (1656–1666), fols. 381, 436, E (1666–1675), fol. 41, E (Orders) (1666–1675), fols. 17, 18, 22, 34, 51, 55, 84, 127; Stephen Saunders Webb, *1676: The End of American Independence* (New York, 1984), 56.

TABLE 32

Crimes and Misdemeanors in Virginia, 1637–1675

	Lower Norfolk Court, 1637–1675		Lancaster Court, 1652–1675	
	No.	%	No.	%
Crimes of Violence				
Murder	13	2.7	6	3.2
Assault (physical)	23	4.8	12	6.5
Assault (threatened)	5	1.0	12	6.5
Rape	1	.2	0	0
Hard usage	11	2.3	10	5.4
Total	53	11.0	40	21.5
Property Offenses				
Theft	29	6.0	7	3.8
Killing livestock	24	5.0	40	21.5
Extortion	7	1.4	0	0
Embezzlement	3	.6	2	1.1
Forgery	1	.2	0	0
Arson	1	.2	0	0
Total	65	13.5	49	26.3
Sexual Offenses				
Adultery	12	2.5	0	0
Bastardy	70	14.5	25	13.4
Fornication	56	11.6	12	6.5
Bigamy	2	.4	1	.5
Cohabitation	4	.8	0	0
Sodomy	1	.2	0	0
Total	145	30.0	38	20.4
Defamation				
Total	113	23.4	26	14.0
Contempt of Court and Challenges to Authority				
Contempt of court	36	7.5	19	10.2
Swearing in court	11	2.3	4	2.2
Drunk in court	1	.2	1	.5

TABLE 32 Continued

	Lower Norfolk Court, 1637–1675		Lancaster Court, 1652–1675	
	No.	%	No.	%
Fighting in court	5	1.0	0	0
Sedition	2	.4	1	.5
Bound to keep the peace	3	.6	0	0
Pew controversy			1	.5
Total	58	12.0	26	14.0
Miscellaneous Offenses				
Misdemeanors (unspecified)	4	.8	1	.5
Absence from divine service	22	4.6	0	0
Breach of Sabbath	9	1.9	0	0
Barratry	1	.2	0	0
Swearing (out of court)	3	.6	0	0
Drunkenness	7	1.4	0	0
Trading with a slave	1	.2	1	.5
Witchcraft	2	.4	0	0
Sale of or lending guns to Indians			5	2.7
Total	49	10.1	7	3.8
Grand total	483	100.0	186	100.0

Sources: Lower Norfolk: Minute Book, 1637–1646 (transcript), Wills and Deeds B (1646–1651), C (1651–1656), D (1656–1666), E (1666–1675), E (Orders) (1666–1675), Deed Book, no. 4 (1675–1686), Order Book (1675–1686). Lancaster: Deeds Etc., no. 1 (1652–1657), no. 2 (1654–1666), Orders Etc. (1655–1666), Orders Etc., no. 1 (1666–1680).

The authority of Lancaster's county court was subjected to fewer challenges. Between 1653 and 1675 only nineteen cases of contempt and defamation of individual justices or the bench were tried. Two serious confrontations stand out. In August 1653, while the court was sitting at Mr. David Fox's house, Captain Thomas Hackett challenged Fox, a justice, to a duel following a dispute about a bill for one hundred pounds. "I wonder you should soe much degenerate from a gentleman," Hackett wrote, "as to Cast such an aspercion on me in open Court makinge nothinge apeare but I know it bee out of malice and an evill dispositicon w[hi]ch remaines in you therefore I desire you if you have anything of a gentleman or of manhood in you to meet me on tewsday morning about eight of the Clock where I shall expect you coming to give me satisfacon." Fox declined the invitation, and the court ordered Hackett to be held in custody "without baile." Richard Denham, Hackett's son-in-law, was convicted of contempt of court for delivering the challenge while the court was in session and received six stripes. Whatever the merits of Hackett's claims, the court would not tolerate its members' being threatened with physical violence while it was sitting.[21]

The second case also involved Fox. The trouble began when Stephen Chilton was "ordered to be laide in the stocks" for "his misdeamenor and affront offered this Court" in March 1666. When Fox attempted to carry out the order, a small riot erupted:

> Mr Davyd Fox high sheriffe of this County being in the p'secucon of the saide order carryeing the saide Chilton to the stocks, the saide Chilton was rescued from the saide Sheriffe by one Symon East and Will Bushee and many threatening words uttered by them and others in Contempt of this Court the p'ticulars not to bee distinguished, by reason of soe great a confusion as then was, whereupon this Cort thought it not safe to sitt any longer, being in a manner forced to adjourne and did thereupon adjourne for the prevencon of any further troubles, which then in all p'bability was likely to follow.[22]

What caused the flare-up is uncertain. Neither Chilton, East, nor Bushee had appeared in court before, and they would not appear again. Court records give no indication that trouble was brewing. Of interest is how the court responded to the fracas. Chilton was fined four hundred pounds of tobacco for allowing himself to be rescued, but the main censure of the court fell on those who attacked the sheriff. East and Bushee were to be sent for trial by the governor and Council, and John Meredith, who had assisted Chilton's escape, was fined one thousand pounds. The court did not attempt to confront the rioters, opting instead to display its magnanimity and impartiality by adjourning to avoid an increase of violence and appealing to a higher authority in Jamestown for a vindication of its actions. In the meantime, local residents were to aid the restoration of order by being ready to form a posse (if necessary) to apprehend East and Bushee. In fact, no more is heard of the affair. The court reconvened in April to carry on with its rou-

21. Lancaster County, Virginia, Deeds Etc., no. 1 (1652–1657), 63–65 (CW, microfilm, reel M 1363-1).

22. Lancaster County, Orders Etc. (1655–1666), 369–370 (CW, microfilm, reel M 117-7).

tine business as if nothing had happened. Order was reestablished almost as quickly as it had been disrupted.

Confrontations with the court and its officers were not common anywhere in the Chesapeake. Only a trickle of cases involving contempt, defamation of justices, or attacks on sheriffs and constables came before Maryland's provincial court annually from the late 1630s to 1675. Kent Island may have been an exception, since resistance to Baltimore's rule seems to have lingered through to the late 1640s. Three planters of "the Ile of Kent" were accused in 1637 of "sedition, pyracie and murther," but no case was apparently brought against them. In 1648, two sheriffs of Kent were beaten up, and Giles Brent, esquire, a member of the Council, was "defamed" by Edmund Lennin "publikely in the howse of one Commins att Kent and otherwhere." The same year, Captain Robert Vaughan, commander of Kent, was alleged to have uttered "divers revyling scoffing speeches . . . animating thereby those people committed to his charge, to sedition and rebellion and to the lessening the power and authority of the Gov[eno]r and gover[me]nt." These examples conform more closely to a pattern of antiproprietary (and anti-Catholic) behavior, which persisted throughout seventeenth-century Maryland, than to a breakdown of the province's law and order. Generally, there appears little sustained resistance to the authority of the province's courts.[23]

Crimes and Misdemeanors

Virginia and Maryland, according to Douglas Greenberg, were "arguably the most violent societies in the American colonies." The Chesapeake "weathered a terrifying degree of conflict that was reflected not only in personal assaults and frequent thefts, but in substantial political violence as well."[24] To what extent was society along the tobacco coast riven by conflict, as manifested in serious crimes, personal violence, feuds between neighbors, and confrontations between different religious groups?

Unlike their European counterparts, American historians have not shown

23. For the background to the dispute between William Claiborne and the Calverts over ownership of Kent Island, see Menard, "Maryland's 'Time of Troubles,' " *Md. Hist. Mag.*, LXXVI (1981), 128–133; *Md. Archives*, IV, 395–396, 402, 419, 439–440, 459. The significance of antiproprietary sentiment will be considered below. For county courts, see *Md. Archives*, LIII, LIV, LX. Records of Maryland's Provincial Court through to 1675 may be found in *Md. Archives*, IV, X, XLI, XLIX, LVII, and LXV.

24. Greenberg, "Crime, Law Enforcement, and Social Control," *Am. Jour. Leg. Hist.*, XXVI (1982), 302.

a great deal of interest in analyzing crime as a means of interpreting attitudes toward hierarchy, order, and community in the early modern period. Considering the almost complete loss of General Court records for Virginia and the patchiness or absence of county court records for both Chesapeake colonies, a reluctance to examine systematically criminal and civil cases that came before local and central courts in the seventeenth century may not be surprising. Yet some such evaluation is necessary if the nature of local and provincial society in the Chesapeake is to be understood. The following section examines cases brought before Lower Norfolk, Lancaster, and Charles county courts and the Provincial Court of Maryland between 1637 and 1675. Scrutiny of similar cases and actions in English courts will place these findings in a broader, comparative context.[25]

The most serious problem confronting historians of crime, which applies as much to early America as to England, is the existence of a "dark figure" of unrecorded offenses, the magnitude of which is unknown. Any change in the incidence of offenses, as one authority points out, "is therefore at least as likely to be evidence of changes in reporting as in crime actually committed."[26] Fluctuating crime rates over time, or an apparently higher number of felonies in one region compared to another, may reflect the efficiency of courts and their officers in prosecuting crimes, the propensity of individuals

25. The literature on crime in early modern England and Europe is extensive and growing. See, for example, J. S. Cockburn, ed., *Crime in England, 1500–1800* (London, 1977); V.A.C. Gatrell *et al.*, eds., *Crime and the Law: The Social History of Crime in Western Europe since 1500* (London, 1980); J. A. Sharpe, *Crime in Seventeenth-Century England: A County Study* (Cambridge, 1983); Sharpe, *Crime in Early Modern England, 1550–1750* (London, 1984); J. M. Beattie, *Crime and the Courts in England, 1660–1800* (Princeton, N.J., 1986); Peter Linebaugh, *The London Hanged: Crime and Civil Society in the Eighteenth Century* (London, 1991). Studies of the Chesapeake have tended to focus more on court procedures than on criminal activity: Philip Alexander Bruce, *Institutional History of Virginia in the Seventeenth Century: An Inquiry into the Religious, Moral, Educational, Legal, Military, and Political Condition of the People . . .* , 2 vols. (New York, 1910), I, pt. 3; Scott, *Criminal Law*; Hugh F. Rankin, *Criminal Trial Proceedings in the General Court of Colonial Virginia* (Charlottesville, Va., 1965). Raphael Semmes, *Crime and Punishment in Early Maryland* (Baltimore, 1938), is impressionistic but useful. Our knowledge of how county courts functioned and the kinds of routine business they dealt with will be broadened by David Konig's forthcoming study of justice in colonial Virginia. Philip J. Schwarz examines the fate of slaves in *Twice Condemned: Slaves and the Criminal Laws of Virginia, 1705–1865* (Baton Rouge, La., 1988). Generally, see Eric H. Monkkonen, ed., *Crime and Justice in American History*, I–II (Westport, Conn., 1991).

26. Sharpe, *Crime in Early Modern England*, 44, 48, and chap. 3.

to seek arbitration in the courts as opposed to informally within the community, the different perceptions of what constitutes criminal activity, or a different tolerance of antisocial behavior.

Comparisons between different areas of the tobacco coast over different periods are far from straightforward, but more problematic are comparisons between colonial societies and England. Maintenance of law and order in the parent country depended on an array of courts from King's Bench, Chancery, and Star Chamber in London, which dealt with all manner of criminal and civil cases, to the assizes and quarter and petty sessions that supervised the shires. In addition, manorial courts and liberty and borough jurisdictions regulated local affairs while church courts dealt with moral and spiritual offenses besides having important supervisory functions. Estimating the total number of offenses that came before all these courts is virtually impossible even when one concentrates on a single community.[27] Contextual material will therefore rely on assizes, quarter sessions, and church courts, which among them dealt with the bulk of serious offenses as well as much petty crime.

As discussed already, county courts in Virginia and Maryland adopted the powers traditionally assigned to quarter sessions in England. In 1629 the Virginia Council stated that monthly courts were "to decide Controversies of *meum et tuum* under one hundred weight of tobaccoe and to take into their Chardge the conservacon of the peace soe far as is belonging to the Quarter Sessions of the justices in England life only excepted."[28] County courts absorbed the jurisdictions of a range of local courts in England, notably quarter and petty sessions, church, and manorial courts. The General Court of Virginia and Provincial Court of Maryland assumed the powers of English assizes in that they dealt with serious crimes and sat as a court of appeal, but, as in England, there was often a good deal of overlap between the higher and lower courts. For the purposes of this study, what should be emphasized is the simplification of the judicial system in the Chesapeake, which led the county courts to function as sessions, church, and manorial courts all rolled into one. This has an important bearing on the type and volume of offenses that they routinely considered. Although county courts could not try felonies that involved the loss of life or limb, they generally inquired into

27. *Ibid.*, chaps. 2–3. The biggest problem is the patchy survival of records during the period, although there is considerable variation from one region to another, depending on the particular courts concerned.

28. H. R. McIlwaine, ed., *Minutes of the Council and General Court of Colonial Virginia*, 2d ed. (Richmond, Va., 1979), 193.

TABLE 33

Crimes and Misdemeanors in Maryland, 1637–1675

	Charles Co. Court, 1658–1674		Maryland Provincial Court, 1637–1675	
	No.	%	No.	%
Crimes of Violence				
Murder	4	2.5		
Guilty			11	4.8
Not guilty			15	6.6
Verdict unknown			3	1.3
Manslaughter			7	3.1
Assault (physical)	8	5.1	27	11.8
Assault (threatened)	7	4.4	1	.4
Hard usage	4	2.5	0	0
Rape	2	1.3	2	.9
Total	25	15.8	69	30.1
Property Offenses				
Theft	10	6.3	37	16.2
Killing livestock	10	6.3	0	0
Extortion	1	.6	1	.4
Embezzlement	2	1.3	0	0
Forgery	1	.6	4	1.7
Arson	0	0	0	0
Piracy	0	0	2	.9
Total	24	15.2	44	19.2
Sexual Offenses				
Adultery	1	.6	6	2.6
Bastardy	22	13.9	11	4.8
Fornication	4	2.5	7	3.1
Bigamy	1	.6	1	.4
Cohabitation	3	1.9	3	1.3
Abortion	1	.6	0	0
Total	32	20.3	28	12.2
Defamation				
Total	57	36.1	55	24.0

TABLE 33 Continued

	Charles Co. Court, 1658–1674		Maryland Provincial Court, 1637–1675	
	No.	%	No.	%
Contempt of Court and Challenges to Authority				
Contempt of court	6	3.8	4	1.7
Swearing in court	1	.6	1	.4
Drunk in court	1	.6	3	1.3
Fighting in court	0	0	0	0
Sedition	1	.6	12	5.2
Breach of the peace	3	1.9	0	0
Rebellion	0	0	2	.9
Total	12	7.6	22	9.6
Miscellaneous Offenses				
Breach of Sabbath	3	1.9	1	.4
Malicious mischief	2	1.3	0	0
Blasphemy	0	0	1	.4
Barratry	0	0	1	.4
Disturbing divine service	0	0	1	.4
Drunkenness	1	.6	4	1.7
Witchcraft	2	1.6	3	1.3
Total	8	5.1	11	4.8
Grand total	158	100.1	229	99.9

Source: William Hand Browne *et al.*, eds., *Archives of Maryland*, 72 vols. to date (Baltimore, 1883–), IV, X, XLI, XLIX, LVII, LX, LV.

serious crimes such as homicide, grand larceny, treason, and rape in order to decide whether the offender should be sent to the higher court for trial. In other words, lower courts took on the role of grand juries screening cases for the General or Provincial Court. Both serious and petty crimes therefore came under the scrutiny of local justices.

By far the greatest amount of business that came before the county courts of Lower Norfolk, Lancaster, and Charles counties between 1637 and 1675 concerned recording land patents, sales, transfers, debt transactions, and the supervision of local affairs from looking after orphans to maintaining the highways and licensing taverns. Civil actions involving the recovery of debts, disputes over land, and regulative offenses such as the failure to maintain roads are not addressed here. Only offenses that threatened peace and order in local society are of concern, divided into six categories: interpersonal violence, property offenses, sexual offenses, defamation, offenses against order, and miscellaneous offenses (Tables 32, 33). No claim is made that this analysis is exhaustive (given the nature of the evidence, it is difficult to see how any study could be), but certain generalizations can be made.

The incidence of violent crimes, including homicide, assault, rape, and hard usage (excessive beating of wives or servants) averaged 11.0–21.5 percent of all offenses dealt with by the county courts and 30.1 percent brought before Maryland's Provincial Court (Tables 32, 33). Figures include accusations as well as proven felonies and are therefore substantially higher than for convicted offenses alone. Of 36 homicides dealt with by the Provincial Court between 1637 and 1675 (including 10 cases of infanticide), 11 persons were found guilty, 7 were convicted of manslaughter, 15 were found not guilty, and the verdicts of 3 cases are unknown. Homicide composed no more than 2–3 percent of all offenses in the county courts (15.7 percent in the Provincial Court), assaults (physical and threatened) ranged between 6 and 13 percent, and hard usage between 2 and 5 percent.[29]

To put these figures into perspective, homicide and infanticide made up 3–16 percent of serious crimes brought before various English assizes and sessions between 1550 and 1709. Just fewer than 300 homicides committed in Essex, for example, came before the assizes and King's Bench between 1620 and 1680, which represented 3.4 percent of all Essex indictments (including quarter sessions) during the period.[30] Maryland's population rose from a few hundred in the 1630s to about 19,000 fifty years later; thus 38 murder cases indicate a higher homicide rate than for Essex with a population of about 110,000 in the same period. County populations in Virginia were initially comparable to medium-sized English villages, and even by the end of the century many were only about the size of an average market town. The 13 murder and 28 assault cases that came before Lower Norfolk's

29. *Md. Archives*, IV, X, XLI, XLIX, LVII, LXV.

30. Sharpe, *Crime in Early Modern England*, table 1, 55; Sharpe, *Crime in Seventeenth-Century England*, table 19, 183, chap. 8; J. S. Cockburn, "The Nature and Incidence of Crime in England, 1559–1625: A Preliminary Survey," in Cockburn, ed., *Crime in England*, table 1, 55; Beattie, *Crime and the Courts*, chap. 3; J. S. Cockburn, "Patterns of Violence in English Society: Homicide in Kent, 1560–1985," *Past and Present*, no. 130 (February 1991), 76–79.

court between 1637 and 1675 should be set in the context of a population that ranged from under 1,000 to about 2,500. Homicide rates may have been higher in the Chesapeake than England, but the figures hardly support the view that early Chesapeake society "weathered a terrifying degree of conflict" or that serious interpersonal violence was of a different order compared to England.[31]

Motives for murder and assault were varied. A number of cases involved the beating to death of servants. John Dandy, a blacksmith of Newtown, "in the County of Potomake," appears to have had an unusually violent temperament. In 1643 he was found guilty by the Provincial Court of murdering an "Indian ladd" but managed to avoid capital punishment. Seven years later he assisted his wife in beating up Thomas Maidwell. The cause of the assault is unclear, not least to Maidwell, but he was first struck on the head with a "Smithes Cindar" by Mrs. Dandy and then hit on the head again by her husband wielding a three-pound hammer. Dandy's violent career came to an end in 1657 with his conviction for murdering his servant, Henry Gouge. Pope Alvey and Francis Carpenter, of Maryland, were found guilty of killing their servants but were both convicted of manslaughter and acquitted on benefit of clergy. The pattern of violence exhibited in these cases took a common form: frequent and excessive beatings that led to serious injuries and eventually death, sometimes by a single fatal blow that killed the servant outright or after a protracted period of beating.[32]

Less frequently, servants and slaves turned the tables and struck back at their owners. William Page of Lancaster "did strike at his sd. Master

---

31. Population figures are drawn from Sharpe, *Crime in Seventeenth-Century England,* 134; Russell R. Menard, "Immigrants and Their Increase: The Process of Population Growth in Early Colonial Maryland," in Aubrey C. Land *et al.,* eds., *Law, Society, and Politics in Early Maryland* (Baltimore, 1977), 90–99; Aubrey C. Land, *Colonial Maryland: A History* (Millwood, N.Y., 1981), 58–59; Morgan, *American Slavery, American Freedom,* table 3, 412–413. The quote is from Greenberg, "Crime, Law Enforcement, and Social Control," *Am. Jour. Leg. Hist.,* XXVI (1982), 302. Of the 13 homicides that came before the Lower Norfolk court between 1637 and 1675, 8 were referred to the General Court in Jamestown, 4 were dismissed, and 1 verdict is unknown. Homicide rates (homicides per thousand of the population) are difficult to estimate because of the problem of constructing reliable annual population figures for Virginia and Maryland counties.

32. *Md. Archives,* IV, 254, 260, X, 31, 524–525, 534–545, XLIX, 230, 234–236, LVII, 60–65 (see also XLI, 190–191, XLIX, 304–314); Lower Norfolk County, Wills and Deeds D (1656–1666), fol. 358.

[Mr. Edward Dale] w[i]th a howe swearing (God damme hym) if his master stroke hym hee would beate out his braynes," for which he was ordered to serve an extra year. Three servants and a slave belonging to John Hawkins of Elk River, Baltimore County, were convicted of petty treason in 1671 for murdering their master and ordered to be hanged by another of Hawkins's slaves, who had been acquitted. Violence was met with violence. Margery Biddle, servant to Sarah Jones of Lower Norfolk County, told the court in 1664 how she had been sent by her mistress "to the Cow penn, (she hearinge some noyse there) to see what ayled the Cattle and when she returned to the dwellinge house of the sd. Joanes shee sawe her through the windowe, to lye uppon the ground and her head and ground about it to be all bloudy and a servant man of hers named Robert goinge upp and downe the house wth a Candle lighted in his hand, whereuppon supposed her the sd. Joanes to be dead, she departed from the house and acquainted the Neighbours wth what had happened." The accused, Robert Challicome, argued that Jones had struck him and that he "tooke upp the iron pestle and strocke his sd. mistresse two blowes on the head and that her head bledd and that after the sd. blowes he . . . did not see her stirr and . . . he this Examinant stayed all night in the house and the next morning fledd away." Challicome was sent to Jamestown for trial.[33]

A number of murders were the outcome of domestic quarrels or what appears to be senseless violence. In a case already alluded to, Captain William Carver stabbed to death Thomas Gilbert while "troubled wth frantick fitts," in the presence of several witnesses who had gathered at Carver's house for dinner. Although some of his neighbors doubted whether he had been "out of his witts" that night, he was successful in pleading his innocence before the General Court and was acquitted of murder. Patrick Due of Calvert County, Maryland, shot and killed a seaman and wounded others, crying, "Damme mee you Dogges I will kill you, If there bee noe more Sea Dogges in the world," for nothing more (apparently) than that they ate some of his oysters. Despite unequivocal evidence of guilt, he was convicted of manslaughter. On a hot summer's night in mid-June 1682, a row developed between Edward Husbands and his wife Elizabeth concerning her deceased father, Mr. David Miles. Elizabeth's mother was also in the house and, hearing the words that passed between them, "arose saying doe nott abuse my dead husband," at which, as Elizabeth describes it, "hee layd vyolent hands on her, w[hi]ch Caused her to crie out murder." John Wilford, his wife, and a

33. Lancaster County, Orders Etc., no. 1 (1666–1680), 200; *Md. Archives*, LXV, 2–8; Lower Norfolk County, Wills and Deeds D (1656–1666), fols. 398–399.

servant arrived on the scene, and Wilford asked, "Do you intend to murther her[?]" Husbands then attacked Wilford and in the fight that ensued picked up a knife, saying, "You dogg I will be avenged on you," and stabbed him to death. Husbands was sent for trial and subsequently executed.[34]

Infanticide represents a distinctive category of homicide. English law had been tightened up in 1624 (21 Jac. I, c. 27) to make not only the murder of a newborn child but also the concealment of stillbirths capital offenses. Presumption of guilt revolved around concealment because whether a child was dead on delivery or had been murdered was often difficult to prove. The allegations made by Anne Gaskins about Anne Foster's "mischance" could have led Foster to the gallows, the finality of which might account for the justices' reluctance to prosecute.

How common infanticide was in seventeenth-century England is problematic. Only seven cases came before the Kent assizes between 1603 and 1625 (compared to eighty-six other cases of homicide), whereas eighty-three cases were prosecuted at the Essex assizes from 1620 to 1680, nearly 30 percent of all homicides in the period. A much larger number, however, may have never come to the courts' attention. The accused were usually young women, often servants, who could not support, emotionally or financially, a bastard child. They would have been well aware of the community's opprobrium and the shame that would fall upon them, which might wreck their chances of ever securing a respectable marriage, and they would have known also of the severe or humiliating punishments that courts meted out: whipping, confinement in a house of correction, and public confession. Panic and confusion and the dread of public disgrace may have overwhelmed a tiny minority of women who perhaps saw no alternative apart from doing away with the baby as quickly as possible. Neonaticide, the murder of a child within twenty-four hours of its birth, was for some of these unwed mothers "a deliberate form of delayed abortion."[35]

34. Lower Norfolk County, Wills and Deeds E (1666–1675), fols. 127–128; *Md. Archives*, XLIX, 10–16, 230, 233–234; Lancaster County, Orders Etc., no. 2 (1680–1686), 93–94, 103, 237 (CW, microfilm, reel M 117-7).

35. J. S. Cockburn ed., *Calendar of Assize Records: Kent Indictments, James I* (London, 1980), nos. 175, 248, 289, 597, 628, 790, 795; Sharpe, *Crime in Seventeenth-Century England*, 135–137; G. R. Quaiffe, *Wanton Wenches and Wayward Wives: Peasants and Illicit Sex in Early Seventeenth Century England* (London, 1979), chaps. 8–10; R. W. Malcolmson, "Infanticide in the Eighteenth Century" in Cockburn, ed., *Crime in England*, 192–197. Peter C. Hoffer and N.E.H. Hull discuss individual motivation from the perspective of modern psychopathology in *Murdering Mothers: Infanticide in England and New England, 1558–1803* (New York, 1981), 147–148, 151–153, 154.

Ten cases of infanticide, more than a quarter of all homicides, came before Maryland's Provincial Court between 1637 and 1675. Four women were found guilty, and at least two, Elizabeth Greene from near "Norwitch" (probably Norwich) and Isabella Yausley, were sentenced to hang. All of the accused were either servants or single women. Their motives are obscure, since the courts were less interested in what caused them to murder their newborn than in ascertaining whether a felony had been committed. In view of the one or two years of extra service that female servants could be forced to serve for bearing an illegitimate child, it might seem surprising that infanticide was not more common. Possibly the majority of neonaticides went undetected, or possibly women servants found pregnancy and child rearing welcome relief from the tedious routine of household chores and field work. Bastardy was not condoned, but in a society where men outnumbered women by two or three to one, having an illegitimate child was unlikely to prevent a women from eventually marrying.[36]

Finally, a category of violence that had no parallel in England was English-Indian conflict, which took the form not only of periodic hostilities (wars) between the two peoples but also of sporadic frontier killings. The apparent lack of motive behind some of the killings may be deceptive, since there is little evidence of the general background to the outbreak of violence. What lay behind the murder of Roger Oliver, whose throat was cut in a fight with an Indian in 1643, is unclear. Equally puzzling is the shooting of the "king of Yowocomoco" by John Elkin earlier that year. But what caused English settlers the greatest anxiety were unpredictable lightning Indian raids on individual plantations or outlying settlements. In 1665, for example, the Maryland Provincial Court voiced its concern about "the dayly incursions of the Indian Enemy into this province." A few months later the court dealt with a case that graphically illustrates the horror of such attacks. Agatha Langworth of St. John's, Charles County, recounted how in August as she

Lay sick on her Table . . . [there] came ffower Indians and knock'd att the doare. The wench by name Lewis Good told this Depont That shee thought it had beene the Children But Cryed Indians and flung open the doore, wth th[a]t this Depont turned about, and made to the doore and fownd one of the 4 Indians by name Chotyke wthin the roome and the Dogge keeping a barking att him, hee made some blowes att itt, still Looking uppon this Depont, and made a back blowe att her wth a Tomahauke,

36. *Md. Archives*, X, 456–458, XLI, 430–432, XLIX, 212, 217, 231–236, LVII, 74, 99, 123, 251, 598, LXV, 9–11, 12–14, 30, 31, 32–33.

but mist her whereuppon hee retreated out of the roome. . . . Then shee went to a window next to a neighbors of hers and hollowed and Cryed Indians, Indians. Wth th[a]t the neighbors came, In wch interim this Depont heard her Children cry out saying, Good nindians, good nindians, After wch this Depont did againe see the foresd ffower Indians, and after that fownd Two of her children murthered.

Elizabeth Brumley informed the court that she was

in the Cornefeild of her mistresse, Agatha Langworth, when shee heard her sd mistresse Cry out Indians, whereuppon this Depont did strive to gett the Children together, who did cry Extraordinarily, And this Depont called the Boy John and sayd Peace Jonny, and this Depont turned about and saw ffower Indians, making towards her, Two of wch Indians was th[a]t Indian called Bennett, now in custody, as allsoe th[a]t Indian called the ffisherman, But for the other Two shee did not know, And th[a]t the aforesd Bennett did then make towards one the Children, wch was a Boy, and knockd him downe wth his Tomahauke, Whereuppon shee asked him in Indian *Kaquince machissino Chippone* why hee did soe? Who answered in Indian, Because hee would. Uppon th[a]t this Depont run away wth the Girle, and this Indian Bennett made after her, shooting Arrowes, but missed her, and came up to her wth the Boyes head under his arme, And shee saw the old ffisherman passe her, and this Indian Bennett came into the weeds and lay downe the Childs head and sayd in Indian *Pops inna-hayo* A woman with Child, and struck att her wth his Tomahauke, three times, wch made three Cutts in her Cap and two cutts in her head, and thereuppon left her for Dead.

Two of the four Indians, Maquamps als Bennett and Chotkye of the "Matta-woman" of Charles County, were found guilty and sentenced to hang; the others were never captured.[37]

This was the kind of incident—the seemingly callous and indiscriminate killing of women and children—that inflamed planter hostility against all Indians, friend and foe, and that ten years later was a major factor in the eruption of Bacon's Rebellion in Virginia. The king's commissioners, Herbert Jeffreys, Sir John Berry, and Francis Morryson, who were charged to inquire into the cause of the rebellion, reported that "within this 14. or 15. months, it is conceaved, there hath beene near 300 Christian persons, barbarously murthered by the Indians," probably a gross exaggeration but indicative of

37. *Ibid.*, IV, 177, 180–181, 210, XLIX, 465, 481–484.

the widespread fear of Indian attacks. On the other hand, the half a dozen homicides that came before the Provincial Court involving Indians are not an accurate reflection of Anglo-Indian hostilities. Far more killings by either side never came to the court's attention because the culprits were unknown or the circumstances surrounding the murder were unclear. Bearing in mind that some counties, like those in the Northern Neck of Virginia, were affected much more than others, this was an aspect of crime and disorder that set Chesapeake society apart from England.

Another contrast with English patterns of crime lies in the incidence of property offenses, notably theft. In late Tudor and in Stuart England, between 70 percent and 93 percent of indictments for felony were for property offenses, but in Maryland and Virginia accusations of and convictions for theft were comparatively rare.[38] Property offenses in general, including theft, illicit killing of livestock, forgery, embezzlement, extortion, and arson, made up between 14 and 26 percent of cases in the county courts and 19 percent in the Provincial Court (Tables 32, 33). Theft ranged from 4 to 6 percent in the county courts to 16 percent at the provincial level. Whereas in English shires, at the quarter sessions and assizes, the great majority of indictments related to the theft of livestock, crops, clothing, cloth, money, food, and all sorts of household goods, along the tobacco coast such offenses were much less frequent. John Bedford of Lancaster, described by the court as "a loose person," was convicted in 1673 of stealing a pair of breeches belonging to one of Mr. David Fox's slaves, and William Crompe of the same county was arrested for trial for allegedly breaking into Richard George's house and "taking hence twelve bags of Indian corne." Occasionally, food and clothing were filched from neighbors' houses or merchandise and tobacco stolen from merchants. Runaway servants stole various goods from their owners— boats, food, and clothing—to facilitate their escape.[39] But the small, face-to-face communities of the tidewater were not characterized by high rates of theft.

The explanation lies in a combination of factors that can only be suggested here. Chesapeake society was less attenuated by extremes of wealth and poverty than England; standards of living for the vast majority were much lower (in material terms), and thus the ownership of valuable household

38. Billings, ed., *The Old Dominion*, 280; Sharpe, *Crime in Early Modern England*, table 1, 55.

39. Lancaster County, Orders Etc., no. 1 (1666–1680), 184, 249; Lower Norfolk County, Wills and Deeds B (1646–1651), fols. 72, 149, D (1656–1666), fols. 201, 243, 306, E (Orders) (1666–1675), fols. 14, 17, 127.

items was less common; and, most important, the very intimacy of community life made the prospect of getting away with a theft undetected difficult, if not impossible. It is hard to imagine how someone who stole plate, money, or some other kind of valuables could have escaped detection except by sailing for England. Most thefts related to stealing or killing hogs, where there was a better chance of success, either because the owner might not notice that one of his hogs was missing or because the marks could be changed.[40]

As in England, serious sexual crimes, such as rape, bestiality, and sodomy, were extremely rare; no more than a handful of cases exist during the period 1637–1675. Far more common were moral offenses that in England were dealt with by church and manorial courts as well as by petty and quarter sessions: adultery, fornication, cohabitation, and bastardy. Moral offenses made up 20–30 percent of the cases that came before Charles, Lancaster, and Lower Norfolk county courts, of which bastardy was by far the most numerous. The number of bastardy cases that came before English courts in this period has been little studied. Sixty-one women (20 percent of all indictments) were accused of bearing bastards in Kent quarter sessions papers between 1651 and 1672 (Table 34). Presentments for fornication and adultery (including bastardy) that came before the church courts of Wiltshire, 1615–1629, numbered 33–137 annually, which in practice meant that individual parishes presented 1 or 2 offenders every few years. The churchwardens of six parishes in the deanery of Sutton, Kent, brought 8 cases to the attention of the consistory court of Canterbury in 1621 and 10 between 1632 and 1636, most of which related to prenuptial fornication. Similarly, in the Vale of Berkeley there was a steady, if relatively small, number of cases every year throughout the century.[41]

Neither in England nor in the Chesapeake was local society overwhelmed by sexual immorality, but the problem was nevertheless a vexing one for local justices and parish worthies. Some idea of its local impact in Virginia can be judged from the grand jury presentments of Lower Norfolk County. In October 1678, for example, the jury charged John Powell with living with his brother's wife "in adultery," Nich Wise "for Lying wth his Sister," Thomas Potts "for deluding mens wifes the wch Causes a great strife betwixt

---

40. Semmes, *Crime and Punishment*, chaps. 3–4.

41. Martin Ingram, *Church Courts, Sex, and Marriage in England, 1570–1640* (Cambridge, 1987), table 10, 258, chaps. 4, 7–8; Consistory Court, Ex Officio, Comperta et Detecta, Deanery of Sutton, 1620–1635 (X.6.4), Canterbury Cathedral Library; Gloucester Diocesan Registers (GDR), volumes for the period 1619–1687, Gloucestershire Record Office.

TABLE 34

Crimes and Misdemeanors, Kent Quarter Sessions, 1651–1672

	No.	%
Crimes of Violence		
Murder	5	1.7
Murder (attempted)	1	.3
Assault (physical)	22	7.3
Assault (threatened)	1	.3
Rape	3	1.0
Abduction	1	.3
Ill-treatment	3	1.0
Total	36	12.0
Property Offenses		
Theft	168	56.2
Smuggling	1	.3
Poaching	6	2.0
Arson	2	.7
Total	177	59.2
Sexual Offenses		
Adultery	2	.7
Bastardy	61	20.4
Fornication	3	1.0
Bigamy	2	.7
Sodomy	1	.3
Total	69	23.1
Defamation		
Total	0	0
Offenses against Authority		
Sedition	4	1.3
Miscellaneous Offenses		
Disturbing divine service	1	.3
Illegal conventicles	5	1.7

TABLE 34 Continued

	No.	%
Witchcraft	6	2.0
Good behavior	1	.3
Total	17	5.7
Grand total	299	100.0

Sources: Calendar of Quarter Sessions Records, Sessions Papers, 1639–1677 (KAO, Q/SB 1–12), Kent Archives Office.

men and their wifes," Francis Plomer and a woman for having "unlawfully married her husband being alive," and Robert Woody and Daniel Lenier's wife "who by Report are as Comon man and wife." The following May, two women were presented for having bastards, Laurance Arnold was charged with "haveing of two wifes and his wife for haveing another husband," and Eliza Whitly was accused of "Runing away wth Thos Potts, and being taken in bed together." [42] The problem was not that the social order was threatened by such offenses or that marriage and family would eventually break down; rather, the issue (from the courts' point of view) was how to deal with a persistent small minority of offenders who flagrantly defied prescribed moral standards of the day.

Closely related to acts of immorality were imputations of immorality by word. Sexual slander was one of the most common offenses dealt with by English church courts in the seventeenth century and was also commonly prosecuted in Chesapeake courts (Tables 32, 33). Two general points are worth making, since they appear to apply equally to English and colonial society. First, as James Sharpe suggests, "considerations of honour, good name, and reputation" were of vital concern at all levels of society in the seventeenth century. Prosecution of defamation in the courts reflected an alacrity to defend reputation that "ran from the top to very near the bottom of English society in this period." [43] Defending one's good name was essential to credit and standing in the community, both in maintaining re-

42. Lower Norfolk County, Deed Book, no. 4 (1675–1686), fols. 40, 48 (CW, microfilm, reel M 1365-1).

43. J. A. Sharpe, *Defamation and Sexual Slander in Early Modern England: The Church Courts at York*, Borthwick Papers, no. 58 (York, 1980), 1, 3.

spectability and social rank and in the more tangible sense of being able to carry on one's work within the community or perhaps finding a suitable marriage partner. Loss of reputation could lead to public disgrace and social ostracism. Little wonder, then, that a preoccupation with issues of honor and shame was particularly intense in the small societies of English villages and newly founded colonial settlements.

Second, defamation cases developed out of a constant commentary on the activities and reputations of neighbors and social superiors in the context of what one historian calls a milieu of gossip. Gossip, it has been argued, was typically neither idle nor trivial; besides being a principal means by which news was exchanged, it served as a mechanism for regulating and enforcing social and moral norms within the community. Unacceptable behavior, public or private, would be commented upon and the individual's social standing brought into question. Gossip laid down the limits of acceptable behavior and attitudes and voiced the community's displeasure when these informal rules were breached.[44] Having said that, one should not underestimate the relish with which some protagonists slandered their neighbors or overlook the fact that defamation might ensue from long-standing feuds within the community.

Honor and reputation were at the heart of the vast majority of cases that came before the courts in Maryland and Virginia. Henry Hawkins deposed before the Lower Norfolk court in 1637 "that being at the Warrikesquiake plantation they were there jesting concerning rare ripe pumpkins whereupon George Locke told him that Thomas Davis had the use of Ann Clarke once and that he could not do it again, and further this deponent sayeth that Thomas Davis told him likewise that he did ask said Anne Clarke to lie with him and her answer was she would not but three weeks hence she might better do it." The court found in favor of the plaintiff and in consideration of "the great impeaching and scandalizing of her credit" ordered Davis to "ask the aforesaid Anne Clarke's forgiveness here now in Court and the next ensueing Sabbath at Capt. John Sibsey's at the time of divine service." Jacob Lumbrozo, defending John Gould and his wife of Charles County, was sufficiently moved to put his case into verse: "Gils Glover," he claimed, "hath much defamed your Petitioners wife in Calling of her whore and in saying that hee woold prove her a whore which is the greatest infamy that a malitious toung Can Cast on a woman seeing that Shee lives for ever in eternal shame / that lives to see the death of her good name." Major

---

44. *Ibid.*, 18–19; Ingram, *Church Courts*, 318–319; Mary Beth Norton, "Gender and Defamation in Seventeenth-Century Maryland," *WMQ*, 3d Ser., XLIV (1987), 5.

Thomas Lambert, a justice of Lower Norfolk, was fined the extraordinary sum of five thousand pounds of tobacco for calling Matthew Fassett a "rascall, Knave and foole in the open Co[u]rt" in 1654. The fine was evidently based on an assessment of the damage done to his livelihood by Lambert's slander, whereby Fassett "hath beene grossely abused and scandalized in his good name and reputacon . . . to the greate ympeachment of his good name and creditt, not only in this Country, but it may be farr more in forraine ptes where the sd. Fassett may come to the losse of his voyages or his utter undoeing."[45]

Defamation cases embraced a variety of types. As we have seen, much abuse was aimed at prominent men and their wives, especially in the early years of county formation. Margaret Harrington, servant to William Julian, a justice, was presented to the Lower Norfolk court in 1638 for having "most infamously and maliciously scandalized and defamed her mistriss, Sarah Julian, by reporting that she had often seen Cornelius Lloyd use her said mistress in carnal copulation." William Whitby deposed in the same case that Harrington had told him that her mistress "had often misused her but now she would be even with her." She was sentenced to one hundred lashes. Rows between women occasionally developed into bitter slanging matches. Joan Nevill called Mary Dod "whore and th[a]t shee woold Prove her a whore and that shee woold Prove her Captayne Battens whore . . . and that the sayd Dods wife lay with Capt Batten at Patuxon in the sight of six men with her Coats up to her mouth." Elizabeth, wife of Walter Herd of Lancaster, was accused of having "very much defamed the wife of Thomas Powell by ill language tendinge to the bastardizing of the childe of the saide Thomas Powell." The court ordered her to "publiquie aske the said Powell and his wife forgivenes, and shall at the next Co[u]rt for the lower pte of this Countie stand during the sitting of the saide Co[u]rt stand wth Capital l[et]tres fixed on her breast expresseing her saide offence."[46]

Language and invective were much the same as used in England. On a "publique Streete" in Dursley, Gloucestershire, for example, Anne Reeve said that Anne Turner "was a Whore a common Whore and that the Childe she now hath was and is a bastard." Susan Short of Harrietsham, Kent, called Sarah Coachman "a great belly'd whore," and John Cary, of Maid-

---

45. Lower Norfolk County, Minute Book (1637–1646), I, fol. 4, Wills and Deeds C (1651–1656), fol. 72; *Md. Archives*, LIII, 319.

46. Lower Norfolk County, Minute Book (1637–1646), I, fols. 15–16; *Md. Archives*, LIII, 377; Lancaster County, Deeds Etc., no. 1 (1652–1657), 288. See also Semmes, *Crime and Punishment*, chap. 9.

stone, began a brawl with Deborah Whiting by shouting after her, "You old whore, you old lecherous jade, where are you[r] two bastards . . . lecherous bitch."[47] The language of the streets was transferred directly to the tidewater.

In some instances, the exchange of insults could lead to more serious allegations, such as witchcraft. A spate of "scandalous speeches . . . concerneing sev'all women" in Lower Norfolk County, "termeing them to be Witches, whereby theire reputations have beene much impaired, and theire lives brought into question," persuaded the court in 1655 to impose a heavy fine on anyone making false or malicious accusations. Nevertheless, Mrs. Mary Batts was charged by George Beasely the following year "of having familiarity wth incleane Spreritts," and Ann Godby slandered the "good name and Creditt of Mic[hae]l Robinsons wife terming her a witch" a few years later. Goody Michell of Charles County brought a number of suits to court after she had been accused by Mistress Hatche of bewitching her face. "Wheras your Poor Petitioner," she testified in 1661,

> is most shamfully [sic] and her good name taken away from her shee doath desire that shee may bee righted and that shee may bee searched by able woemen whether she bee such a person or no which thos persons say I am. . . . I desire th[a]t Mr Francis Doughty [a minister] may bring thos Persons to light that have raysed this schandalous reports of mee for hee sayd that I salluted a woman at Church and her teeth fell a Aking as if shee had bin mad and I desired him to tell mee who had raysed this report of mee and hee woold not and so from one to an other my good name is taken away that I Cannot bee at quiet for them for it is all their delight and table talke how to doe mee a mischief beeing a poore distressed widow but my trust is in God that hee will plead my Case for mee and will never suffer the poor and innocent to perish by the hands of their Enemies.[48]

Women played a prominent part in defamation proceedings, both as litigants and witnesses. Mary Beth Norton has estimated that, of about two thousand civil actions brought before Maryland courts in the seventeenth century, women appeared in only 19 percent of cases, whereas in defama-

47. GDR B4/1/879, GRO; Consistory Court, Depositions, 1664–1682 (X.11.18), 24–25, 78, Canterbury Cathedral Library.

48. Lower Norfolk County, Wills and Deeds C (1651–1656), fol. 157, D (1656–1666), fols. 6, 237; *Md. Archives*, LIII, 55, 142. For a general discussion of scolds and witches in 16th- and 17th-century England, see D. E. Underdown, "The Taming of the Scold: The Enforcement of Patriarchal Authority in Early Modern England," in Fletcher and Stevenson, eds., *Order and Disorder*, 116–136.

tion suits women participated in more than half of them. In Lower Norfolk County, between 1637 and 1675, women were the targets of slanderous abuse in forty-five cases, compared to fifty-eight cases involving men, and initiated about half the litigation that came to court. Where the nature of the slander could be determined, about half referred to sexual misconduct, just under a quarter to terms of abuse (such as rogue, base fellow, and knave), and a sixth to theft.[49]

Defamation cases expressed the anxieties of local communities: the honesty and creditworthiness of men in their dealings with neighbors, the impartiality of commissioners, and the sexual propriety of women, single and married. At times litigation reached epidemic proportions. In Charles County more than fifty cases were heard between 1658 and 1666. As local societies coalesced along the Bay, there appears to have been an initial period of social competition in some counties during which residents vied with each other in the courts to defend their reputations and respectability. In this way, rank within the community was either challenged or confirmed. But perhaps the most important point to emerge from this analysis is that a means of channeling social friction through the courts was quickly established by adopting English precedents, and potentially bloody contests over honor, rank, and status were for the most part avoided.[50]

The incidence and types of criminal offenses and misdemeanors that came before Maryland and Virginia courts in the seventeenth century do not suggest that society was chronically unstable and disorderly, at least at the local level, when compared to contemporary English society. Indeed, study of offenses heard before English manorial courts would likely show English local society to be more turbulent than the above discussion has indicated. If England, through its different hierarchies of courts, was "a much-governed country," the same could be said of the Chesapeake, if for different reasons. Plantation society had no need of the complex array of jurisdictions of the

---

49. Norton, "Gender and Defamation," *WMQ*, 3d Ser., XLIV (1987), 4–5. Of approximately 108 defamation suits, only 31 are sufficiently detailed to allow slanderous language to be categorized; see Kathleen Mary Brown, "Gender and the Genesis of a Race and Class System in Virginia, 1630–1750" (Ph.D. diss., University of Wisconsin–Madison, 1990), 146–147.

50. *Md. Archives*, LIII, for the Charles County cases. For different procedures concerning defamation cases in England and the Chesapeake, see Norton, "Gender and Defamation," *WMQ*, 3d Ser., XLIV (1987), 7–8; Clara Ann Bowler, "Carted Whores and White Shrouded Apologies: Slander in the County Courts of Seventeenth-Century Virginia," *VMHB*, LXXXV (1977), 411–426; Sharpe, *Defamation and Sexual Slander*, 4–9; Ingram, *Church Courts*, 292–300.

parent country, but the creation of a decentralized system of county courts meant that relatively small populations by English standards had access to justice dispensed locally. For most of the century, one or two thousand inhabitants in each county were governed by, and sought redress of their grievances in, their own courts. This feature of early Maryland and Virginia society was crucial to the maintenance of order.[51]

Protest and Rebellion

In the fifty-five years after its foundation, Maryland experienced armed clashes with Virginians in the 1630s, near collapse during Ingle's Rebellion of 1645, a pitched battle in 1655 between Lord Baltimore's forces and those of the parliamentary government established three years earlier, an antiproprietary coup in 1660, an abortive uprising in 1676, and the overthrow of Baltimore's rule in Maryland's Glorious Revolution of 1689. These events would seem to lend powerful support to Bernard Bailyn's assertion that Chesapeake political structure "was too new, too lacking in the sanctions of time and custom, its leaders too close to humbler origins and as yet too undistinguished in style of life" to provide lasting political stability.[52] Although there is some truth in this statement, such an interpretation does not account for the persistence of antiproprietary sentiment that was a major factor in Maryland politics throughout the century and makes little reference to the link (if any) between periodic political upheavals and widespread social discontent.

The most important sources of political instability in Maryland were constitutional and religious. Baltimore's title to rule was founded on the charter of June 1632, which empowered him to "ordain, Make and Enact Laws, of what kind soever" with "the Advice, Assent, and Approbation of the Free-Men of the same Province, or the greater part of them, or of their Delegates or Deputies whom We will shall be called Together for the Framing of Laws." Although George and Cecilius Calvert both subscribed to England's ancient

51. W. A. Roberts, ed., *Elizabethan Court Rolls of Stokenham Manor [Devon], 1560–1602* (Kingsbridge, Devon, 1984). The quote is from Sharpe, *Crime in Early Modern England*, 39.

52. Carr, "Sources of Political Stability," *Md. Hist. Mag.*, LXXIX (1984), 44; Menard, "Maryland's 'Time of Troubles,'" *Md. Hist. Mag.*, LXXVI (1981), 125; Bailyn, "Politics and Social Structure," in Smith, ed., *Seventeenth-Century America*, 102. In fairness to Bailyn, his article focuses on the causes of political instability in Virginia leading to Bacon's Rebellion and does not address Maryland.

constitution and the pivotal role played by the king-in-Parliament, neither believed that their native country's mature form of government was a suitable model for governing a fledgling colony in America. Hence the inclusion of the bishop of Durham's clause in the first charter, which invested the lord proprietor with executive authority unfettered by popular institutions.[53]

It is important to bear in mind the political context in England. The grant of Charles I to Baltimore and the early years of political formation in the new colony took place against a background of growing consternation at home: notably with the king's religious policies, his refusal to convene Parliament, a pacific foreign policy that did nothing to assist the Protestant struggle in Europe against ascendant Catholic forces, the perceived arbitrary imposition of taxes, developments in Ireland under Wentworth, and the growing influence of Catholics at court. Antipopery played a major role in the disaffection of large numbers of the ruling class and populace from the king and was a critical factor in the crisis of the 1640s, not only because to English Protestant sensibilities Catholicism reeked of idolatory, superstition, and ignorance but, crucially, because it was associated with tyranny, absolutism, and the destruction of individual liberties. Catholicism, it was widely believed, was inimical to the rights of English people guaranteed by Magna Carta, the common law, and Parliament.[54]

Baltimore may have genuinely believed that he needed the extensive executive powers allowed him by his charter if he was successfully to establish authority and order in Maryland, but it can be easily seen why opponents viewed these developments with misgivings, especially considering Baltimore's Catholicism. Neither is it surprising, in this context, that the Provincial Assembly quickly tried to assert its claim to be considered a form of provincial parliament, the principal guardian of traditional English rights and liberties against the feudal privileges of the proprietor.

Political conflict between successive proprietors and settlers, as David Jordan suggests, revolved around the precise nature of the rights and privileges of each. The Calverts saw their task as initiating and enacting legislation on behalf of the people with their advice and consent, but they did not believe they were bound by the Assembly, which was merely a conciliar body. This view was emphasized by Phillip Calvert in an address to the lower house in 1669:

53. Jordan, *Foundations of Representative Government*, 2–7.

54. Caroline M. Hibbard, *Charles I and the Popish Plot* (Chapel Hill, N.C., 1983); Anthony Fletcher, *The Outbreak of the English Civil War* (London, 1981); John Miller, *Popery and Politics in England, 1660–1688* (Cambridge, 1973), chap. 4.

They are not to Conceive that their privileges run paralell to the Commons in the Parliament of England, for that they have no power to meet but by Virtue of my Lords Charter, so that if they in any way infringe that they destroy themselves; for if no Charter there is no Assembly, No Assembly no Privileges. Their power is but like the common Council of the City of London which if they act Contrary or to the overthrow of the Charter of the City run into Sedition and the Person Questionable.[55]

Settlers based their claims on the explicit reference in the charter to an assembly of freemen or their representatives whose consent was required for the passage of laws and on the fact that colonists were to be considered English subjects with "all the privileges, franchises and liberties" of the kingdom of England. All the major upheavals of the century reflected this constitutional struggle to one degree or another.

Ingle's Rebellion and the troubles of the 1650s were a direct outcome of civil war in England. Richard Ingle, a London shipmaster, was arrested in 1644 for treasonable words against the king, "viz [the king (meaning or Sovereigne Lord king Charles) was no king, neither would be a king, nor could be a king, unles he did joine wth the Parlamt]." Armed with letters of marque authorizing him to seize any vessels in the king's service, he returned to Maryland in February 1645 to settle old scores and, after capturing St. Mary's City, proceeded to plunder Catholics and Protestants alike who refused to take an oath of loyalty to Parliament. The outcome was catastrophic. Governor Leonard Calvert fled to Virginia, and Baltimore's government collapsed, leaving the colony in the hands of Ingle and William Claiborne (one of Baltimore's most potent political adversaries). Unchecked pillage followed, encouraging many planters to move across the Potomac or to the Eastern Shore. Only late in 1646, with the aid of a force from Virginia, was Calvert able to restore his authority.[56]

Anti-Catholic sentiment was in evidence before and during the rebellion. Thomas Bushell complained to the Provincial Court in 1643 that he had been slandered by Michol Harker, spinster, who alleged that he said "he hoped there would be nere a Papist left in maryland by may day: to the damage of the pl[ainti]f and the quaestioning of his life." Ingle justified his plundering not only by appealing to the rules of war but also to the fact that his enemies were Papists. "It pleased God," he wrote, "to enable him to take divers places

---

55. Quoted by Jordan, *Foundations of Representative Government*, 97.
56. Menard, "Maryland's 'Time of Troubles,'" *Md. Hist. Mag.*, LXXVI (1981), 124–140; *Md. Archives*, IV, 241 (brackets in source).

from them." A decade later, antipopery manifested itself in the erection of a Puritan government in Maryland under the leadership of William Fuller. In the Puritan tract *Babylon's Fall*, Leonard Strong objected to Baltimore's "Arbitrary and Popish Government" and to the oath of loyalty imposed on settlers that upheld "Antichrist." He also charged the governor, William Stone, and Council with popery and fomenting rebellion against Cromwell's authority in the colony. A force raised by Stone to reestablish proprietary government was repulsed on the river Severn in March 1655 to the great rejoicing of the Puritans.[57]

Similar sentiments, fear of popery and arbitrary government, persisted after the Restoration and the collapse of Josias Fendall's short-lived attempt to elevate the Assembly to sovereign power in the province. In 1676 the writers of "Complaint from Heaven with a Huy and crye and a petition out of Virginia and Maryland" charged Baltimore's regime with gross corruption, nepotism, arbitrary taxation, and mismanagement. "Wee doe not exclaime against reall and necessary Taxes and Duties, without which the Country can not subsist," the petitioners wrote, "but against sutch Fines and leavis that are onely to maintaine my Lord and his Champions in their princeship, and not the peoples good nor the Country's welfare." They warned of an international conspiracy: "Pope Jesuit [is] determined to over terne Engl[an]d with feyer, sword and distractions, within themselves, and by the Maryland Papists, to drive us Protestants to Purgatory within our selves in America, with the help of the French spirits from Canada. . . . Unmask the Vizard, and y[o]u will see a young Pope and a New Souveraigne pepe out of his [Baltimore's] shell."[58]

On the eve of the overthrow of the government of Maryland in 1689, rumors circulated along the lower Western Shore that Catholics were inciting the Senecas to "kill the Protestants before the shippes come in For after the shippes come the protestants would kill all the papists." Other rumors told of nine thousand French and Indians landing in Maryland to hold the colony for Baltimore and James II. When Captain Richard Smith sought to raise troops to support the proprietor, he found that his men were unwilling "to fight for the papists against themselves." In an appeal sent to the English government in November, the revolutionaries emphasized that they were driven to act by the "Injustice and Tyranny under which we groan" and the

57. *Md. Archives*, IV, 234; Land, *Colonial Maryland*, 46; Leonard Strong, *Babylon's Fall* (1655), in Clayton Colman Hall, ed., *Narratives of Early Maryland, 1633–1684*, Original Narratives of Early American History (New York, 1910), 235–244.

58. *Md. Archives*, V, 134, 141, 145.

pernicious consequences of Baltimore's "Unlimited and Arbitrary pretended Authority." They reported how "Churches and Chappels (which by the said Charter should be Built and Consecrated according to the Ecclesiastical Laws of the Kingdom of England) to our great Regret and Discouragement of our Religion are erected and converted to the use of Popish Idolatory and Super-stition. Jesuits and Seminary Priests are the only Incumbents . . . as also the chief Advisers and Councellors in Affairs of Government."[59]

Fundamental constitutional issues were at stake: was the government to be arbitrary, or representative? What was the role of religion in state and society? Political instability in Maryland was a consequence of the persistent struggle over these vital questions and was generated both within the colony itself and in England. Aside from Ingle's Rebellion and the challenge posed by Claiborne's claim to Kent Island, the most serious threats to Baltimore's government came from the colony's ruling classes (or those that aspired to be part of the governing clique) rather than from below. There were no popu-lar rebellions in Maryland during this period.[60] As discussed earlier, class hostilities were voiced in the "Huy and crye," and conditions for poorer planters worsened considerably after 1680, but lower-class discontent was not the major cause of upheavals at the provincial level. Apart from the mid-1640s, daily life for the vast majority of the population was little disturbed by the power struggles that accompanied periodic changes of government in Maryland.

Bacon's Rebellion is rightly seen as one of the key moments of Virginia's history. What began as an unauthorized attempt to raise a militia led by Nathaniel Bacon, Jr., to fight the Indians rapidly turned into rebellion and civil war. In less than a year, between summer 1676 and spring 1677, the country erupted into armed insurrection, and the authority of Sir William Berkeley, who had governed the colony for nearly thirty years, crumbled in the face of widespread popular hostility that eventually forced him to return to England a disgraced and ruined man. In the fighting between Bacon's and Berkeley's forces, marauding soldiers and sailors plundered indiscrimi-nately, destroying thousands of pounds worth of property. On Septem-ber 20, Jamestown itself was put to the torch by Bacon's men. An uneasy peace was restored only by the arrival from England of a squadron of six

59. Carr and Jordan, *Maryland's Revolution of Government,* 47, 59; Charles M. Andrews, ed., *Narratives of the Insurrections, 1675–1690,* Original Narratives of Early American History (New York, 1915), 305, 307–309.

60. The abortive uprising in Calvert County in late August 1676 was the closest Maryland came to a popular revolt.

men-of-war, eight transports, one thousand redcoats, three hundred officers and staff, and three royal commissioners charged with suppressing the revolt and inquiring into the factors that had caused it.[61]

What does Bacon's Rebellion reveal about law, order, and constituted authority in Virginia? Was the violence unleashed during the upheaval symptomatic of an immature society, unstable and half-formed, where bitter and pervasive hostilities lurked just beneath the surface? Was the exploitation of servants, slaves, and poor planters by the elite bound to lead to an explosion of lower-class resentment at one time or another? Or is the crisis best conceived of as an intraelite struggle between those, like the Ludwells, Lees, and Beverleys, who benefited from Berkeley's regime and those who did not?[62]

Bacon's Rebellion is quite unlike any other revolt in the Chesapeake during the seventeenth century, both because of the scale of support given by the lower and middle classes to the gentry (militia officers, burgesses, and Baconians) who challenged Berkeley and the scope of reforms they demanded. In this respect, it comes closer to a popular uprising than any of the other revolts. From the beginning the rebellion had two distinctive facets. First was a determination to carry an offensive war against all Indians to make the frontiers safe for English settlement. Second was a broad-ranging program of reforms designed to undo the perceived injustices of Berkeley's regime, notably the high taxes that fell inequitably on poorer planters, the engrossment of profitable offices by small, privileged cliques favored by the governor, the unaccountability of officeholders to taxpayers, and the embezzlement and waste of public funds.

The underlying causes of the rebellion were evident a decade earlier. Henry Norwood, former royalist and Virginia's treasurer, outlined complaints that were common hearsay in 1667. First were the "extream and greivous taxes" that planters "ly under Continually and yet the tobbaccoes that are Raised not Expended to the desired end": several hundred thousand pounds had been raised for building forts, "and yet no forts that are any

---

61. Webb, *1676*, 101.

62. Classic accounts of the rebellion are Thomas J. Wertenbaker's *Virginia under the Stuarts, 1607–1688* (Princeton, N.J., 1914), 115–224; and *Torchbearer of the Revolution: The Story of Bacon's Rebellion and Its Leader* (Princeton, N.J., 1940); Craven, *Southern Colonies*, chap. 10. See also Wilcomb E. Washburn, *The Governor and the Rebel: A History of Bacon's Rebellion in Virginia* (Chapel Hill, N.C., 1957); Jane D. Carson, *Bacon's Rebellion, 1676–1976* (Jamestown, Va., 1976); Billings, ed., *The Old Dominion*, 243–249; Webb, *1676*, bk. 1; and Warren M. Billings, John E. Selby, and Thad W. Tate, *Colonial Virginia: A History* (White Plains, N.Y., 1986), chap. 4.

wayes serviceable built in the Country." A similar amount had been levied for "maintaining of agents in England," but "yet no businesse effected." Two million pounds had been raised for building forts "at the heads of the Rivers *upon great mens plantations and settlements*." Fourth were complaints about the "great Injuryes that is done in the Courts by the Insinuation of some that Make advantages by the governors passion, Age, or weaknesse" and "the great Sway that those of the Councell bear over the Rest of the Assembly in matter of Lawes." Finally, there were objections to Berkeley's Indian policy of "tollerating and lycensing some to trade with the Indians though barbarous Enemyes whereby they were furnished with powder and Shot." In Norwood's opinion, "the main Cause of those tumults" was "the not tymely Suppressing the Incursions of those formidable Savages whereby many men were Cut off and severall plantations deserted."[63]

High taxation, Stephen Saunders Webb comments, was "the great grievance" of planters throughout the Chesapeake, but it was the use to which public money was put, rather than taxes per se, that was the main source of unrest. Levies had been raised on specious grounds merely to line the pockets of the "Grandees" at the expense of the poor. Where the need for taxes was evident, as for example to provide defenses against Indian attack, the money had been wasted or frittered away, leaving planters on the frontier vulnerable to lightning raids. In fact, there was a general suspicion that both Berkeley and Baltimore were more sympathetic toward the Indians, with whom they traded, than toward their own people. So in 1676 the people fought on two fronts against "oppressive grandees and the dangerous Indians." It was, as the petitioners acknowledged, "a miserable extremity the poore inhabitants are and see themselves [in,] viz. with oppression and warr from within and Hazard of life and Estate by Indians from without and at hom."[64]

Grievances drawn up in Virginia in the aftermath of Bacon's Rebellion reveal the same concerns. Complaints from Isle of Wight County stressed the "great oppressions" of recent years: the people "evrie year being more and more opprest with great taxes . . . and unnecessarie burdens." "*Whereas* formerly it was accounted a great leavie that was 40: or 50: pounds of tobacco *per* each," now "two hundred a head yearly" was paid, "but for what we know not." It was demanded that the uses to which annual levies were put be made public, "and that ther may noe more gifts be given to noe particular

63. H[enry] Norwood to Joseph Williamson, 17 July 1667, CO 1/21, fol. 158 (my emphasis), Public Record Office, London.

64. Webb, *1676*, 70–75.

person or persons whatsoever nether in publick or by private, which hath been, one only means to make us poore and miserable." Besides the usual grievances about heavy taxes, government mismanagement, and Indians, residents complained of the cupidity of local "great men" who profited from handouts or perks of office at the expense of the majority of planters. Colonel Joseph Bridger, with several other "Gentlemen," spent "forteen or fifteen thousands pounds of tobacco from our countrie" in negotiations during two or three days about county boundaries, "which wee humbly conceave is on great oppression." Bridger had several men fined for not attending militia musters, but no one knew what had happened to the money. It was supposed that "Corll *Bridger* makes use to his own private Interest." Similarly, Major Powell received twelve pounds per poll to purchase ammunition for the county, "which wee never had." Members of the local elite scrambled for office because "they doe find such a great benefit by it" and "predominate over the poor comentrie." [65]

Plenty of examples from other counties of complaints about the frequency and profligacy of assemblies, nepotism, favoritism, and corruption could be given. A report of June 1676 informed Whitehall that most people believed that the main reason for high taxes was that "the Assembly meets so often and that the members have such high allowances." There was also widespread discontent about the inequity of taxation: "A poor man who has only his labour to maintain himself and his family pays as much as a man who has 20,000 acres." Giles Bland told Sir Joseph Williamson a few months earlier that the people had many grievances and there was "little respect for the [colony's] government." [66]

As the price of leaf tumbled and tobacco became increasingly a poor man's crop, money made from office became more and more attractive to unscrupulous provincial magnates: Attractive not only because the rapid rise in the number of tithables produced (potentially) an enormous increase in revenue but also because of the absence of the traditions and restraints of England. Colonial elites thus had much greater opportunities to embezzle personal fortunes from the public purse. Men like Colonel Bridger, Edmund Scarborough and John Custis of the Eastern Shore, John Carter of Lancaster, the Ludwells of James City, Robert Beverley and Richard Lee of Middle-

65. H. R. McIlwaine, ed., *Journals of the House of Burgesses of Virginia, 1659/60–1693* (Richmond, Va., 1914), 101–103.

66. *Ibid.*, 105–113; CO 1/36, fols. 109–110, 111–112, Public Record Office (CW VCRP, 657); Webb, *1676*, 29–30, 41–42, 160–162; Morgan, *American Slavery, American Freedom*, chap. 13.

sex wielded far more power as justices, sheriffs, and burgesses in their respective counties than their peers in English shires.[67]

In England, the reconstruction of traditional political order after the restoration of Charles II was based firmly on an appeal to law. "The reaction towards authority," Paul Seaward argues, "was not so much towards the personal power of the Crown as towards the impersonal authority of the law, towards all that the Crown stood for against the confusion of the last twenty years: legalism and legitimacy, the ancient ways of the English constitution." While Restoration gentry were determined to reassert their social and political prominence in the localities, they were obliged to do so within the confines of the law and constitution that governed the entire settlement. Strengthening of gentry power was brought about, for the most part, by strictly constitutional means. Berkeley and the Calverts, on the other hand, were less restricted by this consideration and had much more license than English provincial rulers to interpret their powers as they felt fit. In this respect, complaints about arbitrary government during the Civil War and Interregnum somewhat resemble complaints in the Chesapeake between 1660 and 1690. Far removed from the agencies of central government—the court, Privy Council, offices of state, Parliament, the king's courts, and assizes—which checked the power of overmighty subjects in English counties, the grandees of Maryland and Virginia had almost free rein to run colonial affairs as they wished. The Restoration desire to return to just laws and the ancient constitution had little bearing on the relationship between colonial elites and ordinary people in the Chesapeake after 1660, as many of the latter's complaints testify.[68]

A neglected aspect of the rebellion is the degree to which Bacon and his followers initially tried to cast their opposition to the governor's authority in legitimate constitutional forms. Even before Bacon was adopted as their

67. Webb provides a graphic account of the problems encountered by royal officials in dealing with "Berkeleyans" after Bacon's Rebellion (*1676*, 127–163). Morgan has a rather different view but also stresses the problems that central government in England faced trying to control Virginia's ruling class (*American Slavery, American Freedom*, chap. 14).

68. Paul Seaward, *The Cavalier Parliament and the Reconstruction of the Old Regime, 1661–1667* (Cambridge, 1989), 45; Alan Everitt, *The Community of Kent and the Great Rebellion, 1640–1660* (Leicester, 1966), 219–225; J. S. Morrill, *The Revolt of the Provinces: Conservatives and Radicals in the English Civil War, 1630–1650* (London, 1976). For a later interpretation of the relationship between English local and central government, see Anthony Fletcher, *Reform in the Provinces: The Government of Stuart England* (New Haven, Conn., 1986).

leader, the frontiersmen of the upper parts of the James River had petitioned the governor for a commissioned officer to lead them against the Indians whose "Murders, Rapines and outrages" throughout the colony had been met by indecision in the Council chambers at Jamestown. Bacon, too, sought a commission and later justified his defiance of Berkeley in terms of preserving "his Majesties Honour and the Publick good without any reservation or by Interest." His manifesto denied that "wee have in any manner aimed at subverting the setled Government," but, rather, his actions had been forced upon him by the "Oppressions" and self-interest "of those whom wee call great men." "How much wee abhorre those bitter names" of "Traitor and Rebell," he wrote. "May all the world know that we doe unanimously desire to represent our sad and heavy grievances to his most sacred Majesty as our Refuge and Sanctuary, where wee doe well know that all our Causes will be impartially heard and Equall Justice administered to all men." [69]

Bacon's Oath, which purportedly required those taking it to resist even the troops dispatched to quell the revolt, stated: "1. You are to oppose what Forces shall be sent out of England by his Majesty against mee, till such tyme I have acquainted the King with the state of this country, and have had an answer. 2. You shall sweare that what the Governor and councill have acted is illegal and destructive to the country, and what I have done is according to the Lawes of England. 3. You shall sweare from your hearts that my comission is lawfull and legally obtained." [70]

Backed by a commission wrung from Berkeley at gunpoint and supported by the majority of burgesses and some of the Council, Bacon "found ready cooperation" from the people generally. A report that reached England in October stated that Bacon played "Rex" in the colony and that most people, if not joining him, favored his pretenses. Although his army was mainly composed of poorer men, including in the later stages servants and slaves, he also enjoyed the support of middle- and upper-class planters who had considerable influence locally. Bacon's Oath, for example, was put to the commons by county justices and militia officers. [71]

Many believed they were not in rebellion but did the king's will in resisting attacks of enemy Indians. Others argued that Berkeley and the Council had abrogated their authority by their manifest failure to defend the colony from

69. Billings, ed., *The Old Dominion*, 267, 278–279; "Narrative of Bacon's Rebellion," *VMHB*, IV (1896–1897), 121.

70. Andrews, ed., *Narratives*, 122.

71. Craven, *Southern Colonies*, 386; SP 29/385, Public Record Office (CW VCRP, 6268, item 248).

outside aggression. At a convention held at Middle Plantation (the future Williamsburg) in early August, it was asserted that "whereas Sir Wm Berkeley Kt, late Governor, hath absented himself from the Governmt and Care of this his Ma[jes]ties distracted Country of Virginia," an assembly should meet the following month to remedy the colony's "Blood and Confusion." This was not a "revolutionary replacement for the colonial assembly," Stephen Saunders Webb argues, but an appeal to tradition in seeking to restore the colony's welfare by placing their faith in the bastion of their liberties, an assembly elected by "housekeepers and freemen."[72]

Bacon's only chance of success was convincing the king that he had taken up arms to defend settlers from the ravages of Indian attack and the gross exploitation of Berkeley's clique of grandees. Reports circulating in England by the autumn, however, branded him a rebel, and he was never able to free himself from that stigma. The belief that armed resistance to Berkeley, the crown's representative, was justified because of the old governor's incompetence was hardly likely to appeal to a king whose own father had died on the scaffold at the hands of revolutionaries. Moreover, as Bacon's measures became more extreme—such as the freeing of servants and slaves recruited into his army and talk of declaring independence from England— he gradually lost the loyalty of the bulk of the planters who had supported him earlier. By the time of his death in late October his cause was doomed.[73]

The rebellion was not intended, as Bacon's critics alleged, "to Levell all." Class hostility was in evidence on both sides, but there was no attempt to overturn the social order: the plundering and destruction of property was opportunistic rather than a coherent plan to redistribute the estates of the rich among the poor. Neither did county government irrevocably break down. How often courts met during the worst of the troubles is uncertain, since, for most counties, including Lancaster and Lower Norfolk, records for the crucial months have not survived. But most benches were operating by the spring of 1677, busy collating the grievances required by the royal commissioners for their report to the crown.

The rebellion is best interpreted, not as indicative of the inherent fragility of Virginia society, but as a massive protest against the failures of Berkeley's second term that attempted to sweep away a corrupt elite and restore the traditional rights of Englishmen. As in most provincial or village revolts in England and throughout Europe in this period, participants saw themselves as conserving old liberties and defending the status quo, not overturning it.

72. Webb, *1676*, 48–49.
73. Craven, *Southern Colonies*, 388–389.

The ancient tradition of resistance to tyranny, censured by Tory Anglicans who elevated passive obedience to an article of political faith, resurfaced in Virginia in 1676 as it was to do in England twelve years later during the Glorious Revolution. Berkeley was charged with breaking the cardinal principles that bound all rulers to their subjects in an implicit contract: defense of the realm, provision of justice according to law, moderation of arbitrary power and self-interest, and the protection of individual rights. The revolt of 1676–1677 was an attempt to bring the grievances of settlers to the king's attention as a preliminary to seeking redress. Insofar as the upheaval precipitated the demise of Berkeley's regime and forced the crown to scrutinize the affairs of the colony more closely than at any other time since the collapse of the Virginia Company in the 1620s, they succeeded.[74]

Until 1676, according to Jon Kukla, "Virginia experienced no episodes of internal collective violence or civil disorder." In 1624, when the colony came under the control of the crown, in 1652 when Berkeley handed over power to parliamentary commissioners, and in 1660 at the Restoration "major transfers of political authority occurred in potentially explosive circumstances without disruption of the polity."[75] During Bacon's Rebellion, Virginia experienced harrowing months of violence and pillage, but colonial society was not permanently disfigured by the upheaval. The accepted social hierarchy, gentry rule, and law and order were not fatally undermined, nor were their institutional expressions.

Judged by the standards of contemporary England rather than New England, neither Virginia nor Maryland appears to have been a chronically violent and unstable society. In England, men of Kent participated in anti-enclosure riots during the late 1540s and early 1550s, Wyatt's Rebellion against Mary Tudor in 1554, and sporadic food riots from the 1580s through the 1630s. Gloucestershire and Kent experienced pitched battles, sieges, plundering, anti-Parliament insurrections, and military occupation during the English Revolution. Within forty years, one Stuart king had been beheaded and another forced to flee from the country never to return. Instead of viewing early modern England as congenitally unstable, however, social historians have interpreted riot and rebellion as responses to complex and rapid social, economic, and political change. In fact, far from condemning the period as disorderly, English historians have been impressed by the durability of traditional notions of hierarchy and the capacity of governing

---

74. Yves-Marie Bercé, *Revolt and Revolution in Early Modern Europe: An Essay on the History of Political Violence*, trans. Joseph Bergin (Manchester, 1987), 4–9, 28–33, 35.

75. Kukla, "Order and Chaos," *AHR*, XC (1985), 296.

institutions to survive the recurrent crises of the sixteenth and seventeenth centuries.[76]

Considered in this light, the periodic challenges to proprietary rule in Maryland and Bacon's Rebellion in Virginia appear less dramatic. Rather than being symptoms of chronic social and political instability, they, like events in the parent country, were reflexive adjustments to far-reaching changes in the Anglo-American world. Life in the colonies could be hard and brutal, and we should not underestimate the difficulties that settlers encountered in adjusting to novel conditions, but perhaps we should be more impressed by their successes in creating a social order that reflected many traditional English assumptions about wealth, birth, rank, and the reciprocal obligations of the rulers and the ruled. During the second half of the century, Chesapeake society lost the contingent character that had marked the early years of settlement. The primacy of the law in governing and regulating social relations and the establishment of local and provincial institutions that reflected the basic premises of governance practiced at home ensured that Maryland and Virginia, like England, were intensely governed societies. This was a lasting achievement.

76. Peter Clark, *English Provincial Society from the Reformation to the Revolution: Religion, Politics, and Society in Kent, 1500–1640* (Hassocks, 1977), 79–89, 229–251; Barrett L. Beer, *Rebellion and Riot: Popular Disorder in England during the Reign of Edward VI* (Kent, Ohio, 1982), 152–153; Peter Clark, "Popular Protest and Disturbance in Kent, 1558–1640," *Economic History Review*, 2d Ser., XXIX (1976), 365–382; Andrew Charlesworth, ed., *An Atlas of Rural Protest in Britain, 1548–1900* (London, 1983), 8–81; Everitt, *Community of Kent and the Great Rebellion*, chaps. 6–8; J. P. Kenyon, *The Civil Wars of England* (New York, 1988), 80–82. For food riots and popular protest against the enclosure of wastes and forest in Gloucestershire, see Buchanan Sharp, *In Contempt of All Authority: Rural Artisans and Riot in the West of England, 1586–1660* (Berkeley, Calif., 1980), 15, 42, 82–96, 218–220; Roger B. Manning, *Village Revolts: Social Protest and Popular Disturbances in England, 1509–1640* (Oxford, 1988), 127–129.

On durability of traditional notions, see Fletcher and Stevenson, eds., *Order and Disorder*, 38; Brewer and Styles, eds., *An Ungovernable People*, 17–20; E. P. Thompson, *Customs in Common* (London, 1991).

9

Inner Worlds: Religion and Popular Belief

In 1645 the parliamentary newssheet *Mercurius Civicus* reported an unusual story from America. "God's goodnesse hath beene lately very eminent in delivering me and my family from the Indian massacre," the correspondent wrote.

> Upon the first day of April my wife was washing a bucke[t] of clothes, and of a sudden her clothes were all besprinkled with blood from the first beginning to the rincing of them, at last in such abundance as if an hand should invisibly take handfuls of gore blood and throw it upon the linnen. Where it lay all of an heape in the washing-tub, she sent for me in, and I tooke up one gobbet of blood as big as my fingers end, and stirring it in my hand it did not staine my fingers nor the linnen: Upon this miraculous premonition and warning from God having some kinde of intimation of some designe of the Indians (though nothing appeared till that day) I provided for defence, and though we were but five men and mistrusted not any villiany towards us before: yet we secured our selves against 20 savages which were three houres that day about my house. Blessed be the name of God.[1]

At first sight the story appears another example of the remarkable providences experienced by Puritan settlers on God's errand in New England. In fact, the miracle that saved the writer's life and his family took place, not in the Bible Commonwealth, but in Virginia on the eve of the Indian uprising of 1644.

That Virginia seems an unlikely setting for such an occurrence owes in large part to the scholarly emphasis given to the precocious secularism of

---

1. Joseph Frank, ed., "News from Virginny, 1644," *Virginia Magazine of History and Biography*, LXV (1957), 86–87.

early Chesapeake society, contrasted to the "aggressive, reforming Protestantism" and "deep Christian religiosity" of New England. Immigrants went to Virginia and Maryland to make money, not to contemplate their spiritual welfare. The weakness of the Anglican church in Virginia and its absence in Maryland appear to confirm that most settlers were unconcerned about formal religious practice. But although religious issues were not as prominent in the lives of settlers as in the northern colonies, one ought not infer that religion was unimportant or that colonists quickly shed their beliefs as irrelevant baggage. A dozen Anglican churches were established in Virginia by 1634 and another fifty by 1668. The vestry became an important feature of local society and, despite a chronic shortage of clergymen, was able to provide at least rudimentary instruction by the appointment of lay readers. Nonconformists established flourishing congregations in Lower Norfolk, Nansemond, Isle of Wight, Charles, and Anne Arundel counties as well as along the Eastern Shore, areas that later became fertile ground for Quakerism. Catholics, Anglicans, Independents, Presbyterians, Anabaptists, and Quakers lived side by side in Maryland. Further, a range of traditional beliefs relating to witchcraft and magic also survived the transatlantic crossing.[2]

2. The quotations are from Jon Butler, *Awash in a Sea of Faith: Christianizing the American People* (Cambridge, Mass., 1990), 55. On weakness of Anglican church, see the introduction to Lois Green Carr, Philip D. Morgan, and Jean B. Russo, eds., *Colonial Chesapeake Society* (Chapel Hill, N.C., 1988), 1–46; Darrett B. Rutman, "The Evolution of Religious Life in Early Virginia," *Lex and Scientia: Journal of the American Academy of Law*, XIV (1978), 191; Philip Alexander Bruce, *Institutional History of Virginia in the Seventeenth Century: An Inquiry into the Religious, Moral, Educational, Legal, Military, and Political Condition of the People . . .* , 2 vols. (New York, 1910), I, pt. 1; George Maclaren Brydon, *Virginia's Mother Church and the Political Conditions under Which It Grew*, 2 vols. (Richmond, Va., 1947–1952); William H. Seiler, "The Anglican Parish in Virginia," in James Morton Smith, ed., *Seventeenth-Century America: Essays in Colonial History* (Chapel Hill, N.C., 1959), 119–142; Lawrence C. Wroth, "The First Sixty Years of the Church of England in Maryland, 1632–1692," *Maryland Historical Magazine*, XI (1916), 1–41; William Hand Browne *et al.*, eds., *Archives of Maryland*, 72 vols. to date (Baltimore, 1883–), V, 130–132 (hereafter cited as *Md. Archives*).

On establishment of Anglican churches, see Warren M. Billings, ed., *The Old Dominion in the Seventeenth Century: A Documentary History of Virginia, 1606–1689* (Chapel Hill, N.C., 1975), 71–72.

On lay readers and non-Anglicans, see Butler, *Awash in a Sea of Faith*, 37–55; Babette M. Levy, "Early Puritanism in the Southern and Island Colonies," American Antiquarian Society, *Proceedings*, LXX (1960), 122–157; Michael Graham, "Meetinghouse and Chapel: Religion and Community in Seventeenth-Century Maryland," in

The full complexity and richness of England's religious heritage was not transferred to Maryland and Virginia, no more than to New England or any other part of the Anglo-American world in the seventeenth century, but important elements of the religious spectrum were established and undoubtedly made a significant contribution to the development of society along the Bay. This chapter assesses settlers' attitudes toward the church, religious doctrine, magic, and popular belief. More so than previous chapters, it explores the mind of seventeenth-century colonists: how they perceived the afterlife, their attitudes toward sin and salvation, and their awareness of a supernatural world where the invisible forces of good and evil were ever present around them.

Religion, Church, and Society

In view of the role played by national churches in the process of European state building during the sixteenth century, it is hardly surprising that the crown believed the transfer of the Church of England to America was essential for the maintenance of social order. It was axiomatic to the founders of Virginia that there could be no settled government without organized religion; church and state were the twin pillars of civilized society. Consequently, Anglicanism arrived with the first colonists. Early governors were required by James I to ensure that "the true word, and service of God and Christian faith be preached, planted, and used, . . . according to the doctrine, rights, and religion now professed and established within our realm of England." Ministers and civil authorities alike were determined that settlers should not fall into "ungodly disorders." Services were to be held every Sun-

---

Carr, Morgan, and Russo, eds., *Colonial Chesapeake Society*, 242–274; Kenneth L. Carroll, "Maryland Quakers in the Seventeenth Century," *Md. Hist. Mag.*, XLVII (1952), 297–313; *Md. Archives*, V, 133.

On witchcraft and magic: Bruce, *Institutional History*, I, 278–289; Francis Neal Parke, "Witchcraft in Maryland," *Md. Hist. Mag.*, XXXI (1936), 271–298; Richard Beale Davis, "The Devil in Virginia in the Seventeenth Century," in Davis, *Literature and Society in Early Virginia, 1608–1840* (Baton Rouge, La., 1973), 14–42; Jon Butler, "Magic, Astrology, and the Early American Religious Heritage, 1600–1760," *American Historical Review*, LXXXIV (1979), 317–346; Rutman, "Evolution of Religious Life," *Lex and Scientia*, XIV (1978), 193–202. No attempt is made to consider Indian and African religious beliefs in this chapter, but for suggestive accounts see Helen C. Rountree, *The Powhatan Indians of Virginia: Their Traditional Culture* (Norman, Okla., 1989), 130–139, 186–191; and Mechal Sobel, *The World They Made Together: Black and White Values in Eighteenth-Century Virginia* (Princeton, N.J., 1987), 171–225.

day, and attendance was compulsory. Sir Thomas Dale's *Lawes Divine, Morall, and Martial* of 1612 laid down stringent punishments—loss of food rations, whipping, a stint in the galleys, and ultimately, for persistent offenders, the death penalty—for absence from church, blasphemy, and disobedience.[3]

In 1619, Virginia's first Assembly, held in the "Quire of the Church" in Jamestown, formally recognized the church's spiritual and temporal responsibilities by enacting a series of measures relating to the exercise of ministerial functions in conformity with "the Ecclesiastical lawes and orders of the churche of Englande." In addition to conducting divine service every Sunday morning, ministers were enjoined to "Catechize suche as are not yet ripe to come to the Com[munion]" in the afternoon. They were responsible also for disciplining those who "will not forbeare . . . skandalous offenses, as the suspicions of whoredomes, dishonest company keeping with woemen and suche like." Five years later the Assembly reiterated its intention that "there be an uniformity in our church as neere as may be to the canons in England; both in substance and circumstance, and that all persons yeild readie obedience unto them under paine of censure." Desiring, Jon Butler has argued, to "sacralize the landscape in traditional English ways," the Assembly ordered the "Comander of every Plantatione" to provide "some decent howse or sittinge roome be erected and builte for the service of God" and to ensure that "theire severall Plantacons had" "a place stronglie paled or fenced in for the buriall of the dead." In succeeding years, the organization of the church and clerical duties were brought more closely into line with the mother church in England: vestries were empowered to levy assessments for the maintenance of the church and minister; procedures were established for the submission of presentments for moral and spiritual offenses to the county courts; ministers were required to keep parish registers of christenings, marriages, and burials; churches were to be provided with a Bible, Book of Common Prayer, and ornaments; and vestries were ordered to take care of the parish poor.[4]

---

3. Perry Miller, *Errand into the Wilderness* (Cambridge, Mass., 1956), 106; Seiler, "Anglican Parish," in Smith, ed., *Seventeenth-Century America*, 121–123; Butler, *Awash in a Sea of Faith*, 38–40.

4. "Proceedings of the Virginia Assembly" (1619), in Lyon Gardiner Tyler, ed., *Narratives of Early Virginia, 1606–1625*, Original Narratives of Early American History (New York, 1907), 271–272; William Waller Hening, ed., *The Statutes at Large: Being a Collection of All the Laws of Virginia . . .* , 13 vols. (1809–1823; Charlottesville, Va., 1969), I, 69, 123, 144, 155, 180, 240–243; Butler, *Awash in a Sea of Faith*, 40; H. R. McIlwaine, ed., *Minutes of the Council and General Court of Colonial Virginia*, 2d ed. (Richmond, Va., 1979), 105; Virginia Bernhard, "Poverty and the Social Order in Seventeenth-Century Virginia," *VMHB*, LXXXV (1977), 141–155.

As a result of this legislation two enduring principles were established: first was the primacy of Anglicanism and the liturgy of the Church of England, "for the administration of the word and sacrament, . . . duely performed according to the booke of common prayer, allowed by his Ma'tie and confirmed by consent of parliament"; and second was an alliance between church and state to enforce social and moral discipline. The traditional duty of the English church to supervise and regulate moral and spiritual matters was directly transferred to Virginia.[5]

Yet in important respects the colony's leaders failed in their effort to create a strong and unified church. Despite the exhortations of early missionaries, propagandists, and pious governors like Dale, Virginia did not emerge as a "new Jerusalem." There was no sustained Anglican crusade to convert the multitude of "savages, heathens, infidels, idolaters etc." who inhabited America; and neither, after an initial burst of enthusiasm, were qualified and respected ministers recruited in sufficient numbers to keep pace with population growth and the spread of English settlement. William Castell believed that, far from converting the "natives" to Protestantism, English settlers "for want of able and conscionable Ministers . . . are become exceeding rude, more like to turne Heathen, then to turne others to the Christian faith." John Hammond observed that "Virginia savouring not handsomely in England, very few of good conversation would adventure thither, (as thinking it a place wherein surely the fear of God was not), yet many came, such as wore Black Coats, and could babble in a Pulpet, roare in a Tavern, exact from their Parishioners, and rather by their dissolutenesse destroy than feed their Flocks." Even the Assembly was forced to recognize the poor character of the clergy and ordered that "mynisters shall not give themselves to excesse in drinkeing, or riott, spendinge theire tyme idellye by day or night, playing at dice, cards, or any other unlawfull game." By the early 1640s only five to ten clergymen were resident in the colony, a figure that increased little if at all over the next quarter of a century despite the massive surge of immigration and an increase in population from about eight thousand in 1640 to approximately thirty thousand by 1670.[6]

5. Hening, ed., *Statutes at Large*, I, 241; Martin Ingram, *Church Courts, Sex, and Marriage in England, 1570–1640* (Cambridge, 1987), Seiler, "Anglican Parish," in Smith, ed., *Seventeenth-Century America*, 128–129, 142.

6. Wesley Frank Craven, *The Southern Colonies in the Seventeenth Century, 1607–1689* (1949; Baton Rouge, La., 1970), 177–182; Butler, *Awash in a Sea of Faith*, 38–46; Richard Eburne, *A Plain Pathway to Plantations* (1624), ed. Louis B. Wright (Ithaca, N.Y., 1962), 23–26; Patricia U. Bonomi, *Under the Cope of Heaven: Religion, Society, and Politics in Colonial America* (Oxford, 1986), 16–17; *Petition of W[illiam] C[astell] Exhibited to the High*

Just as at home, the Church of England's brand of Anglicanism did not evolve as a fiery evangelical creed, and settlers who yearned for an all-consuming religious experience turned to Puritanism, Quakerism, and, in Maryland, Catholicism. Disputes over payment of ministers' salaries, induction or contracts of "hiring," and the upkeep of the glebe occupied church-state relations far more than theological issues. While the ruling elite wished to create a robust religious presence in the colony, they had no intention of erecting a church sufficiently strong to challenge their own power: hence their resistance throughout the century to the establishment of church courts in Virginia and to the notion of a resident bishop. In the context of the opposition to Laudianism in the 1630s and the emergence of an increasingly latitudinarian temperament in the Church of England after the Restoration, their intransigence was perhaps understandable, but the result was a seriously weakened church, subordinate to the magistracy.[7]

Despite these difficulties, by 1640 parishes and vestries were firmly in place and constituted a framework for the provision of religious observance, moral discipline, and pastoral care in Virginia. By contrast, settlers arriving in Maryland encountered a very different attitude toward religion. In trying to secure a haven for Catholics, George and Cecil Calvert adopted a policy of toleration that eschewed a state-supported church and turned instead to a privatistic view of religion where one's beliefs, whether Catholic or Protestant, were one's own affair so long as the public peace was not disturbed. The Act concerning Religion of 1649 spelled out that individuals were not to be "troubled, Molested, or discountenanced" because of their religious convictions. Rather than a bold new formula for social and religious

---

Court of Parliament Now Assembled, for the Propagation of the Gospel in America, and the West Indies; and for the Setling of Our Plantations There . . . (London, 1641), 10; John Hammond, *Leah and Rachel; or, The Two Fruitfull Sisters Virginia and Mary-land* (1656), in Clayton Colman Hall, ed., *Narratives of Early Maryland, 1633–1684*, Original Narratives of Early American History (New York, 1910), 287; James P. Walsh, " 'Black Cotted Raskolls': Anti-Anglican Criticism in Colonial Virginia," *VMHB*, LXXXVIII (1980), 21–36; Hening, *Statutes at Large*, I, 158.

7. R. G., *Virginia's Cure; or, An Advisive Narrative concerning Virginia* (1662), in Peter Force, comp., *Tracts and Other Papers, Relating Principally to the Origin, Settlement, and Progress of the Colonies in North America*, 4 vols. (1836–1846; Gloucester, Mass., 1963), III, no. 15, 3–4; *Md. Archives*, V, 130–132; Craven, *Southern Colonies*, 177–182; Bonomi, *Under the Cope of Heaven*, 41–43; G. R. Cragg, *From Puritanism to the Age of Reason: A Study of Changes in Religious Thought within the Church of England, 1660 to 1700* (Cambridge, 1966), chaps. 2–4; Arthur Lyon Cross, *The Anglican Episcopate and the American Colonies* (New York, 1902), chap. 1.

harmony, toleration resulted from a pragmatic concern for the well-being of Catholics in a colony where they were heavily outnumbered by Protestants. Since it was politically impossible for the Calverts to establish the Roman Catholic church in Maryland, an acceptance of Catholicism was achieved by disassociating "matters of Religion" from the government.[8]

An important aspect of this policy was that settlers were not obliged by law to pay tithes for the support of a church and ministry. Individuals could make voluntary donations for the construction of private chapels and churches and for the payment of clergymen, but, unlike anywhere else in the Anglo-American world of the seventeenth century, these were left entirely to their discretion. Shorn of state support, public worship withered, and a large proportion of the population became "essentially unchurched." On average, until 1675, only one Anglican minister served the province, and altogether only six ministers are known to have served in Maryland from its foundation until 1690. In the absence of an established church and with the adoption of toleration, several Protestant Nonconformist denominations sought to fill the spiritual vacuum left by the decay of Anglicanism. Hundreds of Puritans left Virginia to settle in Anne Arundel and Somerset counties in the 1640s and 1650s. Three Presbyterian ministers, Church of England clergy before their ejection from English benefices, were active for varying periods in Charles County between 1659 and 1679, and Presbyterian churches were also formed in Somerset County. The first Quakers arrived in 1655 or 1656 and quickly established meetings on both sides of the Chesapeake Bay. Within twenty-five years, at least fourteen meetings were scattered throughout the colony. Even so, when Lord Baltimore informed the Privy Council in 1676 that three-quarters of Maryland's settlers were "Presbiterians, Independents, Anabaptists, and Quakers," he was undoubtedly exaggerating. No certain figures exist, but it is unlikely that Catholics and Nonconformists together made up more than about a quarter to a third of the province's twenty thousand inhabitants. The rest, nominally Anglicans, had to make do without organized religion.[9]

8. Bonomi, *Under the Cope of Heaven*, 22–23; John D. Krugler, "Lord Baltimore, Roman Catholics, and Toleration: Religious Policy in Maryland during the Early Catholic Years, 1634–1649," *Catholic Historical Review*, LXV (1979), 49–75; John Tracy Ellis, ed., *Documents of American Catholic History* (Milwaukee, Wis., 1955), 115–117.

9. Lois Green Carr, lecture delivered to St. Mary's College, 1984; Butler, *Awash in a Sea of Faith*, 52–53; Graham, "Meetinghouse and Chapel," in Carr, Morgan, and Russo, eds., *Colonial Chesapeake Society*, 256–260; Levy, "Early Puritanism," AAS, *Procs.*, LXX (1960), 130–131, 133, 140; Wroth, "The First Sixty Years," *Md. Hist. Mag.*, XI (1916),

It is worth emphasizing that English immigrants who settled north of the Potomac encountered a very different religious landscape than did their counterparts in Virginia. Because the Church of England was not established in Maryland until after the Glorious Revolution, the fundamental unit of English local society, the parish, was entirely missing during the first sixty years of the colony's history. For many immigrants, whether deeply religious or not, this void must have represented a radical break with the past. Equally perplexing to many settlers was the attempt to encourage religious pluralism and toleration in a period when a state church was universally held as the sine qua non of orderly and peaceful government. The attempt was certain to be viewed with suspicion by Anglicans who saw it principally as a means to invigorate Catholicism at the expense of the true Protestant church, hence the periodic outbursts of antipopery sentiment throughout the century. Moreover, while Sir William Berkeley proscribed Nonconformity and enforced Anglican supremacy in Virginia, the Calverts seemed content to allow the proliferation of all sorts of sects and the steady spread of paralyzing apathy. So little effort was "taken or Provision made for the building up Christians in the Protestant Religion," wrote the Reverend John Yeo from Maryland to the archbishop of Canterbury in 1676, that "not only many Dayly fall away either to Popery, Quakerism or Phanaticisme but alsoe the lords day is prophaned, Religion despised, and all notorious vices committed soe th[a]t it is become a Sodom of uncleaness and a Pest house of iniquity."[10] Both Chesapeake colonies experienced difficulties in establishing organized religious observance and recruiting able ministers, but developments in Virginia and Maryland exhibit important contrasts.

Lower Norfolk, Lancaster, and Middlesex counties illustrate how individuals and communities coped with the problem of constructing a religious context for their lives in the New World. Thus, Anglican services were held in Lower Norfolk from the county's inception, initially at the houses of Captain John Sibsey and Captain Adam Thorowgood before the first church was constructed at Sewell's Point. Mr. John Wilson served as minister of Elizabeth River Parish until his death in 1640. Little is known about him apart from a complaint early in 1639 that he had "received great loss and damage by not

1–41; Louis Dow Scisco, "The First Church in Charles County," *Md. Hist. Mag.*, XXIII (1928), 155–162; J. William McIlvain, *Early Presbyterianism in Maryland* (Baltimore, 1890), 6–18; Rufus M. Jones, *The Quakers in the American Colonies*, 2 vols. (London, 1923), I, 267–278.

10. See Chapter 8, above; *Md. Archives*, V, 131.

receiving his corn due the last year for tithes." Those who had "denied the payment" were ordered to pay, but their refusal may be a hint that they did not like him. He was succeeded by a young Calvinist minister, Mr. Thomas Harrison. The wording of the parishioners' agreement with him is significant: "Whereas the Inhabitants of this Parrishe being this day convented for the p[ro]vidinge of themselves an able minister to instructe them concerninge their soules health mr Thomas Harrison tharto hath tendered his service to god and the said Inhabitants . . . wch his said tender is well liked." To "testifie their zeale and willingness to p[ro]mote gods service," they agreed to pay him the generous sum of one hundred pounds a year.[11]

By the time of Harrison's appointment the county had divided into two parishes—Elizabeth River and Lynnhaven, each with its own vestry and minister—but the split involved more than a recognition of the two major areas of settlement. During the late 1640s Elizabeth River became the scene of a bitter struggle between Puritans and Anglicans for control of the parish.[12]

Several hundred Puritans led by Captain Christopher Lawne and the Bennett family had settled along the southern bank of the James River in the 1620s and 1630s, principally in Isle of Wight and Nansemond counties. The proximity of a strong Puritan presence on the east side of the Nansemond River, adjoining the county boundary of Lower Norfolk, probably encouraged the growth of an Independent congregation in Elizabeth River Parish. William Durand, John Gookin, and John Hill, prominent in the early development of Puritanism in Lower Norfolk, all had connections with the Bennetts of Nansemond. John Hill had been a cosigner, with Richard Bennett, Daniel Gookin, and sixty-eight others, of a letter to the "Pastors and Elders of Christs Church in New-England" bemoaning "their sad condition for the want of the means of salvation." Edward Johnson of Massachusetts recalled: "About the yeer 1642 the Lord was pleased to put it into the heart of some godly people in Virginia, to send to N. E. for some of the Ministers of Christ, to be helpfull unto them in instructing them in the truth, as it is in Jesus. The Godly Mr. Philip Bennit coming hither, made our reverend Elders acquainted with their desires, who were very studious to take all opportuni-

11. Lower Norfolk County, Virginia, Minute Book, transcript of Wills and Deeds A, 2 vols. (1637–1646), I, fols. 1–5, 18, 27, 50 (Colonial Williamsburg, microfilm, reel M 1365–2; references to CW microfilm will be given only with the first citation); George Carrington Mason, "The Colonial Churches of Norfolk County, Virginia," *William and Mary Quarterly*, 2d Ser., XXI (1941), 143.

12. Lower Norfolk County, Minute Book (1637–1646), I, fols. 55, 59. Mr. Robert Powis officiated at Lynnhaven from 1640, or possibly a year or two earlier.

ties for inlarging the kingdome of Christ." These men, Jon Butler observes, "were as 'Puritan' as the New Englanders to whom they were writing." William Durand heard the Puritan divine John Davenport preach in London in the 1630s and kept notes of his sermons, which he later found a source of great spiritual comfort in "this desolate place" in Virginia. He described in a letter to Davenport, now of New Haven, the "wreched and miserable condition" in which they lived and expressed a fear that without godly ministers many ("sinners and backesliders") would fall away from the true path: "Scattered in the cloudy and darke day of temptation, beeing fallen from their first love, and are even as the wife of youth forsaken and desolate . . . for if ever the lord had cause to consume the citties of Sodom and Gomorrah he might as justly and more severely execute his wrath upon Virginia, swoln so great with the poison of sin, as it is become a monster, and ready to burst."[13] Like their counterparts in England and New England, Virginia's Puritans desired a godly society, where the true word was the basis of a pure church, spiritual nourishment, and a reformed laity.

Against the background of the first civil war in England and the attack upon the Church of England, Sir William Berkeley initiated the first of a series of measures to ensure that "Phanaticisme" did not take root in Virginia. Shortly after his arrival, the Assembly, for "the preservation of the puritie of doctrine and unitie of the church," enacted that "all ministers whatsoever which shall reside in the collony are to be conformable to the orders and constitutions of the church of England, . . . and not otherwise to be admitted to teach or preach publickly or privatly." Berkeley and the Council were empowered to expel from the colony all Nonconformists who refused to abide by the legislation. Two years later, Thomas Harrison, who had been persuaded to remain as minister of Elizabeth River, was presented by the churchwardens of the parish "for not reading the book of common prayer and for not administering the Sacrament of Baptism according to the Canons and order presented and for not catechisinge on Sundays in the afternoon according to act of Assembly." The court ordered him to appear before the governor and Council at the next quarter court in Jamestown to

13. John Bennett Boddie, *Seventeenth Century Isle of Wight County, Virginia* . . . (Chicago, 1938), 26–31, 54–59; [Edward Johnson], *Johnson's Wonder-Working Providence, 1628–1651*, ed. J. Franklin Jameson, Original Narratives of Early American History (New York, 1910), 265 (*Wonder-Working Providence of Sion's Savior in New England*, written about 1650–1651 but not published until 1654 [as *A History of New England*]); Jon Butler, *Awash in a Sea of Faith*, 47; Butler, ed., "Two 1642 Letters from Virginia Puritans," Massachusetts Historical Society, *Proceedings*, LXXXIV (1972), 105–109.

answer the charges. Berkeley's insistence on conformity must have been especially irksome, considering the collapse of the state church in the parent country.[14]

Although Harrison may have promised Berkeley that he would conform, it is evident that in practice the Elizabeth River church clung to its Puritan convictions. Eventually the county's high sheriff, Mr. Richard Conquest, together with Captain John Sibsey and Mr. Thomas Ivy, prompted by the governor and Assembly, attempted decisive action. At the end of May 1648 they gave

> publique Notice to the Inhabitants of Elizabeth River . . . to forbeare and desist from theire frequent meetings and usuall assembling themselves togeather, contrary to the lawes and Government of the Collony: And thereupon wee . . . did fynd one named William Durand with much people (men woemen and children) assembled and mett together in the Church or Chapell of Elizabeth River aforesaid, (in the forenoone of the said day) and wee did see the said William Durand goe into and sett the deske, or the Reading place of the said Church, which as alsoe in the pullpitt he hath customarily by the space of three months last past, upon severall Sabboth dayes (as by certaine and credible informacons to us given) preached to the said people.

Conquest, in the name of the king, commanded the congregation to disband immediately and "retorne to theire severall dwellings, or habitations." However, two justices, Mr. Cornelius Lloyd and Mr. Edward Lloyd, together with John Fernihaugh and "divers others (whose names are not yet certaynly to us knowne) . . . not onely denyed and refused to ayde and assist the said high sheriffe to suppresse the said faction and sedition . . . but alsoe they . . . did goe about to rescue the said William Durand from and after Arrest." Berkeley, having lost all patience, banished both Harrison and Durand from the colony, and Cornelius Lloyd was fined by the county court three thousand pounds of tobacco for having "very much abused his Ma[jes]t[y]s Com[mission]ers in words, as alsoe in not obeying theire Comands."[15]

14. Hening, ed., *Statutes at Large*, I, 277; Lower Norfolk County, Minute Book (1637–1646), II, fol. 39. Butler suggests the Elizabeth River vestry that cited Harrison was installed by Governor Sir William Berkeley (*Awash in a Sea of Faith*, 47). William Durand hoped that events in England would soon lead to the establishment of the "true profession and practise of religion" (Butler, ed., "Two 1642 Letters," MHS, *Procs.*, LXXXIV [1972], 108).

15. Lower Norfolk County, Wills and Deeds B (1646–1651), fols. 74–75, 82, 89, 92, 103 (CW, microfilm, reel M 1365–17).

The departure of Harrison for England and Durand to Maryland did not reconcile Puritan parishioners to the established church. Edward Lloyd, Mr. Thomas Meares (another justice), Mr. Thomas Marsh (who had stood security for Durand), Edward Selby, Richard Day, George Kemp, Richard Owens, John Norwood, and others, described by the sheriff as "seditious sectaries" and "schismatics," were presented to the court the following year for "obstinately" refusing to attend divine service. The court admonished them for breaching several statutes requiring attendance at church (carrying a fine of twenty pounds per month) and warned them that their refusal to obey the sheriff was "in disdaine and great Contempt of his Highnes Lawes and very much tends to the p'nitious [pernicious] example of all other Malefactors."[16]

No doubt Lloyd and other Puritans would have argued the contrary. By the summer of 1649 a republic had been proclaimed in England, the monarchy and the House of Lords had been abolished, and the Church of England had been abandoned. It was the governor, Council, and courts, not Lloyd and his group, who were out of step with events by refusing to recognize the new regime and by their determination to maintain Anglicanism even though its government, liturgy, and ritual had been proscribed in England. Nevertheless, as long as Berkeley held Virginia loyal to the Stuarts, the courts continued to enforce legislation against Nonconformists. Lloyd and the others were given a couple of months "to Informe theire Judgem[en]ts and to Conforme themselves, according to the Lawes establish'd." Tiring of the struggle, they chose not to confront Berkeley again and, encouraged by the newly appointed governor of Maryland, Captain William Stone, moved to a more congenial religious climate up the Bay.[17]

The departure of Harrison, Durand, and their followers was a severe loss to the county. As the authorities recognized, Harrison and Durand were popular preachers and had served Elizabeth River continuously for almost a decade. Lloyd and his fellow justice, Thomas Meares, had represented the county in the Assembly on several occasions in the mid-1640s, and both, along with Thomas Marsh and Durand, went on to hold important

16. *Ibid.*, fols. 120–121.

17. Claire Cross, "The Church in England, 1646–1660," in G. E. Aylmer, ed., *The Interregnum: The Quest for Settlement, 1646–1660* (London, 1972), 99–120; Lower Norfolk County, Wills and Deeds B (1646–1651), fols. 120, 148, C (1651–1656), fols. 111, 143, D (1656–1666), fol. 154 (CW, microfilm, reel M 1365–17, 18); Boddie, *Isle of Wight County*, 59–60. Edward Lloyd moved to the "Seavern in An arrandell County" (Providence), along with Thomas Marsh, Thomas Meares, and others. Durand was already there.

offices in Maryland. Independency was removed from Lower Norfolk, but the cost was great, as events were to prove. In May 1649 Elizabeth River's vestry, "with the free and full consent of all the freemen," chose Mr. Sampson Calvert to be their minister. Less than six months after his arrival he confessed to committing the "fowle offence" of adultery with the wife of Laurence Phillipps and subsequently quit the parish. The county's problems worsened with the death of Robert Powis in the winter of 1651–1652, and for several years neither parish had a minister. In December 1654 members of a "Grand Inquest" informed the court of a "gen'all breach of the Sabboth day through out the whole County, wch we conceive is most chiefly occasioned through want of a godly Minister." Fearing that church discipline might soon collapse, the court ordered both vestries to meet with parishioners after Christmas to decide on a course of action. The following year the court asked Captain Thomas Willoughby, who planned a visit to England, to "p[ro]vide a Minister of Gods word for us." When that came to nothing, they sent an invitation to a Mr. Moore in "mannadus" [Manhattan], in "New England," which also proved unsuccessful.[18]

County rulers, such as those of Lower Norfolk, found themselves in an impossible position. They were obliged to enforce the Assembly's laws against Nonconformists and hence expel Puritan preachers like Harrison and Durand, but there were insufficient Church of England ministers willing to replace them. Exiling religious enthusiasts only served to weaken further the tenuous hold exerted over the religious lives of inhabitants. Lancaster County's leaders encountered similar difficulties in securing and retaining a minister during the 1650s and early 1660s. Mr. Alexander Cooke agreed to serve from March 1653, but whether he arrived or how long he remained is a mystery. The Reverend John Gorsuch, who replaced him, died in 1656, and Mr. Samuel Cole, appointed a year later, died in 1659, at which time the county was left without a minister. In October 1661 the court, "takeing into consideracon the great want of the Ministry, that hath beene in this Countie and conceiving it to arise from the smallnes of the p'ishes, not able to give such a competency as might invite Mynisters to officiate amongst us," ordered the constables of each parish to summon inhabitants to "the usual place of meeting" to consider whether they would be willing to share

18. Edward C. Papenfuse *et al.*, eds., *A Biographical Dictionary of the Maryland Legislature, 1635–1789*, 2 vols. (Baltimore, 1979, 1985), I, 290, II, 534, 574–575, 593–594; Lower Norfolk County, Wills and Deeds B (1646–1651), fols. 88, 115, 129, 209, C (1651–1656), fols. 113–114, 117, 158, D (1656–1666), fol. 29.

a minister between them until such time as they could afford their own.[19] The two parishes south of the Rappahannock, however, decided to seek their own incumbent, perhaps fearing that a minister who served the entire county would spend more time on the northern side of the county than on the southern side.

If Lower Norfolk's justices believed that the removal of the Independent faction would solve the problem of religious schism in the county, they were to be sorely disappointed. Along with difficulties raised by the failure to find a suitable minister to replace Robert Powis and a spate of witchcraft allegations in the late 1650s, a new threat to the peace emerged. In August 1660, the newly reinstated governor, Sir William Berkeley, wrote to the county's sheriff, Richard Conquest, admonishing him for "not stopping the frequent meetings of this most pestelent sect of the quakers." He was ordered "not to suffer any more of theire meetings or Conventicles." Quakers were described in an act passed by the Assembly in March as "An unreasonable and turbulent sort of people . . . teaching and publishing, lies, miracles, false visions, prophesies and doctrines, which have influence upon the comunities of men both ecclesiasticall and civil endeavouring and attempting thereby to destroy religion, lawes, comunities and all bonds of civil societie." Severe penalties were imposed on anyone bringing Quakers into the colony, on householders holding meetings in their homes, and on those who attended. Quakers could be fined, imprisoned, and banished.[20]

There is no evidence that Conquest took any immediate action, but in June of the following year Benjamin Forby was arrested for "admitting and suffering assemblies of quakers at his house" and was sent to James City for trial. He was imprisoned for twenty-one days and ordered to pay twenty-five pounds of tobacco for each day of his captivity. Later that summer, Isabel Spring called Mr. Thomas Browne, who had just been reappointed to the bench, "traitor" when he came to her house "to suppresse the quakers." Browne had first been commissioned in 1648 but left the bench two years later "because he would not engage nor would not serve under the rebels"

19. Lancaster County, Virginia, Deeds Etc., no. 1 (1652–1657), 41–42, Orders Etc. (1655–1666), 1, 91, 153, 158 (CW, microfilm, reels M 1363–1, 117–8); Brydon, *Virginia's Mother Church*, I, 133.

20. Lower Norfolk County, Wills and Deeds C (1651–1656), fol. 157, D (1656–1666), fols. 6, 237, 264; Hening, ed., *Statutes at Large*, I, 532–533; Kenneth L. Carroll, "Quakerism on the Eastern Shore of Virginia," *VMHB*, LXXIV (1966), 172; Jones, *Quakers in the American Colonies*, I, 270–271.

during the Interregnum. In restoring him to the commission in 1661, Berkeley made it clear that a principal factor had been "the manifestacon of his loyalty to his Ma[jes]tie" in the 1650s. The upheavals caused by the revolution in England and the demise of royal government in Virginia in 1652, followed eight years later by the Restoration, served to complicate religious differences in the county and sharpened political antagonisms between Anglicans, Nonconformists, and religious radicals.[21]

Over the next few years the court's campaign against Quakers intensified. Twenty individuals, including the daughter of the incumbent sheriff, were presented to the court in December 1662 and fined 200 lbs. of tobacco each. In June 1663, Berkeley wrote to the justices urging them "to p[ro]vide t[ha]t the abominated seede of the Quakers spread not in yo[u]r County" and added four new men to the bench to assist in their suppression. Accordingly, Richard Russell was fined £100 for holding a meeting in his house, and Richard Yates, Robert Spring (husband of Isabel), and Benjamin Forby were each fined £20 for not attending church. Other fines during 1663 amounted to more than 20,000 lbs. of tobacco. In the same year it was reported to the Assembly that John Porter, burgess for Lower Norfolk, was "loving to the Quakers and stood well effected towards them, and had been at their meetings, and was so far an Anabaptist as to be against the baptising of children." He was expelled from the House after refusing to take the oath of supremacy. In November, thirty-five people who had gathered at Richard Russell's were arrested, and ten days later the sheriff broke up another meeting "aboard the Shipp Blessinge rideing at anchor in the southerne branch of Elizabeth River."[22]

Prosecutions declined sharply after 1664. The heavy fines and continual disruption of meetings may have led to a fall in Quaker numbers and discouraged people from joining. Elizabeth Emerson, for example, fined 200 lbs. of tobacco for attending a meeting, appeared before the court in 1664 "absolutely renouncinge the sd. sect of the Quakers" and promised "her obedience for the future." But, possibly, Quakerism did not seem such a threat to local society by the mid-1660s, and the court may have decided to live and let live. The sect had not been suppressed, as Berkeley desired, but neither had it flourished.[23]

---

21. Lower Norfolk County, Wills and Deeds B (1646–1651), fol. 75, D (1656–1666), fols. 302, 305–307, 312–313, 328.

22. *Ibid.*, D (1656–1666), fols. 360, 373–374, 380, 392, 396; Boddie, *Isle of Wight County*, 113–114.

23. Lower Norfolk County, Wills and Deeds D (1656–1666), fols. 380, 400, 435–436.

About 40 individuals had been named as Quakers or had been cited for attending meetings in the early 1660s, not a large figure compared to the rapid growth of the county's population from slightly more than 400 tithables in 1660 to 590 four years later (600–900 adults, assuming a ratio of 2 men for every woman)—but not insignificant.[24] From what sort of backgrounds did they come?

They were not drawn from a particular social stratum, such as the middling rank, for example. Among them were representatives from the county's ruling class, like John Porter, Sr., and his son, both commissioned in 1655, and Mr. William Robinson, who was appointed to the bench in 1660. John Porter, Jr., was sheriff in 1659–1660 and burgess in 1663. He was married to the daughter of another justice and sheriff, Colonel John Sidney. Mrs. Mary Emperor was the wife of Captain Francis Emperor, a justice, sheriff, and surveyor of Virginia. Further down the social scale were more modest planters: Nicholas Seaborne had been transported to the colony in 1636 as an indentured servant; Thomas Halloway and his wife worked a small plantation of 150 acres; Richard Yates, son of a shipwright, owned 350 acres at Deep Creek on the Southern Branch of the Elizabeth River. Three men, William Gouldsmith, Richard Joanes, and John Johnson, served as constables in the 1650s. Others may have been less respectable. Anne Godby was involved in several defamation cases from 1648 onward, including an accusation of witchcraft against a neighbor's wife in 1659. When John Joncks called her a "whore" in the following year, the bench found itself unable to disagree and declared her behavior to be "very unhansome and not becoming a Civill woman." Bitteras Barnaby was presented to the court on three occasions, suspected of fornication and adultery with another Quaker, William Chichester. Chichester was ordered to "fortwith put [her] away . . . from his house, and for the future not to keepe or frequent her company." [25]

It is difficult to assess their wealth. Of sixteen individuals whose landholdings could be traced, nine had small estates of 150–400 acres, four of 400–750 acres, one of 750–1,200 acres, and two of more than 1,200 acres. None of the five men whose inventories survive died rich. Mary Emperor's plantation was valued at 2,000 lbs. of tobacco (£12–£13) at the time of her husband's death in 1662; the rest of his movable estate came to £96. Richard Russell, who was given the heaviest fines by the court, died in 1668 worth about £123. Robert Spring's estate was valued about £150 a decade later, but

24. Individuals attending Quaker meetings are listed *ibid.*, fols. 302, 305–307, 328, 360, 373–374, 386, 392, 396, 400. For numbers of tithables, see fols. 268–269, 412–413.

25. James Horn, Biographical Files (Quakers), Lower Norfolk County, Virginia.

he was heavily in debt. Two small-to-middling planters, James Johnson and Nicholas Seaborne, were worth £70 and £60, respectively.[26]

Men and women who attended Quaker meetings in Lower Norfolk came from a broad cross section of county society, embracing justices and sheriffs, large and small planters, recent immigrants and longtime residents. There is little to distinguish them from the wider population except for one characteristic. All of those whose area of residence could be traced were from the western half of the county and lived along, or near, the three main branches of the Elizabeth River. None was from the Lynnhaven River region or the broad tract of land running from Sewell's Point to Lynnhaven Bay. Quakerism took root where Puritanism had earlier flourished. A similar pattern can be found elsewhere in the Chesapeake. Quaker meetings spread along the Eastern Shore of Maryland and Virginia, in Nansemond, Isle of Wight, Surry, and Anne Arundel counties, all areas with strong Puritan connections. As in England, many men and women who were attracted to separatism in the 1640s were later converted to Quakerism in the 1650s and 1660s.[27]

There is little direct evidence of Quaker experience in Lower Norfolk, but a confrontation in York County gives a glimpse of Quakers' hostility to the official church and of the county elite's fears. In August 1661, Mr. Thomas Bushrod called two Anglican ministers, Mr. Justinian Aylmer and Mr. Phillip Mallory, "a Couple of Espicopall knaves" and "Antichrists" who "preceeded from the pope." He also challenged "the Magestrates to apprehend the Quakers at their meetinge if they durst." That same month the York court noted that there had been several meetings of Quakers in the county, "especially by Women," and, following Berkeley's instructions, ordered that "all Woemen who . . . continue their said unlawfull meetings, and broach their schismaticall and hereticall Doctrines and opinions, should by the adjoyn-

26. Lower Norfolk County, Wills and Deeds D (1656–1666), fols. 346, 389, 404, E (1666–1675), fols. 33, 156, Deed Book no. 4 (1675–1686), fols. 57–58 (CW, microfilm, reel M 1365-1, 18).

27. Levy, "Early Puritanism," AAS, *Procs.*, LXX (1960), 122–123, 133, 156–157. Of the 21 individuals traced in Lower Norfolk, 8 were from the Western Branch, 7 from the Southern Branch, and 6 from the Eastern Branch. Quaker meetings also developed in Henrico, Warwick, and York counties; see "Proceedings in York County Court," *WMQ*, 1st Ser., XI (1902–1903), 29–33; Colonial Williamsburg, York County Project, DOW (3), 66, 125, 131; B. Reay, "Quakerism and Society," in J. F. McGregor and Reay, eds., *Radical Religion in the English Revolution* (Oxford, 1984), 141–143. Thomas Meares, Thomas Marsh, Richard Owens, and possibly William Durand became Quakers in the 1650s (J. Reaney Kelly, *Quakers in the Founding of Anne Arundel County* [Baltimore, 1963], 24–28).

ing Magistrate be tendred the oathes of Supremacy and Allegiance, and the refusers to be Imprisoned according to Law." Nevertheless, Mrs. Mary Chisman and "Two or Three negroes belonging to hir husband," together with other Quakers, subsequently met "in the woods."[28]

This was the kind of social leveling that the authorities feared most. The meeting of women, slaves, servants, gentlemen, and ordinary planters on equal terms to worship together was not only to the great "dishonour and disservice of God" but would inevitably lead, in their view, to the overturning "of the Countreys peace." The prominence of women, which seems to have been particularly disturbing to the colony's leaders, reflected their role within the Quaker movement in England. "Quaker women" according to Barry Reay, "preached, proselytized, wrote and printed tracts, participated in church government (though in separate meetings and mainly in the area of welfare), and assumed a militant role in the sect's various campaigns." Nearly half of the Quaker missionaries to arrive in America between 1659 and 1663 were women, and the first Quaker to preach in Maryland was a woman, Elizabeth Harris.[29] Quakerism gave women an opportunity to participate more fully in the religious life of their community; the same was true of other less-privileged members of society, servants and slaves.

The attraction of Quakerism lay in its direct appeal to God for spiritual nourishment (freely granted to all men and women willing to open their hearts), the simplicity of ritual, an emphasis on the intrinsic equality of believers, and the importance placed on religious community. These virtues were especially significant in the early Chesapeake, where the lack of ministers and absence of an established church in Maryland eviscerated Anglicanism. Quakerism, according to Michael Graham, "solved the chronic problem of the scarcity of ordained Protestant clergy in the province by emphasizing the priesthood of all believers." There was no need for churches, since meetings could be held in Friends' houses and barns, on shipboard, or in the woods, and there was no need of ministers, since they had their own lay speakers. "Meetings provided a religious environment in which marriages could be solemnized, God worshipped with apostolic purity, and children

28. CW, York County Project, DOW (3), 131, Aug. 26–27, 1661; "Proceedings in York County Court," *WMQ*, 1st Ser., XI (1902–1903), 29–30.

29. CW, York County Project, DOW (3), 66; Reay, "Quakers and Society," in McGregor and Reay, eds., *Radical Religion in the English Revolution*, 144–145; Kenneth L. Carroll, "Elizabeth Harris, the Founder of American Quakerism," *Quaker History*, LVII (1968), 96–111. Of the 40 or so Quakers of Lower Norfolk County, 19 were women, 2 of whom held meetings in their homes.

raised in a vibrant Protestant atmosphere."[30] Vital rites of passage—conversion, marriage, and burial—as well as the humdrum events of everyday life took place against the background of a community of Friends that provided support, guidance, a sense of moral order, and spiritual discipline: virtues that took on greater significance on the frontier.

Religious life in Lancaster and Middlesex counties was much less troubled by doctrinal controversies. In the early years most disputes concerned parish boundaries and the payment of tithes rather than differences over the liturgy or Anglican ritual. Richard Bennett, Daniel Gookin, and William Durand considered the Rappahannock as a possible site for a future Puritan settlement in the early 1640s but later decided prospects were brighter in Maryland. While several of Lancaster's original settlers were from Isle of Wight, Nansemond, and Lower Norfolk counties, they do not appear to have been Nonconformists. Christ Church's vestry, on the south bank, had a firm grip on parochial affairs and was represented by some of the most powerful men in the county. Similarly, on the north side of the Rappahannock David Fox and John Carter, two of the region's wealthiest planter-merchants and both prominent justices, played an important part in the establishment and organization of Whitechapel and Christchurch parishes. Middlesex and Lancaster counties were bypassed by Puritanism and Quakerism, and the Church of England developed unchallenged.[31]

The vestry records of Christ Church Parish illustrate how Middlesex settlers organized church affairs. Mr. Henry Corbin, a justice and vestryman, as a temporary measure until a minister could be found, kept the register of christenings, marriages, and burials. In January 1664, the vestry engaged the services of Mr. Richard Morris, "a Minister now come to Reside wth us"; but although he served "according to Agreement," the parish chose not to retain him, and he was dismissed in 1666. Three "readers" were appointed in his stead to lead divine service every Sunday at the mother church and

30. Graham, "Meetinghouse and Chapel," in Carr, Morgan, and Russo, eds., *Colonial Chesapeake Society*, 260.

31. Nell Marion Nugent, comp., *Cavaliers and Pioneers: Abstracts of Virginia Land Patents and Grants*, 2 vols. (Richmond, Va., 1934, 1977), I, 138–139. Christ Church's vestries of the 1660s and early 1670s included Henry Corbin, Lt. Col. Cuthbert Potter, Maj. Gen. Robert Smith, Sir Grey Skipwith, Sir Henry Chicheley, Robert Beverley, and Capt. Christopher Wormeley; see C. G. Chamberlayne, ed., *The Vestry Book of Christ Church Parish, Middlesex County, Virginia, 1663–1767* . . . (Richmond, Va., 1927), 1–21; Lancaster County, Virginia, Orders (1655–1666), 158, Orders Etc., no. 1 (1666–1680), 81 (CW, microfilm, reels M 117–7, 8).

the upper and lower chapels. The appointment of readers offered a convenient means of maintaining services and had the appeal of being sanctioned by English precedent. In "all parrishes destitute of incumbents," an act of 1661 stated, "there may be for the present necessity readers appointed of sufficient abilities to reade the prayers and homilies of the church . . . and to catechise children and servants according to that excellent forme presenting the church of England as hath beene used in times of queene Elizabeth when there was a scarcity of orthodoxe reformed ministers to supply the congregations."[32]

Christ Church continued to employ readers at the upper chapel and the lower Piankatank church after a new minister, John Shepherd, moved to the parish in 1668, thereby ensuring that services were held at all three locations each Sunday. The arrangement suited the new incumbent, who did not have to divide his time between the three precincts, and suited the parishioners who could attend their own local place of worship. Readers (or clerks) became a permanent presence in the parish and were appointed throughout the ministries of Shepherd and his successors. Other major responsibilities of the vestry included the provision of care for bastard children and the poor and sick and the maintenance of the church and chapels.[33]

Did the unchurching of the bulk of the population in Maryland and the weakness of Anglicanism in Virginia lead to indifference, skepticism, and atheism? How many would have agreed with Thomas Newhouse of Lower Norfolk that "a great part of the Bible was false" or with Captain William Mitchell of Maryland, who, "being amongst a Company of Gentlemen told them that he wondred the world had been Soe many hundred Years deluded with a Man and a Pigeon which . . . [he] attributed to our Saviour Christ and the holy Ghost"? To what extent did "Maryland's decaying Christian presence" engender a "stunning secularity" in the second half of the century?[34]

A variety of factors contributed to the "desacralization" of Chesapeake

32. Chamberlayne, ed., *Vestry Book of Christ Church Parish*, 1, 2, 9; Hening, ed., *Statutes at Large*, II, 29–30, 46–47.

33. Chamberlayne, ed., *Vestry Book of Christ Church Parish*, esp. 16–17. Shepherd served the parish for 15 years until his death in 1683 and was replaced by Duell Pead (see esp. 38, 41). The Reverend Morgan Godwyn was critical of the use of readers, describing them as "leaden Lay-Priests of the Vestries ordination" in a letter to Sir William Berkeley in the late 1660s (quoted in Brydon, *Virginia's Mother Church*, I, 188).

34. Bruce, *Institutional History*, I, 277; *Md. Archives*, X, 173; Butler, *Awash in a Sea of Faith*, 53, 54.

society. The scarcity of ordained ministers meant not only that "settlers heard few sermons and participated in little liturgical exercise" but also that the sacraments of baptism and communion were rarely practiced, burials became private affairs and were increasingly seen as opportunities for heavy drinking and feasting, and church attendance (where churches existed) was sporadic. A "Memorial of what abuses are crept into the Churches of the Plantations," written in 1677 by the bishop of London, complained of the clergy's being "hired (as they terme it) by the yeare and sometimes by the Sermon." In Virginia, vestries "pretend an authority to be intrusted with the sole managem[en]t of Church affairs and so exercise an arbitrary power over the Ministers themselves." Parishes were kept vacant, and the tithe was diverted to uses unrelated to the church. Both church-building and the provision of public burial grounds were neglected. In Maryland, there was "no settled maintenance for the Ministers at all, the want whereof does occasion a totall want of Ministers and divine worship except among those of the Roman beliefe."[35]

The Puritan Durand feared that he and others would soon fall away from the true faith "in this land of darknesse" without the succor of a reformed ministry. "If we continue under these wreched and blind Idoll shepards the very bane of this land," he wrote of the Anglican clergy in 1642, "we are like to perish." For men and women of similar convictions, it was not so much the weakness of the Church of England per se that concerned them as the existence of "so much corruption and false worship." Some Anglicans feared that colonists' profanity had already brought down God's wrath on their heads. The Reverend Roger Green attributed "their long languishing improsperous condition" to "the Curse of God," placed on them because they continued "to rob God in a great measure of that publick Worship and Service, which as Homage due to his great name, he requires to be constantly paid to him, at the times appointed for it, in the publick Congregations of his people in his House of Prayer." Private piety was not enough. In stressing the necessity of public ceremony in the prescribed manner, Green addressed the problem of insufficient churches, the lack of ministers, and nonattendance at divine service and also attacked individuals or groups who had broken away from Anglicanism. Only collective worship, according to the established liturgy in properly constructed churches, would lift God's curse and ensure the colony's future well-being.[36]

35. Butler, *Awash in a Sea of Faith*, 54; PRO CO 1/41, fols. 48–49, Public Record Office, London (CW VCRP, 662).

36. Butler, ed., "Two 1642 Letters," MHS, *Procs.*, LXXXIV (1972), 108; R. G., *Virginia's Cure*, in Force, comp., *Tracts and Other Papers*, III, no. 15, 4–5.

To settlers of strong religious convictions, no doubt the venality and materialism of society represented the "rotten fruits" of colonial life, but what of
the experiences of the majority of inhabitants who were less zealous? Many
men and women presumably developed a casual attitude toward the church.
Nominally Anglican, they paid the parish rate and attended services when a
minister was resident or when vestries enjoined them to do so. Distance from
a church or chapel had an important bearing on the frequency of attendance.
The thrust of Roger Green's letter of 1662 was that the large size of Virginia's
parishes and dispersed settlement pattern discouraged planters from going
to church regularly. Many "of the more remote Families," he wrote, "being
discouraged, by the length or tediousnesse of the way, through extremities
of heat in Summer, frost and Snow in Winter, and tempestuous weather in
both, do very seldome repair thither." Before the construction of a chapel
on the Southern Branch of the Elizabeth River in 1666, for example, planters
would have had to travel seven to eight miles to the chapel near the entrance
of the Eastern Branch and nearly ten miles to the parish church at Sewell's
Point. The development of upper and lower chapels, flanking the mother
church of Christ Church Parish, Middlesex County, is another example of
how local congregations came to be served by their own places of worship.[37]

The chronic shortage of ministers undoubtedly encouraged householders
to look after their own religious needs. John Seaverne of Accomack mentioned in a court case of 1641 seeing Liveing Denwood and his family "att
his house they being att prayers." Thirty years later, in response to inquiries
by the Lord Commissioners of Foreign Plantations about religious instruction in Virginia, Berkeley replied that colonists took "the same course that is
taken in England out of towns; every man according to his ability instructing his children." Some support for Berkeley's observation is found in the
incidence of Bibles, sermons, and pious works found in household inventories. Books appear far more frequently in the inventories of Chesapeake
planters than in inventories of their counterparts in England (see Tables 28–
30). Although titles are not usually given, it is probable that many were
Bibles and religious tracts. In Lower Norfolk County, a fifth of planters' inventories, 1640–1680, explicitly mentioned Bibles. They also owned prayer
books, psalms, and catechisms as well as popular devotional works like *The
Practice of Piety* and *The Whole Duty of Man*. Mrs. Sarah Willoughby's library

37. R. G., *Virginia's Cure*, in Force, comp., *Tracts and Other Papers*, III, no. 15, 4;
Mason, "Colonial Churches of Norfolk County," *WMQ*, 2d Ser., XXI (1941), 141; Darrett B. Rutman and Anita H. Rutman, *A Place in Time: Middlesex County, Virginia,
1650–1750* (New York, 1984), 59, 63.

reflected an orthodox Anglican piety and included a large Bible in folio, two Bibles in quarto, a Latin Bible, two testaments, *The Souls Progress to the Celestial Canaan, Preservation against Sin, The Epistles of St. Anthony, An Exposition on the Ten Commandments, An Exposition on the Lords Prayer, A Treatise of the Divine Essence*, and a book of sermons, besides various practical manuals and classical works.[38]

The ownership of Bibles and prayer books does not necessarily mean that householders conducted their own services or that they even read them. They may have been kept as a form of totem to ward off danger, bad luck, and evil spirits. But men and women who wanted to refresh their spiritual lives by reading the Scriptures could do so, either by acquiring their own copies or by borrowing a Bible from a neighbor.[39]

Wills provide further evidence of individual piety. Although the majority of testators adopted a short preamble bequeathing their souls to God and their bodies to the earth, some were moved to express themselves more fully. Rowland Rowley of Lancaster County, "calling to remembrance the uncertaine estate of this transitory life and that all flesh must yeilde unto death when it shall please God to call," committed his soul "unto Almighty God my Saviour and Redeemer in whom and by the meritts of Jesus Christ I trust and beleeve assuredly to be Saved and to have full Remission of all my Sins and that my Soule with my body at the Gen[era]ll day of resurrecon shall rise againe with Joy and through the meritts of Christs death and passion possess and inheritt the Kingdom of heaven prepared for his electe chosen." Elizabeth Keeling of Lynnhaven trusted "through the meritts of my dearest Saviour Christ Jesus to rest wth him Eternally in glory." Lawrance Plumer of the same parish commended his soul "to God th[a]t gave it me In hope of A Joyfull resurrection through the free grace and mercy of Jesus Christ my onely Lord and Saviour," and Richard Starnell of Elizabeth River affirmed his belief that his body would be "raised againe at the generall day of Judgmt." Joan, wife of John Beale, who recognized her bastard son in her will, confessed "to a sin of wch I am ashamed and do heartily repent and humbly begg Gods gratious pardon and the worlds Pitty." She asked Mr. John Halles to instruct her children "in Litterature, good manners and the fear of God."[40]

38. Susie M. Ames, ed., *County Court Records of Accomack-Northampton, Virginia, 1640–1645* (Charlottesville, Va., 1973), 59; Butler, *Awash in a Sea of Faith*, 45; Lower Norfolk County, Wills and Deeds E (1666–1675), fols. 168–169. Mrs. Willoughby was the widow of Thomas Willoughby II.

39. See, for example, Ames, ed., *County Court Records . . . 1640–1645*, 62.

40. Lancaster County, Virginia, Wills and Deeds no. 5 (1674–1689), 59 (the wills of

Some wealthier planters out of "pious Zeale and love to the Church" made bequests or gifts. John Lloyd, a Catholic of St. Mary's County, bequeathed the bulk of his property to his wife, but in the event of her dying intestate his land and personalty were bequeated to "the s[ai]d Colledge of secular Preists att Doway in ffanders." Luke Gardiner provided in his will to disinherit any of his children who rejected the Catholic faith before the age of twenty-one. He gave twenty-two hundred pounds of tobacco to four priests because he desired "the prayers of the Holy Roman Catholic Church." His fellow resident of St. Clement's Manor, William Brittaine, "To the greater honor and Glory of Almighty God the ever immaculat Virgin Mary and all Saints," freely gave to the Catholic inhabitants of St. Clement's Bay and Newtown sufficient land for the construction of a "Church or Chappel" and a churchyard. Similarly, devout Anglicans donated plate, Bibles, ornaments, and linen to their churches.[41]

How prevalent was indifference? In 1712, Colonel William Churchill of Christ Church Parish left a bequest of £125 for ministers to preach "against the four reigning vices of atheism and irreligion, of swearing and cursing, fornication and adultery and drunkeness." The Reverend Nicholas Moreau of St. Peter's Parish, New Kent County, complained to the bishop of Coventry and Lichfield in 1697 that he had "the very worst parish of Virginia and most troublesome," but added there was an "abundance of good people who are very willing to serve God, but they want good Ministers. . . . If ministers were such as they ought to be," he continued, "I dare say there would be no Quakers nor Dissenters." Lower Norfolk's grand jury reported a general breach of the Sabbath throughout the whole county in 1654, caused chiefly "through want of a godly Minister." Three years later, the bench, noting "severall inormities and transgressions are Comitted agt. God and Man and the parties seldome or never questioned nor Punished," ordered that all such offenses in future would be dealt with by the court. Even so, only a

---

Edward Grimes of the same county and Francis Finch of Lower Norfolk use language the same as or similar to Rowley's: Lancaster County, Deeds Etc., no. 1 [1652–1657], 124–125; Lower Norfolk County, Wills and Deeds E [1666–1675], fol. 133); Lower Norfolk County, Wills and Deeds C (1651–1656), fols. 98, 179, E (1666–1675), fol. 90; will of Joan Beale, 1675 (St. Mary's City Commission transcript of wills, no. 295).

41. *Md. Archives*, XLI, 116, 531; will of Luke Gardiner, 1674 (SMCC transcript of wills, no. 271) (see also Graham, "Meetinghouse and Chapel," in Carr, Morgan, and Russo, eds., *Colonial Chesapeake Society*, 246–253); C. G. Chamberlayne, ed., *Vestry Book of Christ Church Parish*, 25, 27, 35; Chamberlayne, ed., *The Vestry Book of Petsworth Parish, Gloucester County, Virginia, 1677–1793* (Richmond, Va., 1933), 10, 25; Lower Norfolk County, Wills and Deeds D (1656–1666), fol. 77.

few cases of nonattendance and working on Sundays were presented each year by churchwardens and grand jurors. James Githery and John Steele, for example, were reported in 1666 for "not coming to heare divine service," and Richard Joanes and Cornelius Johnson were charged with "Grindeing on the Sabbath day." During the next twelve years there was little concern with enforcing church discipline, but in 1678 the grand jury made another blanket presentment:

> Wee present the ministers of the County and other officers Exersising Ecleseasticall Jurisdiction for nott Loocking that the people Come to Church on the lords day to heare divine service according to the Cannons of the Church of England . . . by wch neglect the lords day is much profaned by Ill disposed people who make noe accompt of the lords day butt what their pleasures Lead them too.

Again, no sustained action appears to have resulted. In succeeding years, one or two parishioners found themselves before the court for fighting, fishing, or working when they should have been in church, but there does not seem to have been much of an attempt to address the disregard of the Sabbath.[42] The clergy of Lower Norfolk probably gave up trying to coerce families who, either because of the distance to church or their convictions, had no intention of attending services every Sunday, if at all.

Parishes with an energetic vestry, a conscientious minister, and a court determined to enforce church discipline were able to maintain a strong Anglican presence in the community. Yet it is improbable that they represented a majority of the colony's parishes in the second half of the century. Every county had its "troublesome" parishioners or "ignorant and undisciplin'd" people who showed little interest in attending church regularly. The net result was a decline in the importance of communal Anglican worship (the close association of community with church) and an increasing emphasis on individual or sectarian responses to religious observance, a trend even more advanced in Maryland. But this was not just a consequence of the chronic shortage of Church of England ministers in the Chesapeake; it was also a reflection of broad changes in the religious complexion of English

42. Bishop [William] Meade, *Old Churches, Ministers, and Families of Virginia*, 2 vols. (Philadelphia, 1857), I, 369; C. G. Chamberlayne, ed., *Vestry Book of Christ Church Parish*, 132, 135; Chamberlayne, ed., *The Vestry Book and Register of St. Peter's Parish, New Kent and James City Counties, Virginia, 1684–1786* (Richmond, Va., 1937), 621; Lower Norfolk County, Wills and Deeds D (1656–1666), fols. 435–436, Deed Book no. 4 (1675–1686), fols. 40, 48, 119, 169, 202.

society: splits within Anglicanism, the appearance of radical religious groups during the 1640s and 1650s, and the rise of dissent after 1660. Neither in England nor in the colonies was the ideal of one church and one nation achieved. Increasingly after the Restoration, the Anglican church was one church among many.[43]

To appreciate the extent of change in the religious lives of settlers, it is important to consider their backgrounds in England. How would colonists from Gloucestershire and Kent, for example, have adapted to conditions in the Chesapeake? Perhaps the most obvious difference was the physical presence of the church in England. Whereas the English countryside was covered with parish churches built of sturdy materials that had stood for half a millennium or more, Virginia's and Maryland's early churches bore a closer resemblance to tobacco barns and lasted about the same length of time, perhaps twenty to twenty-five years. Later churches built of brick were more durable, but they tended to be small by English standards, more like chapels than parish churches. No Norman towers or gothic spires graced the skies of the seventeenth-century tidewater.[44]

New arrivals would have missed the familiar landmarks of parish churches and the equally familiar sound of bells calling parishioners to prayer or marking the important events of the year. They would have quickly realized that the colonial church had been sheared of its courts, officials, and customary functions, most of which were taken over by the vestries and county courts. Missing was the prominent role played by church leaders in politics and government at both the local and national levels. Missing, too, was the conspicuous consumption of archbishops, bishops, and their retinues in cities and cathedral towns. The weakness of the Anglican church in the Chesapeake was therefore reflected by the poverty of both fabric and personnel. Although the parent church in England had suffered severe financial setbacks following the Reformation, it was still a great landowner and was incomparably wealthier than its poor American relation.[45]

43. Chamberlayne, ed., *Vestry Book and Register of St. Peter's Parish*, 621; William Stevens Perry, ed., *Historical Collections Relating to the American Colonial Church* (Hartford,.Conn., 1870), I, 326; Christopher Hill, *Religion and Politics in Seventeenth-Century England* (Brighton, 1986), vol. II of *The Collected Essays of Christopher Hill*, 19.

44. Dell Upton, *Holy Things and Profane: Anglican Parish Churches in Colonial Virginia* (Cambridge, Mass., 1986).

45. Christopher Hill, *Economic Problems of the Church: From Archbishop Whitgift to the Long Parliament* (Oxford, 1956); Rosemary O'Day and Felicity Heal, eds., *Princes and Paupers in the English Church, 1500–1800* (Leicester, 1981).

Despite the fears of commentators such as William Castell and Roger Green, pious settlers did not suddenly apostatize in the colonies. But it would be mistaken to assume that most immigrants were devout believers who shared the established view of liturgy and who uniformly supported the role of the church in English society. Government and church officials were concerned that settlers who had been only loosely committed to Anglicanism in England might abandon it altogether in Virginia and Maryland. It seemed possible that the Chesapeake, like English wood-pasture and forest districts, would become a refuge for all sorts of seditious radical religious sects.

Little is known about colonists' religious backgrounds, but popular attitudes toward church and religion provide a basis for speculating generally about the experiences of settlers before they emigrated. While Anglicanism retained the nominal allegiance of a great majority of men and women in the seventeenth century, it is clear that significant sections of the population had only a vague understanding of state credo. In extreme cases, a motley of beliefs and traditions garnered from pre-Reformation and pre-Christian periods was woven together with contemporary theology to form an eclectic form of religion that owed little to established doctrine. Despite improving clerical standards and the evangelizing efforts of the church, there remained considerable indifference to Anglicanism among the masses, represented by a sheepish lip service to liturgy, nonattendance of divine service, and frequent breaches of church discipline. In studying Wiltshire parishes, Donald Spaeth argues that popular, or "village," Anglicanism—"a simple form of Protestantism" that cared little for church rituals and rigorous religious instruction—was widespread among the laity. No more than half of parishioners received Communion ("the central sacrament of the Church of England") at any time during the year. Parishioners usually turned up at church on Sundays and observed the major holy days such as Christmas, Easter, and Whitsunday, but they did not attend services on all the holy days prescribed by the church, which, including Sundays, would have amounted to more than a quarter of the year. In church, some of the congregation followed the service closely in their own Bibles and prayer books, but others had little idea of what was expected of them and passed the time sleeping or talking.[46]

46. Keith Thomas, *Religion and the Decline of Magic: Studies in Popular Beliefs in Sixteenth- and Seventeenth-Century England* (London, 1971), 189–206; Barry Reay, "Popular Religion," in Reay, ed., *Popular Culture in Seventeenth-Century England* (London, 1985), 96–103; Geoffrey Parker, "Success and Failure during the First Century of the Reformation," *Past and Present*, no. 136 (August 1992), 43–82; Donald Arragon Spaeth,

Kent furnishes numerous examples of lay skepticism and dissent. A lighterman of Ramsgate, told that he must attend divine service, declared that it "was never merry England since we were impressed to come to church." In 1626 Warham Turner, a chandler from Sutton Valence, challenged the minister of his parish to answer him whether the Book of Common Prayer was "subject to the word, or the word to it?" Ten years later, Archbishop Laud was informed that there were "very many refractory persons to the government of the church of England about Maidstone and Ashford and some other parts." So many radical sects existed by midcentury that contemporaries believed it "necessary to distinguish between Christendom and Kent." Anabaptists, Brownists, Muggletonians, Independents, and Quakers all appeared before or during the Revolution. After the Restoration, Nonconformity continued to exert a strong influence in the county. Colonel Thomas Culpeper observed in 1662 that sectaries were "secure and insolent" in "the wilds of Kent," and seven years later episcopal returns drew attention to Anabaptists, Quakers, and Independents, some of whom had been "very active in the late Rebellion." In the early 1680s, James Wilson, vicar of Leeds, wrote to Archbishop William Sancroft that there "is great reason to complain of many of the meaner sort of people besides dissenters from the church who absent themselves from the publick worship, and this is the generall complaint of all parishes amongst us."[47]

During the seventeenth century, many urban centers and ports in Kent, such as Canterbury, Maidstone, Tenterden, Cranbrook, Dover, and Sandwich, developed large congregations of Dissenters, and in numerous villages

---

"Parsons and Parishioners: Lay-Clerical Conflict and Popular Piety in Wiltshire Villages, 1660–1740" (Ph.D. diss., Brown University, 1985), 76–96, 353.

47. Arthur Hussey, "Visitations of the Archdeacons of Canterbury," *Archaeologia Cantiana*, XXVII (1904), 32; Canterbury Cathedral Library, Consistory Court, Ex Officio, Comperta et Dectecta, Deanery of Sutton, 1620–1635 (X.6.4), 100, 255; William Page, ed., *The Victoria History of the County of Kent*, II (London, 1926), 93; Hill, *Religion and Politics*, 92; McGregor and Reay, eds., *Radical Religion in the English Revolution*, 35–36, 38, 144; Mary Anne Everett Green et al., eds., *Calendar of State Papers*, Domestic Series, *of the Reign of Charles II*, 27 vols. (London, 1860–1938), II, *1661–1662*, 107, 555–556; G. Lyon Turner, ed., *Original Records of Early Nonconformity under Persecution and Indulgence*, 3 vols. (London, 1911–1914), I, 13–19. Samuel Parker, archdeacon of Canterbury, observed in 1676 that "the Heads and Preachers of the severall Factions are such as had a great share in the late Rebellion" (II, 27). Wilson is quoted in C. Everleigh Woodruff, "Letters Relating to the Condition of the Church in Kent, during the Primacy of Archbishop Sancroft [1678–1690]," *Arch. Cant.*, XXI (1895), 183.

judging by the Compton Census returns of 1676 large numbers of people were so unenthusiastic about the church they had stopped going altogether.[48]

Gloucestershire's religious landscape was equally varied. Puritanism became increasingly influential in the early seventeenth century, and lectureships were established in Gloucester and several clothing towns, including Dursley and North Nibley. Its development was partly a response to the poor state of the established church. Bishop Godfrey Goodman told Laud in 1635 that the county was full of impropriations (church property held by laymen) and "very mean ministers," whose poverty made them "fall upon popular and factious courses." John Smyth of Nibley agreed. "Appropriacions," he wrote, are "yet suffered to live in this day light of the gospell, to the great hindrance of learninge, the impoverishment of the ministery, decay of hospitallity, and infamy of our religion and profession." Religious conflict intensified during the Revolution with the strengthening of the Puritan party and the arrival of Independents, Anabaptists, Antinomians, Quakers, and Ranters. The Puritan John Corbet, commenting on opponents to the parliamentary cause, observed that the "superstitious adoring of their old way imbittered their spirits against reformed Religion, which to them seemed a peevish affectation of novelty, besides, the hatred and feare of Ecclesiasticall Discipline." Gloucestershire, however, "was more happy than many other parts of the Kingdome by meanes of a practicall Ministry, which hath not onely its powerful working in Divine things, but doth also inable vulgar capacities more fitly to apply themselves to such things as concerne the life of a morall man."[49]

Unsurprisingly, given its growth over the previous half-century, Nonconformity did not quickly wither away after the restoration of the Church of England in 1660. Quakerism in particular "spread mightily" throughout the Southwest and became entrenched in Bristol and the surrounding region,

---

48. The most thorough study of the Compton Census is Anne Whiteman, ed., *The Compton Census of 1676: A Critical Edition*, British Academy, Records of Social and Economic History, New Ser., X (London, 1986); CCL, MSS. Cat. 114, H. Z.; Turner, ed., *Original Records of Nonconformity*, I, 27.

49. William Page, ed., *The Victoria History of the County of Gloucester*, II (London, 1907), 32, 34; John Smyth, *A Description of the Hundred of Berkeley in the County of Gloucester and of Its Inhabitants*, vol. III of *The Berkeley Manuscripts*, ed. Sir John Maclean (Gloucester, 1883–1885), 88; Hill, *Religion and Politics*, 96–97; John Corbet, "A true and impartiall History of the Military Government of the Cities of Gloucester from the beginning of the civil war . . ." (London, 1647), 7, 10, Thomason Tracts, microfilm, reel E402, British Library, London.

notably in the market towns and clothing villages of the Vale of Severn and Cotswolds Edge, the Puritan parishes of northern Somerset, and around Glastonbury. Presbyterianism also remained strong. The bishop of Gloucester reported in 1669 that two hundred Presbyterians attended conventicles at Marshfield, in the southeastern corner of the county. In the Vale of Berkeley, Presbyterian meetings were established at Berkeley, Wotton under Edge, Cam, Thornbury, and Rangeworthy. At Wotton, when Thomas Wither, a tithingman, and Sir Gabriel Lowe, a justice, attempted to enforce the law prohibiting Nonconformist meetings in 1670, they were confronted by "a very numerous conventickle of neere 300 persons" who refused to disband and go home peacefully. Rangeworthy's conventicle drew upon not only its own inhabitants but also "the greatest p[ar]t" of the neighboring parish of Iron Acton. By the 1670s, meetings—mainly Presbyterians, Independents, Baptists, and Quakers—existed in at least forty-four parishes throughout the county, and Dissenters were present in no fewer than 60 percent of Gloucestershire parishes.[50]

How many people joined dissenting groups or did "not goe to any place" of worship will never be known. But in Kent and Gloucestershire, as in many other parts of the country, Nonconformity was a vital facet of religious experience. By the time of the great surge in emigration during the middle decades of the century, dissenting congregations were well established in the cities, market towns, clothing villages, and wood-pasture districts of southern and central England, communities and regions from which the great majority of settlers were drawn. England's religious heterogeneity was transferred to the Chesapeake: Nonconformity in Virginia and Maryland was not an aberration or a peculiar throwback out of tune with mainstream social

---

50. Christopher Hill, *The World Turned Upside Down: Radical Ideas during the English Revolution* (London, 1972), 79; D2052, Gloucestershire Record Office; Turner, ed., *Original Records of Nonconformity*, I, 9–12; David Underdown, *Revel, Riot, and Rebellion: Popular Politics and Culture in England, 1603–1660* (Oxford, 1985), 251; Add. MSS, 33589,75, 78, BL; Green *et al.*, eds., *Cal. State Papers, Dom. Ser., of Charles II*, XIII, *May 18th to September 30th, 1672*, 44, 197, 578, 677; Quarter Sessions Order Books, 1672–1692 (Q/SO3), GRO. The Compton Census returned about 5% of the adult population as Dissenters in 1676, but this is undoubtedly a gross underestimate. Wotton under Edge reported only 14 Dissenters out of more than 1,700 adults; Berkeley only 3 out of 1,100. In Cam, Dursley and Stinchcombe, where Presbyterian and Quaker meetings took place, only 14 Dissenters were listed in 1676 out of nearly 1,500 people. Photocopy of the Compton Census, 37/7, D2052, GRO; Whiteman, ed., *Compton Census*, 527; Frank Bate, *The Declaration of Indulgence, 1672: A Study in the Rise of Organized Dissent* (London, 1908), appendix 7, xxviii–xxix, lxvii–lxviii.

developments, but represented, like Catholicism in Maryland, an expression of the complexity of religious life and the rapidly shifting political and religious scene of the seventeenth century. Similarly, anticlericalism, a lack of enthusiasm for the established church, nonattendance of services, ignorance, and skepticism, accentuated by conditions along the tobacco coast, had long existed to varying degrees in the parent country. While the course of religious life in the Chesapeake was not predetermined—much depended on particular circumstances—it continued to be enormously influenced by developments in England.[51]

Magic and Witchcraft

"Most men and women in seventeenth-century Britain," Christopher Hill remarks, "lived in a world of magic, in which God and the devil intervened daily, a world of witches, fairies and charms." That close interconnection between the natural and supernatural—the immediacy of a world of spirits and invisible forces that acted upon the lives of everyone—did not spawn autonomous systems of belief and practice that existed outside of, separate from, conventional religion in the form of Christianity.[52] Christian doctrine and magic (embracing sorcery, witchcraft, magical healing, conjuring, divination, astrology, prophecy, and fortune-telling) represented, as Darrett Rutman suggests, two variants of the same impulse: "a thirst to systematize the unknown." Religion and magic, far from being incompatible, coexisted side by side and were intimately linked in the minds of people.[53] Little attention has been given to this aspect of settlers' religious lives. To what

51. See, for example, Butler, *Awash in a Sea of Faith*, chap. 1.

52. Hill, *World Turned Upside Down*, 87; Thomas, *Religion and the Decline of Magic*, chaps. 14–18; Alan Macfarlane, *Witchcraft in Tudor and Stuart England: A Regional and Comparative Study* (London, 1970); Christina Larner, *Witchcraft and Religion: The Politics of Popular Belief* (Oxford, 1984); Geoffrey Scarre, *Witchcraft and Magic in Sixteenth and Seventeenth Century Europe* (London, 1987); Brian P. Levack, *The Witch-Hunt in Early Modern Europe* (London, 1987); G. R. Quaife, *Godly Zeal and Furious Rage: The Witch in Early Modern Europe* (London, 1987). Older studies include Wallace Notestein, *A History of Witchcraft in England from 1558 to 1718* (1911; New York, 1965); and George Lyman Kittredge, *Witchcraft in Old and New England* (New York, 1929).

53. Rutman, "Evolution of Religious Life," *Lex and Scientia*, XIV (1978), 192; Reay, "Popular Religion," in Reay, ed., *Popular Culture*, 92; Ingram, *Church Courts, Sex, and Marriage*, 96–97. David Hall writes, "Magic stubbornly resists our efforts to distinguish it from religion," in Steven L. Kaplan, ed., *Understanding Popular Culture: Europe from the Middle Ages to the Nineteenth Century* (Berlin, 1984), 8.

extent did contemporary beliefs in magic, cunning folk, witches, spirits, and demons reappear in the Chesapeake?

Colonists certainly believed in witchcraft and the real presence of the devil. William Crashaw, referring to the Indians, wrote of Virginia in 1613, "Satan visibly and palpably raignes there, more then in any other known place of the world," and Alexander Whitaker thought that Indians had some "great witches among them" and were "very familiar with the Devill." The first reported allegation of witchcraft practiced by an English settler was made against "good wiefe Wright" in 1626, described by two witnesses as "a very bad woman." She was accused of prophesying the death of several colonists, causing sickness, and killing poultry and crops. Rebecca Graye informed the General Court that Wright said to her "That by one Token wch this deponent had in her forehed she should burye her Husband, And Fourther sayeth that good wiefe Wright did tell this deponent that she told Mr ffellgate he should bury his wiefe (wch came to pass)." Lieutenant Giles Allington described how he had asked Wright

> to bringe his wife to bed, but the saide goodwiefe being left handed, his wiefe desired him to gett Mrs Grave to be her midwiefe, wch this deponent did, and sayeth that the next daye after his wiefe was delivered, the said goodwiefe Wright went awaye from his howse very much discontented, in regarde the other midwiefe had brought his wiefe to bedd, shortlie after this, this deponents wiefes brest grew dangerously sore of an Imposture and was a moneth or 5 weeks before she was recovered, Att wch tyme This deponent him selfe fell sick and contynued the space of three weeks, And further sayeth that his childe after it was borne fell sick and soe contynued the space of two moneths, and afterwards recovered, And so did Contynue well for the space of a moneth, And afterwards fell into extreme payne the space of five weeks and so departed.

Despite evidence from eight witnesses testifying to her occult powers, Goodwife Wright was not convicted.[54]

Although "accompted for a witch," she may well have been a cunning woman. Mrs. Isabell Perry recounted that Wright had told her that, when

54. Davis, *Literature and Society in Early Virginia*, 17; Bruce, *Institutional History*, I, 278; Capt. John Smith, *A Map of Virginia, with a Description of the Countrey* . . . (1612), in Philip L. Barbour, ed., *The Complete Works of Captain John Smith (1580–1631)*, 3 vols. (Chapel Hill, N.C., 1986), I, 169; McIlwaine, ed., *Minutes of the Council and General Court*, 111, 114.

she lived in Hull, England, she had been churning butter when a woman came to her mistress's house who was believed to be a witch. Following the instructions of her "dame," she "Clapt the Chirne [churne] staffe to the bottom of the Chirne and clapt her hands across uppon the top of it by wch means the witch was not able to stire owt of the place where she was for the space of six howers." The witch was released only after asking her mistress's forgiveness. Wright appears to have been taught magic by her dame in Hull while in service, but the point to stress here is that magic was used to ward off evil, not to cause harm or damage. Mrs. Perry stated that, when accused of witchcraft by some of her neighbors, she had made light of it and had said, "God forgive them." Her magical powers and ability to see into the future were evidently feared, but, significantly, no one accused her of a compact with the devil or of being familiar with evil spirits. The charge of witchcraft was based solely on the misfortunes she had allegedly caused those who crossed her; and, since nothing positive could be proved against her, the case was dropped.[55]

Of the two dozen cases that occurred in Virginia and Maryland during the rest of the century, the majority fell into two categories. About half arose from defamation suits and may have involved little more than name-calling. Jane Rookens of Lower Norfolk, for example, accused the wife of George Barker of being a witch, but, when the case came before the General Court in April 1641, she claimed that she did not remember what she had said. Nevertheless, she apologized for her offense. In the mid-1650s a number of witchcraft allegations compelled the Lower Norfolk court to impose a fine of one thousand pounds of tobacco for anyone making a false accusation. On the other hand, several cases were more serious and clearly incorporated elements of contemporary thinking about witchcraft in England. In every instance where the basis for the charge is known, the allegation revolved around *maleficium*: causing the physical injury or death of persons or damage to their property, usually crops and livestock, by occult means. No Chesapeake witches were accused of devil worship, engaging in wild sexual orgies, cannibalism, or congregating at sabbats. Neither were they accused of elabo-

---

55. McIlwaine, ed., *Minutes of the Council and General Court*, 112. The devil is not mentioned once in the reported proceedings. For the legal background to witchcraft in England, see Thomas, *Religion and the Decline of Magic*, chap. 14; Macfarlane, *Witchcraft in Tudor and Stuart England*, chap. 2; Clives Holmes, "Popular Culture? Witches, Magistrates, and Divines in Early Modern England," in Kaplan, ed., *Understanding Popular Culture*, 85–111.

rate pacts with the devil. The increasingly "sophisticated demonology" that developed in Europe during the sixteenth and seventeenth centuries largely bypassed Virginia and Maryland.[56]

Chesapeake witchcraft took a relatively simple form. In a case referred to earlier, Joan Michell of Charles County was accused in 1659 of bewitching Mistress Hatche's face, causing her "abundance of Miserie by the soarnes of her mouth." Two years later she brought a number of suits against her neighbors, including the minister, Mr. Francis Doughty, who, she claimed, persisted in calling her a witch. Mistress Long told Richard Tarlin that the chickens she had bought from Michell "did die in such a strang manner that she thaught sum old witch or other had bewitched them." To clear her name, Michell demanded to "bee searched by able woemen [to determine] whether she bee such a person or no which thos persons say I am." A quarrel between Edward Cole and Mrs Neal of Northumberland County in 1671 led to an allegation that she had cursed him, causing all the people on his plantation, including his wife, to fall sick. A similar accusation made against Alice Cartwright of Lower Norfolk County, charged with casting a spell over John Salmon's child, led to the impaneling of a jury of women who "delegently Searched the body of the sd Alice" but could "find noe Suspitious marks whereby they can Judge her to be a witch butt onely what may and Is usuall on women." Rebecca Fowler of Calvert County was presented in 1685 for "being led by the instigation of the Divell [to practice] certaine evil and dyabolicall artes called witchcrafts, inchantments, charmes, and sorceryes" leading to the injury of Francis Sandsbury, laborer, and others, whose "bodyes were very much the worse, consumed, pined and lamed." She was found guilty and sentenced to hang. Hannah Edwards, spinster, also of Calvert County, charged with the same crime, was acquitted.[57]

The social impact of witchcraft on Chesapeake society should not be exaggerated. A couple of dozen cases, half of which were really defamation suits, hardly add up to a witch craze. There was nothing on the scale of the Essex witch-hunt in England or the Salem outburst in Massachusetts.[58] Chesapeake

56. McIlwaine, ed., *Minutes of the Council and General Court*, 476; Lower Norfolk County, Wills and Deeds C (1651–1656), fols. 157, 237; J. A. Sharpe, *Early Modern England: A Social History, 1550–1760* (London, 1987), 313.

57. *Md. Archives*, LIII, 55, 142–145; Bruce, *Institutional History*, I, 282; "Witchcraft in Virginia," *WMQ*, 1st Ser., I (1892–1893), 128; Parke, "Witchcraft in Maryland," *Md. Hist. Mag.*, XXXI (1936), 283, 285–286.

58. Macfarlane, *Witchcraft in Tudor and Stuart England*; John Putnam Demos, *Entertaining Satan: Witchcraft and the Culture of Early New England* (New York, 1982); Chadwick Hansen, *Witchcraft at Salem* (New York, 1969); Paul Boyer and Stephen Nis-

witchcraft strongly resembled simple English patterns: allegations generally involved "village maleficium" (harming neighbors or enemies by the use of magic). The great majority of the accused were women (only two men were convicted of sorcery and witchcraft), and most were acquitted. Three witches were put to death at sea en route to Maryland and Virginia, but only one, Rebecca Fowler, may have been executed in the Chesapeake. Although the majority of those involved in trials were ordinary planters and their wives, belief in witchcraft was not confined to the lower classes. Magistrates were reluctant to execute alleged witches, but they were not reluctant to try them according to English law, and they followed English practice in looking for the physical characteristics of witches. Thus when "Jone the wife of Lazarus Jenking" of Lower Norfolk was charged with "being familiar wth Evell Speritts and useing witchcraft" by Mr. William Carver, a justice, the court ordered her to be searched by a special jury "according to the 118 Chapter of Doulton."[59]

Yet if occurrences of witchcraft were relatively rare in Maryland and Virginia, they nevertheless testify to a rich vein of beliefs in the supernatural. Settlers believed that witches could harm them and their children, livestock, and crops. Anne Ball of Essex County alleged that Eleanor King "had ridden her during several days and nights until she was wearied nearly to death." Edward Cole believed that his sick wife had been saved from the evil intentions of a witch only because the witch had passed under a horseshoe nailed to his front door as she entered his house while making a visit. William Eale not only accused Phyllis Money of casting a spell over Henry Dunkin's horse, causing injury to its master, but he also charged that she had taught her daughter to be a witch, who in turn taught her husband to be a wizard. The daughter, he said, "had boasted to him that she was a sorceress; that she had betwitched his cow, and was herself regularly sucked by the Devil."

senbaum, *Salem Possessed: The Social Origins of Witchcraft* (Cambridge, Mass., 1974); Frederick C. Drake, "Witchcraft in the American Colonies, 1647–62," *American Quarterly*, XX, (1968), 694–725; Richard Weisman, *Witchcraft, Magic, and Religion in Seventeenth-Century Massachusetts* (Amherst, Mass., 1984); Carol F. Karlsen, *The Devil in the Shape of a Woman: Witchcraft in Colonial New England* (New York, 1987).

59. Sharpe, *Early Modern England*, 313 ("village maleficium"); Rutman, "Evolution of Religious Life," *Lex and Scientia*, XIV (1978), 193–194; Parke, "Witchcraft in Maryland," *Md. Hist. Mag.*, XXXI (1936), 283–284; Lower Norfolk County, Wills and Deeds E (Orders) (1666–1675), fol. 129 (CW, microfilm, reel M1365–18); "Grace Sherwood, the Virginia Witch," *WMQ*, 1st Ser., III (1894–1895), 190–193, 242–244, IV (1895–1896), 18–19. "Doulton" is Michael Dalton, *The Countrey Justice . . .* (London, 1618, and many later eds.).

Witches sometimes rode their victims merely for sport. Charles Kinsey and John Potts of Princess Anne claimed in 1698 that they had been ridden by two witches, one from his land to Elizabeth Russell's and the other "along the seaside and home to his own house." Similar ideas about witches circulated in England.[60]

Witchcraft was the most common expression of popular belief in the occult, but one finds other evidence of the close connection between the natural and supernatural worlds. In February 1649, two weeks after the execution of Charles I, Daniel Hoare saw an apparition at Blunt Point on the James River "which Lasted about halfe an hower" and took the form of "a whight fire paralel to the Horrison." He made no attempt to interpret the vision but was sufficiently impressed to make a drawing of it. Unusual happenings—apparitions, comets, violent thunderstorms, floods, large numbers of wolves and vermin, harvest failures—were frequently interpreted as portents of things to come or a sign of God's wrath. Spectral gobbets of blood found in the washing bucket of a Virginia settler, as we have seen, proved an omen of the Indian uprising of 1644. From Rappahannock County, twenty years later, Colonel John Catlett wrote to his cousin in Kent: "Wee have had many prognosticks of Gods Judgments . . . very apparent to such as note the wayes of providence, first a very Unseasonable yeare so th[a]t I can say nothing did prosper of the fruits of the earth, 2ly The coming down of wilde beast amongst us more than ordinary such as bears and woolves . . . 3ly The treachery of the heathen, the manner too long to relate . . . 4ly At this very Junction of time there was a combination of severall servants, who had complotted first to arm themselves with their Masters armes and then 2ly to make their owne termes which was their freedom and in case of denial to kill all that should oppose them." Nicholas Perrey of Virginia, in a petition to the king in 1667 for five or six pounds to return to England, claimed that "the dreadfull fireing of that fatall Cittie of London" in the previous year was God's punishment for "such a high rebelion . . . Chiefly by th[a]t Cittie ag[ain]st y[ou]r sacred father." These last examples reveal the compatibility

60. Bruce, *Institutional History*, I, 282–286; Davis, *Literature and Society*, 36–37; Thomas, *Religion and the Decline of Magic*, chaps. 14–17; Macfarlane, *Witchcraft in Tudor and Stuart England*; J. S. Cockburn, ed., *Calendar of Assize Records: Kent Indictments of James I* (London, 1980), nos. 31, 71, 100, 139, 552, 577; QS/B 2/12–14, QS/B 4, Kent Archives Office, Maidstone, Kent; [David Webster, comp.], *A Collection of Rare and Curious Tracts Relating to Witchcraft in the Counties of Kent, Essex, Suffolk, Norfolk, and Lincoln, between the Years 1618 and 1664* (London, 1838). A skeptical, but revealing, account of witchcraft is to be found in Reginald Scot, *The Discoverie of Witchcraft* . . . (London, 1584), 5–6, 18–19.

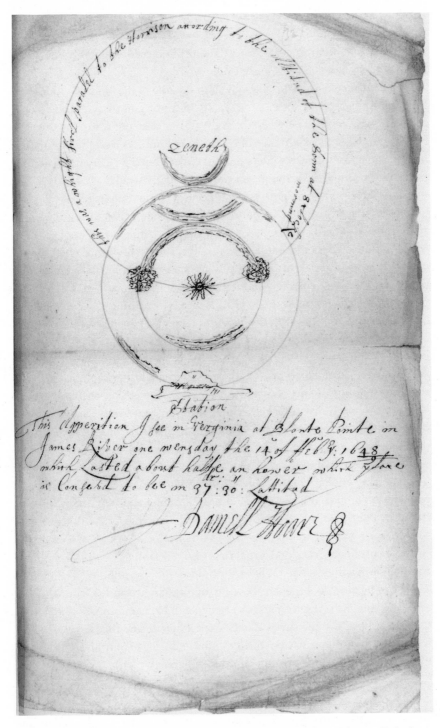

9. Apparition Seen by Daniel Hoare. *Permission of the Bodleian Library, Oxford, Ms. Ashmole. 242, fol. 126*[R]

of supernatural occurrences with Christianity and established religion. God, like the devil, had a real presence in the world.[61]

Either because of the emphasis given to the role of the "tobacco industry" in shaping Chesapeake society, the search for the origins of chattel slavery, or the traditional contrast between the godly northern colonies and the ungodly South, the religious experience of colonists has not received the attention it merits. Most Chesapeake settlers did not seek to build a "Citty upon a Hill," but neither were they harbingers of the increasingly secular age to come. Immigrants' beliefs were in large part a reflection of the complexity of religious life in seventeenth-century England, embracing skepticism, orthodoxy, and zeal. If the weakness of the Church of England in Virginia and its absence in Maryland gave further impetus to the indifference to and uninterest in official credo already apparent among sections of the population in England, one ought not infer that colonists suddenly became irreligious. A small but important minority assuaged their spiritual needs by turning to Catholicism or Nonconformity, but the majority reverted either to a form of "village Anglicanism" or to an eclectic form of popular belief that drew upon a hotchpotch of sources and traditions—Protestant, Catholic, pre-Christian, and occult— that had been a principal concern of the Anglican Church in endeavoring to root out "ignorance" and "superstition" from the lower classes following the Reformation. In terms of bringing the laity into conformity with Anglican doctrine, the evisceration of the Church of England in the Chesapeake put the clock back a hundred years.

A consideration of religion, including the occult, is important not only for its own sake, giving a more rounded picture of society, but also because it provides a glimpse into the minds of ordinary men and women: what they thought about their relationship with God, the afterlife, and the cosmos. It serves as a reminder that colonists had other imperatives besides the concerns of earning a living and providing for their families; and it suggests a common link with systems of belief, orthodox and unorthodox, in England. There can be little doubt, even allowing for indifference and skepticism, that efforts to establish Anglicanism, the struggle of Nonconformists, the persistence of antipopery, the survival of household piety, and the range of beliefs in magic and the supernatural testify to the enduring significance of religion in the lives of most seventeenth-century settlers.

61. Ashmolean MS 242, fol. 126, Bodleian Library, Oxford; Frank, ed., "News from Virginny," *VMHB*, LXV (1957), 87; Original Letters, John Catlett to Thomas Catlett of Hollingborne, Kent, Apr. 1, 1664, Colonial Williamsburg Library; CO 1/21, 126–127, Public Record Office. See also Thomas, *Religion and the Decline of Magic*, 103–105.

10

English Society in the New World

This study has sought to uncover the experiences, values, and attitudes of the men and women who moved from England to a small but important part of the Anglo-American world of the seventeenth century. An English perspective has been emphasized. Settlers down to the final decades of the century were overwhelmingly English (not British) by birth and brought with them a miscellany of English traditions, customs, and attitudes that were enormously influential in shaping their responses to conditions encountered in the Chesapeake. Cultural continuities—their national characteristics and assumptions—were more important than environment in shaping the societies that emerged in Maryland and Virginia. Colonists viewed the landscape and the people who lived there through English eyes. What they saw was in large part what they wanted or expected to see: an Eden or a wilderness, innocent children of the Garden or barbarous savages, abundance or dearth, a superfluity of free land for the taking, and a vast fund of natural resources to be exploited. To understand why immigrants responded to the New World as they did, it is necessary to understand the dominant cultural assumptions that lay behind their actions and perceptions: the cultural language employed to make sense of their experiences.

Opportunities in the Old World and the New were closely related. The exodus of hundreds of thousands of poor laborers to Ireland and America in the sixteenth and seventeenth centuries can be explained only by the growing levels of poverty and emiseration of the lower classes in England. Poverty was reflected by the rapid rise in poor relief in town and country alike, the spreading slums of cities, spiraling mortality rates, the massive increase in vagrancy, and the steady tramp of the young and out-of-work from one part of the country to another in search of subsistence. "Enforced migration," Peter Clark asserts, "was a disease endemic among most poor people." In hard times, the poor stole clothes to keep warm, pulled down fences for firewood, and filched bread, cheese, and milk from wealthier neighbors. Official poor, those recognized as deserving by the parish, usually received some help, but pauper migrants were rarely so fortunate and could expect short shrift from most parish authorities.[1] Churchwardens and overseers of the poor were only too glad to see the backs of strangers who might become a burden on the parish.

These points should be kept in mind when considering the social backgrounds of indentured servants. Migration within England and immigration to America were of the same piece. The poor man "in great waunte" given sixpence by the churchwardens of Chatham, Kent, in the summer of 1638 might well have moved on to London or Gravesend and been picked up as a vagrant and shipped out to the colonies. Some of the poor who moved to wood-pasture villages of the Severn Valley (of whom John Smyth complained testily in 1639) later ended up in Bristol and thence went to Ireland and America. Forests and woodlands, such as Dean, Kingswood, Neroche, and Frome-Selwood, served as temporary shelters, staging posts, for poor people who subsequently moved to the ports and then overseas. Indentured servants composed a small minority of the tremendous flow of people who migrated to London, Bristol, and other cities in this period and cannot be distinguished from the majority by their foresight or vision in opting to emigrate.[2]

The emphasis placed on poverty and the limited opportunities for the young and displaced in England should give us pause when considering the plight of servants in the Chesapeake. Would they have fared better if they had remained at home? There can be no conclusive answer, but their chances of getting on in England, by working their own smallholding or securing a living from a recognized trade, must have been slight. The analogy of a lottery has been used to describe the experiences of settlers in Virginia and Maryland. Large numbers, perhaps as many as a third, died within the first couple of years after arriving. Like the men and women who flooded into London during the seventeenth century, immigrants who moved to the tide-

---

1. Peter Clark, "The Migrant in Kentish Towns, 1580–1640," in Clark and Paul Slack, eds., *Crisis and Order in English Towns, 1500–1700: Essays in Urban History* (London, 1972), 138. For an example of treatment of official poor, in Thornbury, Gloucestershire, regular disbursements were made to men and women in "sicknes and miserie" and "in want in Cold and hard times," during the 1650s and 1660s (Thornbury, Overseers of the Poor Accounts, 1655–1670, D688/1, Gloucestershire Record Office).

2. St. Mary's, Chatham, Churchwardens Accounts, entry for June 15, 1638, P85/5/1, Kent Archives Office, Maidstone, Kent.

water risked disease and early death. But for those who survived there was a possibility, at least down to the 1670s in some regions, that they would eventually be able to establish themselves as small planters. If one must be cautious not to exaggerate opportunities for ex-servants, their prospects were probably a little brighter than those of the destitute in England.

It is harder to generalize about the social origins of free emigrants. They were a diverse group, ranging from men who had little more than the cost of their passage, fleeing from creditors or misfortune and hoping for better luck in the colonies, to wealthy merchants, gentry, and royal officials. Following the end of military campaigns in Flanders and Ireland in the late sixteenth and early seventeenth centuries, conquest and plunder beckoned in the New World, attracting gentry soldiers of fortune and seasoned campaigners. The failure of Virginia to yield the riches of Mexico or Peru and the adoption of large-scale tobacco production by the 1620s, however, led most of the early soldier-pioneers to abandon the colony. Thereafter, a fusion of merchants and minor gentry formed the ruling class.

Notable were the close connections between merchants and mariners in the two major colonial ports, London and Bristol, and planter-merchants in the Chesapeake. Atlantic commerce, unrestricted by mercantile monopolies and regulated companies, allowed all sorts of petty traders—retailers, wholesale merchants, ship captains, seamen, and victuallers—to dabble in the tobacco trade. In the early 1660s John Bland described Virginia merchants of London: "They are no Merchants bred, nor versed in foreign, or any Trade, but [that] to those Plantations, and that from, [being] either Planters there or Wholesale Tobacconists and Shop-keepers retailing Tobacco here in England." The number of London tobacco importers rose from 264 in the late 1620s to 573 by 1676. By the latter date, 60 big firms (importing 50,000–1,000,000 lbs. per annum) accounted for 70 percent of total imports (by weight), but the strength of the middle tiers is revealed by the presence of 98 firms importing 10,000–50,000 lbs., and 181 importing 2,000–10,000 lbs. Bristol tobacco merchants numbered 338 in 1680, and a much greater proportion (59 percent, compared to London's 27 percent) fell into the middling category. Small merchants, factors, and mariners frequently took up land in Virginia and Maryland, temporarily for speculative purposes or permanently as settlers. Occasionally, large merchants such as Edward Bennett and John Bland visited to supervise their affairs personally, but small and middling traders constituted the backbone of the planter-merchant class who resided in the tidewater. They were men such as James Turpin, a tobacconist of the Liberty of the Tower of London, who migrated to Virginia in 1675 and died there a few years later; Edmund Goddard, citizen and cooper of London, originally from Suffolk, who emigrated in 1662/3; and Thomas Jarvis, who described himself in his will of 1684 as "late of Virginia and now of London, merchant."[3] Unquestionably, the expansion of the tobacco trade and its accessibility to small men stimulated a steady flow of free emigrants from London and the outports.

Sons of gentlemen and minor gentry were another important category of free emigrants. Promoters of colonization and colonial leaders actively encouraged the gentry to move to the New World, believing them the natural rulers of society and finding it inconceivable that the new colonies could be brought under orderly rule without persons of mark to govern them. Mismanagement of Virginia's affairs in the early years was blamed partly on the poor quality of the colony's leaders. George Sandys wrote in 1623 that some of the councillors were "no more than Ciphers" and described others as "miserable poor." With an eye to creating a Maryland aristocracy, Lord Baltimore offered lordships and manors, "with all such royalties and priviledges" usual in England, to anyone transporting five or more men. The *Relation of Maryland* of 1635 contained a list of "Gentlemen adventurers that are gone in person to this Plantation," which was doubtless intended to encourage others to do the same. Most gentry, however, were attracted to the tobacco coast, not from a high-minded desire to offer themselves for public service or because they wanted to erect feudal lordships in America, but because they perceived opportunities to make money. John Pory's remarks about Sir George Yeardley set the tone: "The Governour here, who at his first coming, besides a great deale of worth in his person, brought onely his sword with him, was at his late being in London, together with his lady, out of his meer gettings here, able to disburse very near three thousand pounde to furnishe himselfe for his voiage. And once within seven yeares, I am persuaded . . . that the Governors place here may be as profittable as the lord Deputies of Ireland." This is not to imply that public office was seen purely in terms of sinecures that offered substantial financial perks, but colonial leaders adopted the conventional view that there was nothing contradictory about private gain from public office.[4]

3. Jacob M. Price and Paul G. E. Clemens, "A Revolution of Scale in Overseas Trade: British Firms in the Chesapeake Trade, 1675–1775," *Journal of Economic History*, XLVII (1987), 3, 11, 27; Colonial Williamsburg, VCRP, nos. 3716, 3727, 3729 (many other examples of small and middling traders could be given).

4. Bernard Bailyn, "Politics and Social Structure in Virginia," in James Morton Smith, ed., *Seventeenth-Century America: Essays in Colonial History* (Chapel Hill, N.C., 1959), 90–91; *A Relation of Maryland* (1635), in Clayton Colman Hall, ed:, *Narratives of Early Maryland, 1633–1684*, Original Narratives of Early American History (New

The majority of gentry did not emigrate with the intention of becoming part of a permanent office-holding class. Provincial politics was important, but more important was earning money from tobacco plantations, merchandising, and other entrepreneurial activities. From this perspective, gentry are hard to distinguish from merchants. County rulers, like Henry Fleet and John Carter of Lancaster County and Thomas Willoughby and Adam Thorowgood of Lower Norfolk, were both. Their genteel origins gave them an immediate introduction into the higher echelons of colonial society, yet first and foremost they were planter-merchants who owned large plantations worked by large numbers of servants and slaves. Younger sons of gentry, such as Maurice Thompson and Henry Corbin, like so many of their peers, sought their fortunes in trade, moving first to London or Bristol and then to the colonies.

Emigration was highly selective. Mainly the young, single, and male emigrated. Across the century, the overwhelming majority of colonists (about 80 percent) were indentured servants; predominantly they were the poor from southern England's towns, cities, and wood-pasture regions. Emigration was also highly diverse. If the majority of settlers came from central and southern parts of the country, few regions, nevertheless, did not have some people leaving. Virtually the entire social spectrum was represented, from vagrants and petty criminals to the gentry, together with a broad range of occupational groups from rural and urban communities. Among indentured servants were the impoverished and desperate from city streets and slums and inmates of bridewells as well as those who were better off and had decided, for one reason or another, that their prospects were brighter overseas. Many free emigrants, as we have seen, were petty merchants and retailers who had garnered sufficient capital to pay for their transportation and set up their own plantation. Most emigrants were therefore from England's lower and middle classes; relatively few of the *nobilitas major* were attracted to the tobacco coast.

Diversity is worth highlighting. First, it underlines that emigration should not be viewed as a single massive flow of people from one side of the Atlantic to the other, but as a series of migrations, the character of which was

York, 1910), 91, 101; "Letter of John Pory" (1619), in Lyon Gardiner Tyler, ed., *Narratives of Early Virginia, 1606–1625*, Original Narratives of Early American History (New York, 1907), 285. See Sir Francis Wyatt's letter of 1623/4 for an example of a governor who took his duties seriously but was concerned about his private affairs ("Letter of Sir Francis Wyatt, Governor of Virginia, 1621–1626," *William and Mary Quarterly*, 2d Ser., VI [1926], 114–121, esp. 121).

shaped by developments in Virginia and Maryland, conditions in England, and the individual motivations of the emigrants themselves. Virginia society down to the mid-1620s, dominated by the Virginia Company, for example, had a very different tone from the succeeding period, which was heavily influenced by the expansion of the tobacco industry and consequent demand for labor. Successive waves of settlement emphasize that the composition of migrants might vary considerably and that timing of departure from England and arrival in America had a crucial bearing on their opportunities. Second, to understand the subsequent development of Chesapeake society, it is vital to recognize the mixing together of English people from very different backgrounds—different parts of the country, different occupations, and very different local and provincial contexts.

How did settlers respond to their new environment? Arrivals would have been impressed initially by the major physical characteristics: the immense stretch of water of the Bay, the spacious waterways of the four great rivers, the intricate network of smaller rivers and creeks, the low-lying terrain covered by extensive woodland, broken here and there by Indian clearings. If they arrived during the summer months, doubtless they would have been struck by the heat (as "hot as in Spaine") and humidity. "The Natural Temperature of the Inha[bit]ed part of the Country," Robert Beverley remarked of Virginia, "is hot and moist." Winters, on the other hand, were short "and no worse" than in England. Climate and health were closely related in the minds of colonists. Heat and "Moisture . . . occasion'd by the abundance of low Grounds, Marshes, Creeks, and Rivers" were believed harmful and, in part, accounted for the heavy mortality of the region. Like certain estuarine areas and marshlands in England, the tidewater early gained a reputation for sickness and death.[5]

Depending on where and when they arrived, colonists might have soon come into contact with some of the strange peoples they had heard about before leaving England: Indians and Africans. How settlers reacted was very much influenced by particular circumstances as well as by the attitudes

5. *Relation of Maryland*, in Hall, ed., *Narratives of Maryland*, 77; John Hammond, *Leah and Rachel; or, The Two Fruitfull Sisters Virginia and Mary-land* (1655), *ibid.*, 290; Robert Beverley, *The History and Present State of Virginia*, ed. Louis B. Wright (Chapel Hill, N.C., 1947), 296, 303–304; Karen Ordahl Kupperman, "Fear of Hot Climates in the Anglo-American Colonial Experience," *WMQ*, 3d Ser., XLI (1984), 213–240. Despite the summer heat, Hammond and Beverley both stressed the temperate nature of the climate.

they brought with them. Whether, for example, they first met local Indians through war, trade, disputes over land, or in the courts, whether they first saw black slaves on the plantations of wealthy neighbors, when working with them side by side, or as purchasers, first impressions had an enormous impact, confirming or challenging existing prejudices. Cross-cultural "conversations," T. H. Breen and James Merrell have argued, were influenced not simply by English assumptions of superiority and ethnocentrism but also by the specific context of interaction. Race relations were hammered out in myriad face-to-face encounters. Whatever the local consequences of these meetings, there can be no doubt that the presence of Indian and African peoples in the Chesapeake constituted a major difference between colonial and English society, one that all colonists were forced to confront.[6]

Differences between tidewater and English society can be measured in terms of *presence* and *absence*. Explorers and settlers exhibited considerable curiosity in the strange peoples, plants, and animals that they encountered in America, and early accounts are full of descriptions of New World exotica. Thomas Hariot's description and John White's drawings of the Indians, fauna, and flora of Roanoke are outstanding examples, but pamphlets and letters containing all sorts of information about the American environment continued to arouse interest in England throughout the colonial period. Some of this material took the form of tracts commissioned to encourage settlement, and some fell into the category of travel literature, one of the most popular genres of the day. What was missing from the American landscape received less attention but, arguably, was more important. Settlers would have been immediately aware that much of what was familiar and taken for granted in their native communities was absent in the Chesapeake. There were no market towns full of the hustle and bustle of market day, no busy roads carrying goods and people from one part of the region to another, no compact villages surrounded by open fields, no county towns where the pomp of court days and civic ritual punctuated the cycle of the year, no cathedrals, no stone or flint churches, no castles or grand country houses built in the latest style. There was nothing in the landscape, to English eyes, that represented the antique—symbols of tradition and the past, of continuity—that pervaded everyday life in England. Men and women from Berkeley and surrounding villages had an ever-present reminder of the long

6. T. H. Breen, "Creative Adaptations: Peoples and Cultures," in Jack P. Greene and J. R. Pole, eds., *Colonial British America: Essays in the New History of the Early Modern Era* (Baltimore, 1984), 197–203, 215–221; James H. Merrell, "Some Thoughts on Colonial Historians and American Indians," *WMQ*, 3d Ser., XLVI (1989), 118.

rule of the lords Berkeley in the shape of the massive red sandstone castle that had stood for five hundred years guarding the border with Wales. Scattered throughout the Vale, as in other parts of England, country seats and game parks symbolized the power and wealth of the gentry and aristocracy, a testament to their prestige and elevated status. The survival of manors in many parts of the country recalled a previous age, when the local lord's will was virtually absolute. In parishes over the length and breadth of England, sturdily built churches represented half a millennium of public worship, celebration, and seasonal festivities, a natural meeting place and focus for parish life.

There was much different about the Chesapeake environment—differences that persisted throughout the century—but we should not assume that immigrants were intent on reproducing the ordered landscapes and densely populated urban communities of central and southern England. The view that English settlers desired to recreate colonial society in the image of the society they had left behind is only partially valid. Tidewater Virginia and Maryland were perceived as a vast woodland and fenland susceptible to exactly the same kinds of improvement from which it was thought marginal areas in the parent country would benefit. Settlers flocked into the region following the same impulse that attracted projectors and poor migrants to woodlands and newly claimed marshlands in England. The author of "A True and Natural Description of the Great Level of the Fens" wrote in 1685:

> And ye, whom hopes of sudden Wealth allure,
> Or wants into Virginia, force to fly,
> Ev'n spare your pains; here's Florida hard by.
> All ye that Treasures either want, or love,
> (And who is he, whom profit will not move?)
> Would you repair your fortunes, would you make,
> To this most fruitful Land yourselves betake.[7]

Manufactures and crops that were introduced into the English countryside were subsequently transferred to Virginia and Maryland, along with similar ideas about the efficacy of putting the poor to work. The Chesapeake was a new and distinctive English province. Apart from the vision of a few early governors, evidenced in the attempt to establish colonial capitals as cities and large tracts as manors, there is little to suggest that the great majority of immigrants were interested in recreating the complex provincial and urban societies they had left behind. No more than migrants in newly claimed

---

7. Quoted in Keith Lindley, *Fenland Riots and the English Revolution* (London, 1982), 4.

lands in England sought to introduce manors and Norman churches, Chesapeake settlers for most of the century were unconcerned about reproducing
the material fabric of Old World society in America. Apart from an abortive attempt in St. Mary's City in the middle decades of the century, not
until the 1690s, with the founding of Williamsburg and Annapolis, was a
sustained and self-conscious effort to mirror the grandeur of civic building,
public facilities, and formal space of European towns and cities attempted.[8]

If the Chesapeake's landscape and climate were unfamiliar, nevertheless
conventional attitudes about the social order, the locus of political power,
hierarchy, government, justice, property, marriage, the family, gender relations, and religion left immigrants in no doubt that they had arrived on
"English ground in America." The fabric of English society and culture was
maintained by the transfer and adaptation of English values, norms, and
attitudes, which represented the major continuities between life in the Old
World and the New. In this view, the disruption caused by environmental
factors has been given too much emphasis by historians seeking to construct
a developmental model of Virginia and Maryland society that proceeds from
chronic social and political instability in the seventeenth century to a golden
age of prosperity and consensus in the eighteenth. While the outlines of the
peculiar demographic regime—the skewed sex ratio and youthfulness of immigrants, high mortality rates, and comparatively late age of marriage—are
generally acknowledged, their actual impact on local society has been given
far less attention. How were they mediated, for example, by the inherited
attitudes and local experiences of English settlers? What specific factors influenced settlers' adaptation to these conditions? More generally, while the
rebirth of Chesapeake studies has seen an outpouring of work on demographic and economic structures, considerably less interest has been shown

8. John W. Reps, *Tidewater Towns: City Planning in Colonial Virginia and Maryland*
(Williamsburg, Va., 1972), chaps. 2–3, 6–7; Carter L. Hudgins, "Robert 'King' Carter
and the Landscape of Tidewater Virginia in the Eighteenth Century," in William M.
Kelso and Rachel Most, eds., *Earth Patterns: Essays in Landscape Archaeology* (Charlottesville, Va., 1990), 59–70; Mark P. Leone, "Rule by Ostentation: The Relationship between Space and Sight in Eighteenth-Century Landscape Architecture in the
Chesapeake Region of Maryland," in Susan Kent, ed., *Method and Theory for Activity
Area Research: An Ethnoarchaeological Approach* (New York, 1987), 605–632. For parallel
developments in England, see Michael Reed, *The Georgian Triumph, 1700–1830* (London, 1983), chaps. 4–7. My point is that a symbolic landscape—of well-constructed
public buildings in the latest metropolitan fashion, sturdy stone or brick churches,
and impressive brick mansions belonging to wealthy gentry and merchants—was
largely missing in the Chesapeake until the early 18th century.

in social, cultural, and institutional developments, which have been left, for the most part, to previous generations of historians.[9]

In Lower Norfolk, Lancaster, and St. Mary's counties, as elsewhere along the Bay, the well-born and wealthy governed. There was greater opportunity for men from humble or middling backgrounds to climb into the elite than in England, but, as provincial society matured during the second half of the century, substantial wealth and inherited status became the usual criteria for entry into the Chesapeake squirearchy. Except in some frontier regions, members of the bench who had arrived as servants were a rarity in Virginia after 1660 and in Maryland after 1680. Men from humble backgrounds were chosen to hold positions of power only when there were insufficient numbers of men of proven rank and quality. Opportunities for the poor to improve dramatically their social standing in their own lifetime were relatively short-termed, confined to perhaps a single generation (twenty to thirty years) in both colonies. By the Restoration there appear to have been a strengthening of traditional English attitudes toward social hierarchy in Virginia and a hardening of attitudes toward the poor. Social divisions widened and became increasingly fixed.[10]

The adoption of English law and, where possible, English institutions and procedures enabled Virginia and Maryland rulers to appeal to the weight of

9. An excellent summary of the research produced during the last 20 years can be found in the introduction to Lois Green Carr, Philip D. Morgan, and Jean B. Russo, eds., *Colonial Chesapeake Society* (Chapel Hill, N.C., 1988). There are, of course, notable exceptions to these generalizations, such as Allan Kulikoff, *Tobacco and Slaves: The Development of Southern Cultures in the Chesapeake, 1680–1800* (Chapel Hill, N.C., 1986); Edmund S. Morgan, *American Slavery, American Freedom: The Ordeal of Colonial Virginia* (New York, 1975); and Mechal Sobel, *The World They Made Together: Black and White Values in Eighteenth-Century Virginia* (Princeton, N.J., 1987). For earlier histories, see the work of Thomas Jefferson Wertenbaker and Philip Alexander Bruce. Thad W. Tate discusses Chesapeake historiography in "The Seventeenth-Century Chesapeake and Its Modern Historians," in Tate and David L. Ammerman, eds., *The Chesapeake in the Seventeenth Century: Essays on Anglo-American Society* (Chapel Hill, N.C., 1979), 3–50.

10. For example, 18 men served as justices of the peace in Charles County, 1658–1661, of whom 5 were illiterate and 8 were former servants. By contrast, of 27 justices who lived in Prince George's County, Maryland, 1695–1709, all were literate and 3 or 4 were sons of English gentlemen. None had entered the province as a servant. Russell Robert Menard, "Economy and Society in Early Colonial Maryland" (Ph.D. diss., University of Iowa, 1975), 431–433; Lorena Seebach Walsh, "Charles County, Maryland, 1658–1705: A Study of Chesapeake Social and Political Structure" (Ph.D. diss., Michigan State University, 1977), 442, 444; James R. Perry, *The Formation of a Society on Virginia's Eastern Shore, 1615–1655* (Chapel Hill, N.C., 1990), 195–200.

custom to justify their decisions and actions. Virginia and Maryland courts were consequently part of a hierarchy of jurisdictions that led eventually to the central courts in London and ultimately Parliament, the Privy Council, and the king. The highest echelons of government and the judiciary were located in England, a fact that emphasized the subordination of colonial polities to English political developments. Virginia and Maryland governors spent almost as much time in London defending their policies as in Jamestown and St. Mary's City. Westminster and Whitehall formed the political cockpit of the seventeenth-century English empire, just as London was its economic hub.

Gentry rule in the Chesapeake can be interpreted as an extension of gentry rule in England. New World squires self-consciously modeled themselves on their counterparts at home in dominating local as well as provincial politics. They claimed the sanction of tradition—an appeal of considerable force in the rapidly changing society of the early Chesapeake—and they counted, as did their English counterparts, on the approbation and cooperation of those they governed. All had a duty to assist in upholding the king's peace. As in England, the gentry could not expect the unconditional obedience of the commons; an implicit contract was at the heart of the relationship between rulers and ruled. In return for obeying their superiors and maintaining the peace, people expected government to be reasonably equitable, just, and impartial. They did not believe that public office should be used for the relentless exploitation of subjects or for flagrant self-interest, and, when rulers fell short of these expectations, opposition to their continuance in office arose. Perhaps more than a formal legal code, these unwritten assumptions were of signal importance in shaping relations between the people and their governors in this period.

Maintenance of order was a collective responsibility binding together the lowest to the highest. Heads of household were held responsible for the behavior of members of their family and, at the most intimate level of domestic politics, were empowered to exercise direct authority over wives, children, and servants. Family discipline and assumptions that governed family relations were vital to the upkeep of the peace and were little different from those prevalent in England. Despite the shortage of women in the Chesapeake, gender relations do not appear to have been fundamentally altered. The move to America did not undermine patriarchalism, the theoretical basis of male dominance, or alter in practice the somewhat more ambiguous social relations between men and women. So long as the political power of men was not publicly challenged, minor breaches of domestic discipline could be overlooked, but outspoken attacks by women on male authority were met

in both societies with a variety of punitive measures, notably shaming rituals such as ducking or being forced to confess the offense before the parish
congregation.

Sexual relations were equally difficult to regulate in both societies. In
theory, sexual union was not permitted outside of marriage, but in England
and the Chesapeake betrothal was frequently construed as legitimizing sex
for a consenting couple who intended to marry. Indeed, as has been argued,
betrothal constituted an integral part of marriage and was itself sometimes
believed to be a form of marriage. Parish and church officials for the most
part turned a blind eye to such practices, which, judging by the rate of prenuptial pregnancies in England, were common. What could not be tolerated,
however, were illicit sexual relations that threatened the social and moral
welfare of the community. Fornication could lead to unwanted children,
adultery, disrupted marriages, and conflict between neighbors, threatening
the integrity of the family and ultimately the entire social order. Hence,
church and secular courts waged an unremitting campaign against sexual
offenders, reserving their heaviest punishments (outside of felonies such as
rape or sodomy) for women bastard-bearers. In England usual punishments
were public confession, whippings, or confinement in a house of correction.
Where punishments other than a pledge to support the child were meted
out, whipping was most common, frequently in the marketplace or public
thoroughfare, "for the example of others to avoid the like offence." Justices
in Maryland and Virginia adopted the same punishments—whipping, fines,
and public penance—but in the case of female servants added the sanction
of extra service to compensate the master for the woman's lost labor and for
the support of the child. In both societies women tended to be punished far
more severely than men for sexual offenses.[11]

Attitudes toward sex and marriage and the roles that husbands and wives
were expected to play did not differ greatly in the two societies, despite different demographic contexts.[12] Men were expected to provide economic sup-

11. S. D. Amussen, "Gender, Family, and the Social Order, 1560–1725," in Anthony
Fletcher and John Stevenson, eds., *Order and Disorder in Early Modern England* (Cam-
bridge, 1985), 197–210; G. R. Quaife, *Wanton Wenches and Wayward Wives: Peasants and
Illicit Sex in Early Seventeenth Century England* (London, 1979), 216–224; Kathleen Mary
Brown, "Gender and the Genesis of a Race and Class System in Virginia, 1630–1750"
(Ph.D. diss., University of Wisconsin–Madison, 1990), 339–353.

12. For different interpretations, see Brown, "Gender and the Genesis of a Race
and Class System"; Terri Lynne Snyder, " 'Rich Widows Are the Best Commodity This

port and to treat their partners with care and respect. Wives were expected to devote themselves primarily to raising children, keeping house, and supplementing the family income. In the crucial area of passing on family property to heirs and maintaining the family after the death of the male head of household, widows played a pivotal role. Husbands in both societies generally turned to their wives to administer their estate after their death. Higher mortality rates in the Chesapeake do not appear to have undermined this basic aspect of male testamentary practice. Patterns of bequests were influenced by the variety of methods of transmitting property (for example, laws governing intestacy, manorial customs, and inter vivos settlements such as marriage portions), the age and sex of the children, and the economic status of the parents. In both societies, however, testators were concerned to provide support for their wives during widowhood and to ensure that the bulk of the estate remained in the family; hence, sons were usually favored over daughters with respect to the main landholdings while daughters were compensated with household goods, livestock, money, and, in the Chesapeake, servants or slaves. The assumptions that underpinned this pattern, whether in the Vale of Berkeley or the tidewater, were patriarchal and patrilineal, but the great majority of testators desired to provide for as many of the children as possible, not just firstborn males. Affective relations between spouses and parents and children appear to have altered little in the move to the Chesapeake. There is no evidence that shorter marriages and early parental death significantly weakened emotional ties between family members.

   In both societies, friends and neighbors provided the basic social cement for binding together the local community (hence their frequent appearance in wills). This was especially so in Maryland, where important local institutions (the parish, for example) that might have strengthened local society were missing. In form and function the local communities in pastoral districts of England, such as the Vale of Berkeley, and in the tidewater exhibited many similarities: their geographical extent was about the same, generally no more than five miles in radius; they were usually composed of a number of smaller units, neighborhoods; and they served essentially the same purposes in providing individuals with companionship, help in times of need, credit, witnesses for ceremonies, rites of passage, legal documents, and, in some cases, marriage partners. The local community was a small-scale theater in which most people acted out their lives, the most important social

Country Affords': Gender Relations and the Rehabilitation of Patriarchy in Virginia, 1660–1700" (Ph.D. diss., University of Iowa, 1992).

unit beyond the family and the essential context of everyday life. In England and the Chesapeake, community was organized, not around extended kin groups, but around individual households unrelated by blood, linked to one another by ties of neighborliness and friendship.

English attitudes were fundamental to shaping the response of seventeenth-century colonists to conditions in the New World, but they did not impose on Anglo-American society a bland, uniform English culture. English culture was itself a diverse and highly variegated complex of provincial and local cultures, and colonial societies of North America and the Caribbean contributed a new dimension to that diversity. The key to reconciling the impact of English and American cultures on colonial society lies in the relationship between dominant and variant cultures. English language, laws, government, religion, institutions, economic organization, heritage, and self-identity, together with the perceptual and ideological frameworks that underpinned them, constituted the essence of a dominant or national culture and influenced to varying degrees all parts of the English empire of this period.[13]

Different colonies drew upon this common culture in different ways, but all, consciously or unconsciously, were heavily influenced by it. The relationship with the dominant culture was continuous and exerted a powerful influence throughout the colonial period; it was not broken at the point of departure of emigrants or the creation of new societies in America. English colonies were not culturally isolated from the parent society and did not evolve in a vacuum. There was a constant correspondence between English and American society embracing not only trade and politics but also social and cultural developments. Wealthier settlers returned to England periodically to attend to business and perhaps see friends and relatives. Some retained property there, and a steady, if relatively small, number eventually returned for good. Together with foodstuffs and manufactured goods transported from English provinces, the flow of shipping to the colonies brought the latest news of current affairs as well as letters from friends, family, and partners. The exchange of news and gossip not only was important in keeping settlers in touch with events in their native society but also provided a welcome sense of continuity with their past.[14]

13. Bernard Bailyn and Philip D. Morgan, eds., *Strangers within the Realm: Cultural Margins of the First British Empire* (Chapel Hill, N.C., 1991), 1–17.

14. David Cressy, *Coming Over: Migration and Communication between England and New England in the Seventeenth Century* (Cambridge, 1987), chaps. 7–11; James Horn,

The evolution of variant cultures in America depended on a number of factors: the nature of the environment, the pattern of immigration, demographic regimen, the mix of settlers from different English regions and from elsewhere, the development of colonial economies, the adaptation of English laws and institutions, the creation of new laws and procedures (or customs), relationships with other cultures (such as African and Indian), and the gradual emergence of a sense of local history or heritage. They complemented, and were embraced by, the overarching context of English national culture, allowing individuals to locate themselves as Virginians or Barbadians and also as English subjects.[15]

The rough outlines of a Chesapeake culture, as it emerged during the seventeenth century, are reasonably clear. Settlers were keenly aware of the physical and environmental distinctiveness of the region. The whole of the second book of Robert Beverley's *History and Present State of Virginia*, for example, was devoted to what he termed the "Natural Product and Conveniencies of Virginia," where detailed consideration is given to "the Waters," soils, wild fruits, fish, fowl, and game. Book III is given over to a description of the Indians and their way of life. But, significantly, Beverley included a narrative of the colony since the first coming of the English. By the time of publication in 1705, English settlement in Virginia was nearly a century old. English Virginia had its own local history, its own myths replete with heroes and villains, stretching from the glorious days of Elizabethan discovery and conquest, through massacres and Indian wars, revolution and rebellion, and conflicts with the Dutch, to the foundation of Williamsburg and the eve of the golden age at the beginning of the eighteenth century. We need not concern ourselves with the accuracy of Beverley's account, or the particular story it tells; what is important is that the region had its own history, a sense of its own past. Just as English county historians, such as Sir Robert Atkyns, William Dugdale, and others sought to create a narrative of their native counties, so Beverley, self-mockingly calling himself "an Indian," constructed an early history of Virginia.[16]

Awareness of place and a sense of history were two vital aspects of the for-

---

" 'To Parts beyond the Seas': Free Emigration to the Chesapeake in the Seventeenth Century," in Ida Altman and Horn, eds., *"To Make America": European Emigration in the Early Modern Period* (Los Angeles, 1991), 85–130.

15. I am indebted to T. H. Breen for this insight; see *Puritans and Adventurers: Change and Persistence in Early America* (New York, 1980), 107–108, and, more generally, "Creative Adaptations," in Greene and Pole, eds., *Colonial British America*, 195–232.

16. Beverley, *History and Present State of Virginia*, ed. Wright, 9.

mation of a provincial culture, but also important were shared experiences. Tobacco culture and plantation husbandry provided a common context for the lives of all settlers—rich and poor, slaves and freemen—even the few men and women not primarily involved in raising leaf. Seasonal rhythms of cultivation, the ebb and flow of English shipping, the price of leaf in Bristol, London, and Amsterdam, and the rise and fall of demand were features of life familiar to planters from the Virginia capes to the mouth of the Susquehanna. Through to the final years of the century the Chesapeake was unified economically by a common dependence on tobacco and a transatlantic marketing system centered on the major English colonial ports and financed by a multitude of English merchants.

Other shared experiences can be mentioned briefly. The majority of inhabitants were immigrants and consequently faced a common challenge in adjusting to their new society. A pragmatic attitude toward local government was adopted; English laws and institutions were simplified and amended to suit their own purposes. Although important differences emerged between Maryland and Virginia, both colonies were represented by provincial assemblies that also served as central courts of appeal, and both relied on county courts and gentlemen justices to run local affairs. Working lives were similar from one part of the region to another, and domestic conditions had much in common. For the most part, traditions of architecture and consumption were similar in different parts of the tobacco coast. Throughout the region, domestic conditions were uniformly basic. The simplicity and crudeness of agrarian society and the absence of ways of life taken for granted in England must have been apparent to all new arrivals. Finally, there may have been a range of shared attitudes—hopes of making money and returning to England, a sense of being cut off from friends and family left behind, hostility toward local Indians, a desire to establish a smallholding and become an independent planter—that bound together planters from different parts of the Bay.

A broad spectrum of common experiences and attitudes, therefore, united settlers throughout the Chesapeake and was the basis of a provincial culture unique to the region. Many of its principal ingredients were present in the early decades of the century and were included in early descriptions, travel literature, and polemics that emphasized the distinctiveness of the environment, flora and fauna, climate, and indigenous peoples. Tobacco husbandry was firmly established by the 1620s and spread rapidly throughout the region over the next fifty years. The evolution of a calendar that marked special days of deliverance from Indian uprisings and servant rebellions testifies to a recognition of local events deemed worthy of public celebration that could be added to the traditional English calendar. In other words, an interpretation of the English history of the region was being shaped during the period itself. While most settlers who arrived during the great surge of immigration in the middle decades of the century were probably unaware of the ways of life they shared with settlers in other parts of the tobacco coast, a bird's-eye view of society reveals the unmistakable outlines of a Chesapeake-wide culture in formation.

Local subcultures that existed below the provincial level have been little studied in either Virginia or Maryland, and a few general remarks are worth making. If colonists' lives had much in common throughout the tidewater, important local variations nevertheless exerted a substantial influence on individual experience. Local cultures emerged gradually as new areas of the tidewater were settled and can be associated with particular locales, such as the river basins of the James, York, Rappahannock, and Potomac or parts of the bayside, such as the Eastern or the Western Shore.[17] Development of local cultures was conditioned by differences in soils and lines of communication and, consequently, by the quality and quantity of tobacco that could be profitably cultivated, which in turn influenced the type of social structures that emerged. Areas of high-quality soils in the upper James basin, the Northern Neck, and lower Western Shore of Maryland saw the development of large estates worked by large numbers of servants and slaves. Poorer regions, such as south of the James, parts of the Eastern Shore, and frontier counties such as New Kent, tended to be dominated by smaller planters who worked their own holdings. These were the first areas to turn away from tobacco cultivation in the latter years of the century. Timing of settlement had an important bearing on economic development and patterns of immigration and distinguished core areas from frontiers.[18]

Social differences are more difficult to identify. Areas like the Southside, parts of the Eastern Shore, and Anne Arundel County were heavily influenced by Puritan immigration and later by Quakerism while St. Mary's County had a disproportionately high number of Catholics, yet it is uncertain what long-term impact different religious temperaments had on local

17. For example, *ibid.*, 243.

18. Morgan, *American Slavery, American Freedom*, 225–230; Gloria L. Main, "Maryland and the Chesapeake Economy, 1670–1720," in Aubrey C. Land *et al.*, eds., *Law, Society, and Politics in Early Maryland* (Baltimore, 1977), 134–152, and Paul G. E. Clemens, "Economy and Society on Maryland's Eastern Shore, 1689–1733," 153–170; Lois Green Carr, "Diversification in the Colonial Chesapeake: Somerset County, Maryland, in Comparative Perspective," in Carr, Morgan, and Russo, eds., *Colonial Chesapeake Society*, 342–382.

cultures. Interaction between English settlers and local Indians differed from place to place depending on time and circumstance, but notably on whether it was a frontier or an old, established area. Some Chesapeake counties had closer ties with English outports than others, but, again, how different trade links influenced particular localities is unclear. What is certain is that no direct correspondence between particular regions in England and particular parts of the tobacco coast can be demonstrated. Emigrants from the Bristol region did not uniformly end up in counties on the south bank of the James, no more than Kentish settlers all went to York or the Northern Neck. Imported English local and provincial cultures did not last long in the Chesapeake.

English society in Maryland and Virginia between the 1620s and 1690s was distinctive. Connections with England were closer than during any other period. Most settlers were English by birth. They established an infrastructure based on English laws, government, and economic organization. They brought traditional English attitudes toward the social order, religious practices, and the afterlife. They endowed the Chesapeake landscape with familiar English names reminiscent of home, and they established and maintained close commercial as well as social ties with England. At the same time, the settlers' experience was mediated and powerfully influenced by adaptation to local conditions, creating a unique blend of English and Chesapeake ways of life. Anglo-Chesapeake society was molded by a variety of influences: the dominant English culture, the early emergence of a regionwide provincial culture, and the more gradual evolution of local subcultures that distinguished one part of the Bay from another. None of these influences was constant—they varied in nature and intensity throughout the century— but from their dynamic interaction the region's history unfolds.

By the turn of the century, signs of profound change were in the air. As the flow of immigrants from England rapidly diminished, the balance of population shifted decisively toward a majority of native-born inhabitants. A crucial direct link with English ways of life was permanently severed as emigration from the parent country dwindled and the rate of natural population increase in the Chesapeake grew. The tidewater was no longer an immigrant society by the second decade of the eighteenth century. Second, the large numbers of black slaves imported into the region and the commitment to chattel slavery by planters large and small represented a fundamental and irrevocable break with the parent society. Some Chesapeake counties in 1750 bore a greater resemblance to the plantation societies of South Carolina and the West Indies than to English rural society. Attempts by provincial elites to bring institutions and laws into a closer conformity with English equivalents and to imitate metropolitan fashion exhibited an increasingly artificial tone. Rather than drawing directly upon the experiences of settlers from England, English dominant culture in the eighteenth-century Chesapeake relied more and more on imitation and self-conscious replication. At the same time, inhabitants' growing awareness of their provincial identity was encouraged by the spread of settlement into the interior and a rapidly expanding population that had little sustained contact with English culture other than the marketing of tobacco and purchase of English goods. Despite the mimetic impulse of the Chesapeake gentry and the rising volume of Anglo-American trade, at the popular level tidewater society was less dependent culturally on England than ever before. Whereas seventeenth-century colonists were first and foremost English and then Virginians or Marylanders, in the following century roles were reversed.[19]

Colonial historians have tended to ignore the English context of Chesapeake social development, as if conditions encountered along the Bay necessarily imply a radical break with the past. But, as this study has shown, the evolution of Maryland and Virginia society is incomprehensible without an awareness of English social development in the seventeenth century. Only a transatlantic perspective can comprehend the complexity of interaction between the various cultural horizons of settlers and their creativity in preserving and adapting English traditions and customs to life along the tobacco coast. In this way, we may achieve some idea of what was lost and what gained in the transfer of English society to America.

19. These developments are surveyed by Jack P. Greene in *Pursuits of Happiness: The Social Development of Early Modern British Colonies and the Formation of American Culture* (Chapel Hill, N.C., 1988), chap. 4, although he comes to different conclusions about their impact. Despite the work of Edmund Morgan, Greene, Isaac, Kulikoff, Clemens, the Rutmans, Main, Land, Carr, Walsh, Beeman, and Breen, among others, there is still no comprehensive synthesis of the 18th-century Chesapeake.

Index